STUDIES IN EARLY MODERN INDO-ARYAN LANGUAGES, LITERATURE AND CULTURE

ALAN W. ENTWISTLE (1949-1996)

पानीं केरां बुदबुदा, अस मानस की जाति।
देखत ही छिपि जाइंगे, ज्यौं तारे परभाति॥ – कबीर

This life of ours is like a bubble of water;
As soon as you see it, it disappears,
Like the stars at dawn. – KABIR

Studies in
Early Modern Indo-Aryan Languages, Literature and Culture

Research Papers, 1992-1994, presented at the Sixth Conference on Devotional Literature in New Indo-Aryan Languages, held at Seattle, University of Washington, 7-9 July 1994

Edited by
ALAN W. ENTWISTLE and CAROL SALOMON
with
HEIDI PAUWELS and MICHAEL C. SHAPIRO

MANOHAR
1999

First published 1999

ISBN 81-7304-269-1

Published by
Ajay Kumar Jain for
Manohar Publishers & Distributors
2/6, Ansari Road, Daryaganj
New Delhi 110002

Typeset by
A J Software Publishing Co. Pvt. Ltd.
305, Durga Chambers,
1333, D.B. Gupta Road,
Karol Bagh, New Delhi 110005

Printed at
Rajkamal Electric Press
B 35/9 G T Karnal Road Indl. Area
Delhi 110033

Contents

Preface

The Sixth International Conference on Early Literature in New Indo-Aryan Languages convened between 7 and 9 July 1994 at the University of Washington, in Seattle, Washington (USA). The conference followed previous meetings that had been held at Leuven/Louvain (1979), Bonn (1982), Leiden (1985), Cambridge (1988) and Paris (1991). The Seattle conference was attended by approximately one hundred participants from fourteen countries of North America, Europe, and Asia. During the three days of the conference 34 papers were presented, of which 28 are included for publication in this volume.

Although the papers delivered in Seattle touched upon many distinct topics, several subjects served as central themes of panels. These topics were hagiography, oral traditions, text criticism, Islam in the Indian context, and metaphors. Although the majority of papers examined aspects of 'medieval' texts and textual traditions, several other papers dealt with the treatment of devotional themes in modern folklore traditions and in twentieth century literatures in New Indo-Aryan languages.

The idea of hosting what has informally come to be known as the 'Bhakti' conference in Seattle was the brainchild of Alan Entwistle. It was Alan who proposed to bring the conference to Seattle, who secured from various administrators at the University of Washington the money to put on the conference and to pay for some of the publication costs of the conference papers, who corresponded with participants, and who fussed endlessly about what food and libations should be served at the conference receptions and banquet. Alan was involved in every aspect of the conference and, it is safe to say, Alan loved every aspect of hosting it.

The death of Alan Entwistle on 28 March 1996, after a decade-long battle with brain cancer, has made the publication of these conference papers a much sadder occasion than it might otherwise have been. It is obvious to anyone who has worked in the field of

Early New Indo-Aryan textual studies, that Alan, by virtue of his masterful publications, but equally much by his unassuming and gracious personality, total dedication to his field, and position as a superb teacher and colleague, contributed greatly to Early New Indo-Aryan studies. For us at the University of Washington the loss of Alan has been particularly hard. For approximately a decade, the study of early Hindi at the University of Washington was inexorably linked to Alan's presence and guidance.

Regrettably, Alan's death delayed considerably the publication of these papers. No doubt, had Alan lived to complete the editing of the volume, some things would have been done differently. Certainly, there would have been a greater degree of standardization of format than was eventually achieved. The delays in the publication of this volume are very much regretted by the editors. They would like to thank all the contributors for their patience in what has, of necessity, been a long-drawn-out process.

The hosting of the 1994 conference and the publication of this volume would not have been possible without the assistance of many persons and organizations. At the University of Washington, financial support was provided by the Department of Asian Languages and Literature, the South Asia Program of the Henry M. Jackson School of International Studies, the Graduate School, the Center for the Humanities, and the College of Arts and Science. The past Divisional Dean for the Humanities, Richard J. Dunn, was especially supportive of the conference and provided encouragement and financial support. Thanks are also due to Rebecca Manring, who assisted in the early editing of some of the papers.

A special word of thanks is due to Manohar Publishers & Distributors, and particularly its director, Ramesh Jain. Manohar's work in bringing out this work, under difficult circumstances, has been exemplary. The editors are most grateful to Ramesh Jain and his associates for their patience and their professionalism.

CAROL SALOMON
HEIDI PAUWELS
MICHAEL C. SHAPIRO

Between Pestle and Mortar: Women in the Marathi Sant Tradition

VIDYUT AKLUJKAR

Introduction

The Sant tradition of Maharashtra (*c.* thirteenth to seventeenth century AD) records women's contribution on many levels. On the one hand, some women were Sants in their own right, and even today are fondly remembered and venerated for their steadfast Bhakti and beautiful poetry. Two of the most prominent females who are celebrated as Sants are Janābāī (*c.* thirteenth century), who was an orphan maidservant in Sant Nāmdev's house, and Bahiṇābāī (AD 1628-1700), who was a Brahmin housewife and the first female to have written an account in verse of her entire life. The names of other females such as Muktābāī or Kānhopātrā appear in some *abhaṅgas* and occupy a place in the larger circle of Sants. On the other hand, there are other women, i.e. women in a male Sant's life, his mother, sister, wife or daughter, who are remembered mainly for their nuisance value to the Sant, or as his stepping stones towards his world-weariness. In addition to the portrayals of these women in the Sants' lives, there are stories and anecdotes of women that appear in the poems of the Sants. And finally, there are some female stereotypes that are used by the Sants as paradigms of virtue or vice. To my knowledge, there is no attempt anywhere, either in English or in Marathi, to take into account all sides of the representation of women in the Sant tradition of Maharashtra. There are studies of particular female Sants, but no comprehensive study of the female contingent has been published. In order to obtain a comprehensive vision of the female collective consciousness, we need to look at all these pictures and caricatures of women in the Sant literature of Maharashtra. Although an exhaustive account of each and every female is an impossibility given the space limitations of this paper, I propose to survey and analyse in the first part of this paper, the portrayals of women on either side of the Bhakti fence in the Marathi Sant tradition, with special reference to the lives of women related to or associated with Nāmdev (AD 1270-1350) and Tukārām (AD 1598-1649). The latter part of this paper will survey the literary representations of various types of females, through stories and anecdotes preserved by the Sant tradition.

My choice of these two Sants is influenced by practical considerations. These two are chronologically as well as influentially central figures in the extensive Sant tradition of Maharashtra. Nāmdev's influence was felt all the way up to the Punjab, and for centuries, Tukārām's proverbial *abhaṅgas* have been the most used coinage in everyday Marathi by both the masses and the elite alike. Associated with the names of both Nāmdev and Tukārām are exquisitely preserved records of women who tried to turn the Sants away from the path of Bhakti. At the same time, both these male Sants have been associated in the popular tradition with kindred spirits who were women Sants, i.e. Nāmdev with Janābāī, and Tukārām with Bahiṇābāī. In short, they offer us the most colourful examples of male Sants associated, on the one hand, with female Sants and on the other hand, with other females. In addition, they furnish us with many stories and anecdotes of women whom they use as stock examples of virtue or vice. Hence, although I will occasionally draw upon the other Sants, I will concentrate mainly on the cluster of women around Nāmdev and Tukārām.

Sources

My sources of information for this study are the five volume compilation of Sant verses or *abhaṅga-gāthās, Sakala santa gāthā,* which is based on the Vārkarī sect's traditional canon. There are no seperate critical editions of the works of Janābāī or of Bahiṇābāī. All information about the women of the Sant tradition comes to us mainly through *abhaṅgas* in their names incorporated in the *abhaṅga* collections of male Sants, or through *abhaṅgas* about these women by the male Sants. Therefore in order to study all these females, the only choice is to look at the traditional canonical collection of all Sants' poems. For a detailed discussion of the various manuscripts, partial editions, and an attempt at a critical edition of Tukārām's works, I refer the reader to the 1950 edition published by the Government Central Press in Bombay under the editorship of Purushottam Mangesh Lad. I have used his edition as an additional resource along with the standard canonical edition of the works of all Sants which is the five volume text of the *Sakala santa gāthā* (hereafter *SSG*), edited in 1983 by R.C. Dhere. Apart from the *SSG*, which is essentially based on the 1908 edition of the canonical *Santagāthā* text of Nānā Mahārāj Sākhare, I use the occasional hagiographical accounts that appear in the extensive Sant literature. Often, in *abhaṅgas* in the names of minor Sants or in the name of a Sant's wife, son or daughter, we find accounts of incidents in a major Sant's life that are essentially hagiographical. I have used these, as well as the standard hagiographical works such as the *Bhaktavijaya,* written in 1762 by Mahīpati (AD 1715-90). For the texts of Bahiṇābāī's verses which are not included in the above canonical text, I use *Bahīṇābāīcā gāthā* (second edition, 1956) published by the Chitrashāḷā Press, Pune. All translations in this paper are mine.

PART ONE

We will examine the works of Nāmdev's maidservant Janābāī and Tukārām's disciple, Bahiṇābāī, later in part one. But first, who are the women we consider to be on the other side of the Bhakti fence? They are Nāmdev's mother Goṇāī and his wife Rājāī, and Tukārām's second wife Āvalī. A brief introduction to these women is in order here. Sant Nāmdev was the only son of Goṇāī and Dāmājī, who were tailors by caste and profession and lived in Pandharpur. His mother, Goṇāī, and his wife, Rājāī, are the two women who figure in the story of Nāmdev's early conflicts with the mundane. There are *abhaṅgas* in their names, and they are mentioned in *abhaṅgas* by other members of Nāmdev's family, as well as in the verse-stories of the later hagiographer Mahīpati Taherabadkar. Sant Tukārām, a merchant of Dehu, mentions his mother, first wife, and daughter occasionally when referring to the bonds of worry, desire, and delusion that he has severed,[1] but his second wife, Āvalī, was his major adversary. Her trials and tribulations in her marriage to Tukārām have been immortalised in many of the *abhaṅgas* in Tukārām's name. The oral tradition in Maharashtra remembers her name as Āvalī, or sometimes as Jijā'ī. However, in Tukārām's verses, she is mentioned only as *strī* 'woman', or as *pisī, lānsī,* or *rāṇḍa,* 'madwoman', 'slut', or 'bitch'. Even in Mahīpati's *Bhaktavijaya,* other Sants' wives or mothers are mentioned by name, but Tukārām's harassed wife remains a nameless woman, a *strī*. This is surprising in view of the fact that Mahīpati claims to be a disciple of Tukārām and devotes three and a half chapters of his *Bhaktavijaya* (Chs. 48, 49, 50 and part of 51) to Tukārām's life. In Chapter 49, he chooses to expound at length on the eleven verses composed by Tukārām in which Tukārām instructs his contrary wife on the significance of his lifestyle steeped in Bhakti. In short, although Tukārām's domestic life and its strife remains of central importance to his major hagiographer, the main thrust in Mahīpati's account is to exalt Tukāram, and true to that spirit, the Sant's wife remains nameless. I shall start by examining in chronological order the roles of these lesser known women in the lives of the two Sants.

In a prologue to Nāmdev's biography in verse at the beginning of his *abhaṅga gāthā* are several sections in which conversations are recorded between Goṇāī and Nāmdev, Goṇāī and God, God and Nāmdev, and all three together. I am not concerned here with the issue of the authorship of these *abhaṅgas*, since to me, it is enough that they record the popular tradition of conflict between Nāmdev and his family. There seems to be little doubt that there was conflict resulting from the Sant's uncompromising worship and his failure to perform his household duties. Many of the incidents here find mention again in the *abhaṅgas* in the names of Nāmdev's sons, in those of Janābāī, and in Chapter 4 of Mahīpati's *Bhaktavijaya*. My discussion essentially follows the accounts as they appear in the *abhaṅgas* attributed to Nāmdev. These *abhaṅgas* tend to be repetitious, and many times they express the same thoughts in slightly different words, in a manner consistent with recording multiple versions of an oral tradition. But the human drama emerging from these story-poems is fascinating.

Nāmdev was a child Sant. According to traditional accounts, he experienced the grace of God early in his life. God used to eat from his hands, and Nāmdev would share food in God's house. Naturally, as he grew up, Nāmdev became thoroughly immersed in God and started to live in the temple, singing and dancing in ecstasy instead of minding his tailor shop. His parents married him to Rājāi, hoping to cure him of his excessive addiction to God, but to no avail. Finally, his mother confronted him and poured out her heart in an effort to make him see the light.

Goṇāī is a concerned mother, and although she is herself worshipful of God, she has her feet firmly on the ground and believes in fulfilling her daily duties to the best of her abilities before immersing herself in worship. Her arguments stem from her well-defined sense of duty and are quite consistent with her place in this world as understood by her and her society. At first, she praises her son. She tries to remind Nāmdev of her bond to him ever since she carried him in her womb, and of her pride in him when he was blessed as a child by God: 'When you were born, I was so happy. My heart was full of joy, full of delight. You earned a good name among our family and relations. The God of Paṇḍharī was pleased with you.'[2] She is not averse to worship, but she believes that excess of even a good quality is to be avoided. She praises his intelligence and uses his peers as examples. She says:

'Nāmyā, you are no longer a child.[3]

'Look at other people's sons; they may not be as bright as you are, but they look after their parents.'[4]

'They do something worthwhile with their lives. Look at you on the other hand. Why, you don't even glance at the house, let alone the shop. You are at the feet of this God all day long, singing, dancing, and forgetting yourself altogether. We have seen plenty of devotees, but you are totally mindless of your own good. What kind of other-worldly worship is this? Nāmyā, it has burnt your family to ashes.'[5]

'Cure this addiction to God; why are you bent on total destruction (lit., drowning) of home?'[6]

To this, Nāmdev simply confesses that he is fed up with the world which is nothing but poison and that therefore, his only hope is God. He advises Goṇāī to join him and stay there in God's Paṇḍharī rather than leave for that strange place she calls home. Of course, the battle of wits is unresolved, and she answers by expressing her firm resolve to succeed in her mission and take him home instead. Now she turns to address God and demands that He give her back her son. In this appeal to God in fourteen *abhangas*, she makes requests, accusations, and threats. She resorts to provocation and finally, out of exasperation, she gives in to her son (*SSG* 2: 39-40, 42, 44, 45-9, 51-2, 55, 57-8). God tries to tell her in many words why the matter is no longer in His hands (*SSG* 2:41, 43, 50, 53, 54). He describes Nāmdev's God-centred attitude, acquired as a result of deeds in many births, his utter distaste for the world, his firm resolve not to leave God, and his true devotion which makes him realise all his worldly relations in God. This is no news to Goṇāī. That is what she is fighting at the moment, and with a woman's logic, when her son leaves her side for God, she tries to make God her ally. She asks God:

'You are the Lord in possession of the whole universe, what do You lack?'[7]

'Why must You snatch away the one and only son that I have? Are You tired of being the One and Only? If You are thirsty for company, must You take away the only son of a poor tailor? Have You forgotten who called You here to Paṇḍharī in the first place, and for ages to come, who made You stand steady on this brick? It was Puṇḍalik, the devotee who was so good to his old parents that even when You came to his door, he would not get up from the service of his old father, and threw You a brick to stand upon while You were waiting for him'. (*SSG* 2: 51)

'God, why don't You smarten up? Why do You hanker after someone else's wealth?'[8]

'Why should You lure away other people's children? Now remember Your reputation as a merciful God, and unite me with my stray calf'. (*SSG* 2: 42)

She threatens to sit at God's door and go on a hunger strike if He does not comply.[9] God showers her with praise and congratulations for giving birth to a great devotee (*SSG* 2: 54), but she is not flattered. At last God asks Goṇāī how He can abandon a devotee who has come to Him in good faith. Who will then believe in Truth (*SSG* 2: 54)? When she fails to bring God to her side, Goṇāī begs the other Sants to put some sense in Nāmdev, but they, too, echo God and praise her for her good fortune instead. Her resolve to go home with Nāmdev or stay there indefinitely and reason with God is undiminished. Finally, God cannot take it anymore and says to Nāmdev, 'Your mother has set her heart on you, go back to her. After all, she has raised you on her own milk, you should not abandon her' (*SSG* 2: 68). Nāmdev answers that God is not being fair. Nāmdev had turned to God in the first place out of fear of his mother, so now how can God send him back to her?[10] When neither the headstrong mother nor her stubborn son listens to God, He resorts to a miracle. He tells Goṇāī to take back Nāmdev, and when she gladly does so and starts to walk away, she finds God in her hands instead. God and Nāmdev have become one and the same. This miracle is supposed to have enlightened her; but according to another version, Goṇāī remains a worldly woman to the core and resists 'enlightenment' based on a miracle with characteristic wit. This is how the incident is related (*SSG* 2: 69):

God became Nāmā and Nāmā became God in order to test the attitude of Goṇāī. (God said,) 'Here, take back your Nāmā, who cares for him?' She was ecstatic with love. She took him with her by the hand, and as she turned to look, there was God in her hand. She flipped. 'Oh my Father, who wants You? What would I, frail as I am, do with You? All those sixteen thousand women of Yours, with the eight superior ones, all of those would come running to finish me off. By the way, You gave Your word to Puṇḍalik once, remember? You can't come with me, You rascal!'

She refers here to the traditional belief that God promised to remain for ever in Pandharpur, standing still on a brick thrown to him by his earlier devotee, Puṇḍalik.

We do not know whether or not Goṇāī gave up her mission to try and tame Nāmdev's Bhakti. There are contradictory accounts recorded in the tradition (*SSG* 2: 69-70; *SSG* 2 Janābāī 138). It is more than likely that she had to give up and that Nāmdev's all-encompassing Bhakti went on without regard to his householder's duties. There is ample evidence to believe that Nāmdev was unaffected by his mother's arguments. So, on to the next chapter in the war of *Weltanschaungs*. When the mother fails to bring back her son, the wife takes over (*SSG* 2: 84-97; also in *SSG* 2 Gonda's *abhaṅgas* 9-14). Rājāī has been a dutiful wife to Nāmdev and has already given him four sons and two daughters. But Nāmdev is no longer there. He is lost in his Bhakti. At first, Rājāī tries to reason with her husband and tells him to listen to his mother. She tries to convey to him her worries, her loneliness, and her sense of having failed the older generation. When he turns a deaf ear to her, she resorts to something quite logical. Mother Goṇāī, as we saw earlier, had directly appealed to God, the cause of her son's obsession. There is a rationale behind Goṇāī's choice. Nāmdev, as a child-Sant, often indulged in calling God Viṭhobā in the feminine gender as his mother Viṭhāī. In keeping with Nāmdev's attitude, Goṇāī tries to reason with God in broad daylight as a mother to Mother. Rājāī is Nāmdev's wife, she has no such leverage as she remains on a lower rung of the household-hierarchical ladder. She is clever though, and more subtle than her mother-in-law in choosing the time and the person for her message. Therefore, in the darkness of midnight, she seeks out the better half of God. Her message to Viṭhobā, given to Goddess Rakhumā (i.e. Rukmiṇī, also known as Rakhumābāī, Rukmābāī, Rukmāī, etc.) to deliver, is recorded in five *abhaṅgas* in her name (*SSG* 2: 85-9). In what follows, I offer a partial translation, enough to set the tone:

'Oh Rakhumābāī, ask your husband why He has fooled my husband. He has no clothes, no pot, nothing to eat, but he goes on dancing day and night like a shameless man. I've got fourteen mouths to feed[11] in my house, and I have to go from door to door in order to feed them. You better realise this and convince Him to find a better way, or else this Rājāī of Nāmā won't remain good any more'. (*SSG* 2: 85)

'How can I describe the ways of these fools? They all become crazy at the feet of God. All become charmed and dance like ghosts in bliss. They are all useless in the world; they bow at each other's feet, and sway in their joy of Brahman.' (*SSG* 2: 86)

'Look! My poor naive mother-in-law gave birth to a bright gem. And he has joined hands with the God who reclines over the serpent Śeṣa. What is poor Rājāī to do?' (*SSG* 2: 86)

'Listen Rukmābāi, you sit in these fine silks, but poverty does not leave me. What am I to do? Fortunate women wear jewelry, but I am an unloved woman. What can I do? Some get to wear divine robes, and all I have are these worn out rags. It seems that poverty has come to rest forever with us, Mother. Who will listen to my complaints? The hut is broken, the wind howls from all sides. I have a lot to suffer, Mother. Whom shall I tell? Never mind a bed of flowers or a mattress, all I have for a bed is a torn quilt. My son and my daughter are ready for marriage, but my husband never comes home. All the neighbours are laughing at us. They say Nāmā has gone crazy.' (*SSG* 2: 88)

'Please ask your husband why He makes us poor ones suffer so much. What are we to do, Mother? Under whose roof shall we sit? He has lured my husband away from me; He does not let him go even for a moment. We are poorer because of contact with you; how can you not feel for us? I cannot fathom the entire misery of this world. You better do whatever is to be done.' (*SSG* 2: 89)

The heartfelt agony of a dutiful wife at her wit's end in these *abhaṅgas* is hard to miss, but her message falls on deaf ears. Nāmdev does not change his ways. Her gentler efforts in vain, Rājāī becomes desparate and resorts to the only course available to her. With her son Viṭhā in her hand and another son Nārā on her hips, she goes to the river Bhivarā at Pandharpur, and tying her children to her, jumps in the river and almost drowns in a whirlpool. Nāmdev still does not heed, but now God takes action. God wakes up from his yogic trance, uplifts all three of them and brings them to meet Nāmdev who is still at his temple. Nārā calls out to his father Nāmdev, but Nāmdev tells his son to go back home, and Rājāī, in total disgust, once again attempts suicide. This time she finds a dead serpent, cuts it to pieces, cooks it in its own poison, and starts to eat it and feed it to her children. But when she lifts the lid, the pot is full of gold. According to one account, this miracle enlightens Rājāī (*SSG* 2: 90).

There are a couple more accounts of Rājāī's miseries and her attempts to resist or confront the situation. Although the details of her difficulties may differ, it is noteworthy that the resolution of the conflict always enlists the help of a miracle. Another account (*SSG* 2: 92-7) in five *abhaṅgas* in Nāmdev's name mentions Nāmdev's inadvertent mistreatment of Rājāī's brothers as the cause of Rājāī's sorrow. In this story, Rājāī's brothers come to visit their sister. When Nāmdev appears, they get up to pay their respects, but Nāmdev is so engrossed in his God that he fails to acknowledge their presence, and this upsets Rājāī. Like a good wife, she somehow swallows it and asks Nāmdev to arrange for a feast for the brothers. Nāmdev reminds her that it is the tenth of the month which is designated as a half day fast for all Vaiṣṇavas, and that the day after is the eleventh, another day-long fast. Her brothers had gotten up early in the morning and had walked quite a distance to visit their sister. They are worried and cannot sleep due to hunger. After reminding her of her religious duties, Nāmdev retires to the temple. Rājāī becomes very sad at heart at the prospect of spending that day and the next in Hari *kathā* and *bhajan* on an empty stomach, and not being able to entertain her brothers at her house. She wonders, 'Why did my father give me in marriage to such a man? No meals, no snacks, no jewels, no clothes. The only thing I am chosen to enjoy in this life is misery' (*SSG* 2: 94).

Now God sees that the beloved of his *bhakta* is worried and comes in disguise to drive away her misery. He comes as a merchant when Nāmdev is not at home, delivers a sack full of gold coins, and then leaves. Nāmdev returns and learns that a merchant called Keśavarāj came and delivered this sack full of wealth. He recognises the deed of God for what it is. Nāmdev goes out, brings back some needy Brahmins, and distributes the wealth brought home by God. Suspecting Nāmdev's sweeping generosity, Rājāī had hidden some coins from him, but when she recovers them, she finds that they had turned into charcoals. She then confesses her sin to Nāmdev. As he glances at the charcoals, they turn back into gold coins. Nāmdev again gives them away to the needy Brahmins. This triple miracle is the occasion for Rājāī's enlightenment and conversion to Bhakti in some accounts.

The *abhaṅgas* in the name of Gondā, one of the four sons of

Nāmdev, contain an account of the incidents involving Goṇāī and Rājāī similar to the one described above. However, in this account the Sant's childhood exploits with the God convince Goṇāī of his greatness; and the two stories of Rājāī's plight are confused, so that it is the gold coins in the pot in which she cooked the serpent that Nāmdev distributes among needy Brahmins. When Rājāī scolds him and curses her fate, God appears before her in disguise and once again offers her some wealth. This tale also culminates in God's triple miracle and Rājāī's enlightenment. In Chapter 18 of Mahīpati's *Bhaktavijaya*, another account appears of the conflict between Rājāī's attempts at fighting poverty and Nāmdev's resistance to these attempts. Rājāī borrows a philosopher's stone, a *parisa,* from the wife of a neighbour, Parisā Bhāgvat, who had been granted the stone as a boon by Viṭhobā's consort Rukminī. Rājāī hopes to use the stone to put an end to her poverty, but when Nāmdev discovers her plans, which he deems unsuitable for a *bhakta's* wife, he takes the stone and throws it into the river. Both Rājāī and Parisā's wife, Kamaljā, are heartbroken and start to cry. When Parisā Bhāgvat learns of this incident from his wife, he demands the stone back. Nāmdev simply takes a handful of pebbles from the river-bed and claims that all of them are philosopher's stones. The villagers test this claim and find it to be true. Parisā Bhāgvat becomes enlightened, accepts Nāmdev's greatness, and shuns worldly wealth. Mahīpatī does not mention whether the wives were convinced or not.

Even if we discount these miracles leading to the women's conversions as standard motifs found in any Sant hagiography, we cannot miss the sincerity in Goṇāī's and Rājāī's earlier appeals to Nāmdev and to God. Unlike the women in the life stories of other Sants,[12] these two are not just nameless women serving as bonds of Māyā, making the Sant's lot difficult. Nor do they resemble the typical wailing women of renouncer husbands in north Indian folk-tales such as those about King Bhartharī or King Gopī Chand (A. Gold 1992). For unlike these typical wailing women, the Marathi Sant's mother and wife have no intention either of making the Sant give up his worship completely or of joining him in his total disregard for the family. We see them taking their social roles of mother and wife very seriously and wholeheartedly. Between the two of them, they have used practically all possible arguments to make the Sant assume his share of the household responsibility.

Coming from good, intelligent, God-worshipping, strong women, their arguments are impeccable and hard to refute by reason alone. Therefore, the dispute between the divine and the domestic remains unresolved at the rational and social levels. I think it significant that nothing short of a miracle converts them to the path of total abandonment in Nāmdev's style of Bhakti. Even then, as we shall see in part two of this paper, they are seen as impediments to the Sant's progress in the self-sacrificing path of Bhakti.

Both these women pale in comparison to Tukārām's second wife, Āvalī, who is portrayed by Tukārām as a sharp-tongued nag. She has a lot more to complain about. Tukārām himself describes why he chose to become a renunciate. He was unhappy with his low caste, and his profession as a shop-keeper. His mind was not on his shop. He was troubled by a pseudo-righteous Brahmin, Sālomālo, who used to plagiarise Tukārām's *abhaṅgas,* and incite Brahmins against the low-born Tukārām. Due to Sālomālo's malice as well as some natural disasters such as famine, Tukārām suffered many a loss in his life. The notebooks of his *abhaṅgas* were thrown into the river by his rivals. Moreover, he went bankrupt, lost his shop, and lost his parents, his first wife, and his children in a famine. This loss turned him wholeheartedly towards God. He gave away whatever he had to the needy, and went on singing and dancing in God's name. Of course, the second wife was at home. Without the husband's support she was left to her own resources and naturally, started to complain, curse, and finally resort to abuses and violence. Tukārām gives a running commentary on her in eight *abhaṅgas* as she talks (*SSG* 4: 3766-73). He also relates in eleven *abhaṅgas* how he advised her to change her perspective, put her faith in the God, stop worrying, and live totally immersed in Bhakti (*SSG* 4: 3774-84). We find a clear mention of and a gloss to these eleven *abhaṅgas* by Tukārām in Mahīpati's *Bhaktavijaya* (Chapter 49 verses 57-116), indicating that the tradition of a conflict between Tukārām and his wife was well-known as early as in Mahīpati's times. The earlier eight *abhaṅgas* in Tukārām's *gāthā* are full of emotion and real-life drama. It is as if a candid camera is recording the confrontation scene as it happens. The wife is presented to us through her accusations, curses, and her hysterics as related by her husband, who is at once the cause of her misery, the witness of her outburst, and the reporter and record-keeper of the incident. However, the *abhaṅgas* are also like a three-sided-mirror reflecting the scene from different angles. In the speeches attributed by Tukārām to his wife, we get a vivid picture of the Sant himself from his wife's angle, and come to know of her trials. In the remarks at the end of these verses, we hear Tukārām, the Sant, responding to his wife, the householder, and aggravating her misery by his calm quiet demeanor. To my knowledge, these *abhaṅgas* are unparalleled in the entire Sant tradition for their life-like presentation of the tensions between the domestic and the divine. Each *abhaṅga* starts with the woman's speech and ends with a comment by Tukārām. My partial translations retain this format.

'How long can I carry on being a wife? How many more calamities must I endure? Shall I offer my body to these children to tear into morsels? They would be better off dead. My husband does not let me save anything in this house. He robs me outright. I don't even have dung to sweep my floors with.' Tukā says, 'The bitch does not think. She carries a burden on her shoulders and whines.' (*SSG* 4: 3766)

'Who knows? He must have been my mortal enemy in a past life. That is why he has become my husband in this life. How am I to endure this misery all the time? How many people am I to beg? What good has the mother-fucker God ever done for anyone in this world?' Tukā says, 'The wife is breaking down with hysterical seizures. She cries, she laughs, she sobs, and rants on and on.' (*SSG* 4: 3767)

'The sack (of grains) has arrived (at our) home, and still he won't let my children eat the grains. He has to fill other people's bellies. Damn the rogue, the robber, the sucker.' 'The madwoman is outraged and drags me by my arms like a witch.' Tukā says, 'The bitch is bankrupt in merit from the past.' (*SSG* 4: 3768)

'What will you eat now, my son? The husband is mad after that God. He claps his head and wears those garlands, and has given up his business altogether. He does not fill his own belly nor does he worry about ours. *Tāḷ* in hand and mouth opened wide, he sings in the temple of that God. What are we to do now ? Leave home, go to the forest?' Tukā says, 'Have patience, nothing has happened yet.' (*SSG* 4: 3769)

'He can't work. Why would he? He gets to eat without lifting a finger. As soon as he gets up, he starts to clammer with the *ṭāḷ*. He doesn't let anyone sleep. From dawn to dusk, it is *chini chini chini*. He makes a racket all the time. He is a living corpse. It is as if he has percolated all shame and drunk it. He does not even bother glancing at his family. His widow is in pain here. She is throwing stones at the mention of his very name.' Tukā says, 'Here, woman, I wrote it all down.' (*SSG* 4: 3771-2)

We witness here an outburst of a cornered woman whose situation is similar to the women in Nāmdev's house, but whose spirit and language are quite different from theirs. The story of Tukārām's wife remains essentially different from the cluster of stories about women in Nāmdev's house. Unlike in the story of Nāmdev, no miracle takes place here to convince Āvalī of her husband's greatness. Unlike the two in Nāmdev's house, Tukārām's wife has no direct dialogue with God. Later on, Mahīpati in Chapter 49 of his *Bhaktavijaya* narrates an incident in which Āvalī runs to the temple with a stone in her hand, intending to hurl it at the divine feet of God. Rukmiṇī, however, listens to her complaint against the Sant and grants her wealth, which, of course, Tukārām does not allow her to enjoy. But in no other incident in Tukārām's *abhaṅgas* or elsewhere does she not deal directly with her husband. She comes across as a disenchanted, bitter, essentially helpless woman, faced with an unsympathetic, unproviding, and adamant husband, who is obsessed by a God she does not understand nor care for. All we have is this record of her passionate breakdown reported candidly by Tukārām. Unlike Nāmdev's mother and wife, we do not get any *abhaṅgas* in her name praising God. Even Mahīpati portrays her as a cantankerous wife who does not understand the magnanimity of her Sant husband and does not flinch at cursing, foulmouthing, and even once hitting Tukārām with a sugarcane. In his *Bhaktavijaya*, as in Tukārām's *abhaṅgas*, she remains a nameless woman. All of this, coupled with the fact that these *abhaṅgas* concerning the conflict between the Sant and his wife are found in all the oldest manuscripts from Dehu, Pandharpur and Talegao traditions and have been preserved in the critical edition by P.M. Lad, give us strong reasons to believe in the authenticity of the story. Tukārām later tries to convince his wife of the futility of her short-sighted expectations and to instruct her in his path. We do not know whether or not she changed her outlook. There is no indication in the *gāthā* of Tukārām that she did. Even if she did, it was probably because she had no other choice, short of giving up the ghost. Her outrage and her desperation at the total lack of sympathy from her husband are what haunt us in her most life-like description of her suffering at the hands of her husband.

Of course, elsewhere we hear more unkind words about her short-tempered nature from her husband, the Sant. Tukārām thanks God many times for giving him all the miseries in life, since, like Kuntī, he believes that the sorrows and miseries of this world constantly remind him of God and anchor him firmly in Bhakti.[13] His wife gets an honourable mention among his miseries:

'God, it's good that You made me a peasant. Or else false pride would have killed me.' (*SSG* 4: 63)

God, it's a good thing that I went bankrupt in this famine. That is what nauseated me towards this world and reminded me of You. I'm glad that my wife is a shrill nag and that she embarasses me in public. I'm glad that I'm humiliated in this world. It's a good thing that I lost all my wealth, all cattle, and all shame. That is what made me come to you for help.' (*SSG* 4: 3763)

We know that in the eyes of Tukārām, his wife is useful to him only as a painful reminder of worldly misery.

Rājāī, Goṇāī, and Āvalī are typical examples of disempowered women. These women are seen as trapped in a society which assigns them the role of nurturing their family, but offers no protection against a husband who refuses to share the load. When they try to assume their assigned traditional roles, they are accused of being obstacles in the path of worship by their *bhakta* husbands. A woman's natural concern for her husband, her children, and her family is criticised and ridiculed by her God-centred husband. She is mostly ignored, but sometimes rebuked and belittled by her Sant husband who preaches equality for all beings. Is the situation any different if a woman abandons tradition and wants to become a *bhakta* herself ? Hardly. If she herself wants to follow the path of Bhakti, but her husband is a worldling, then she is opposed by the husband, scorned by her family as a loose woman, and often abandoned or abused by society. The predicament of a female Sant has been mentioned several times so far, so I will not belabour it. It is sufficient to look at two examples of women Sants, Janābāī and Bahiṇābāī, separated from each other by more than three centuries. They differ in every respect: in their family life, their status, their attitude towards God and towards the society in which they live, and also in their poetry. The only thing they have in common is their maltreatment by society.

Sant Janābāī was an orphan maidservant living in Nāmdev's house. She was a sensitive and imaginative poet in her own right, and so she managed to surpass the habitual neglect coupled with hard physical labour that was her lot. The fact that Janābāī often speaks of herself as Nāmdev's Janī and talks about Nāmdev's family in her verses whereas Nāmdev does not even mention her once may indicate her lowly position in her master's family. Very modestly, she gives credit for her good fortune to her association with her master, Sant Nāmdev. She says, 'Along with the bride, the guests also get to eat delicacies at the wedding. Similarly, since Janī is a servant of Nāmyā, she too has been able to join with Viṭhobā' (*SSG* 2: Janābāī 31). She does record, however, her harrassment at the hands of the priestly establishment of the temple. The reason for this harassment is precisely Janābāī's choice of the path of Bhakti. As a person immersed in passionate worship of Viṭhobā, she has risen above her station and conveyed through her poems her exalted status as the beloved friend of God. For example, in one place she says:

> 'My mother and my father are both dead now. You have to take care of me, Viṭṭhala! Hari, I have no one, and my head is itching.' Viṭṭhala said to His consort Rukmiṇī, 'Poor Janī of mine, she has no one.' So He grabbed some oil and a comb and combed my hair and braided it. When He tied a knot at the end of my braid, Janī said to Him, 'Now how about a back-rub?' Janī said, 'O Gopāḷā, You will celebrate with a weakling like me.' (*SSG* 2: Janābāī 133)

In other places, she relates how God, her buddy, eases all her tasks by giving her a hand (*SSG* 2: Janābāī 83-4, 86-90, etc.). When she has a washload to finish on an empty stomach, God comes running behind her and uses all four of his hands to finish her task (*SSG* 2: Janābāī 129 and 135). When she goes to the woods to collect dung, God goes with her and not only collects dung, but helps her make patties, ties them in a bundle, and lifts it to his head while Janī has only to walk behind (*SSG* 2: Janābāī 130). When she has mountains of grains to grind at a grindstone, God sits opposite her and makes light work of her formidable task (*SSG* 2: Janābāī 125-6, 128, 135). Janābāī does not limit herself to these descriptions of God as her associate, her helper, and her buddy. Her devotion to God sums up all her emotions, all her passions, and is forcefully expressed as in the following verse: 'I eat God, I drink God. I sleep on God. I give God. I take God. I deal with God. Here God, there God. There is no place empty of God.' Janī says, 'Viṭhābāī has filled everything inside and out, and has remained besides' (*SSG* 2: Janābāī 198).

All such descriptions of her mystic experiences are interpreted as boasts by the temple priests, and they find a way to humiliate her. They try to accuse her, of stealing the ornaments of God's idol, convict her, and prepare to impale her on a stake (*SSG* 2: Janābāī 154; Mahīpati's *Bhaktavijaya*, Chapter 21). She wonders whether God is dead, but is saved from her fate by divine intervention when the *sūḷ* or 'stake' turns to water.

Finally, she revolts, and in defiance of the society which does not allow her to swim against the current, she proudly proclaims that her liberated ways are tantamount to those of a prostitute:

'Instead of covering my head with modesty, the end of my saree has fallen to my shoulders. I am preparing to enter the market as I am, with *ṭāḷ* in my hands and *vīṇā* on my shoulders. Who can stop me now?' Janī says, 'God, I have become a whore. I have opened a shop in this marketplace of Paṇḍharī. You can pour oil on my wrist (and I will howl in Your name). I have come to Your house now.' (*SSG* 2: Janābāī 232)

Bahiṇābāī (1628-1700) is another example of a woman who wanted to embrace the path of Bhakti and had to suffer for it. Although Janābāī is more celebrated in the Sant tradition than Bahiṇābāī, specific dates cannot be ascribed to Janābāī, and all we know is that she is said to be a contemporary of Sant Nāmdev. Bahiṇābāī's case is different. We have sufficient details available to us concerning her life, thanks to her own feat of recording them in verse. Hagiographers like Mahīpati are frugal in their words when it comes to female Sants. Mahīpati devotes just a chapter of his *Bhaktavijaya* to Janābāī whereas he devotes six full chapters and portions of a few more to Nāmdev's stories, and a similar number to sing Tukārām's glories. But Mahīpati has no story to tell of Bahiṇābāi who was the closest to him in time, and only mentions her in passing in the summary verses of the epilogue of his *Bhaktavijaya.* Bahiṇābāī was perhaps the first woman Sant who narrated her own life in detail in 78 *abhangas,* and has given us the exact date of her birth, etc. At the age of three she was married off to a thirty year old Brahmin widower. From the age of eleven, she was subjected to the demands of married life although her heart was not in it. Sant Tukārām's appearance in her dream guided her to the path of Bhakti and to chanting the name of Viṭhobā. Of course, her husband tried to change her mind. 'We are Brahmins who chant the Vedas all the time,' he said. 'Why do you need this lower caste Tukārām to come in your dream and instruct you?' (*Bahiṇābāīcā gātha* 32) Bahiṇābāī tried to reconcile to the demands of her husband and find pleasure in being a dutiful housewife, but neither succeeded in draining herself of her powerful emotion of Bhakti nor in pleasing her hard-to-please, hot-tempered husband. So she tried to engage in her pursuits of Bhakti while remaining a dutiful wife to her husband. Soon her fame began to spread and the husband began to be upset. At one point in Bahiṇābāī's *abhaṅgas,* we find that she reads accurately the thoughts of her husband, who was in all likelihood just jealous of the attention and fame she was getting. This is how she describes what was going on in his mind: 'They will now all come and bow at her feet, and she will treat me as a straw. All these people come to consult her, and here I am a Brahmin turned fool. They all call her the Gosāvīṇ, but no one remembers me while she is around' (*Bahiṇābāīcā gātha* 33). He is said to have abused, beaten, and confined her to their cattle-shed. When neither words nor physical abuse won her back, he prepared to leave her, but suffered a sensation of burning limbs for a whole month, and finally was convinced of her sincerity in her chosen path.

Even after this, until she died at the age of seventy-two, Bahiṇābāī lived a split life, torn between the cruel demands placed on her woman's body by her mismatched marriage, and her own urge towards renunciation and Bhakti. Her mental torment is powerfully expressed:

'The Vedas call out, the Purāṇas roar: "There is no merit in the company of a woman." I was born with a woman's body. So how do I arrange for a better life, for *paramārtha*? Idiocy, possessiveness, temptation and illusion, all these make a woman's company disastrous.' Says Bahiṇī, 'Thus is a woman's body deemed treacherous. How on earth can I aspire for a better goal?' (*Bahinābāīcā gāthā* 63)

Bahiṇābāī is all the more tormented since she does not want to follow the path of Bhakti in place of her social duties. She wants to have her cake and eat it too. She chooses not to abandon her husband or her family as many women Sants before her were forced to do. She calls out to God for help in this enterprise, and says, 'Hari, You alone are my friend, my brother. You are Pāṇḍu-raṅga, the resort of the weak. Arrange it so I can worship You and fulfill my duty as a good wife' (*Bahiṇābāīcā gāthā* 68). But even with God's help, it is not easy, and we find her recording her trials as an aspiring soul trapped in a woman's body:

'What sins have I committed in my past lives that I was abandoned by the Best Man, by God? I acquired birth as a human being, but with this female body. My untold sins must have ripened. I am not entitled to listen to the meaning of the Vedas, and the Brahmins have hidden the *Gāyatrī mantra* as well. I cannot utter the sound of *praṇava.* I cannot listen to the utterance of a *bīja mantra.* I cannot talk with another man, since my husband is as hot-tempered as Jamadagnī incarnate.' Bahinī says, 'My life is torture, but God takes no pity on me.' (*Bahiṇābāīcā gāthā* 64)

Finally, she reconciles herself to her lot as a woman by embracing the doctrine of *karma* and *prārabdha.* She says, 'Many miseries have I endured, my friend. I have been humiliated to the core. This misery is my lot. I incurred it in a previous life. This is how I try to console my mind. Even Brahmā and the others could not escape suffering their sorrows, and the rest are nobodies compared to them.' Bahiṇī says, 'Such is the fate of my body. I brought it on myself, so what can God do about it?' (*Bahiṇābāīcā gāthā* 70).

We see in these examples that a woman in the Marathi Sant tradition is at fault no matter which way she turns. Whether she defies the tradition or follows it faithfully, a woman is not free of blame. Why is this so? The answer lies in society's denial of free-will to a woman. A woman, married or unmarried, is to follow only the path her mentor dictates. If she has no husband and is an orphan like Janābāī, she may take to Bhakti, inspired by her master, but even her choice is not entirely free of obstacles. Not only does society accuse her and abuse her, but she also senses partiality even in God's graces. She feels that God has accepted Rājāī and Goṇāī quite wholeheartedly, but He is not as generous with her. She accuses God: 'Rājāī and Goṇāī get to stay always at Your feet, but You treat me as a lowly person and therefore keep me only at the door' (*SSG* 2: Janābāī 70). Perhaps it is in response to this complaint of Janābāī's that Chapter 21 of Mahīpati's *Bhaktavijaya* narrates a story in which God comes to her hut in secret in compensation for his lack of consideration. Nevertheless, an orphan like Janābāī somehow finds solace in God's Bhakti and gets over her handicap at being born a woman: 'One should not get despondent at being born as a woman. The Sants have showed a way out. I am a servant branded as one of the house of the Sants, so Viṭhobā has granted me an aspect of His love' (*SSG* 2: Janābāī 181). But if she is married, a woman has no other choice than that of following her husband. She is to follow only the path that he chooses for her. If he is a Sant, then she is not free to be a traditional housewife, as we saw in cases of Rājāī, and Āvalī; and if he is a traditional husband, and she chooses to be a Sant, as Bahiṇābāī did, then heaven help her.

PART TWO

When we turn from the portraits of these individual women to the sketches and caricatures of women in the Sants' poems, a similar fragmented pattern emerges. In general, the Sants praise women as mothers and revile them as temptresses. Nāmdev offers a very simplistic bilateral division of all women based on the virtue or vice (!) of their physical beauty. He says:

'The beautiful woman, the pretty woman, the desirable woman should be recognised as a sinner. When one sees her, the desire to be with her is strong, and that destroys the merit that a *bhakta* gains from chanting.' Nāmā says, 'One should not glance at her face, since such a bitch is a sinner, and she destroys a man as well.' (*SSG* 2: 1943)

'The ugly woman, of inferior body, is a woman to be congratulated as a mother. No one can ever be attracted to her, and thus she is no threat to one's worship. Such a matron is in fact kind and beneficial to a man as she does not destroy his *bhajan*.' Nāmā says, 'One should look at her face, regarding her as a mother, and bow at her feet.' (*SSG* 2: 1943, 1944)

Even though we understand that it is his urge to worship without distractions which prompts him to divide women in two such sweeping categories, it is difficult to accept his convoluted reasoning which transfers the blame for the weak aspirant's wavering mind to the beauty of the woman he beholds. In this manner of reasoning, the physical attributes of ugliness or beauty are somehow transformed into moral attributes of virtue and vice, or in even stronger terms, into merit and sin. This fateful division of women based on the effect of their existence on men permeates the psyche of the whole society, which then finds it easy to blame a woman for all the evils in the minds of men.

The temptress/nurturer dichotomy prevails throughout Sant literature, with many variations on the theme. Although Nāmdev the child-Sant brands all beautiful women as sinners and therefore deems them disastrous to the worship of a *bhakta*, Tukārām shows a mature Sant's response to the tempting beauty of women. Even the temptress can sometimes be transformed into a mother and cease being a temptress. The *gāthā* of Sant Tukārām records the story of a woman who approaches Tukārām in order to seduce him. Tukārām addresses her as 'mother' and thus distances her effectively. This is what he says to her:

'Any other woman is like the Goddess Rakhumāi to me. This is the eternal rule I follow. Go away, dear mother. Do not exert yourself; we, the servants of Viṣṇu are not of that type. I cannot bear to see you fall. Please don't say the wicked words.' Tukā says, 'If you want a mate, is there a lack of other men?' The formula practiced by the Sants at all times and prescribed to those who want to follow the path of Bhakti is: 'Treat women belonging to others as your mothers.' (*SSG* 2: 1941, *SSG* 4: 3785-6)

When is a woman regarded as a temptress? She does not have to be 'the other woman' or a prostitute; even a dutiful housewife, or a concerned mother can be seen as a temptress by a Sant because, as we saw in the life-story of Nāmdev, insofar as she cares for the Sant and binds him with worldly love, she proves to be an impediment to his path of unconditional worship. Here we notice a contradiction in the Sants' treatment of women. Although Nāmdev worships God in the form of mother and in general upholds mother's love as the ultimate selflesss love, he deserts his own mother in favour of God. Any woman can be regarded as a temptress and no woman is as motherly as God. Tukārām praises the selfless love of a mother (*SSG* 4: 2180), and sees both the Sants and God as mothers (*SSG* 4: 1994, 2058, 2096, 2180-1, 2183-5, 2197-8). In fact, a Sant is sometimes said to be better than a mundane mother, since a mother brings you into this world, whereas a Sant shows you the way to be rid of this world. When parents raise a child, they have a vested interest in him. God is always better than parents since God's love for a devotee has no strings attached.[14]

Further subdivisions are introduced into the above two-fold division. When the Sants regard a woman as a wife, they see her role as that of a devoted wife, *pativratā*, or a deceitful wife, *śindaḷī*, or *vyabhicāriṇī*. It is no surprise to find the Sants sympathetic to the devoted wife. On the whole, a deceitful woman, a *vyabhicāriṇī*, is censured and cursed to an afterlife in hell (*SSG* 4: 2336). She is said to destroy due to her misconduct both her father's family and the one into which she is married (*SSG* 4: 2338). The Sants have further used these two types of women as analogies for the Sant and for the householder. At one point, Nāmdev has effectively used the *vyabhicarī nārī* as a prescriptive model for the householder. He says that if you are engaged in mundane affairs, you must still concentrate on the Lord. You should behave like an adultress in her own household who all the while keeps the other man in mind (*SSG* 2: 1848). As steadfast *bhaktas* of God, the Sants regard themselves as *pativratās* or faithful women towards the Puruṣottama, the Best Man, God. When some deceitful householders criticize Tukārām for his outspokenness, he remarks, 'When an adultress hears praise for a faithful woman, she gets a headache. Our comments on the world are spontaneous. We do not ask others for permission to say what we say' (*SSG* 4: 2353).

Here is one curious point worthy of note. When the Sants preach general norms of morality to householders, they unequivocally curse a woman who cheats on her husband. However, the prostitute (*gaṇikā* or *kuṇṭaṇī*) is given different treatment in real life than in the literature of the Sants. Within the realm of Bhakti, the Sants were supportive of all outcastes, and anybody, however low his or her status in the society, was welcomed into their fold as long as he or she chose to embrace the path of true Bhakti. Consistent with this spirit, Sant Kānhopātrā, a prostitute who lived near Mangaḷveḍhe, is included in the list of Marathi Sants without any hesitation.[15] Perhaps, because the Sants recognise the helplessness of a prostitute in the male-dominated societal order, or perhaps, because they were using an inherited stock of traditional Vaiṣṇava stories, they cite the prostitute as an example of someone truly downtrodden yet deserving who is saved by the merciful God (*SSG* 2: 1218, 1220, 1228, 1316-17, 1323, etc. *SSG* 4: 306, 1812-13, 1826, 1871, etc.).

It is no wonder that the Sants praise the devoted wife as the paradigm of virtue, and often use her as a symbol of the *bhakta's* concentration on the Almighty Lord.[16] However, even a wife who does not hanker after another man may prove to be detrimental to her husband by making excessive demands on him. Tukārām presents many pictures of such women and warns people against them (*SSG* 4: 2327-32). A willful woman who makes her husband dance to her tune is despised by the Sants. She is caricatured as the worst kind of temptress. Her fault seems to lie in the fact that she not only severs a man from his own family, but she also makes him worship her rather than God, and thus deprives him of the chance to be enlightened. Correspondingly, a man who is under the thumb of his woman is ridiculed over and over again (*SSG* 4:

2327-8). He is like an insipid dog who eats without discretion, like a monkey on the rope of a street-player. He is a jackass as long as he lives and goes to hell after he dies. These pictures are quite consistent with the overall attitude of society which denies free will to women and considers a man as the prime candidate for enlightenment.

Unlike Nāmdev, who places the blame for an aspirant's failure squarely on the shoulders of women, Tukārām is usually fair to both sexes within the constraints of his society and his Bhakti. Whether male or female, if a person worships God, then that person is like God to him.[17] He ridicules both men and women who, deluded by *māyā*, misbehave (*SSG* 4: 2343-4). Somehow his pictures of misguided women are more vivid and full of humourous details than those of misguided men and hence are quoted and remembered by generations after him. For instance, one well-known sketch of a woman about to go to Panḍharpur on a pilgrimage has become so famous in Maharashtra that one of its lines, i.e. 'āvā nighālī panḍharapurā', is used as a proverb in Marathi to describe a person who cannot make up his mind about what is good for him. I offer a full translation of the *abhaṅga*:

> 'Listen, daughter-in-law, don't waste milk or curds.' Āvā started to go to Pandharpur, but she turned back from the town's boundary and came home again. 'Daughter, pay attention to what I say. Look after the chipped half of the grinding stone. The *kaḷavaḍu* (a drinking pot) that I always use—don't break it in my absence. The curds are set solid; don't disturb them without me. This mortar, this pestle, this grinding stone, this is where my mind hovers. When beggars come to the door, tell them that I have gone to Pandharpur. Eat in moderation. Don't waste.' The daughter-in-law said, 'Very well, you proceed on your pilgrimage and be happy. Mother, you look after your own merit and leave all such desires behind.' When she heard this speech of her daughter-in-law, the mother-in-law was doubtful. She thought, 'The witch is putting on an act. She wants me to vanish. Why should I go on a pilgrimage? What will I see there? Children, grandchildren, the home and the yard: this is where my Pandharpur lies.' Tukā says, 'Thus are the people engulfed in Māyā.' (*SSG* 4: 2343)

Tukārām is a great social commentator. He is extremely critical of anyone who sells his daughters, his cows, or his *kathā*, God's praise in the form of a story (*SSG* 4: 2316). The nouns he uses for all these, *kanyā, go,* and *kathā*, are feminine in Marathi. Although society condones the practise of taking two wives, he does not and yet many Sants such as Tukārām himself and Gorā Kumbhār are said to have had two wives (*SSG* 4: 2333). This discrepancy between what he practices and what he preaches might not indicate hypocrisy on the part of Tukārām, as it may seem to on the surface. Rather, it perhaps points to an evil in society to which he himself had fallen victim at the wishes of his elders. All kinds of mismatched couples are described by Tukārām with equal criticism. Just as he notices the helplessness of a man whose wife is infertile, he talks about the plight of a woman who is married to an impotent man (*SSG* 4: 2782). He has no sympathy, however, for the infertile woman who wraps rags around her belly and pretends to be pregnant. That is hypocrisy, pure and simple, according to him. Tukārām depicts the miseries of a man sandwiched between two wives (*SSG* 4: 2333), and shows awareness of the pain women suffer as a result of the cruel marriage practices prevalent in his society. Since girls were married off by their elders, sometimes even before they were born, and often to over-ripe husbands twice their age, women were subjected to mismatches of all types. Here are two such sorry friends as seen and described by Tukārām:

> Two friends. One has a boyish husband, the other is married to a widower. It is the perpetual tale of this world.
>
> 'My husband is so young, he constantly runs away to play with the kids. He spends the whole evening playing and stays outside the house while I wait for him in bed. I don't have enough merit accumulated in my past lives. How can I describe my sorrow?'
>
> 'Friend, you want to hear about my misery? The old man coughs all the time. If I take the initiative and go near him, he won't let me touch him. He is too tired.'
>
> Tukā says, 'Women, this is how your karma rewards you. Why do you blame God?' (*SSG* 4: 4405)

Of course, since Tukārām concludes that women have themselves to blame for their misfortune in this life, he does not feel the need to challenge society on their behalf. His answer to all such miseries of this life would be to discard the passion which ties one to this miserable world and to immerse the mind in Bhakti of God.[18] That is what he did when he was troubled by the miseries of this world. But we saw earlier how that choice was not open to married women unless their husbands also became *bhaktas* with them and abandoned everything in this world. Therefore, all these miserable women whom we witness in the Sants' poems and who influenced their lives remain rooted in their respective miseries.

Conclusion

The condition of women in the Marathi Sant tradition can be summed up in the words of Bahiṇābāī. As a disciple of Sant Tukārām, she too believed that her lot in this life as a woman was a result of her sins in her past lives, her *prārabdha*, and that she had to endure all her trials patiently. However, as his true disciple, she also wanted to follow the path of Bhakti as he did. As we saw above, that was not so easy. Tukārām's advice to his wife to follow the path of Bhakti became celebrated in the tradition, and was quoted by others like Mahīpati as exemplary. In contrast, Bahiṇābāī could not give advice to her husband that he would be able to accept, let alone that he and others would praise in her lifetime and, as a result, had to endure a split personality all her life. She has crystallised her hard-earned lifelong wisdom in the following two lines: 'A woman's body is a body controlled by someone else. Therefore, the path of renunciation is not open to her.'[19] I submit that as we look at the various lives of individual and archetypal women, married, unmarried, widowed or orphaned in the long Sant tradition, the only truth that emerges is that 'a woman's body is a body controlled by someone else, and therefore, no path is open to her without permission of another'.

NOTES

1. bāila melī, mukta jhāl' / deveṁ māyā soḍavilī // poreṁ melīṁ, bareṁ jhāleṁ / deveṁ māyāvirahita keleṁ // *SSG* 4: 65
2. upajalāsī taiṁ maja jālā santoṣa / ānanda ullāsa vāṭe jīvā // gaṇa gotā mājī kele bāre nāva / panḍharīcā deva prasanna kelā // *SSG* 2: 37
3. are nāmadevā navhesī lekarū / *SSG* 2: 31
4. tujahūna loka āhetī ājñāna / na visaṁbatī kṣaṇa māyabāpā // *SSG* 2: 30
5. kaisī tujhī bhaktī laukikāvegaḷī / sasārācī hoḷī kelī nāmyā // *SSG* 2: 29
6. sāṇḍī devapiseṁ karū nako aiseṁ / baḷeṁ ghara kaiseṁ buḍavīsī // *SSG* 2: 28
7. tuja kāya uṇeṁ brahmāṇḍa nāyakā / navhesī maja sārikhā ekadesī // *SSG* 2: 48
8. goṇāī mhaṇe devā hoī kāṁ śahāṇā / vāṁyāṁ kāṁ paradhanā dharisī lobha // *SSG* 2: 38
9. tujhe dvārī baisonī upavāsa karīna / nāmā gheuna jāīna guṇa rāśī // *SSG* 2: 62

10. nāmā mhaṇe śaraṇa ālorṁ jicyā bheṇeṁ / tice hātī deṇe ucita navhe // *SSG* 2: 68
11. This fact is corroborated by Janābāī in one of her *abhaṅgas* (*SSG* 2: Janābāī 137).
12. For example, the two wives of Gorā, the potter, in Mahīpatī's *Bhaktavijaya*, Chapter 17.
13. Kunti's speech in the *Bhāgavatapurāṇa* 1: 8-25: vipadaḥ santu naḥ śaśvat tatra tatra jagadguro/bhavato darśanam yatsyād apunarbhavadarṣanam//
14. māyabāpeṁ sāṁbhāḷitī / lobhākāraṇeṁ pāḷitī // taisā navhe devarāva/ yācā kṛpāḷū svabhāva // *SSG* 4: 3007
15. Mahīpati's *Bhaktavijaya* allots her the entire chapter 39.
16. *SSG* 4: 415; pativrate jaisā bhratāra pramāṇa / āmhāṁ nārāyaṇa taiśā par // *SSG* 4: 416
17. ho kāṁ nara athavā nārī / jyāñcā āvaḍatā hari // te maja viṭhobā samāna / *SSG* 4: 2129
18. prapañcācā chanda ākhniyāṁ govā / dharāveṁ keṣavā hṛdayāñta // *SSG* 4: 2349
19. striyece ṣarīra parādhīna deha / ne cāle ūpāva viraktīcā // Bahiṇābāīcā gāthā : 60

REFERENCES

Bahiṇābāī. *Bahiṇābāīcā gāthā*. 2nd ed. Pune: Citrashala Prakashan, 1956.

Bhāgavatapurāṇa. 9th ed. Bombay: Nirnayasagara Press, 1950.

Dhere, R.C., ed. *Sakala santa gāthā* (*gāthā pañcaka*). 5 Vols. Pune: Varada Books, 1985 (1908).

Gold, Ann Grodzins. *A Carnival of Parting: The Tales of King Bharthari and King Gopi Chand as Sung and Told By Madhu Natisar Nath of Ghadiyali, Rajasthan*. Berkeley: University of California Press, 1992.

Inamdar, Hemant Vishnu. *Santa Nāmadeva (Nāmdev: The Saint-poet of Maharashtra)*. Pune: Kesari Prakashan, 1970.

Mahīpati. *Bhaktavijaya*. Ed. S.R. Devale. Pune: Sharada Prakashan, 1989.

Schomer, Karine and McLeod, W.H., eds. *The Sants: Studies in a Devotional Tradition in India*. New Delhi: Motilal Banarsidass, 1987.

Sheorye, Indumati. *'Santa Kavayitrī'* in *Strī muktīcyā Mahārāṣṭātīla pāulakhuṇā* by Tata Institute of Social Sciences. Bombay: Popular Prakashan, 1989.

Tukārām. *Śrī Tukarāma bāvāncyā abhangāñcī gāthā*. Ed. P.M. Lad. Bombay: Government Central Press, 1955 (1950).

Zelliot, Eleanor and Berntsen, Maxine, eds. *The Experience of Hinduism: Essays on Religion in Maharashtra*. Albany, N.Y.: State University of New York Press, 1988.

The *Cūdaḍī* Type of Songs in the Oral and Written Traditions of Northern India

H.C. BHAYANI

The word *cūdaḍī,* variously spelt in Gujarati, Rajasthani, Hindi, etc., as *cūdaḍaī, cūnarī,* etc., commonly refers to a costly fine *sārī,* dyed deep red to shades of saffron, with a spotted design. It has always been prized and coveted by women who wear them on ceremonial, festive or auspicious occasions.[1] Many lyrical songs in Rajasthani and Gujarati oral (as well as medieval written) traditions describe and praise the *cūdaḍī* (see M.R. Majumdar 1954, pp. 364-429; A. Nahta 1962; N. Rajyaguru 1993, p. 67). They depict its beauty and employ the form of a wife's pressing request to her husband to purchase a *cūdaḍī* of a famous variety for her. But both these traditions put the theme equally to metaphorical, allegorical, or symbolic use.[2] In the terms of the *alaṅkāra* theory, the *rūpaka* (metaphor) may be *niraṅga* (straight), *sāṅga* (extensive) or even *ekadeśavivartin* or *samastavastuviṣaya* (a full-fledged, completely worked out allegory).[3] Shyam Parmar (1961, pp. 67-89) recorded such a metaphorical *cūdaḍī* song from the Malvi-Nimadi elegiac songs belonging to oral tradition. Similarly, *cūdaḍī* songs with the *nāma-mudrā* of *bhakta* poets like Mūldās, Morār, Mīrābāī, Dayānand-Svāmī, or Amrabāī are currently sung as *bhajans* in the oral tradition of Gujarat, such as Mīrābāī's popular *pad*: 'Ho syāma piyā morī raṁga de cūnarīya'. Some *cūdaḍī pads* are attributed to Kabīr (H.P. Dvivedi 1970, pp. 247, 259, 260; *Kabīr racnāvalī* nos. 166, 167, 172):

Kauṇa raṁgarejavā raṁgai mor cūdarī,
Naihar mẽ dāga lagāya aī cunarī,
Bhījata cunariyā prema-rase būdana,
Morī cūnarī mẽ parī gayo dāga piyā.

We know of the manuscript of a medieval Gujarati Jain poem entitled *Cuṁdaḍi-ḍhāla* (dated VS 1839/AD 1783) by Āśakaraṇa, and in the *c.* mid-eighteenth century *Cauvīśī* of Mohanavijaya, the first line of a popular song is quoted as 'Cūnaḍī to bhīje ho sāhibā' (M.D. Desai 1944, vol. 3, p. 1897).

A thirteenth century cūdaḍī

The publication, however, of an Apabhraṃśa poem, a few years back, pushes the date of the first occurrence of a *cūdaḍī* back to the thirteenth century AD. The poem entitled *Cūnaḍiyā*, written by Muni Vinayacandra, a disciple of Udayamuni of the Mathura-saṃgha of the Digambara Jain sect, and edited by Bhamvarlal Polyaka on the basis of a single manuscript belonging to the collection of the Jainvidya Sansthan of Digambar Jain Atishay Kshetra Shri Mahavirji in Rajasthan, was first published in the 1984 issue of the half-yearly *Jainvidyā* and later separately as a booklet. It consists of thirty-three six-line stanzas. The language seems to be late Apabhraṃśa somewhat modernized. The manuscript obviously contains numerous scribal mistakes. And the printed text is equally unsatisfactory on different accounts, and several passages are wrongly translated.[4] In spite of all these shortcomings, the publication is valuable because it establishes the fact that the ancestry of the *cūdaḍī* type goes back to the late Apabhraṃśa period. The *Cūnaḍiyā* presupposes non-Jain models, and possibly folk songs, with the same theme and mode of treatment. The original form of the word was *cunnaḍiya* (or *cuṇṇaḍiya*) which became modernized to *cūnaḍīya/cūnaḍīyā*.

Actually, the present poem *Cūnaḍiyā* has as its subject a real *cūnaḍī* to be produced by a real dyer for a real lady to wear. As such it is not a metaphorical poem, not of the type we find in the poems of Kabīr, Mīrā and other poets (as quoted earlier). The difference, however, from the usual *cūnaḍiyā*, consists in the fact that instead of the usual design of the spots, flowers, birds, etc., the *nāyikā* of the poem wants a *cūdaḍī* printed with all the tenets, beliefs and practices of Jain religion and philosophy, and therefore the poem deals with the principles, tenets, dogmas, beliefs and practices of Jainism, with its cosmography, mythology, and the observances prescribed for the ascetic and the layman (vv. 5 to 30). The *nāyikā* requests her husband to get such a *cūdaḍī* printed and to present it to her, so that she could go to worship at a Jina temple (v. 4.7) wearing it. The husband has the *cūdaḍī* prepared, and the *nāyikā* puts it on and goes home (v. 3.3-4).[5]

On the metrical structure of the Cūnaḍiyā

The metrical form of the *Cūnaḍiyā* is interesting. The poem has thirty-three stanzas, each containing six lines followed by a refrain. After stanza 33, there is an extra line which is obviously a later interpolation (it unnecessarily repeats what is already expressed in the fifth line of the stanza). The metre is a *ṣaṭpadī* with six lines each composed of two halves. The *mātrā* structure of the six lines is: 16, 16, 14, 16, 13, 16. The lines a, b, d, and f have 16 *mātrās* divisible as 6 + 4 + 4 + ∪∪/—; the lines c, e, and the refrain have 13 *mātrās* divisible as 6 + 4 + ∪∪∪; line *a* rhymes with line *b*, line *d* rhymes with line *f*. The *gaṇ* scheme of the 16-moraic *pād* is the same as that of the *Vadanak pād* and that of the 13-moraic *pād* is the same as that of the odd *pāds* of the *dohā* (see H.C. Bhayani 1953, introduction, pp. 87 and 96).

In Apabhraṃśa verse texts the metrical form is well regulated. The rules are usually strictly observed. Hence the scribal changes, orthographical and others, which we find invariably in the manuscripts can be detected and restored with little difficulty. The poems were sung to some popular melody. In songs the short final syllable of a line could be lengthened as required. In the manuscripts, these short final syllables were generally written as short but sometimes as long (final *ū* as *o*). In our text as a rule it is written short. The exceptions are *cūnaḍīyā* (v.1.5; 4.5), *jimā* (v. 2.3), *maho* (v. 3.5), *juyā* (v. 5.3), *guṇā* (v. 6.3; 1.3), *tiyā* (v. 9.5), *ṇayā* (v. 13.3), *sayā* (v. 13.5), *dijjaī* (v. 15.2), *maṇā* (v. 15.3).

In this connection we may note that the metre of the first section of the *Bharahesara-bāhubali-ghora* of Vajrasena-sūri (*c.* AD 1166) and that of the first section of the *Bharateśvara-bāhubali-rāsa* of Śālibhadra-sūri (AD 1185), the two earliest known poems in old Gujarati, are a *tripadī* with the same metrical structure as that of the first half of the meter of the *Cūnaḍiyā*.[6]

Concerning the word cūdaḍī

The meaning of the word *cūdaḍī* (Raj. H. *cūnrī, cunnī,* etc.), i.e. the type of garment it stands for, its social function and symbolic significance, have all varied considerably over the centuries, and also regionally. The variations relate to the material and texture, colour, design, process of production, as well as the customary ceremonial and auspicious occasions for wearing it, and the class of the wearer.

The word is used in slightly varied forms in Rajasthani (*cunaḍī, cūnaḍī, cūnaḍī, cūunaḍī, cunaḍ, cūdaḍī*), in Gujarati (*cūdaḍī*), in Hindi (*cunaḍī, cunarī, cūdaḍī, cunnī*), in Panjabi (*cunarī, cunanī*), in Nepali (*cunarī, cūndarī*), and in Sindhi (*cunī*). Originally, it seems it was a silken *sārī*, dyed red or deep saffron, with a spotted design prepared either by means of the tie-and-dye process (i.e. the *paṭṭadūkula* or *paṭolā* type), or block-printed with a leaf and flower design, with birds (like the peacock, swan, etc.) on the border and in the corners. Later on all this changed. The garment that is produced by the tie and dye process is called *bāndhaṇī* in Gujarati.

The *cūdaḍī* is customarily not to be worn by widows. It was worn on auspicious, ceremonial, or festive occasions. Different customs prevailed, or prevail at present, in the different northern regions and castes. For example, in some Baniyā castes of present-day Gujarat, the *cūdaḍī* is ceremonially put on the fiancée by the ladies from the side of the fiancé to symbolize that the betrothal is fixed. In Rajasthan the *cūnarī* is ceremonially put on the bride by her maternal uncle prior to the nuptial ceremony of hand-taking in the marriage pandal, and relevant conventional wedding songs are sung on that occasion.

In the poem *Cūnaḍiyā* discussed in the present paper, the designs are to be 'written' (*lihāvahi* v. 1, *lihivi* v. 31, *lihahi* vv. 15, 17, *lihi* vv. 19, 22, 27, etc., *lihāvaṇa* v. 5), i.e. drawn or 'printed' on the cloth (*chiṁpāvahi* v. 4) with a painter's brush (*lehiṇī* v. 15) by the dyer or colour-printer (*chiṁpulada* v. 5). Pk. *chiṁpaya* 'a dyer' is recorded in the *Deśīnāmamālā* (ed. R. Pischel 1938, 1, 98), and in the *Pāialacchīnāma-mālā* (ed. B.J. Doshi 1960, 236/770); *chiṁpā* is recorded in the *Deśīśabdakośa* (ed. M. Dulaharaj 1988, p. 184) from Pk. literature. Note also H. *chipnā* 'to print on calico', *chīpī* 'dyer', 'cloth-printer', G. *chīpo* with the same meaning, and M. *śimpī* (R.L. Turner 1966, no. 4994), etc.

From Prakrit literary and lexicographical sources we gather that the terms *navaraṁgaya-* (*navaraṁga*)-(n.), *raggaya-*(n.) and *ghaṭṭa-*(m.) were synonymous. In Hāla's *Gāhākosa* dating from the early centuries of the Christian Era, a peasant woman is described as proudly displaying the much-coveted *navaraṁgaya* (v. no. 241). In another verse (no. 328), a young girl in love is described as going about presenting sweets to the neighbours and relatives on a festive occasion, wearing the *navaraṁgaya*. In a third verse (no. 461) a wanton woman is said to have carelessly left her *navaraṁgaya* on a tree at her tryst after making love with her lover. Etymologically *navaraṁgaya* means 'newly dyed [cloth]'. But it came to mean a 'costly upper garment, i.e. a *sārī* dyed in Indian madder and worn by women (especially rustic women) on auspicious or festive occasions' (Bhuvanapāla on no. 461, i.e. GS 462; Haripāla on *Gauḍavaho* v. 598).

Raggaya also is explained as referring to a garment dyed in Indian madder (Haripāla on *Gauḍavaho* [ed. N.G. Suru 1975], v. 402; Hemacandra on *Deśīnāmamālā* [ed R. Pischel 1938], 7. 3) and is given as synonymous with *navaraṁga-* (*Pāilachhīnāmamālā* [ed. B.J. Doshi 1960], 915).[7] Etymologically *ragga-* is given as equivalent to *rakta-* 'dyed' (*Siddhahema,* 8. 2. 10). Actually, it is the analogically formed past passive participle of *raṁjai* 'colours, dyes (red)', on the model of *bhaṁjai* = *bhagga.* It became specialized in the sense of 'a woman's upper garment freshly dyed in Indian madder'.

In *Deśīnāmamālā* (ed. R. Pischel 1938, 7. 3), *raggaya-* is noted with the meaning *ghaṭṭa-* which in the commentary (and independently at 2. 111) is said to have the meaning of a red garment dyed in Indian madder; *kausumbha-vastram, kausumbha-rakta-vastram.* The word *ghaṭṭaṁsua-* occurs in Hemacandra's *Kumārapālacarita* (5. 79). The verse describes the orange trees with oranges as the *ghaṭṭaṁsuas* worn by the sylvan beauty. The commentator Pūrṇakalaśagaṇi explains *ghaṭṭaṁsua* as garments dyed in Indian madder and having small, pot-shaped cloth cut-outs decoratively sewn on the borders. Gujarati has *ghāṭ* 'a costly silken *sārī* worn on special occasion', and *ghāṭḍī* = *cūdaḍī.*

The earliest form of the word occurring in the poem *Cūnaḍiyā* discussed here is *cūṇiyā* (v. 31) and *cūnaḍīya* (vv. 1, 3, 4, 33). Most probably these are comparatively late variants of the original *cunniya* and *cūṇṇaḍiya* respectively. And this can be supported by the occurrence of the word *cuṇṇī* which I unexpectedly came across in an Apabhraṃśa text probably datable to the twelfth century AD. In the *Harivaṃśapurāṇa,* the huge epic of Dhavala, a Digambara Jain poet, a passage describes cowherd women who, wearing festive costumes come to Nanda's house to celebrate Kṛṣṇa's birth; some of them are said to wear *cuṇṇīs* with floral designs.

> kāsu-vi sīse liṁja dharālī,
> kāsu-vi cunni phullaḍiālī.
>
> (*Sandhi* 53, *Kaḍavaka* 17) (see H.C. Bhayani 1979, p. 171)

The work has not been published as yet. The NIA forms are

derivable from *cuṇṇī* and *cuṇṇaḍiya.* The forms with *d* resulted from the phonological process of the interpolation of a voiced stop homo-organic to the nasal that precedes a trill (cf., e.g. Pk. *pannarasa,* H. *paṁdrah,* G. *paṁdar,* etc.; Prakrit *vannara,* H. *baṁdar,* G. *vā̃dar,* etc.). It is not clear whether Apabhraṃśa *cuṇṇīya* derives from *cuṇṇ-* 'to pucker' (compare H. *cunnā,* etc.) or 'to select, pluck' (see R.L. Turner 1931 under *Cunnu*).

Conclusion

Leaving aside the Classical period, throughout the Middle Ages (i.e. until pre-modern times), there has been a continuous give and take between written and the orally transmitted texts. This was quite natural in a society with a low rate of literacy in all Indian languages. We know of long poems (including whole epics) incorporating the narratives of the *Mahābhārata,* the *Rāmāyaṇa,* the tenth book of the *Bhāgavatapurāṇa* and numerous Purāṇic *ākhyānas* and folktales that are preserved in writing as well as in oral tradition. The *cūdaḍī* songs are another instance.[8]

In this context one may recall that medieval written texts as well as the current oral types of devotional poems frequently put an object, a customary activity, or an event in the world of everyday life to metaphorical if not allegorical use. Thus, songs of the Sant *bhakta* traditions by poets like Kabīr and Mīrābāī, as well as metaphorical or allegorical orally transmitted texts made (and continue to make) use of terms like *pyālo* (bowl), *kaṭārī* (dagger), *hoko* (hukkah), *nīsaraṇī* (ladder), *carakho/rẽṭiyo* (spinning wheel), *baṁsarī/moralī* (flute), *jhālarī* (gong), *taṁburo* (drone), *khaṁjarī* (a type of percussion), *cādar* (sheet), *paṭoḷī* (a costly silken *sārī* the threads of which are dyed through a tie-and-dye process before being woven), *cūdaḍī, mā̃ḍavo* (marriage pandal), *vivāh* (wedding), *hāṭaḍī* (shop), *vaṇajāro* (trader leading a caravan), *vāniyo* (merchant), *naṭavo/ bajāṇiyo* (rope-dancer, bamboo-dancer), *khel* (drama show), *ā̃bo* (mango tree), *khetī* (farming), *varasād* (rains), *vāhaṇ* (ship), *devaḷ* (temple), *baṁgalo* (bungalow), *haṁsalo* (swan), *moralo* (peacock), etc.

NOTES

I am very grateful to Professor Dr. (Mrs.) F. Mallison for suggesting some useful changes which I have incorporated in this final version.

1. See above, '*concerning the word* cūdaḍī' for a detailed discussion of the various types and functions of the *cūdaḍī* as well as of the meanings of the word.
2. It is a well-known fact that there is a solidly established literary tradition of major and minor allegorical works of poetry, fiction, and drama on this theme in more or less all the Indian languages.
3. M.R. Majumdar 1954, pp. 364-429; A. Nahtā 1962; N. Rajyaguru 1993, p. 67.
4. Here are a few samples of the changed orthography:
   1. *n* instead of *ṇ*: *dinayara* (v. 1.1), *vakhānu* (v. 3.6);
   2. Sanskritization: *svāmī* (v. 1.3), *sārada* (v. 2.21), *māthura* (v. 3.1), *sundrara* (v. 4.3);
   3. Simplification of a cluster with lengthening of the preceding vowel: *sāmuhu* (v. 2.5), *dūgamu* (v. 3.4), *volai* (for *vollai*) (v. 4.2), *lājahu* (v. 3.5), *saṁpūṇī* (v. 33.2), *cūnaḍīya* (v. 1.5; 4.5), *cūṇaḍīya* (v. 3.6), *cunaḍīya* (for *cūṇṇaḍiya*) (v. 33.1), *cūṇiya* (for *cuṇṇiya*) (v. 31.4), *rākheveṁ* (for *rakkhevaiṁ*) (v. 13.6);
   4. Wrong nasalization: *pabhaṇaiṁ* (v. 1.6), *sarasauṁ* (v. 2.6), *laiṁ* (v. 15.1);
   5. Omission of the mark of nasalization: *hau* (v. 4.6), *kālai* (v. 7.1);
   6. Simple consonant for a cluster: *tiṇi* (v. 5.3), *uḍhatteṁ* (v.5.4), *pariṭhiya* (v. 6.2), *aja milecha* (v. 6.4);
   7. Miscellaneous: *daṁti* (for *daṁta*) (v. 4.1), *viṇai* (for *viṇaya*) (v. 3.3), *sarasaiṁ* (for *sarāsai*) (v. 2.6), *thiū* (for *ṭhiu*) (v. 14.4), *āyaū* (for *āyau*) (v. 32.2), *vaḍḍha* (for *vaḍha*) (v. 15.2), *rākheveṁ* (for *rākhevaiṁ*) (v. 13.6).

   Editorial errors: Wrongly split stems and endings and compound words: *jambūdīva ho* (v. 6.1), *lihi vi* (v. 31.3); many a compound is wrongly separated.

   Misprints: *guṇatilaḍa* (for **au*) (v. 1.2), *sivayuri* (for **puri*) (v. 33.4), *lahara* (for *lahai*) (v. 33.4). These lists are incomplete. The text needs re-editing.
5. The line as it stands in the printed text, is out of order, metrically as well as grammatically. The textual confusion has obscured the meaning.
6. It is noteworthy that the editor of the *Cūnaḍiyā* has given at the end of the text the musical notation for the refrain and the first two lines in accordance with the popular melody to which the Rajasthani folksong 'Dhaṇa ne maṁgāyā dijyo pomaciyo pyārā' is traditionally sung at present.
7. Another synonymous word, *sulasa*, is also recorded by the *Deśīnamamālā* (8.37) with the sense of 'cloth dyed in Indian madder'.
8. The Apabhraṃśa Academy of Jaipur, which has brought out the *Cūnaḍiyā*, can also take credit for publishing another text, viz., the

Buddhirasāyaṇa or *Oṇamacaritu* (*Rāmaṇa-caritu*), which is the earliest *Rāvaṇa-mandodarī-saṁvāda* that has come to light in the New Indo-Aryan regional literatures. See H.C. Bhayani, 1992, introduction, pp. 9-10; texts, pp. 87-91.

REFERENCES

Bhayani, H.C. 'Apabhraṁśa sāhitya meṁ Kṛṣṇa-kāvya'. In *Bhāratīya bhāṣaoṁ-meṁ Kṛṣṇa-kāvya,* ed. Bhagiratha Mishra. Part I, pp. 138-78. Bhopal: Madhya Pradesh Sahitya Parishad, 1979.

———. 'Bharahesara-bāhubali-ghora'. In *Prācīn Gūrjar kāvya sañcay,* ed. H.C. Bhayani and A.C. Nahta, pp. 15-18. Ahmedabad: L.D. Institute of Indology, 1975

———, ed. *Kṛṣṇa-bāḷacaritra* of Kīku Vasahī. Bombay: Forbes Gujarati Sabha, 1992.

———, ed. *Paumcariu.* Part I. Bombay: Singhi Jain Shastra Sikshapith, Bharatiya Vidya Bhavan, 1953.

Desai, M.D., ed. *Jain Gūrjāra kavio.* Vol. 3. Bombay: Sri Jain Svetambar Conference Office, 1944.

Doshi, B.J., ed. *Pailachhīnāmamālā,* Bombay: 1960.

Dulaharaj, Muni, ed. *Deśīśabdakośa.* Ladnun (Rajasthan): Jain Vishva Bharati, 1988.

Dvivedi, H.P., ed. *Kabīr.* 6th reprint. Delhi: Rajkamal Prakashan, 1970.

Jinavijaya, Muni, ed. *Bharateśvara-bāhubali-rāsa.* Bombay: Bharatiya Vidya Bhavan, 1940.

Lalas, Sitaram, ed. *Rājasthānī sabad kos.* Jodhpur: Rajasthani Shodh Sansthan, 1961-78.

Majumdar, M.R. *Gujarātī sahitya-nā svarūpo.* Vadodara: Acharya Book Depot, 1954.

Nahta, Agarchand. *Prācīn bhāṣā-kavyoṁ-kī rūp-paraṁparā.* Bikaner: Bharatiya Vidya Mandir Shodh Pratisthan, 1962.

Parmar, Shyam, 'Saṁtoṁ-kī rahasyonmukhī pravṛttioṁ-kā lokjīvan par prabhāv'. In *Sammelan-Patrikā* 46.4 (1961): 67-89.

Patwardhan, M.V., ed. *Gāhākosa.* Ahmedabad: Prakrit Granth Parishad, 1980.

Pischel, R., ed. *Deśīnāmamālā.* 2nd ed. revised by P. Ramanujaswami. Bombay: Dept. of Public Instruction, 1938.

Polyaka, B.L., ed. *Cūnaḍiyā.* Rajasthan: Digambar Jain Atishay Kshetra Sri Mahavirji, 1984.

Rajyaguru, N. 'Cetana-vara-ni cūṁdaḍī'. *Phārbas Gujarātī Traimāsik* 58.2 (1993): 67-73.

Sheth, H., ed. *Pāiasaddamahaṇṇavo: A Comprehensive Prakrit-Hindi Dictionary with Sanskrit Equivalents and Complete References.* Reprint. Prakrit Text Series 7. Varanasi: Prakrit Text Society, 1963.

Suru, N.G., ed. *Gauḍavaho.* Ahmedabad: Prakrit Text Society, 1975.

Turner, R.L. *A Comparative Dictionary of Indo-Aryan Languages.* London: Oxford University Press, 1966.

———. *A Comparative and Etymological Dictionary of the Nepali Language.* London: Routledge, 1931.

Vaidya, P.L., ed. *Prakrit Grammar of Hemacandra.* Poona: Bhandarkar Oriental Institute, 1958.

Weber, A., ed. *Ueber das Saptaçatakam des Hāla.* Abhandlungen für die Kunde des Morgenlandes 7.4. Leipzig: E.A. Brockhaus, 1881.

Early Sant Tradition and Sufism in Medieval India

NETTY C. BONOUVRIÉ

Scholars studying texts of the Sant tradition have regularly pointed to similarities between this tradition and Sufism. Some of them have ascribed those similarities to Sufī influences on the Sant tradition; however, none of these studies has given evidence for such an influence.

In this paper I would like to inform you of my own research on the relation between the Sant tradition and Sufism, which is the subject of my Ph.D. thesis. I have decided to analyse and compare the three constituent parts of the Sant path with their Sufī equivalents, making use of Sant and Sufī texts and studying them from a religious-historical point of view. The three constituent parts of the Sant path as they have been mentioned by Ch. Vaudeville (1987, p. 31) are (1) importance and position of the spiritual guide (*guru*), (2) the practice of prayer (*nāmsumiran*), and (3) the importance of the religious community (*satsaṅga*). If my research achieves its goal, I hope it will not only give a better understanding of the Sant tradition and Indian Sufism, but it will also contribute to a better understanding of interaction between the religious traditions.

This paper starts with a short survey of the different opinions concerning the relation between the two religious traditions. The main part of the paper consists of an analysis and a comparison of one of the three parts of the Sant path, viz., *nāmsumiran*, with the *dhikr* of Sufīs. This will finally lead to a discussion of the relation between the Sant tradition and Sufism.

Different opinions

From the thirteenth century onwards Sufism came to be firmly established in the northern part of the Indian subcontinent, mainly by means of the various *ṭarīqas* (brotherhoods). Two centuries later, northern India was immersed by the teachings of Bhakti. When, in the present century, scholars started studying the various Bhakti *saṃpradāys*, the presence of Islam, particularly Sufism, and the possible influences from it on the flourishing of these *saṃpradāys,* also became objects of their interest. F. Mujtabai (1978, pp. 92-110), for example, has pointed out the many similarities between Sufism and Indian Bhakti on the philosophical, devotional and popular level. According to him, similarities exist between the doctrines of *advaita* (non-dualism) and *waḥdat al-wujūd* (unity of being). Both traditions stress the equality of all people, and reject the caste-system.

With regard to the relation between Sufī Islam and the Sant tradition, it is not surprising that most information has been provided by scholars studying Kabīr. Remarkably, scholars hold almost opposite opinions with regard to this relation, as the following examples will make clear. According to P.N. Ojha (1978, pp. 1-39), Kabīr was deeply influenced by Sufī thought. Tara Chand (1954, pp. 143-65) holds that Kabīr's verses were shaped by the language and expressions used by Sufī saints and poets; he has also pointed out the close resemblance between the importance of the guru, and his position in the Sant tradition and that of the *shaykh/pīr* in Sufī *ṭarīqas.* S.H. Sharda (1974, pp. 212-49), on the other hand, has totally rejected any influence of Sufism on the Sant tradition. In her excellent study on Kabīr, Ch. Vaudeville (1974, p. 85) remarked that 'as the Sufī preaching had spread all over northern India in Kabīr's time, Sufī mysticism had impregnated the whole composite culture of that time. Kabīr's own religious ideas and representations could not but be somewhat influenced by Sufī thoughts and imagery, as suggested by many of his sayings'. M. Thiel-Horstmann, in her study on Dādū (1991, p. 4), has written that Bhakti has profited from Sufism, as both were working in the mixed Hindu-Muslim milieus. Both Kabīr and Dādū are believed to have belonged to castes that were converted to Islam. However, none of these studies has mentioned in which respect and to what extent the Sants in general, or Kabīr and Dādū in particular, were influenced by Sufism. The only study exclusively dealing with the relation of Sants and Sufīs is, as far as I know, an article by B.B. Lawrence (1987, pp. 359-73). Although Lawrence thinks that Sufism did not have much influence on the Sant tradition, he mentions three points of indirect influence, viz., (1) reference to Sufīs in Sant literature, (2) the use of technical Sufī terms, and (3) thematic innovations closely resembling Sufī themes, like *jap-dhikr, virah-dard,* and *prem-'ishq.*

Analysis of the Sufīs' dhikr

As many non-Indian Sufī texts were well known and used in India,[1] I will first deal with the practice of *dhikr* within Sufism in general. *Dhikr* is an Arabic word meaning 'remembrance', 'mention', and is used by Sufīs to denote a particular kind of prayer, often involving the name of God. In this paper the term *dhikr* is used as 'remembrance of God'. Studies of texts ascribed to early Sufīs make it clear that the practice of *dhikr* was well known within Sufism quite early. Sahl at-Tustarī (d. 896; R.A. Nicholson 1911, part 1, p. 259), for example, is believed to have answered the question of one of his disciples 'O master, what is the food?' with the words 'the recollection of God Immortal.' It has been also related (R.A. Nicholson 1911, part 1, p. 195) that he summoned his disciples to remember God continuously with the words 'O Allah! 'O Allah! 'O Allah!'. At-Tustarī and many other Sufīs and their opinions are mentioned in the text *Kitāb at-ta'arruf* ascribed to al-Kalābādhī (d. 995). In the chapter on recollection, al-Kalābādhī (A.J. Arberry [tr.] 1977, p. 95) introduces this subject saying, 'Real recollection consists in forgetting all but the One recollected. So God says: "And remember thy Lord when thou hast forgotten", that is, when thou hast forgotten what is not God, then thou hast remembered God.'[2]

Referring frequently to verses of the Qur'ān and the Hadīths, and to sayings of other Sufīs, al-Ghazāllī gives extensive information on *dhikr* in his *Iḥyā' 'ulūm ad-dīn.* From this text we learn, for example, that *dhikr* can be performed in all situations and in all positions (Fazul-ul-Karim [tr.] n.d., book I, p. 285), 'Hazrat Ibn Abbas said: "Remember God day and night, on land and water, in journey and habitation, in solvency and want, in health and disease, openly and secretly." ' Al-Ghazalli also emphasized the importance of remembering God. He states that *dhikr* will destroy sins and will give salvation. A person who remembers God often, will enter paradise.[3]

As is clear from Sufī texts various formulae for recollecting God were in vogue. Most Sufīs had a preference for one special formula, and in later times when the *ṭarīqas* were established, the formula used for *dhikr* became one of their distinguishing characteristics. One of the most often recommended formula is the word Allah. We have already seen above that the words 'O Allah! O Allah! O Allah!' were prescribed by at-Tustarī for remembering God. Rāzī seems to have had a preference for the formula '*la ilāha illā Allāh*', for which he refers to the words of the Prophet.[4] The diversity of formulae was already admitted by al-Ghazāllī. He mentions, in addition to Allāh and the first part of the *shahāda,* also *subḥān Allāh* ('glory to God'), *akbar Allāh* ('God is great') and many others formulae. Al-Ghazāllī, however, remarks that the Prophet preferred 'there is no god than God' to other forms of *dhikr,* because this formula was supposed to have been given by God Himself.

Dhikr is normally divided into different stages. A distinction is made between spoken *dhikr* performed with the tongue (*dhikr jalī* or *dhikr lisānī*), and silent *dhikr* in the heart (*dhikr khafī* or *dhikr qalbī*). The latter is often considered better. Also a threefold division is known, consisting of the two types of *dhikr* mentioned earlier and *dhikr* of the *sirr,* the inmost being, where the distinction between the invoker and the Invoked disappears. We may also refer here to Sha'rānī, who in the sixteenth century mentioned a seven-fold *dhikr.*[5] However, aloud or silently, using one of the names of God or other formulae, merely remembering God is not enough, as is clear from the texts. The *Iḥyā'* (Fazul-ul-Karim [tr.] n.d., book I, p. 295) states: 'If there is no attention of mind at the time of Zikr, there is little benefit therein, but constant Zikr with attention or at most times is above all other divine services.' The final goal is to internalize the practice of *dhikr;* not just to utter the formula thoughtfully, but to remember God with attention in one's heart till the God-given knowledge is received. At this final stage the distinction between the invoker, the invocation and the Invoked disappears, and what remains is God speaking in the heart of His servant.

The texts of Indian Sufis give more or less the same information on *dhikr* as those of non-Indian Sufis. For example, *dhikr* must be practiced always, or, as the *Khayr al-Majālis* remarks, the tongue should never be free from the *dhikr* of God.[6] A story about saints continually absorbed in remembering God is related in the *Fawā'id al-Fu'ād* (Lawrence [tr.] 1991, p. 320): 'Once a person approached such a saint with this request: "When you are beseeching God, if memory of me comes to mind, please offer a prayer on my behalf." Replied that dervish: "Woe to that time when memory of you comes to mind!".'

How remembering God by repeating His name was integrated in the daily life at a *khānqāh* is clear from the *Siyar al-'auliyā.* The night was considered the best time for meditating on God, but also at day *dhikr* was performed. In fact, every minute that was not spent at prayers, in listening to discourses of the spiritual master or in reading from the Qur'ān and other Islamic works, had to be devoted to the remembrance of God by the repetition of His name.

Indian Sufīs, too, made a distinction between loud *dhikr* and mental *dhikr.* The *Khayr al-Majālis* (K.A. Nizami [ed.] 1959, p. 92) mentions *dhikr* with the tongue (*zabān*) and in the heart (*qalb*), of which the latter is preferred. And, as other Sufīs, the Indian Sufīs mentioned different formulae. Both the *Merṣād* and the *Khayr al-Majālis* mention the formula '*la ilāha illā Allāh*', while in the Fawā'id (B. Lawrence [tr.] 1991, p. 193) a story is told of Ibrāhīm ibn Adham who, when asked the question 'Do you know the greatest name?,' answered: 'First you should clean your stomach of unlawful food, then you should empty your heart of love of this world, and after that by whatever name you call upon God that is the Greatest Name!'. The texts ascribed to Indian Sufīs do not give much information on the function of *dhikr.* When it is mentioned, stress is laid on its purifying function. No remarks have been found in these texts with regard to the legitimation of *dhikr.* It is possible that *dhikr* was so well known to the Indian Sufīs that they did not feel the need for writing down such a legitimation.

Analysis of the Sants' nāmsumiran

As is clear from texts ascribed to Kabīr, Dādū, Rajab and Sundardās, the remembrance of the name of God was given a central place in the Sants' path. Although the names of Hari and Rām occur most often, in practice it does not matter which name one uses; all names refer to the same One, the Creator, the Infinite. A verse (P.R. Caturvedi [ed.] 1966, 2.20) ascribed to Dādū, for example, says: 'How many names exist of the Creator, the Infinite; take that one that crosses your mind. That is the way how *sādhus* and Sants remember.' Muslim names, like Allah and Rahim, also occur, especially in verses ascribed to Rajab (W.M. Callewaert 1978, 17.42, 2.18). The Sants considered the name as the only support in this *kali yug.* The practice of *nāmsumiran* became thus the only means by which the Unbound, the Supreme One, could be grasped and through which He became more or less concrete. The idea of the name as a connecting link between human being and God is, for example, expressed in the *Sarvāṅgī* (W.M. Callewaert, 1978, esp. *aṃga* 20). This text also speaks of the meeting place of the name, the place where devotees can experience God.

With regard to the actual performance of *nāmsumiran,* various terms are used, such as *jap, ajapā, bhajan* and *ajapājap.* The term *sumiran* (remembrance) can be considered as a general term referring to the activity of remembering. However, a distinction can be made in how this remembrance has to be done. *Jap* and in many cases also *bhajan* point to the real utterance of the name of God while *ajapā* and *ajapājap* refer to inner meditation on the name. That the last form of *sumiran* is also the best one, the one which one has to aim at, is clear from the following *sākhī* (W.M. Callewaert 1978, 19.2): 'Who worships with his mouth is a human being, who worships with his heart a god, who worships with his soul enters the light; Rajab (says) that is true service.' The texts further recommend that the Sant practice *nāmsumiran* always, day and night, and without effort until it becomes a natural part of his existence.

Although the texts cited mention the name of God and discuss how to perform *nāmsumiran,* it is the meaning and function of *nāmsumiran* that they emphasize again and again. Compared with other practices, *nāmsumiran* has been given the utmost importance. Various verses point to the complete irrelevance of, e.g. pilgrimage, fasting and reading holy texts. The most obvious benefit of *nāmsumiran* is, according to the texts, its salvific potency. In this context, terms related to the concept of Samsara are frequently met with, e.g. remembering God will destroy karma (W.A. Callewaert 1978, 19.17) and will take a person across the ocean of existence (H.N. Sharma 1936, 2.9). Because of its salvific quality, man is often warned against neglecting to do *nāmsumiran* (W.M. Callewaert 1978, 2.18).

All Sants explain why the practice of *nāmsumiran* has to be done. Kabīr (P.N. Tivari, 1961, 3.26), for example, refers to Brahmā and Śiv: 'Says Kabīr, as I have said so have Brahmā and Maheś said, the name of Rām is the essence of reality; teach this to all.' Of the *sākhīs* ascribed to Sundardās, the *aṃga sumaran* contains five verses which describe the importance that various earlier saints attached to the name of Rām. In these lines prominent sages and saints are named, starting with the south Indian philosopher Śaṅkara and ending up with Sundardās's guru Dādū.[7] It is obvious that it was felt necessary by Sundardās to legitimize the practice of *nāmsumiran,* which has been done by tracing it back to recognised authorities. *Sākhīs* of the *Sarvāṅgī* of Rajab (W.A. Callewaert 1978, 17.40, 22.39) point to written authorities: 'Whether a Hindu or a Muslim, attaching oneself to the name one will be saved; both Vedas and Koran tell the same, says Rajab.' The way in which the Sants use the name of god closely resembles the use of mantras; in fact, the name is a mantra. As the use of mantras has a long tradition in Hinduism, it is no surprise that the Sants were not the only ones who made use of them. This has been clearly shown by Tulpule (1991) in his study on the divine name. The practice of *sumiran* was already mentioned in the *Bhāgavatapurāṇa* as one of the nine forms of Bhakti, and was propagated by, for example, the Caitanya and Vallabha *sampradāys.*

The Purāṇas mention various types of mantras and describe how to utter them (S.A. Dange 1987, vol. 3, pp. 980-9). *The Encyclopaedia of Puranic Beliefs and Practices,* citing the *Liṅgapurāṇa* I 85.20-2, mentions three types, called (1) *vācika,* in which the *mantra* is uttered very softly, (2) *upāṃśu,* in which the *mantra* is audible to the ears of the mutterer only, and (3) *mānasa,* mental uttering. The last of these three methods is considered the best one. The benefits of uttering *mantras* as disclosed in some of the Upaniṣads and Purāṇas are much the same as those mentioned in the Sant texts. Repeating a *mantra* is believed to destroy sins and to lead to salvation (*mokṣa*).

Evaluation of the findings

Comparing the results of the analysis of *dhikr* and *nāmsumiran,* similarities as well as differences can be distinguished. To begin with, both for *dhikr* and for *nāmsumiran* different formulae can be used, although both traditions have their own preferences. Both, however, stress the efficacy of the use of the name of God. Secondly, the actual practices of *dhikr* and *nāmsumiran* have been divided into three types; saying the name of God out loud, silently and in the heart; both consider the last form to be the best. Next, devotees are encouraged to perform *dhikr* or *nāmsumiran* everywhere and always. Moreover, both *dhikr* and *nāmsumiran* will, if practised with attention and the right disposition of mind, lead to paradise or release from samsara. And finally, both traditions legitimize their practices by referring to recognized authorities, be they the Qur'ān or the Vedas, or gods like Brahmā and Śiv, or the philosopher Śaṅkara.

As we have seen, *dhikr* was already practised by Sufis of the ninth century AD, and *nāmsumiran* is a practice well known within Hinduism. Similar practices are known from other religious traditions also, like the *nembutsu* of Buddhism and the Jesus-prayer in eastern orthodox churches. Obviously, there is no reason to conclude that there has been interaction between the two traditions in this specific case, despite similarities between the two practices. Does this mean, however, that there has not been any interaction with regard to this practice? The answer to this question depends on how interaction is defined. The term often has the connotation of direct influence, the incorporation of a new practice or idea. There are, however, various degrees of interaction. In this context reference should be made to studies on Christianity like that of K. Berger and C. Colpe (1987) which examines the relation between early Christian texts and those of non-Christians in the same geographical area. This study mentions fourteen different categories of interaction between analogous ideas, practices and constructions in literature. Although these catagories have been developed especially for the study of Christan texts, they can, with a few modifications, also be applied to analogous practices like *nāmsumiran* and *dhikr*.

Some final remarks

After analysing and comparing the three chosen parts of the Sant path and their Sufi counterparts, I hope to obtain a better understanding of the interaction between the two religious traditions. The use of the categories mentioned earlier, and more generally, of the science of religion, can hopefully contribute to a deeper understanding of the interaction between religious traditions in medieval India.

NOTES

1. According to the Indo-Muslim historiographer Baranī, books on Sufism became almost fashionable in Delhi in mid-fourteenth century. Among these books were the *Iḥyā' 'ulūm ad-dīn,* the *Kashf al-maḥjūb,* the *Kitāb at-ta'arruf* and the *Merṣād* (A. Schimmel 1975, p. 348).
2. Al-Kalabādhī refers here to *surā* 18.24.
3. Fazul-ul-Karim (tr.) n.d., book I, p. 286: 'The Prophet said: "If anybody wishes to enter the garden of paradise, let him remember much".' According to another tradition the Prophet was asked: 'Which action is the best?' He said: 'Your meeting with death in the condition of your tongue being saturated with Zikr of God'.
4. Algar (tr.) 1982 (*Merṣād*), p. 268: 'The Prophet, upon whom be peace and blessings, said: 'The best zekr is that of lā elāha ellā'llāh, and the best supplicatory prayer is that of al-ḥamdo le'llāh'.'

   The words lā ilāha illā Allāh ('there is no god but God') form the first part of the shahāda, the Islamic profession of faith.
5. Schimmel (1975, p. 174) enumerates, '*dhikr al-lisān* with the tongue; *dhikr an-nafs,* which is not audible but consists of inner movement and feeling; *dhikr al-qalb,* with the heart, when the heart contemplates God's beauty and majesty in its inner recesses; *dhikr ar-rūḥ,* when the meditating mystic perceives the lights of the attributes; *dhikr as-sirr,* in the innermost heart, when the divine mysteries are revealed; *dhikr al-khafiy,* the secret recollection, which means the vision of light of the beauty of essential unity; and, finally, the *dhikr akhfā al-khafī,* the most secret of secret, which is the vision of the Reality of Absolute Truth (*ḥaqq al-yaqīn*)'.
6. K.A. Nizami (ed.) 1959, p. 122: '*ama mibāyad ke zebān tu yekzamān az dhikr khodāye ta'ali khāli nebāshad*'.
7. Sundardās (H.N. Sharma [ed.] 1936, 2.47-50) refers also to, e.g. Śeṣ, Nārad, Druv, and Prahlād.

REFERENCES

Algar, Hamid. *The Path of God's Bondsmen from Origin to Return. A Sufi Compendium.* Persian Heritage Series no. 35. New York: Caravan Books, 1982. Tr. of the *Merṣād* of Najm al-Dīn Rāzī.

Arberry, A.J. *The Doctrine of the Sufis.* Cambridge: Cambridge University Press, 1977 (1935). Tr. of the *Kitāb at-ta'arruf li-madhhab ahl al-taṣawwuf* of Abū Bakr al-Kalābādhī.

Berger, K. and C. Colpe. *Religionsgeschichtliches Textbuch zum Neuen Testament.* Göttingen: Vandenhoeck & Ruprecht, 1987.

Callewaert, Winand M. *The Sarvāṅgī of the Dādūpanthī Rajab.* Leuven: Orientalia Lovaniensia Analecta, 1978.

Caturvedi, P.R. (ed.). *Dādūdayāl granthāvalī.* Varanasi: Nagari Pracharini Sabha, 1966.

Chand, Tara. *Influence of Islam on Indian Culture.* Allahabad: The Indian Press, 1954.

Dange, S.A. *The Encyclopaedia of Puranic Beliefs and Practices.* Vol. 3. New Delhi: Navrang, 1987.

Rizvi, S.A.A. and S. Zaidi. *Alakh bānī or Rushd Nāma.* Aligarh, 1971. Introduction, translation and annotation of Shaikh Abd-ul-Quddus Gangohi's *Rushd Nāma.*

Jackson, P. *Letters from Maneri. Sufi Saint of Medieval India.* New Delhi: Horizon India Books, 1980. Tr. of Maneri's *Maktūbāt-i Sadi.*

Karim, Fazul ul-. *Imām Gazzālī's Iḥyā' 'Ulūm-id-dīn.* 4 vols. Lahore: Sind Sagar Academy, n.d.

Lawrence, Bruce B. 'The Sant Movement and North Indian Sufis.' In *The Sants,* ed. by K. Schomer and W.H. McLeod, pp. 359-73. Delhi: Motilal Banarsidass, 1987.

———. *Nizam ad-din 'Auliya - Morals for the Heart.* New York: Paulist Press, 1991. Tr. of Amir Hasan Sijzi's *Fawā'id al-Fu'ād.*

Mujtabai, F. *Aspects of Hindu-Muslim Cultural Relations.* New Delhi: National Book Bureau, 1978.

Nicholson, Reynold A. *The Kashf al-Mahjūb. The Oldest Persian Treatise on Sufism by 'Alī ibn 'Uthmān al-Hujwīrī.* E.J.W. Gibb Memorial Series. Vol. 17. 1911. Reprint. Leiden: Brill, 1959.

———, (ed.). *Memoirs of the Saints.* London: Luzac & Co, 1959. Tr. of Farid al-Din 'Attar's *Tadhkirat al-'Auliyā* (1905-7).

Nizami, Khaliq Ahmad. *Khayr al-Majālis.* Aligarh: Aligarh Muslim University, 1959. Edition of Maulana Hamid Qalandar's *Khayr al-Majālis.*

Ojha, P.N. *Aspects of Medieval Indian Society and Culture.* Delhi: B.R. Publishing Corporation, 1978.

Schimmel, Annemarie. *Mystical Dimensions of Islam.* Chapel Hill: The University of North Carolina Press, 1975.

Sharda, S.H. *Sufi Thought.* New Delhi: Munshiram Manoharlal, 1974.

Sharma, H.N. (ed.). *Sundardās granthāvalī.* Calcutta: Rajasthan Research Society, 1936.

Thiel-Hortsmann, Monika. *Dādū Lieder.* Beiträge zur Südasienforschung, Südasien-Institut, Universität Heidelberg, Band 138. Stuttgart: Franz Steiner Verlag, 1991.

Tivari, P.N. (ed.). *Kabīr granthāvalī.* Allahabad: Hindi Parishad, Prayoga Vishvavidyalaya, 1961.

Tulpule, Shankar Gopal. *The Divine Name in the Indian Tradition.* Simla: Indian Institute of Advanced Study, 1991.

Vaudeville, Ch. *Kabīr.* Oxford: Oxford University Press, 1974.

———. 'Sant Mat: Santism as the Universal Path to Sanctity.' In *The Sants.* Ed. K. Schomer and W.H. McLeod, pp. 21-40. Delhi: Motilal Banarsidass, 1987.

Rabindranath and the Poetic Heritage of Bhakti

MANDAKRANTA BOSE

Among those modern Indian writers in whose works the Bhakti tradition has survived, the most notable is Rabindranath Tagore. It will not be an overstatement if we claim that Rabindranath's love of poetry and music had its roots not only in Vaiṣṇava poetry but also in the paintings of the Pahari and Mughal schools which were themselves outcrops of the Bhakti tradition. Although by Rabindranath's own admission the spirituality of Bhakti left him untouched, its perception of the natural and the human worlds moulded his entire response to nature and his conception of emotional states, while its rhetoric formed his poetic mode. That, to this day, half a century after Rabindranath's death, Bengal still finds its voice largely in his imagery and sentiments, affirms the vitality of the Bhakti tradition. In Rabindranath, then, we find the paradox of a cultural phenomenon that gained a renewed life even as its primary, spiritual hold weakened.

Rabindranath's first exposure to Vaiṣṇava poetry was through Jayadeva's *Gītagovinda,* which he read before he reached his teens (R. Tagore 1912, pp. 42-3) and his first experience of Indian paintings came through his grandfather Dwarakanath Tagore's collection of Rajput, Pahari and Mughal paintings (S. Chatterjee 1978, pp. 80-1). The impression of these experiences is stamped on virtually every one of his vast body of poems and songs of *prem* (romantic love) and *prakṛti* (nature) as well as on his musical plays and dance-dramas.[1] The genesis and course of these encounters tell us as much about the imaginative force of Bhakti as about the capabilities of an imaginative genius.

In *Jībansmṛti,* his principal memoirs, Rabindranath tells us how, as a young boy, he was attracted to the rhythm and imagery of Vaiṣṇava poetry. Speaking of his father in the section entitled 'Pitṛdev', he recalls how he found an old edition of *Gītagovinda* on a river trip with his father and how he was drawn to Jayadeva's '*madhurakāntakomalapadāvalī*' by melodic, sweet and gentle verses. Here is one example of such a verse:

> nibhṛtanikuñjagṛhaṃ gatayā niśi rahasi nilīya vasantaṃ
> (*Gītagovinda,* 2.11)
>
> I reach the lonely forest hut where he secretly lies at night
> (B.S. Miller 1984, p. 80)

He copied *Gītagovinda* in its entirety so that he might read it again and again to himself. Since the edition gave the text without punctuation, no doubt following the common practice of manuscript orthography, Rabindranath had to work out the voicing of the poem by laboriously scanning the entire poem. He recorded his delight when he was able to do so (1912, p. 41). This apprenticeship was the basis not only of his astonishing metrical inventiveness but also of his skill as a song writer.

Few works of literature have left as deep and lasting a mark on a nation as Jayadeva's *Gītagovinda.* Soon after its appearance in the twelfth century, it swept through India, and in the succeeding centuries Vaiṣṇava songs came to occupy the minds of the masses of eastern India. At least forty poems were written following Jayadeva's style on the love of Rādhā and Kṛṣṇa both in Sanskrit and in vernacular languages all over India. By the thirteenth century the fame of Jayadeva had spread to west and south India and to Nepal (B.S. Miller 1984, pp. 3-7). Under Caitanya's influence, Bengal, already influenced by Vaiṣṇava devotionalism, became a centre of Bhakti, and all over eastern India, in Assam, Bihar, and Orissa, the celebration of the love of Rādhā and Kṛṣṇa became a strong religious force which found expression in the literature, dance and music of these regions. The influence of *Gītagovinda* extended to art as well. Between the seventeenth and nineteenth centuries five sets of paintings on *Gītagovinda* alone were produced. Hundreds of paintings on the Kṛṣṇa and Rādhā theme from the *Bhāgavatapurāṇa* and other Vaiṣṇava poems written around this time were produced. Paintings representing different *rāgs* with the *rāgadhyāna ślokas* were also produced around the Kṛṣṇa and Rādhā theme. Even the Mughal school of painting was influenced by that theme. In music in particular, Jayadeva's influence was strong and to this day, Jayadeva's songs may be heard in Bengal.

Not surprisingly, young Rabindranath's imagination was most powerfully stirred by Jayadeva, in whose poetry he discovered an entire realm to explore. This interest was reinforced when he was introduced to more poems from the *padāvalī* genre by friends of his elder brother, Jyotirindranath, who were themselves poets. They often discussed the writings of the Vaiṣṇava poets and two of Jyotirindranath's friends, Akshaychandra Sarkar and Saradacharan Mitra, brought out collections of poems by Vidyāpati, Caṇḍīdās and several lesser lights of the Vaiṣṇava school. Often the obscurity of the Maithili phrases was a special allure and he systematically studied them to get a feel for the language (1912, pp. 64, 76-7). This fascination deepened when he saw the paintings of the Rajput, Pahari and Mughal schools in the collection of his grandfather, Dwarakanath Tagore. A great number of paintings from these schools portrayed the love of Rādhā and Kṛṣṇa. *Gītagovinda* furnished the themes of many such paintings from medieval to early modern times in India.

The twin experience of Vaiṣṇava poetry and corresponding paintings remained a lasting influence throughout Rabindranath's entire life. So deep was this influence that he encouraged his nephew, the artist Abanindranath Tagore, to study these paintings (S. Chatterjee 1978, pp. 80-1) along with Vaiṣṇava *padāvalī* (A. Tagore 1977, vol. I, p. 305). A number of Abanindranath's paintings show how powerful this advice proved to be (Shankar 1991).

Rabindranath's first exposure to Jayadeva was at the age of eleven, and at age fourteen he came across more Vaiṣṇava poetry. Although he also began to read and enjoy classical Sanskrit poetry at this time—his favourite was *Kumārasambhavam*—he took Vaiṣṇava verse as his model. He had access to no reliable guide to the language of the *pads*, thought by many contemporary scholars to be a language derived from Maithili and termed Brajabuli (N. Gupta 1935, vol. 2, introduction, pp. 2-3). But by patiently studying the diction of the *pads*, he was able to write in a style close enough to theirs, although he believed it was a made-up language. He mentioned that the difficulty of understanding Brajabuli made him concentrate on sound and rhythm. The first two lines that he wrote imitating the *pads* are as follows:

gahana kusuma kuñja mājhe,
mṛdula madhura vaṁṣī vāje

(*Bhānusiṅgher Padāvalī* 1977, poem 1, p. 5)

In the dense flower grove,
The gentle and sweet flute plays on.[2]

Shortly thereafter, he published an entire cycle of poems in the same style, attributing them to a mythical Vaiṣṇava poet called Bhānusiṅgha and entitling the collection *Bhānusiṅgher Padāvalī*. He disclosed his authorship immediately and admitted that it was a lighthearted attempt to emulate Chatterton's similar pretence of discovering the imaginary ancient poet Rowley. Rabindranath was given the idea unwittingly by his brother's friend Akshaychandra Sarkar, who told him about the boy poet (R. Tagore, 1912, p. 76).

Rabindranath completed this set of twenty poems celebrating the love of Radhā and Kṛṣṇa at the age of eighteen, when he was quite unsure of his poetic ability. Later he altered the arrangement of the poems and added two more. The youthful need to imitate what had enthralled him was later viewed by him with some embarrassment, as is attested by his introduction to *Bhānusiṅgher Padāvalī* in his collected works. He deplores what he considers to be the inadequacies of the poems, saying that *Bhānusiṅgher Padāvalī* merely imitated the language of the Vaiṣṇava poets but had no kinship with the Vaiṣṇava worldview (R. Tagore 1961, vol. I, p. 127). While true in reference to Vaiṣṇava spirituality, this judgement must not be allowed to detract critical attention from Rabindranath's lifelong attachment to Vaiṣṇava poetry, both in regard to style and to emotional definition.

In retrospect, Rabindranath's interest seems to have been more than youthful infatuation, for he made a sustained effort to collect and publish the vast body of Vaiṣṇava poetry. In 1885, at the age of twenty-four he finally brought out, jointly with Srishchandra Majumdar, a collection entitled *Padaratnāvalī* , containing poems by Vidyāpati, Caṇḍīdās, Govindadās, Jñānadās, Balarāmdās, Rāi Śekhar, Rāi Vasanta, Anantadās, Yadunandandās, Yadudās, Narottamdās, Uddhavdās, Vaṁśīdās, Narasiṃhadās, Vipradās Ghoṣ, Yādavendra, Mādhavdās, Premdās, Vaṁśīvadan, Śrīnivāsdās, Jagannāthdās, Vṛndāvandās, Narahari and Locandās. The editors depended on a number of already published collections for this edition, *ŚriŚrīpadakalpataru,* edited by Satishchandra Roy being one major source. In the same year, Rabindranath brought out a second edition, adding a hundred more *pads.* He continued to enlarge his collection, and one result of his efforts was a manuscript collection of forty *pads* with annotations, now in the Visvabharati archives at Shantiniketan. Some *pads* from his later collection have been included in a recent edition of *Padaratnāvalī* along with some of his Bengali renderings (R. Tagore and S. Majumdar 1990, introduction, pp. 9-11). After *Padaratnāvalī* Rabindranath turned his energies to translations of Vidyāpati and Caṇḍīdās's *padāvalī*, as reported in the *Englishman* in 1915 (M.A. Qaium 1992, p. 11). This, however, was never published in his lifetime despite continued efforts on his part (R. Tagore and S. Majumdar 1990, p. 336).

This constant interest was certainly not due to any identification with the Vaiṣṇava religious life. Rabindranath's religious convictions were strong but they grew out of his knowledge of the *Bhāgavadgītā* and the Upaniṣads to which he had been introducted by his father Devendranath when he was about ten. The songs known as *brahmasaṅgīts* are impregnated with the spirituality of the *Bhāgavadgītā* and the Upaniṣads. The Krṣṇa worship of Jayadeva or Vidyāpati forms no part of *Bhānusiṅgher Padāvalī* or any other work of Rabindranath. Vaiṣṇava poetry in general and Jayadeva in particular served him as sources to be mined for the enchantment of rhythm, diction and imagery. This was the motivation that led to the publication of *Padaratnāvalī,* about which Bimanbihari Majumdar comments in his *Rabīndrasāhitye padāvalīr sthān* (quoted in R. Tagore and S. Majumdar 1990, introduction, p. 9) that it was the first collection of Vaiṣṇava poetry which was not presented as a text pertaining to the Vaiṣṇava faith, a judgment that echoes Rabindranath's own disclaimer about *Bhānusiṅgher Padāvalī* and his rhetorical question, 'Does the Vaisṇava sing only to reach Vaikuṇṭha?' (R. Tagore and S. Majumdar 1990, ms. fascimile facing p. 2).

If we are to go by Rabindranath's own testimony, it was the music of Jayadeva's verse that held him the most closely. While he learnt his craft from many sources, Indian and European, Rabindranath derived much of his skill with syllabic measures, alliteration and assonance from *Gītagovinda*. Among many examples is the poem (and popular song) '*Śeṣ minati*':

kešara kīrṇa kadamba bane,
marmara mukharita mṛdu pavane,
varṣaṇa harṣa bharā dharaṇī,
virahaviśaṅkita karuṇakathā. . . .

(*Gītabitān* 1961, vol. 2, pp. 462-3)

In the pollen-strewn kadamba forest,
The murmuring voice of the gentle breeze,

The earth brimming with the joy of rain
Trembling with a sad tale of parting. . . .

The balanced flow of the lines is achieved here both through alliteration and a four-beat structure varied by emphasised measures in the first and third lines. As examples of metrical brilliance Rabindranath frequently cited Jayadeva. For instance, in his treatise on metre, *Chanda,* he uses the line, '*viharati haririha sarasavasante*', (*Gītagovinda,* 1.27) as an illustration; again, in *Jībansmṛti,* he recalls the lilt of '*nibhṛtanikuñjagṛhaṃ gatayā niśi rahasi nilīya vasantam*' (*Gītagovinda,* 2.11) (cited by S. Bhattacharya 1984, p. 311).

The truth, however, is that the influence of Jayadeva on Rabindranath was by no means limited to metrical manipulation but helped to form his perception of the world at a deeper level. This is not surprising, for over and above their musical movement, the lines quoted earlier show the resonance between human experience, and landscape and atmosphere, which is characteristic of Vaiṣṇava poetry, particularly *Gītagovinda.* Both the movement of the verse and the imagery of separation echo Jayadeva's portrayal of lovers suffering separation in spring:

lalitalavaṅgalatāpariśīlanakomalamalayasamīre,
madhukaranikarakarambitakokilakūjitakuñjakuṭīre,
viharati haririha sarasa vasante
nṛtyati yuvatijanena samaṃ sakhi virahijanasya durante
(*Gītagovinda,* 1.27)

Soft sandal mountain winds caress quivering vines of clove.
Forest huts hum with droning bees and crying cuckoos.
When spring's mood is rich, Hari roams here
To dance with young women, friend—
A cruel time for deserted lovers.
(B.S. Miller 1984, p. 74)

The world of nature painted by Jayadeva created an entire convention for the representation of love, marked by physical signifiers such as *kadambaban* (kadamba grove), *varṣaṇ* (rain), *megh* (cloud), *kuñjakuṭīr* (forest bower), *abhisār* (tryst). As an aesthetic construct this convention was powerful enough to flourish even when divested of its spiritual content. It determined the designs of Rajput and Pahari paintings on the Rādhā-Kṛṣṇa theme and reappears as the formative principle of Rabindranath's romantic landscape, becoming the essential correlative of passion not only in his overt *padāvalī* imitations, but also in all his explorations of love in poetry. Not only was nature's beauty a value in itself, it also set Rādhā and Kṛṣṇa in a human setting. Like Jayadeva, Rabindranath could see them as metaphors for all human lovers, but unlike Jayadeva, he could not or would not extend the metaphor to a metaphysical symbolization of the love of Rādhā and Kṛṣṇa as the yearning of the human soul for the divine. Rabindranath's Rādhā and Kṛṣṇa are unambiguously human figures and he has a direct personal engagement with the emotional events revolving around them, whereas Jayadeva's are divine beings in human form whom he worships from a distance. This also explains why the speaker in *Bhānusiṅgher Padāvalī* is an insider, a participant, such as Rādhā herself or one of her companions. By contrast, the speaker in *Gītagovinda* is Jayadeva himself who observes and narrates an evolving action. Rabindranath's direct engagement with his creation makes his poems lyrical distillations of moods, but the very power of the experience underlying each poem keeps it distinct and separate from the others, while Jayadeva's distance allows him to develop a dramatic narrative out of emotional events, each leading to the next and evolving into an unified and sequenced action.

Yet the same rhetoric drives the work of both poets and they tread paths that run parallel much farther than Rabindranath's comments suggest. As in Jayadeva and the paintings, so in Rabindranath the sylvan scenery of spring and monsoon appear as the only proper settings for ecstasy. In poem after poem, not only in the immature *Bhānusiṅgher Padāvalī*, but also in later works that Rabindranath held in much higher regard, he recalls the world of Jayadeva:

nīlāñjanachāyā praphulla kadambabana. . . .

(*Gītabitān* 1961, vol. 2, p. 375.)

The shadow of the blue-black sky and the smiling kadamba forest. . . .

oi āse oi ati bhairava haraṣe
jalasiñcita kṣitisaurabha rabhase
ghanagaurabe navayauvanā varaṣā
śyāmagambhīra sarasā. . . .

kuñjakuṭīre oi bhāvākulalocanā
bhūrjapātāy navagīta kare racanā. . . .

('Varṣāmaṅgal' in *Gītabitān* 1961, vol. 2, pp. 437-9)

There she comes, in thunderous joy,
Bearing the sweeping fragrance of the rain-soaked earth,

Monsoon in her budding youth with cloud-filled grandeur,
Dark, heavy and water-laden. . . .

That young maiden with contemplative eyes,
Sitting in the forest grove,
Is composing new songs on *bhūrja* leaves. . . .

These lines not only echo Jayadeva's lilt, but reproduce the world Jayadeva creates in *Gītagovinda,* which begins with the verse:

meghairmedurambaraṃ vanabhūva śyāmāstamāladrumair
naktaṃ bhīrurayaṃ tvameva tadimaṃ rādhe gṛhaṃ prāpaya
(*Gītagovinda,* 1.1)

Clouds thicken the sky.
Tamāla trees darken the forest.
The night frightens him.
Rādhā, you take him home!
(B.S. Miller 1984, p. 69)

This verse in particular appears again and again in Rabindranath's poetry. In a poem in *Mānasī* he recalls the poet Jayadeva who on

a similar day of rains
Saw over the *tamāla* groves on the horizon
This dark shadow, swelling clouds covering the sky.
('Meghadūta', *Mānasī, Sañcayitā* 1959, p. 101)

In 'Rūpāntar' he gives another rendering of the same lines:

ambara ambude snigdha,
tamāle tamisra vanabhūmi
timir śarvarī e ye
śaṅkākula-saṅge laho tumi.
(quoted in S. Bhattacharya 1984, p. 310)

The sky softened by clouds,
The groves of tamāla trees darkened,
The night black, he is
Fearful—take him with you.

In another poem, from *Sonār Tarī,* he refers again to the same line:

Opening the first page of the songs of Gītagovinda,
I sing, '*meghe ambara medur*'.
('Varṣāyāpan', R. Tagore 1961, vol. 1, p. 358)

The debt here cannot be solely metrical. The cultural imaginary that was Jayadeva's forest groves by the river Yamuna is Rabindranath's literary template for the whole experience of love. That template, its details enriched by the Kangra and Gurjar paintings inspired by the Vaiṣṇava aesthetic—including illustrations of *Gītagovinda*—was as much a shaping tool for the young poet's growing romantic sensibility as for its expression.

The parallels to *Gītagovinda* in Rabindranath's poetry are obviously persuasive. Equally prominent, though not always noticed, is the correspondence between Rajput and Pahari paintings and *Bhānusiṅgher Padāvalī* and other poems of Rabindranath. The following verses, for example, are explicit responses to paintings from these schools, in particular from the series of paintings illustrating *Gītagovinda*.

Paintings

1. Abhisārikā (woman going to a love tryst):
W.G. Archer 1954, pl. 2, 'The Lady at the Tryst,' *c.* 1775, Fitzwilliam Museum, Cambridge, P.C. Manuk and Miss G.M. Coles bequest, P.D. 126-1948; pl. 5, 'A Night of Storm,' *c.* 1780, British Museum, P.C. Manuk and Miss G.M. Coles bequest, O.A. 1948-10-9-0138; M.S. Randhawa 1963, pl. 1.

śāṅana gagane ghora ghanaghaṭā nīśīthayāminī re
kuñjapathe sakhi kaise jāoba abalā kāminī re
(*Bhānusiṅgher Padāvalī* 1977, vol. 21, p. 26)

Dark, rumbling clouds in the monsoon sky, the night deep,
How will you tread the forest paths, Friend, helpless maiden that you are?

sur kare bārbār
paḍi varṣā-abhisār:
andhakār yamunār tīr,
niśīthe navīnā rādhā
nāhi māne kono bādhā
khuñjiteche nikuñjakuṭīr.
('Varṣāyāpan', *Sonār Tarī*, R. Tagore 1961, vol. 1, p. 358)

Again and again (I) sing and recite (the tale of the) monsoon tryst,
The dark banks of Yamunā, (where) ignoring every obstacle, young Rādhā
Searches for the flower grove.

āṣāḍh hateche śeṣ
miśāye mallār deś,
raci 'bharā vādarer' sur.
khuliyā pratham pātā
gītagovinder gāthā
gāhi 'meghe ambar medur' (ibid.)

The month of Āṣāḍh is coming to an end,
By blending *mallār* and *deś* (*rāgs*)
I create the melody of monsoon,
After opening the first page
Of the lyric Gītagovinda
I sing 'the sky is full of clouds'.

2. Radha abandoned by Kṛṣṇa:
   M.S. Randhawa and J.K. Galbraith, *Indian Painting* (Boston: Houghton Mifflin Co., 1968), pl. 2.

śunalo śunalo bālikā
rākha kusumamālika
kuñje kuñje pheranu
sakhi, śyāmacandra nāhi re!
(*Bhānusiṅgher Padāvalī* 1977, vol. 21, p. 20)

Listen, o my friend
Put away your flower garland
We searched every grove
My friend, Śyāmcandra cannot
be found.

3. Grieving Rādhā:
   M.S. Randhawa 1963, pl. 88.

hṛdayaka sādha miśāolo hṛdaye, kaṇṭhe śukhāolo mālā
(op. cit., p. 29)

My heart's desire has withdrawn into my heart and the garland has dried.

4. Love in springtime:
   M.S. Randhawa 1972, pl. 3, and pl. 7.
   Kangra, *c.* 1775-80, Victoria and Albert Museum.

vasanta āolo re!
madhukara gun gun amuyā mañjarī
kānana chāolo re!

śuna śuna sajanī hṛdaya prāṇa mama
harakhe ākula bhela. . . .

(R. Tagore 1961, vol. 1, p. 129)

The spring has arrived
The bees are humming around the buds
Covering the entire grove.
Listen my friend,
My heart and soul are ecstatic with joy.

āju sakhi muhu muhu
gāhe pika kuhu kuhu
kuñjabane duhuṃ duhuṃ
dohāra pāne cāy

(*Bhānusiṅgher Padāvalī* 1977, vol. 21, p. 11)

My friend, the cuckoo is singing away today incessantly,
In the forest grove the lovers are gazing at each other.

5. Monsoon clouds:
Kangra, *c.* 1775-80. Lalit Kala Series on *Gītagovinda,* portfolio no. 3, pl. 3.

āmi base āchi śyāmbaṅgadeśe
yethā jaydeva kavi kon varṣādine
dekhechilā diganter tamālavipine
śyāmacchāyā, pūrṇameghe medura āmbar

('Meghadūta', *Mānasī,* included in *Sañcayitā,*
R. Tagore 1959, p. 101)

Here I am in the green land of Bengal
Where on some rainy day Jayadeva
Saw in the tamala groves on the horizon
Dark shadows, the sky darkened by swelling clouds.

ogo, nadīkūle tīratṛṇadale ke base amala vasane, śyāmala vasane?

('Navavarṣā', *Sañcayitā,* R. Tagore, 1959, p. 421)

O, who is sitting on the grassy riverbank clad in brilliant verdant raiment?

As these correspondences show, Rabindranath's emphasis on the exclusive influence of metre notwithstanding, the aesthetic of Bhakti acted as one of the prime modulators of his poetic identity. In turn, the central position of Rabindranath in Bengali culture ensured a renewed life for that aesthetic although its base shifted from the religious to the secular. This is a shift that marks both the connection and the distance between Rabindranath and Jayadeva but it is not one that can conceal the continuity of the Bhakti tradition in the cultural life of India.

NOTES

1. Cf., *Gītabitān, Mānasī, Kaṛi o Komal,* etc.
2. This and other translations, unless otherwise noted, are mine.

REFERENCES

Archer, W.G. *Garhwal Painting.* London: Faber & Faber, 1954.

Bhattacharya, Sukhamay. *Saṃskṛtānuśīlane Rabīndranaṭh.* Calcutta: Aruna Prakashani, 1984.

Chatterjee, Sudhananda. *Kācher mānush Abanīndranath.* Calcutta: Gurudas Chattopadhyay, 1978.

Das, Anathnath and Visvanath Roy, ed. *Padaratnāvalī.* New edition of the original edition by Rabindranath Tagore and Srishchandra Majumdar. Calcutta: Ananda Publishers, 1990.

Gupta, Nagendranath, ed. *Vidyāpati racanāvalī, Vaiṣṇava mahājana padāvalī.* Calcutta: Vasumati Sahitya Mandir (*c.* 1935). Vol. 2.

Miller, Barbara Stoller, ed. and trans. *The Gītagovinda of Jayadeva.* Delhi: Motilal Banarsidass, 1984.

Qaium, M. A. *Sāmayikpatre Rabīndraprasaṅga: dhākāprakāś.* Calcutta: Tagore Research Institute, 1992.

Randhawa, M.S. *Kangra Paintings of the Gītagovinda.* New Delhi: National Museum, 1963.

———. *Kangra Valley Painting.* Rev. ed. New Delhi: Publication Division, 1972.

Shankar, ed. *Ṭhākurbarir citrakalā.* Calcutta: RPG Enterprises and Dey's Publishing, 1991.

Sinha, R.P.N. *Geeta Govind in Basholi School of Indian Painting.* New Delhi and Calcutta: Oxford Book and Stationary Co.; Bombay: D.B. Tarapurwala, 1958.

Tagore, Abanindranath. *Jorāsaṅkor dhāre. Works of Abanindranath Tagore.* Vol. 1. Calcutta: Prakash Bhavan, 1977.

Tagore, Rabindranath. *Rabindra racānavalī* (Collected Works, birth centenary ed.). Vol. 1 Calcutta: Government of West Bengal, 1961.

———. *Bhānusiṅgher Padāvalī.* In *Svarabitān.* Vol. 21. Calcutta: Visvabharati Publication, 1977.

———. *Gītabitān.* Vol. 2. Calcutta: Visvabharati Publication, 1961.

———. *Jibansmṛti.* Calcutta: Visvabharati Publication, 1912.

———. *Sañcayitā*. Calcutta: Visvabharati Publication, 1959.

Tagore, Rabindranath and Majumdar, Srishchandra, eds. (new ed. by Anathnath Das and Visvanath Roy) *Padaratnāvalī*. Calcutta: Ananda Publishers, 1990.

Victoria and Albert Museum, Kangra Paintings Collection.

Images of the Last Day: Muḥammad Jāyasī's *Ākhirī Kalām* and Indian Islam

THOMAS DE BRUIJN

One of the best-known stories from the *Paracāī*, one of the hagiographic sources on the life and death of the poet Kabīr, is that in which his followers debate on a proper funeral. The Hindus want to cremate him, the Muslims have a burial in mind (see D. Lorenzen 1991, pp. 40-2). This episode touches on an essential point in Muslim belief. The burial of the dead has a meaning deeply rooted in Islamic faith, that of preserving the body for the resurrection on the Last Day. This belief in afterlife is, as illustrated by the *Paracāī*, incompatible with the cremation of the body.

This difference in belief and ritual is problematic if one interprets the religious outlook represented in early Indian Sufi literature (thirteenth-sixteenth century AD) as an attempt to integrate religious traditions of Hinduism and Islam in a syncretic doctrine. Syncretism has been projected too easily onto early Sufi poetry as a whole and onto the epic romances in Avadhī in particular.[1]

The works of Malik Muḥammad Jāyasī have also been interpreted in this way.[2] The poet is well-known for his texts on the theme of mystical love, such as *Padmāvat* and *Kanhāvat.* He is also the author of a text, *Ākhirī Kalām,* which describes the events on the Last Day. In this paper I will try to illustrate how he connects several layers of Islamic traditions in this text, to construct a rhetoric which can be described without reference to the idea of syncretism.

Ākhirī Kalām (Discourse on the Last Day), is a relatively small work in the *caupāī-dohā* style, dated by the poet AH 936 or AD 1529/30.[3] This makes it earlier than both *Padmāvat* and *Kanhāvat.*

The work starts with an introduction in *masnavī*-style including the usual topoi, such as praise of Allah, his creation and the Prophet Muhammad. It also includes praise of Sultan Bābur and a eulogy of the *pīr* Sayyid Ashrāf Jahāngīr.[4] A description of the devil's evil deeds and a trick to frighten him sets the tone for the theme of the Last Day. The date of the poem is embedded in a warning about the unavoidable coming of the end of time.

The first signs of the Last Day are described as a strong earthquake, the sun coming up in the west, and division and strife spreading among the people. The four archangels Gabriel, Michael, Isrāfīl and Azrael cause earthquakes and torrential rains that leave no one alive. Then Gabriel comes to wake up the dead from their graves and take them to where Muhammad has returned. The Prophet guides the believers to the *pūl-i ṣirāṭ*, the narrow bridge over the pools of Hell, thousand *kośas* long, but so narrow that only an ant can cross it. This crossing is the first test of strength for the Muslims; each will have to find his own way of getting to the other side.

Then God[5] will summons the survivors to his presence to judge them severely. The sun will rise for six months and scorches the believers. Even the prophets will have no shade. As Allah only grants the sinless access to paradise, Muhammad asks pardon for the whole of the *'umma.* He turns to the prophets Adam, Moses, Abraham and Jesus to ask them to intercede with Allah on behalf of his people. They all turn down the request, declaring themselves incapable and scorned by God's anger in the past. Muhammad cannot change God's mind and takes the burden of his people on himself. Then Fatima is summoned before Allah, and she crosses the narrow bridge. She is furious and demands justice for the death of her sons Ḥasan and Ḥusayn and admittance to heaven for her followers. As she threatens to burn the world with the fire of her rage, Allah accepts the requests. Yazīd, the murderer of 'Alī, is brought forward and killed.

After the final judgement, the sins of the believers are removed, they are offered a banquet and taken to paradise in a wedding-procession led by Muhammad who is seated on a horse. The Prophet asks for a *darśan* of God before entering paradise. This is granted and God shows himself in the form of a bright light. The believers take up residence in the heavenly palaces and marry the *ḥūris* who surpass *padminīs* in beauty.

The last stanzas describe the palace of Kailāś where the queen sits on her throne, her body radiant like a pearl. The beholder becomes absorbed in her beauty and finally reaches mystical union through eternal love.

tahā̃ na mīcu na nīdu dukha raha na deha mā̃ roga/
sadā ananda muhammada saba sukha māte (mānai?) bhoga//
(*AK* 60.8-9)

There is no death, no sleep, no suffering or disease in the body, Muhammad says, there is always joy and everyone is drunk with happiness.

The text of the *Ākhirī Kalām* is sometimes difficult to understand, probably due to its editorial state.[6] Jāyasī uses, apart from terms like *pul-i silāvat* (*AK* 22.4; 27.1), *ummat* (*AK* 24.5; 25.1, etc.), *rasūl* (*AK* 24.2; 24.6, etc.), *bībī* (*AK* 38.6; 39.1, etc.) a vocabulary that is entirely Avadhi. Some of the images are Indianised, like the figure of the devil, who appears as Nārad (*AK* 6.5; 11.1), and that of Yam.[7]

Although there is no evidence linking the *Ākhirī Kalām* to any specific historical event, one could relate the text to Jāyasī's contacts with the Mahdawi movement. Among the *pīrs* who claimed to be inspired by Sayyid Muḥammad of Jaunpur, the self-proclaimed *mahdī* of the end of time, was Shaykh Burhānuddīn. Jāyasī had been a pupil at his *dargāh* in Kālpī. The Mahdawis began as an Islamic reformist movement, but had, by Jāyasī's time, become a network of *pīrs* and *murīds* not dissimilar to a Sufi-*ṭarīqa*.[8]

Speculation on the coming of the Last Day at the end of the first millennium of Islam also led to greater sensitivity for eschatological predictions. Apart from the specific historical background, the descriptions in the *Ākhirī Kalām* reflect general Islamic traditions and eschatological speculations.[9] The mystical element is present in the scene of the *darśan* of the light of Allah and the ascent to the heavenly throne. The queen of heaven is portrayed as the divine spirit or the ultimate beauty of monistic speculations. This makes the description of the voyage of the souls from the grave to the final union with this celestial beauty, a metaphor for the return to its divine origin.[10] The fulfilment of *pirīti* and *ananda* are put forward as the ultimate goal of religious life in this world and the next.

The exposition of mystical symbolism though, was not the main objective of the poet. The theme of the Last Day has a special significance in Islamic tradition because of the role of the Prophet Muhammad in the events. This figure has, in the course of the development and spread of Islam, become the centre of a devotional undercurrent that is much greater than his role in the canonical tradition would justify.[11] The veneration of the Prophet has been very important in shaping popular Islamic traditions and has influenced religious literature in the whole of the Islamic world. Any treatise dealing with the events of the Last Day is therefore foremost a representation of popular beliefs and legends connected with the figure of Muhammad.

Another important feature of popular Islam in India was the worship of the *dargāh* and the *barakāt* of the Sufi *pīr.* This had, from the sixteenth century onwards, become an increasingly popular form of devotion which attract both Muslims and Hindus.[12] From the *Ākhirī Kalām* it is evident that Jāyasī was thoroughly familiar with both spheres of Islamic devotion. In his representation of Judgement Day, the local background of *pīr*worship and popular mystical symbolism is an important frame of reference. By using this language and metaphoric idiom, he tries to bring this theme from the heart of Islamic tradition to his own audience of devotees who frequented the Sufi-shrines.[13]

Let me illustrate this by showing how two motifs connected with the figure of Muhammad in the *Ākhirī Kalām,* that of the divine light of Muhammad and that of the *shafa'a,* the role of the Prophet as intercessor at the final judgement, are represented.

In the first reference to Muhammad, in the introductory stanza, this image of light is part of the usual praise of the Prophet of Islam.

ratana eka bidhanai avatārā/nāvā muhammada jaga ujiyārā//
cāri mīta cahū̃ disi gajamotī/mā̃jha dipai mani mānika motī//
jehi hita sirijā sāta samūda/sātahu dīpa bhare eka bundā//
tā para caudaha bhuvana dasāre/bicạ bica khaṇḍa bikhaṇḍa sāvāre//
...
sahasa aṭhāraha duniyā serī/āvata jāta jātarā pherī//
jei nahī linha janama mā̃ nāū̃/tehi kahā kīnha naraka mā̃ ṭhāū//
so asa daiva na rākhā jehi kārana saba kīnha/
dahū̃ tuma kāha muhammada ehi prithimī cita dīnha//

(*AK* 7)

God created a jewel, his name was Muhammad, he brightened up the world.
He is the *gajamotī* pearl in the midst of his four friends and the four directions, He radiates between pearls, rubies and jewels.
For him the seven oceans were created, and were filled with the seven islands, as with one drop.

...
Eighteen thousand have, by coming and going, completed their journey in this world.
He who does not honour his name in this life, for him he created a place in Hell.
God, why did You not save such a man for whom You have done all this. Muhammad says, Why have You ever given attention to this world?
(cf. Jāyasī's *Padmāvat* 11, 1-3. V. Agraval 1961, pp. 10-11).

Although these are stock images for praising Muhammad, they have here the specific function of introducing themes which will appear in the rest of the work. The image of the light of Muhammad as proof of his prophethood and as theophanic emanation for the Muslims in this world comes back in the scene at the entrance of paradise. After the judgement Muhammad refuses to enter paradise without obtaining visual proof of God's presence in the form of a *darśan*.

kahaba rasūla bihista nā jāū̃/jaba lai darasana tumhāra na pāū̃//
ughara na naina tumahī binu dekhē/sabahi aṃbirathā more lekhe//
tau lai keu baikuṇṭha na jāī/jau lai tumharā darasa na pāī//
karu dīdāra dekhaū̃ maĩ tohī̃/tau pai jīu jāi sukha mohī̃//
dekhe darasa naina bhari leū̃/sīsa nāi pai bhuī̃ kahā deū̃//
janama mora lāgā saba thārā/paluhai jīu jo gīu ubhārā//
hoi dayāla karu disṭi phirāvā/tohi chā̃ṛi mohī aura na bhāvā//
sīsa pāi bhuī lāvaū̃ jo dekhaū̃ tohi āṅkhi
darsana dekhi muhammada hiye bharaū̃ tori sāṃkhi//

(*AK* 49)

The Prophet will say, I shall not go into paradise as long as I have not obtained a *darśan* of You.
Everything there will appear worthless to me, without seeing You with my own eyes.
As long as I have not beheld You, I will not go to paradise. Show Yourself so I can see You; only then happiness will come in my heart.
I will fill my eyes with this vision and bring my head to the ground.
My whole life I have been your friend. My heart will blossom when I stretch out my neck.
Be compassionate and let your image circulate. Besides You no other appeals to me.
I will bring my head to the ground when I behold You with my eyes.
Muhammad says, Having seen the *darśan,* my whole heart will be a witness of You.

Allah grants the request and praises Muhammad as the aim of creation. He shows Himself in the form of a bright light which blinds and dazzles the believers.

sunau rasūla hota phuramānū/bola tumhāra kīnha para-mānū//
tahā̃ huteũ jahā̃ huteu na ṭhāū̃/pahile raceū̃ muhammada nāū̃//
tuma binu abahũ na paragaṭa kīnheũ/sahasa aṭhāraha kā jiu dīnheũ//
caudaha khaṇḍa utara ka rākheũ/nāṃda calāi bheda bahu bhākheũ//
cāra phiriste baṛe autāreũ/sāta khaṇḍa baikuṇṭha saṁvāreũ//
...
tuma tana eta sirijā āi kai antara heta/
dekhahu darasa muhammada āpani umata sameta//

(*AK* 50.1ff.)

There was an order: Listen Prophet, I have made your word authority in the world.
I was there where there is no place, and first I created the name Muhammad.
Without you I would not have made myself known right now. I have given life to eighteen thousand already.
I have created the fourteen parts and preserved them. I have spread my message and have spoken in many ways.
I have made the four great angels incarnate. I have made paradise with seven storeys.
...
I have created you with this body. I have put love inside it.
Muhammad says, Behold this vision together with your people.

suni phuramāna harakha jiu bāṛhe/eka pāvā se bhae uṭhi tāṛhe//
jhāri umata lāgī taba nārī (tārī?)/jevā sirijā purukha au nārī//
lāgai saba se darasana hoī/ohi binu dekhe rahai na koī//
eka camakāra hoi ujiyārā/chapai bīju tehi ke camakārā//
cāṃda suruja chapihaī bahu jotī/ratana padāratha mānika motī//
so mana dipē̃ jo kīnha thirāī/chae so raṅga ghāta para āī//
ohu rūpa niramala hoi jāī/aura rūpa ohi rūpa samāī//
nā asa kabahū̃ dekhā na keū ohi bhāṃti/
darasana dekhi muhammada mohi pare bahu bhāṃti//

(*AK* 51)

Hearing this command joy rose in their hearts, they got up in one motion.
The whole '*umma* watched intensely, all the men and women that were in the created world.
A *darśan* became visible for everyone, no one was excluded from the sight of Him.

There was a bright flash, the lightning was hidden by its brightness.
The moon and the sun, the gems and diamonds, rubies and pearls were hidden—so much light was there.
He who made his mind firm was covered with this colour as in one blow.
He became spotless through seeing His form, and his own form merged with His.
No one has ever seen Him in this way.
Muhammad says, after seeing this *darśan*, the people were perplexed in many ways.

This image of the *darśan* of light returns in the final stanzas of the text, in the mystical symbolism of the entrance into paradise. The vision of the merging of the soul with the beloved is clearly related to the *darśan* Muhammad was given. The divine light which was unveiled there is here the radiance of absolute beauty.[14]

sātaũ pavāri nakhata mana bhekhata (pekhaba?)/sātau āya [āi] su kaukuta dekhaba//
cale jāba āge tehi āsā/jāi paraba bhītara kailāsā//
takhata baiṭhi saba dekhaba rānī/jībahi saba cāhi pāṭa baru mānī//
darasana joti uṭhai camakārā/sakala bihista hoi ujiyārā//
bāraha bānī sari ho subaranā/tehi kā cāhi rūpa ati lonā//
niramala badana candana kai jotī/sabakai sarīra dipai jasa motī//
bāsa subāsa tasa chūvai bedhi bhāvara kahi jāta/
bara so dekhi muhammada hiradai mā̃ na samāta//

(*AK* 59.2ff.)

At the seventh porch one will behold the stars in the mind. After reaching the seventh (floor) one will see this wonderful display.
One will go further with this expectation, and come to the inner part of this Kailasa.
There all will see the queen sitting on her throne and will experience that this throne is larger than their soul.
There will arise a flashing vision, and the whole heaven will be bright.
Although she is beautiful like gold of twelve colours, her beauty is even more lovely than that.
Her face is spotless and shines like sandalwood; the bodies of all radiate like pearls.
Her fragrance is so attractive, it is said that the bee can only touch it by impaling himself.
Muhammad says, The sight of this greatness can not be contained in the heart.

The motif which seems to connect these different scenes is that of the *nūr-i Muḥammad*, the light as emanation of the divine nature of Muhammad's prophethood and a central theme in Islamic belief. The light as manifestation of the mystery of creation and of Allah has a long history in Islamic tradition, going back to places in the Qur'ān like the so-called Light Sura.[15] This concept of Muhammad as receptacle of the light has led to extensive light imagery in both mystical speculation and Islamic folk-poetry. Both these elements are present in the *Ākhirī Kalām*. There is also a third element in the light image in Jāyasī's text, which links the concept to his own background. The terms the poet uses to describe the spectacle of theophany, like *darśan* and *camakar*, refer to the worship of the Sufi *pīr*. The goal of the devotee of the *dargāh* is to get a share of the *barakāt*, the metaphysical power the *pīr* has acquired through penance and divine grace. The ritual of the *darśan*, seeing the tomb of the *pīr* in the heart of the *dargāh*, is the way to partake of this *barakāt*.

The image of light as the materialization of the *darśan* and of divine inspiration can be found in various contexts in Jāyasī's work and is an important part of the metaphoric idiom of his *Padmāvat*. The use of this light imagery in the praise of his *pīr*, Sayyid Ashrāf Jahāngīr, in the introduction demonstrates the power of the image in Jāyasī's own religious background.

mānika eka pāeũ ujiyārā/saiyada asarapha pīra piyārā//
jahaṃgīra cistī niramarā/kula jaga mā̃ dīpaka bidhi dharā//
au nihaṅga dariyā jala māhā̃/būrlata kahā dhari kāṛhatabāhā̃//
samũda mā̃jha jo bohita phirāī/letai nāvā sahū̃ hoi taraī//
tina ghara haũ murīda so pīrū/sāvarata bina guna lāvai tīrū//
kara gahi dharama pantha dekharāeu/gā bhulāi tehi māraga lāeu//
jo asa purusai mana cita lāe/icchā pūjai āsa tulāe//
jo cālisa dina sevai bāra buhārai koi/
darasana hoi muhammada pāpa jāi saba dhoi//

(*AK* 9)

I have obtained a shining ruby, Sayyid Ashrāf, my beloved *pīr*.
Jahāngīr is a Chishtī, God has made this spotless one a guiding light for the whole world.
He grabs the arm of the lonely drowning man in the water of the stream and pulls him out.
The boat that is adrift in the ocean will get across if he guides it.
In his house I am a pupil, and he is the *pīr*. Without virtues, only by remembering him, I reached the shore.

He took my hand and showed me the path of dharma. When I got lost, he brought me back on the track.
He who concentrates on such a man, his wishes will be fulfilled and his hopes will be rewarded.
He who serves for forty days, or someone who sweeps the door (once)—Muhammad says, when there is a *darśan*, the sins of all will be washed away.

Similar references can be found in Jāyasī's other works. The poet introduces here the images which will return later in the text, the light of God reflected in the *pīr*, the *darśan* which removes sin and purifies the soul.[16] The tomb of Sayyid Ashrāf Jahāngīr was a flourishing centre in Kichaucha. The house Jāyasī refers to may well have been the *khānqāh* in Jais which was headed by a son of the *pīr*.[17] The cited verses show how Jāyasī uses his imagery to connect the spheres of mystical symbolism and of popular traditions on Muhammad with the devotional practice of the *dargāh.*

The fact that Jāyasī uses images to represent the predictions of the Last Day does not imply a syncretic intention on the part of the poet. More likely it is an attempt at expressing a central Islamic tenet, using the local dialect and the metaphoric idiom of the Muslims who came to Sufi shrines. As the *dargāhs* must also have attracted many non-Muslims one can also see a rhetoric of propaganda in the text. This was not so much aimed at converting people to Islam as at showing the prestige and powerful *barakāt* of the *pīr,* who was, through these properties, connected to strong figures of popular Islam.

The emphasis in the stanza on Sayyid Ashrāf Jahāngīr on the power of the *pīr* to save lost souls echoes the description of the efforts of both Muhammad and Fatima to gain admittance to paradise for their followers. In the Islamic tradition this motif is known as the *shafa'a* ('intercession', 'advocacy'). One of the privileges of Muhammad over the other prophets is that he is entitled to ask pardon for the sinners on the Last Day. Part of the *shafa'a* motif is that he first visits the other prophets in the chain from Adam up to Jesus to ask them to mediate for his people. Their refusal and inability to intercede with God, because of their former mistakes and imperfection, emphasizes the special position of Muhammad.

Like the *nūr-i Muḥammad,* the *shafa'a* has inspired various levels of Islamic tradition. According to the mystical interpretation of this voyage to the prophets, it is a metaphor for the journey of the soul to its divine origin.[18] At the end of the voyage the soul realizes that though it cannot count on others to lead it, it has the divine in itself. On another level *shafa'a* motif represents the protective power of Muhammad when he saves the believers at the judgement. This image of hope and comfort for the believers, even for the sinners, is also present in the *Ākhirī Kalām*.

sabai bhāra asa meli uṛāuba/phira phira kahaba utara nā pāuba//
puni rasūla jaihaī darabārā/paiga māri bhuī karaba pukārā//
taī saba jānasi eka gosāī̃/kou na āva mori umata ke tāī̃//
jei se kahaū̃ so cupa hoi rahaī/umata lāi keu bāta na kahaī//
more cā̃ṛa keū nahī̃ cā̃ṛā/dekhā dukha sabahī̃ mohī chāṛā//
mohī asa tuhī̃ lāga karatārā/tuhi hoī bhala soi nistārā//
jo dukha cahari umata kā dīnhā/so saba maī apane sira līnhā//
lekhi jokhi kahiyāvana (?) marana gañjana dukha dāhu/
so saba sabhai (sahai?) muhammada dukhī karau jani kāhu//
(*AK* 37)

He will take the burden of all with him and lift it up, but every time he asks, he will not get an answer.
Then the Prophet will go to the court. He will strike the floor and shout:
Oh Lord, know all to be the same. Nobody will come and help my people.
Whomever I turn to remains silent. Nobody says anything to help my people.
Nobody has fulfilled my wish. Having seen the suffering they all have deserted me.
Oh Creator, I am so much attached to You. Let this be ended properly, by Your doing.
Whatever suffering or joy is given to my people, I will take it all upon me. The crush of death, the fire of suffering, all that is written in fate, Muhammad says, He will bear it for all, so he will not make anyone unhappy.

Another character Jāyasī stages in this scene is Fatima. Like Muhammad she has also become the object of a devotion which expands her role more than orthodox Islam would allow. Especially in Shī'ī tradition her role as widow of 'Alī and mother of Ḥasan and Ḥusayn has led to a cult in which her position in religious life is not much inferior to that of her father.[19] This strong and decisive role is what Jāyasī wants to present to his audience in his version of the Last Day. Her world-threatening anger and claim for justice for the killing of her sons and husband make her into a figure who will protect the believers and gain entrance into paradise.

These images of Muhammad and Fatima have much in common with the saving power of the Sufi *pīr*. For an audience captivated by the miraculous power and protective might of the *pīr* as described in Jāyasī's own verses on Ashrāf Jahāngīr, this must have made the predictions of the Last Day very appealing. Such images are not only the stuff hagiographic sources connected with the saints of northern India are made of, they also form the metaphoric language Jāyasī uses to describe his own religious background.

The exposition of the theme of the Last Day in the *Ākhirī Kalām* illustrates that syncretism is not the core of Jāyasī's rhetoric. It does more justice to his images and rhetoric to see it as an appeal to fellow Muslims in his audience. The Sufi outlook of the poet is present in the allusions to mystical symbolism but is not the dominant aspect of the representation. The theme of the *Ākhirī Kalām* presents Jāyasī with a set of images that not only have great significance in mystical theories, but that also appear in the traditions of veneration of the Prophet and his daughter Fatima. Muhammad is depicted as *nūr-i Muḥammad, shafi'ī* and bridegroom. His daughter Fatima is represented as the fearsome woman, who, after her revenge on Yazīd, will safeguard the entrance of the believers into paradise.

Jāyasī presents these figures in the metaphoric idiom of popular *pīr* worship and combines well-known figures as Muhammad and Fatima with the images of miracle-working and protection which are present in the cult of the *barakāt* of the *pīr*. In this way he brings the central Islamic theme of the Last Day to that sphere of popular, localized Islam which had become a dominant feature of this religion in India.

The rhetoric in this poetry is not that of syncretism or conversion. Surely he must have been aware that his audience consisted of lower class Muslims and Hindus who frequented the Sufi *dargāhs* and other devotional centres in northern India. In the depiction of the Last Day he warns with images of final destruction and shows that the power of the *pīr* can compete with the great figures of Islam. In the medieval north Indian situation all sorts of popular religious movements like the Nāth Yogīs, the Sants and the Sufis, appealed to the vast audience of the lower class masses. In this environment which could best be described as a highly competitive religious market, this rhetoric was good marketing.

The conclusions based on the *Ākhirī Kalām* can also be extended to Jāyasī's other works, and I hope to publish more extensively on these matters with respect to his *Padmāvat.* The main point is that in the fifteenth and sixteenth centuries around the Sufi *dargāhs,* a localized, Indian form of Islam developed, which absorbed all kinds of Indian elements and attracted lots of Hindus. Research into this development by scholars like Richard Eaton and Bruce Lawrence (see, e.g. R. Eaton 1978 and 1982; B. Lawrence 1982; A. Schimmel 1982; C. Ernst 1992) has shown that this is not a degeneration of Islam or of Sufism. Rather, it should be considered an adaptation to changing conditions.

The Sufis became intermediaries between the different discourses in Indian Islam, that of the local shrine and that of the political centre. In the works of Muḥammad Jāyasī one can see how a poet, by using imagery and rhetoric, can communicate with all parties involved: Hindu and Muslim devotees at shrines, Rajput and Muslim local rulers, and the uncertain world of central political power. This does not have to affect the basics of his Islamic persuasion. The only hope for release from worldly entanglements, after all, is the afterlife in paradise. That is why the Muslims wanted Kabīr to be there with them.

NOTES

1. Ths issue of the confluence of Islamic and Hindu tradition in medieval Indian poetry has been the subject of a number of papers at earlier conferences on early NIA literature, e.g. H. van Skyhawk, 'Sufi Influences in *Ekanāthī-bhāgavat:* Some Observations on the Text and its Historical Context', in R.S. McGregor 1992, pp. 67-79; P. Gaeffke, 'How a Muslim Looks at Hindu Bhakti', ibid., pp. 80-8; F. Mallison, 'Muslim Devotional Literature in Gujarati: Islam and Bhakti', ibid., pp. 89-100; A.S. Asani, 'The Ismaili *Gināns* as Devotional Literature', ibid., pp. 101-12; D. Matringe, 'Krisnaite and Nath Elements in the Poetry of the Eighteenth Century Punjabi Sufi Bulhe Shah', ibid., pp. 190-206. See also Ch. Vaudeville 1974, pp. 84-110.
2. For examples of this interpretation of the works of Jāyasī, see the introductions to the text editions by M. Gupta 1952 and V. Agraval 1961, and the translation by Shirreff 1944. These views have been adapted by many other commentators.

3. *Ākhirī Kalām* (*AK*) 13.1: nau sai barasa chatīsa jo bhae/taba ehi kabitā ākhara kahes//. Note the pun on *ākhara/ākhira*.
4. Mīr Sayyid Ashrāf Jahāngīr probably lived in the fifteenth century, and was in his lifetime a famous Sufi and after his death a renowned *pīr*, whose grave in Kichaucha became a place of worship. The sons of Ashrāf Jahāngīr continued the tradition of the *barakāt* of their father and one of them headed a *khānqāh* in Jais. See also note 17.
5. The Avadhī-words used are: *daiu* (*AK* 1.1), *bidhātā* (*AK* 3.8; 34.7), *bidhi* (*AK* 3.4; 4.3; 8.1; 9.2; 32.9, etc.), *gosāī̃* (*AK* 21.1; 37.3; 38.1; 46.3); Allah is not used by Jāyasī.
6. The verses quoted in this paper are from the edition by M.P. Gupta, with some help from the scanty notes in R.C. Shukla's edition. This text is based on only a few manuscripts. Many of the problems have to do with the right transliteration of the Persian script of the manuscripts. The name of the text poses such a problem. In this paper I have used Gupta's title. To my knowledge there is no translation or extensive commentary of the text available. There is some secondary literature: see D. Sethi 1970, pp. 91ff and D. Saksena 1974, pp. 23-6.
7. *AK* 20.5; 20.8. Cf. also Jāyasī's *Akharāvaṭ*.
8. See S. Rizvi 1965, pp. 68-134. In Jāyasī's *Padmāvat* and *Kanhāvat*, Sayyid Muḥammad is mentioned as one of the *pīrs* in the *silsilāh*. The *mahdī* is a figure predicted in eschatological speculation who will come just before the end of time and will act as a perfect ruler. He will restore the pure faith and justice to give the believers an impression of what paradise has in store for them. The combination of the tenth century of Hijra and this claim presented a challenge to the Muslim rulers.
9. Eschatological speculation is a vast subject in Islamic tradition; for an overview of literature see *EI*, s.v. *qiyām* (*ḵiyāma*), *al-hisāb* and *ma'ād*.
10. This is known in the traditional literature as *ma'ād*, or *radja'a*, return. This is an interpretation of the resurrection as a return to origins and new beginning. Cf. Qur'ān, 28.85. Some Shi'ite traditions also hold on to this idea of return under the guidance of the *mahdī* at the end of the first millennium of Islam. See *EI*, s.v. *ḵiyām*.
11. Important work on this has been done by A. Schimmel 1981. A standard monograph is: T. Andrae 1918.
12. A similar development took place in other parts of India. See on this, e.g. C. Ernst 1992 and S. Bayly 1989.
13. The audience I refer to in this paper is similar in religious outlook to the *outer circle*, as described by Richard Eaton (1978) in his studies of the Sufis of Bijapur.
14. Cf. the images with which the beauty of Padmāvatī is described in several places in the *Padmāvat*.

15. Qur'ān 24:35: God is the light of the heavens and of the earth..., etc. See A. Schimmel 1981, pp. 108-23.
16. Cf. *AK* 43-4, where the judgement is described. The whole body will be witness of sins, but in the end the sins and duality will be rinsed off with water from the Kausara well.
17. The *dargāh* of Sayyid Ashrāf Jahāngīr was divided between his five sons. Shaykh Ḥāji Aḥmad became *sajjāda* in Jais. See: S. Rizvi 1978, pp. 266ff. Records of land-grants to the *khānqāh* have been found. See: R. Bilgirami 1972, pp. 298-335ff.
18. This interpretation has been the basis for the use of these images in Persian Sufi-poetry. An example is 'Āṭṭār's *Muṣībat-nāma,* where the *shafā'a* motif is elaborated. See: H. Ritter 1955. For the tradition on *shafā'a* see T. Huitema 1936.
19. See *EI,* s.v. *Fāṭima,* on the various traditions of Fāṭima devotion and further references.

ABBREVIATIONS

AK: *Ākhirī Kalām.* In: *Jāyasī Granthāvalī,* ed. Mataprasad Gupta, pp. 685-708. Allahabad: Hindustani Academy, 1952.

EI: *The Encyclopaedia of Islam.* New Edition and Supplement. Leiden: E.J. Brill, 1954ff.

REFERENCES

Agraval, V.S. *Padmāvat, Malik Muhammad kṛt mahākāvya.* Cirgāv: Sahitya Sadan, 1961.

Andrae, T. Die Person Muhammeds in Lehre und Glauben seiner Gemeinde. Stockholm: P.A. Norstedt, 1918.

Asani, Ali S. 'The Ismaili Ginān s'. In *Devotional Literatures in South Asia: Current Research, 1985-1988,* ed. R.S. McGregor, pp. 101-12. Cambridge: Cambridge University Press, 1992.

Bayly, S. *Saints, Goddesses and Kings: Muslims and Christians in South Asian Society 1700-1900.* Cambridge: Cambridge University Press, 1989.

Bilgirami, R. 'Some Mughal Revenue Grants to Family and Khanqah of Saiyid Ashraf Jahangir'. In *Medieval India: A Miscellany.* Vol. 2, pp. 298-335. Aligarh and London: Asia Publishing House, 1972.

Callewaert, Winand M., ed. *Early Hindi Devotional Literature in Current Research: Proceedings of the International Middle Hindi Bhakti Conference (April 1979).* Leuven: Departement Oriëntalistiek, Katholieke Universiteit Leuven, 1980.

Eaton, Richard M. 'Court of Man, Court of God'. In R. Martin, 1982, pp. 44-61.

———. *Sufis of Bijapur.* Princeton: Princeton University Press, 1978.

Ernst, Carl W. *Eternal Garden, Mysticism, History and Politics at South Asian Sufi Center*. Albany: State University of New York Press, 1992.

Gaeffke, Peter. 'Alexander in Avadhi and Dakkhini Mathnavis'. *JAOS* 109.4 (1989): 527-32.

Gupta, Mataprasad, ed. *Jāyasī Granthāvalī*. Allahabad: Hindustani Academy, 1952.

Huitema, T. De *Voorspraak (shafa'a) in den Islam*. Leiden: E.J. Brill, 1936.

Lawrence, Bruce B. 'The Function of Institutional Sufism'. In R. Martin, 1982, pp. 27-43.

Lorenzen, David N. *Kabīr Legends and Ananta-das's Kabīr Prachai*. Albany: State University of New York Press, 1991.

Martin, Richard C., ed. *Islam in Local Contexts*. Contributions to Asian Studies 17. Leiden: E.J. Brill, 1982.

McGregor, Ronald Stuart, ed. *Devotional Literatures in South Asia: Current Research, 1985-1988*. Cambridge: Cambridge University Press, 1992.

Ritter, H. *Das Meer der Seele: Welt und Gott in den Geschichten des Farīduddīn 'Aṭṭār*. Leiden: E.J. Brill, 1955.

Rizvi, S.A.A. *History of Sufism in India*. Vol. 1. New Delhi: Munshiram Manoharlal, 1978.

———. *Muslim Revivalist Movements in Northern India: 16th-17th Centuries*. Agra: Agra University, 1965.

Saksena, Dvarika Prasad. *Padmāvat mẽ kāvya saṃskṛti aur darśan*. Agra: Vinoda Pustaka Mandir, 1974

Schimmel, Annemarie. *Und Muhammad ist Sein Prophet: Die Verehrung des Propheten in der Islamische Frommigkeit*. Düsseldorf-Köln: Diederichs, 1981.

———. 'Reflections on Popular Muslim Poetry'. In R. Martin, 1982, pp. 17-26.

Sethi, Darshan Lal. *Jāyasī ka kāvya śilpa*. Dehradun: Sahitya Sadan, 1970.

Shireff, A.G. *Padmāvati of Malik Muhammad Jaisi*. Bibliotheca Indica 267. Calcutta: Royal Asiatic Society of Bengal, 1944.

Shukla, Ram Chandra. *Jāyasī granthāvalī*. Varanasi: Nagri Pracarini Sabha, 1935.

Theil-Horstmann, Monika. *Bhakti in Current Research, 1979-1982: Proceedings of the Second International Conference on Early Devotional Literature in New Indo-Aryan Languages, St. Augustin, 19-21 March 1982*. Berlin: Dietrich-Reimer Verlag, 1983.

Vaudeville, Ch. *Kabīr*. Vol. 1. Oxford: Clarendon Press, 1974.

The Bottom of the Page: Representing Variation in an Oral Tradition

KENNETH E. BRYANT

This is the last, I very much hope, in the series of progress reports delivered in this forum over the years, progress reports dealing with the Sūrdās critical edition project. The central concern of the paper is a very mechanical one: the time has come to settle on a format for presenting the edited text, and more important, for presenting the critical apparatus. But while the original intention was to restrict discussion to something quite pedestrian, other concerns have insidiously wormed their way into the paper: concerns which are abstract, almost ideological; and not merely concerns, but doubts and frustrations about the whole enterprise of editing such texts.

As many of you know, Jack Hawley and I have worked for years now with the early manuscript collections of poems attributed to the medieval Braj poet Sūrdās. Throughout most of that research Jack and I have avoided referring to 'the poems of Sūrdās', but have instead referred to 'the poems of the Sūrdās tradition', in recognition of a fact which the manuscript evidence makes inescapable: the poems circulating for centuries under the 'Sūrdās' *chāp* are the product of a very fluid oral tradition, rather than being the written oeuvre of a single poet. The early manuscripts differ from one another enormously, and the least important of these differences are the 'scribal errors' of copying which dominate more traditional textual criticism. The dozen or so earliest manuscripts represent about ten distinct collections, presumably transcribed from the repertoires of various singers at various times and places. Typically any two collections show a 30 to 50 per cent overlap in the poems contained: that is, typically half or two-thirds of the poems contained in collection A will not appear in collection B. Beyond the differences in poem inventories lie still more interesting differences in the readings given for individual poems: for these readings differ in ways which reveal, not the copyist's errors of a written tradition, but the exuberant improvisations of many singers over a period of generations.

In my wanderings through these tangles, it has frequently proved necessary to reexamine the original intention, which was to produce a critical edition of the Sūrdās materials. Two questions plagued me above others. The first was: What exactly is this critical edition supposed to represent? Certainly it is not supposed to represent the original works of a man named Sūrdās. While there is no reason to doubt that one of the earliest of those many singers bore such a name, the questions we would most like to ask about him simply have no answers: Did the poet Sūrdās sing this song? And if so, was he the first to sing it, or did he hear it from someone else? And if he sang it, did he sing it in this version, or that, or the other; or, perhaps, did he sing all three versions on different days of his life? We are not going to know these things.

But we can know something about the poetry of his times, or at least of the times tradition ascribes to him. Sūrdās is said to have lived and composed in the sixteenth century; and the manuscripts do permit the reconstruction of a sixteenth-century stratum of the Sūrdās tradition—a stratum which looks very different, as Jack Hawley has long since established, from the largely nineteenth-century stratum available in the currently standard edition. To present this sixteenth-century stratum, then, is the aim of the critical edition project, and the answer to the first question.

But present it how? This is the second question. Here I have felt a constant tug of war between the very notion of a critical edition on the one hand, and my sense of what the manuscripts showed me on the other.

A critical edition traditionally strives to reconstruct the true text, and cut away the untrue deviations. Actually it doesn't dispose of these deviant readings entirely; it squeezes them dry and then compacts them into little pellets called a critical apparatus. I am told that an eminent Indologist once referred to a critical apparatus as 'the shit at the bottom of the page'. If she didn't really say it, then perhaps I imagined the line myself; certainly its emotional tenor matches my own whenever I think about the dilemma of presentation. Within a tradition as fluid as that of the Sūrdās materials, no single reading, however reconstructed, really deserves the privileged status conferred, in a critical edition, by the top of the page; conversely the oral variants, the improvisations of other early performances, deserve a fate far better than that conferred by the bottom.

All such doubts and frustrations will be familiar to those of you who have worked with orally transmitted texts; they will sound especially familiar to those who have worked with Sukthankar's critical edition of the *Mahābhārata.* Here, obviously, is the great Indian oral text, the grandparent of them all, and Sukthankar's monumental project will inevitably be one paradigm for those of us who try to make sense of other oral traditions from the subcontinent. The introduction to the first volume, published in 1933, contains a piece of wisdom which has become almost a mantra for me:

> The *Mahābhārata* is not and never was a fixed rigid text, but is fluctuating epic tradition, a *thème avec* variations, not unlike a popular Indian melody. Our objective should consequently not be to arrive at an archetype (which practically never existed), but to represent, view and explain the epic tradition in all its variety, in all its fullness, in all its ramifications. Ours is a problem in textual dynamics, rather than in textual statics. (V. Sukthankar 1933, p. cii)

While I won't press too far the comparison between *Sūrsāgar* and *Mahābhārata*—*kahā̃ ye aur kahā̃ vo*—what Sukthankar has to say here is perfectly applicable to our own case: I should like to think that we too deal with a problem in textual dynamics. Sukthankar goes on to apply the notion of 'textual dynamics' to the question of the format in which his critical edition is to be presented: '[T]he *Mahābhārata* is the whole of the epic tradition: the entire critical apparatus. Its separation into the constituted text and the critical notes is only a static representation of a constantly changing epic text' (ibid.).

What is the true *Mahābhārata* then? Sukthankar says, it is the *entire* critical apparatus; the top of the page, and also the bottom of the page. It intrigues me how easily this discussion from the 1930s shades off into some of the more fashionable of today's academic battlefields. We hear much about 'margins', and 'centres'; the academic climate is generally one of suspicion for that which has been canonized, centered, pushed to the top of the page; the deconstructive maneuver is to invert such hierarchies, open the canon, recenter that which has been banished to the margins.

Sukthankar, half a century ago, could almost have been speaking for Derrida.

And yet I fear I must perform a deconstructive act myself, and read Sukthankar's two sentences again; because it seems to me that there is a whole story trapped in the tension between them, and it is a story in which I too am enmeshed. 'The *Mahābhārata* is the whole of the epic tradition: the entire critical apparatus.' So far, a triumphal pronouncement: the critical apparatus is the epic; the bottom of the page is given parity; nothing is thrown out, all is preserved. But then, alas, Sukthankar cautions: 'Its separation into the constituted text and the critical notes'—in other words, the top of the page and the bottom—'is only a static representation of a constantly changing epic'.

What he means is: don't take this separation seriously; look at the whole page as if all of it were equally important; where you see 'static', think 'dynamic'. And yet we all know it doesn't work that way. We read, study, translate, assign to our classes the constituted text at the top of Sukthankar's page; now and then, on special occasions, we stir a stick in the stuff at the bottom.

Having vented my angst at the dilemma, it's going to be an anticlimax when I confess that I have found no radical solutions. Rather, I have reached into the same bag of tricks used by other frustrated editors before me, and cobbled together an uneasy compromise. In the long term, electronic publication, in some kind of hypertext format, will undoubtedly serve us better, and I am beginning to experiment with such formats now. But hypertext authoring systems suitable for such a task do not yet appear to exist, and in any case there is still a large proportion of the potential readership that can only be reached by print. For the moment, any solution must be a compromise, constrained by the dimensions of a flat sheet of paper, and by the economics of book publishing.

One purpose of the present paper, then, is simply to enlist the help of colleagues in working out the terms of that compromise. This paper will present one possible format for such an edition; hopefully some among you will have suggestions for ways to make that format better serve its aims.

Let me direct your attention to the three pages of Nāgarī text at the end of this paper, which present mock-ups of three *padas* from the critical edition. The general idea of the format is that of parallel texts; but whereas it would often be useful to have eight or ten parallel texts across the top of the page, practical considerations get in the way. There are 440 poems in the edition; I have attempted to arrive at a format which will average one page per poem, including critical apparatus. The compromise which seems possible is three parallel texts for each poem, one given in full and the other two in the margins. I'll explain each of the three in a moment, but the important point to grasp is that taken together, the variants at the top of the page are intended to illustrate briefly the range of variation which the poem exhibits in the early manuscript corpus.

As a typographical convention, variants in the left margin are italicized, and keyed to the italicized words in the central reading; variants in the right margin are underlined, and keyed to the underlined words in the central reading.

Let's ignore that over-privileged center for a moment and talk about the margins. The left margin reports the readings from an early manuscript of what I shall call the 'courtly' recension; the right margin, an early manuscript of what I shall call the 'Braj' recension. I have elsewhere discussed the recensions of the corpus (See K. Bryant 1982, pp. vii-xx; 1983; J. Hawley 1979, 1984, Ch. 2). In brief, the claim is that the readings recorded in the early Sūrdās manuscripts were transmitted through three main lines, presumably representing three or more families of singers: one line centered at the Rajput courts; another centered in the Braj country itself; and a third, less important because it preserves only the '*vinay*' style of *pad*, appearing in collections made by the Dādū Panth. The important thing to note at this juncture is that the two marginal readings are intended to illustrate the range of difference across this spectrum; and while the manuscript used for the left-hand reading is chosen by a fixed set of criteria to be discussed in a moment, the manuscript used for the right-hand is always selected with only that display of difference in mind: that is, the manuscript chosen is, of the early mss., the one which seems best to illustrate the *divergence* of the three families.

With divergent readings tugging at the margins, what then is that reading in the center supposed to be? It doesn't claim to be the true and original words of a man named Sūrdās. It does claim to be the earliest retrievable version of the poem. In most cases this earliest retrievable reading won't look very different from the 'courtly' reading; this edition generally regards the 'courtly' line as the older, for two reasons: first and most important, simply because the two oldest surviving manuscripts belong to this line;

second, because the 'courtly' line appears to have been the more conservative (cf. Sukthankar's arguments for the Śarada version of the *Mahābhārata*); the 'Braj' line shows evidence of much more rapid change.

The copy text used as the basis for the central reading is in most cases one of those two earliest mss.: the one written at Fatehpur in northern Rajasthan, in AD 1582; the other written in Burhanpur in the Deccan in 1624. In certain cases I have chosen to go outside the copy text for the central reading. Where this change has been significant—that is, not simply an orthographic change, or the correction of an obvious scribal error—the original copy text reading appears in the left margin.

At this point I feel the need to caution once again: the central reading doesn't matter very much more than others. It is a peg upon which to hang variations, a device permitting us to grasp how much stayed the same from performance to performance, and how much was open to creative change. Likewise, the left and right margins are only two streams among many, a feeble attempt, constrained by paper, to remind us that not far away lies the ocean.

In an electronic, hypertext format we would at least not be restricted to two dimensions: a poem could have as many margins as it pleased. Alas, in paper, for those interested in the full range of variations, the next step is, inevitably, to the bottom of the page.

It is here that things always get messy, and that messy decisions have to be made. My early versions of a critical apparatus format attempted to display every smidgin of difference among the various readings recorded—oral variant, scribal clumsiness, marginal emendation, minor orthographic variation, all mechanically reproduced. The result was much longer than any publisher was likely to accept; economics aside, while the mind-numbing body of detail would have served some purposes well, it would have entirely defeated others. Specifically, such a wealth of detail would probably serve well the purposes of linguistic research, in which each deviant spelling might provide evidence useful for a reconstruction of sixteenth-century Braj; but for the literary scholar, and particularly for those interested in the dynamics of oral improvisation, the forest was being obscured by the trees. I attacked this problem with a blunt weapon; now, as you can see, the bottom of the page has developed a bottom of its own (and down there the print gets very small). The upper bottom contains that information which seems relevant for understanding the thematic and stylistic transformations of the text; the bottom bottom contains information which seems primarily linguistic in nature. Finally, there are certain distinctions which I have allowed to slip quietly off the page altogether: variations which involve only a distinction between the graphs for v and b, or s and sh, or a shift between nasalized and unnasalized vowels, are no longer recorded.

I can feel Stuart McGregor's eyes on the back of my neck as I say this, and as I contemplate how insidiously political such seemingly trivial decisions become: in my efforts to privilege the oral tradition, I risk marginalizing the linguist!

Once we have delegated phonetic or orthographic variation, and scribal errors, to the bottom of the bottom, the oral variants that remain are surprisingly orderly. The tricky bit is to decide in each case what metrical context most clearly displays the major variations—that is, do we compare word with word, or line with line, or at the level of some metrical subset of a line? What the parsing of such variants reveals, again and again, is the central role of a system of metrical patterning which I discussed in another paper before this body, six years ago at the Cambridge conference (K. Bryant 1992). I'd like to return briefly to that discussion and show how it applies to the present case. This requires, first, that I summarize that six-year-old paper for all who have forgotten it.

The metres dealt with here are based on a cycle of sixteen *mātrās,* much like *tīntāl* in Indian music. A long syllable counts as two *mātrās*; a short syllable counts as one. A line of poetry is divided into two uneven segments: the first segment is a complete cycle of sixteen *mātrās,* followed by a caesura; the second segment is a partial cycle—in the examples here, of eleven or twelve *mātrās.*

There have been several different schemes proposed for dividing that cycle of sixteen into smaller functional units. Those of you who read the earlier paper will remember that the division proposed there was based, in the first instance, on the evidence of patterns made by the words themselves. What emerged was a system of prefabricated slots for words of different metrical dimensions: slots for two-*mātrā* words, slots for three-*mātrā* words, slots for four-*mātrā* words and so forth. What is important for our purposes is that this system is in fact far more restrictive than the traditional rules of Hindi metre would make it seem: words can be moved about in a line, but only within well-prescribed limits. This means that, as we look at the variants on the bottom of the page, all is not as chaotic as we might expect. More often than not, the metrical pattern of a line will not change, or will change very little, even across a wide range of variation in the words and their sequences.

Let me again return briefly to that earlier paper to explain what I mean by a metrical pattern. The data presented in the paper was developed from a computer scansion of 1600 lines of the Sūrdās corpus. The metrical scansion of each line was mapped against two other variables: word boundary in the first instance, and stressed syllable in the second. By either measure, the two most frequent patterns in the corpus for dividing sixteen *mātrās* turned out to be: first, 3-3-2 3-3-2; second, 4-3-3-2-4. Below are some recycled examples from the earlier paper:

A. 3-3-2 / 3-3-2:
sūra adhama kī / hota kauna gati...[1]
kāma krodha mada / lobha grasita hvai...[2]
mudita badana aru / udita sadana tai...[3]

B. 4 / 3-3-2 / 4:
māgadha / mathana hatana nṛpa / bandhana...[4]
besyā / putra sobha nahi / pāvai...[5]
kampita / trāsa sāsa ati / mukulita...[6]

It is not surprising that the two most common patterns contained only words of two, three, and four *mātrās*: this is simply linguistic fact: words of those three lengths account for something like 85 per cent of the corpus. What was surprising was the prevalence of one particular sequence: 3-3-2. This is a very common way of dividing up an eight-beat rhythmic cycle in many musical systems of the world, including those of India; but the pattern has no 'official' sanction in the traditional prescriptive prosody of Hindi.

Those of you who read the other paper will remember that, as we moved down the list of patterns, a general system emerged in which the rules were the following. First, the underlying division of a cycle of sixteen was in fact the obvious one: four by four. But this underlying system of four-*mātrā gaṇs* is comparable to the bars of Western music in 4-4 time: that is, a base upon which to build variations. The first rule for variation was that any two consecutive four-*mātrā* units could be replaced by a sequence of 3-3-2. If you look at the following example—again cribbed from the earlier paper—you will see how those two most frequent patterns can be mapped onto an underlying cycle of 4-4-4-4. In each case, two adjacent four-*mātrā gaṇs* are replaced by a sequence 3-3-2: in pattern A, this replacement occurs in the first and second *gaṇs,* and again in the third and fourth; in pattern B, it occurs in the second and third:

<table>
<tr><td>Pattern A:</td><td colspan="2">3 3 2</td><td colspan="2">3 3 2</td></tr>
<tr><td>'regular' line:</td><td>4</td><td>4</td><td>4</td><td>4</td></tr>
<tr><td>Pattern B:</td><td>4</td><td colspan="2">3 3 2</td><td>4</td></tr>
</table>

There were some other important substitutions as well, but not many: one obvious one, for example, divides a four-*mātrā* slot into two twos; another creates a sequence 3-3-4. For our immediate purposes, the most important principle was that three-*mātrā* words almost always stick together—that is, threes come in pairs—and that there are only three very restricted slots in a cycle of sixteen *mātrās* where such a pair-of-threes can begin: at the beginning of the line; at the beginning of the second four-*mātrā gaṇ*; at the beginning of the third four-*mātrā gaṇ.*

It is not my intention to recapitulate that paper in its entirety. What I'm leading up to is a brief practical illustration of the metrical system, while at the same time demonstrating the relative transparency of a critical apparatus format which focuses on the dynamics of oral variation. I call your attention to the second line of the first illustration. The central reading—the lemma—gives four two-*mātrā* words: *saba sukha nidhi pada.* Of the four variants that follow, three retain this same 2-2-2-2 pattern, even though they juggle the words: *saba sukha nidhi hari, tava pada sukha nidhi, saba sukha kī nidhi.* Only the last variant changes the pattern, and then to the familiar 3-3-2: *parama kṛpā nidhi.*

So far we've looked at the first eight *mātrās* of the line; the next variation covers the second eight *mātrās*—that is, up to the caesura. Here, the theme is entirely 3-3-2; every variation maintains that pattern: *kamala bisari śrama; carana kamala taji; chāḍi kavala śrama; kavala chāḍi śrama; carana chāḍi kai.* It is also interesting to note certain variations which do *not* occur, variations which are otherwise perfectly plausible but which would violate the metrical patterning hypothesis: for example, in the first eight *mātrās* we will never see *taji carana kamala.* Similarly, we might expect a variation transposing *pada* and *kamala* to their more natural sequence, thus rendering the first sixteen *mātrās* as *saba sukha nidhi kamala pada bisari śrama*; but this divides the sixteen in an unacceptable fashion: 2-2-2-3-2-3-2.

I'd like to discuss one last example; this comes in illustration 3, at the beginning of line 4. There's a twofold purpose to this illustration: first, to show again the alternation between a 3-3-2 division and a 4-4 division; second, to demonstrate a final convention of the apparatus format. In this case, the various manuscripts display five variations for the first eight-*mātrā* segment of the line: *parama dīna janu; parama dīna manu; parama dīna jyū; parama dīna ati*; and *mānhu nalinī.* It is obvious that the first four of these variations are close cousins, varying only in a single word; but that the fifth variation marks a significant departure. The question is how we are to capture such facts in a critical apparatus entry: that is, how to display both variations and subvariations. The convention I have adopted in such cases uses subscripting: in the present case, there are two main variations presented—*parama dīna janu,* with a metrical division of 3-3-2, and *mānhu nalinī,* which divides 4-4; subvariations within the first major variation are indicated in subscript: i.e. for the word *janu* is substituted *manu, jyū,* and *ati* :

[परम दीन जनु *मनु J4; ज्यूं J2; अति M1*] मानहु नलिनी *A1, B3*

It only remains to present, on the following pages, the text of the three illustrations; and to earnestly solicit suggestions, from those who are likely users of the edition, as to ways to make the format more serviceable.

Illustration 1

	मेरौ मन मतिहीन गुसाई	
करै	सब सुष निधि पद कमल बिसरि श्रम *करत* स्वान की नाई	परम कृपा निधि चरण कमल तजि
	फिरत बृथा भाजन अवलेहन सूनै सदन समसान	बुथा फिरचौ; अवलेहत
ता	*तिहि* लालच कबहू कैसी बिधि त्रिपति न पावत प्रान	ऐसी बिधि कहि धौ इह लालिच
	जहं जहं जात तहां तहं त्रासत असम लकुटि पद त्रान	जही जही जाइ तहीं तहीं पावत
	कवल कवल कारन कुबुद्धि सठ सहत इतै अपमान	कारन ग्रास आस त्रिष्णा कै
	परम दयाल बिस्व पालक हरि अषिल ह्निदै निज नाथ	दीन; प्रभु; लोक
दास भव	ताहि छाडि यह सूर *महा सठ* भ्रमत भ्रमनि के साथ	सूरदास अब ताहि बिसारै

Meter: 16/12, 16/11. **Mss.:** *B2:405;* B4:88; G1:422; J4:276; J8:430; U1:167; V1:5. NPS:103.

2 सब सुष निधि पद] सब सुष निधि हरि *U1;* तव पद सुष निधि *B4;* सब सुष की निधि *J8;* परम कृपा निधि *G1.* **कमल बिसरि श्रम]** चरण कमल तजि *G1;* छाडि$_a$ कवल$_b$ श्रम *J4,V1$_{ba}$;* चरण छाडि कैं *U1, J8.* **करत]** करै *B2;* श्रम करत G1; फिरत *J4, U1;* भ्रमत *J8.* **स्वान]** स्याम *J4.;* स्वाति *B2.* **3 फिरत$_a$ बृथा$_b$]** *G1$_{ba}$, J4$_{ba}$.* **फिरत]** करत *B2;* फिरचौ *G1.* **अवलेहन]** अवलेहत *G1, J4, J8, U1;* अवलोकत *V1.* **समसान]** अग्यान *V1.* **4 तिहि...बिधि]** ऐसी विधि कहि धौ इह लालिच *G1.* **तिहि]** ता *B2;* यहु *J4.* **कैसी बिधि]** कैसेहु *U1, V1;* कैसे करि *B4, J4, J8.* **त्रिपति न]** नृपति *V1.* **पावत]** पावन *B2;* मानत *J4:* **5 जात]** जाइ *G1, J8, J4.* **तहां तहं]** तहीं तहीं *G1, J8, U1, V1;* तहा तन *B4;* तहा *B2.* **त्रासत]** भय त्रासत *V1;* पावत *G1.* **6 कवल...सठ]** कारन ग्रास आस त्रिष्णा कै *G1.* **कवल कवल]** कौर कौर कै *J4, J8, V1.* **कारन]** काज *J4;* काजि *U1.* **सठ]** सरु *B2;* जड *J4, V1;* अब *B4.* **सहत** *सहित U1* **इतै]** किते सहत *B4, J4, J8, V1.* **7 परम दयाल]** परम कृपाल *U1;* दीन दयाल *G1;* तुम सरवग्य *B4, J4, V1.* **बिस्व पालक हरि]** विस्व परिपूरन *B4;* सकल विस्व पूरन *J4;* सकल बिधि पूरन *V1;* सबही बिस्व पालिक *J8;* बिश्व पालक प्रभु *G1.* **ह्निदै]** लोक *G1;* भुवन ,*V1,* **8 ताहि...सठ]** सूरदास अव ताहि बिसारै *G1.* **ताहि]** तिनहि *J4, J8, U1, V1.* **सूर महा सठ]** सूरदास भव *B2.*

2 ***सब]*** *सन B2.* ***कमल]*** *कंवल B2, J4.* ***बिसरि]*** *विसारै B2.* ***श्रम]*** *विश्राम B2; स्रम J4, V1.* 3 ***फिरत]*** *फिरति U1.* ***बृथा]*** *ब्रिथा J8; थिथा B2.* ***सूनै]*** *सून G1, J8; सूनोहुं U1; सूदन B4.* ***सदन]*** *मदन U1.* ***समसान]*** *सुमसान J8, U1; समान B4.* 4 ***पावत]*** *पावति U1, J8; पावतु B4.* 5 ***जहं]*** *जहां B2, B4, J4, J8; जाहां V1; जही G1, U1.* ***जात]*** *जातु B4, U1.* ***त्रासत]*** *त्रासतु B4; त्रासित J8.* ***लकुटि]*** *लकुट B4, J4, V1.* 6 ***कवल]*** *काल B2; कौर J4; कोर V1; कवन U1; कुवर B4, J8.* ***कारन]*** *कारनि J8.* 7 ***सरवग्य]*** *सरवगि B4; सरवज्ञ V1.* ***बिस्व]*** *बिस B2; बिसु B4.* ***ह्निदै]*** *ह्रदै B4; हिदै B2; हिरदै J8. निज] जिन U1.* 8 ***तिनहि]*** *तिनहीं J8; तिनह V1.* ***भ्रमत]*** *भ्रमति J4, U1.*

Illustration 2

उहि भूमि | चकई री चलि चरण सरोवर जहां न पैम बियोगु
जहं *भ्रम* निसा होत नहिं कबहू वह साइरु सुष जोगु — होति; सो
[जहं] सनक स हंस मीन सिव मुनि जन नष रवि प्रभा प्रकास — गन
प्रफुलित कमल निमषु नहि ससि डरु गुंजित निगम सुबास
जिहि सर सुभग मुकति मुकता फल सुकृत बिमल जल पीजै — उहि; मुकति मुकत; हल नृमल; रस
सो सर छाडि कुबुद्धि बिहंगम इहां कहा रहि कीजै — सोई; त्यागि
सहज | जहं श्री सहित *करत* नित क्रीडा प्रणमत सूरिज दास — उहि सर सषा सहित; सब सुष
अब न सुहाइ बिषै बन छीलर वा समुद्र की आस — भई

Meter: 16/11, 16/12. **Mss:** A1:163; B2:13; B3:112; B4:107; G1:447; J1:4(10); ***J1:44(16);*** J2:397; J4:297; J5:24; J6:302; J8:430; M1:747; U1:198; U5:190; V1:23. NPS:337.

1 री चलि] चलहि न री हरि *J2;* चलि चलि *J6.* **जहां**] तहां *J6.* **न**] नहि *B3.* **2 जहं**] तहं *A1, J4, J6;* उहि *B2, J1B, J2, U1;* जिहि *M1.* **भ्रम**] भूमि *J1B, M1.* **होत**] होइ *M1.* **वह** *सो B2, B4, G1, J6, M1, U1, U5; वे A1, B3, J4; सुष J8* **साइरु**] सोभा पर *V1.* **3 जहं**] Ø *A1, B3, G1, J6, M1, V1.* **स** *सुक U1; सु A1, B3; से J4, V1* **हंस**] सनदन *J8.* **जन**] गन *A1, B3, B4.* **नष**] नव *V1.* **प्रभा**] प्रभू *J8;* प्रवहा *J2.* **4 कमल निमषु**] विमल कमल *J1A.* **गुंजित**] गुंजन *M1.* **5 जिहि**] उहि *B4.* **सर**] सूर *J1B;* सरि *J4, J8, U5.* **सुभग मुकति**] सुधा चुनत *J1A;* चुनत मुकति *J4;* चुगति मुकति *J8;* सषी मुकति *B2, U1;* मुकति मुकत *B4.* **मुकता**] निगम *U5.* **फल**] हल *B4, J1A, J6, J8, M1.* **सुक्रित]** नृमल *B4, J4.* **बिमल**] अम्रित *J5, J8, V1.* **जल**] रस *B4, G1, J5, J8, U1, V1;* जस *B2.* **6 सो**] सोई *A1, B3, B4, J2.* **सर**] जल *J1A.* **छाडि**] तजत *J1A;* त्यागि *B4;* छाडि अब *J2.* **कुबुद्धि**] अबुधि *J6.* **कहा रहि कीजै]** ब रहि काहा लीजै *J2.* **7 जहं श्री** *श्रीपति U5; आनंद J8* **सहित करत** *होत J2; सहज J1B, G1*] जिहिं *उहि B4* सर सषी *सषा B4* सहज *सहित B4* *B2, U1, B4;* सुनि ससि सिरी करति *J1A;* श्रीपति सहित सबै *J6.* **नित** *निज U5; दिन J1A* **क्रीडा**] क्रीडा रस *J6.* **प्रणमत**] सोभित *J5, J1A, J2, B3, J4, A1, M1, J8;* सोहत *J4;* प्रगटित *B2, U1;* पूणवंत *J6;* सब सुष *B4.* **सूरिजदास**] सूर सुदास *J4, M1.* **8 अब न सुहाइ**] यह किना तजहु *J1A.* **बन**] जल *J5;* रस *J4, J6, J8, U5;* जौ *J1A;* भयौ *A1, B3, M1;* भई *B4;* कौ *G1;* छीयो *J2.* **वा**] उध *B2.* **समुद्र**] सरबर *J4, U5.* **आस**] प्यास *G1.*

1 ***पैम*** *] प्रेम A1, B3, B4, J4, J5, J6, J8, M1, U5, V1.* ***बियोग*** *] बिवोग B4, J4, J6, J8, U5; बिजोग V1. 2* ***होत*** *] होति A1, B3, B4, J1A, J2, V1; होतु J1B;.* ***नहि*** *] नही B2, G1, J2, J5, J6, J8, U5.* ***साइरु*** *] साइर B2, B4, G1, J5, J6, U5; सायर A1, B3, J2, J4, J8, U1. 3* ***सिव*** *] स्यौ U5.* ***प्रकास*** *] प्रगासै J1A; प्रकाशा B3. 4* ***प्रफुलित*** *] प्रफूल्लित G1; प्रफूलित J2, J6, J8, M1, U5.* ***कमल*** *] कंवल J2, J4, J6, G1, J8, U5.* ***गुंजित*** *] गुंजत G1, J2, J4, J8, U5, V1; गुंजति U1;.* ***निमषु*** *] निमष J2, B2, B4, J6, G1, J8, U5; निमिष B3, A1, V1; निमुष J4; निमषि M1.* ***नहि*** *]* ***नही*** *B2, J2, J4, J5, J6, J8, U1.* ***सुबास*** *] सुवासै J1A. 5* ***सुक्रित]*** *सुकृत J1A, U1, B3, J1B, M1, G1, V1.* ***अम्रित*** *] अमृत V1. 6* ***सर*** *] सरु A1, B3, J1B.* ***कुबुद्धि*** *] कुबुधि J1, J5, U1, A1, G1, U5; कुबधि B2; कुवद्धि J4; कुवुध्ध M1.* ***बिहंगम*** *] बिहंगनि A1, B3, J2; बिहंगिमि J4; बिहंगिनि A1, B3. 7* ***प्रणमत*** *] प्रणमति G1; प्रणवंत U5. प्रगटित] प्रगटीत U1; प्रकटित B2. 8* ***सुहाइ*** *] सुहाय J2, B3, J4, A1, J8.* ***बिषै*** *] विषय A1, B3.* ***समुद्र*** *] समूंद J2.*

Illustration 3

कहां लौं कहिये ब्रज की बात

बनि सुनहु स्याम तुम बिनु *उन* लोगनि जैसै द्यौस बिहात कैसै

गोपी गाइ ग्वाल गोसुत सब मलिन बदन कृस गात गाय गोप गौसुत गोपी

परम दीन जनु सिसिर हेम हत अंबुज गन बिनु पात ज्यूं ससिही

जा कहु आवत देषत सब मिलि पूछत है कुसरात ता सों; om.

चलन न देत प्रेम आतुर उर फिरि चरननि लपटात परम अति आतुर

पिक चातक बन बसन न पावत बायस बलिहि न षात पावें; बलिहू

स्वामि सूर *स्याम* संदेसनि कै डर पथिक न उहि मघ जात दास

Meter: 16/11. **Mss.:** A1:116; B3:79; G1:21; ***J1:144(79);*** J2:62; J4:189; M1:655; U1:117. NPS: 4736. **Line order:** ...5,6,3,4... A1, B3, G1, J2.

2 उन] बनि *J1;* उहि *J2.* **जैसै**] कैसै *J2, M1.* **3 गोपी गाइ**$_a$ **ग्वाल**$_b$ **गोसुत**] *M1 ba;* गाइ ग्वाल *गोप J2* गोसुत गोपी *A1, B3, J2.* **सब**] *om. J2, M1.* **मलिन**] बिलषि *A1, B3, G1.* **बदन**] बसन *M1.* **कृस**] अस *M1.* **4 परम दीन जनु** *मनु J4; ज्यूं J2; अति M1*] मानहु नलिनी *A1, B3.* **सिसिर**] ससिही *J2.* **हेम हत**] हिमंत मै *M1.* **अंबुज गन**] ज्यौ अंवुज *M1.* **पात**] प्रात *A1, J2.* **5 जा** *यो B3* **कहु** *काहु A1, B3, J2, U1*] जो कोनहूं *कोउ M1* *J4, M1.* **देषत** *देषति A1* **सब** *हें A1; हीं B3* **मिलि**] देष दुर ते *J4;* पथिक जनन सौ *M1.* **है**] *om. A1, B3, J2, U1.* **6 न**] *om. J2, J4.* **देत**] देति *A1, B3, J2;* देहि *M1, U1.* **प्रेम**] परम *J2, U1;* विरह *G1.* **आतुर उर**] अति आतुर *व्याकुल G1, M1* *A1, B3, G1, J2, M1;* व्याकुल तन *U1.* **7 पावत**] पावति *U1;* पावें *J2;* पावहि *J4.* **बलिहि**] बलिहु *J2, U1.* **8 स्याम**] स्वामि *J1;* दास *G1, J2, J4, M1.* **कै डर**] डरपत *M1.* **पथिक न उहि मघ**] पथिक न आवत *J4;* कोन उही पथ *M1.*

1 ***कहां*** *] काहां J2.* ***लौं*** *] लुं U1.* ***कहिये*** *] कहीये G1, J2, J4, U1; कहिऐ M1.* ***ब्रज*** *] वृज M1. 2* ***स्याम*** *] शाम B3.* ***तुम*** *] तुम्ह A1.* ***बिनु*** *] बिन G1, J2, J4, M1, U1.* ***उन*** *] उनि G1.* ***लोगनि*** *] लोगन M1.* ***द्यौस*** *] दिवस M1. 3* ***गाइ*** *] गाय A1, B3, J2, J4.* ***ग्वाल*** *] गोवाल A1.* ***मलिन*** *] मिलन J4.* ***बिलषि*** *] बिलिषि B3.* ***कृस*** *] कृश A1, J1; क्रिस J2. 4* ***सिसिर*** *] ससिर J1, J4. 5* ***पूछत*** *] बूझत M1; पूछती J2.* ***कुसरात*** *] कुसलात G1, J4, M1. 6* ***फिरि*** *] फिर M1.* ***चरननि*** *] चरनन M1; चरननु U1. 7* ***चातक*** *] चात्रिग J2, U1.* ***बायस*** *] बाइस G1, J1, M1. 8* ***संदेसनि*** *] संदेसन M1.* ***उहि*** *] वैही G1; वहि J1.* ***मघ*** *] मग B3, G1; मघू J2.*

NOTES

1. For a published version see *Sūrasāgara*, ed. Nandadulare Vajpeyi, 1972, *pad* 52 line 6.
2. Ibid., *pad* 111 line 8.
3. Ibid., *pad* 613 line 2.
4. Ibid., *pad* 17 line 5.
5. Ibid., *pad* 34 line 4.
6. Ibid., appendix *pad* 94 line 5.

REFERENCES

Bryant, Kenneth E. 'The Manuscript Tradition of the *Sūrsāgar*: The Fatehpur Manuscript'. In *The Padas of Sūrdās*, ed. G.N. Bahura, pp. vii-xx. Jaipur: Maharaja Sawai Man Singh II Museum, 1982.

———. 'The Fatehpur Manuscript and the Sūrsāgar Critical Edition Project'. In *Bhakti in Current Research 1979-1982*, ed. M. Theil-Horstmann, pp. 37-52. Berlin: Dietrich Riemer Verlag, 1983.

———. 'Three-three-two verusu four-by-four-: material frames for the padas of Sūrdās'. In *Devotional Literature in South Asia*, ed. R.S. McGregor, pp. 209-24. Cambridge: Cambridge University Press, 1992.

Hawley, J.S. 'The Early *Sūr Sāgar* and the Growth of the Sūr Tradition'. *Journal of American Oriental Studies* 99.1 (1979): 64-72.

———. *Sūrdās: Poet, Singer, Saint.* Seattle: University of Washington Press, 1984.

Sukthankar, Vishnu S., ed. *The Mahābhārata.* Poona: Bhandarkar Oriental Research Institute, 1933.

Vajpeyi, Nandadulare, ed. *Sūrasāgara.* 4th edn. Varanasi: Nagari Pracharini Sabha, 1972.

The Apabhraṃśa *Cariu* as Courtly Poem

RICHARD J. COHEN

Śrīdhara's *Pāsaṇāhacariu* (*PC*) or 'Life of Pārśvanātha' (Skt. *Pārśvanāthacarita*) is a hagiography of the twenty-third Jain *tīrthaṅkara.* The text, composed at Delhi at the behest of one Naṭṭala Sāhu, was finished on the eighth day of the dark-half of *Agrahāyaṇa, Vikram Saṃvat* 1189, which corresponds to 12 November AD 1132. Structurally, and stylistically, the *PC* belongs to the category of Jain 'Purāṇa' which are patterned after Vimalasūri's *Paumacariya* and Jinasena's *Ādipurāṇa.* The language of the text is western Apabhraṃśa, also known as Śaurasenī Apabhraṃśa, a late form of Middle Indic or Prākrit, patronized mainly by Digambar Jains between the ninth and fourteenth centuries AD. This is a period when various sects of Jains were experiencing political and economic ascendancy throughout western India, in Gujarat, Rajasthan, Haryana and parts of Uttar Pradesh. Indeed, the boundaries existing between Hindus and Jains were not clearly drawn as we tend to perceive them today. The presence and influence of Jain merchants in fortified towns and other places where representatives of the king lived was widely felt.

Copies or 'versions' of biographies of the sixty-three *śalākā-puruṣas* or 'great heroes' of the Jain faith were most often composed in response to a commission offered by a pious layperson. These texts were usually written by talented Jain *sādhus* who studied grammar, rhetoric, and exegetics from an accomplished master, and who were recognized for their skill at weaving an artful story, albeit twice-told, often using a bewildering array of languages, literary devices and meters. Such a talented individual was Śrīdhara.

The author who calls himself 'the Wise Śrīdhara' *buha-sirihara* (Skt. *budha-śrīdhara*) in the *PC* and 'the Wise Good Poet Śrīdhara' *vibuha-siri-sukai-sirihara* (Skt. *vibudha-śrī-sukavi-śrīdhara*) in the *Vaḍḍhamāṇacariu* (Skt. *Vardhamāṇacarita*) is definitely the same person (R. Jain 1975). In both texts he gives the name of his mother and father as Vīlhā and Golha (*Pāsaṇāhacariu* 1.2.3-4; *Vaḍḍhamāṇacariu* 1.3.2 and 10.41.5). We learn from *PC* 1.2.3 that he was an Agravāla Digambar Jain. Futhermore, in *PC* 1.2.1. Śrīdhara mentions that he has already erased the karma of past deeds by composing a *Candappahacariu* (Skt. *Candraprabhacarita*). In *Vaḍḍhamāṇacariu* 1.2.6. Śrīdhara's patron requests the poet to compose the text as beautifully as he did the *Candappahacariu* and *Sāntiṇāhacariu* (Skt. *Śāntināthacarita*). Manuscripts of these texts have so far not been located. Since the dates of the *PC* and *Vaḍḍhamāṇacariu* are respectively AD 1132 and AD 1133, we may conclude that the order of composition of the four works was *Candappahacariu*, *Pāsaṇāhacariu*, *Sāntiṇāhacariu* and *Vaḍḍhamāṇacariu*, with the possibility of the *Sāntiṇāhacariu* being composed before the *Pāsaṇāhacariu*.

Two more texts have been attributed to Śrīdhara, namely, a *Sukumālacariu* (Skt. *Sukumālacarita*) and *Bhavisayattacariu* (Skt. *Bhaviṣyadattacarita*). The name formula in both of these texts is the same as that at the end of the *Vaḍḍhamāṇacariu*, i.e. *vibuha-śrī-sukai-sirihara*. Dated AD 1151 and AD 1173 respectively, they can conveniently be placed within the productive period of Śrīdhara. The most suggestive evidence, however, which links these two works with the Śrīdhara of the *PC* is the style of their closing *praśasti*, and more specifically, the use of particular locutions.

In addition to the stylistic argument, geographical/historical references in the four extant texts point to a circumscribed area appropriate for the activities of our poet. We know that the *PC* was composed in Ḍhillī, that is, modern Delhi. The author mentions that the city lies in the country of Hariyāṇa (1.2.14-15) and that he crossed the Yamunā River in order to get to it (1.2.13). This would imply that he came from an easterly direction. In *Vaḍḍhamāṇacariu* 10.41.1-4, we learn that Śrīdhara wrote the work in a village called Asuhara, which so far has remained unidentified. A possible clue to the locale of this village, however, is the fact that Śrīdhara mentions that his patron, Nemicanda, was born in the city of Bodāuva (modern Budaun), now a district headquarters in Uttar Pradesh, some 120 miles SSE of Delhi.

In *Sukumālacariu* 1.2.1-2, Śrīdhara mentions that he composed the text in a village called Valaḍai, during the reign of a king named Govindacanda (R. Jain 1975, p. 299). Hiralal Jain, in 1942, was the first scholar to bring to notice this composition (H. Jain 1942, pp. 84-6). He established a theory, tenuous at best, concerning the identification of Valaḍai and Govindacanda. He identified Valaḍai with the modern village of Valad, near Ahmedabad, and Govindacanda as the 'local' king who ruled there when the text was composed in AD 1151. Taking Jain's lead, Nemicandra Shastri further develops the argument, suggesting that Valaḍai is an early name for Ahmedabad, and that three separate but contemporary poets with the name 'Śrīdhara' are responsible for the four texts (N. Shastri 1974, pp. 137-50). Neither does he give details in support of his assumption, nor have I been able to confirm it. The old name of Ahmedabad seems to have been Asaval (*Imperial Gazetteer of India*, vol. 5, p. 106) and the ruling king at the time, that is, *c.* AD 1151, was Kumārapāla of the Cālukya dynasty, situated at Aṇhillavāḍa. Collectively, the data has led me to the conclusion that the Govindacanda mentioned by Śrīdhara in the *Sukumālacariu* is none but King Govindacanda of the Gāhaḍavāla dynasty of Kannauj, who ruled from *c.* AD 1114-54. Inscriptional evidence supports the thesis that the Gāhaḍavālas were the major power between Benares and Delhi at this time, and that the Rāṣṭrakūṭas of Budaun and the Tomaras of Delhi, although rulers in their territories, were nevertheless subject to the will of the Gāhaḍavālas (R. Niyogi 1959, pp. 20-4; 84-5, 97 and 100).

The *Bhavisayattacariu* was written in AD 1173 for a patron who resided in a town called Candavāra, and who was a *Māhura* Jain (i.e. connected with the town of Mathura) (K. Kaslival 1950, p. 150). H.G. Raverty (1973, vol. 1, pp. 470, 516, 518) and Roma Niyogi (1959, pp. 107-12), identify the modern town of Candwāl, a few miles SE of Etawah (Uttar Pradesh) as the site of the decisive battle of Candvār in AD 1193 between Qutb-ud-dīn Aibak and the Gāhaḍavāla king, Jayacandra, which set the stage for a complete Pathan take over of north India. The more likely identification is, however, with the modern Candwāṛ in Agra District, near Firozabad, on the Yamunā River. Ruins at this site in Agra District confirm that Candwāṛ was a sizeable fortress in early times, and, more significantly, an important centre of Jainism (*Uttar Pradesh District Gazetteers,* pp. 23, 25, 30-8). There is also evidence that Candwāṛ (the medieval spelling being Candavāḍa) was also a centre of Jain literary activity (H. Jain 1942, pp. 89-91; Kaslival 1950, p. 144; R. Jain 1974, 170; 578-99).

Since Candwāṛ is only twenty-two miles from Agra, the namesake of the Agravāl Jains, Śrīdhara's community (*kula*), since it is most likely that the Govindacanda mentioned in the *Sukumālacariu* is the great Gāhaḍavāla ruler of Kannauj-Benares, and since the four dates of the texts fall within a time span of forty-one years (AD 1132-73), the data are persuasive enough to attribute all four extant texts to the same author.

An error which has crept into the biographical scholarship on Śrīdhara is the belief that he was born in the country of Hariyāṇa (R. Jain 1975, p. 7 of the introduction; H. Kochar 1962, p. 210; N. Shastri 1974, p. 138). This assumption is based solely on the fact that in *PC* 1.2.13-15, the poet mentions he crossed the Yamunā River and came to the city of Ḍhillī, situated in the country of Hariyāṇā. A literal reading of the text does not allow one to assume Śrīdhara originates from Hariyāṇa. Although our knowledge concerning the boundaries of the country of 'Hariyāṇa' at this time is incomplete, it is safe to say that the Yamunā constituted the eastern boundary of the country, just as it delimits the border between the states of Haryana and Uttar Pradesh today. It must have served as a natural boundary between the Tomaras based at Ḍhillī and the Rāṣṭrakūṭas at Budaun. As Śrīdhara crossed the Yamunā in order to reach Ḍhillī, he must have come from an easterly direction. This points to the same area of which we find geographical references in the *Vaḍḍhamāṇacariu* and *Sukumālacariu*, i.e. Budaun and Candwāṛ (near Agra).

The person who gave a commission to Śrīdhara to write the *PC* was a resident of Ḍhillī called Naṭṭala Sāhu. We may assume from the element of *sāhu* in his name that Naṭṭala was a respected and influential member of society, a merchant or banker. Indeed, we are told in *PC* 1.9.1-5 that Naṭṭala built a temple to the first *tīrthaṅkara*, Ādinātha. He belonged to the same *kula* of Digambar Jains as Śrīdhara, i.e. the *Agravāla* (1.5.6). His father's name was Jejā (1.5.8), his mother's Memaḍiya (1.5.7), his wife's Saivālī (1.9.6), and his two older brothers Rāhau (1.5.10) and Soḍhala (1.5.12). Śrīdhara explains how he came to meet Naṭṭāla Sāhu through a mutual friend, Alhaṇa Sāhu. He recited portions of his *Candappahacariu* for Alhaṇa who, as it is made clear in the text, was quite impressed with Śrīdhara's work (1.4.7-10). Alhaṇa extols the virtues of Śrīdhara's poetic abilities and remarks that it is appropriate for one to spend his wealth on poets who fill the earth and its inhabitants with the glory of their poetry (1.4.1-

1.5.4). Alhaṇa then proceeds to praise the virtues of Naṭṭala and convinces Śrīdhara to meet with him. The interview goes well. Śrīdhara speaks of the potential for ill will amongst those around them, and wonders if jealousy will drive someone to speak poorly of him to Naṭṭala. All of this, of course, is to neutralize the 'evil eye' and to highlight the purity of the poet's creation. Out of consideration for Śrīdhara, the patron clears the room of visitors. Now safe from rivals and those whose ears would not be fit for the type of story he was about to relate, Śrīdhara confesses to Naṭṭala that after a careful study of language and the devices of literary composition, he felt incompetent and confused. This is, of course, the obligatory confession of the poet which sets the stage for an invocation to Sarasvatī, the goddess of inspiration and wisdom, who, in the final analysis, makes it possible for the poet to articulate his craft.

Without interrupting the sacred context of the *PC* itself, Śrīdhara incorporates into the text, measured but explicit praise of his patron Naṭṭala Sāhu. He achieves this by associating the name of Naṭṭala with the main characters in the story. At the end of Book One, when Śrīdhara closes by mentioning the birth of the Jina, he states (1.21.16), 'Naṭṭala praises this statement of Śrīdhara'. At the close of Book Two, while describing Hayaseṇa, the father of Pāsaṇāha, he remarks (2.18.14) that the king, 'was full of perfect happiness like Naṭṭala'. Likewise, Book Four closes by mentioning that Naṭṭala is adorned with glory like King Ravikitti, the uncle of Pāsaṇāha. A dramatic example of the scholarly erudition of Śrīdhara and the mixed linguistic nature of the text is the *āsīvāya* (Skt. *āśīrvāda*) or benediction which occurs at the end of each *sandhi* or book. It is written in Sanskrit, often displaying rare grammatical forms, and is given over to unabashed praise of the patron, Naṭṭala:

> yasyābhāti śaśaṃka-sannibha-lasatkīrtirdharetrītale;
> yasmādvaṃdījano babhūva sakalaḥ kalyāga-tulyārthiṇaṃ.
>
> (1.22.2a)
>
> yenāvāci vacaḥ prapaṃca-racanā-hīnaṃ janānāṃ priyaṃ;
> saśrīmānjayate sudhīranupamaḥ śrīnaṭṭalaḥ sarvvadā.
>
> (1.22.2b)

May Śrī Naṭṭala, whose fame, appearing like the moon, shines on the earth; because of whom bards have become seekers of the wish-fulfilling-tree; by whom speech is uttered free of error; who is beloved of the people, illustrious, pious, and incomparable, be victorious!

It is stated in *PC* 12.20.7-9 that Naṭṭala travelled extensively and was well-known to many kings. In his travels as an important merchant, banker or handler of caravans, he could have become acquainted with the rulers of other countries, but this notion must remain a speculation. What is not speculation is that Naṭṭala was a rather prominent resident of the city, more properly speaking a fort, called Ḍhillī. He built a temple to the first *tīrthaṅkara,* Ādinātha. In any case, the place-name, Ḍhillī, finds its first textual expression in the *PC* of Śrīdhara, in AD 1132. I have written elsewhere about the characterization of Ḍhillī in Śrīdhara's text, and will not go into it here (R. Cohen 1989). Stylistically, the *PC* is informed by a number of traditions. One is tempted to call it a poem of courtly society, inasmuch as it employs the kind of sophisticated literary devices associated with the Sanskrit *kāvya* tradition. It was written by a trained poet for a patron who occupied a high position in society; who may have had access to the Tomara Rājpūt court at Ḍhillī. On another note, the *PC* reflects the historic and complex environment of Jain didacticism and its world of stories within stories. More than anything else, for me, this is what is fascinating about Jain literature, and what holds the most potential for productive study. Last, but not least, are the variety of meters found in such a text, their skillful deployment by the poet, and the possibility of their representing contemporary, popular musical rhythms.

Let us take a look at some of the many literary devices employed in the *PC.* At the outset of the text, Śrīdhara constructs a standard invocation to the twenty-four *tīrthaṅkaras,* filled with alliteration and paranomasia:

1.1.1. pūriya-bhuanāsaho pāva-paṇāsaho ṇiruvama-guṇa-maṇi-gaṇa-bhariu toḍiya-bhava-pāsaho paṇavevi pāsaho puṇu payaḍami tāsu ji cariu.

1.1.2. jaya risaha parīsaha-sahaṇa-sīla; jaya ajiya parajjiya-para-dusīla.

1.1.3 jaya saṃbhava bhava-bhaṃjaṇa samattha; jaya saṃvara-ṇiva-ṇaṃdaṇa samattha.

1.1.4. jaya sumai samajjiya-sumai-poma; jaya paumappaha paha pahaya-poma.

1.1.5. jaya jaya supāsa pasu-pāsa-ṇāsa; jaya camḍappaha pahaṇiya-saṇāsa.

1.1.6. jaya suvihi suvihi-payaḍaṇa-pavīṇa; jaya sīyala parama-yasa-ppavīṇa.

1.1.7. jaya sėya seya-lacchī-ṇivāsa; jaya vāsupujja parihariya-vāsa.
1.1.8. jaya vimala vimala-kevala-payāsa; jaya jaya aṇaṃta pūriya payāsa.
1.1.9. jaya dhamma dhamma-maggāṇuvaṭṭi; jaya saṃti pāva-mahi-maiya-vaṭṭi.
1.1.10. jaya kuṃthu parikkhiya-kuṃthu-satta; jaya ara arihaṃta mahaṃta-satta.
1.1.11. jaya malli malli-pujjiya-pahāṇa; jaya muṇi suvvaya suvvaya-ṇihāṇa.
1.1.12. jaya ṇami ṇamiyāmara-khayara-viṃda; jaya ṇemi ṇayaṇa-ṇihayāravimda.
1.1.13. jaya pāsa jasāhaya-hīra-hāsa; jaya jayahi vīra parihariya-hāsa.
1.1.14. iya ṇāṇa-divāyara guṇa-rayaṇāyara vittharaṃtu mahu mai pavara; jiṇa-kaccu kuṇaṃtaho duriu haṇaṃtaho sara-kuraṃga-māraṇa-savara. ||1|| ghattā.

Bowing to Pārśva, Hope of All the Worlds, Destroyer of Evil, Breaker of the Noose of Existence, I once again relate his deeds, which are full of immeasurable benefits. (1.1.1) 'Hail to Ṛṣabha who patiently endured the vexations.[1] Hail to Ajita who overcame the evil behaviour of others. (1.1.2) Hail to Sambhava who was able to end rebirth. Hail to the able son of King Samvara.[2] (1.1.3) Hail to Sumati who received the benevolence of Padma.[3] Hail to Padmaprabha whose splendour is like the expanded lotus. (1.1.4) Hail to Supārśva who removes the chains which bind the soul.[4] Hail to Candraprabha who achieved self-annihilation.[5] (1.1.5) Hail to Suvidhi who was skilled at teaching the rules. Hail to Śītala who succeeded in achieving the highest glory.[6] (1.1.6) Hail to Śreyāṃsa, the abode of happiness and good-fortune. Hail to Vāsupūjya who renounced clothing. (1.1.7) Hail to Vimala, the pure light of omniscience.[7] Hail to Ananta, the fulfilment of man's hope. (1.1.8) Hail to Dharma who followed the path of righteousness. Hail to Śānti who was of a high-minded nature. (1.1.9) Hail to Kunthu who inspected carefully for small insects.[8] Hail to the noble Arihanta, Ara.[9] (1.1.10) Hail to Malli, the eminent one, worshipped with the *malli* flower. Hail to Munisuvrata who maintained strict adherence to religious vows. (1.1.11) Hail to Nami whom gods and divine beings[10] reverence. Hail to Nemi whose eyes are more beautiful than the lotus. (1.1.12) Hail to Pārśva whose splendour is more brilliant than a diamond. Hail, O Hail to Mahāvīr who has abandoned pride. (1.1.13) O Excellent Ones, Illuminators of Knowledge, Depositories of Virtue, extend your wisdom to me, (so that I may) emulate the Jinas and destroy evil, O Deer-Slaying Hunters of Smara![11] (1.1.14).

In the next example, our poet provides a description of the environs and banks of the Yamunā River, as he crossed it on his way into the country of Hariyāṇa and his destination, the city of

Ḍhillī (Delhi). The country-side is likened to a courtesan, the river her necklace, and aspects of the riverine environment various *guṇas* of the courtesan:

1.2.2 viharaṃtem koūhala-vaseṇa; parihacchiya vāesari-raseṇa.
1.2.3 siri-ayaravāla-kula-saṃbhaveṇa; jaṇaṇī-vīlhā-gabbhubbhaveṇa.
1.2.4 aṇavaraya-viṇaya-paṇayāruheṇa; kaiṇāvuha-golha-taṇūruheṇa.
1.2.5 payaḍiya-tihuaṇa-vai-guṇa-bhareṇa; maṇṇiya-suhi-suaṇeṃ siri-hareṇa.
1.2.6 jauṇā-sari sura-ṇara-hiyaya-hāra; ṇaṃ vāra-vilāsiṇi-paura-hāra.
1.2.7 ḍiṃḍīra-piṃḍa-uppariyaṇilla; kīlira-rahaṃga-thovvaḍa-thaṇilla.
1.2.8 sevāla-jāla-romāvalilla; vuhayaṇa-maṇa-pariraṃjaṇa-chailla.
1.2.9 bhamarāvali-veṇī-valaya-lacchi; papphulla-pomadala-dīharacchi.
1.2.10 pavaṇāhaya-salilāvattaṇāhi; viṇihaya-jaṇavaya-taṇu-tāva-vāhi.
1.2.11 vaṇamaya-gala-mayajala-ghusiṇa-litta; dara-phuḍiya-sippiuḍa-dasaṇa-ditta.
1.2.12 viyasaṃta-saroruha-pavara-vatta; rayaṇāyara-pavara-piyāṇuratta.
1.2.13 viyulāmala-puliṇa-ṇiyaṃva jāma; uttiṇṇī ṇayaṇahiṃ diṭṭha tāma.
1.2.14 hariyāṇae dese asaṃkha-gāme; gāmiyaṇa-jaṇiya-aṇavaraya-kāme.
1.2.15 para-cakka-vihaṭṭaṇu siri-saṃghattaṇu jo suravaiṇā parigaṇiuṃ; riu-ruhira-āvaṭṭaṇu paviulu paṭṭaṇu ḍhillī-ṇāmeṇa ji bhaṇiuṃ. || 2 || ghattā.

While roaming about out of curiosity, with a fondness for the Goddess of Speech, Śrīdhara viewed the Yamunā River, which charms the hearts of gods and men, seeing her as a courtesan's beautiful necklace. (1.2.2-1.2.6) Her upper garment was the globules of foam and her glorious breasts the sporting geese.[12] The line of hair above her navel, effective in distracting the minds of learned men, was the network of algae. Her beautiful ringlets of braided hair were the rows of bees, and her long eyes, the petals of the blossomed lotus. Her navel, dispelling the heat of those with fever, were the whirlpools churned by the wind. The saffron smeared (on her body) was the ichor of the wild elephant, and her shining teeth, the half-open oyster shells. Her excellent face was the blossoming lotus. She is affectionate to her lover as the Pravarā is to the ocean.[13] Her buttocks were the wide, glistening sand banks. When Śrīdhara crossed the river, he saw her with his eyes in this manner. (1.2.7-1.2.13)

In the region of *Hariyāṇa*[14] which has numerous villages and whose inhabitants are ever happy, there is the large city called Ḍhillī, favoured by Surapati,[15] destroying hostile armies, a mass of wealth making the blood of the enemy boil.[16] (1.2.14-1.2.15)

Next, we come across one of the more important sections of

the *PC*, from the point view of history. It is a description of the Tomara fort and the market place within it. Some architectural remnants of the fort can still be seen on the perimeter of the complex known today as Qutb Minar. One can find the moat and the bastions alluded to in the text; as well as the Ananga Saru or Ananga's Lake, now a *tāl* outside the village of Mehrauli.

1.3.1. jahiṃ gayaṇa-maṃḍala-ālaggu sālu; raṇamaṃḍava-parimaṃḍiu visālu.
1.3.2. goura-siri-kalasa-āhaya-payaṃgu; jala-pūriya-parihā-āliṃgiyaṃgu.
1.3.3. jahiṃ jaṇa-maṇa-ṇayaṇa-āṇaṃdirāiṃ; maṇiyara-gaṇa-maṃḍiya-maṃdirāiṃ.
1.3.4. jahiṃ caudisu sohahiṃ ghaṇa-vaṇāiṃ; ṇāyara-ṇara-khayara-suhāvaṇāiṃ.
1.3.5. jahiṃ samaya-karaḍi ghaḍaghaḍahaḍaṃti; paḍisaḍaḍeṃ disi vidisi viphuḍaṃti.
1.3.6. jahiṃ pavaṇa-gamaṇa-dhāvira-turaṃga; ṇaṃ vārirāsi-bhaṃgura-taraṃga.
1.3.7. paviulu aṇaṃga-saru jahiṃ vihāiṃ; rayaṇāyaru saiṃ avayariu ṇāiṃ.
1.3.8. jahiṃ tiya-payaṇeura-rau suṇevi; harisem sihi ṇaccai taṇu dhuṇevi.
1.3.9. jahi maṇaharu rehai haṭṭamaggu; ṇisesa-vatthu-saṃciya-samaggu.
1.3.10. kātaṃtaṃ piva paṃjī-samiddhu; ṇava-kāmiṇi-jouvaṇam'iva saṇiddhu.
1.3.11. suraramaṇiyaṇu va varaṇetta-vattu; pekkhaṇayaram'iva vahu-vesavaṃtu.
1.3.12. vāyaraṇu vā sāhiya-vara-suvaṇṇu; ṇāḍaya-pekkhaṇayam piva sapaṇṇu.
1.3.13. cakkavai va vara-pūaphalillu; saccuṇṇu ṇāiṃ saddaṃsaṇillu.
1.3.14. dappūbbhaḍa-bhaḍa-toṇu va kaṇillu; saviṇaya-sīsu va vahu-gorasillu.
1.3.15. pārāvāru va vitthariya-saṃkhu; tihuaṇavai-guṇa-ṇiyaru va asaṃkhu.
1.3.16. ṇayaṇam'iva satārau saruva-sahārau paura-māṇu kāmiṇiyaṇu va; saṃgaru va saṇāyau ṇahu va sarāyau ṇihaya-kaṃsu ṇārāyaṇu va. || 3 || ghattā.

The immense wall, adorned all around with bastions and encircled by a moat filled with water, touches the vault of the sky, the radiant pinnacle of its city gate brighter than the sun.[17] The buildings, studded with a multitude of gems, delight the minds and eyes of the people.

Dense forests, pleasing to the city-dwellers and demigods, beautify the entire locality; where rutting elephants forcefully clash, splitting all the directions with reverberation, and galloping horses, swift as the wind, are like ocean waves about to break. The wide Ananga Lake seems like the ocean.[18] The peacock, its body trembling, dances with delight, hearing the tinkling sound of women's anklets. (1.3.1-1.3.8) The fascinating marketplace glitters with a collection of every commodity. Like Kātantra's grammar, it abounds in *pañjī*,[19] and is friendly like the youthfulness of a young girl. It possesses precious cloth like goddesses,[20] numerous guises like a public spectacle, eloquent speech like a grammar and connoiseurs like the performance of a drama. It possesses the best betel-nut as the general possesses the advantage of superior troops.[21] It possesses an honest appearance as one full of truth possesses the six systems of philosphy.[22] It is filled with grain as the quiver of a proud, excellent warrior is filled with arrows and with many milk preparations as the well-trained student is filled with the sweetness of eloquent speech. Like the ocean, its size is vast, immeasurable like the multitude of virtues of a 'Lord of the Three Worlds.'

It is radiant like the eyes, enchanting like a lake, very capricious like a woman in love, full of elephants like a battle,[23] colourful like the sky, and whose *kansa* is struck like Nārāyaṇa's.[24] (1.3.16)

Let us now turn to a section which involves the actual *cariu* (*caritra*) or story of Pāsaṇāha (Pārśvanātha). It is a battle scene in which a king, Ravikitti (Ravikīrti), uncle to Pāsaṇāha, is engaged in a fight with a Yavana king, who has demanded Ravikitti's daughter for marriage. The use of an abbreviated meter, containing half the usual amount of *morae*, is an interesting technique to create the feeling of quick motion and fighting passion:

4.6.1. ravikitti caḍevi rahe hayavare kovi ṇariṃ'duddhare; mayajala-vuḍiya-karaḍa-kari-kaṃdhari kovi mayāri-kaṃdhare.
4.6.2. eehiṃ avarehiṃ; jīya-bhūri-samarehiṃ.
4.6.3. sohai jiṇo pāsu; ṇimmahiya-bhava-pāsu.
4.6.4. ahiya-maṇa-jūreṇa; saṃgāma-tūreṇa.
4.6.5. iya sayalu āvaṃtu; vāhuvalu dāvaṃtu.
4.6.6. kara-kaliya-karavālu; ravikitti bhuvālu.
4.6.7. ṇāūṇa sahasatte; pekharevi vara-patti.
4.6.8. jauṇo vi sampattu; raṇaraṃga-siri-rattu.
4.6.9. agaṇaṃtu siva-saṭṭu; dāhiṇauṃ aṇa-bhaṭṭu.
4.6.10. haya-puccha-saṃjalaṇu; vahu-jīva dara malaṇu.
4.6.11. ruhiroha-varisaṇauṃ; jasa-rāsi-ṇirasaṇauṃ.
4.6.12. puṇu puṇu vichiṃkiyau; maṃtīhiṃ saṃkiyau.

4.6.13. ahiṇāha khaṃḍiyau; pahu ruhira-maṃḍiyau.
4.6.14. aikaruṇu rovaṇauṃ; vala-lacchi-lovaṇauṃ.
4.6.15. vāyasaho kaḍu-rāu; saṃhariya-aṇurāu.
4.6.16. ṇiya-maṇaho kaya-tāu; paḍikūla-sābhāu.
4.6.17. samaraṃgaṇe raṇatūraim haṇevi dūrujjhiya-majjāyaim tāvaiṃ; abbhiḍiyaiṃ ṇiru viṇṇivi valai khaya-mariu periya-jalaṇihi ṇāvai. || 6 || ghattā.

Ravikīrti mounted a chariot, another, a tall horse, another, the shoulders of an elephant whose temples were covered with ichor, still another, the shoulders of a lion. (4.6.1) Along with those who had won many battles, Pārśva, the Jina, who destroyed his noose of existence, appeared with a battle-drum, extremely disturbed. Thus, all the strong-armed (warriors) advanced and rushed forward, sword in hand. King Ravikīrti quickly understood (the situation) and prepared his fighting-unit. (4.6.2-4.6.7) The Yavana also approached, impassioned with the splendor of the battefield, paying no attention to the exchange of heads, or the other skillful leaders. (4.6.8-4.6.9) The fierce energy of a horse's hindquarters half-trampled many people, raining a flood of blood, washing away the amassed glory (of the event). Repeatedly separated, feared for by his ministers, a king was wounded; his path adorned with blood. The great lamenting and crying (which followed), reduced the effectiveness of the army. The death-song of the crow crushed the will (of the warriors).[25] (4.6.10-4.6.15)

Then, flashes of hostility ignited in the warriors' hearts. Beating war-drums on the battlefield, far away from their borders, both armies then resolutely clashed; like the ocean churned by the Wind of Destruction.[26] (4.6.16-4.6.17)

Finally, our attention is drawn to an aspect of the text which some would be surprised to find in a Jain composition. The poet sets no limits to the detailing of the violence associated with the battle. Repetition and alliterative strings are used to heighten the feeling of clashing armies, soldiers and animals:

4.8.1. keṇavi matta-kuṃbhi-kuṃbhattahalu karavāle ṇa dāriū; keṇa vi karu dharevi acchoḍiu keṇa vi moḍi māriū.
4.8.2. keṇa vi kaṭṭivi kosaho vālo; āhau bhīma-bhaḍ'oha-kavālo.
4.8.3. ṇiggau ratta-pavāhu bharaṃto; bhūmiyalaṃ raya pūru haraṃto.
4.8.4. jāya-suṇimmala-diṭṭhi bhaḍāṇaṃ; ṇiddaliya-ari-kariṃda-ghaḍāṇaṃ.
4.8.5. tuṃga-turaṃgahaṃ tuṃga-turaṃga; matta-mayaṃgahaṃ matta-mayaṃgā.
4.8.6. pakkala-vīrahaṃ pakkala-vīrā; bhūhara-dhīrahaṃ bhūhara-dhīrā.

4.8.7. kuṃta-karaggahaṃ kuṃta-karaggā; vaggiya-khaggahaṃ vaggiya-khaggā.
4.8.8. cāru-rahohaṃ cāru-ṛahohā; dujjaya-johaṃ dujjaya-johā.
4.8.9. bhāmiya-cakkahaṃ bhāmiya-cakkā; ema bhaḍā avaroppparu thakkā.
4.8.10. saṃaraṃgaṇa-tūra-raveṇa raṇe pekkhevi suhaḍahaṃ suhaḍa bhiḍaṃtaiṃ; bhaggaiṃ bhaya-bhariyaiṃ kayaraiṃ pāṇa laeviṇu radaṃtaiṃ. || 8 || ghattā.

The skull of an enraged elephant was split open by someone's sword. A grasping hand was pulled, twisted and broken by someone. Someone cut off the hair from the scalps of a multitude of warriors and broke their skulls. A stream of blood spilled forth, quickly covering the ground and settling the dust. A completely clear view was afforded the warriors who had crushed the heads of the enemy's elephants. These were tall horses against tall horses; enraged elephants against enraged elephants; powerful warriors against powerful warriors; the resolution of kings against the resolution of kings; spear-tip against spear-tip; brandished sword against brandished sword; droves of rushing chariots against droves of rushing chariots; invincible soldiers against invincible soldiers; discus against discus. (4.8.1.-4.8.9) Thus, warriors mutually exhausted, observed the battlefield, amidst the roar of the war-drums, champion warriors fighting against champion warriors, taking the lives of those who were beaten, who were full of fear, had become faint-hearted and were disconsolately crying. (4.8.10)

NOTES

1. Cf. Skt. *parīṣahā*, Apa. *parīsaha.* A technical term referring to twenty-two 'vexations' which were liable to detrimentally influence the proscribed conduct of the wandering monk whose behaviour was based on the metaphysical notion of *saṃvara*, i.e. 'shutting out of the external world', in order to check the accumulation of *karma.* Canonical enumerations of the vexations are found in the second chapter of the *Uttarādhyāyansūtra* and the fiftieth *sūtra* of the *Samavāyāṅgasūtra. Tattvārthasūtra* 9.8-17 also discusses the vexations.
2. The name of the *tīrthaṅkara* Abhinandana is not mentioned, although it is alluded to by a pun on 'son' (*nandana*).
3. Upon his initiation into monkhood, Sumati broke a nine-day fast by accepting rice from Padma, king of Vijayapura.
4. A reference to the bonds of karma.
5. A reference to his death-fast (*saṃlekhanā*) which he performed as a final act before achieving *nirvāṇa.*
6. The author's selection of *yaśa* is based on the connotation of Śītala's

name 'cold', by extension to 'clear', 'bright', 'glory'. His gold color and the whiteness of his symbol, the *Śrīvatsa*, also project the concept of 'glory'.

7. I.e. *kevala-jñāna* 'omniscience', the fifth and final degree of knowledge, the possession of which qualifies the *jīva* or soul to sever all connection with the cycle of rebirth.
8. In accord with the notion of non-violence, Jainas follow a proscription to wear a filtering cloth over one's nose, and to care-fully inspect clothing, bedding, food and ground underfoot so as not to kill insects inadvertently.
9. Arihanta 'destroyer of enemies', is an epithet for *tīrthaṅkara*, similar in meaning to the more often used epithet Jina 'victor'.
10. Cf. Skt. *khacara* 'moving in the air'. A class of semi-divine, mostly benevolent demigods who fly about in the intermediate world between Heaven and Earth.
11. The author compares the Jinas' ability to slay Smara, the god of passion, with the bow-using ability of the Śabara, a tribal group of eastern India.
12. The ruddy goose, Skt. *rathāṅga*, synonymous with the *cakravāka*. These birds, usually found in pairs, were often used in Indian literature to epitomize love and the amorous couple. It was believed that they truly mourned when separated from a mate.
13. The Pravarā is a tributary of the Godāvarī which flows into the Bay of Bengal.
14. A toponym referring to the area west of the Yamunā River, roughly between the towns of Karnal, Sirsa, Hansi and Delhi. The modern form of the name is Haryana, now a state of the Indian Union.
15. An epithet of Indra. Indraprastha, 'Indra's Plain', is an area in Delhi, early associated with the god Indra, and mentioned in the *Mahābhārata*.
16. The reference to 'hostile armies' and the 'enemy' probably refers to military threats from Rājpūt clans such as the Chauhans, and also the Muslim Pathan armies which had begun to pose a threat and which eventually captured Delhi under the leadership of Muhammad ibn Sām (Muhammad Ghūrī) in AD 1192.
17. A reference to Lāl Koṭ, the fort constructed by King Anaṅgapāla II (*c.* AD 1051-81), a Tomara king of Delhi. One can still see the remnants of the bastions and moat, associated with the Qutb Minar complex, situated due north of the present village of Mehrauli.
18. King Anaṅgapāla II constructed this lake. It is adjacent to Lāl Koṭ, and must have served as a watering and pleasure spot.
19. The *Kātantra*, a Sanskrit grammar by Śrīsarvavarman. The pun is on the word *pañjī*, meaning both 'commentary' and 'account-book'. Also cf. Tamil *pañci* 'cotton'.
20. Śrīdhara's use of *suraramaṇīyaṇu* is unattested elsewhere. It can be

explained as Skt. *suraramaṇījana* 'wives or mistresses of the gods'. My translation 'goddesses', is tentative. The usage may be meant as a synonym for Skt. *apsaras* 'a class of female divinities', 'wife of a *gandharva*'.

21. *varapūaphalillu* (cf. Skt. *varapugaphalavat*) is a pun: 'possessing the best betal-nut' and 'possessing the advantage of superior troops'.
22. Namely, Mimāṃsā, Vedānta, Nyāya, Vaiśeṣika, Sāṃkhya, and Yoga.
23. A three-fold pun is possible: Apa. *sanāyau* may be construed as a *tadbhava* of Skt. *sanāda* 'possessing loud noise', *sanāga* 'possessing elephants', or *sanyāya* 'possessing logic'.
24. The pun is made possible by Apa. phonology, but is almost impossible to render in grammatical English. Apa. *kansa* is comparable to Skt. *kansa* 'the demon whom Kṛṣṇa slayed', and Skt. *kānsya* 'a bell', the sound of which fills the market.
25. The large, black crow is considered to be of evil nature and a bad omen. See Angelo do Gubernati, *Zoological Mythology*, vol. II, pp. 253-4.
26. Cf. Skt. *kṣaya-vāyu* 'the wind which occurs at the end of the world'.

REFERENCES

Cohen, Richard. 'An Early Attestation of the Toponymn Ḍhillī'. *Journal of the American Oriental Society* 109.4, 1989: 513-17.

de Gubernatis, Angelo. *Zoological Mythology, or the Legends of Animals.* London: Trubner, 1872.

Imperial Gazetteer of India. Vol. 5. New ed. Delhi: Today & Tomorrow's Printers and Publishers, 1972.

Jain, Hiralal. 'Some Recent Finds of Apabhraṃśa Literature'. *Nagpur University Journal*, 8, 1942: 81-92.

Jain, Rajaram. *Raidhū: Sāhitya kā ālocanātmak-pariśīlan.* Vaishali: Prakrit Jainshastra aur Ahimsa Shodh Sansthan, 1974.

———. *Vibhua-Sirihara-viraiu Vaḍḍhamāṇa-cariu.* New Delhi: Bharatiy Jnanpith Prakashan, 1975.

Kaslival, Kasturcand. *Praśasti-saṅgrah,* Jaipur: Digambar Jain Atishay Sri Mahavirji, 1950.

Kochar, Harivamsh. *Apabhraṃśa-sāhitya,* Delhi: Bharati Sahitya Mandir, 1962.

Niyogi, Roma. *The History of the Gāhaḍavāla Dynasty.* Calcutta: Calcutta Oriental Book Agency, 1959.

Raverty, Henry. G. *Ṭabaqāt-i-Nāṣirī.* Reprint. New Delhi: Munshiram Manoharlal, 1973.

Shastri, Nemicandra. *Tīrthaṅkar Mahāvīr aur unkī ācārya-paramparā,* Sagar: Shri Bharatvarshiya Digambar Jain Vidvatparishad, 1974.

Uttar Pradesh District Gazetteers: Agra. Lucknow: Government of Uttar Pradesh Publications, 1965.

Representations of 'Alā'uddīn Khaljī

ALAN W. ENTWISTLE

It has now become commonplace to deny the possibility of objective historiography and to assert that any account of historical events is inevitably coloured in order to reaffirm preconceptions or preach a moral message. This is certainly true of literary works based on incidents associated with 'Alā'uddīn Khaljī, one of the most famous, or one might say 'infamous', of India's Muslim rulers. In many ways his reign (1296-1316) was the highpoint of the Delhi Sultanate. He was successful in repelling Mongol invasions and, before he became sultan, was the first Muslim to lead forces south of the Narmada and into the Deccan, where he defeated the Yādavas of Deogir (later renamed Daulatabad). In the third year of his reign his armies plundered Gujarat and brought the main idol (or *liṅga*?) from Somnath to be desecrated in Delhi. In 1301 he persevered with a long and troublesome siege of Ranthambhor which ended in a *jauhar* and the death of Hammīrdev. Two years later he took Chittor, sparing the life of the defeated king; in 1305 he captured Mandu and annexed Malwa, and in 1311 defeated Jalor. His forces plundered Maharashtra and the Deccan and exacted tribute from the Kakatiyas of Tilangana and the Pandyas of Tamilnadu. Few of these conquests, however, were easily accomplished and towards the end of his reign parts of the empire broke away, and there was growing discontent among his courtiers.

'Alā'uddīn in the works of muslim historians

As opponent and conqueror of so many Hindu rulers, 'Alā'uddīn features as the antagonist in several quasi-historical works composed by Hindus and Jains, as well as by the Sufi Muḥammad Malik Jāyasī. Before discussing the way 'Alā'uddīn is characterized in these texts, we might pause to consider how he is represented in the chronicles of Muslim historians. The principal accounts are those of Amīr Khusrau (*Khazā'in al Futūḥ*, which describes events up to AD 1311), 'Abdul Malik 'Iṣāmī (1350), and Ẓiyā'uddīn Baranī (completed in 1357).[1] As one might expect from someone who resided at 'Alā'uddīn's court, Khusrau gives a flowery encomium in which he passes over his patron's more ruthless actions and praises him for maintaining law and order. Although Khusrau is impressed by the valour, courtesy, hospitality, and sense of honour of the Hindu Rājas, he extols 'Alā'uddīn's iconoclasm and victories against infidels (*kāfirs*) who, despite their bravery, are doomed to hell. A.M. 'Iṣāmī admires 'Alā'uddīn's ability to conquer and maintain power, says that in his reign the art of government reached its zenith, and praises him for the purity of his coinage, ability to keep down prices, bounteousness towards his subjects, renunciation of alcohol, and massacre of heretics (n.d. vol. 2, pp. 475-7, 491-2). Ibn Bāṭṭūṭah, who arrived in Delhi in 1333, endorses this favourable assessment by saying that 'Alā'uddīn was one of the best sultans and was still acclaimed by the inhabitants (trans. C. Defrémery 1877, p. 184).

Baranī grew up during the reign of 'Alā'uddīn and was a nephew of one of his principal advisers. While he acknowledged the achievements that were lauded by contemporary historians, he was much less effusive and places more emphasis on the tyrannical side of his character. It is not surprising that he should wish to defame 'Alā'uddīn, since he was concerned to proclaim the virtues of the ruling Sultan, Firoz Shāh Tughlaq. Among the more notorious incidents mentioned by Baranī is the manner in which 'Alā'uddīn seized power by assassinating his uncle and father-in-law, Jalāluddīn Firoz Shāh, and parading his head around on a spear. Supporters of Jalāluddīn and others who might oppose him, including their wives and children, were blinded or killed. Seeing this as a new downturn in ethical standards, Baranī comments that 'up to this time no hand had ever been laid upon wives and children on account of men's misdeeds' (trans. H.M. Elliot n.d., p. 164).

Throughout his reign, 'Alā'uddīn resorted to blinding, torture, and ruthless extermination of opponents and their families. In the course of his campaign to drive back the Mongols, he not only had thousands of soldiers trodden under the feet of elephants, but also ordered the massacre of many more newly converted Mongols who had settled in Delhi during the reign of his predecessor. He is also reported to have imprisoned Mongol ambassadors and to have had several of their attendants trampled by elephants.[2] He introduced secret agents and oppressive economic and social measures in an attempt to stifle rebellion and curtail public drinking and conviviality among the nobility, which he believed fostered conspiracy. Prices were held down, but the economy was geared to supporting a large standing army. Hindus, in order 'to grind them down' and keep them impoverished, were heavily taxed and forbidden certain luxuries such as the right to possess horses and bear arms (H.M. Elliot and J. Dowson n.d., p. 182).

'Alā'uddīn is characterized as a stern and determined ruler, but as having a violent temper that worsened as the years went by. Baranī notes (ibid., pp. 168f.) that his early successes made him reckless and even more arrogant; he considered himself capable of conquering the world, assumed the title of 'Alexander the Second', and likened himself and his four chief commanders to Muḥammad and his companions. For a while, until restrained by his advisers, he fancied that he had the power to establish a new universal religion that would immortalize his name. According to Baranī, 'Alā'uddīn's advisers encouraged him to attack Chittor in order to detract him from such hubristic schemes. He had no education and never associated with men of learning, even though his court was attended by scholars such as Amīr Khusrau;[3] nor was he regular in attending the mosque or saying his prayers (trans. A.R. Fuller and A. Khallaque 1967, p. 92) and he based his policies on expediency and pragmatism rather than on the dictates of religion. During his campaign in Gujarat he had acquired a converted young slave and eunuch named Kāfūr Hazārdīnārī (Malik Kāfūr) whom he later appointed as military commander. He allowed his infatuation for him to influence his actions and, towards the end of his reign, replaced experienced administrators with 'young slaves who were ignorant and thoughtless, and with eunuchs without intelligence' (trans. H.M. Elliot and J. Dowson n.d., p. 207).

The early historians mention 'Alā'uddīn's infatuation for Malik Kāfūr, but give us no tales about his romantic attachment to any Hindu princess. The oldest accounts of his obsession for Padmiṇī or Padmāvatī, wife of the ruler of Chittor (Ratansen), belong to the sixteenth century. The first Muslim historian to refer to a version of this legend is Firishta (1829, pp. 362-3), writing in 1606, who refers to Ratansen, his imprisonment after the fall of Chittor, 'Alā'uddīn's offer to release him in exchange for his fabulously beautiful daughter, and her ruse to secure her father's release. In the earliest sources, the only mention of a royal romance involves 'Alā'uddīn's eldest son, Khiẓr Khān, who is said to have fallen in love with Deval Rānī (or Deval Devī), daughter of Karaṇ Rāī of Gujarat, a romance that is celebrated by Amīr Khusrau in his *'Āshīqah.*[4] Khiẓr Khān was placed in charge of Chittor after it was conquered, which may partly explain how the story of 'Alā'uddīn's passion for the Rāṇā's queen came about.

Although many of 'Alā'uddīn's actions were unexceptional for their times, Baranī seems to have set the tone for the denunciations of later historians. Firishta is inclined to present 'Alā'uddīn's career as an example of retribution. After noting the misfortunes that soon befell the assassins 'Alā'uddīn set upon his uncle, he adds that 'even Alla-ood-Deen himself, though fortune smiled on him at first, yet in the end he suffered great distress of mind, being obliged to imprison his own children, and to put to death, one after another, the friends whom he had loved most, and in whom he most confided' (1829, p. 319).

Literary adaptations of the deeds of 'Alā'uddīn

The picture that emerges from these sources has led to the characterization of 'Alā'uddīn as a cruel and arrogant despot and an oppressor of Hinduism who eventually got what he deserved. J. Tod refers to the 'remorseless brutality' of his attack on Chittor (1920, vol. 1, p. 307) and notes that he was known by the epithet *khūnī* ('bloodthirsty, murderous', 1920, vol. 2, p. 809, 1920, vol. 3, p. 1698). The bard Sūryamall Miśraṇ in his *Vaṃś bhāskar,* an extensive history of the Hāḍā Rajputs of Bundi written in the mid-nineteenth century, introduces 'Alā'uddīn as the 'cruel' and 'wicked' nephew of Jalāluddīn, compares him to a serpent, describes him more than once as 'unbearable' and characterizes his rule as *ugra* ('fierce', 'harsh', 'cruel').[5] A common non-Muslim view of 'Alā'uddīn's reign is that it marks the nadir of Muslim rule. For example, in his introduction to *Hammīramahākāvya* (Nayacandra Sūri 1968, p. 3), Muni Jinvijay says that 'Alā'uddīn was responsible for a cataclysm (*pralaya*) in Indian history. His aim in life was to annihilate Indian culture and prosperity: 'Everywhere he ignited a dreadful forest fire in order to destroy India's nationhood to the very root.' Because Ranthambhor was such a significant conquest for him, it was only natural that the blazing fire of 'Alā'uddīn's cruel gaze should fall on it in order to bring it under his control as well. [Hammīr] was no figurine of crude iron that would simply melt in the glare of 'Alā'uddīn's cruel fire of anger.

Elsewhere (introduction to Hemratan 1966, p. 3) he refers to 'Alā'uddīn as the

mega-barbaric (*mahāmlecch*), most wicked (*duṣṭatam*) Muslim Sultan of Delhi . . . a perversely lustful (*viṣam-lolup*), infatuated (*madāndh*), sacrilegious (*dharma-dhvaṃsak*), murderous Muslim Turk intent on destroying the integrity (*satītva*) of superlative Hindu women.

We do not find such outright condemnation of 'Alā'uddīn in the quasi-historical works composed between the fifteenth and early nineteenth centuries that deal with his confrontations with the rulers of Deogir, Jalor, Ranthambhor, and Chittor. The campaign against Kānhaḍde of Jalor is described in Padmanābh's *Kānhaḍde prabandh* (*KDP* 1456, a work usually classified as being in Old Gujarati, though the language might arguably be termed 'Old [Western] Rajasthani'). A brief but interesting prose account of the siege of Jalor is given by Mūhto Naiṇsī in his Rajasthani (i.e. Marwari) *khyāt,* written in the mid-seventeenth century. The love of 'Alā'uddīn's daughter for the son of Kānhaḍde is told in the anonymous *Vīramde Sonīgarā rī vāt,* which has been edited on the basis of manuscripts dating from 1704.

The heroic stand of Hammīr at Ranthambhor is recounted in Nayacandra Sūri's Sanskrit *Hammīramahākāvya* (*HMK*), composed before or around 1400,[6] and in a series of vernacular accounts, of which the most important are Bhāṇḍau's *Hammīrāyaṇ* (*HA,* also titled *Hammīrde caupaī,* 1481, in Rajasthani), Amṛtkalaś's *Hammīr prabandh* (*HP,* 1518, in Old Gujarati/Rajasthani), *Hammīr rāso* by Maheś Kavi (early seventeenth century), and an expanded version with the same title by Jodhrāj (1828), both in Brajb Bhāṣā, or rather the modified version of the language that is referred to in Rajasthan as 'Pingal'.[7]

The campaigns against Deogir and Chittor are associated with more romantic legends, the first involving a princess named Chitāī—which has been narrated by Nārāyaṇdās in *Chitāī vārtā* (*CV,* early sixteenth century?, in Braj Bhāṣā/Pingal).[8] The second features the celebrated story of Padmiṇī/Padmāvatī, which forms the subject of Jāyasī's *Padmāvat* (*P,* 1540, in Awadhi), Hemratan's

Gorā Bādal Padminī caupaī (*GBPC*, 1588, in Rajasthani),[9] Jaṭmal Nāhar's *Gorā Bādal caupaī* (*GBC*, 1623, in Pingal), Labdhoday's *Padmiṇī caritra caupaī* (*PCC*, *c.* 1650, in Rajasthani), and the sixth *khaṇḍ* of *Khumāṇ rāso* (*KR*), composed in Rajasthani in the first half of the eighteenth century by a poet named Dalpat or Daulatvijay.[10]

All of these works, especially those dealing with Chitāī and Padmiṇī, are free literary adaptations of the basic historical material. In them the sieges and various characters are confused or conflated and names and other details vary from one version to another.[11] Some incidents are no doubt borrowed from folklore and earlier heroic and romantic legends. The representation of 'Alā'uddīn in all of these works is not as negative as one might expect, given the way in which he is characterized by Baranī and his successors. For instance, very little mention is made of his iconoclasm. *Chitāī vārtā* (*CV* 260-1) does say that, on the way to Deogir, he destroyed temples and erected mosques on their sites, but this is given merely as an incidental detail. His seizure of the *linga* from the temple of Somnath and his attempt to drag it through the territory of Jalor is part of the reason for the conflict with Kānhaḍde, but the act of iconoclasm itself does not provoke much comment.

Somewhat more is made of his violent temper, which is described by various metaphors of which the most common is that of him flaring up like ghee thrown into in a fire.[12] Jodhrāj says that he rose up like a cobra when he heard that one of his men had taken refuge at Ranthambhor, and in *Padmāvat* (*P* 494), when rebuffed by Ratansen, he blazed in anger like the summer sun and his gaze set everything on fire wherever it fell. The poets do not resort to such metaphors on the few occasions when the Rajput protagonists lose their temper; on the whole, their stance is one of dignified defiance in the face of 'Alā'uddīn's impetuosity.

A clash of cultures

The most common term used to identify Muslims in this type of literature (apart perhaps from the simple epithet 'Turk') is not *mleccha* ('barbarian') but *asura* ('demon', 'devil'). As this term suggests, the confrontation is not seen as a clash of specific individuals, but rather a contest between opposing principles. The manner in which the conflicts are narrated encourages us to view them as epic struggles between Hindu culture and a demonic force that seeks to destroy it, or between *dharma* and *adharma.* For example, Naiṇsī says (1960, vol. 1, p. 213) that when the cart on which the uprooted *liṅga* of Somnath was placed refused to budge, the obstinate 'Alā'uddīn had five hundred oxen harnessed to it. This was to no avail: the *liṅga* emitted fire that required five hundred water carriers to extinguish. Although Śiv displayed such miraculous power, the 'demons' (*dānavas*) prevailed and, albeit at the rate of only one *kos* per day, managed to drag the *liṅga* as far as Jalor.

In *Kānhaḍde prabandh* (*KDP* 4.297), Kānhaḍde urges his men to fight and kill the *mlecchas* in a battle like that of the *Rāmāyaṇa.* Amṛtkalaś (*HP* 676) says that Hammīr's stand against 'Alā'uddīn in this Kali Age corresponds to the battle between the Pāṇḍavas and the Kauravas in the Dvāpar Age, Rām and Rāvaṇ in the Tretā Age, and the great battle of Mandhātā in the Kṛta Age. Bādal likens himself to Hanumān in the service of Rām when he explains to his mother why he must fight to defend Ratansen and Padmiṇī (*GBC* p. 201, v. 100), and *Khumāṇ rāso* [*KR* p. 181, (28) 53] compares Bādal, Ratansen, and Padmiṇī to Hanumān, Rām, and Sītā. The implication here, of course, is that 'Alā'uddīn represents Rāvaṇ, and as such is a latter-day representative of a perennial antagonistic principle.

Sometimes Hindu and Jain poets bring in the theory of *karma* in order to explain why such exemplary Rajput heroes should be on the losing side. In *Kānhaḍde prabandh* and *Vīramde Sonīgarā rī vāt,* 'Alā'uddīn's daughter falls in love with Vīramde, the son of Kānhaḍde. She explains to her father (*KDP* 3.194ff.) that she had been married to Vīramde in six previous lives, some of which ended with her becoming a *satī.* Because of a sin committed in her sixth life, she was reborn in the seventh as a 'Turk'.[13] Later on (*KDP* 3.212-22) she explains that Kānhaḍde was once a *dev* while 'Alā'uddīn was reborn an *asur* as a result of karmic retribution, but he would eventually be released.

Naiṇsī (1960, vol. 1, pp. 213-16) gives a more elaborate explanation in which 'Alā'uddīn and Kānhaḍde are reborn from two halves of a Brahmin who commited ritual suicide at Kasi by means of some kind of sawing apparatus (*karot, karvat*). This Brahmin had been a devotee of Śiv, but was disaffected when his hands were amputated as a result of being falsely charged with murder (whereby hangs another tale of karmic retribution). The person administering the *karvat* told the Brahmin that by giving up his present life he could wish for anything he desired in the next. The Brahmin, wishing to avenge Śiv for failing to protect him, said that one half of his body should be born as someone who would uproot the *liṅga* of Somnath and bind it in wet leather, while the other should be born as someone who would rescue it. This story encourages us to regard 'Alā'uddīn and Kānhaḍde as actors in a conflict that transcends the historical moment and the span of their mortal lives, that is attributed to supernatural causes, and will ultimately be resolved. Alternatively, the situation can be the result of a curse. In *Chitāī vārtā* (*CV* 211-20), Saūrsiṃh forfeits his wife Chitāī to another man when, while pursuing his passion for deer hunting, he disturbs and is cursed by the sage Bhartṛhari.

A striking resolution of the Hindu-Muslim conflict is found in the two versions of *Hammīr rāso* (Maheś Kavi 22-5; Jodhrāj 99-171). In the eleventh century, there was an ascetic named Padma who was instrumental in the founding of Ranthambhor. He was seduced by nymphs sent by Indra and so, to atone for this shameful lapse, performed a sacrifice in which he divided himself into five parts. His head became 'Alā'uddīn, his chest Hammīr, his arms Mahimāśāh (i.e. Muḥammad Shāh, a fugitive from 'Alā'uddīn harboured by Hammīr) and his brother Gabharū, and his feet the woman who was to become 'Alā'uddīn's begum. At the end of the story, when 'Alā'uddīn offers terms for peace, Hammīr reminds him that they are both partial incarnations (*aṃśas*) of Padma Riṣi and should fight in order to reunite themselves in death (Jodhrāj 852ff., cf. Maheś Kavi 239ff.). As the battle rages, Hammīr says that so much blood is being spilled that he and 'Alā'uddīn should fight each other hand to hand. 'Alā'uddīn consults with his advisers, who tell him that, since he is bound to lose, he should sue for peace. Hammīr rejects 'Alā'uddīn's cowardly offer and orders his warriors to stop using missiles and demonstrate their true valour by fighting only with swords and daggers or by wrestling. When they attack in this way, the Muslims flee and 'Alā'uddīn is captured on his elephant. Hammīr says that he should be set free and allowed to rejoin his troops.

'Alā'uddīn returns to Delhi and the Rajputs pick up the banners of the defeated Muslims, which they brandish as they march back to Ranthambhor. Seeing the enemy's banners, the women throw themselves into the fire, thinking that the Muslims have won and are advancing to claim the fort. Hammīr, when he learns of this, cuts off his head and offers it to Śiv. When 'Alā'uddīn arrives on the scene to pay his respects, the severed head tells him to go and drown himself in the ocean. 'Alā'uddīn instructs his wazir to enthrone his son then goes to Rāmeshwaram, does *pūjā* of the *liṅga*, and plunges into the sea. In this way 'Alā'uddīn, Hammīr, and Mahimāśāh are all reunited in heaven. *Kānhaḍde prabandh* (*KDP* 2.131-8) presents another way of mythologizing the conflict. The Rajput hero Sā̃tal is shown around the enemy camp at night by his patron goddess. He sees that the sleeping 'Alā'uddīn possesses all the trappings of Śiv and wonders how he can fight an opponent who has taken on the form (*avatariu*) of Rudra, yet decides he must do so since he cannot abandon his honour. Later in the story (*KDP* 3.163-6), 'Alā'uddīn sees Kānhaḍde in a dream as an incarnation of Viṣṇu.

Rajput ethics

In the Hammīr narratives particularly, 'Alā'uddīn serves as a foil against which the superiority of Rajput *dharma* can be demonstrated. The keystones of the Rajput ethic are loyalty, keeping one's word—here specifically the refusal to hand over fugitives, and not giving away one's women in marriage in order to placate barbarians. In all of these legends death is preferable to dishonour. Rajput women, for example, choose to kill themselves rather than fall into the hands of the enemy. Likewise, Hammīr decapitates himself after declaring that posthumous reputation is more important than any concerns of worldly life.

The Rajputs are seen as protectors of Hindu society. *Kānhaḍde prabandh* contains two descriptions of Jalor as a Hindu utopia, the first when 'Alā'uddīn's daughter surveys the citadel and the second when she describes it to her father (*KDP* 3.242ff., 4.5ff.). Amṛtkalaś begins his narrative with a description of Ranthambhor as a place where Brahmins and cows are protected, merchants conduct thriving businesses, culture flourishes, etc. Jodhrāj says that men and women maintained their respective duties (338: *apanai apanai dharmma maĩ rahaĩ sabai nara nāri*), and both he (336-7) and Maheś Kavi (70-1) remark that there was no trace of Islam at

Ranthambhor. In *Padmāvat* (*P* 501-2) Chittor is said to be a bastion of Hinduism, and when Hindu kings plead with 'Alā'uddīn not to attack it, he graciously gives them betel as a sign that they should go there to defend it. One of the stipulations made by Kānhaḍde's son in his negotiations with 'Alā'uddīn (*KDP* 3.239) is that he should desist from his assaults on temples, Brahmins, and cows.

A true Rajput can be relied on to keep his word. Even in death, Vīramde keeps his vow never to look at 'Alā'uddīn's daughter. Padmanābh tells us that his severed head turned away when it was presented to her on a tray (*KDP*, 4.323-5) and Naiṇsī (1960, vol. 1, p. 224) says that as the head was carried round the fire in a marriage ceremony, it swivelled so as to keep its gaze averted. After her marriage to the severed head, 'Alā'uddīn's daughter had herself cremated along with it, thus showing that she had absorbed the Hindu principles of wifely fidelity. *Vīramde Sonīgarā rī vāt* concludes by saying that Vīramde's head turned towards her when she declared that she would become a *satī*, and afterwards the two of them are reconciled (Anonymous, 1960, p. 99: *sāh vegamrai nai Vīramderai rūsṇo bhāgo*).

'Alā'uddīn is vengeful against those who flout his authority, but he is also just and respectful to Nālh, Hammīr's bard. Following the *jauhar* and death of Hammīr and his warriors, 'Alā'uddīn arrives on the scene with Nālh to pay his respects (*HA* 297ff.). Nālh delivers a eulogy of Hammīr and the heroes who fell with him, including the Muslim rebels to whom he had given shelter and who had served him loyally. He also praises 'Alā'uddīn and is granted a boon by him. He demands the execution of the Hindu traitors Raypāl and Raṇmal. Amṛtkalaś tells how, after flaying the traitors and rewarding the bard, Alā'uddīn cremated Hammīr's body and immersed his remains in the Ganges (*HP* 675).

Sometimes 'Alā'uddīn is depicted in a surprisingly favourable light. After his opening paean to the Hindu city of Ranthambhor, Amṛtkalaś lavishes praise on 'Alā'uddīn's Delhi for its law and order, fair dealings in the market, and freedom to practise different religions (*HP* 51-82). 'Alā'uddīn is said to be charitable and to believe in all the six schools of Hindu philosophy, and the description ends with a line comparing him to Indra (*HP* 82: *pahuvi iṃda ki avataru alāvadīna suritāṇa*). Such compliments are endorsed by later poets, such as Labdhoday, who says that Brahmins and *paṇḍits* are well received at 'Alā'uddīn's court (*PCC* pp. 26-7).

Some of the Rajput ethic seems to rub off on 'Alā'uddīn. In *Chitāī vārtā* he is shown to be chivalrous in his treatment of Chitāī's father, Rāmdev, when he comes to Delhi after they have concluded peace. He became good friends with 'Alā'uddīn (*CV* 74-5) and stayed in Delhi for three years.[14] Later on, 'Alā'uddīn is shown to be as scrupulous as any Rajput in keeping his word. When he entered the fort in disguise and was recognized by one of Chitāī's maids, he promised her that he would lift the siege the next day if she agreed not to reveal his identity. Assuring her of his trustworthiness, he promises that if he is still there by the next mealtime, then he would eat pork (*CV* 456). Later he declares that, just like Hariścandra and Bali, he must keep his word (*CV* 489-90). In *Kānhaḍde prabandh* (*KDP* 4.112) he is confident that Kānhaḍde will never break his promise and launch a night attack and, correspondingly, instructs his troops to fight the Hindus fairly (*KDP* 4.115-17).

Alongside these commendations, there are also references to 'Alā'uddīn's deceitfulness. The defensive stance taken by Hindu and Jain writers is based on notions of purity and moral superiority (valour, honour, chivalry), which contrast with the rapaciousness and opportunism of alien culture. Jāyasī shows us that 'Alā'uddīn is untrustworthy, as when Gorā and Bādal warn Ratansen about the craftiness of the Turks (*P* 558). Jaṭmal is fond of the word *kapaṭ* to describe 'Alā'uddīn's cunning, as when he exploits the invitation into the fort as a means of capturing Ratansen (*GBC* p. 195, v. 71). Hemratan and Dalpat both repeat a line saying that while Ratansen's heart is free of guile, 'Alā'uddīn harbours excessive animosity.[15] Dalpat attributes this quality to Hindus in general, who are said not to resort to duplicity (*bheda*), and when Ratansen is captured he remarks that a Muslim is not to be trusted [*KR* p. 147, v.(25)56: *asura taṇo keho visavāsa*]. It is only after 'Alā'uddīn acts dishonestly (by seizing his host while being escorted out of the fort), that Gorā and Bādal decide that the only way they can free Ratansen is by adopting the same kind of crafty tactics as the Turks (e.g. *P* 621). In order to free Ratansen, they follow the celebrated ruse of bringing into 'Alā'uddīn's stronghold palanquins that purport to convey Padmiṇī and her handmaidens, but in fact contain a force of armed men. Realising that he has been deceived by Gorā and Bādal, 'Alā'uddīn acknowledges that he was the first to play false when he captured Ratansen (*GBPC* 556).

In *Padmāvat*, 'Alā'uddīn showers gifts on Ratansen before capturing him, then submits him to incarceration and torture—which happens to be the only direct reference to his cruelty (*P* 574ff.). Jāyasī does however show that 'Alā'uddīn has some decency: when Rāghav Cetan tries to get him to look up at Padmāvatī, he expresses his reluctance to do so because he is a guest in the palace (*P* 561). Generally, in the various narratives, 'Alā'uddīn resorts to trickery only when force fails, and then it is usually at the instigation of a Hindu traitor.

The real villains

'Alā'uddīn is the antagonist of the Rajput princes, but he is not really the villain. Since he is a *mleccha*, he can be expected to behave in a barbaric manner, hence the authors do not dwell on his predictable defects. There is not much explicit criticism of his lust, cruelty, or other moral failings—he is a benighted *asur* after all. The real villains are not the barbarians, but treacherous Hindus who should know better. Motivated by rancour and untrue to their *dharma*, they are the ones who are criticized and punished. Muslims succeed not only because of their superior power, but also because they are aided by traitors.

One of the villains in *Kānhaḍde prabandh* is Mādhan Mahuto (*KDP* 1.13ff.), a disgruntled Brahmin minister of Sāraṅgde of Gujarat, who is blamed for leading the *mlecchas* into Hindu territory. He goes to Delhi and incites 'Alā'uddīn to invade Gujarat and demand that Kānhaḍde allow him to pass through Jalor. There is also a palanquin bearer (*sejvāḷ*) named Vīkau, who is motivated by greed to show the Muslims a way into the fort, but is killed by his outraged wife when she learns of his treachery (*KDP* 4.185ff.).

In *Hammīramahākāvya* (*HMK* 9.151ff.), Dharmasiṃh is disaffected when Hammīr mutilates and disgraces him for his mishandling of an attack led by 'Alā'uddīn's brother. Hammīr replaces Dharmasiṃh with his bastard brother Khāṇḍadhar Bhoj, but he is also persuaded to defect. The chief villain in the Hammīr legend is his envoy Ratipāl (or Rāypāl), later joined by Raṇmal, whom 'Alā'uddīn wins over with bribes and by plying him with drink (see *HMK* 13.49-82, cf. *HA* 223ff.). They reveal the secret passage into the fort—a devastating act of betrayal towards Hammīr for which 'Alā'uddīn eventually puts them to death since they cannot be expected to be faithful to him either.

In the Chitāī and Ratansen-Padmiṇī legends, the villain is the Brahmin Rāghav Cetan.[16] In *Gorā Bādal Padmiṇī caupai* (*GBPC* 94-135) and subsequent versions of the story, Rāghav Cetan incurs Ratansen's anger by walking into a private apartment where he and Padmiṇī are making love. When Ratansen orders his eyes to be put out, he flees to Delhi, ingratiates himself with 'Alā'uddīn, and instigates his search for a *padmiṇī* that eventually takes him to Chittor. Rāghav Cetan gets his revenge by stimulating 'Alā'uddīn's desire for Padmiṇī and devising the scheme by which he gets invited into the fort and subsequently captures Ratansen. In *Padmāvat* (*P* 446-9), Rāghav Cetan is disaffected when he is found to have used his magic to alter the appearance of the moon in order to cover up an astrological miscalculation he had made. In *Chitāī vārtā* (*CV* 330-43) there are mitigating circumstances for Rāghav's treachery. 'Alā'uddīn, having decided to resort to trickery after other means have failed, tells Rāghav Cetan that he will have him flayed the next day unless he can devise a stratagem. Rāghav prays to his patron goddess, who suggests the ploy of going into the fort accompanied by two female spies and 'Alā'uddīn disguised as a servant.

Motivated by greed, desire for revenge, or simply because they are mean-spirited, these traitors all find fertile soil for their treachery by joining up with the Muslims. In contrast, Rajput ethics are assimilated by Muslim defectors to the side of Hammīr. Mahimāśāh and the others who seek refuge with him are not spoken of with disapproval. In *Hammīramahākāvya* (*HMK* 13.148ff.) Mahimāśāh demonstrates that he is as staunch as any Rajput by killing his womenfolk and then fighting to death on the side of his protector. In later versions (Maheś Kavi 224-5, Jodhrāj 830-1), 'Alā'uddīn offers to forgive Mahimāśāh and reward him with land grants and a bride. Mahimāśāh declines, saying that even in his next birth he will remain loyal to Hammīr.

'Alā'uddīn in love

In the legends about Chittor and Deogir, 'Alā'uddīn's motivation for investing the fort is to capture a supremely beautiful woman. This motive, evidently chosen for its romantic appeal, is not mentioned by any of the Muslim historians. As emperor, 'Alā'uddīn considers it a matter of pride that he should have the best of everything and get whatever he wants. In *Padmiṇī caritra caupaī*

'Alā'uddīn wonders how the Hindus can dare to compete with him and angrily declares that he will destroy Chittor simply by blowing at it and will snatch Padmiṇī from the Rāṇā like a bird.[17] In the Gorā-Bādal narratives, 'Alā'uddīn is aroused by Rāghav Cetan's description of the *padmiṇī* type of woman. When Rāghav Cetan is invited to inspect the women of the harem (in most versions by looking at their reflections), he declares that none of 'Alā'uddīn's women belongs to the *padmiṇī* category. In Labdhoday's version, 'Alā'uddīn expresses his disappointment by asking what the purpose of his incarnation is, for without a *padmiṇī* an emperor has no real sovereignty and all other women seem insipid.[18] His failure to bring back a *padmiṇī* from the island of Singhala adds to his embarrassment and results in his being taunted by his begum. Rāghav Cetan then suggests launching an attack on Chittor in order to capture Ratansen's Padmiṇī (*GBPC* 228-41).

In the Chitāī story, 'Alā'uddīn is shown to be a sensitive soul who responds to the charms of music, which Chitāī's father had taught him to appreciate (*CV* 74). 'Alā'uddīn swoons when he is shown portraits of Chitāī made by a painter who himself had swooned whenever he caught sight of her at Deogir. 'Alā'uddīn's falling for Chitāī is not portrayed negatively, rather it is presented as the way any full-blooded man would react on seeing such a beauty, just as in *Padmāvat* both he and Ratansen swoon when they behold or merely hear descriptions of Padmiṇī.

Chitāī, however, is already betrothed to a prince named Saũrsiṃh, one of whose qualities is that, contrary to 'Alā'uddīn, he does not have an eye for other men's women (*CV* 154: *para tīā para driṣṭa navi karaï*). 'Alā'uddīn immediately begins to suffer the pangs of *viraha* and, despite the princess's engagement and his friendship with her father, sends an army to abduct her from Deogir (*CV* 247-8). Eventually he manages to have her captured during one of her daily visits to a Śiv temple. He feels ashamed when she says that she is like a daughter to him, but none the less installs her in his harem so as not to lose face (*CV* 535-8). He does what he can to cheer her up, giving her fifty dancing girls to whom she can teach music in the southern style. He ceases to cast his evil gaze (*pāpadriṣṭi*) on her and places her in the care of Rāghav Cetan (*CV* 552).

'Alā'uddīn is moved when he hears Saũrsiṃh, now a Yogī

wandering in search of his bride, play a *vīṇā* that Chitāī had left with a musician in the hope that one day her fiancé would turn up and play it. 'Alā'uddīn asks Saũrsiṃh to perform for Chitāī and is deeply touched when he sees how overcome she is by the music (*CV* 668). Recognizing their true love, his heart melts and he allows them to marry, entrusting Chitāī to Saũrsiṃh 'like a father giving away his daughter' (*CV* 727-8).

Hemratan portrays 'Alā'uddīn as a victim of *virah,* his desire inflamed by Bādal's words (*GBPC* 518-22). In Dalpat's version, 'Alā'uddīn declares that he feels incomplete after catching a glimpse of Padmiṇī; he is 'like a cloud without water', etc., and will become a fakir if he has to go back to Delhi without her (*KR*, p. 144, v. (25)32). According to Labdhoday (*PCC* pp. 101-2), 'Alā'-uddīn explains his defeat by saying that the Hindus were able to trick him only because he had fallen under the spell of Padmiṇī. His begum, reminding him of how Rāvaṇ lost his kingdom for the sake of a woman, replies that he has now learned his lesson and should concentrate on God and rule contentedly.

Padmāvat is distinctive for the way in which it presents Ratansen's pursuit of Padmāvatī as a spiritual quest. Jāyasī, who belonged to the Chishtī spiritual lineage of Niẓāmuddīn Auliyā (the preceptor of Khusrau and Baranī), saw how the legend could serve as a vehicle for describing the Sufi mystic's journey. Moreover, the legend had probably become topical following a recent *jauhar* at Chittor when it was attacked by Bahādur Shāh of Gujarat in 1534. Readers of the poem are inevitably struck by the disjunction between the first two-thirds of the work, in which Ratansen pursues Padmāvatī, and the last third, which describes events after his return to Chittor. Vaudeville notes that the first part is self-sufficient and, true to the Persian *masnavī* genre, is an allegorical account of the hero's spiritual quest for a vision of the divine, whereas the latter is more of a pseudo-historical 'roman de chevalerie' that relies more on the tropes of the Indian *mahākāvya* and folklore traditions.[19]

Jāyasī is the only author to develop the theme of the need to become a Yogī in order to win Padmāvatī. The closest we come to this in other versions is in Labdhoday (*PCC* pp. 9-10) and Jaṭmal (*GBC* p. 184, vv. 13-14), where Ratansen meets a Yogī who, by asking him to assume the guise of a Yogī, helps him reach the island of Singhala by flying over the sea on an antelope skin. In *Chitāī vārtā* Saũrsiṃh becomes a Yogī when he wanders in search of Chitāī, but in none of these cases is the need for renunciation developed to anything like the extent it is in *Padmāvat.* In the other versions the motive for Ratansen's search is more down-to-earth, or even flippant: Ratansen one day jests about his wife Prabhāvatī's cooking, to which she retorts with words to the effect 'If you don't like my cooking, then go to Singhala and find yourself a *padmiṇī* !'[20]

Jāyasī does not pass judgment on 'Alā'uddīn or condemn him explicitly for his lust or deceitfulness, but simply allows poetic justice to take its course. Both Ratansen and 'Alā'uddīn set out on an ardent quest, but while the former does so honourably, the latter resorts to devious means—his love for Padmāvatī is carnal. In terms of love symbolism, Ratansen is like the sun and Padmāvatī like the moon, but in terms of temporal power, Ratansen is like the moon in comparison to 'Alā'uddīn, the effulgent sun-king. Their final battle is described as one between the sun and the moon (*P* 515-24). Solar imagery is often used with reference to 'Alā'uddīn. He is a bounteous sun who rewards his feudatories (*P* 566-7); by day he is as brilliant as the sun, an intelligent and glorious monarch who knows and understands everything, while at night he disguises himself as a Yogī in order to roam about and check up on the welfare of his subjects (*P* 457-8). When Rāghav Cetan is rebuked by Ratansen, he seeks the munificent patronage of 'Alā'uddīn. By describing the beauties of the lotus Padmāvatī, he plans to make him rise up like the sun, leaving Ratansen like a mere fish in the water (*P* 456; see also solar imagery in 490), which recalls the feat by which he used his knowledge of magic to manipulate the moon.

The ending of *Padmāvat* seems somewhat perfunctory after the detailed narrative of the preceding episodes, but Jāyasī does give us a few poignant lines about 'Alā'uddīn when he goes into the fort to view the remains of the *jauhar* (*P* 651). He casts a handful of ashes from the pyre into the air, now aware of the vanity of worldly striving and realizing that craving is not extinguished until one is covered in ashes. There is nothing like this in any of the other accounts. The closest thing to it is at the end of Amṛtkalaś's somewhat earlier version of the Hammīr story (*HP* 663ff.) where 'Alā'uddīn arrives at the scene of the women's *jauhar* and Hammīr's suicide. When he witnesses the destruction, he throws down his weapons, having realized that honour and reputation are more long-lasting than worldly success.

Women and honour

In *Kānhaḍde prabandh* (*KDP* 2.71) 'Alā'uddīn, in the course of boasting about his conquests, mentions that Rāmde of Deogir gave him his daughter. It is therefore not surprising that he should reject his own daughter's request to marry Vīramde, the son of Kānhaḍde, saying that she should marry a Muslim prince instead (*KDP* 3.123ff.). When she praises the refinements and admirable qualities of Hindu culture as opposed to that of the Turks, 'Alā'uddīn agrees to the match. However, Vīramde says that he would never forfeit his honour by marrying a Turk and mocks 'Alā'uddīn for attempting to make territorial gains through a marriage alliance rather than warfare; shame would befall the entire Rajput race if he were to agree—such a thing is unprecedented and could never happen, for a Cauhān Rajput never relinquishes his honour (*KDP* 3.140: *cāhuāṇa navi mū̃kai mā̃ṇa*). In Naiṇsī's account, 'Alā'uddīn's daughter falls for Vīramde when she sees him perform in a wrestling contest. She goes on hunger strike in order to force her father to consent to the marriage. Vīramde, however, rejects 'Alā'uddīn's offer and returns to Jalor, which causes 'Alā'uddīn to send an army to avenge the slight.

In the Hammīr, Chitāī, and Padmiṇī narratives the question of giving Hindu women to 'Alā'uddīn is a central issue, one that is of course related to cultural notions about the inferiority of bride-givers to bride-takers. In the Hammīr narratives, one of 'Alā'uddīn's demands when he sues for peace is Hammīr's daughter Devalde[21]—a proposal that Hammīr naturally declines (*HMK* 11, *HP* 411-17, etc.). She is mentioned along with gold mohurs, elephants, horses, etc., and the surrender of the fugitive rebel chiefs. Later (*HMK* 13.105-29), Ratipāl spreads the rumour in the women's quarters that all 'Alā'uddīn had really demanded was the hand of Hammīr's daughter. This leads the women to express their willingness to let the girl be handed over, but Hammīr replies that to surrender her to sinful, base, beef-eating Muslims would bring disgrace upon him and result in a miserable afterlife.

'Alā'uddīn's readiness to compromise the honour of his women is demonstrated by the way in which he wins Ratipāl over to his side by allowing him to enter his harem and enjoy the company of his sister (*HMK* 13.81). Another incident involving women is one in which dancing girls are used to taunt 'Alā'uddīn, as when Hammīr stages a dance performance on the battlements of Ranthambhor in which one or two of his female dancers (the number and names vary) insult 'Alā'uddīn by turning their backs or pointing their feet at him while he watches from below. He puts a stop to this by having an archer wound the dancer(s), upon which Mahimāśāh fires back an arrow that knocks down 'Alā'uddīn's crown or parasol.[22]

In the Chitāī and Padminī stories the issue of handing women over to 'Alā'uddīn is a major concern. Chittor was an important symbol because the ruler of Mewar, Mahārāṇā Pratāp, had put up a valiant fight against the Mughals. Hemratan wrote his version of the Gorā-Bādal story twelve years after Pratāp's heroic stand against Akbar at Haldī Ghāṭī and two years after he had regained all of his territory except Chittor (*GBPC* intro., p. 22). Some manuscripts of *Gorā Bādal Padminī caupaī* conclude with a *praśasti* mentioning Mahārāṇā Pratāp, who was still alive and resisting the Mughals. They also inform us that the poem was commissioned by a prominent Jain businessman who was a brother of one of Pratāp's governor's (see *GBPC* pp. 98-9). The message is that while some may be prepared to concede 'Alā'uddīn's demands, true warriors like Gorā and Bādal do not trade their women for peace in the manner suggested by Vīrbhāṇ, the son of Ratansen (*GBPC* 392-4). As the son of Ratansen's first wife, he sees Padminī as the reason why his mother has been deprived of her husband. Padminī seeks the assistance of Gorā and his nephew Bādal, proclaiming more than once that she would sooner destroy her tongue or burn herself than go to the house of *asura*.[23] At first Bādal's mother is opposed and sends his wife to dissuade him, but the young bride gives him her support when she sees his determination to fight. Bādal suggests that Gorā should stay behind in the fort, but Gorā objects, saying that by doing so he would ruin his noble character.[24] Vīrbhāṇ eventually agrees to resist 'Alā'uddīn when Bādal comes up with the idea of smuggling soldiers inside palanquins.

Hemratan's purpose, therefore, appears to have been to inspire those who, like Gorā and Bādal, were prepared to defy the Mughals and to criticize those who, like Vīrbhāṇ, were prepared to submit and come to terms with them (for negative references to Vīrbhāṇ, see *GBPC* 97, 107). Hemratan presents Gorā and Bādal as upholders of Rajput martial values (*khitravaṭa rīti, GBPC* 376ff.) who repeatedly express concern for their reputation as loyal *kṣatriyas.* Possibly his intention was also to criticize indirectly those Rajputs who had rendered brides to the Mughals, as the Kachvāhās of Jaipur had done to Akbar.

'Alā'uddīn had set a precedent by accepting the daughter of Rāmdev of Deogir in exchange for peace and protection. The question of whether he should be allowed to take Rajput brides remained the dominant theme in all later versions of the Padmiṇī legend. Dalpat frequently refers to Gorā and Bādal's concern for their Rajput honour (*khatrīvaṭa*) and loyalty to their feudal lord (*sā̃madharama*), mentions their dedication to protecting the honour of the Hindus (*KR* p.153: *māṇa rakhkhahū̃ hiṃdavā̃ṇa*), and, in his final line, declares that Hindu *dharma* proved its worth and the kettledrums of glory resounded [*hī̃dū dhrama sata parimāṇa, vājyā suja (sa) taṇā nīsā̃na*]. In *Vīramde Sonīgarā rī vāt* (Anonymous 1960, p. 97) the mortally wounded hero declares before 'Alā'uddīn that Rajputs follow *hindu khatrī dharam* and that mouths that have repeated the name of Rām cannot pronounce the Muslim *kalimah.*

Though he was a Muslim, Jāyasī's sympathy seems to have lain with the Rajputs and he shows us the hollowness of 'Alā'uddīn's victory (A. Ahmad 1963, p. 475). Among the literary works featuring 'Alā'uddīn, *Padmāvat* is exceptional in that it is concerned not so much with the historical confrontation as with the difference between worldly and spiritual love, pointing out the moral superiority of the true lovers' *Liebestod* and exposing the vanity of carnal desire. In the other literary works, historical legends are freely adapted to reaffirm Hindu cultural values in the context of a stirring romance. These works belong to a type that Aziz Ahmad has called 'counter-epic'. Some of them have an obviously apologetic purpose in that they explain the defeat of Hindu kings as the result of fate or *karma.* None of them is particularly concerned with pointing out specific flaws in the character of 'Alā'uddīn, nor do they demonize him as a representative of Muslim tyranny; in fact they may be simply neutral (e.g. *Vīramde Sonīgarā rī vāt*) or even sometimes depict him favourably. 'Alā'uddīn plays a more generalized role in situations that demonstrate the inherent superiority of Hindu culture, in particular that Rajput chivalry is morally superior to the power of the Sultanate.

ABBREVIATIONS

CV	: Nārāyaṇdās, *Chitāī vārtā* (early sixteenth century?)
GBC	: Jaṭmal Nāhar, *Gorā Bādal caupaī* (1623)
GBPC	: Hemratan, *Gorā Bādal Padminī caupaī* (1588)
HA	: Bhāṇḍau, *Hammīrāyaṇ* (1481)
HMK	: Nayacandra Sūri, *Hammīramahākāvya* (*c.* 1400?)
KDP	: Padmanābh, *Kānhaḍde prabandh* (1456)
KR	: Dalpat, *Khumāṇo rāso* (first half of the eighteenth century)
HP	: Amṛtkalaś, *Hammīr prabandh* (1518)
P	: Jāyasī, *Padmāvat* (1540)
PCC	: Labdhoday, *Padmiṇī caritra caupaī* (*c.* 1650)

NOTES

1. Namely, A. Khusrau trans. M.W. Mirza, A.M. 'Iṣāmī trans. A.M. Husain n.d., vol. 2, pp. 418-525, and substantial translation of Baranī by H.M. Elliot and J. Dowson n.d., vol. 3, pp. 148-210, and more extensive translation by A. R. Fuller (*JASB* 1869, pp. 181-220, and 1870, pp. 1-51) which was completed and reprinted by A. Khallaque. Most of the information given by Baranī is repeated by the later historians Badā'ūnī (trans. G.S.A. Ranking, pp. 232-69) and Firishta (trans. J. Briggs, pp. 303-82).
2. 'Abdullah Wassāf, *Tazjiyatu-l Amsār wa Tajriyatu-l Āsār* (1300-28), H.M. Elliot n.d., vol. 3, pp. 51-2, cited as proof of his having been 'a tyrant [who]. . . never used to hesitate at slaughter, burning, [etc.] . . . and was quite overcome by his disposition towards temerity and oppression'.
3. Firishta, however, does say (p. 348) that 'Alā'uddīn made efforts to educate himself and pay more attention to the learned men at his court.
4. This work, written in 1316, is summarized in H.M. Elliot and J. Dowson n.d., pp. 544-57. A.M. 'Iṣāmī n.d., vol. 2, pp. 500-13, 516-17, gives a fairly romanticized account of the love affair, which is also mentioned by Badā'ūnī 1898, pp. 256, 266, and Firishta 1898, pp. 365-9. See comments by A. Ahmad 1963, p. 471.
5. Sūryamall Miśraṇ, *Vaṃś bhāskar,* 1963, vol. 3, p. 1650: *krūra bhatījā sāhako duṣṭa alābuddīna* (4.37.54) and comparison to a *vyāla* (4.37.56); vol. 4, pp. 1678 and 1688: *dusaha alā(v)uddīna* (5.1.11, 5.2.1); vol. 3, p. 1651: *ugratā* (prose passage) and *ugra, ugra nidesa* (4.37.59-60); vol. 4, p. 1744 (prose passage): *ugrasāsan.*
6. Various dates have been proposed for this work. K.R. Qanungo 1971, p. 9, says 1336; in his introduction to the edition (1968), Muni Jinvijay, p. 28, says *c.* 140; B. Nāhṭā, in his introduction to Bhāṇḍau's *Hammīrāyaṇ,* p. 23, places it during the reign of Vīram Tomar of Gwalior, 1401-22.

7. M.G. Bhārgav, in his introduction to Maheś Kavi's version, 1988, pp. 8-24, refers to other earlier and later texts that mention or deal with Hammīr, including two entitled *Hammīr haṭh* by Gvāl Kavi (1826) and Candraśekhar Vājpeyī (1845)—neither of which was available to me. Maheś Kavi's work has also been edited by A. Nāhṭā, Jodhpur: Oriental Research Institute, 1982. The appendices to B. Nāhṭā's edition of Bhāṇḍau's *Hammīrāyaṇ* contain a passage about Hammīr from Vidyāpati's *Puruṣaparīkṣā* and some short sequences of verses by Mall and Bhāṭ Khem, and from *Prākṛta-paiṅgalaṃ.*
8. R.S. McGregor 1984, p. 61, assigns *CV* to the early sixteenth century. It seems that an original version by Nārāyaṇdās was expanded by a later poet called Ratanraṅg. In his introduction to *CV*, p. 11, M.P. Gupta proposes a date of 1526 (citing a line in the manuscript), though later on, pp. 24-6, he suggests a date as early as 1423 for Nārāyaṇdās' version and 1493 for Ratanraṅg's. A.M. 'Iṣāmī refers to Chitāī as Jhatayāpalī; a suggested derivation for her name is Kṣitipālī (see introduction by M.P. Gupta). Another work on this theme is *Kathā Chītā kī* (1636) by the Sufi poet Jān Kavi, which is referred to in the introduction to *CV*, p. 6, and P. Caturvedi, pp. 148-53, 162-3.
9. An enlarged version of this work was produced (in 1703?) by Bhāgvijay, which also included verse by a certain Saṅgrāmsī (*GBPC*, intro. pp. 5-6). Hemratan's text was reprinted, without critical apparatus but with a lengthy introduction by Muni Jinvijay, under the title *Gorā Bādal caritra.*
10. B. Nāhṭā's edition of *PCC*, pp. 109-28, also contains a sequence of *kavittas* (by a certain Mall Kavi?) that would appear to pre-date Hemratan and Labdhoday since they incorporate some of them (see ibid., pp. 20-1 for correspondences).
11. See M.P. Gupta's introduction to *CV*, pp. 36-45, for comparison of its narrative with that of historians. See K.R. Qanungo's article refuting the historicity of Padmiṇī, and also T.S. Tomar 1956, pp. 191-200, and K.S. Lal 1967, pp. 102-11.
12. *HP*, 270: *alāvadīna rosai dhaḍahaḍyu, jāṇe ghṛta vaisvānara ḍhaliu*; see also 280, 383; *PCC*, p. 44: *bhabhakati āga mẽ jāṇi ghṛta bhelīyo*; see also p. 42: *dhamadhamīyo kopyo ghaṇo ati amarasa mana māhi*; Jodhrāj vs 2006, 264: *prajure patisāhi su kopa kiyā / manu jvāla bisāla sughṛtta diyā.*
13. In *Vīramde Sonīgārā rī vāt* (Anonymous 1960, p. 85) it is said that she was reborn as the daughter of 'Alā'uddīn because she stumbled over a cow bone while on her way to commit ritual suicide.
14. A.M. 'Iṣāmī n.d., vol. 2, pp. 459-60, says that after the second campaign against Daulatabad (Deogir), Rāmdev and his associates were taken to Delhi, where they were treated well by 'Alā'uddīn.
15. *GBPC*, 284: *nṛpa mani koi nahī chala bheda, khurāsānī mani adhikaü kheda*; cf. *GBPC*, 339, *KR*, pp. 140 v.(24)98, 145 v.(25)43.
16. In *PCC*, Rāghav and Cetan are the names of two Brahmin preachers.

17. *PCC*, p. 45: *karaī mukha ragata yuvagata ālimadhaṇī, ḍāri dyū̃ phū̃ki thakī gaḍha cītoṛa / rāṇa sū̃ padamaṇī ciḍī jima pākaḍū̃, kavaṇa hiṃdū karai hama taṇī hoṛa?*
18. *PCC*, p. 34: *eha bāta suṇī ālimapati kahai re, kyā merā avatāra / kaisī patisāhī viṇa padmaṇī re, aürati aüra asāra.*
19. Ch. Vaudeville 1962, pp. 355-6. On p. 316 she comments that 'l'inspiration religieuse [sem]ble tarie et l'on retombe dans un romanesque assez conventionnel: l'histoire de Ratansen et Padmāvatī continue, mais l'histoire de l'âme humaine sur le chemin de l'union divine est finie'.
20. For example *KR*, p. 130 v.(24)31: *rā̃dha na jā̃ṇā̃ bhojana bhaṇī, paraṇo the sī̃ghala padamaṇī*; cf., *Gorā Bādal kavitt*, ed. B. Nāhṭā, 9, p. 110; *GBPC*, 28-36; *PCC*, 5-6 .
21. The name Devalde seems to have been borrowed from accounts of Deval, daughter of Karaṇ Rāī of Gujarat.
22. *HMK*, 13.1-38; *HP*, 459ff.; Maheś Kávi 171-4; Jodhrāj 631-43; cf. the song and dance staged by Ratansen on the battlements of Chittor, pp. 527-8, and by Sā̃tal Siṃh at Siwana, *KDP*, 2.116ff.
23. *GBPC*, 367: *khaṃḍū jībha dahū nija deha, piṇa navi jāū̃ asurā̃ geha*; see also 374, 406, and *KR*, p. 152 v.(25)97.
24. *GBPC*, 478: *tū jāvaï hū pāchaü rahū, taü hū rāvata paṇaü nija dahū.*

REFERENCES

'Abdullah Wassāf. *Tazjatu-l Ansār wa Tajriyatu-l Āsār.* In Elliot and Dowson, Ch. 11, pp. 24-54.

Anonymous. *Vīramde Sonīgarārī vāt*, included in *Rājasthānī sāhitya-saṃgrah, bhāg 2.* Ed. Puruṣottamlāl Menāriyā. Jodhpur: Rajasthan Oriental Research Institute, 1960, pp. 68-99.

Ahmad, Aziz. 'Epic and Counter-Epic in Medieval India,' *Journal of the American Oriental Society*, 83.4 (1963): 470-6.

Amṛtkalaś. *Hammīrāprabandh.* Ed. Bhogilal J. Sandesra and Somabhai Dhu. Parekh. Prācīn Gurjar Granthmālā, 11. Vaḍodarā: Maharaja Sayajirav Visvavidyalay, 1973.

Badā'ūnī (Bādāyūnī), 'Abdul Qādir. *Muntakhabu-t-tawārīkh by 'Abdu-l-Qādir ibn-i-Mulūk Shāh known as Al-Badāonī.* Trans. George S.A. Ranking. vol. 1. Calcutta: Baptist Mission Press, 1898.

Baranī, Ziya'uddīn. *Tarikh-i Firoz of Ziau-d Din Barni.* In Elliot and Dowson. Ch. 15, pp. 93-373.

Bhāṇḍau. *Hammīrāyaṇ.* Ed. Bhavarlal Nahta. Bikaner: Sadul Rajasthani Research Institute, vs 2017.

Chaturvedi, Parashuram. *Sūfī kāvya saṃgrah.* Prayag: Hindi Sahitya Sammelan, 1965.

Dalpat/Daulatvijay. *Khumāṇo rāso, khaṇḍ 6,* in Labdhoday (q.v.), pp. 129-81.

Elliot, H.M. *The History of India as Told by its Historians.* Ed. John Dowson. Reprint. Vol. 3. Allahabad: Kitab Mahal, n.d.

Firishta (Mahomed Kasim Ferishta). *History of the Rise of the Mahomedan Power in India, till the Year A.D. 1612, from the Original Persian of Mahomed Kasim Ferishta.* Trans. John Briggs. Vol. 1. London: Longman, Rees, Orme, Brown, and Green, 1829.

Fuller, A.R. and A. Khallaque, *The Reign of 'Alāuddīn Khiljī,* Translated from Zia-ud-din Baranī's *Tarīkh-i-Firūz Shāhī.* Calcutta: Pilgrim Publishers, 1967.

Hemratan. *Gorā Bādal Padmiṇī caupaī.* Ed. Udaysimh Bhatnagar. Jodhpur: Rajasthan Oriental Research Institute, 1966.

Gorā Bādal caritra. Ed. Muni Sri Jinvijay. Jodhpur: Rajasthan Oriental Research Institute, 1968.

'Iṣāmī, 'Abdul Malik. *Futūḥu's Salāṭīn, or Shāh Nāmah-i Hind of 'Iṣāmī.* Trans. Agha Mahdi Husain. 3 vols. Bombay, London, etc.: Asia Publishing House, n.d.

Ibn Bāṭṭūṭah. *Voyages d'Ibn Batoutah.* Trans. C. Defrémery and B.R. Sanguinetti, vol. 3. Paris: Imprimerie Nationale, 1877.

Jaṭmal Nāhar. *Gorā Bādal caupai,* in Labdhoday (q.v.), pp. 182-208.

Jāyasī, Malik Muhammad. *Padmāvat.* Ed. Mataprasad Gupta. Allahabad: Bharati-Bhandar, 1963.

Jodhrāj. *Hammīrrāso.* Ed. Shyamsundardas. Kasi: Nagari Pracarini Sabha, vs 2006

Khusrau, Amīr. *Khazā'in al-Futūḥ of Ḥazrat Amīr Khusrau Dihlawī.* Trans. Mohammad Wahid Mirza. Bibliotheca Indica, Work No. 275. Calcutta: Asiatic Society, 1953.

Labdhoday. *Padminī caritra caupaī.* Ed. B. Nahta. Bikaner: Sadul Rajasthani Research Institute, vs 2018.

Lal, Kishori Saran. *History of the Khaljis, A.D. 1290-1320.* Calcutta: Asia Publishing House, 1967.

Maheś Kavi. *Hammīr rāso.* Ed. Manahar Gopal Bhargav. Allahabad: Anubhuti Prakashan, 1988.

McGregor, Ronald Stuart. *Hindi Literature from its Beginnings to the Nineteenth Century* (Jan Gonda, ed., *A History of Indian Literature.* Vol. 8, Fasc. 6). Wiesbaden: Otto Harrassowitz: 1984.

Nahta, Agarchand. 'Kavi Hemratan kṛt Gorā Bādal caupāī tathā anya racanāẽ', *Śodh patrikā, varṣ 26 aṅk 1* (1975), pp. 55-6.

Naiṇsī. *Mūhtā Naiṇsī Feṇt Mūhtā Naiṇsī rī khyāt.* Ed. Muni Jinvijay. Vol. 1, Rajasthan Prachyavidya Pratishthan, 1960.

Nārāyaṇdās. *Chitāī vārtā.* Ed. Mataprasad Gupta. Kasi: Nagari Pracarini Sabha, vs 2015.

Nayacandra Sūri. *Hammīramahākāvya.* Ed. Muni Jinavijaya. Jodhpur: Rajasthan Oriental Research Institute, 1968.

Padmanābh. *Kānhaḍde prabandh.* Ed. Kantilal Baldevram Vyas. Jodhpur: Rajasthan Oriental Research Institute, 1953.

Qanungo, Kalika Ranjan. *Studies in Rajput History.* 2nd ed. New Delhi: S. Chand & Co., 1971.

Sūryamall Miśraṇ (Sūrajmal Mīsaṇ). *Vaṃś bhāskar.* Ed. R.K. Asopa. Jodhpur, 1902(?).

Tod, Lieut.-Col. James. *Annals and Antiquities of Rajasthan.* Ed. William Crooke. 3 vols. 1920. Reprint. Delhi: Motilal Banarsidass, 1971.

Tomar, Ṭīkamsiṃh. *Hindī vīrkāvya (1600-1800 ī.).* Allahabad: Hindustani Academy, 1956.

Vaudeville, Charlotte. 'La Conception de l'amour divin chez Muhammad Jāyasī: *viraha* et '*ishq*', *Journal Asiatique, tome CCL, fasc. no. 3* (1962): 351-67.

Kṛṣṇa Plays of the Parsi Theater

PETER GAEFFKE

The Parsi Theater originated from the English theatrical companies which visited India, especially Bombay, in the middle of the nineteenth century. Parsi businessmen who observed the financial success of these enterprises decided to make a buck by establishing their own companies, and when this was a success they traveled with the performance through the country. The language of these plays was Hindustani, which most people understood, at least in north and central India, and the themes were drawn from Muslim folklore. We have plays on Lailā and Majnūn, Amīr Ḥamzā, etc.

Around 1900, under the influence of the Hindi movement and because some of the managers were Hindus, a shift occurred to themes taken from Puranic stories. And, obviously by popular demand, some Hindu playwrights became permanent members of some of the companies. The most well-known of these playwrights was Radheshyam Kathavachak (1890-1955?) who for many years wrote plays for the New Alfred Company in Lahore, whose director was Kavasji Khatau.

How did Radheshyam get this position? He grew up as the son of a Brahmin who made his living telling Puranic stories. His father prepared him for the same profession. Soon it appeared that Radheshyam was a very successful *kathāvācak* and one day he decided to use his knowledge to write a play for a traveling Parsi theater group and out of that developed a long relationship.

Radheshyam and a handful of his colleagues filled the repertoire of the Parsi theater with Hindu plays. For our purpose we have chosen two plays of Radheshyam which deal with the Kṛṣṇa story, namely *Kṛṣṇa-avatār* (1925; hereafter *KA*) and *Rukmiṇī-Kṛṣṇa* (1928; hereafter *RK*).

While working on this material, I looked in vain for a book like Camille Bulcke's *Rāmakathā*, which follows the development of the Rām story through times and various languages, or something similar to Paul Hacker's magisterial studies of the Prahlād myth.

Because no such comprehensive history of the Kṛṣṇa story exists, judgment on the dependence of Radheshyam on intermediate sources is not easy to make. We, therefore, have to start with the story as told in *Bhāgavatapurāṇa*, which would be a good place to start in assessing the repertoire of a *kathāvācak*. There are, however, two major deviations which we will mention here but not deal with in this paper. The first is, of course, the prominent role of Rādhā in these plays, for which there is no evidence in the Purāṇa. The second is the absence of the particular philosophical approach so typical for the Purāṇa, which contains long passages of this nature.

Here one could raise the issue that such philosophical pondering does not fit into the pace of a drama. But this leads us directly to the question of dramatic requirements shaping the story. We shall search for an explanation of these changes beyond technical necessities and try to find out what sort of Kṛṣṇa is presented here. This will be facilitated by numerous passages responding more to the needs of the time than to devotional necessities.

The dependence of Radheshyam's plays on European drama traditions is obvious from his use of technical terms for the divisions of his plays such as *aṅk (act), sīn* (scene), *ḍrāpsīn, ḍrāp* or *pardā* (*KA* p. 150). This terminology comes also from the mouths of the mythological characters in the dialogue, even in the lines given to Nārad (*RK* p. 160). However, the drama does not follow the five act pattern. *Kṛṣṇa-avatār* has only three acts of 8, 8, and 3 scenes, respectively, and *Rukmiṇī-Kṛṣṇa* contains also three acts of 8, 7, and 3 scenes. However, from the point of view of general dramatic action one can invoke the Aristotelian rules concerning the difference between tragedy and comedy. *Kṛṣṇa-avatār* definitely lacks a tragic hero. The whole play deals with the fight with the monster Kaṃs. It starts with the famous *ākāśvāṇī* and ends with Kaṃs's death. This Kaṃs has nothing but flaws while his adversary has no flaws at all and, therefore, does not succumb to them or to destiny. All this fits very well in Aristotle's definition of a comedy and that may come as a surprise to the devotees of Kṛṣṇa.

The second play, *Rukmiṇī-Kṛṣṇa*, consists of three acts each of which forms a separate story, first Uddhav and the Gopīs, then Rukmiṇī's marriage, and finally, the return of Pradyumna. These are actually independent one-act plays held together by the common hero Kṛṣṇa.

From the above it appears as if the *Kṛṣṇa-avatār* is more a Kṣatriya story, and indeed most of the scenes are either filled with the cruelty and violence of Kaṃs and the measures taken against him while, at the same time, we see a transformation of Kṛṣṇa into a war hero. The drama starts with the statement that only when violence by a tyrannic ruler causes a certain degree of suffering among the oppressed Hindus is God willing to come down to earth as an *avatār* (*KA* p. 8). Therefore, Nārad interferes with Akrūr, who wants to save the sixth son of Vasudev, because the violence has not yet reached the ultimate degree (*KA* p. 51). So the people of Braj, especially Devakī, Vasudev and Ugrasen, have to suffer. For example, schools in Braj are destroyed but liquor factories are opened, grazing fields for cows are made into amusement parks (*pramod-ban*, *KA* p. 30), etc. But the *avatār* happens only when the violence is directed against women (*KA* p. 8). In particular, the suffering of Devakī will trigger it. In the meantime we get pictures of the lost manliness (*kṣatriyatā*) of the people of Braj, their helplessness, and the imprisonment of anyone who tries to resist the ruler (*KA* p. 46). On stage we see Kaṃs giving orders to kill the sixth child by suffocating it, but when Akrūr interferes, Kaṃs kills it himself with his sword. Furthermore, Kaṃs tries to kill the seventh, a girl substituted for Kṛṣṇa, by throwing her against a rock (*KA* pp. 49-53).

Instead of displaying the *bālā līlā* in detail, Radheshyam incorporates it in the form of a report of Akrūr to Kaṃs (*KA* p. 80), who had ordered the killing of male infants of his country and now boasts of his power to rule heaven and earth (*KA* p. 84). The picture of this tyrannical, violent ruler would be incomplete if Radheshyam had not also pointed out that he is a secularist and a rationalist. When Akrūr reveals his innermost conviction before his king that Kṛṣṇa is Nārāyaṇ, Kaṃs shouts: 'You have no *buddhi*, *vicār*, and not a shred of *vivek*' (*KA* 177).

Now look at what appears when Kṛṣṇa's story is transferred to the stage. Especially difficult for Radheshyam is the integration of the erotic passages of the *Bhāgavatapurāṇa* story into this Kṣatriya drama. Kṛṣṇa states quite clearly in the beginning that Rādhā is the *sār* (essence) of his life and *ādhār* (foundation) of his *līlā* (*KA* p. 88). Also, in her first words Rādhā says that their love is not that of husband and wife (i.e. sexual). Rather, she compares it with the love of the waves for the ocean, of the peacocks for the clouds, of a Hindu wife for the *tīrtha* of a *parvā* day (*KA* pp. 91f.). Strangely enough, Kṛṣṇa answers: 'Your words make me crazy' (*bāvalā, KA* p. 92). And when Rādhā complains about his playing the flute because it attracts the Gopīs, he answers that playing the flute is good for it helps to digest the butter which Yaśodā has fed him (*KA* p. 94). The explanation for this de-erotization of the Vrindavan episodes is given in the treatment of the *rāslīlā*.

Before this, we have to look into the butter-stealing episode (*KA* pp. 96ff.) and the Kālīdah (*KA* pp. 116ff.) and Govardhan (*KA* pp. 126ff.) episodes. Kṛṣṇa encourages the Gops to steal butter because it gives them the ability to fight Kaṃs, their enemy (*KA* p. 100). In this context, Kṛṣṇa teaches them the importance of *go-mātā* and of mothers in general. He says that every Indian has four mothers: India's cows, his real mother, India as *janma bhūmi* and finally, the rivers that nurse his ashes after death. Among these mothers, the cows are most important because they are also mothers of gods and therefore, their importance is paramount for the whole of creation (*KA* pp. 101ff.).

The Kālīdah episode gives the playwright an opportunity to speak about the importance of learning how to swim. Kṛṣṇa teaches the Gops this *vidyā*, but he remains the best swimmer; he therefore survives the dive into Kālīdah, and when he emerges from it, he dances on the head of the subdued snake. And this is to show to the world, as the play maintains, how important the art of dance is (*KA* pp. 122).

Moreover, the Govardhan episode gives occasion to speak about irrigation. Kṛṣṇa stops the Gops worshipping Indra for rain because it would prolong their dependence on nature and make them forget self-help, i.e. digging wells and irrigation channels (*KA* p. 130). No wonder that the audiences of this play conceived of it as a nationalist, anti-British enterprise.

And now, finally, the *rāslīlā*. Traditionally, it is placed before Kṛṣṇa's departure to Mathura. Radheshyam leaves it in this position but says Kṛṣṇa needed it in order to collect from the Gopīs his *śakti*s, the power that only the women could give him to overcome Kaṃs (*KA* p. 143). And when the Gopīs appear in a deranged and dishevelled state, searching for their lover, Kṛṣṇa jokes with them saying that it was not right for them to be with a *parpuruṣ*. They ask him: 'What *puruṣ*? Who calls you a "man"? You are only a boy of eight years!' [puruṣ? puruṣ? tumhẽ puruṣ kahtā hī kaun hai? tum to abhī āṭh varṣ ke bālak ho (*KA* p. 148)].

After this scene the balance turns; instead of children murdered, the enemies of Kṛṣṇa die on stage. There are three dead bodies in the last scene of the third act: Kaṃs and two of his bodyguards.

In the second play, *Rukmiṇī-Kṛṣṇa,* the issue is clearly the role of the Hindu woman. Therefore, the emphasis is shifted from the erotic scenes in the *Bhāgavatapurāṇa* and the literature that followed it. Medieval authors, especially, exploited the erotic possibilities of the Rukmiṇī episode. Not so here. First we hear of Uddhav addressing Mahāmāyā (i.e. Rādhā) and Kṛṣṇa's *śaktis* (i.e. the Gopīs) in Vrindavan, in what is generally known as the *bhramar* episode. The *Bhāgavatapurāṇa* explains through the mouth of Uddhav how less advanced the Gopīs are in their love of the absent Kṛṣṇa for, in truth, the inconceivable Nārāyaṇ is everywhere. Here, however, the scene brings out different forms of devotion in men and women. Rādhā tells Uddhav: āp prem kā tattva jānte hī nahī̃, gopiyā̃ hī jāntī haī̃ ('You do not know the essence of love. Only the Gopīs know').

For them there exists no *bhītar* and *bāhar* (*RK* p. 34) and, therefore, their erotic attitudes and expressions mean the same as what *jñāna* and *yoga* teach. And again Rādhā is called a niṣkām prem kī pavitra pratimā (*RK* p. 31) ('The sacred image of desireless love').

Rukmiṇī, a more mortal woman, fights for her right to choose her own husband. She is lucky that her astrological chart points to Kṛṣṇa and that her parents agree. But it is her brother who objects to this marriage and swears to fight Kṛṣṇa. This situation elicits great words: Rukmiṇī declares that she is a girl of *ārya varta* and when she has made up her mind she will not give up that man for the rest of her life (*RK* p. 100). Her brother is told that when a girl sheds her demure (*lāj*), she will become Durgā (*RK* p. 108). Furthermore, he is told that it is a sign of narrow-mindedness if a man is startled by the *svatantratā* of a girl (*RK* p. 64). But he holds that a woman should follow her parents' and brothers' wishes like a cow. Rukmiṇī's friend Sulekhā answers: 'On the day women are held to be chattel (*paśu*), *ārya vart* will turn into a hell' (*RK* p. 65).

But her brother puts Rukmiṇī under house arrest, and she writes a letter to Kṛṣṇa which a Brahmin brings secretly to Dvārikā. Now we see Kṛṣṇa display Brahmin Bhakti by pressing his feet, feeding him, and fanning him. Uddhav calls this an *adarś* for which Kṛṣṇa himself is called a Brahmin (*RK* pp. 116ff.).

In the last act Rukmiṇī, after becoming mother of Pradyumna, then losing and regaining him, has come across a picture of Kṛṣṇa with another woman (Rādhā), and she iş as startled as any woman would be in such a situation. Kṛṣṇa explains, as any man would do in such a situation, 'With her I have a completely different relationship.' He calls it *niṣkām, akhaṇḍa, pavitra*; for him Rādhā is his *mahāmāyā*, while Rukmiṇī is for the body, his *paṭrānī*, and because of Rādhā's *śakti*, Rukmiṇī is able to see the *yugal jhāṅkī* ('vision of the pair'). With this the drama ends.

Much of the above foreshadows the ideals admired recently in the Rām story. Therefore, one has to look at Radheshyam's Kṛṣṇa plays as conscious attempts to bring the Kṛṣṇa story into the mainstream of *sanātan dharma* and Hindu Mahāsabhā teachings. I assume it will not take long before the now completely forgotten Radheshyam will get his place in the intellectual history of the BJP.

REFERENCES

Bulcke, Camille. *Rāmakathā: utpatti aur vikās.* 3rd ed. Prayag: Hindi Parishad, 1971.

Hacker, Paul. *Prahlāda: Werden und Wandlungen einer Idealgestalt: Beiträge zur Geschicte des Hinduismus.* 2 vols. Abhandlungen der geistes-und sozialwissen-schaftlichen klasse. Jg. 1959, Nr. 9 and 13. Wiesbaden: Franz Steiner, 1960.

Radheshyam Kathavachak. 1925. *Śrīkṛṣṇa-avatar.* 8th ed. Bareilly: Sriradheshyam Press, 1970.

———. *Rukmiṇī-Kṛṣṇa.* 1928. 3rd rpt. by Ramnarayan Pathak. Bareilly: Sriradheshyam Press, 1966.

Ramsimha and Suryakaran Parik, eds. *Veli Krisan Rukmiṇī rī.* Allahabad: Hindustani Academy, 1931.

Simh, Ranavira, ed. *Pārsī Thiyeṭar.* Jodhpur: Rajasthan Sangit Natak Academy, 1990.

The Yogī who Pissed from the Mountain

DANIEL GOLD

Stories of the great Nāth Yogīs—Gorakh, Matsyendra, Gopīcand—are told throughout northern India, but particular Indian regions also have their own Nāth heroes. In Rajasthan, the stories of great Yogīs and local legendary figures are preserved in separate traditions; the main exponents of both, however, are the householder Nāths, who are settled as a caste in villages throughout the region. The great Yogīs are the subjects of epics recited by Nāth bards in extended public performances. The legends of local heroes are, by contrast, told in a casual anecdotal manner, as asides from everyday discourse. The epics are likely to highlight the more poignant existential issues faced by village Nāths—the tensions, say, between their householders' life and renouncers' identity explored in the recent work of Ann G. Gold in the epic of Gopīcand (1992). The legends, by contrast, frequently reveal the village Nāths' more practical concerns, such as land-rights and power. It is with these more down-to-earth issues that I will deal here, examining one of the best-known legends of eastern Rajasthan: that of Gehlā Rāwal Nāth, who has an establishement dedicated to him at Gailpur, near Kisangarh, south of Jaipur.[1]

Living largely as settled farmers, not wandering ascetics, householder Nāths nevertheless share more than legendary and magical lore with the ideally celibate Nāth Yogīs who are still to be found in the region. In many cases, these may well have been their physical as well as spiritual forbears. When asked about their beginnings, householder Nāths in Rajasthan frequently mention a great Nāth Yogī who, through the strength of his miracles, received land from a local ruler. That great Yogī remained celibate and his first few generations of disciples remained celibate. Eventually, however, one of those disciples had a female disciple, 'and that's how we came into being'. Since this narrative seems more frank than flattering, we may take its main lines seriously, particularly for groups who live near a major shrine. And although most householder Nāths today expend most of their energy in farming, they are still seen to retain some of the magical power of their Yogic forbears, an esoteric knowledge that is passed down through the generations. In their villages, they serve some particular ritual functions for the peasant castes and the community as a whole. The story of Gehlā Rāwal Nāth speaks to their situation as a well-settled caste of hereditary magical specialists.

'*Gehlā*' is a Rajasthani word for crazy, while '*rāwal*' is a Nāth lineage name that is also used for kings.[2] So Gehlā Rāwal's name itself suggests the anomalous, slightly crazy or at least contradictory place of the householder Nāths in the Rajasthani domains of family lineage and royal power. The Rajasthani Nāths, moreover, have had real experience of those domains. In the past, Nāth Yogīs served royal patrons as both gurus and soldiers, developing a tough, effective, image that could bring together physical Yoga and alchemical mystique with the wrestler's cultivation of his body.[3] Some of the religious and economic clout of the past Yogīs has been retained by their present-day descendants, who have clearly *not* been transformed into low-status performers as many comparable castes have been in other parts of India.[4] Today, householder Nāths in Rajasthan are for the most part respectable middle-caste peasants, farmers of their own land who mix freely and interdine with other clean, peasant castes. The story of Gehlā Rāwal Nāth reveals the practical significance that the rough spiritual identity of the past Nāth Yogīs can have for present householder Nāths concerned with family, society, and land.

I heard the story—or parts of the story—in different places and on different kinds of occasions. The first time was in a village not far from where I was living in Ajmer District;[5] it was narrated by Rām Nāth, an elderly farmer of Rāwal *gotra,* known for being able to tell the tales of the Rāwal Yogīs. The longest version was told by an old energetic householder named Bhāgaṛ Nāth at the monastery in Gailpur, still an imposing presence on the small mountain referred to in this paper's title. I also heard variants from Ugmā Nāth, my principal informant; Sukhā Nāth, the main Nāth genealolgist of the area; and Rūp Nāth, a distinguished Nāth householder guru who was visiting a monastery founded by a lineage brother of Gehlā Rāwal Nāth. While some of the variants of the legend had more embellishment and added episodes, the main lines of the story were more striking in their similarities than in their differences, and those are what I will focus on here. And in all the longer versions of the story, the most striking image, to which the story built up and over which everyone chuckled, was the image I have used in the title: the Yogī taking a piss off the top of the mountain.

In its contexts, moreover, I think this image is emblematic as to what the story is about. For Gehlā Nāth didn't piss off of the mountain simply because he had to relieve himself. His pissing was, instead, an eminently territorial act. Gehlā had reached an agreement with a *bād<u>sh</u>āh* whom he had impressed through a miracle that he could have all the land his piss could encircle. The amount, to the *bād<u>sh</u>āh's* dismay, was remarkably large. We thus get a very graphic image of the Nāth's corporeal nature as at once powerfully unrefined and entitiled to land—and full of surprises, too. The story of Gehlā Rāwal Nāth as a whole, I think, more than the legends of Gorakh or Gopīcand, speaks to the identity of the Rajasthani Nāth as a landed Hindu peasant who sees the place he has in the world deriving from a coarsely envisioned, inherited magical power, yet who, like everyone else, is beset by family and social concerns.

Two episodes revealing complementary dimensions of this socio-religious persona lead up to the denouement on the mountain. The first is the account of Gehlā Nāth's inherited body and familial upbringing, which reveals the power of contrasting extremes: valiant gentry and vulgar ascetic nurturance; pitiful crying humanity and the highest divine tutelage. The second is the story of Gehlā's mature encounters with Hiṅglāj Mā, the Devī in Baluchistan that has been a vital place of pilgrimage for western Indian Yogīs but is now practically inaccessible. This episode suggests the way in which the Yogī's power can encompass his land and community. These two episodes will be examined in their contemporary cultural contexts.

Gehlā Rāwal Nāth, they say, was of the lineage of one Rājā Amīr Singh, but he was not exactly his son. Before going off to fight the armies of the *bād<u>sh</u>āh* (as the adversary in this story is usually called), the *rājā* gave the following instructions to his *rānī*, 'When our force returns, look at the pennant bearers. If there is a red flag, we won, and you will be *rānī* of a great realm. If there is a green flag, we lost, and you will have to join the *bād<u>sh</u>āh's* harem.'

He said this and forgot, and even though he won the battle, he returned flying a green flag, not a red one. The *rānī*, pregnant, decided to take drastic action when she saw the accidentally displayed signal of defeat. She went to Rājā Amīr's guru, a Nāth *sādhu*, and pointing to the foetus in her stomach said: 'I have something of your *śiṣya's*.' He told the *rānī* to cut open her stomach (as pregnant *satīs* are wont to do), and then to hide the foetus in the big jar in which he kept his *bhāṅg*, the intoxicating hemp drink. After the foetus was thus deposited, the *rānī* killed herself and the ascetic sat down in meditation for twelve years. When he woke up, he looked in his *bhāṅg*-jar for a little something, and what did he see? A boy happy in the *bhāṅg*-jar, sucking his thumb and playing, whom he made his disciple.

So Gehlā himself is of the seed of a valiant, if forgetful, *rājā* and his brave, if mistaken, wife—both demonstrating their hereditary virtues, but appearing a little foolish too. A respectable Rājpūt lineage can thus be claimed for Gehlā, even though, as the story shows, Rājpūts are not really so smart anyway. An orphan, Gehlā needs some surrogate parents. Who might these be? In making Gehlā his disciple, the *rājā's* guru becomes his spiritual father, so to speak; but if he is Gehlā's father, than who is Gehlā's mother? Throughout this part of the story, Gehlā is referred to as the *bhāṅg*-jar boy, so perhaps his mother is none other than the *bhāṅg*-jar, the guru's solace and companion, who kept Gehlā alive and happy for twelve years, womb-like and full. Certainly, she nurtured him for longer than his natural mother did. Yet the guru and his *bhāṅg*-jar finally do not give him everything that is his due, and new divine guardians enter the scene.

The guru had another disciple, older than Gehlā, who used to gather wood in the forest. Gehlā one day decided that he should go, too. The guru said: 'No, you're too little'. Gehlā, however, was stubborn, and finally the guru agreed—but with conditions: he should stack the wood on his head to one-and-a-quarter arm-lengths; and he shouldn't tie the pieces of wood together. Then the two disciples went into the jungle and split up. Gehlā was having a difficult time. It was hard enough for him to lift that much wood onto his head, and then when he started to walk without having tied it up, the wood would inevitably fall off. He got very frustrated and started to cry loudly.

Who should hear little Gehlā but the great god Śiv and goddess Pārvatī, who happened to be strolling nearby. Pārvatī then asked

Śiv to find out why the boy was crying. Śiv didn't want to. 'Look, Pārvatī,' he said, 'the world is full of human children who cry. How can I help them all?' Pārvatī got angry. 'I'm not talking about them all,' she retorted: 'You make *that one* happy.' Śiv told the boy simply to order the wood to do what he wanted it to 'by Śaṅkar's name' and, of course, it worked. Meanwhile the first disciple had brought back wood, but not Gehlā. The guru was surprised and angry: 'Where's my crazy *bhāṅg*-jar boy,' he asked. So while Gehlā was busy with Śiv and Pārvatī, he got his adult name, which means crazy.[6]

Each of Gehlā's parent figures, then, seems to have added something to his corporeal nature. The story of his natural parents, somewhat ambivalently, gives him a respectable Rājpūt lineage and makes a dig at Rājpūts too. From his Nāth guru he gets initiation—which implicitly entails getting the cartilages of his ears cut—and from his *bhāṅg*-jar mother, a birthright for cannabis, which many householder Nāths continue to enjoy. Śiv and Pārvatī then give him the magical powers that bring him to young adulthood. For after his encounter with those deities, Gehlā was told by his *guru* to go live alone on Gailpur mountain.

Gehlā would then have further encounters with the goddess, particularly in her form most exalted by the Nāths of western India, Mother Hiṅglāj. The shrine to Hiṅglāj Mā is located on the Hingool River in Baluchistan (D.C. Sircar 1973, p. 85), where she is locally known as Bibi Naṇi. Always distant in the far western reaches of Islamic India—and now virtually inaccessible in Pakistan—Hiṅglāj Mother is not a well-known goddess through most of the north today. But she is frequently found in the longer lists of Śākta Pīṭhas, which enumerate the sites where Brahmā, Viṣṇu and Śani scattered the parts of Satī's body to quell Śiv's rage (D.C. Sircar 1973, pp. 5-7). For Yogīs, moreover, she can understandably become the most important site, for she is said to represent Satī's *brahmarandhra*, the top of the head through which Yogīs aim to escape the world. Hiṅglāj has thus been a very important place of pilgrimage for Nāths, her distance in the rugged west no doubt increasing her fabled allure for Yogīs of the northern deserts and plains. Briggs frequently mentions the importance of the pilgrimage to Hiṅglāj for Nāths and the increased status of those who have returned.[7]

So great was the attraction of Hiṅglāj Mother, they say, that Gehlā Rāwal Nāth had gone to visit her six times and had started on his seventh trip. On the way an old woman appeared in his path. She asked him who he was and where he was going. Gehlā Rāwal was a little annoyed, but told her, somewhat anachronistically 'I am going to Pakistan to see Hiṅglāj'. 'Go no further,' she said. 'I am Hiṅglāj'. Gehlā wasn't sure he believed her. If you're really Hiṅglāj, he said, you'll fulfil my vow. She agreed, and he went home to his mountain where he asked her to give him *darśan* for an eighth of the day (one *pahar*), half in the morning, and half in the evening. Since then, daily *sevā* has been offered to Hiṅglāj Mā at Gailpur, and she is said to come for the *ārati*. Today, the monastery at Gailpur has one of the more important shrines to Hiṅglāj in the area.

While establishing the sanctity of the Gailpur shrine, this story is also known to householder Nāths in a fairly wide area beyond it, for whom it carries broader meanings.[8] First of all, it shows the Nāths bringing the powerful presence of the goddess to Rajasthan. Still distant and mysterious, she is now seen as a deity more indigenous to the area than she seems to have been in the past. This partial transplantation may be even more necessary given the political realities of 'Pakistan' that are now invoked. And as a more locally regional deity, Hiṅglāj is very much under the hegemony of the Nāths, their own cherished goddess whom they also mediate to a good-sized segment of the local peasant community in a crucial rite. For Hiṅglāj is the focus of worship in an esoteric regional funeral cult of which the Nāths are leaders.[9] Both in the eyes of peasant participants in the cult and in those of Nāth adepts, leadership in this cult is probably the most revered socio-religious role a Nāth can have.

We now come to the climactic acts of Gehlā on Gailpur mountain. These explicitly make the links between the Nāths' very physically embodied magical prowess and their rights to land. Indeed, contemporary Nāths are still aware of these links. Since their magic has been seen to be particularly effective against calamities affecting the community as a whole—hail, drought, and especially locusts—Nāth families were often lured to villages with no Nāth population through grants of land from local *ṭhākurs*, resulting in a generally sparse dispersion of the caste across villages in the region. There are also, however, some villages where Nāths are plentiful, if not the most numerous caste. These, like Gailpur, have all been the sites either of yogic establishments that are still visibly substantial or of locally well-remembered Yogīs with endowments from *rājās* certified by copper-plates. Most of those Yogīs are said to have performed miracles that materially aided a *rājā* or village: protecting the former from enemies, say, or the latter from hail, although not all are said to have established their land claims with the magical aplomb shown by Gehlā Rāwal Nāth.

Beyond the claims for land, the story of Gehlā's encounter with the *bādshāh* has other implications for householder Nāth socio-religious identity, some more overt, some more subliminal. Claiming territory though piss suggests a dog, and an extraordinarily powerful piss suggests a magical dog. The latter is an ambivalent figure throughout the world religions, at once a dirty, lonely scavenger but sometimes domestically loyal, too. This combination of domestic fidelity and powerful unrefined aloofness presents a tension generally endemic to householder Nāth identity: most are loyal family men who also cherish their image as detached and powerful Yogīs. More specifically, dogs are associated with Bhairav, the effective instrument of the goddess' power—a being with whom Nāths unambiguously identify. In a succinct summation of householder Nāth identity that I heard late in my last stay from a genealogist, and which struck me as particularly apt, Nāths are Śiv *rūp,* because they wear thick earrings like him; Hiṅglāj is their *iṣṭa,* especially important in funeral rites; but their *pūjya* is Bhairav. In fact, most of the practical magic they perform for villagers is done through Bhairav's agency. And Bhairav, in Rajasthani as well as in other regional iconographical traditions, is regularly depicted with dogs.[10]

While the story of Gehlā's powerful piss clearly presents some of the more unrefined aspects of Bhairav, it also introduces images of mundane domesticity into the narrative, appropriate for householder Nāths concerned with land. For in the process of testing Gehlā's powers, the *bādshāh* invokes the image of his somewhat testy wife. Making camp with his army on the way to Kishangarh, the *bādshāh* saw Gehlā's fire on the mountain and sent some scouts there to look for water. Gehlā gave them his water pot, which was able to quench the thirst of all the soldiers and the horses in the camp. The next morning the *bādshāh* himself went to greet the great *mahātmā* with the magical pot. Asking Gehlā to accept him as a disciple, he gave him a finely embroidered shawl, which Gehlā promptly threw into his fire.

The *bādshāh's* officers, annoyed with the whole scene, goaded the *bādshāh* to test Gehlā further. He returned saying he had made a terrible mistake. The shawl he had given Gehlā was actually his wife's, who would get very angry if she found out it had been given away. Could Gehlā please give it back to him? The *bādshāh* would give him another, even better one. The *mahātmā* spoke to the fire, put his hand in it, and pulled and pulled: the shawl kept coming out—perhaps we are supposed to recall Draupadī's *sārī* (*Mahābhārata* 2.27.61, see J.A.B. Van Buitenen 1975, p. 146). At this point, the *bādshāh*, embarrassed and apologetic, said: 'Let me give you everything as far as you can see.' When Gehlā told him that he could see everything from Delhi to Udaipur, the *bādshāh* hesitated. At this point Gehlā suggested: 'Well then, how about as far as I can piss?' To this the *bādshāh* readily agreed, thinking that maybe he'd have to give as much as a large corral for horses. But Gehlā, instead, through his piss, claimed land for miles around.

The image of a one-upped *bādshāh* with a wife people believe will harry him is echoed in Bhāgaṛ Nāth's long retelling of the story, where we are given a rambling and very amusing account of a soldier who was pressured by the *begum* to cuckold the *bādshāh*, and, when found out, joined the army of Amīr Singh, Gehlā Rāwal's natural father. The wife is presented as domineering and a little wily; the *bādshāh* as a bit of a sissy, but angry and calculating. The *bādshāh* is driven to fight Amīr Singh because of the adulterous soldier, and loses.

But these representations of weak *bādshāhs* with importuning wives leading them to ill-conceived schemes, in addition to talking about the husband's plight, also say something about the image of Muslims. While the *bādshāh* is not portrayed as particularly evil, as the recurring adversary in the story he is clearly depicted as the other, and he has a definite Muslim identity. Regularly outwitted and bested by Nāths and their disciples, he thus makes them all the more gloriously Hindu—an element of Nāth social identity that in non-Rajasthani context may be at issue. In several north Indian regions, some Yogī castes are considered Muslims, and in the Punjab the same term Rāwal that is found in Gehlā's full name has referred specifically to Muslim Yogīs (see G.W. Briggs 1938, p. 2). Today in Rajasthan, however, the Nāths seem to be exclusively identified as Hindu. Nevertheless, some ambiguity as to their authenticity remains, with one Rajasthani Nāth lineage, the Hāṇḍī Varaṅgs, remembered to have Muslim origins. Indeed, in order to become a Nāth, the founder of this lineage had to undergo severe physical transformations.

I have come across several versions of the Haṇdi Varaṅg Nāth origin story. One of them takes up our narrative of Gehlā where we left off. The *bādshāh,* impressed by Gehlā's many miracles, asked to become his disciple. Gehlā agreed—with conditions. Since the *bādshāh* was a Muslim he really had to become *pukka,* 'fully developed', here taken in its more etymologically precise sense as 'thoroughly baked'. Gehlā put a little unbaked jug (*hāṇḍī*) around the *bādshāh's* neck. 'When this is baked,' he said, 'you'll be my disciple; otherwise, you'll remain a Muslim.' The *bādshāh* was then buried in the earth, and twelve years later dug up; the jug had hardened and he was renamed Hāṇḍī Varaṅg Nāth. Yet even after having undergone such transformations, the former *bādshāh* is still kept at a distance by contemporary householder Nāths of Hāṇḍī Varaṅg *gotra*: it was not he himself who eventually took a wife, the story goes, but two of his disciples, brothers identified as Jāṭs (see G.W. Briggs 1938, pp. 70-1). It is these Hindu Jāṭs who are the physical progenitors of the Hāṇḍī Varaṅgs, not the former Muslim. Another version of this story adds a vivid detail of Muslim otherness most pertinent to our central image. This one takes place in the more distant past, with the curse of a royal Hindu father to have his son reborn as a Muslim *bādshāh.* The *bādshāh* remembers his past and realizes he can only find liberation by encountering a true Yogī. Then Gorakh Nāth comes along, who, when importuned, tells him: 'How can you become a Nāth, you're circumcised!' But if he stayed underground for twelve years his circumcision would be restored. (Ugmā Nāth's interpretation was that this meant he would get a new birth.) In any event, however Hāṇḍī Varaṅg Nāth Yogīs were once religiously identified in Rajasthan, both versions of this story emphasize that today householder Nāths of Hāṇḍī Varaṅg *gotra* have identifiably Hindu bodies.

In fact, the image of Muslim otherness may well have been less of an issue for Rajasthani Nāths of some past eras than it is now, with the rise of Hindu nationalism and the control of Hiṅglāj by Pakistan. Nevertheless, the whole legend of Gehlā Nāth seems to focus on immediate issues of social identity: land, socio-religous role, Hinduness. In this it differs from the epic story of Gopīcand. Gopīcand, the king who was born to be a Yogī, is, in the Rajasthani account, distraught with his fate, attached to his wealth and family, and regularly calling out for help to his guru. Accompanied by musical performance in a specific setting, the story of Gopīcand incorporates elements of social identity to be sure, but focuses on the emotional tension between the householder and Yogic realities experienced by Nāths: Gopīcand is regularly in tears. The legend of Gehlā Rāwal Nāth, by contrast, forges elements from the two sides of householder Nāth awareness into a viable image that the Nāths can present to themselves and the world. Focusing on more practical socio-religious concerns, the story of a local hero like Gehlā can be told informally by Nāths as an aside from current gossip about local politics, land, and power, without much shift in mindset. It thus needs no special performative space that promises the epic vision and dramatic pathos of a story like Gopīcand. While that story may speak more poignantly to the householder Nāths' ambivalent hearts, the story of the Yogī who pissed from the mountain helps them better situate their bodies in their immediate earthly realms.

NOTES

1. Considerable work on the oral traditions of the Rajasthani Nāths has already been done by A.G. Gold: a translation and analysis of the epic of Gopīcand (1992); and a treatment of the salvational songs (1988, pp. 99-123). A short treatment of the Rajasthani Nāths in their contemporary contexts can be found in Gold and Gold 1984. On related traditions in Nepal, see V. Bouillier 1979; 1986; 1989; 1991. G.W. Briggs 1938 describes north Indian Nāth traditions at the beginning of the century.
2. *The Rājasthāni sabad kos* (Lalas 1962-75, p. 4150) says that Rāwal was first a yogic term that was later applied to some royal houses through their association with that lineage of Nāths. The term is also used to refer to Nāths in the Punjab, particularly Muslims (see G.W. Briggs 1938, p. 2). Rāwal is listed as one of the 'twelve panths of the Nāths' by both Briggs (p. 66) and Srivirnathji (1988, p. 297), who also names the *panth's* major shrine as Gailpur, Rajasthan. Srivirnathji's work is a compendium of Nāth lore that circulates widely today among literate Nāth ascetics; it briefly notes one Gehlāravāl as a Nāth Siddha who lived after the eighty-four classical Siddhas and had disciples in western India (1988, p. 315).
3. On the Nāths in Jodhpur see P. Sharma 1972 and D. Gold 1995; on the relationships between Nāths and kings in Nepal see V. Bouillier 1989; on wrestling culture in north India see J. Alter 1992.
4. In a flyer, the Akhil Bhāratīya Nāth Samāj, a national caste association, lists the names by which the wider community is known in thirty-one

Indian regions. Jogī (or Yogī) is the most common, followed by Nāth—usually perceived as a more respectable design-ation. In a general petition dated 24 June 1993, the association's president, Mahinder Nath Goswami, made a case for special protections for the community as a 'Religious Nomadic Tribe', a status needing more protection than the other 'backward classes' among which it is listed in the Mandal Report. The national association has counterparts in a number states, including Rajasthan, where its members are active mostly in cities and towns. Its publications, however, do find their way to literate Nāths in the villages.

5. The research on which this paper is based was done in the Spring and Summer of 1993 under a grant from the American Institute of Indian Studies.
6. *Rājasthā̃nī sabad kos* (Lalas 1862-75, pp. 760, 763) glosses *gehlāu* as a variant form of *gailau*, 'crazy' or 'stupid' (*pāgal, nāsamajh*). Most related terms show the Rajasthani retroflex *ḷ*: *gaiḷ* 'light intoxication' (*halkā naśā*); *gaiḷak* 'someone who forgets' (*bhūlnevālā*).
7. See G.W. Briggs 1938, pp. 10, 107-10. A useful piece of research on Hiṅglāj, presenting accounts of early pilgrimages, has been prepared by F. Pannebaker 1983. On Hiṅglāj in the context of Śakti worship in general see D.C. Sircar 1973, and K.M. Erndl 1993, p. 35.
8. Thus, I first heard the story of Gehlā Nāth's encounter with Hiṅglāj from a village Nāth living outside the immediate environs of Gailpur, who was not a frequent visitor to the temple there.
9. On the cult see A. Gold 1988, pp. 99-123; and Gold and Gold 1984.
10. For the broader significance of the dog in world religions see D.G. White 1991. See also M. Leach 1961, an interesting compendium of dog-lore from around the world. She treats Bhairav specifically on pp. 11, 175. The most extensive easily accessible study of Bhairav specifically is E. Chalier-Visuvalingam 1989.

REFERENCES

Alter, J.S. *The Wrestler's Body: Identity and Ideology in North India.* Berkeley: University of California Press, 1992.

Bouillier, V. *Naître renonçant: une caste de Sannyāsi villageois au Népal central.* Recherches sur la Haute Asie 5. Nanterre: Laboratoire d'ethnologie, 1979.

———. 'Le Caste Sectaire des Kānphaṭā Jogī dans le Royaume du Népal: l'Example de Gorkha'. *Bulletin de l'École Française d'Extrême Orient* 75 (1986): 105-47.

———. 'Des Prêtres du Pouvoir: Les Yogī at la Fonction Royale'. *Puruśārtha* 12 (1989): 193-213.

———. 'Growth and Decay of a Kanphata Yogi Monastery in South-west Nepal'. In *Indian Economic and Social History Review* 28.2 (1991): 151-70.

Briggs, G.W. *Gorakhnāth and the Kānphata Yogīs.* 1938. Rpt. Delhi: Motilal Banarsidass, 1973.

Chalier-Visuvalingam, E. 'Bhairava's Royal Brahmanicide: the Problem of the Mahābrāhmaṇa'. In *Criminal Gods and Demon Devotees: Essays on the Guardians of Popular Hinduism,* ed. Alf Hiltebeitel, pp. 157-229. Albany: State University of New York Press, 1989.

Erndl, K.M. *Victory to the Mother: The Hindu Goddess of Northwest India in Myth, Ritual, and Symbol.* New York: Oxford University Press, 1993.

Gold, A.G. *Fruitful Journeys: The Ways of Rajasthani Pilgrims.* Berkeley: University of California Press, 1988.

———. *A Carnival of Parting: The Tales of King Gopi Chand and King Bharthari as Sung and Told by Madhu Natisar Nāth of Ghatiyali, Rajasthan, India.* Berkeley: University of California Press, 1992.

Gold, D. 'The Instability of the King: Magical Insanity and the Yogis' Power in the Politics of Jodhpur, 1803-1843'. In *Popular Religion and Political Dissidence in North India,* ed. David Lorenzen, pp. 120-32. Albany: State University of New York Press, 1995.

Gold, D. and A.G. Gold. 'The Fate of the Householder Nāth'. In *History of Religions* 24 (1984): 113-32.

Lalas, S. *Rājasthā̃nī sabad kos.* Jodhpur: Rajasthani Shodh Sansthan; Upasamiti Rajasthani sabad kos; Chaupasani Siksha Samiti, 1962-75.

Leach, M. *God Had a Dog.* New Brunswick, New Jersey: Rutgers University Press, 1961.

Pannebakker, F. 'Hiṅglāj: A report of the research carried out in connection with an excursion to London, Spring 1983'. In *Devi: The Worship of the Goddess and its Contribution to Indian Pilgrimage,* eds. Hans Bakker and Alan Entwistle. Pp. 71-85. Groningen: Institute of Indian Studies, State University of Groningen, 1983.

Sharma, P. *Maharaja Man Singh of Jodhpur and his Times (1803-1843 AD).* Agra: Shiva Lal Agarwala and Company, 1972.

Sircar, D.C. *The Śākta Pīṭhas.* 2nd ed. Delhi: Motilal Banarsidass, 1973.

Srivirnathji. *Śrīnāthcarit.* Haridwar, U.P.: Akhil Bharatvarshiya Avadhut Bhesh Barah Panth Yogi Mahasabha, 1988.

Van Buitenen, J.A.B., tr. and ed. *The Mahābhārata: The Book of the Assembly Hall.* Chicago: University of Chicago Press, 1975.

White, D.G. *Myths of the Dog-Man.* Chicago: University of Chicago Press, 1991.

A Theology of Place: Pilgrimage in the *Caurāsī Baiṭhak Caritra*

DAVID L. HABERMAN

My intention in this paper is to explore the journey depicted in the *Caurāsī baiṭhak caritra,*[1] a text written in Braj Bhāṣā in the seventeenth century by Gokulnāth, a grandson of Vallabhācārya, the sixteenth century saint and founder of the Vaiṣṇava sect the Puṣṭimārg. Gokulnāth, the fourth son of Vallabha's son and successor Viṭṭhalnāth, lived in the Braj town of Gokul during the reign of Jahāngīr. Although he composed several important works in Sanskrit, he is best known for popularizing the Puṣṭimārg by using Braj Bhāṣā. In fact, he is the first Puṣṭimārgī leader to write in Braj Bhāṣā. Three texts written by him in that language are well-known and often discussed by Puṣṭimārgīs: *Caurāsī Vaiṣṇavan kī vārtā* or *The Lives of the Eighty-four Vaiṣṇavas* (e.g. disciples of Vallabha), the *Do-sau-bāvan Vaiṣṇavan kī vārtā* or *The Lives of the 252 Vaiṣṇavas* (e.g. disciples of Viṭṭhalnāth), and the *Caurāsī baiṭhak caritra* or *The Stories of the Eighty-four Seats* (of Vallabha).

Structurally the *Caurāsī baiṭhak caritra* is divided into eighty-four sections, each being comprised of a description of one of the eighty-four *baiṭhaks,* or seats, established by Vallabha during three pilgrimages around India in which he visited many of the famous holy places. The work does not provide detailed information about Vallabha's life, nor does it follow any strict chronological order, but the text functions significantly in the pilgrimage culture of the Puṣṭimārg. Vallabha's followers have tended to emphasize his travels as represented in this text and have constructed monument-shrines called *baiṭhaks* at each place where some important event in his life occurred. Although not all of the *baiṭhaks* now exist as physical shrines, these form a skeletal structure for Puṣṭimārgī pilgrimage. My present concern, however, is with the journey itself. What is the purpose of Vallabha's journey as it is recorded in the *Caurāsī baiṭhak caritra*?

Gokulnāth tells us numerous times that the main purpose of

Vallabha's travels throughout India is to 'break' (*khaṇḍan*) the Māyāvād and establish the Brahmavād or Bhaktimārg. He presents Vallabha's journey explicitly as a *digvijaya* aimed to convert the Māyāvādīs and others to Kṛṣṇa Bhakti. Who are these Māyāvādīs? The term 'Māyāvādī' in Gokulnāth's text refers specifically to the followers of Śaṅkara's Advaita Vedānta; they are portrayed as worshippers of Śiv and wearers of *rudrākṣa*. Śaṅkara himself is identified in the *Caurāsī baiṭhak caritra* (*CBC* p. 176) as an *avatār* of Śiv. The Puṣṭimārgī debate with the Māyāvādīs is complex and vehement. Presumably, the *Caurāsī baiṭhak caritra* itself was written to further the cause of defeating the Māyāvādīs and establishing the Brahmavādī world view of Kṛṣṇa Bhakti, wherein everything is accepted as Brahman. The *Caurāsī baiṭhak caritra*, however, does not present a sophisticated philosophical argument to defeat the Māyāvādīs; we will see that this text portrays a very different strategy toward this end.

Among the many points of contention between the Māyāvādīs and the Puṣṭimārgīs, what stands out perhaps most sharply is a major difference with respect to their perspectives on the world. Whereas for Śaṅkara—at least as he is understood by Puṣṭimārgī philosophers—the differentiated world as *māyā* is ultimately unreal, in contrast Vallabha clearly states that the world is real. Moreover, from the Brahmavādī perspective of the pure non-dualism of Vallabha's *śuddhādvaita*, Śaṅkara's rejection of the world reveals a problematic dualism: if absolutely everything is considered to be Brahman or Kṛṣṇa, the world itself is non-different from Kṛṣṇa. Within the pilgrimage culture of the Puṣṭimārg this is taken in a literal sense as is evident in much of the pilgrimage activity of the Puṣṭimārg. For example, Puṣṭimārgī pilgrims in Braj worship the natural forms of rocks, trees, rivers, and ponds as earthly forms of Kṛṣṇa.[2] Puṣṭimārgīs, then, most specifically reject Śaṅkara's notion of *māyā*; thus their identification of his followers as Māyāvādīs. From a Puṣṭimārgī perspective divinity should be present in every form of nature, and especially evident in places known for their sacrality. Direct revelation of the divine form of a place could therefore be used to undermine the opposing position that the natural world is ultimately unreal and thus unrelated to the ultimate reality of Brahman.

The Puṣṭimārgī founder Vallabha himself had developed and expressed this theology of place. In a Sanskrit work entitled the

Siddhāntamuktāvalī, he identifies three perspectives by which one may perceive anything within the world. (Gokulnāth himself wrote an important commentary on this text.) Vallabha uses the example of the Ganges to illustrate these three perspectives, which are concomitant with three forms of Kṛṣṇa. The first perspective involves viewing the physical form of the river: the water which corresponds to the earthly form of the Ganges, called by the Puṣṭimārgīs, the *ādhibhautika*. Vallabha uses this example to illustrate the earthly form of Kṛṣṇa, more commonly known as the world. The second perspective by which one may view the Ganges is to see it as a holy pilgrimage site that will cleanse one's sins; this corresponds to the spiritual form of the Ganges, called by the Puṣṭimārgīs, the *ādhyātmika*. Vallabha uses this example to illustrate the spiritual or formless form of Kṛṣṇa, known as *akṣara* Brahman, the form of Brahman that Puṣṭimārgīs claim the Māyāvādīs are fixed on exclusively. The third and highest possible perspective by which the Ganges can be viewed is as the divine form of the goddess. One does not come to worship for one's own benefit from this perspective, but comes rather as a devotee, without thought of reward, to praise Gaṅgā Mā. The goddess corresponds to the divine form of the Ganges, called by Puṣṭimārgīs, the *ādhidaivika*. Vallabha uses this example to illustrate the divine form of Kṛṣṇa, known as Bhagavān, which yields the highest joy (*ānanda*).

Although within the non-dual frame of *śuddhādvaita* all three forms are accepted as Kṛṣṇa, they are ranked hierarchically. The second perspective and concomitant form encompass the first, and the third encompass the other two. In this sense, the third perspective is more complete. The Puṣṭimārg, then, as a 'path' can be viewed as a movement from the first perspective of the *ādhibhautika* (earthly forms) through the second perspective of the *ādhyātmika* (formless), and then on to the more complete perspective of the *ādhidaivika* (divine forms). Richard Barz (1976, p. 15) concurs: 'The step from the *ādhibhautika* view (which is the *laukika* view) to the *ādhyātmika* (which is removed from the ordinary material view and so is *alaukika*, but is still not the vision of the complete truth) and the step from the *ādhyātmika* attitude to the *ādhidaivika* point of view (which is the perfect *alaukika* attitude) brings one to the goal of the Puṣṭimārga.' But it is important to realize the importance of the first level for any further advancement. Vallabha indicates that the *ādhidaivika* vision is available only for one who understands the non-difference between the *ādhibhautika* form and the others; that is to say one can arrive at the highest *ādhidaivika* level only through the *ādhibhautika*. One modern teacher of the Puṣṭimārg explained this to me by using the metaphor of a television. He said that the *ādhibhautika* is like the material substance of the television, the glass, wires, and plastic; the *ādhyātmika* is the electrical power; and the *ādhidaivika* is the resulting visual picture. The point being that one cannot see the picture without the material substance of the television; likewise one cannot arrive at the highest level of *ādhidaivika* by abandoning the world as recommended by the Māyāvādīs, but rather by going through it, while understanding that the world itself is divine.

The realization of *ādhyātmika*, then, is a step in the right direction, but to get stuck at the *ādhyātmika* level—for any reason—would be a mistake. Moreover, if one were to hold firmly to the second level, defending it as the only and final position, then that would be a mistake of spiritual arrogance bordering on a tragedy that keeps one from experiencing the highest joy. This is precisely how the Māyāvādīṣ, who hold all differentiated form to be unreal, are pictured in Puṣṭimārgī literature. From this perspective they are not necessarily on the wrong path, but are simply stuck at the *ādhyātmika* level and need to get moving. (For those who know the text, I am reminded of the *Lotus Sutra's* depiction of the haughty Arhats who had assumed that they had achieved final *nirvāṇa*, which consequently made them closed to the Buddha's ongoing teaching intended to show them that their journey had not yet ended.) 'Conversion', then in this context, means dislodging the Māyāvādīs from their solid foothold in the *ādhyātmika* level and moving them on to the higher, ever-changing and more delightful *ādhidaivika* level. This would result in a perspectival shift to Bhakti wherein the world is real and divine and the highest joy of Bhagavān is experienced in everything, even in the seemingly ordinary level of the *ādhibhautika*. But, we might ask at this point, what is the method of conversion used by Vallabha in Gokulnāth's text to bring about this perspectival shift?

The *Caurāsī baiṭhak caritra* does not present a sophisticated argument. How then does Vallabha dislodge the Māyāvādīs from their firm foothold in the *ādhyātmika*? The answer to this is twofold: he performs a *saptāh* and he reveals the divine form of a particular place.

A *saptāh* involves a seven-day reading of the *Bhāgavatapurāṇa*. The textual justification for this ritual act is found in the *Bhāgavata* itself. We read in the opening book that King Parīkṣit was out hunting one day and became thirsty. Arriving at the hermitage of Śamika, he came upon the sage in meditation and asked him for water. Because Śamika was in a yogic trance he did not hear Parīkṣit. Thinking that the sage was rudely ignoring him King Parīkṣit became enraged. He picked up a dead snake with the end of his bow and threw it onto the shoulder of the sage. When the sage's son discovered this unjust act he cursed the king, announcing that Parīkṣit would die in seven days from a snake bite. King Parīkṣit realized his mistake and now understood he had only seven days to live. He sat down on the bank of the Ganges and took a vow not to drink or eat anything for his remaining seven days, striving ardently to become enlightened. He called upon various teachers to show him the way to liberation within seven days, but only when Veda Vyāsa's son, Śukadeva, appeared before him did he find his answer. Śukadeva told him that for seven days he would speak of the stories and glories of Kṛṣṇa that were taught to him by his father, and that by hearing them Parīkṣit's goal would be realized. A seven-day reading of *Bhāgavata*, then, is an opportunity for all involved to realize the benefits that were made available to King Parīkṣit.

Among the many benefits of the *Bhāgavata*, one of the most important for Braj Vaiṣṇavas is the affirmation of the limitations of the Māyāvād, specifically its theoretically final goal of *mokṣa*. Kṛṣṇa says in the third book of the *Bhāgavata* (3.29.13), for example:

> Even if the five kinds of *mokṣa* are offered, namely, coresidence in the same world, equality in power, proximity, similarity in form, or even union, my devotees do not accept anything but my service.[3]

Such statements are very important for Braj Vaiṣṇavism where the higher goal of Bhakti is to taste and enjoy the ravishing sweetness of the Lord of Forms, not to merge into a formless Brahman wherein all experience is rendered null and void.

Although Vallabha is presented in Gokulnāth's text as one skilled in scriptural debate, and although other Puṣṭimārgī texts greatly highlight this quality, it seems to me that the *Caurāsī baiṭhak caritra* emphasizes something quite different. At the seventy-third *baiṭhak* site of Avantikā Purī (*CBC* pp. 171-7), Vallabha successfully converts a group of Māyāvādīs who had previously been worshippers of Śiv. Śiv, who himself had been present for this event, approached Vallabha and expressed surprise at Vallabha's method. He remarks that he had expected him to convert the Māyāvādīs through scriptural debate; instead Vallabha chose to give a direct vision—a *sākṣāt darśan*—of divinity. The activities that are given by far the most attention by Gokulnāth in the *Caurāsī baiṭhak caritra* are the numerous divine showings that occur as a consequence of Vallabha's itinerant presence. This seems to be the method of theological contest most preferred by Vallabha as he is portrayed by Gokulnāth, and is the most important and effective device Vallabha uses in his encounters with the Māyāvādīs. I will therefore spend the remainder of my time examining this method and its theological implications.

Vallabha's journey through the sacred sites of India can be read as a revelation of the divinity of everything, especially of the divine forms of particular places. An example of this is found in the story recorded for the fourth *baiṭhak* (*CBC* pp. 7-10), located near Baṃsībaṭ in Vrindaban. There Vallabha encountered one Prabhūdās Jaloṭā and offered him *mahāprasād*. Prabhūdās, however, resisted saying: 'O Mahārāj, I have not taken a bath, so how can I accept *mahāprasād*?' From the Puṣṭimārgī perspective of *śuddhādvaita* this demonstrates a misleading dualism based on a negative sense of the world. Vallabha responded to Prabhūdās's resistance by revealing to him the divine form of Vrindaban wherein he saw Kṛṣṇa in every leaf of every tree. Vallabha's disclosure seems to be a direct means of implying the undermining question: Where is there any place for pollution within a world wherein everything is Kṛṣṇa? His dualistic perspective shattered by this divine revelation, Prabhūdās happily accepted the *mahāprasād* from Vallabha.

Throughout the *Caurāsī baithak caritra* Vallabha gives his disciples divine visions that enable them to have access to the *ādhidaivika* perspective on a place. For example, at the seventh *baiṭhak* site of Kamodban (*CBC* pp. 15-17), Vallabha tells a story about how the place got its name. He explains to his disciples that upon the request of Rādhā, Kṛṣṇa created a beautiful forest here of Kamoda and Kamodanī trees along with two ponds filled with lovely lotuses. When his disciples complained that they could not see this scene, Vallabha repeated the *śloka* from the *Bhāgavadgītā* where Kṛṣṇa says to Arjuna: 'I give you divine eyes (*divyacakṣu*) so that you can see my lordly form', and then gave his disciples 'divine eyes' that enabled them to see the divine form of Kamodban. Likewise, he gave them 'divine eyes' (*divyacakṣu*) at Mānasī Gaṅgā (*CBC* p. 22), a sacred pond located on Mount Govardhan in Braj, so that they could have sight of the divine form (*ādhidaivika sarūpa*) of the pond.

The story told at the eighth *baiṭhak* site of Bahulāban (*CBC* pp. 17-19) presents another challenge to the Brahmavādī perspective of Vallabha in the form of the Muslim prohibition on worshipping any form. Although there is obviously a great difference between Islam and Advaita Vedānta, from a Puṣṭimārgī perspective both make the mistake of limiting ultimate reality to the realm of the formless. The local Muslim ruler of the area had prohibited the worship of an image of Bahulā, a sacred cow whose temple is located in this forest. In the presence of the Muslim ruler Vallabha offered the image grass and the cow ate it. Witnessing this the ruler realized the limitations of his own perspective and begged to be initiated into Vallabha's. The resistance of the Muslims, however, is of little concern in the *Caurāsī baiṭhak caritra*; the main targets of Vallabha's transformative activities are the Māyāvādīs.

Another kind of story commonly told to demonstrate Vallabha's effectiveness in establishing the Brahmavādī view of Bhakti involves Vallabha performing a *saptāh* at some site, usually beneath a *chõkar* tree near some body of water. While he is reading the *Bhāgavata*, a beautiful woman or unusual man appears. When questioned as to the identity of the being, Vallabha informs those gathered that the being is the divine form of the site itself. Sanketban Devī appears to fan Vallabha at the eighteenth site of Sanket (*CBC* pp. 35-6) and the divine form of the Tāpī River appears to fan him at the fifty-third site of Surat (*CBC* pp. 137-8); the goddess of the Narmadā River appears to request Vallabha to bathe in her at the fifty-fourth site of Bharuch (*CBC* p. 139); at the fifty-eighth site of Śrī Piṇḍatārak (*CBC* pp. 143-5) the pilgrimage site appears in his divine form of a Brahmin; likewise the divine forms of Kedārnāth (Seventy-eighth *baiṭhak*, *CBC* pp. 182-3), Himācal Mountain (eightieth, *CBC* pp. 184-5) and the Ganges (eighty-first, *CBC* pp. 185-6) appear respectively as a Yogī, a Brahmin, and a beautiful woman. Divine forms seem to appear everywhere in Vallabha's presence. Rādhā and Kṛṣṇa appear on a number of occasions throughout Braj and elsewhere; the deity of a particular temple appears and is identified with Kṛṣṇa. And perhaps most importantly, throughout the book Vallabha himself is revealed to be an *avatār* of Kṛṣṇa. This, in fact, proves to be the most convincing way that Vallabha has of converting the Māyāvādīs.

The text describing the seventy-third *baiṭhak* site of Avantikā Purī (*CBC* pp. 171-7), modern Ujjain, gives a better understanding of the role that these divine revelations played in converting the Māyāvādīs. The text informs us that Vallabha arrived in Ujjain and set up his camp under a *pīpar* tree. He bathed in the Kṣiprā River, sat down above Gomatī Pond, and then began to instruct his faithful companion, Dāmodardās. Vallabha explained that this site is the city of Mahādev and is therefore an important site of the Māyāvādīs. Vallabha told Dāmodardās that it was therefore necessary to refute the Māyā-mat and establish the Brahmavād. To do this they prepared a *saptāh,* since the *Bhāgavata* is the text that proves that the Māyāvādī's goal of *mokṣa* is limited. The Māyāvādīs soon heard that the one who had defeated many Māyāvādīs in a *digvijaya* had arrived in their area, but they were afraid to meet him. Two pundits favored by Mahādev, however, happened to live nearby. Mahādev, who himself had a desire to hear Vallabha speak *Bhāgavata,* explained to them that previously he was commanded to establish the Māyā-mat, but now was the time to end this *mat,* move on to the Brahmavād, and realize Vallabha as an *avatār* of Kṛṣṇa. Mahādev then went to meet Vallabha who bowed to him and greeted him as the master of Avantikā Pūrī. Vallabha told Mahādev to call the Māyāvādīs for a meeting with him. That night Mahādev visited them all in a dream and urged them to confront Vallabha. He informed them that since he was on their side they would be protected. Many Māyāvādīs came to Avantikā Pūrī; Mahādev joined them, but remained hidden. While conversing with the Māyāvādīs, Vallabha suddenly smiled and revealed his divinity. The Māyāvādīs realized that they had achieved a direct vision of an *avatār* of Kṛṣṇa, were converted by this encounter, and requested shelter with Vallabha. He told them to remove their *rudrākṣas* and bathe in Gomatī Kuṇḍ. He then initiated them with a *mantra* and gave them *tulsī mālās* to wear.

In a similar vein, at the fifty-first *baiṭhak* site of Totādrī Mountain (*CBC* pp. 134-6), Vallabha revealed the presence of a divine lake. When the local Māyāvādīs saw this lake they were amazed and acknowledged that here was a reality that had always been present but had previously escaped their perception because of mistaken belief. Moreover, they now admitted the lake to be an *aṃśa,* or particle, of the divine form. Realizing the limitations of their previous perspective, they asked to be initiated by Vallabha. They too then removed their necklaces of *rudrākṣa* and Vallabha replaced them with *tulsī.*

Having revealed the divine form of each place, in order to be consistent with *śuddhādvaita,* it is necessary to affirm the oneness or non-duality of all divine forms. And this too is an important aspect of Vallabha's itinerant activity: he traveled about revealing the identity of Kṛṣṇa and the divinity of a particular place. For example, at both Citrakūṭ and Ayodhya, the twenty-fourth (*CBC* pp. 50-2) and twenty-fifth *baiṭhak* sites (*CBC* pp. 52-4), Vallabha revealed the identity of Rām and Kṛṣṇa. At Citrakūṭ Vallabha prepared a food offering to Rām. When questioned by his disciple Kṛṣṇadās Meghan as to why a Kṛṣṇa *bhakta* would make an offering to another deity, Vallabha replied that Rām was not different from Kṛṣṇa. At Ayodhya, Rām told Hanumān to bring food for Vallabha. Hanumān hesitated, since he considered himself solely a Rām *bhakta.* None the less, Hanumān obeyed Rām's instruction; when he presented the food to Vallabha he saw Vallabha as Rām, making the identification of the two explicit. Kṛṣṇa of Braj is identified again and again with various divinities throughout the text: Viṭṭhalnāth at Paṇḍharpur (*baiṭhak* 35, *CBC* pp. 82-8), Varadrāj at Kāñcī (*baiṭhak* 40, *CBC,* pp. 98-102), as well as many others.

The picture of the world one gets reading the *Caurāsī baiṭhak caritra* is a world alive with divinity. The purpose of pilgrimage in this text is to reveal the divinity present in each place visited, as a way of establishing the Brahmavād of Kṛṣṇa Bhakti and breaking the limiting boundaries of the Māyāvād. The Māyāvādīs are apparently aware of the specialness—the *ādhyātmika*—of a pilgrimage *tīrth;* what Vallabha reveals to them is the *tīrth-devatā* of a pilgrimage site and thereby opens the *ādhidaivika* realm to them. The world, as revealed by Vallabha, is a world fully divine. His travels as depicted in the *Caurāsī baiṭhak caritra* reveal the ever-present reality of Kṛṣṇa, a non-dual reality that is none the less multi-dimensional: it is present everywhere, but takes unique form from place to place. The Māyāvādīs dismiss the diverse world of place as an ultimate illusion, but from a Puṣṭimārgī perspective this means missing an important form of Kṛṣṇa. What Vallabha accomplishes by a continual series of revelations is to give access to a view of the extraordinary *ādhidaivika* in the seemingly ordinary *ādhibhautika*. The chief lesson that Vallabha teaches the Māyāvādīs that enables them to move on from their obstinate foothold in the *ādhyātmika* level, is that the world itself—each and every place—is fully divine. This opens their eyes to a reality that is ever-present, but was previously blocked from perception because of firm but finally mistaken belief. The shattering of this limited viewpoint and the opening into this new world view leads on to the highest perspective of the *ādhidaivika*. More than any other means, a direct revelation of the divine form of a particular place brings about the perspectival shift that leads to the conversion from Māyāvād to Brahmavād. And this after all is what Gokulnāth tells us is the chief design of Vallabha's pilgrimage.

NOTES

1. The edition of this text I refer to is one edited by Niranjandev Sharma, hereafter cited as *CBC*.
2. See my *Journey Through the Twelve Forests,* especially Chapter 3.
3. This is one of the verses quoted by the Gauḍīya Vaiṣṇava leader Rūp Gosvāmin to illustrate the inferiority of *mokṣa* compared to Bhakti. See his *Bhaktirasāmṛtasindhu*, 1.2. 28.

REFERENCES

Barz, Richard. *The Bhakti Sect of Vallabhācārya.* Faridabad: Thomson Press, 1976.

Haberman, David L. *Journey Through the Twelve Forests.* New York: Oxford University Press, 1994.

Sharma, Niranjandev. *Caurāsī baiṭhak caritra.* Mathura: Sri Govardhan Granthmala Karyalaya, 1967.

The Snake-bite Episodes in *Candāyan*: A Journey within a Journey

NASEEM HINES

Candāyan, completed in AD 1379, is considered to be the first Indo-Islamic Sufi *masnavī*. It is the earliest Indo-Sufi *masnavī* we have, and as such it is considered the pioneering work of the genre in Hindi and seems to serve as a model for the later works of this style. Maulānā (or Mulla Dāūd) (d. 1395) of Dalmau, the author of *Candāyan* is believed to be one of the disciples of Nizāmuddīn Auliā of Chisht. He composed the *masnavī* during the reign of Firoz Shāh Tughlaq (AD 1351-88), dedicating it to his prime minister, Jaunā Shāh. Unfortunately, very little else is known about Maulānā Dāūd.

Candāyan is based on the folk legend of 'Canainī' or 'Cāndā-Lorik'. Lorik and his devoted wife Mainā live in Govar, but when Lorik and Cāndā see each other, they fall in love and elope. After a long journey and many adventures, Lorik returns home with Cāndā. Initially, there is a conflict between Cāndā and Mainā, but Lorik intervenes to resolve it. In all, 452 stanzas of this composition are available but, since the text is incomplete, we do not know the precise conclusion of the story.

This paper focuses on the two 'snake-bite' episodes which in Parmeshwarilal Gupta's edition begin from stanza 333 and end on stanza 360. Eloping with Cāndā, on his way to Hardi Patan in the Kalinga region, where he hopes to visit with some kinsmen, Lorik puts up at a Brahmin's house. Here, in the night, Cāndā is bitten by a snake and dies. Later, she is revived by a Gunī's or Gāruḍī's *mantras*. Lorik offers the ornaments of his wrists and arms to the Gāruḍī, but the Gāruḍī asks for the rest of Lorik's ornaments and takes them away with him.

Cāndā and Lorik resume their journey the next day, and when night falls, they take shelter under a large tree. Here, once again, Cāndā succumbs to a fatal snake-bite. For two days and a night, Lorik cries in anguish for her. He constantly weeps, laments and recalls the various risks they took to be with each other. He describes how miserably hopeless it is for him to be without her. He blames himself for the tragic incident and repents for his sins. Finally, he comes to the decision that he cannot live without her any more and decides to sit on the funeral pyre, holding her in an embrace. With this plan in mind, he begins to cut wood. However, a Gunī comes along and Lorik implores him to revive Cāndā. In return, he pledges all his belongings and promises to serve the Gunī for as long as he lives and also in the next life. Once again Cāndā is brought back to life, and they continue on their journey.

Now, the first question is, why did Maulānā Dāūd choose to have two snake-bite episodes? And secondly, why are the episodes placed one right after the other? Mataprasad Gupta and Parmeshwarilal Gupta both agree that the second snake-bite episode is entirely Maulānā Dāūd's own creation and that the original folk tale of Mainā-Lorik or Canainī has only one snake-bite episode. My explanation is that when Maulānā Dāūd composed *Candāyan*, he selected a story, i.ĕ. the folk-tale of Canainī, merely as a point of departure. The changes Maulānā Dāūd brought into the story and the sophisticated form he gave his composition altered its focus. It is transformed from a simple entertaining folk tale into an elevated literary work and a vehicle for transmitting Sufi doctrine. The journey of Lorik in *Candāyan* is essentially a journey of the individual self in search of The Universal Self and the two snake-bite episodes represent the pivotal point in this quest, for with them the story embarks upon the spiritual journey within Lorik's physical journey. Since the literary genre of *masnavī* is an allegorical mystical poem, the story must be understood on a different level and the Sufi symbols must be closely examined.

The first step a novice must take towards his mystical journey is in the direction of the *maqām-i-khalwat,* a place of retreat and vigil. Discussing the importance of this first step, Laleh Bakhtiar, in her book *Sufi Expressions of the Mystic Quest* (1976, p. 94) says that to retreat to an isolated cell in order to 'remember' God is considered by many orders to be the most significant step for all Sufi disciples. It is an aid in achieving a state of permanent inward retreat. Observing the traditions of the Prophet, who used to retreat to caves in the mountains, some orders still recommend one to retreat to the solitude of nature. Many Sufi orders have isolated cells for the practice of the *khalwat.*

The premise or logic behind entering *khalwat*, the gateway to the subsequent stages of the mystical journey, is that respite from daily routine and distance from one's immediate surroundings provide the seeker with a different perspective. In both snake-bite episodes, Lorik is away from the two places he is most preoccupied with, i.e. his home and the battlefield. In the first episode, he is at a Brahmin's place and in the second, he is in a leafy arbor beneath a large tree. Here the association of the 'tree of knowledge' comes to mind, as for example, in the account of Buddha's enlightenment. According to the Sufis, as Mir Valiuddin says in his book, *The Quranic Sufism* (1987, p. 152), the stage of the spiritual retreat, if entered into and embraced with sincerity, has the potential to open the door to the next stage of the mystic journey.

Defining the spiritual stations of the internal experiences in Sufism, Carl Ernst writes in *Eternal Garden* (1992, p. 10): 'The Sufi Sarraj gives the meaning of stations as "the station of the creature before God, in terms of where one stands from devotions, exertions, meditations, and concentrating on God. Repentance (*tawba*), asceticism (*zuhd*), poverty (*faqr*), patience (*sabr*), trust in God (*tawakkul*) and satisfaction (*rida*) are some of the principal stations".'

In the light of the above understanding, let us briefly trace Lorik's journey through a few of the stations mentioned earlier. The first station is repentance (*tawba*). In the snake-bite episodes, Lorik repents for his sins again and again and blames only himself for his present predicament, saying that he got what he deserved (M.P. Gupta 1967, p. 313): जस कीन्हेउं, तस पायउं. Asceticism (*zuhd*) is the next station: comparing his condition to Rām's when he was living an ascetic's life in Pañcavaṭī, Lorik says that he too is enduring Ram's circumstances (ibid., p. 317): लोरहि राम अवस्था परी.

When Lorik arrives at the next station, poverty (*faqr*), he first gives away all his material possessions in the first snake-bite episode and in the second episode is willing to serve the Gāruḍī all his life and the next if only the Gāruḍī can bring Cāndā to life. Lorik says (ibid., p. 324): हाथ क मुंदरी, खरग कटारा, कान क कुन्डर, चांद गियं हारा—तौरै कहें चांद जो लहउं—दुहौ जरम चेर होइ रहउं. The next stations are patience and the mystic's trust in God (*sabr* and *tawakkul*). The novice expects mercy from God alone. Lamenting bitterly for Cāndā, Lorik says (ibid., p. 313): दया गुसाई सिरजनहारा, तोहि छाडि कस करउं पुकारा. ('Oh my maker, have mercy on me. Except you, who else should I call upon.')

When a novice enters seclusion, *maqām-i-khalwat,* he is also supposed to engage in constant *zikr,* i.e. repeated mentioning of God's attributes. During both the snake-bite episodes, Lorik keeps recalling the splendor of the joy he had in Cāndā's company and repeats her name over and over again (ibid., p. 320): संग न साथी, भे भे रोवा, मीत जो होत, से दई बिछोवा—कर गहि, चांद चांद गुहरावइ, धुनि धुनि सीस नारि पै लावइ. ('Deprived of his companion, Lorik was beside himself and wept aloud shamelessly, bemoaning the loss of his love. Holding Cāndā's arm, he called out 'Cāndā, Cāndā', leaning over her body and beating his head over and over again.') At this point Lorik is engaged in *zikr.*

The practice of *zikr* helps the disciple to disengage from his present and immediate surroundings and move from his self to concentrate on the divine. At this point, I am reminded of a mystic story I heard from one of my Persian Sufi friends. It goes as follows: A man falls in love with a beauty. He wants to see her and so approaches her abode and knocks at the door. The person within asks: 'Who is it?' 'It is I', came the reply. 'Turn away, it is not the right time to see the one you seek', said the person from within. The lover left and returned the next day at a different time, but the same incident was repeated, and he had to leave. In this way, the lover would visit the house of the beloved over and over again. One day, when the lover knocked at the door, from within came the same question: 'Who is there?' From the lover came the answer: 'You, it is you.' 'Enter now', came the command from within.

Studying the final stages of Lorik's journey, we realize that Lorik actually arrives at that station where he could distinguish the difference between the true essence and the mirror which merely reflects the divine reality. In the second snake-bite episode, when Lorik prepares to go on the funeral pyre, embracing Cāndā, he proclaims (ibid., p. 312): भई बात अब जानेउं चांदा, तोरैं मरन निदान—जो जिउ जाइ कया कस देखहि, मै का करब अबान. ('Only after your demise, Cāndā, have I realized that if the life departs, it is impossible for the form to remain intact. I have no say in this matter nor any other recourse.') Lorik is now prepared to make the ultimate sacrifice: the sacrifice of one's own self or ego. At this moment, he is without carnal desires and his mind is pure. In actively embracing self-annihilation, the ultimate sacrifice, he is actually moving towards his goal of union with the Eternal Joy and life everlasting. *Fanā',* the phenomenon of 'naughting the self' according to

William Chittick (1983 p. 173), is essentially the result of true love, already tested by sacrifice.

Not long ago, a Sufi master Janāb Amīr 'Alī's young daughter asked him: 'How may I differentiate and identify true love?' The teacher replied: मुहब्बत तो कुरबानियां चाहती है, तहे तेग़ पेशानियां चाहती है—जो डर जाए राहे वफ़ा में, मेरी जां, कोई और शै है, मुहब्बत नहीं है. ('Really, it is not very difficult to recognize love because it demands many sacrifices and enjoys putting the heads of the lovers through the test of the scimitar. Then, my darling, that which trembles in the path of total commitment, is surely something other than love.')

Elaborating on the subject of a mystic's journey through the various stations (*maqāmāt*), Laleh Bakhtiar says (1976, p. 52):

> The spiritual stations are degrees of ascent, reached through certain rites and certain difficulties. They are permanent acquisitions, as opposed to states, which are gratuitous gifts that come and go with the attraction of the Divine (difference between *ḥāl, aḥwāl* and *maqām, maqāmāt*). The ultimate station (*fanā'*) is reached when the seeker loses his self in The Self. His final orientation is towards total receptivity: spiritual death. One of the most famous sayings of the Prophet, peace be on him, is 'Die before you die'. The tomb room in Konya of Jalāl ad-Dīn Rūmī, the founder of the Mevlevi Order, is actually the place of his wedding for the night of his death is celebrated with all the joy that surrounds a wedding.

The *urs* or the wedding of Sufi saint is actually his death anniversary celebrated as the day of his annihilation (*fanā'*) in the Unity of Being (*waḥdat al-wajūd*).

Once again, the success of the individual soul in attaining union with The Universal Soul lies in the seriousness of one's pursuit and one's complete commitment and readiness to sacrifice everything to achieve this goal. Unconditional sacrifice, then, is the key to *fanā'*. A *sākhī* attributed to the poet saint Kabir says (B. Tiwari 1985, p. 490): जिन ढूंढा तिन पाइयां, गहरे पानी पैठि—मैं बूढ़ा, बूड़न डरा, रहा किनारे बैठि. ('Only those who sink clear to the base of the sea find what they seek. Scared of sinking and frail, I remain sitting on the sidelines.')

The presence of the Gāruḍī or the Gunī in both snake-bite episodes and the significance of the Brahmin's presence in the first episode, which are symbolic of the spiritual guide or *hādī,* should also be recognized at this point. In Sufism, the novice's relationship with the teacher (*murshid mūrīd*) is of great significance because without the guidance of the teacher it would be difficult for the mystic to realize his ultimate goal of *fanā'*, the last stage. Annemarie Schimmel (1992, p. 103) defines it as 'de-becoming'.

In both the episodes, the time of the snake-bite is late in the night, or rather when the day is about to break (M.P. Gupta, 1967, p. 313): '"पाछिली" राति होत भिनुसारा'. This time is considered to be auspicious in many traditions. Symbolically, the veil of darkness or ignorance is about to be lifted and the light of knowledge is beginning to shine.

With respect to the second question, 'Why are the two snake-bite episodes arranged back to back?', my explanation is that in the mystic journey the seeker has to move from one state to the other without a major break. The *maqāmāt* have to follow each other closely without a major gap. According to Laleh Bakhtiar (1976, p. 94), after one leaves the *khalwat,* the spiritual retreat, one's position within the *maqāmāt* can remain effective only on the condition that the novice continues to practice *zikr.* In *Islam: An Introduction,* Annemarie Schimmel (1992, p. 104) says that 'in the uninterrupted struggle against the *nafs,* not only are poverty and fasting, nightly vigils and, often, silence required, but also constant introspection'. The key words here are 'continuation', 'uninterrupted', and 'constant'.

The first snake-bite episode, therefore, is symbolic of Lorik's setting forth on his spiritual journey and his arrival at that particular *maqām* where he is willing to part with all his material possessions. According to the Sufis, the seeker's successful arrival at this stage naturally leads him to the next logical state. Thus, the subsequent states are symbolized in the second snake-bite episode where Lorik arrives at that high point of his spiritual journey where he willingly relinquishes his desire to live in exchange for the eternal happiness he seeks in death.

In this way, in the snake-bite episodes we watch Lorik move successfully through the prescribed stages on his mystic journey. When he first faces separation from Cāndā, he is distraught with anguish and pain (M.P. Gupta 1967, p. 307): लोरक बीर बहु कारन करई-चाहि कपारै कुन्त दै मरई. ('Brave Lorik bemoaned and wept; taking an ax to his head he wished to die.') Then taking the vow of poverty he gladly gives up all his worldly belongings in order to get Cāndā back (ibid., p. 309): कर कंगन अभरन सभ दीन्हा. But when he loses her the second time, he does not wish to continue to live in a world without her and says (ibid., p. 322): कोउ भान्त न जीवंत देखेउं, परै पिरम के चेलि पिरम खेल सो नै खेलै, सो सर सेतै खेलि. ('The one who follows the dictates of love, is never seen to stay alive. Those who love their lives should not play the game of love.')

In *Studies in Islamic Mysticism* Nicholson says (quoted in L. Bakhtiar 1976, p. 95):

> The relationship between the two stations has been expressed by Ibn Farid in the following way: 'Existence is a veil in the beginning of the mystic life, and also in its middle stage, but not in its end. The mystic is veiled in the beginning by the outward aspect of existence (created things) from the inward aspect (God), while in the middle stage, he is veiled by its inward aspect from its outward aspect. But when he has reached his goal, neither do created things veil him from God nor does God veil him from created things, but God reveals Himself to the mystic in both His aspects at once as the Creator and as the universe of created things, so that the mystic sees with his bodily eye the beauty of the Divine Essence manifested under the attribute of the Outward.

In conclusion, when I was studying the available texts of *Candāyan*, it was amazing to find that in the story, there is actually a significant break after the above discussed snake-bite episodes. The composer-narrator pauses for a moment and allows his peer Maulānā Natthan to step into the narrative and express his opinion of the snake-bite episodes of *Candāyan* (M.P. Gupta 1967, p. 327): आखिर बिसहर खन्ड चन्द सुखन फरमूदने मौलाना नत्थन. The gist of the exchange between them is as follows: Maulānā Natthan says, 'Maulana Dāūd sang this song and whoever heard it was visibly moved' (जे रे सुना सो गा मुरझाई). 'Blessed are the words and blessed is the author, and those who recite it and those who mull over and contemplate the real meaning of it' (धनि रे सबद, धनि लेखनहारा, धनि ते बोल धनि अरथ बिचारा). To this praise, Mullā Dāūd modestly responds, तोर कहा मै यह खन्ड गावडं . . . . ('On your request, I sing this chapter, reciting to people, the story in verse: Lady Cāndā was going to Hardi and was bitten by the snake—I merely narrated that story.') In the courtly manner expected of Mullā Dāūd, he credits Lord Natthan for his own accomplishments: 'Really, it is Lord Natthan who brings forth the tragic emotion' (नथन मलिक दुख बात उभारी). Mullā Dāūd politely concludes the conversation with the words, 'In deference to your wish, I shall compose more poems, contemplating deeply in my mind. I bow my head and join my hands in supplication.'

After this exchange, the narrative of *Candāyan* continues much along the established path of the folk-tale. For example, in the next stanza, Lorik bids good-bye to the Gāruḍī, but somehow, the reader is left with the impression that after Maulānā Natthan has left, the narrator is saying to the rest of the audience who is still waiting to hear the remainder of the story, 'And so where was I?, Oh, yes, and then. . . .' Perhaps the truth is that Maulānā Dāūd, Maulānā Natthan and those who are initiated, informed, and experienced quickly arrive at the true meaning of the snake-bite episodes and for them the story has already arrived at a successful conclusion. The true understanding of the knowledge of the divine can never be logically explained. One experiences and interprets the spiritual phenomemon according to one's own purity and depth.

Ghālib, in the fourth chapter of the opening *ghazal* of his *dīwān* says: आगही दामे शुनीदन जिस तरह चाहे बिछाए, मुद्दआ अन्का है अपने आलमे तकरीर का. ('No matter how Learning may spread her trap of reference, understanding the true meaning of my world of expression by logic is like capturing *ankā* [the legendary rare bird]).'

REFERENCES

Bakhtiar, Laleh. *Sufi Expressions of the Mystic Quest.* New York: Thames & Hudson, 1976.

Chittick, William. *The Sufi Path of Love: The Spiritual Teachings of Rumi.* New York: State University of New York Press, 1983.

Ernst, Carl. *Eternal Garden.* New York: State University of New York Press, 1992.

Gupta, Mataprasad, ed. *Candāyan.* Agra: Pramanik Prakashan, 1967.

Gupta, Parameshvarilal, ed. *Candāyan.* Delhi: Hindi Granth Ratnakar, 1964.

Schimmel, Annemarie. *Islam, an Introduction.* New York: State University of New York Press, 1992.

Tiwari, Bholanath. *Bṛhat Hindī lokokti koś.* Delhi: Shan Printers, 1985.

Valiuddin, Mir. *The Quranic Sufism.* 3rd ed. Delhi: Motilal Banarsidass, 1987.

The *Rasik* Concept of Transcendental Sexuality

ALLAN M. KEISLAR

1. INTRODUCTION

Artists and poets had been presenting Kṛṣṇa's *gopīlīlā* for centuries, but by the early seventeenth century[1] both Gauḍīya and Rāmānandī *rasiks*[2] had developed elaborate theories explaining that the love affairs of their favorite deities, Kṛṣṇa and Rām respectively, were transcendental. Not only did they hold that their worshipful Lords eternally perform *līlās* of spiritual sexuality, but *rasik* devotees, who were often celibate, would enthusiastically contemplate[3] and even participate in these conjugal activities by meditation.[4]

How could orthodox[5] Vaiṣṇavas claim that the explicitly sexual affairs of Kṛṣṇa or Rām with their female lovers are spiritual, fundamentally different from mundane sexuality, despite appearing so similar? Why would celibate monks absorb themselves in such apparently erotic texts? There have been and continue to be many contradictory answers to these questions, and this paper will attempt to present as clearly as possible the explanation given in a number of *rasik* texts that describe transcendental sexuality.

The *Bhāgavatapurāṇa*, generally dated in the ninth or tenth centuries of the common era, is one of the earliest texts dealing with this theme. In the famous tenth canto of the *Bhāgavata*, answering a question about the propriety of Kṛṣṇa's conjugal dalliance with other men's wives, the sage Śukadeva explains that this apparently adulterous affair is not actually so, but is a manifestation of pure love of God, transcendental to all material conceptions of piety and impiety and devoid of any selfish motive. The text indicates that the bodies of Kṛṣṇa and the Gopīs are different from ordinary material bodies; they are eternal, spiritual forms.

Kṛṣṇadās's *Caitanyacaritāmṛta*, the early seventeenth century Bengali classic that is a standard text of Gauḍīya Vaiṣṇavism, posits that mundane and transcendental sexuality are as different as night and day, or as iron and gold; the former is based on self-centered lust, while the latter is pure, selfless love of God—but nevertheless characterized by amorous encounters of the soul in feminine form with God, who is Kṛṣṇa, the supreme male.

The *Bhuśuṇḍi Rāmāyaṇa,* one of the earliest Rām *rasik* texts available, probably written during the mid-sixteenth or early seventeenth century, introduces Rām performing a *rāslīlā* with Gopīs[6] and many other *līlās* associated with Kṛṣṇa. This innovative work is not generally accorded canonical status outside the esoteric *Rāmrasik* school, as it does not establish the consonance of its account with Vedic or Purāṇic texts, nor with the Vālmīki *Rāmāyaṇa* itself; yet it also holds that the bodies and desires of Rām's Gopīs are divine, and that Rām's enjoyment of their divine beauty constitutes the true reality of lust. B.P. Singh has studied many texts of this school, and has summarized their teachings in *Rāmbhakti mẽ rasik sampradāy.* Even more insistently than the Kṛṣṇaite literature, these texts exhort that this subject matter should only be revealed to initiates, and that others can never understand it.

The *Mānaspīyūṣ,* a voluminous *rasik* commentary on the *Rāmcaritmānas,* published in the twentieth century but compiled from a longstanding oral tradition of *kathāvācaks,* further emphasizes the spiritual nature of Sītā and Rām: their bodies, their ornaments, their love for each other, including even Rām's apparent erotic attraction to Sītā's feminine beauty, all are transcendental.

Writing early in this century, Siddhanta Sarasvati, founder of the Gauḍīya Maṭh, presents the same doctrine in a more philosophical format. For example, he writes in *Shri Chaitanya's Teachings* (1989, pp. 604-5):

> So long as we continue to look upon sex with an eye of longing we can never think of it in any other way. But this longing is also part of our present acquired nature and cannot leave us till we are enabled to lay this secondary nature itself. With this reform of nature our relation to the principle of sex also undergoes a complete transformation which is, however, otherwise incomprehensible to our present understanding. The female form of the human soul is not a material form. The relation between the human soul and Shri Krishna is not the relation between the material female form and its corresponding male form. The amorous Pastimes of Shri Krishna with spiritual milkmaids of Vraja are not the amorous Pastimes between male and female of this world.

Finally, contemporary *rasiks* provide intriguing glimpses into their understanding of the doctrine of transcendental sexuality. These devotees generally remain anonymous and carefully guard the confidentiality of their realizations—which nevertheless are sometimes made public, such as in the famous *rāslīlā* dramas, performed especially in Vrindaban. But they can provide valuable insight into the living meaning of transcendental sexuality, today as well as in the past.

These selected texts, among a host of others, describe a sexuality that is transcendental. This does not mean that human sexuality is made sacred, but rather that the purely spiritual love between God and his devotees is expressed in exchanges of conjugal affection in spiritual bodies.[7] As Norvin Hein puts it (1982, p. 120), 'The mating of Rādhā and Krishna is presented by theologians as a transcendental event not related to the carnal couplings of human beings.'

Indeed, *rasiks* assert that sexuality, in its pure, transcendent form, is quite the opposite of what we experience as sexuality in our temporary, painful material bodies, but is the original and ideal[8] loving relationship of the eternally blissful individual spirit (*ātmā*), which has a spiritual female form, with the supreme spirit (*paramātmā* or *parabrahman*), whose eternal, original form is masculine.[9] However, the argument is made (reminiscent of—but extending further—Plato's theory of ideal forms) that the sexuality so prominent in this world could not exist at all if it were not present in ideal form in the soul's relationship with God (S. Sarasvati 1989, p. 605):

> The amours of this world could have no existence unless the substantive principle exists in Shri Krishna. But no one denies the existence and importance of the principle of amour in the Realm of the Absolute in the perfectly wholesome form.

One may certainly account for this extraordinary conception of primeval erotics in a variety of ways, but this brief paper will not seek social or psychological explanations.[10] Nor will it trace the historical development of the concept of transcendental sexuality, except to note that the understanding given in the *Bhāgavatapurāṇa* became increasingly elaborated over the centuries, and that by the beginning of the seventeenth century the theory had been elaborately presented in written form in both Kṛṣṇaite and Rāmite texts.[11]

Indeed, due to the highly confidential nature of the concept of transcendental sexuality, it is extremely difficult to know at what period, historically speaking, this subject was first discussed by *rasiks* (not to speak of when it was first contemplated by individuals who may not have shared their ideas with anyone else). We must primarily rely, of course, on written records, but these confidential ideas are usually never written at all.[12]

Therefore, this paper will focus on trying to present, as clearly as possible, a basically consistent[13] account of transcendental sexuality given by a wide range of *rasiks* from the sixteenth century until today, but which may have originated during a much earlier period, at least as early as that of the *Bhāgavatapurāṇa.*

2. TRANSCENDENTAL SEXUALITY AS EXPLAINED IN *RASIK* TEXTS

In the *Bhāgavatapurāṇa* (10.33.27), after hearing the description of Kṛṣṇa's *rāslīlā* dance with the Gopīs, Parīkṣit asks Śukadeva, 'How could Kṛṣṇa, the upholder of moral laws, have violated them by touching other men's wives?' In the *Bhāgavata* itself Śukadeva gives several answers: first, the great *isvaras* (here, exalted and powerful personalities) are not touched by apparent immorality (10.33.20) for they do not engage in such activities out of any selfish personal motive (10.33.32). Kṛṣṇa is within the Gopīs and their husbands—and all embodied beings—as their controller (10.33.35); he appears as a human being simply for their benefit, to give them the chance to be attracted to himself, the all attractive Lord (10.33.36). Finally, the *Bhāgavata* maintains, the husbands of the Gopīs who were dancing with Kṛṣṇa, being bewildered by his *māyā,* perceived their wives all along at home beside them, so were not jealous of him (10.33.37). Here the seventeenth century *rasik ācārya* Viśvanāth Cakravartī comments that the women with whom their Gopa husbands slept were not the divine women who consorted with Kṛṣṇa, but duplicates of them fabricated by *māyā.*[14]

A. Transcendental sexuality must be love for God

Still, what is the difference between the Gopīs' love for Kṛṣṇa and the love of any woman attached to her lover? Śukadeva answers this exact question of Parīkṣit by reminding him[15] that Śiśupāla obtained liberation by hating the Lord, who is eternal, immutable, infinite, immeasurable, transcendental to all material qualities,[16] but the essence of all qualities, and who liberates the entire world: 'Persons who constantly direct their lust, anger, fear, protective affection, feeling of oneness, or friendship toward Lord Hari are sure to become absorbed in him' (*Bhāg* 10.29.15). Thus, the steady desire to associate with God in conjugal love (or fear, or anger, etc.) leads to liberation.

This assertion is not elaborated in any detailed way in the *Bhāgavata*, but commentators introduced further explanations in an effort to ensure that students of the *Bhāgavata* would not misunderstand this statement.[17] Madhvacarya, for example, cites a number of passages from the Purāṇas that establish the difference between the Gopīs' devotional love for Kṛṣṇa and material lust, stressing that ordinary people should not try to worship Viṣṇu or Kṛṣṇa as a conjugal lover, but rather as the transcendent God.[18] Nevertheless, the *Bhāgavatapurāṇa's* main point here is to establish that if one somehow or other, even in lust, approaches Kṛṣṇa, he or she will become purified, and the motive in approaching the Lord will become transformed from selfish lust to selfless love, for Kṛṣṇa is the all-powerful transcendent Lord.

Thus, transcendental sexuality is conceived of as the opposite of mundane erotics, for—far from aggravating the desire for sensual enjoyment—it replaces the urge for personal gratification with *mādhurya*, the sweet, but intense, desire to serve the Lord.[19] This love is so total in its self-abandonment that the devotee may even joke and argue lovingly with God. In a *rāslīlā* drama recorded by John Hawley (1981, pp. 208-9), one of the Gopīs tells Kṛṣṇa that they have left behind all worldly concerns to be with him:

KRISHNA: Girls, if you left worldly things behind, what were you doing coming to me? I'm a sensual being too, you know. You can see me, smell me, taste me, touch me—if you've left everything worldly and sensory behind, what are you doing here?

SAKHĪ 1: No, no, Lord, you're not sensual, you're the one who wipes away every disease, the wholesome food that will drive it away. Are you thinking of withholding that medicine now? Is that just?

KRISHNA: First you lie down with your husbands and then you come sidling up to me: it's all nothing but self-interest.

SAKHĪ 1: (*offended, enraged*) What is this? You keep taking the role of the sensualist and seeing things from the wrong perspective. Over and over again you say the same things. And over and over there's only one answer. If it were sensual pleasure we wanted, then that would be desire. But it's *you* we want, and that's not desire (*kām*), it's love (*prem*). Desire serves the senses, but love serves only you; ultimately desire results in nothing but destruction, but love leads to playing in the eternal circle dance.

From this it is apparent that not only must transcendental sexuality be in relationship with God, but it must be based on selfless love.

B. Love and lust

This second characteristic of transcendental sexuality is that it has no personal interest. The *Caitanyacaritāmṛta*, which may be one source of the ideas expressed in the *rāslīlā* drama just quoted, stresses the difference between mundane love (*kāma*) and the love of the Gopīs for Kṛṣṇa (*prem*)—the latter involves no selfish motive.

The love of the Gopīs . . . is pure and spotless. It is not at any time lust. . . . Lust and love have different characteristics, just as iron and gold have different natures. The desire to gratify one's own senses is *kāma* (lust), but the desire to please the senses of Lord Kṛṣṇa is *prema* (love). . . . Therefore lust and love are quite different. Lust is like dense darkness, but love is like the bright sun. Thus there is not the slightest taint of lust in the Gopīs' love. Their relationship with Kṛṣṇa is only for the sake of His enjoyment.[20]

In other words, the Gopīs' love for Kṛṣṇa, even their desire to embrace him, etc., is simply to give pleasure to him, not themselves. Of course, *rasiks* do not deny that sensual pleasure is present in transcendence, but contend it is totally different from material sense enjoyment; neither is it the motive for transcendental sexuality nor is it the highest satisfaction, for there is far more pleasure in service than in direct enjoyment. The Gopīs, therefore, enjoy far greater bliss by serving Kṛṣṇa than he does by accepting their service:

There is another wonderful feature of the emotion of the Gopīs. Its power is beyond the comprehension of the intelligence. When the Gopīs see Lord Kṛṣṇa, they derive unbounded bliss, although they have no desire for such pleasure. The Gopīs taste a pleasure ten million times greater than the pleasure Lord Kṛṣṇa derives from seeing them. The Gopīs have no inclination for their own enjoyment, and yet their joy increases. That is indeed a contradiction. For this contradiction I see only one solution: the joy of the Gopīs lies in the joy of their beloved Kṛṣṇa.[21]

Similarly, in the *Bhuśuṇḍi Rāmāyaṇa*, Rām's Gopīs, who are said to have divine forms and divine desires, are enjoyed by Rām with transcendental desire, or the reality of lust (*kāmatattva*):

When the Sārasvata Age arrived, the residents of the Daṇḍaka forest, and the Śrutis as well, were born in the form of Gopīs in Gokula. They, female inhabitants of Pramodavana, who were very dear to Jānakī, obtained Rām's form on both banks of the Sarayu. Having obtained the reality (*tattva*) of Rām, they were infatuated, filled with desire (*kāma*). Other divine women, possessing divine forms (*divyarūpa*), having performed austerities and having obtained a boon, achieved their divine desire (*divya manoratha*). Therefore, the great Rām, to fulfill the boon he had given, enjoyed all those Gopīs with transcendental desire (*kāmatattva*).[22]

Thus, the *rasik* concept of transcendental sexuality requires that the devotee possess a female spiritual form, and direct her selfless love towards God, who has a male form.[23]

C. Spiritual form

This idea of a divine form, or spiritual body,[24] composed not of matter but of *sat, cit,* and *ānanda* (eternity, transcendental consciousness and unrestricted spiritual bliss) is of utmost importance in *rasik* thought. *Rasik* commentators take every opportunity to stress this point. For example, in the *Rāmcaritmānas,* Tulasīdās contrasts Sītā's body with that of material (*prākṛt*) women, and *rasik* commentators eagerly explain that her body is transcendental (*aprākṛt* and *cinmay*).[25]

Commenting on Sītā's body and the sound of her anklets, bracelets and other ornaments, which Tulsīdās tells us bewitch the mind of Lord Rām, the *Mānaspīyūṣ* commentary reads: 'Just as Lord Rām's body and all his ornaments are transcendental (*cidānandmay*),[26] in the same way Lady Sītā's body and the sound of her ornaments are all transcendental.'[27] These divine bodies and ornaments are thus *not* an allegory, but are the naturally blissful and fully conscious ideal forms of which mundane bodies and ornaments are miserable and dull reflections. A little later the *Mānaspīyūṣ* explains: 'The sound of mundane bracelets, etc., cannot enter Lord Rām's heart. Lady Sītā's ornaments are the very embodiment of consciousness in form.'[28]

Yet it is not only the body and ornaments that are transcendental, but the erotic attraction as well. The *Mānaspīyūṣ* commentary stresses the transcendental nature of Rām's attraction to Sītā. Referring to Rām Bahādur Laṃgoḍajī's commentary on *Bālkhaṇḍ, dohā* 230, Sharan writes, 'By using the word "*prabhu*" (Lord), he (Tulsīdās) . . . is informing us that Lord Rām has not fallen in love due to any material motive, nor because of any external beauty.'[29] And Sharan explains in his *ṭippaṇī* on the second *caupāī* following *dohā* 230, in which Rām says, 'My heart, which is pure by nature, is agitated on seeing her transcendental beauty',[30] that '"*sahaja punīta*" means one who is by nature pure from birth, without having undergone any *sādhan* to achieve it, that is, who can never possibly become sexually or otherwise agitated'.[31] Laṃgoḍajī writes on this same *caupāī*:

Persons who really understand the subtleties of love know that in pure love a spiritual relationship is absolutely essential. How mysterious this is: Rām and Lakṣmaṇ are both together, but Sītā's overwhelming beauty affects only Rām, and not Lakṣmaṇ! Rām spoke the truth when he said, 'Only God knows why this is happening!'—(from *Mādhurī*). 'My heart is agitated' here indicates that primeval spiritual relationship.[32]

So the bodies of the Lord and his consorts, as well as their ornaments and their mutual attraction, are considered spiritual, not material. In the same *rāslīlā* drama mentioned above (J. Hawley, pp. 205-6), a Gopī, using a pun, tells Kṛṣṇa:

The husbands (*pati*) we have left behind are the former (*vipati*—defiling husbands, or *vipatti*, a disaster), husbands of mud, and you are the latter (*vipati*—the special husband), the husband of consciousness. They are husbands of the body and you are the husband of the soul. They are the husbands of this one birth, but you are the husband of every age—past, present, and future.

According to the *Caitanyacaritāmṛta*, the body of the purified devotee is similarly *aprākṛta*, spiritual: 'When the devotee's body is thus transformed into spiritual existence, the devotee, in that transcendental body, renders service to the lotus feet of the Lord.'[33]

Stressing the importance of this concept, Siddhanta Sarasvati writes (1989, p. 621):

The real difficulty in the way of our realisation of the nature of transcendental Amour is that we cannot have the necessary basic conception of the nature of the spiritual body itself. We are thus under the necessity of the physical body to the relationships of pure souls who are not encumbered by the grossness and limitations of the defective physical coils.

Therefore, to approach the concept of transcendental sexuality on the *rasiks*' terms, we must first clearly understand this concept of a spiritual body, its physiology as well as anatomy, and its difference from the material body.

D. Spiritual physiology

Rasiks assert that the spiritual body is not different from the soul, and is characterized by and indeed composed of *saccidānanda*, eternity, full consciousness and bliss; the material body, on the other hand, different from the real self, is temporary, full of ignorance and plagued by miseries and anxieties. The material body is a machine, and depends on muscles for movement, bones for support, and nervous, digestive, circulatory, excretory, and reproductive systems, etc., to perform various functions, but the spiritual body requires none of these internal mechanisms.[34]

The physiology of the material body depends on certain processes, among which movements and excretions of bodily fluids are notable, and the spiritual body also exhibits the presence and excretion of various bodily fluids, but they serve completely different functions. Indeed, according to the *rasik* concept of the ideal or original spiritual body, all the unpleasant and necessary material bodily excretions are perverted reflections of highly pleasurable spiritual substances which are produced by the spiritual body simply to enhance the loving exchanges between the Lord and the devotee.

A highly secret topic which I have never seen in writing, but have been confidentially told by *rasiks*, is that the fluids involved in material sexual reproduction are perverted reflections of superficially similar but very different spiritual fluids. For example, the blood emitted from the vagina, either due to menstruation or the rupture of the hymen, is considered the reversed image of a spiritual substance which has the pleasurable taste and intoxicating properties of the finest wine.[35]

The *Bhuśuṇḍi Rāmāyaṇa* hints at this, after describing the first love of Rām and Sītā: 'It was as if that lusty lover had forcibly harassed her, and indeed the bed became reddened, as if by moist red lac.'[36] This reddened bed evidently refers to the bleeding resulting from the rupture of the hymen,[37] so I originally assumed this was a very materialistic description. However, I was surprised to learn from a *rasik* that, in his judgment, I was totally wrong. Rather, he opined, this production of a highly fragrant, rich red liquor by the spiritual female genitalia (not, he stressed, to be confused with any type of material vaginal 'bleeding') occurs whenever a transcendental female experiences a certain ecstatic spiritual condition, or it may be voluntarily produced out of love of God and for his pleasure.

Similarly, he assured me, excretions from the transcendental body of the Lord, though superficially homologous to human feces, urine, and semen, are not connected with discharge of bodily waste or purification of the blood by the kidneys, nor are they in any way required for reproduction; further, like the divine females' ambrosial vaginal fluids, they are extremely pleasurable substances in every way. I suggested (with the *rasik's* hearty approval) that this might explain why, when the child Kṛṣṇa defecated and urinated in the neighboring Gopīs' homes, they were internally very pleased, although they outwardly protested to his mother about it, along with complaining about his stealing their butter.[38]

Thus, while we may explain these ideas in the opposite way—God as an idealized projection of our own desires or fears—*rasiks* believe quite literally that 'God created man (and woman) in his (and his consort's) image', although as vastly inferior replicas, even down to the details of bodily fluids.

E. Non-rasiks cannot understand transcendental sexuality

Given the striking similarity yet simultaneous opposition of these detailed descriptions of transcendental conjugal affairs and ordinary sexuality, it is not surprising that *rasiks* assert outsiders cannot but misunderstand transcendental sexuality. The *Bhuśuṇḍi Rāmāyaṇa,* before describing Rām's dancing with his Gopīs, gives severe warnings about revealing the mystery of Rām's *rāslīlā.* Brahmā is speaking to the crow Bhuśuṇḍi:

> The supreme sporting of the Gopīs and Rām, which you have asked about, is totally secret; how can it be told? Someone who explained it would surely go to hell. On the other hand, (it can be told) to one situated in pure goodness (*sattva*), the devotee, the absolutely pure-minded,

by the best *ācāryas*, who, having heard that, would become totally devoted to it. . . . I am not able to understand that extremely mysterious activity. Perform intense self-purificatory ascetic practices for hundreds of eons; then such imperishable devotion will be yours. Then you will be able to hear about Rām's activities in their entirety, otherwise the masters of yoga headed by Śuka will curse me.[39]

'Don't disclose this to the unqualified', the Lord himself told me. Hearing these words of Brahmā, the bird named Bhuśuṇḍa practiced that great, weighty self-mortification up to the end of his life. Then a voice was heard from the sky as the two of them listened: 'O Brahmā! Explain my wonderful activities known as *rāslīlā* in their entirety to this devotee who is in the form of a bird. He is certainly a very great Yogī, very fond of my pastimes of love in a secluded place, peaceful, controlled, tolerant, and he has endeavored for millions of eons. He is my devotee, he has made me his all-in-all, he is peaceful, he has given up all his memories for my sake, he frequents solitary places, he is humble, and he increases the delight of the devotees. Inform him about all the particulars of the wonderful activities of Rām, which he will drink like nectar, and will never divulge to others.' Hearing this divine instruction, Brahmā became enlivened, and, treating that bird respectfully, described the enchanting Rām *līlā*. One who divulges this secret *līlā* to an unqualified person, impelled by his fate, must burn in the most dreadful hell.[40]

Some philosophical texts explain more specifically the reason why those who are not situated in pure *sattva* (goodness or purity) cannot understand transcendental sexuality. Jīv Gosvāmī, in his sixteenth-century *Bhaktisandarbha* (Sec. 338), warns that one whose senses are subject to sexual agitation must not contemplate the confidential affairs (of Kṛṣṇa with the Gopīs).[41]

B.P. Singh writes:[42]

Ordinary persons attached to sensual pleasures are not eligible for it (enjoying the divine sports [*divya raskeli kā upabhog*]), nor, indeed, are they (descriptions [*varṇan*] of the divine sports) made for them. Thinking it is dependent on the ingredients of worldly sexual enjoyment, and imposing an interpretation directly contrary to the intended meaning but according to their own desires, they ridicule it. Understanding this, the *ācāryas* forbid openly preaching the *rasik* literatures.[42]

In other words, the *rasik* claim is that as long as we find mundane sexuality attractive, we will wrongly assume that transcendental sexuality is similar to the sexuality that attracts us; therefore we should not contemplate and further misunderstand it. When, however, we clearly realize that mundane sexuality is a diseased condition of pure, transcendental sexuality, we will be able to appreciate the difference between the two and can then enter the normal, healthy condition without danger of a relapse.

Jīv Gosvāmī explains that mundane sexuality in fact has nothing to do with *mādhurya ras*, but can only produce the *ras* of *bībhatsa*, repugnance (O.B.L. Kapoor, 1977, p. 216).

3. THE PURPOSE OF CONTEMPLATING TRANSCENDENTAL SEXUALITY

Why, then, would celibate *rasiks* absorb themselves in these erotic affairs, claiming them to be transcendental? G.W. Archer suggests (1957, p. 73) that due to the 'tightening of domestic morals' in the early centuries of the second millennium,

> romance as an actual experience became more difficult of attainment. . . . Yet the need for romance remained and we can see in the prevalence of love-poetry a substitute for wishes repressed in actual life.[43]

He ascribes the increasing popularity of Kṛṣṇa's *Gopi-līlā* at this time chiefly to 'an exact sublimation of intense romantic needs'.

Similarly, S.K. De writes (1942, pp. 550-1):

> The Bengal school of Caitanya no doubt condemns direct erotic practice, but it encourages vicarious erotic contemplation. It emphasises the inward realisation of the divine sports in all their erotic implications as the ultimate felicitous state, and thereby promotes the abnormal satisfaction of a highly refined erotico-religious sensibility. . . .

There is sufficient evidence available[44] that a number of Rām and Kṛṣṇa devotees, considering themselves *rasiks*, including followers of Caitanya in a variety of sects, have in fact adopted erotic contemplation for exactly the reason Archer and De suggest—to satisfy a need for romance or eroticism which is repressed in external life. Nevertheless, this practice is contrary to the teachings of *rasik ācāryas*, and anything tending to such activities has been repeatedly curtailed by orthodox Vaiṣṇava *gurus* and institutions.[45]

As we have already noted, Jīv Gosvāmī holds that one whose senses are subject to sexual agitation cannot properly approach Kṛṣṇa's confidential *līlās*; O.B.L. Kapoor (1977, p. 219) translates this statement in the following way, as a pointed reply to De's charge that Caitanya's school encourages vicarious erotic contemplation:

So long as our mind and senses are not purified and there is any possibility of our deriving vicarious erotic pleasure from the contemplation of the amorous pastimes of Kṛṣṇa with the Gopis, we must not contemplate them.[46]

Bhaktivinod Ṭhākur, the father of Siddhanta Sarasvati as well as his spiritual teacher, had written in the nineteenth century:

Those who have acquired unadulterated prema by abstaining from material pleasure are entitled to cultivate rasa. If those who have not acquired pure *rati* (attachment for Kṛṣṇa) and abstinence from worldly objects try to cultivate it, it will end in great failure and they will continue to be engaged in malpractices only. . . . In fact, those who are entitled to rasa are very rare. So rasa is to be kept in secret.[47]

This is, indeed, the *rasik* injunction as found in numerous texts.

Siddhanta Sarasvati more specifically states (1989, p. 605) that while sexuality can never be abolished, encouraging vicarious sexual contemplation while condemning direct erotic practice solves nothing. Rather, he avers, one must understand that mundane sexuality is only the perverted shadow in this world of the transcendental reality of love, Kṛṣṇa's sweet conjugal affairs with the Gopīs:

It is because we choose to regard as material the female form of the soul that we are shocked at what we suppose to be the shameless sensuous proclivities of the transcendentalists. This is inevitable so long as we deliberately choose to nurse the error that the sex of our experience is the real entity and imagine that we have been able to solve the problem of sex by transferring our sensuous activity from the body to the mind and by condemning as impure the excesses of the external sexual act on no consistent principle. Such bungling philosophy has not convinced and will never convince anybody of the real nature and purpose of the sexual act. This is so because the sexual act is the eternal concomitant in this sinful world of the highest function of the spirit which can, therefore, be never minimised or abolished by all our empiric endeavours, but the right understanding of which can alone save us from the terrible consequences of our present suicidal sexual follies.

In other words, according to *rasik* theory, meditation on transcendental sexuality *by qualified persons* (that is, by those who, deeply realizing the purity of the subject matter, do not thereby become sexually agitated) immerses one in the sweetness of real love, freeing one fully from the attraction of mundane sexuality. The *Bhāgavatapurāṇa* (10.33.40), long before Archer and De offered their interpretations of transcendental sexuality, maintained that the purpose of the revelation of Kṛṣṇa's conjugal sports with the Gopīs is to save the conditioned souls afflicted by diseased sexuality by bringing them to the perfectional stage of Bhakti:

> vikrīḍitaṃ vrajavadhūbhir idaṃ ca viṣṇoḥ
> śraddhānvito'nuśṛṇuyād atha varṇayed yaḥ
> bhaktiṃ parāṃ bhagavati pratilabhya kāmaṃ
> hṛdrogam āśva pahinoty acireṇa dhīraḥ
>
> One who faithfully hears about the dealings between Lord Kṛṣṇa and the Gopīs in the *rās* dance, and one who describes these activities, attain to the perfectional stage of devotional service and simultaneously lose the heart disease of material, lusty desires.

The *Caitanyacaritāmṛta* comments on this verse:

> When one hears or describes with great faith the pastimes of Lord Kṛṣṇa, such as his *rāsa* dance with the Gopīs, the disease of lusty desires in the heart and the agitation caused by the three modes of material nature are immediately nullified, and one becomes sober and silent. Tasting the transcendental, effulgent, sweetly ecstatic love of Kṛṣṇa, such a person can enjoy life twenty-four hours a day in the transcendental bliss of the sweetness of Kṛṣṇa's pastimes.[48]

Finally, *rasiks* hold that, since hearing the confidential *līlās* of transcendental sexuality is the path to full liberation, but only a person who is at least basically liberated from material desire can properly hear them, ordinary persons can achieve that stage by chanting the name of Sītā-Rām or Rādhā-Kṛṣṇa. B.P. Singh states that repeating the name of Sītā-Rām nourishes one's tender feelings for the divine couple, brings supreme happiness, and enables one to understand the mystery of Sītā-Rām's *rāslīlā*.[49]

Similarly, Siddhanta Sarasvati writes (1989, p. 606) that the name of Kṛṣṇa delivers the benefit of hearing the Lord's intimate *līlās* to all, without the risk of misunderstanding them:

> The perfect chant of the Name of Krishna is available to all souls, and it is identical with the amorous service of the spiritual milkmaids of Vraja. This is the sum and substance of the Teaching of Shri Krishna Chaitanya. Conversely, those who do not perform the congregational chant of the Name of Krishna in the manner that is free from offence, are not in a position to realise the nature of Divine Amour. Those who miss such realisation, remain subject to the object thraldom of mundane lust.

This is the practical conclusion of the *rasik* theory of transcendental sexuality, and an explanation of its attractiveness to those *sādhaks* striving to transcend mundane sexuality in accordance with this well-established norm of traditional Indian culture. The ultimate goal for a *rasik* is to become free of all mundane sexual desire by relishing the transcendental loving affairs of Rādhā-Kṛṣṇa or Sītā-Rām as one of the Lord's intimate maidservants, and the path is to become qualified to meditate on those spiritual *līlās* by constant chanting of the Lord's name.

NOTES

1. The Gauḍīya theologian Jīv Gosvāmī had written his definitive theological works by this time, and Rām *rasiks* such as Agradās, who were in close touch with developments in Vrindaban, were developing similar ideas (see P. Lutgendorf 1991a, p. 310; 1991b, p. 230). The *Bhuśuṇḍi Rāmāyaṇa,* although difficult to date, also substantiates this.
2. In the context of Vaiṣṇava *rasik* usage, a *rasik* is one who savours *ras* (which may mean juice, relish, taste, essence, sentiment, etc., but in this context refers to a transcendental emotion). In terms of *mādhurya rasa,* the mood of transcendental conjugality, an orthodox (as opposed to Sahajiyā) *rasik* is one who can appreciate the sweetness of spiritual love without confusing it with corresponding sensations involved in mundane sexuality. The *Bhāgavatapurāṇa* (1.1.3; *Śrīmad Bhāgvatam,* hereafter *Bhāg.*) uses the term for those who are able to relish its divine nectar (*rasa*); similarly Jayadeva writes in his *Gītagovinda, śrī jayadevakaver idam uditam/rasikjanaṃ tanutām atimuditam*: 'May this song of the poet Śrī Jayadeva give great happiness to the *rasiks*' (6.9).
3. *Manasā naṭanīyam* in Jayadeva's *Gītagovinda* (4.9) may indicate this meditative practice as early as the twelfth century. This passage is pointed out by Donna Wulff (1984, p. 172). See also P. Lutgendorf (1991a, p. 311, n. 97): 'The *Gītagovinda* admonishes the listener to "mentally enact" its romantic drama.' Lutgendorf (1991a, p. 311) notes a possible antecedent for this practice as early as the ninth century in the Tamil poems of Nammālvār, who sometimes wrote in the voice of a Gopī scolding the child Kṛṣṇa.
4. David Haberman's *Acting as a Way of Salvation* is an excellent presentation of the Gauḍīya *rasik* practice of entering into the divine *līlā,* although he presents it rather too insistently from the perspective of dramatic theory.
5. 'Orthodox', as opposed to 'Sahajiya' Vaiṣṇavas (who tend to equate mundane and transcendental sexuality)—this is Edward Dimock's terminology for these two distinct Gauḍīya groups: 'In no sense did

the two traditions merge into a single stream: their aims are essentially different, their means radically opposed' (E. Dimock 1966, p. 40).

6. Although it is not so well-known, Rāmānandī *rasiks* developed a *rasik* theology and practice similar to that of the Kṛṣṇaite *rasiks,* though later. Yet, as early as 1957, B.P. Singh had discovered almost one thousand Rām *rasik* texts, including about fifty in Sanskrit, eight hundred in Hindi, and over a hundred related books (B.P. Singh 1957, p. 45). Of these, he considered the *Bhuśuṇḍi Rāmāyaṇa* 'the main source for the erotic worship of Ram' (*Bhuśuṇḍi Rāmāyaṇa* hereafter *BR*, Hindi introduction, p. 2). In English, Philip Lutgendorf has written (both in *Life of a Text* and in 'The Secret Life of Rāmchandra', in Paula Richman's *Many Rāmāyaṇas*) about the Rāmānandī *rasiks.* Peter van der Veer has also briefly dealt with them in *Gods on Earth.* Since Rāmite *rasik* schools developed later than the Kṛṣṇaite ones, Rām *rasiks* have been accused of being imitators. Their response, as B.P. Singh points out in his Hindi introduction to the *Bhuśuṇḍi Rāmāyaṇa* (*BR,* p. 5), is that 'the *rāslīlā* is part and parcel of Kṛṣṇa's pastimes when he descended to this world, but in Rām's activities it is only part of his eternal pastimes in the spiritual world'. Therefore, 'the previous *ācāryas* had all considered Rām's erotic pastimes confidential and forbade preaching them openly to the people in general. Lord Rām's amorous pastimes are for practitioners to meditate on, and are not meant for external or general worship'. (cf. P. Lutgendorf 1991b, pp. 228-31).

7. Sahajiyās, of course, did equate the love of a human couple with the transcendental sexuality of Rādhā and Kṛṣṇa (cf. S.B. Dasgupta 1962, p. xxxvii: 'In the Vaiṣṇava Sahajiyā school . . . it is further held that all men and women are physical manifestations of the ontological principles of Kṛṣṇa and Rādhā . . . the love of any human couple becomes transformed into the divine love that is eternally flowing on between Kṛṣṇa and Rādhā'). This is not accepted by orthodox Vaiṣṇavas.

8. Ideal in both the ordinary and the technical Platonic sense. The Sanskrit word is *ādi,* used for example in *ādirasa* (the original *rasa*), while the Urdu word used by some of my north Indian informants is *aslī,* which also means 'pure' or 'real' (e.g. *aslī ghī,* pure or real ghee, unadulterated, or as opposed to vegetable oil which is also now called *ghī*).

9. More accurately, according to *rasik* thought, the original form of Godhead is the transcendental couple, Rādhā-Kṛṣṇa or Sītā-Rām. It is important to remember throughout this discussion that the Vaiṣṇava conception of God and of the individual soul's relationship with God is very different from that of monistic Indian thought. Vaiṣṇavas do not consider the absolute truth to be formless, nor do they strive to

merge the individual into the supreme soul. Rather, they wish to retain their individual existence in a spiritual body to engage in Bhakti; a position they consider far superior and more relishable than losing one's individuality and, along with it, to enjoy the ecstasy of serving the Lord eternally in loving devotion.

10. We may simply note here that *rasiks* have continued to develop and propagate the conception of the spiritual nature of the love affairs of Rām or Kṛṣṇa, often due to a concern that texts they understand to describe transcendental sexuality are being taken as mundane; no doubt this motive was significant in the past as well. J. Hawley (1981, p. 277, n. 7) points out the recent innovation in the *rāslīlā* dramas, where Kṛṣṇa dances as a peacock, clasping 'a halter of peacock feathers to the back of his waist'. Hawley comments, 'It is important to note that particularly in recent times there has been a great sensitivity among Vaiṣṇavas to the danger that Krishna's dance with the Gopīs be understood as sexual in the mundane sense, and the analogy of the peacock is taken as significant in this respect as well. People in Brindavan sometimes say that there is no actual copulation in the course of the peacock's mating rites.' It is not uncommon to hear Vaiṣṇavas deny that there is actual sexual intercourse between Kṛṣṇa and the Gopīs. 'You never heard of the Gopīs becoming pregnant or having abortions, did you?' I have heard several times. When I pressed the issue, one *rasik* politely insisted that non-*rasiks* (including scholars interested in the subject) would do better not to pursue the matter, for they would be sure to misunderstand it, just as a young child cannot understand his or her parents' sex life.
11. My doctoral thesis explores these historical, social and psychological issues, such as the connection between Tantric sects and Vaiṣṇava *rasiks*, and the influence of erotic literary developments on the *rasiks*, especially trying to clarify how *rasiks* understand these questions, some of which have been discussed by many scholars.
12. The fact that the *Bhuśuṇḍi Rāmāyaṇa* existed for centuries, evidently accompanied by practice based on it (the details of which even today are unavailable to us), with minimal knowledge of its contents and even its existence outside a restricted *Rāmrasik* cult, is evidence that written *rasik* accounts may be older than generally believed, while secret oral traditions and especially confidential personal realizations may far antedate the earliest records we have.
13. Of course, there are significant differences between *rasiks* of diverse schools, and even within a single school, but there is substantial agreement amongst a variety of both Kṛṣṇa and Rām *rasiks* on most of the fundamental principles of transcendental sexuality outlined here. This paper glosses over the differences for the sake of brevity, but my doctoral thesis explores these issues, including disagreements

concerning questions of canonicity, the derivative nature of the *Bhuśuṇḍi Rāmāyaṇa,* manifestations of sectarian rivalry in the *Bhuśuṇḍi Rāmāyaṇa,* etc.

14. Viśvanāth quotes from Rūp Gosvāmī's sixteenth century *Ujjvala-nīlamaṇi: māyākalpitatādṛkstrīśīlanenānusūyubhiḥ / na jātu vrajadevīnāṃ patibhiḥ saha saṅgamaḥ.* Cited by Hridayānand in his commentray on *Bhāg.* 10.33.37 (*Śrīmad Bhāgavatam* 1988, pp. 681-2).
15. In *Bhāg.* 7.1.27ff., Śukadeva had related Nārada's explanation of this to Yudhiṣṭhira, e.g. 7.1.29: 'By thinking (even) in enmity of Kṛṣṇa, who is the Supreme Lord but appears like a human being, one is purified of his or her sins and attains him.'
16. *Nirguṇ* may be variously translated, but certainly does not mean here 'without any qualities'.
17. Viśvanāth Cakravartī points out that Kṛṣṇa was only eight years old when the *rāslīlā* took place (cited by Hridayanand in his commentary on *Bhāg.* 10.29.1). This chronology appears correct from the *Bhāgavata-purāṇa,* for it is specifically stated that Kṛṣṇa was seven when he performed the *Govardhanlīlā* (*Bhāg.* 10.26.3, 14), and the *rāslīlā* took place soon after. However, usually Kṛṣṇa is considered to engage in this dance in his early teens (see Rūp Gosvāmī's *Bhaktirasāmṛtasindhu* 2.125-7, which ascribes the *rāslīlā* to Kṛṣṇa's *madhyama* (mid) *kaiśora* age (about thirteen, for the *kaiśora* age is from eleven through fifteen). The explanation of this apparent contradiction is that the *rāslīlā* continued from Kṛṣṇa's eighth through his fifteenth years, that is until he left Vrindaban.
18. Cited by Hridayanand (*Śrīmad Bhāgavatam* 1988, vol. 2, p. 512) in his commentary on *Bhāg.* 10.29.15.
19. See *Bhāg.* 10.33.39 (ibid., vol. 2, pp. 543-67).
20. *Śrī Caitanyacaritāmṛta* 1974 (hereafter *CC*), *Ādi.* 4.164-5, 171-2, translated by A.C. Bhaktivedanta Swami 1984, pp. 198-9. (This important quotation is also in E. Dimock 1966, p. 162, numbered 4.139ff. based on the Rādhāgovinda Nāth edition, in L. Siegel 1992, p. 69, and is referred to by other scholars, including J. Hawley 1981, p. 295, n. 2):
    kāma, prema,—dōhākāra vibhinna lakṣaṇa / lauha āra hema yaiche svarūpe vilakṣaṇa
    ātmendriya-prīti-vāñchā—tāre bali 'kāma' / kṛṣṇendriya-prīti-icchā dhare 'prema' nāma. . .
    ataeva kāmapreme bahuta antara / kāma—andhatamaḥ, prema—nirmala bhāskara
    ataeva gopī-gaṇera nāhi kāma-gandha / kṛṣṇa-sukha lāgi mātra, kṛṣṇa se sambandha
21. *CC* 1.4.185-9: (translated by A.C. Bhaktivedanta Swami 1984, pp. 131-2).

āra eka adbhuta gopībhāvera svabhāva / buddhira gocara nahe yāhāra prabhāva

gopīgaṇa kare yabe kṛṣṇadarśana / sukhavāñchā nāhi, sukha haya koṭiguṇa

gopikādarśane kṛṣṇera ye ānanda haya / tāhā haite koṭiguṇa gopī āsvādaya

tān̐ sabāra nāhi nijasukha-anurodha / tathāpi bāḍhaye sukha, paḍila virodha

e virodhera eka mātra dekhi samādhāna / gopikāra sukha kṛṣṇasukhe paryavasāna

22. *BR* 1.26.3-7ab:

kalpaṃ sārasvataṃ prāpya daṇḍakāraṇyavāsinaḥ / śrutayaś caiva sañjātā gopīrūpena gokule

rāmarūpam anuprāpuḥ sarayvās taṭayor dvayoḥ / pramodavanavāsinyo jānakyāś ca mahāpriyāḥ

rāmatattvam anuprāpya mumuhuḥ kāmabhāvitāḥ / anyāś ca divyalalanā divyarūpasamanvitāḥ

kṛtvā tapo, varaṃ labdhvā divyam āpur manoratham / tato nijavaraṃ satyaṃ karttuṃ rāmo mahāmanāḥ

kāmatattvena tāḥ sarvā rāmayam āsa gopikāḥ

23. This doctrine may suggest the subordination and exploitation of women; such a perception needs to be balanced, however, by awareness of the *rasik* exaltation of Rādhā (or Sītā) to a position fully equal and even superior to that of Kṛṣṇa (or Rām), an attitude especially prominent in Vrindaban. For example, in the Rādhā-vallabha cult, Rādhā is 'the ultimate God' and 'the very ground of being' (C. White, p. 28).
24. Called, among other things, *divyarūpa* in the *Bhuśuṇḍi Rāmāyaṇa* and *siddhadeha* in Gauḍīya texts.
25. Tulsīdās states that similes comparing Sītā's loveliness to the bodies of material women are all inadequate (*Bālkhaṇḍ,* the first *caupāī* after *dohā* 246: siya śobhā nahī jāi bakhānī jagadambikā rūpa guṇa khānī / upamā sakala mohi laghu lāgī prākṛta nāri aṅga anurāgī). Hanuman Prasad Poddar comments, 'Poetic similes are derived from the illusory material world, which is composed of the three *guṇs*; to use them for the non-material, purely spiritual limbs of the Lord's personal *śakti*, Lady Sītā, would be to insult her and make a fool of oneself.' (*Śrī Rāmcaritmānas* 1957-8, p. 254: kāvyā kī upmāẽ triguṇātmik, māyik jagat se lī gayī haĩ; unhẽ bhagavān kī svarūp-śakti śrī jānakījī ke aprākṛt, cinmay aṅgõ ke liye prayukt karnā unkā apmān karnā aur apne ko upahāsāspad banānā hai.)
26. Literally, composed of or full of consciousness and bliss.
27. A. Sharan 1961-2, p. 279: jaise śrī rāmjī kā śarīr aur sab bhūṣan

cidānandmay haĩ vaise hi śrī sītājī kī deh, abhūṣanõ kī dhvani sabhī cidānandmay haĩ.

28. A. Sharan 1961-2, p. 280: laukik kaṅkaṇ-ādikõ kī dhvani rāmji ke hṛdayaṅgam nahī ho saktī. mahārānīji ke ābharaṇ cetan vigrah-svarūp haĩ.
29. A. Sharan 1961-2, p. 289: 'prabhu' śabd de kar . . . vah batātā hai ki śrī rāmjī kisī prākṛtik prayojan vā bāhysaundarya ke kāran premāsakt nahī hue haĩ.
30. A. Sharan 1961-2, p. 292: jāsu biloki alaukika sobhā / sahaja punīta mora manu chobhā. Because the numbering has not been standardized, in the *Mānaspīyūṣ,* this second *caupāī* is numbered 3 and 4; this is line 3.
31. A. Sharan 1961-2, p. 293: 'sahaja punīta' arthāt jo binā sādhan kiye janm se svābhāvik hī pavitr hai.= jismẽ bhūl kar bhī kāmādi kā veg nahī vyapt hotā. Kṛṣṇa is also described in the *Bhāgavata* (10.33.25: *ātmani avaruddhasauratah*) as being unaffected by sex desire. As June McDaniel notes (p. 170), this may also indicate 'one whose semen was held within himself', a concept of considerable importance in a variety of Indian traditions.
32. A. Sharan 1961-2, p. 293: premsambandhī sūkṣmtāõ ko jñātāõ ko yah bhī vidit ho ki sāttvik prem mẽ ātmik sambandh honā atyāvaśyak hai. kaisī rahasyamayī ghaṭna hai ki rām aur lakṣmaṇ donõ sāth haĩ par sītā kā prabhāv keval rām par paṛtā hai, lakṣmaṇ par nahī. rāmjī satya hī kahā hai ki 'so saba kārana jāna bidhātā.'—(mādhurī se). yahā̃ 'mora mana chobhā' se vahī purātan ātmik sambandh sūcit kiyā hai.
33. *CC* 3.4.193 (translated by A.C. Bhaktivedanta Swami 1984, p. 1877):
sei deha kare tāra cidānandamaya
aprākṛtadehe tāṅra caraṇa bhajaya
34. 'The anatomy of a material body must have a mechanical construction with veins and so forth, but the transcendental body . . . has nothing like veins.' Gloss by Bhaktivedanta Swami Prabhupada of *asnāviram* ('without sinews' or 'without veins') in *Śrī Īśopaniṣad,* text 8 (1984, p. 38).
35. I first heard this idea espoused in the late 1970s but found it too strange to take seriously until, recently, a practicing *rasik* (who wishes to remain anonymous) explained a passage in the *Bhuśuṇḍi Rāmāyaṇa* (1.28.54) using the same idea. See not 36.
36. *BR* 1.28.54ab: *haṭhena tena vyathiteva kāminā rarañja śayyāpi yathārdrayāvakaiḥ.* Or, more graphically: 'It was as if that lusty lover had pierced her violently. . . .'
37. A phenomenon better known in a culture where premarital chastity is highly valued (especially for women), and where, on the morning after the first conjugal intercourse, the bride may be sent home and

the marriage annulled if the nuptial bed is not red with virginal blood.

38. He pointed out that the *Bhāgavata* (5.5.33-4) also describes Ṛṣabha's feces as so aromatic that they filled the atmosphere with fragrance. Like Kṛṣṇa, as well as pure devotees including Nārada, the *rasik* went on, Ṛṣabha was considered to possess a spiritual body even within the material world.
39. That is, including his confidential pastimes of transcendental sexuality.
40. *BR* 1.25.24(cd)-26(ab), 36(cd)-46:
yat pṛṣṭhaṃ tu tvayā gopīrāmayoḥ krīḍanaṃ parām
tat sugopyaṃ kathaṃ vācyaṃ vaktāsyān nārakī dhruvam
athāpi śuddhasattvāya bhatāya vimalātmane
vācyam ācāryavaryais tu tac chrutvā tat paro bhavet . . .
tac caritrāṃ mahāgopyaṃ mayā jñātuṃ na śakyate
kuru kalpaśataṃ tīvrāṃ tapaś caryyāṃ svaśodhikām
tadā te tādṛśī bhaktir bhaviṣyaty anapāyinī
tadā śrīrāmacāritraṃ śrotum arhasy aśeṣataḥ
nocen mām eva śapsyanti yogīndrās te śukādayaḥ
anadhikāriṇe mā bruyād ity uktaṃ prabhuṇāpi me
iti brahmavacaḥ śrutvā bhuśuṇḍo nāma vai dvijaḥ
maḥatim ārttim anvārcchat praṇānte 'pi garīyasim
ākāśavāk samudbhūtā tadā saṃśṛṇvatos tayoḥ
brūhi braḥmann aśeṣeṇa mama cāritrām adbhutam
rāsalīlāvinodākhyaṃ bhaktāyāṇḍajarūpiṇe
ayaṃ hi sumahān yogī mamaikāntaratipriyaḥ
śānto dāntas titikṣaś ca koṭikalpakṛtaśramaḥ
madbhakto matparaḥ śānto madarthatyaktasaṃsmṛtiḥ
ekāntacārī vinayī bhaktānāṃ prītivarddhanaḥ
jñāpayāsmai viśeṣeṇa rāmacāritram adbhutam
pītvā pīyūṣavat sarvaṃ nānyasmai kathayiṣyati
iti daivīṃ giraṃ śrutvā brahmā sañjātasambhramaḥ
sampūjya dvijam ācaṣṭe rāmalīlāṃ manoharām
etām aikāntikīṃ līlām yo bruyād anadhikāriṇe
sa pacyeta mahāghore narake daivacoditaḥ
41. *Pauruṣa(-)vikāravat(-)indriyaiḥ rahasyalīlā tu na upāsyā,* quoted in O.B.L. Kapoor 1977, p. 219.
42. B.P. Singh 1957, p. 175: viṣayāsakt sādhāraṇ log na to uske pātr haĩ aur na unke liye unkā ṣrjan hī hotā hai. sāṃsārik viṣayabhog ke upādānõ par āśrit dekhkar ve uddiṣṭbhāv ke viparīt evaṃ apnī vāsanāõ ke anukūl arth lagāyeṅge aur uskī khillī uṛāyẽge, iskā anumān karke hī ācāryõ ne rasiksāhitya ke khule pracār kā niṣedh kiyā hai.
43. Critics often suggest a similar explanation of the erotic mysticism prevalent among medieval Christian monastics; for example, Melville

Kennedy writes (M. Kennedy 1993, p. 250): 'In the sensuous form which the mystic experience took, we see the breaking out of normal human needs and instincts which had been severely repressed in the life of the cloister.'

44. My own contact with some persons who consider themselves *rasiks* amply confirms this (see my paper presented in the 1995 AAR Conference, 'When shall I forsake this male body and become female?'). There is also ample evidence that such erotic contem-plation leads to direct erotic practice—see, for example, Kennedy's account of Caitanyite *vairāgins* (Kennedy 1993, especially p. 168, fn. 1, as well as pp. 170ff. on *vairāginīs*). This is all quite apart from some Sahajiyās, who glorify direct erotic practice as religious ritual.
45. Contemporary examples may be found within the International Society for Krishna Consciousness (ISKCON). About 1975 a group informally called the 'Gopībhāva Club', was started in the Los Angeles ISKCON center and it soon spread to other ISKCON temples in the United States. Dozens of members secretly read and discussed the activities of Kṛṣṇa and the Gopīs, but when Bhaktivedanta Swami Prabhupada, the founder *ācārya* of ISKCON, came to know of it in 1976, he promptly stopped them, disdainfully labelling them 'Sahajiyās' and explaining that 'thinking of Rādhā-Kṛṣṇa *līlā,* that is in liberated stage, not in the conditioned stage' (quoted in K. Dasa n.d., p. 16). Similarly, a number of ISKCON devotees, centered in Vrindaban, recently (1994-5) were studying the conjugal affairs of Kṛṣṇa and the Gopīs under the tutelage of a non-ISKCON guru, Narayan Maharaj of the Keśav Gauḍīya Maṭh, Mathura. ISKCON's Governing Body Commission insisted that they stop meeting and taking such instruction from Narayan Maharaj, and the leaders involved apologized and promised to give up the practice (Hridayananda Goswami, personal communication, 30 March 1995).
46. This is O.B.L. Kapoor's free translation of *pauruṣa vikāravat indriyaiḥ rahasyalīlā tu na upāsyā.* Kapoor also writes (1977, p. 218), 'The view that Bengal Vaisnavism condemns direct erotic practice, but encourages vicarious erotic contemplation is obviously based on the assumption that our mind consists of isolated processes, that our willing is independent of our thinking and feeling, and that the general pattern of our thoughts and feelings may be entirely different from the general pattern of our manifest behaviour. This is altogether a false assumption. . . . It is impossible that a devotee may indulge in vicarious erotic contemplation and be pure in life, or that he may be pure in life and indulge in vicarious erotic contemplation.'
47. *Shri Chaitanya Sikshamrita,* pp. 221, 229; quoted by Jasomatinandan Das of Ahmedabad in a letter to the ISKCON Governing Body Commission, dated 1 February 1995.

48. *CC* 3.5.45-7 (translated by A.C. Bhaktivedanta Swami, 1984, pp. 1888-9): vrajavadhūsaṅge kṛṣṇera rāsādivilāsa / yei jana kahe, śune kariyā viśvāsa
hṛdrogakāma tāṅra tatkāle haya kṣaya / tinaguṇakṣobha nahe, 'mahādhīra' haya
ujjvala madhura premabhakti sei pāya / ānande kṛṣṇamādhurye vihare sadāya

49. B.P. Singh 1957, p. 204: (sītārām ke nām) ke jap se yugalbhāvanā kī puṣṭi aur paramānand kī prāpti hotī hai. dampati kī rāskrīḍā kā rahasya isī ke dvāra jāna jā saktā hai. He refers to the *Śrī Jānakīsaneha hulāsa-śataka,* written by the nineteenth-century saint of Ayodhya, Yugalānanya Śaraṇ.

REFERENCES

Archer, W.G. *The Loves of Krishna in Indian Painting and Poetry.* London: Allen and Unwin, 1957.

Bhuśuṇḍi Rāmāyaṇa, Pūrva Khaṇḍa. Edited by B.P. Singh, Varanasi: Vishvavidyalaya Prakashan, 1975.

Choudhury, B. 'Love Sentiment and its Spiritual Implications in Gauḍīya Vaiṣṇavism'. In *Bengal Vaiṣṇavism, Orientalism, Society and the Arts,* ed. Joseph O'Connell, pp. 1-10. East Lansing, Michigan: Michigan State University, 1985.

Dasgupta, S.B. *Obscure Religious Cults,* 2nd ed. Calcutta: Firma K.L. Mukhopadhyay, 1962.

Dasa, K., ed. *Prabhupāda smaranam.* Vrindaban: Eye of the Bird Books, n.d. (1994?).

De. S.K. *The Early History of the Vaiṣṇava Faith and Movement in Bengal.* Calcutta: General Printers and Publishers, 1942.

Dimock, E. *The Place of the Hidden Moon.* Chicago: University of Chicago Press, 1966.

Haberman, D. *Acting as a Way of Salvation.* New York: Oxford University Press, 1988.

Hawley, J. *At Play with Krishna.* Princeton: Princeton University Press, 1981.

Hein, N. 'Rādhā and Erotic Community'. In *The Divine Consort,* eds. John Hawley and Donna Wulff, pp. 116-24. Berkeley: Berkeley Religious Studies Series, 1982.

Kapoor, O.B.L. *The Philosophy and Religion of Śrī Caitanya.* New Delhi: Munshiram Manoharlal, 1977.

Kennedy, M.T. *The Chaitanya Movement.* New Delhi: Munshiram Manoharlal, 1993 (1925).

Lutgendorf, P. *The Life of a Text.* Berkeley: University of California Press, 1991a.

———. 'The Secret Life of Ramcandra of Ayodhya'. In *Many Rāmāyaṇas*, ed. Paula Richman, pp. 217-34. Berkeley: University of California Press, 1991b.

McDaniel, J. *The Madness of the Saints.* Chicago: University of Chicago Press, 1989.

Miller, B.S. *The Gītagovinda of Jayadeva.* Delhi: Motilal Banarsidass, 1984.

Rūp Gosvāmī, *Bhaktirasāmṛtasindhu.* Kanpur: Saḥitya Niketan, 1965.

Sharan, A. *Mānaspīyūṣ.* Vol. 3. Gorakhpur: Gita Press, SV 2018 (AD 1961-2).

Shri Ramcharitamanasa (with Hindi and English translations by R.C. Prasad), Delhi: Motilal Banarsidass, 1990.

Siddhanta Sarasvati. *Shri Chaitanya's Teachings.* 3rd ed. Madras: Sree Gaudiya Math, 1989.

Siegel, L. *Sacred and Profane Dimensions of Love in Indian Traditions.* Delhi: Oxford University Press, 1992.

Singh (Siṃha), B.P. '*Bhuśuṇḍi Rāmāyaṇa* and its Influence on the Medieval Rāmāyaṇa Literature'. In *The Rāmāyaṇa Tradition in Asia*, ed. V. Raghavan, pp. 475-504. New Delhi: Sahitya Akademi, 1980.

———. *Rāmbhakti mẽ rasik sampradāy.* Balrampur, U.P.: Sahitya Mandir, 1957.

Śrī Caitanyacaritāmṛta of Kṛṣṇadās Kavirāj (with English translation and commentary [by A.C. Bhaktivedanta Swami]). Singapore: Gauranga Pte. Ltd., 1984.

Śrī Īśopaniṣad (with English translation and commentary [by A.C. Bhaktivedanta Swami]). Los Angeles: Bhaktivedanta Book Trust, 1984.

Śrī Rāmcaritmānas (with Hindi translation and commentary [by H.P. Poddar]). Gorakhpur: Gita Press, SV 2014 (AD 1957-8).

Śrīmad Bhāgavatam (with English translation and commentary [by A.C. Bhaktivedanta Swami]). Cantos 1 and 7. Los Angeles: Bhaktivedanta Book Trust, 1987.

Śrīmad Bhāgavatam (with English translation and commentary [by Hridayananda Goswami]). Vol. 2, canto 10. Los Angeles: Bhaktivedanta Book Trust, 1988.

van der Veer, P. *Gods on Earth.* London: Athlone Press, 1988.

White, C. *The Caurāsī Pad of Śrī Hit Harivaṃś.* Honolulu: University Press of Hawaii, 1977.

Wulff, Donna M. *Drama as a Mode of Religious Realization: The Vidagdhamādhava of Rūpa Gosvāmī.* Chico, California: Scholars Press, 1984.

A New Interpretation of the Rāula-Vela Inscription

TIMOTHY LENZ

Ever since a text and translation of the Rāula-Vela inscription was first published by H.C. Bhayani in *Bhāratīya Vidyā* in 1957 and 1959, it has received considerable attention as purportedly the earliest extant composition in a New Indo-Aryan language. Four monographs devoted to the Rāula-Vela inscription have been published since Bhayani's initial publication. The first two, by Mataprasad Gupta (1962) and Kailash Bhatiya (1983) respectively, are primarily detailed studies of the language of the Rāula-Vela inscription. The third monograph, by Ila Rani Sinha (1987), repeats much of the linguistic material given by her predecessors but adds analyses of various literary aspects of the inscription. The fourth and most recent publication is a new study by H.C. Bhayani (1994) which includes revised editions of his previously published text and translation, as well as a grammatical analysis and an informative discussion concerning the literary tradition of describing regional cultural traits. However, no examination of the broader historical implications of the Rāula-Vela inscription has been attempted in any of these studies.

The Rāula-Vela inscription is unique among Indian literary inscriptions. It contains none of the characteristics commonly associated with Indic inscriptions: its text neither mentions a special occasion to be commemorated nor commemorates a donation. There is also no mention of the name of any person connected to the royal household, save the author himself, Roḍa, or of a king's name, even though it is clearly stated in the dedicatory verse that the work was written for a king. Instead, the Rāula-Vela inscription consists of a dedicatory verse followed by a poem divided into six sections of unequal length, and a signature verse. The dedicatory and signature verses are not atypical, but the poem most decidedly is. Each of the poem's six sections consists of a *nakhaśikha* or head to toe description of the clothes, makeup and jewellery of a young woman from a particular region of India. In each *nakhaśikha,* a toponym identifying the home region of the woman being described is mentioned and the language employed for her description is sprinkled with regional dialect features that presumably parody those actually current in that region at the time when the inscription was composed.

Even though the text of the Rāula-Vela inscription is so unlike those of other inscriptions, it does contain a message that is typical of inscriptions: it may be read as a *praśasti,* praising the unnamed ruler to whom it was dedicated. For the identity of this unnamed king, one must look to the Paramāra dynasty.

The Rāula-Vela inscription was found at Dhar in Malwa, which was the capital of the Paramāras who ruled Malwa from approximately the last quarter of the tenth to the end of the twelfth century. Furthermore, it is probable that the inscription came from the Kamala Maula Mosque, which, as far as I am aware, is the only find spot of Paramāra inscriptions in Dhar. Thus it may be assumed that the Rāula-Vela inscription was composed during Paramāra hegemony in Malwa.

The most likely Paramāra king to have sponsored the Rāula-Vela inscription is Bhoja (*c.* the first half of the eleventh century). Oddly enough, the fact that the king's name is not mentioned in the inscription allows one to make this conjecture. Generally in Indic inscriptions, the sponsor's name is mentioned. Since it is not mentioned in the Rāula-Vela inscription, one can surmise that the sponsor's identity was so obvious that it was unnecessary to specify him by name. According to local tradition, the Kamala Maula Mosque was originally a college established by Bhoja; it is still to this day known as Bhojaśālā by the local Hindu population. If this building was Bhoja's college when the Rāula-Vela inscription was composed, then there would have been no need to mention the sponsor's name as he was the reigning sovereign and the one who constructed the edifice upon which the inscription was engraved. Merely stating that the inscription was for 'the king', as is done in the dedicatory verse,[1] would have been enough to let all the inscription's readers know that it was dedicated to the reigning king, Bhoja. Throughout the rest of this paper it will be assumed that the Rāula-Vela inscription was sponsored by Bhoja. However, if Bhoja was not Roḍa's actual patron, the interpretation of the Rāula-Vela inscription as a *praśasti* would still be valid, with but a few obvious minor modifications, for any Paramāra ruler who might have supported Roḍa's literary activities.

In order to see that the Rāula-Vela inscription is a *praśasti*, it is necessary to understand the structural organization of the poem as well as the reasons why regional references, both geographic and linguistic, were used in the poem. Structurally, the Rāula-Vela inscription seems to be more like a dramatic composition than any other type of literary work. The entire composition is set up as a kind of dialogue reminiscent of those found in ancient Indian dramas such as *bhāṇas,* a type of drama in which a single actor holds a dialogue with unseen characters by means of replies to questions he asks and answers himself. As in a *bhāṇa,* the dialogue in the Rāula-Vela inscription is carried on by means of a series of questions and answers. The following excerpts from the end of the fourth and the beginning of the fifth section of the poem, where one character describes a woman from Ṭakka and the other, a woman from Gaūḍa, exemplifies the type of dramatic dialogue employed in the Rāula-Vela inscription:[2]

Character 1

ehā vehu suhāvā Ṭella | ānna tu saṃdā ḍahi paraï volla ||57||	The Ṭakka girl's attire is so lovely that All others are put to shame.
ehī Ṭakkiṇi païsati sohaï | sā nihāli jaṇu malamala cāhaï ||58||	This Ṭakka girl entering here is so beautiful. After seeing her, everybody wants to caress her.

Character 2

kīsa re vaṇḍiro Ṭāka tuṃ [hiṃ] [vo]la[s]i | rāhū āgeṃ vānatu bhūlasi ||59||	Hey you fool, why do you speak of the Ṭakka girl? Have you forgotten that you are in the presence of the king?
tā iṃ kīsa hū vesa re ḍīṭhe | jehara tehara vānasi dheṭhe ||60||	Just how many other costumes have you seen That you can describe such things so brazenly?
gauḍa suāṇu sa taïṃ kata dīṭhe | te dekhi vesa ki bhāvaṃthi mīṭhe ||61||	How many costumes have you seen that are as beautiful as this Gaūḍi girl's? After seeing her costume, does your girl's costume seem pretty at all?

teḍenhu vādhenhu kesaṃ ja laḍahimva | khoṃpa valīe kahu re [tasa] samva ||62||	When bound tightly, her hair is beautiful What is as beautiful as the curls of her hair bun?

In this series of questions and answers, the first character describes the charms of a young maiden from his home region, Ṭakka, while attempting to demonstrate that she is the fairest woman in all the realm, much as if he were promoting a potential beauty queen in a Miss India contest. The second character refutes the first's assertion that the Ṭakka girl is the most beautiful and claims that the Gaüḍī girl is the most charming girl.

If the interpretation of the Rāula-Vela inscription as a beauty contest can be accepted, then the outcome of the contest can easily be predicted, if one bears in mind that the inscription was found at Dhar in Malwa and that its production was most likely sponsored by Bhoja Paramāra. The winner of this central Indian Miss India contest is, of course, none other than the hometown girl, the girl from Malwa.

Roḍa goes to great lengths to ensure that the Malwa girl's preeminent beauty is acknowledged. He stresses her importance by making her description, the final one of the poem, the longest (one-third of the entire composition) and the richest in poetic imagery. He also distinguishes her decription from the others through the use of metre. While the first five sections are in a metre consisting of two feet of sixteen *mātrās*, the sixth section is in unmetred rhyming prose. The following comparison of a couplet from the fourth section with several lines from the sixth and final section will suffice to make the point:

From the Fourth Section

a[ṃ]ghihiṃ [ka]yyalu [ḍa]harā dittā | jo [ni]hāli kari mayaṇūmattā ||49||	A dab of collyrium is applied to [her] eyes. Seeing it, even Kāma would become delirious.

From the Sixth Section

āṃkhi ra phāṭā tīkhā ūjalā taralā te vānati jībhai j[āu]ṃ kh[ū]jhaï ||100||	Her eyes are large, sharp, bright and tremulous. The one describing them becomes tongue-tied.
taïsaü hathiāru pāviü kāmva-deu jagahī kāiṃ karisī	Kāma-deva has a weapon like that (her eyes).

aïsaü Vṛhaspati hīnaü mūjhaï ‖101‖	But Bṛhaspati does not, and he was overcome.
	What will you do?

This portrayal of Miss Malwa as the fairest maiden of all is not merely a happy ending to a fanciful poetic beauty contest created by an imaginative poet. Roḍa strove to imbue his composition, albeit in a unique manner, with the appropriate amount of obligatory flattery due to his patron.

The laudatory content of the Rāula-Vela inscription is hidden behind the guise of a beauty contest, but beyond that the poem tells of glories of quite a different sort; it alludes indirectly to the sponsoring king's military prowess. The inscription may be read as a metaphor. In other words, it says that the most beautiful girl in the world is the Malwa girl, and the most wonderful and powerful ruler in the world is the sovereign of the glorious Malwa region.

This is not an entirely unique metaphor, although it is perhaps a unique way of setting it forth. The glory of a kingdom or the good fortune of a king, known as *rājyalakṣmī* or *rājyaśrī,* is commonly personified as a woman named either Rājyalakṣmī or Rājyaśrī, who is frequently described as the king's bride. In the Rāula-Vela inscription the women are not expressly depicted as the king's brides; rather each woman implicity represents the 'Fortune' of the regional king from each area mentioned in the composition. The significance of alluding to the fortunes of various regional sovereigns may be seen once the geographic regions mentioned in the inscription are located and the political relations between Bhoja and the regional kings are taken into account.

Presumably each section of the poem contained a toponym, but due to textual lacuna, only five are extant—Golla, Kānoḍa, Ṭakka, Gaüḍa and Mālava. Despite some problems involved in the task, it is possible to identify the extant toponyms. Ṭakka and Mālava are the most readily identifiable. Ṭakka is considered to be identical with the area called Tseh-kia, which was described by the Chinese pilgrim Hieun Tsiang (AD 629) as the region between the Pi-po-che (Vipāsa) and Sin-tu (Sindhu) rivers, that is, the Panjab (S. Beal, 1884, I, p. 165). Mālava is, of course, roughly the same as modern Malwa in Madhya Pradesh. Golla designates the Godāvarī River valley region. This ascription is based on two passages that describe a single event, but use different terms to identify where it took place. In the *Prabandhacintāmaṇi,* the fourteenth-century author Merutuṅga describes Bhoja Paramāra's fateful attack upon the Cālukya ruler Tailapadeva. He states that the event occurred at the Godāvarī River (Merutuṅga 1944, p. 33). In the *Bhojacaritra*, however, the fifteenth-century Jain author Rājavallabha uses the synonym Gola instead of Godāvarī with reference to the same event. The toponym Kānoḍa seems to refer to present-day Kanauj and its surrounding environs. The primary evidence for this assumption is phonetic. Two of the ancient appellations for modern Kanauj, namely Kannoja and Kaṇaüjja, are very similar to the term Kānoḍa used in the Rāula-Vela inscription. The toponym Gaüḍa undoubtedly refers to an eastern region, as the term so often carries the sense of 'the East' in Sanskrit and Prākṛit literature.

A careful consideration of these toponyms shows that they were not mentioned arbitrarily. When plotted on a map, it can be seen that Malwa, the home territory of India's most beautiful maiden and Roḍa's patron, Bhoja, is encircled by all the other regions mentioned in the poem (see map on page 205). It seems that this garland of Indian regions around the neck of Malwa is meant to allude to a *digvijaya*. It is, of course, not a *digvijaya* in the true sense of the word; the toponyms in the Rāula-Vela inscription are neither mentioned in the usual clockwise sequential order nor set forth to mark off the usual well-known natural boundaries of the Indian subcontinent, such as the Himalaya or the Indian Ocean, as they would be in a more typical rendering of a *digvijaya*. Nevertheless, the list of Indian regions given in the Rāula-Vela inscription covers all the cardinal compass points of the Indian subcontinent just as in a normal *digvijaya*: Gaüḍa in the east, Kānoḍa/Kanauj in the north-east, Ṭakka/the Panjab in the north-west, Golla/the Godāvarī River basin in the south, and in the centre, Mālava/Malwa. To complete a circle around Malwa we want only a western region. Thus it seems reasonable to speculate that the missing sixth toponym that presumbly would have been mentioned in the composition was Gūrjjara or some other ancient appellation for modern Gujarat, a region which is both a western region and which, like the other toponyms mentioned in the inscription, is adjacent to Malwa.

The pseudo-*digvijaya* outlined by the geographic references mentioned in the Rāula-Vela inscription was meticulously set forth by Roḍa as all the toponyms cited by him are regions into which his patron actually made military forays. Inscriptions such as the

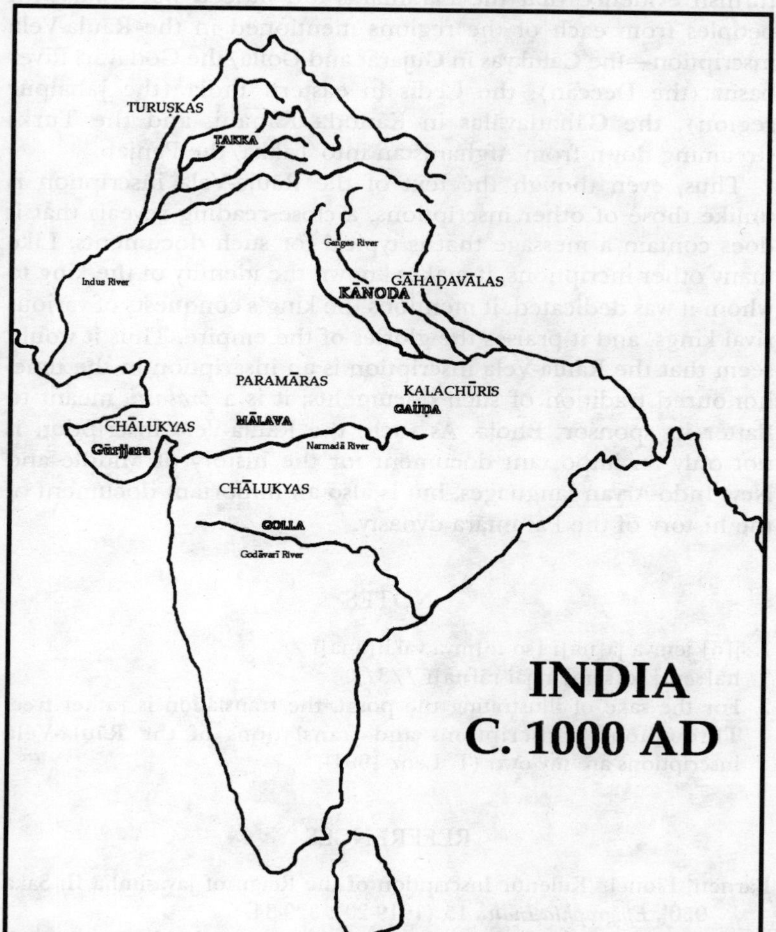
TURUṢKAS
TAKKA
Ganges River
Indus River
GĀHAḌAVĀLAS
KĀNOḌA
PARAMĀRAS
KALACHŪRIS
GAUḌA
CHĀLUKYAS
MĀLAVA
Gūrjjara
Narmadā River
CHĀLUKYAS
GOLLA
Godāvarī River
INDIA
C. 1000 AD

Udaipur Praśasti, the Basahi plate of Govindacandra, the Kuleṇur Inscription of Jayasiṃha II, and various literary works such as Merutuṅga's *Prabandhacintāmaṇi* and Rājavallabha's *Bhojacaritra*, furnish evidence that the Paramāras did indeed wage war with peoples from each of the regions mentioned in the Rāula-Vela inscription—the Cālukyas in Gujarat and Golla/the Godāvarī River basin (the Deccan), the Cedis in eastern India (the Jabalpur region), the Gāhaḍavālas in Kānoḍa/Kanauj, and the Turks streaming down from Afghanistan into Ṭakka/the Panjab.

Thus, even though the text of the Rāula-Vela inscription is unlike those of other inscriptions, a close reading reveals that it does contain a message that is typical for such documents. Like many other incriptions, it makes known the identity of the king to whom it was dedicated, it mentions the king's conquests of various rival kings, and it praises the glories of the empire. Thus it would seem that the Rāula-Vela inscription is an inscription in the time-honoured tradition of such documents; it is a *praśasti*, meant to flatter its sponsor, Bhoja. As such, the Rāula-Vela inscription is not only an important document for the history of Middle and New Indo-Aryan languages, but is also an important document of the history of the Paramāra dynasty.

NOTES

1. j[o] jemva jā[ṇa]ï [so te]mva vakh[āṇa]ï /
   hā[seṃ] to[seṃ] rājaï rā[ṇa]ï //3//
2. For the sake of illustrating the point, the translation is rather free. Throughout transcriptions and translations of the Rāula-Vela inscriptions are my own (T. Lenz 1994).

REFERENCES

Barnett, Lionel. 'Kulenur Inscription of the Reign of Jayasimha II: Saka 950'. *Epigraphia Indica* 15 (1919-20): 329-34.

Beal, Samuel. Buddhist Records of the Western World. Popular ed. London: Kegan Paul, Trench, Trübner, 1884.

Bhatiya, Kailash Candra. *Rāulavela.* New Delhi: Taksasila, 1983.

Bhayani, H.C. 'Prince of Wales Museum Stone Inscription From Dhar'. *Bhāratīya Vidyā* 17.3-4 (1957): 130-46.

———. 'Prince of Wales Museum Stone Inscription from Dhar-II'. *Bhāratīya Vidyā* 19.1-4 (1959): 116-28.

———. *Rāula-Vela of Roḍa (a Rare Poem of c. Twelfth Century in Early Indo-Aryan)*. Ahmedabad: Parshva Prakashan, 1994.

Bühler, George. 'Udepur Prasasti of the Kings of Malva'. *Epigraphia Indica* I (1892): 222-38.

Fleet, Johan Faithfull. 'Sanskrit and Old-Karanese Inscriptions'. *Indian Antiquary* 14 (1885): 101-5.

Gupta, Mataprasad. *Rāula Vela aur uskī bhāṣā.* Allahabad: Mitra Prakashan, 1962.

Lenz, Timothy J. 'A Study of the Rāula-Vela inscription from Dhār, Madhya Pradesh'. Master's Thesis, University Washington, 1994.

Merutuṅga. *The Prabandhacintāmaṇi* [Wishingstone of Narratives]. Ed. C.H. Tawney. *Bibliotheca Indica* 141. Calcutta: Asiatic Society, 1944.

Rājavallabha. *Bhojacaritra.* Ed. B. Chhabra and S. Sankaranarayanan. Calcutta: Bharatiya Jnanpitha Society, 1944.

Sinha, Ila Rani. *Rāula Vela samīkṣā.* Calcutta: Sri Hanuman Mandir Sahityanusandhan Sansthan, 1987

The Life of Kabīr in Legend

DAVID N. LORENZEN

Legendary narratives are neither fish nor fowl. Situated somewhere between myth and history, they partake of the character of both. In one of his novels, Paul Scott has called legend 'fantasy with its roots in fact'. Like the authors of myths, the original authors of legends are mostly anonymous and generally feel free to draw on faith and creative invention to construct their narratives. Like historical discourse, however, legends are about events that happened, or are thought to have happened, to real persons in real (historical) time. When possible, the authors of legends feel obliged to take independent evidence, oral or written, into con-sideration and not rely exclusively on the legend tradition itself. One might say that legends are myths composed keeping in mind the constraints of existing historical tradition, or, looking at them from another perspective, historical texts composed with a creative freedom that carries them into the realm of myth.

Since each retelling modifies the existing legendary tradition, it is virtually inevitable that the original historical kernel of the legends will sooner or later become all but lost among the episodes and details that arise from the chain of creative imaginations of the story-tellers who transmit the legends. In this way legends often become virtually indistinguishable from myths, except that legends are still regarded as historically true in a way that myths are not.

The cycle of legends about Kabīr, the weaver saint of Benares, clearly concerns a historical person. None the less, already in the earliest hagiographic text, Anantadās's *Kabīr paracaī*, the historical kernel is overwhelmed by material that an outside scholarly observer must assume to consist largely of mythological elaboration. Within the *nirguṇī* or Sant tradition, the collection of legends associated with Kabīr is surpassed, in terms of completeness and complexity, only by the collection associated with Gurū Nānak. A few other *nirguṇī* saints including Dādū Dayāl, Haridās Nirañjanī, Pīpā, and Raidās have also acquired fairly extensive hagiographies (D. Lorenzen 1994).

The earliest collection of legends about Kabīr, Anantadās's *Kabīr paracaī*, was written about the end of the sixteenth century. The *Kabīr paracaī* was almost certainly the basic source used by Priyādās for his retelling of the same legends in his influential commentary of AD 1712 on Nābhādās's *Bhaktamāl* (1969). In turn, Priyādās's commentary has served as a basic source for many of the subsequent retellings of the Kabīr legends.

There are, however, several important Kabīr legends that do not appear in the collections of Anantadās and Priyādās. Several of these legends appear to have arisen within the Kabīr Panth. They concern such matters as Kabīr's first appearance in the world and how he acquired his chief disciples. A few other legends have been imported from legend cycles that originally were about other saints and not Kabīr. Finally, some texts associated with the Dharmadāsī sub-sect of the Kabīr Panth tell several legends about Kabīr's earlier incarnations somewhat in the style of the Jātakas about the Buddha.

The authors of most of the collections of Kabīr legends written after those of Anantadās and Priyādās were associated with the Kabīr Panth. The most important exceptions are the *Bhaktamāl* of Rāghavdās (1963), written in about AD 1720, and its commentary by Caturdās (*c.* AD 1800), both of whom were associated with the Dādū Panth, and the *Bhaktavijaya* written in Marathi by the Vārkarī author Mahīpati (1982) in AD 1762. Major Kabīr Panthī collections include Paramānand's massive *Kabīr manśūr* (1984), written in AD 1887; the many relatively short texts of mostly unknown date edited by Swami Yugalanand in the eleven-volume *Kabīr sāgar* (1953), especially the *Kabīr caritra bodh* perhaps written by Yugalanand himself in about the 1930s; Brahmalinamuni's modern *Sadguruśrīkavīracaritam*, a Sanskrit text with the author's own Hindi commentary published in 1960; and Gangasharan Shastri's *Kabīr jīvan caritra*, first published in 1976. The most complete academic study of these legends is my *Kabīr Legends* (1991), in which many of the topics mentioned in this article are treated in more detail and a more complete bibliography is available.

Many academic scholars have attempted to extract a historical biography of Kabīr on the basis of these legends and on the possibly autobiographical references contained in the songs and verses attributed to Kabīr (e.g. Ch. Vaudeville 1974; P. Caturvedi 1964). Unfortunately, there is almost no way to verify the 'facts' of the legends from independent sources. Since many of the legends involve miracles and divine interventions, it is difficult for academic scholars to place much confidence in them. From such a perspective one can say little more than that Kabīr belonged to the Julāhā caste of weavers; that he was raised in a Muslim family in Benares; that he composed many songs and verses in the *nirguṇī* idiom he was instrumental in developing; that he probably became a disciple of Rāmānand, the founder of the Rāmānandī religious order; that he probably was married (something denied by the Kabīr Panth) and had a son named Kamāl; that he was probably a contemporary of the kings Sikandar Lodī and Vīr Siṃh Baghel; that he probably knew several other *nirguṇī* saints who are also said to have been Rāmānand's disciples, especially Raidās and Sen; and that he probably died at Magahar near Gorakhpur in the first part of the sixteenth century.

Two aspects of this biography need some further comment: Kabīr's association with Rāmānand and Kabīr's date. Beginning with Anantadās and Nābhādās, Hindu tradition has unanimously maintained that Kabīr was initiated by Rāmānand. In recent years, however, a few academic scholars, most notably W.H. McLeod (1968, pp. 155-6) and Charlotte Vaudeville (1974, pp. 30-1, 37-40), have expressed doubts about the historical truth of this association. These scholars have argued that the connection between Kabīr and Rāmānand was likely to have been invented in order to give Kabīr and his teaching the legitimacy of approval by a Brahmin guru.

This argument overlooks or downplays several important facts. First is the very unanimity of the Hindu tradition that makes Kabīr Rāmānand's disciple. The earliest authors that make this claim are Anantadās and Nābhādās, both of whom most likely wrote toward the end of the sixteenth century, probably less than seventy-five years after Kabīr's death. An even earlier writer who at least suggests a connection between Kabīr and Rāmānand is Harirām Vyās, who wrote about the middle of the sixteenth century.[1]

Second is the fact that neither Anantadās nor Nābhādās nor Harirām Vyās was a sectarian follower of Kabīr. Anantadās and Nābhādās in fact belonged to the religious order of Rāmānand, and both accepted not only that Rāmānand was Kabīr's guru but also that he was the guru of other low-caste *nirguṇī* saints including the untouchable Raidās. The sectarian affiliation of Harirām Vyās is less clear, but he is associated with Hit Harivaṃśa and Swami Haridās. In stressing the guru-disciple relation between Kabīr and Rāmānand, the two Rāmānandī authors must aim to exalt Rāmānand rather than Kabīr. In point of fact, Rāmānand was a decidedly minor religious and literary figure compared to Kabīr. It is quite possible that later Kabīr Panthī authors were happy to accept that Kabīr had been initiated by a prominent Brahmin teacher, but as far as we can tell it was not the followers of Kabīr who invented the story, if indeed the story was invented.

A third argument that suggests that the relation between Kabīr and Rāmānand is likely to have been historically true is based on the fact that Rāmānand himself, from the few texts attributed to him that have survived (1955), appears to have been a religious radical belonging to *nirguṇī* tradition, notwithstanding his Brahmin caste identity. The early Rāmānandī order was in fact much more 'liberal' in both religious and social terms than it is today, as Peter van der Veer (1989) has clearly shown. The early association of Rāmānand's order with *nirguṇī* tradition is illustrated not only by the genealogical connection between Rāmānand and various *nirguṇī* saints, but also by the fact that Anantadās chose to write hagiographical accounts of the lives of several of these *nirguṇī* saints and that Nābhādās dedicated verses to many *nirguṇī* saints in his famous *Bhaktamāl*. Also significant is the fact that Nābhādās himself reputedly belonged to the untouchable Ḍom caste.

Given all this, I strongly believe that there must have been some actual historical connection between Kabīr and Rāmānand. It is possible that Kabīr was never formally initiated by Rāmānand, and the rather surreptitious character of the initiation in the legendary account in fact suggests as much. None the less, it is highly probable that Rāmānand and Kabīr were contemporaries and that they knew each other and mutually acknowledged the affinity of their respective religious beliefs.

The second historical aspect of Kabīr's biography that merits further discussion is the problem of his dates, and those of his reputed teacher Rāmānand. I have discussed this topic at length in *Kabīr Legends* (1991) and will only repeat the essential points of the argument here. In the Kabīr Panth, the generally accepted dates of Kabīr are from AD 1398 to 1518, a long life span of 120 years. Some modern academic scholars have accepted a date sometime around the traditional one of 1518 as the probable time of Kabīr's death and place his birth around the middle of the fifteenth century. Other scholars, most notably Parashuram Caturvedi (1964, pp. 845-70) and Charlotte Vaudeville (1974, pp. 36-9, 110-17), prefer to place Kabīr's death over a half century earlier, in about the middle of the fifteenth century.

My own view is that four solid arguments, each one independent of the others, clearly establish that Kabīr's floruit must be placed in the first quarter of the sixteenth century. These arguments are based on: (1) the spiritual genealogy of Anantadās, whose *Nāmdev paracaī* was written in AD 1588; (2) the spiritual genealogy of Nābhādās, whose *Bhaktamāl* was probably written in the first quarter of the seventeenth century or even a little earlier; (3) the legendary synchronism of Kabīr with Sultan Sikandar Lodī (r. AD 1488-1512), mentioned by Anantadās and most later sources; and (4) the legendary synchronism of Kabīr with King Vīr Siṃh Baghel (died about AD 1530), also mentioned by Anantadās and most later sources. Whether or not the legends of Kabīr's encounters with these two rulers are true, the synchronisms are still likely to be valid. Most scholars appear not to have realized that Vīr Siṃh Baghel was a historical person whose approximate dates are known. The legendary synchronism of Kabīr and Nānak yields a similar date, but is historically less reliable. The traditional spiritual genealogy of Dādū Dayāl (W. Callewaert 1988, pp. 12-17) suggests that Kabīr's floruit belongs about fifty years earlier, but this tradition is also historically suspect.

The fact that all these four independent arguments put Kabīr's floruit in the first quarter of the sixteenth century suggests that the view that his death took place sometime around the traditional date of 1518 is correct. This also strongly suggests that Rāmānand's floruit should be placed in the latter half of the fifteenth century and not around the considerably earlier dates proposed by a few scholars.

At this point it will be useful to present a summary of the principal Kabīr legends. Given the disparate origins of the individual legends found in the complete collection or cycle of Kabīr legends, however, it is difficult to link them into a single coherent narrative. Logically, one must begin with Kabīr's birth and initiation and end with his death and bodily ascent to heaven, but the relative order of the remaining legends is mostly arbitrary. The summary of the main legends given below mostly follows the order found in the *Kabīr jīvan caritra* of the modern Kabīr Panthī author Gangasharan Shastri (1976). The main sources used for the summary of each legend are noted, but a more complete discussion of the major variants can be found in my *Kabīr Legends* (1991).

The legend of Kabīr's birth is neither found in Anantadās nor in Priyādās. It does figure prominently in most later retellings, however, and several quite different variants exist. Most of the retellings have arisen in the context of the Kabīr Panth and the variants mostly reflect differing efforts to identify Kabīr with divinity and/or deny his low-caste status and Muslim parentage. Most accounts agree that he was found as a baby floating in, or resting on the bank of, the Lahartara pond outside of Benares by a man and his wife who belonged to the Julāhā caste of Muslim weavers. They brought Kabīr to their home in Benares, in the area today known as the Kabir Chaura, where they raised him as their son and taught him the craft of weaving.

While he was still a child Kabīr showed a strong interest in Vaiṣṇava religion. This scandalized his family, especially his mother. At some point, often said to be while Kabīr was still a child, Kabīr decided that he would be initiated by the well-known Brahmin teacher Rāmānand. Since Kabīr was a Muslim, Rāmānand would not agree to initiate him. Kabīr then went out in the early morning darkness and lay down on the path that Rāmānand took on his way to his dawn bath in the Ganges. When Rāmānand stepped on Kabīr, he exclaimed 'Rām! Rām!' and Kabīr took this to be his initiation mantra. When Rāmānand later learned that Kabīr was going about claiming to be his disciple, Rāmānand called him to admonish him. Kabīr reminded Rāmānand of what had happened on the path to the river and impressed his teacher with his religious knowledge and insight. Rāmānand then openly accepted Kabīr as his disciple. Some sources add an incident where Kabīr miraculously told Rāmānand, who was hidden behind a screen, how to solve a problem in placing a garland around the neck of a Vaiṣṇava idol. The legend of Kabīr's initiation is first told in the Nirañjanī Panth recension of Anantadās's *Kabīr paracaī* (1991: section 1) and is found in almost all later legend collections.

One day, when Kabīr was in the market to sell a piece of cloth, God in the form of a poor Brahmin came to test him. The Brahmin begged some cloth from Kabīr who promptly tore his cloth in half and gave half to the Brahmin. The Brahmin then begged the other half and Kabīr gave him that as well. Kabīr was too ashamed to return home without money or cloth and went off to hide (or meditate in some versions) for several days. Meanwhile God, in the disguise of a merchant, came to Kabīr's home and gave Kabīr's mother a bullock cart's load of foodstuffs, saying that it was a gift for Kabīr to give a great feast. This legend is first told by Anantadās and is found in several later sources. It is not particularly popular in the Kabīr Panth, however, perhaps because it shows Kabīr working as a poor weaver.

Kabīr then decided to hold a feast for the devotees (*bhagats*), but this angered the local Brahmins and *saṃnyāsīs* who complained that Kabīr had 'given everything to the Śūdras'. Kabīr agreed to feed the Brahmins and *saṃnyāsīs* as well, but in fact he simply went off to hide (or meditate) since he had no money to buy more food. God came to the rescue again and appeared in the form of Kabīr himself and gave two and one half *sers* (kilos) of food to every Brahmin and *saṃnyāsī.* This legend is told by Anantadās (section 2) and many later writers.

One day the Yogī Gorakhnāth (or one of his followers) came to challenge Kabīr (or his guru Rāmānand) to a debate. Gorakh planted his iron trident in the ground and climbed up and sat on the prongs. He then challenged Kabīr to come up and join him for a debate. Kabīr then threw a thread up into the air and climbed up and sat on that. Gorakh had to acknowledge defeat. This legend is not told by Anantadās and Priyādās but is found in many Kabīr Panthī collections. Paramānand's *Kabīr manśūr* (1956, pp. 111, 166-7) adds two more episodes. In one, Gorakh challenged Kabīr to find him in a pond and changed into a frog. Kabīr grabbed him anyway. Kabīr then successfully hid in the pond by changing himself into the water itself. In the other episode, Gorakh sent two cobras to bite Kabīr, but Kabīr treated them as guests and they did not harm him.

As Kabīr's fame grew, it became more difficult for him to avoid the crowds who came to see him. To rid himself of this problem he went off to the market with his arm around a prostitute while pretending to drink liquor from a jug. When Kabīr came to the court of King Vīr Siṃh Baghel, who had always showed him respect, the king treated him badly. Kabīr then poured out the water from his jug on his own feet. The king asked why he had done this. Kabīr explained that at that very moment a priest of the temple of Jagannāth in the far away city of Puri had dropped a pot of boiling water on his feet. Kabīr had poured out his cool water to save the the priest from getting burned. King Vīr Siṃh Baghel did not believe the story and sent some messengers by fast camel to Puri to verify it. They did so and the king felt obliged to come to Kabīr as a penitent to ask forgiveness. Kabīr happily did so saying: 'There is no anger in my heart. For me there is no question of either hatred or love, nor any difference between king and commoner.' This story is told by Anantadās (sections 4.9-6.6) and most later authors, though some Kabīr Panthī authors such as Brahmalinamuni (1960, pp. 481-96) prudishly omit the episode with the prostitute. This legend is a complex one that involves several interesting social and psychological role inversions (see Lorenzen 1991, pp. 29-32).

A legend about Kabīr, his wife and a libidinous merchant is found in the Muslim *Dabistān-i-Mazāhib* attributed to Muhsin Fāni (1843, vol. 2, pp. 189-91) and in Mahīpati's *Bhaktavijaya* (1982, vol. 1, pp. 178-85, 398-400). Since the *sādhus* of the Kabīr Panth deny that Kabīr ever married, the legend is not found in Kabīr Panthī sources. In actual fact, the legend seems to have been imported from the cycle of legends about the *nirguṇī* saint Pīpā and his faithful wife Sītā and originally had no relation to Kabīr (see Nābhādās 1969, pp. 492-521; Raghavdās 1963, pp. 195-217). According to the *Dabistān*, one day some dervishes arrived at Kabīr's house. Kabīr asked his wife to request a local merchant to give them food on credit. The merchant agreed but only on the condition that Kabīr's wife return at night for a sexual tryst. Kabīr's wife asked Kabīr what she should do, and he agreed to the merchant's condition. That night a rain storm made the roads muddy, and Kabīr carried his wife to the merchant's place so that she would not get dirty. When the merchant asked her how she had avoided the mud, she told him. The merchant was so ashamed that he asked Kabīr's forgiveness, gave away all his goods and became a *sādhu*.

According to Paramānand's *Kabīr manśūr* (1956, pp. 155-6), one day Kabīr, Shaikh Farīd and Kamāl (Kabīr's son) arrived at the house of a poor devotee named Samman. Since there was no food in the house, Samman and his son Seu went out to rob sufficient to feed their honoured guests. They made a hole in the wall of a merchant's house and Seu went in to find what they needed. As Seu was leaving through the hole, the merchant grabbed his foot. Seu then asked his father to cut off his head so that no one would know who had stolen the food. Samman did so and took the food and his son's head home. Samman's wife prepared the food and set out three places for their guests to eat. Kabīr insisted that Samman, his wife and their son Seu eat with them. Kabīr called for Seu to come and the severed head called out that his body was somewhere else. When Kabīr insisted that he come, the headless body came running and replaced its own head. All six of them then sat down to eat. This legend originally seems to have had no connection with Kabīr. Anantadās (1786, fol. 73v.-76v.) made it the theme of another of his *paracaīs* without mentioning Kabīr. In Mahīpati's *Bhaktavijaya* (1982, vol. 1, pp. 98-108), however, the roles of Samman and Seu are played by Kabīr and his son Kamāl.

One of the most popular of all Kabīr legends, told in virtually all collections, is that of his encounter with Sultan Sikandar Lodī. According to Anantadās's version (sections 6.14-9.10), one day Sikandar came to Benares. Kabīr's enemies among the *kāzīs*, mullahs, Brahmins, and Baniyās, and even his own mother, went to complain to Sikandar about his religious activities. Sikandar summoned Kabīr and demanded that he repent his apostasy. Kabīr announced his faith in Rām, and Sikandar ordered him to be chained and thrown into the Ganges. When Kabīr entered the water the chains fell off and he floated unharmed. Next he was tied in a pile of firewood. When the fire was lit the flames were as cool as water. Then Sikandar called for a wild elephant to be brought to trample him. The elephant refused to attack. Sikandar finally accepted Kabīr's innocence and offered him great riches. Kabīr refused the gifts and returned home. Later versions of this legend add many further ordeals and sometimes have Kabīr cure Sikandar of a bad fever. These versions also introduce the figure of Shai<u>kh</u> Takī, who is the principal enemy responsible for instigating Sikandar to subject Kabīr to the terrible ordeals.

Several Kabīr Panthī collections claim that Kabīr accompanied Sikandar to Prayag (Allahabad) where Shai<u>kh</u> Takī challenged Kabīr to revive a dead body floating in the Ganges. When Kabīr called it, the corpse came to life and became Kabīr's adopted son Kamāl. This Kamāl seems to have been a historical person and a religious poet in his own right. Kamālī is said to have originally been the daughter of Shai<u>kh</u> Takī. One day she died and Takī offered to place his faith in Kabīr if he would revive her. When he did so, Kamālī renounced her natural father and claimed Kabīr as her adopted father. Kamāl and Kamālī are not mentioned by Anantadās or Priyādās.

Kabīr Panthī collections contain a number of legends about the travels of Kabīr. During these travels he is said to have met Gurū Nānak, with whom he travelled to Mecca. This exploit of Gurū Nānak is well-known from Sikh sources. These sources do not mention Kabīr's presence on the trip, but several do claim that Kabīr and Gurū Nānak once met. On other journeys Kabīr met a southern Brahmin named Rāmdās, visited the ashram founded by Rāmānuja at Totadri in south India, and traveled to Balkh in Afghanistan where he met the sultan, Shāh Ibrāhīm Adham, the protagonist of a well-known cycle of Sufi legends. None of these legendary journeys of Kabīr need be recounted in detail here. Most of the episodes in these legends seem to be imported from legends originally associated with other religious figures.

During his time as a religious poet and saint, Kabīr is said to have acquired many disciples. One was Kabīr's own 'brother-disciple' Raidās. In Anantadās's *Raidās paracaī* (1982), Kabīr and Raidās, accompanied by their fellow disciple Sen, are said to have had a debate about the relative merits of *saguṇ* ('with attributes') and *nirguṇ* ('without attributes') conceptions of God. Despite the intervention of Viṣṇu on Raidās's side, Kabīr's arguments in favor of a strict *nirguṇ* conception prevailed. Raidās eventually accepted defeat and from then on considered Kabīr to be his guru. The debate itself is recounted in a Hindi text attributed to Sen (1996).

Kabīr's disciple Padmanābh of Benares is first mentioned in Nābhādās's *Bhaktamāl* (1969, pp. 534-6). According to Gangasharan Shastri (1976, pp. 122-4), Padmanābh cured a merchant of leprosy by telling him to bathe in the Ganges and recite the name of Rām three times. Kabīr later admonished Padmanābh for having so little faith, since even a 'hint' of the name would have cured the merchant.

Kabīr's Brahmin disciples Tatvā and Jīvā of Gujarat are also first mentioned in Nābhādās's *Bhaktamāl* (1969, pp. 537-40), but the commentator Priyādās is the first author to explicitly connect them with Kabīr. Tatvā and Jīvā had decided to accept as their guru the first holy man who could pass a certain test. They washed their saintly guests' feet and then poured the water on a dry stick they had planted in the ground. The water that made the stick sprout leaves would identify their future guru. The water from Kabīr's feet instantly had the desired effect, and Tatvā and Jīvā accepted him as their guru. Their caste fellows objected to the fact that Kabīr was a Julāhā, however, and refused to marry into Tatvā and Jīvā's family. They finally relented when Tatvā and Jīvā threatened to marry their own children to each other. Today Tatvā and Jīvā are considered to have been the founders of the Phatuha branch of the Kabīr Panth.

Several other of Kabīr's disciples are said to have been the founders of important branches of the Kabīr Panth. Most Kabīr Panthī sources claim that Kabīr had four principal disciples: Dharmadās, Śrutigopāl, Bhagavāndās Gosvāmī, and Jāgū Sāhab. They are considered to be the founders respectively of the Damakheda-Kharsiya (Dharmadāsī), Kabir Chaura (*mūl gaddī*), Dhanauti (Bhagatāhī), and Bidupur-Shivpur branches of the Panth. None are mentioned by Anantadās or Priyādās. The two most important figures are Dharmadās and Śrutigopāl.

Dharmadās was a pious and well-to-do Baniyā merchant from the town of Bandhogadh in the Baghelkhand region. He first met Kabīr at Mathura where Kabīr performed a minor miracle for him. Eventually both Dharmadās and his wife Āminī Devī became important disciples of Kabīr. Both also became important religious poets in their own rights. One day Kabīr announced that Dharmadās's son Muktāmaṇi was to become the head of the Kabīr Panth and establish his seat (*gaddī*) at Kudarmal (Bilaspur District). The monastery at Kudarmal still exists, but the *gaddī* of the Dharmadāsi branch of the Kabīr Panth has since been moved several times and now is divided between rival branches with their main centers at Kharsiya and Damakheda.

The original name of Śrutigopāl (also called Suratgopāl) was Sarvānand. He was a learned Brahmin pandit from south India. He went about India debating with rival pandits and defeated every one. He then told his mother that she should call him 'Sarvajīt' since he had 'conquered all'. His mother told him he must first debate with Kabīr. Sarvānand came to Benares and challenged Kabīr to a debate. The debate went on for a long time, but Kabīr could not convince Sarvānand. In disgust, Kabīr finally agreed to let Sarvānand write a 'certificate of victory' saying that

Kabīr had been defeated. When Sarvānand got home, however, he found that the certificate said that he himself had been defeated. He returned to Benares two more times to get new certificates, but each time he got home he found the certificate had been magically changed. He finally gave up all his book learning and became Kabīr's disciple, taking the new name Śrutigopāl. The *sādhus* of the Kabir Chaura branch of the Kabīr Panth believe that Kabīr appointed Śrutigopāl to be the head of the Kabīr Panth with his *gaddī* at the site of Kabīr's home in the Kabir Chaura neighborhood of Benares. Today there is still a large monastery at this site.

The last three important legends about Kabīr are told by Anantadās and Priyādās as well as being found in later Kabīr Panthī collections. The first of these legends tells how some Brahmins of Benares once hatched a plot against Kabīr. Four Brahmins disguised themselves as *nirguṇī sādhus* and travelled in different directions, announcing that Kabīr was to give a great feast to which all were invited. When the people began to arrive on the appointed day, Kabīr went away and hid (or meditated). God (Hari) again came to Kabīr's rescue and appeared in the guise of many Kabīrs to greet each guest personally. He gave everyone food to eat and distributed cloth to all the *sādhus.* Today great feasts of this sort are given on different dates at the sites of the principal monasteries of the Kabīr Panth.

The second legend tells how a celestial nymph (*apsarā*) was sent by Hari to test Kabīr's chastity. Kabīr easily resisted all her attempts to seduce him. She returned to heaven and told Hari what had happened. Hari was so pleased he gave Kabīr a *darśan* of himself in his four-armed, *saguṇ* form and offered Kabīr magical powers and limitless treasures. Kabīr said he had no need for such things, and Hari 'made him unaging, immortal, and indestructible'.

The final legend is that of Kabīr's death and bodily ascent to heaven. This is one of the most popular legends about Kabīr. It is told in almost all collections beginning with Anantadās (section 13) and seems to be alluded to in a few verses attributed to Kabīr. When it came time for Kabīr to die, he decided to go to Magahar, usually identified with a town by this name in Basti District near Gorakhpur. It was popularly believed that a person who died in Magahar would be reborn as a donkey. Kabīr went there expressly to prove that Rām could save anyone anywhere. When Kabīr died, his Hindu and Muslim followers argued about what to do with the corpse: burn it or bury it. Later texts make King Vīr Siṃh Baghel the leader of the Hindus and Nawab Bijlī Khān, the leader of the Muslims. All finally agreed to cover the body with flowers. When they later looked for the corpse, they discovered that only flowers remained. Anantadās ends the legend with Kabīr being greeted in heaven by all the gods and divine sages. Viṣṇu told him: 'Heaven is yours! Live here forever!'

This cycle of legends can be analysed from a variety of points of view. We have already noted that many academic scholars have attempted to use the legends to extract a historical biography of Kabīr, but an honest critical approach to this task yields a disappointing minimum of information. Charlotte Vaudeville (1974, p. 46), for instance, laments that 'the legendary life of Kabīr follows well-known patterns of Indian hagiography'. None the less, these patterns are themselves historical products of considerable importance and are not as 'well-known' as Vaudeville suggests. The patterns need to be identified and then compared to the patterns of the legendary lives of saints and heroes from other traditions. Another interesting question is that of the history of these legends themselves—where they come from and how they evolve? Finally, and for me this is the most interesting question, what socioeconomic and religious ideology is expressed by the legends? How do they reflect the religious, social, and economic needs of those who tell and listen to them?

As Vaudeville notes, there do exist 'patterns of Hindu hagiography' in which the cycle of Kabīr legends can be located. In another essay I have attempted to make a detailed comparison of the legend cycles of the seven *nirguṇī* saints who have acquired the most complete cycles: Dādū Dayāl, Haridās Nirañjanī, Kabīr, Nāmadev, Gurū Nānak, Pīpā, and Raidās (Lorenzen 1994). This comparison shows that the basic features common to all or most of these cycles are the following: (1) All the saints belong to non-Brahmin castes. Three belong to Kshatriya castes and four to artisan castes. (2) In at least three of the cycles (Kabīr, Nāmdev and Raidās), legends prominently mention one or more previous lives of the saint. (3) All but two cycles include legends about the unusual events that surround the saint's birth. (4) In all the cycles but one (Haridās), the saint displays evidence of his religious vocation early in life. (5) All the saints have a decisive encounter with either a human guru, divine vision, divine voice, or some combination of these three that leads to their adopting a religious vocation. (6) All the saints were married (although Kabīr remains celibate in Kabīr Panthī texts), but several of them either abandon their families or quarrel with their wives because of their religious vocation. (7) All have various encounters with some combination of petitioners, gods, animals, ghosts, thieves, Brahmins, Baniyās, Muslim holy men, and kings who test the virtues or miraculous powers of the saint. (8) Three of the saints (Dādū Dayāl, Kabīr and Gurū Nānak) are said to have named their own successor before their deaths. Not surprisingly, these are the three whose followers organized the biggest sectarian movements. (9) Unusual events are said to surround the deaths of the same three saints.

Although I will not here attempt to make detailed comparisons of this pattern with the legend cycles of Hindu saints who do not belong to *nirguṇī* tradition or with the cycles of saints and heroes from other religious and national traditions, it should be obvious that both differences and similarities exist. That all the seven *nirguṇī* saints were non-Brahmins undoubtedly reflects historical fact and contrasts markedly with the prominence of Brahmin saints and scholars in more orthodox Hindu tradition. That all seven *nirguṇī* saints were married, and most never totally abandoned their families, also contrasts with the lives of the saints of more orthodox tradition where the saint almost invariably chooses renunciation (*saṃnyās*) over family life. The prominence of the motif of the *nirguṇī* saint being tested by representatives of more orthodox religious tradition and political authority, is a feature that is not absent from the lives of more orthodox Hindu saints, where religious-theological debates are almost always prominently featured. None the less, the high frequency, magical character, and social inequalities of these testing encounters are particularly notable in the legends about *nirguṇī* saints.

As has been noted, several of the Kabīr legends are evidently retellings of specific legends that originally had nothing to do with Kabīr. In earlier versions of the legend of Samman and Seu, the visiting saints were generally anonymous. The legend about Kabīr's encounter with King Ibrāhīm bin Adham of Balkh is clearly borrowed directly from Sufi sources. The legend of Kabīr's encounter with Gurū Nānak and their trip together to Mecca is a simple adaptation of Sikh legend. The legend of Kabīr, his wife and the libidinous merchant, was apparently borrowed from the cycle about Pīpā and his loyal wife Sītā. In the legend of Kabīr's trip to the Totadri ashram in south India, Kabīr makes a buffalo recite the Vedās. This legend (or legend motif) was probably borrowed from a legend about the Vārkarī saint Jñāneśvar. A legend very similar to that of the dispute for Kabīr's corpse and its magical disappearance and replacement by flowers is sometimes told about Gurū Nānak. In this case, however, it is likely that the older version is that of Kabīr. The legend may in fact go back to Sufi sources.

The presence of a common narrative 'pattern', based on similar episodes and motifs, in the legendary lives of *nirguṇī* saints and the existence of notable similarities between that pattern and the common life pattern of Hindu saints, and even of saints and heroes of other societies, strongly suggests the existence of pan-Indian and universal narrative 'archetypes' that must be largely independent of the process of historical diffusion. On the other hand, the transference of quite specific legends and motifs from one saint to another shows that the process of historical diffusion was frequently at work. The process of formation of legend cycles such as that of Kabīr is evidently dependent both on the existence of archetypal patterns and motifs that are somehow biologically given and on the historical diffusion of quite specific legends and legend motifs. Legends, at least in their initial stages, must arise out of the interaction of these archetypes and borrowed elements with the actual historical persons whose life they claim to represent.

Much of the discourse enunciated by any religious movement is ideological. By this I mean that one of its primary purposes is either to legitimize or to protest against the unequal division of social prestige and economic and political power in the society in question. This is particularly true of moral discourse, but is also true of legends and other discursive texts, even those concerned with theology and ritual. This is why there exist fundamental differences between religious movements dominated by upper-class and lower-class persons. In actual practice the ideological discourse of any religious movement usually strikes compromises necessary for the continued survival of the society. The respected and powerful are told to be generous and compassionate and the scorned and weak are told to be patient, fatalistic and obedient. None the less, the ideological messages tend to vary quite markedly depending on the social classes of both the leaders and followers of any given movement or congregation. Within Hindu tradition such an ideological divide is clearly present in the contrasting currents of *nirguṇ* and *saguṇ* Bhakti.

The legends about Kabīr are products of the mostly low-caste, non-Brahmin religious current of *nirguṇ* Bhakti. Their principal ideological messages are those of protest against the exploitation of the poor and weak by the rich and powerful. In these legends the rich and powerful attempt to test or punish Kabīr, who serves as an embodiment of the poor and weak, but in the end they are invariably forced to repent and ask for his pardon.

The stories about Kabīr's birth show him to be 'really' of divine or high-caste status. As a child or youth he outwits his Brahmin guru Rāmānand and secures an initiation and then an honored position among his fellow disciples. The test of Kabīr's generosity by God disguised as a Brahmin beggar ends happily when God disguised as a merchant delivers a large supply of foodstuffs to Kabīr's home. When Kabīr gives this away and the greedy Brahmins complain that they didn't get their share, God again intervenes on Kabīr's behalf. In the legend about Kabīr, the prostitute, the king, and the priest of Jagannāth, Kabīr in effect reverses social roles with the representatives of both political power (the king) and high social status (the priest). In the end the king comes to Kabīr as a penitent. The legend of Kabīr, his wife and the libidinous merchant protests against the sexual and economic exploitation of the poor by merchants, with the merchant finally asking Kabīr for forgiveness. The legend of Samman and Seu has a similar moral. The legend of Kabīr's encounter with Sikandar Lodī has Kabīr magically resist all the tortures devised by Sikandar at the instigation of Kabīr's upper class enemies, both Hindu and Muslim. In the end Sikandar must beg forgiveness. The legends of Kabīr's disciples Tatvā and Jīvā, Śrutigopāl, and Dharmaḍās show Kabīr's spiritual authority being recognized by three Brahmins and a Baniyā. The legend of the unexpected feast has Kabīr again outwit some greedy Brahmins with God's help. The myth of the *apsarā* who cannot seduce Kabīr makes him a master of the sexual desire that low-caste people are often accused of being unable to control. The final legend of Kabīr's apotheosis at his death vindicates all his sufferings and indignities with a bodily ascent into heaven and the homage paid to him by a Hindu king and a Muslim nawab.

All this clearly marks the dominant ideological messages of these legends as those appropriate to the psychological needs of the mostly low-caste followers of Kabīr. Most of the tellers of these legends, at least in their recorded versions, were low-caste *sādhus* from the Kabīr Panth and related *nirgunī* movements whose needs can be considered to largely correspond with those of the lay followers of these movements. Where these tellers' special interests may intrude upon some of the stories is in their insistence that Kabīr was a celibate *sādhu* like themselves, and in their frequent allusions to the duty and value of making generous donations of food and money to the Sants and *sādhus*. In sum, these legends are not simply entertaining stories or edifying religious parables, they also make important statements about the nature and distribution of social prestige and political and economic power in Indian society.

NOTE

1. For an excellent discussion of the song in which Harirām Vyās links Kabīr with Rāmānand, see Pauwels 1994. Although Pauwels bends over backwards to regard the relevant passage with critical skepticism, it is difficult to avoid the conclusion that the phrase '*jākau sevak Kabīr*' ('whose [Rāmānand's] servant, Kabīr. . . .') means that Harirām Vyās regarded Kabīr as Rāmānand's disciple.

REFERENCES

Anantadās. *Saman Seu paracaī*. Manuscript A 12, entitled *Vaisnava Poems*, in the Hindi collection of the India Office Library, London, 1786. Like all of Anantadās's works, it was written about the end of the sixteenth century AD.

———. *Raidās paracaī*. In *Śrī guru Ravidās caritam*, ed. B.P. Sharma. Chandigarh: Sri Guru Ravidas Sansthan, 1982.

———. *Kabīr paracaī*. In *Kabīr Legends and Ananta-dās's Kabīr Parachai*, ed. and trans. David N. Lorenzen (with Jagdish Kumar and Uma Thukral). Albany: State University of New York Press, 1991.

Brahmalinamuni. *Sadguruśrīkavīracaritam*. In Sanskrit with the author's own Hindi commentary. Baroda: the author, 1960.

Callewaert, Winand. M. *The Hindī Biography of Dādū Dayāl*. Delhi: Motilal Banarsidass, 1988.

Caturvedi, Parashuram. *Uttarī Bhārat kī Sant-paramparā*. Allahabad: Bharat Bhandar, 1964.

Lorenzen, David N. *Kabīr Legends and Ananta-dās's Kabīr Parachai*. Albany: State University of New York Press, 1991.

———. 'The Lives of *Nirguṇī* Saints'. In *Bhakti Religion in North India: Community Identity and Political Action*, ed. David N. Lorenzen, pp. 181-211. Albany: State University of New York Press, 1994.

McLeod, W.H. *Gurū Nānak and the Sikh Religion*, 1968. Rpt. Delhi: Oxford University Press, 1976.

Mahīpati. *Bhaktavijaya*. Trans. by J.E. Abbott and N.R. Godbole as *Stories of Indian Saints*. 2 vols. in 1. Delhi: Motilal Banarsidass, 1982.

Muḥsin Fānī. *Dabistān-i-Mazāhib*. Translated from Persian in two vols. by D. Shea and A. Troyer as *The Dabistān or School of Manners*. Paris, 1843. Perhaps written in AD 1665.

Nābhādās. *Śrībhaktamāl*. With the verse commentary of Priyādās (AD 1712) and a modern Hindi prose commentary. 5th imp. Lucknow: Tejkumar Press, 1969.

Paramānand. *Kabīr manśūr*. Short version. Translated from Urdu into Hindi by Sudhadasji Saheb 'Sukavi'. Baroda: Pandit Śrimotidasji Cetandasji, 1956.

———. *Kabīr manśūr*. Long version. Translated from Urdu into Hindi by Madhavacharya. New imp. Bombay: Lakshmivenkateshvar Steam Press, 1984. The date this edition was first published is unknown.

Pauwels, Heidi. 'The Early Bhakti Milieu as Mirrored in the Poetry of Hariirām Vyās'. In *Studies in South Asian Devotional Literature*, eds. Alan W. Entwistle and Françoise Mallison, pp. 24-50. New Delhi: Manohar, 1994.

Rāghavdās. *Bhaktamāl*. With the verse commentary of Caturdās (*c.* AD 1800) and the modern Hindi prose commentary of Nārāyaṇdās. Pushkar: Dadudayalu Mahasabha, 1963.

Rāmānand. *Rāmānand kī hindī rācanāē*. Edited by P.D. Baḍathvāl (Barthwal). Varanasi: Nagari Pracharini Sabha, 1955.

Shastri, Gangasharan. *Kabīr jīvan caritra*. Varanasi: Kabirvani Prakashan Kendra, 1976.

Sen (or Sain). *Kabīr-Raidās kā saṃvād*. Edited and trans. in *Praises to a Formless God*, ed. David N. Lorenzen, pp. 169-203. Albany: State University of New York Press, 1996.

van der Veer, Peter. *Gods on Earth: The Management of Religious Experience and Identity in a North Indian Pilgrimage Centre*. Delhi: Oxford University Press, 1989.

Vaudeville, Charlotte. *Kabir*. Vol. 1. Oxford: Clarendon Press, 1974.

Yugalanand Bihari (ed.). *Kabīr sāgar*. 11 vols. Bombay: Srivenkateshvar Steam Press, 1953. This collection seems to have been first published in the early 1930s. The *Kabīr caritra bodh* is found in vol. 11.

Advaitaprakāś: Questions of Authenticity in Vaiṣṇava Hagiography

REBECCA J. MANRING

Hagiographical materials are not historical documents, but religious texts, commissioned and created by groups of people whose intentions and world views are shaped by the social and political circumstances in which they live. This paper will treat *Advaitaprakāś,* one of the more controversial of the compositions concerned with Advaitācārya, the man considered spiritually responsible for the incarnation of Kṛṣṇacaitanya, founder of the Gauḍīya Vaiṣṇava movement. The controversies surrounding *Advaitaprakāś* arise from early attempts in the secondary literature to treat it as an historical rather than a religious text.

This paper is part of a larger work treating the entire Advaitācārya corpus of texts. Throughout this study the believer's faith is accepted as the appropriate lens through which to examine the texts to learn how members of Advaitācārya's tradition view their leader, and how and why those views may have changed as their beliefs evolved over time. My purpose is not to reconstruct the life of Advaitācārya, although the biographies undoubtedly contain some elements of historical truth. I am not concerned with which, if any, of the biographies reflects the most empirical truth. Historical accuracy is difficult if not impossible to measure in South Asian religious material, as nonsectarian historical records were rarely kept and there is seldom any way to verify names or dates independently of a given tradition. Further, attempts to extract historical fact from hagiographical materials are likely to lead one astray, as will be shown below. My goal rather is to examine *Advaitaprakāś,* purportedly composed in CE 1577, as one of the earliest steps in the process by which the status and identity of Advaitācārya were first established, and then revised and expanded over time.

Advaitācārya, born Kamalākṣa Bhaṭṭācārya, is generally believed by his followers to have lived between CE 1434 and 1559. He was born in the village of Navagrām, 32 km up the Surmā River from Sunāmgañj in what is now Sylhet District of Bangladesh, and relocated at the age of twelve to Śāntipur, about 90 km north of Calcutta in what is now West Bengal, India.

The information we have about Advaitācārya comes from the various biographies of Caitanya, and from about a dozen texts written about him and/or one of his wives, Sītādevī. The earliest biography of Advaitācārya was purportedly written in 1486; the most recent, in 1983. The three main biographies of Advaitācārya are *Bālyalīlāsūtra; Advaitaprakāś* and *Advaitamaṅgal,* and the biography of his wife Sītādevi is entitled *Sītācaritra. Advaitaprakāś* and *Advaitamaṅgal* were composed in middle Bengali. *Bālyalīlāsūtra* is in Sanskrit, and *Sītācaritra* is a Sanskrit text with Bengali elaboration. Along with these texts I have found a number of short works in Bengali concerning Advaitācārya's purported spiritual practices, including *Nitāi-advaita-tattva, Advaitoddeśadīpikā* and *Advaitasvarūpāmṛta*; and a few different texts entitled *Advaitasūtrakaḍacā*. Narahari Das published his *Advaitavilās* in the latter part of the nineteenth century, based on his reading of earlier biographical materials on Advaitācārya. Subal Candra Maitra of Śāntipur published his biography of Advaita (*Advaitācārya*) in 1983. And Amiyakanti Datta's *Advaitācārya,* published in the 1920s, is based on *Advaitaprakāś* and is intended for children.

The material presents a number of questions. First, why does such a relatively large body of biographical material surround Advaitācārya, and by whom was it created? Advaitācārya is the only member of the first generation of Caitanya's devotees about whom extensive biographical material was written. What factors motivated its creation, at this early stage in the Bengali biographical tradition? The texts depict Advaitācārya in quite different ways. What external factors caused their authors to emphasize or de-emphasize various aspects of their subject's life and teachings (mythological or otherwise)? And lastly, why has this particular corpus become controversial during this century?

My first step in solving these problems is to attempt to place the various texts in historical relationship to each other, and thus in chronological relationship to the Caitanya corpus. One goal of examining an entire corpus treating a given religious leader is to chart the changes which that leader's image, and his sect, underwent over time, and to understand those changes in terms of the historical, political, and sociological environments in which they occurred. The date of composition thus becomes significant in the setting of the larger hagiographical context of Gauḍīya Vaiṣṇavism in that its establishment allows one to see how a particular text may have influenced subsequent works, or itself have been influenced by previous works. The issue of the importance of the date of composition is quite distinct from the illusory question of a text's historical accuracy.

Unfortunately, the lack of corroborating evidence from outside the Gauḍīya Vaiṣṇava tradition makes it impossible to establish dates of composition with absolute certainty. While it is possible that *Advaitaprakāś* is a modern (i.e. late nineteenth century) composition as may scholars contend, it is my opinion that there is convincing evidence that it was indeed composed in the late sixteenth century and that it is not a nineteenth-century forgery.

Sometimes corroboration cannot be found even within the tradition. Many events described in the Advaita biographies are either not mentioned, or are depicted differently in the Caitanya biographies. Scholars working at the end of the nineteenth and beginning of the present century dealt with the narrative discrepancies by accepting the Caitanya biographies as the literary and sectarian standard, labelling any deviation from them 'inauthentic', but never clearly defined the word 'inauthentic'. A text could be considered inauthentic if it departed from an orthodox philosophical position or contained ideological, historical or linguistic anachronisms. Or it could be considered inauthentic in terms of historical accuracy, or because of doubts concerning its stated date of composition; but these criteria have not been clearly formulated in the secondary literature up to now.

Gauḍīya Vaiṣṇava theology as codified by Jīv Gosvāmī in his *Satsandarbha* accepts and subsumes its rivals' ideas, thereby neutralizing any possible tension between them while clearly displaying its own beliefs. The question of ideological authenticity does not arise from within the tradition, but seems to have represented an attempt by British-educated scholars to interpret the Vaiṣṇava material in terms of European academic thought.

Sectarian legitimacy, that is, demonstrated connection with an already recognized guru or sect is, however, of great importance in South Asian tradition. Many texts begin with a lengthy exposition of the protagonist's biological and/or spiritual genealogy to establish a relationship of succession. The importance of lineage cannot be overstressed, and was a problematic issue for Caitanya's followers. According to sectarian lore, Caitanya recognized this need for legitimacy and therefore sent the six gosvāmīs from Bengal to Vrindaban to produce a scriptural theology for the sect. The task of the gosvāmīs was to provide a textual base for Gauḍīya Vaiṣṇavism which would legitimate the group in the context of the four classical Vaiṣṇava sects. At the end of the eighteenth century Baladev Vidyābhūṣaṇ formally announced the Gauḍīya Vaiṣṇavas to be affiliated with the Mādhva Sampradāy, a statement which continues to provoke controversy as the philosophies of Madhva and those of the six gosvāmīs are quite different. None the less, the stated affiliation provided the new sect with a legitimacy which permitted them to worship and perform rituals in any Vaiṣṇava temple.

The writings of the gosvāmīs were aimed at orthodox Brahmin Vaiṣṇavas. Their treatises preach the worship of Kṛṣṇa, not of Caitanya, and do not mention the role of Caitanya in introducing the devotional path. The job of delineating Caitanya's personal position fell to Kṛṣṇadās Kavirāj, author of *Caitanyacaritāmṛta*, who lived in Vrindaban and had minimal direct contact with the people concerned with Caitanya's life. He wrote, probably at the instruction of the six gosvāmīs, to paint a picture of the leader and his philosophy conforming to their teachings, which represented sectarian orthodoxy.

Meanwhile, in Bengal a very different type of literature was being produced: devotional poetry and biography. The teachings of Caitanya as displayed in the biographical materials produced in Bengal differ markedly from the orthodox Vaiṣṇavism codified in the scriptures which the gosvāmīs produced. In such compositions as *Caitanyabhāgavat* (1548) and the Advaita corpus, Caitanya is portrayed as opposed to the rigidities of the caste system, and is repeatedly represented as embracing untouchables, and quoted as saying that nobility is a matter of character and behaviour, not a mere accident of birth. He apparently advocated a caste-blind approach to Godhead in which anyone could participate. *Advaitaprakāś* propounds this same approach through the actions of Advaita, and also accepts Caitanya as the incarnation of the age. Thus *Advaitaprakāś* is inconsistent with the conservative framework the gosvāmīs created.

With the preceding as introduction, let us turn now to the matter of the authenticity of the author and date of composition of *Advaitaprakāś*. I have considered three factors in trying to determine whether *Advaitaprakāś* was composed at the end of the sixteenth century, as its colophon claims:

1. Physical evidence.
2. Linguistic evidence.
3. Authorship.

Physical evidence

Advaitaprakāś, written by one Īśān Nāgar, was purportedly completed in 1499 Śaka (*c.* CE 1577). The text appears to have remained undiscovered until Acyutacaran Caudhuri Tattvanidhi introduced it in *Baṅgīya Sāhitya Pariṣat Patrikā* issue No. 4 of 1303 BS (['Bengali Era'] *c.* AD 1897). It was first published and edited in 412 Caitanya Era (*c.* AD 1898) by Keshavalal Ray. A 'new edition' was edited and published by Satishcandra Mitra in 1333 BS (*c.* AD 1927); a second edition edited by Mrinalkanti Ghosh bears no publication date, but the third edition, also edited by Mrinalkanti Ghosh, was published in 1339 BS (*c.* AD 1933). The texts of the published editions are identical.

The only extant manuscript of *Advaitaprakāś* of which I am aware is Ms. No. 4683 in the collection of Dhaka University. The colophon of this manuscript indicates that it was copied in 1298 BS (*c.* AD 1892) from a manuscript dated 1702 Śaka (*c.* AD 1780). The paper and style of handwriting support this date. The manuscript is clearly not an original text, as throughout can be seen examples of the scribe's having lost his place in the exemplar and later corrected his errors. I have no reason to doubt the authenticity of the date given for the prototype from which the scribe copied the extant manuscript. While the manuscript does not differ significantly from the published editions, there are a few *ślokas* in it which do not appear in the published text, and vice versa. Additionally, spellings in the manuscript do not always match those in the published text (not necessarily a significant difference, as editors have been known to regularize or modernize orthography), and one occasionally finds lexical variants in the form of synonyms of similar metrical value. In terms of content, the manuscript does not differ at all from the published text.

Thus available physical evidence tells us that *Advaitaprakāś* predates 1780.

Linguistic evidence

While any good scholar of Bengali linguistics could imitate the language of the sixteenth century, a sixteenth-century writer would not have been able to produce forms not yet in current usage. On the other hand, scribes have been known to 'correct', or modernize, the language of old texts, with the result that their linguistic origins are no longer apparent. Acyutacaran Caudhuri Tattvanidhi discusses this problem in his introduction to *Bālyalīlāsūtra.* Thus linguistic evidence alone is not sufficient to establish a date of composition, but if a text is found to contain no modern usages we must admit the possibility that it might have been composed earlier.

Sukumar Sen (1991, pp. 394-5) states that the language and style of composition of *Advaitaprakāś* are modern, and believes the text to have been composed fairly recently, but does not cite any examples of linguistic anachronism from the work. Ahmad Sharif contends (personal communication) that the language of the text is perfectly consistent with that of other works composed in the late sixteenth century.

I examined the language of the first four chapters of *Advaitaprakāś,* listing all the pronominal and verbal forms found in those chapters because those forms typically reveal the greatest morphological variation, both synchronically and diachronically. I then consulted Suniti Kumar Chatterji's *Origin and Development of the Bengali Language* to determine when those particular forms were first attested in Bengali. My examination of the pronouns revealed a very rich morphology, with considerably more variety than is found in Modern Standard Colloquial Bengali. Several isomorphs seem to have existed in free variation, at least in literary Middle Bengali, and are well-attested in the Caryāgīti (*c.* tenth to twelfth centuries) and in compositions roughly contemporary with the alleged date of composition of *Advaitaprakāś.* For example, *mui, muñi,* and *āmi* were found for the nominative first person singular pronoun; the genitive second person pronoun might be expresssed by *tora, tomāra, tava* or *to.*

The verbal morphology of Advaitaprakāś is similarly consistent with the late sixteenth century. We find past participles in both *-i* and *-iya*, and past tense affixes added to the verb base in *-il-*. As a matter of style, present tense forms are frequently used with past value in historical narrative, as they are in Modern Bengali.

Since the grammar of the text appears to be consistent with the grammar of Middle Bengali of the late sixteenth century, I must reject the contention that the language of *Advaitaprakāś* is modern. A good scholar of Bengali could certainly have produced a work imitating the language of an earlier time, but *Advaitaprakāś* cannot be said to be modern on linguistic grounds. The linguistic evidence, at face value, supports the date of composition given by the author *Advaitaprakāś* in the colophon.

Authorship

One troubling point is that *Advaitaprakāś* is mentioned in none of the other biographies of Advaita or Caitanya, though an Īśān is named in *Advaitamaṅgal* as one of Advaitācārya's disciples. The published edition of *Sītācaritra* (but neither extant manuscript) contains a lengthy section on an Īśān Dās who had come to Advaita's house as a child with his widowed mother. Advaita sent him to Nabadwip as Caitanya's nurse-companion, and after Caitanya's death, Īśān returned to Advaita in Śāntipur. Much later, Sītā urged him to marry and compose Advaita's biography. I suspect the silence regarding the text is due to the fact that *Advaitaprakāś*, like *Bālyalīlāsūtra* and *Sītācaritra*, was produced in the Sylhet area, far removed from the centres of Vaiṣṇava scholarship in Vrindaban and Nabadwip, and remained there until Acyutacaran Caudhuri Tattvanidhi brought them to public attention. These three texts together form a corpus of which scholars are very skeptical, as they seem to have remained unknown until the turn of the present century.

The lack of corroboration regarding the author's identity does not of itself disprove the existence of Īśān Nāgar. One might speculate that his name appears nowhere outside the Advaita corpus because he was a domestic servant who played no role in the life of Caitanya or other sectarian leaders.

The controversies

An examination of which scholars doubt the authenticity of *Advaitaprakāś* and which accept it may provide some insight into the sociological issues surrounding the *Advaitaprakāś* controversy. At least three noted literary scholars reject *Advaitaprakāś* as inauthentic: Bimanbihari Majumdar, Sukhamay Mukhopadhyay, and Sukumar Sen. Bimanbihari Majumdar and Sukhamay Mukhopadhyay may reject *Advaitaprakāś* because they are orthodox Vaiṣṇavas both of whom interpret Caitanya in light of the writings of the Vrindaban gosvāmīs. Sukumar Sen, as mentioned earlier, rejects the text as inauthentic in his *Bāṅglā sāhityer itihās.*

Majumdar's suspicions regarding *Advaitaprakāś* are based on two factors: his acceptance of the Caitanya biographies as true and authentic and his observation that *Advaitaprakāś* contains a profusion of dates.

In his exhaustive *Śrīcaitanyacariter upādān* (1939, pp. 405-89), Bimanbihari Majumdar observes that Īśān Nāgar's accounts of a number of events differ from accounts of the same events in the Caitanya biographies. He further points out that the Advaita works were purportedly written by persons close to Advaita who should not have made such 'factual errors'. All of the authors of these biographies claim to be people who already had some personal connection with Advaita's family before they became devotees. This long-standing close association sets these biographers apart from the writers of the Caitanya corpus, who were devotees first and foremost. Advaita's biographers were in positions which allowed them the sort of intimate access to Advaita's daily life that would not be available to the average devotee: King Divyasiṃha, later known as Lauḍīya Kṛṣṇadās (author of *Bālyalīlāsūtra*), was Advaitācārya's father's employer; Īśān Nāgar was a household servant boy; Haricaraṇ Dās (author of *Advaitamaṅgal*) was a disciple of Advaita's son Acyuta. He bases his account of Advaita's early life, he tells us, on the eyewitness testimony of Īśvar Purī.

The author of *Advaitaprakāś* describes events in Advaita's household as only an insider, particularly a kitchen servant, could: preparations for feeding guests, Sītā's recipes, her manner of cooking. Yet Majumdar refers to various 'factual errors' in the text which he says no one as close to Advaita as Īśān Nāgar should have been, could have made. But Majumdar's conclusion, as mentioned above, is based on the false premise that some texts are more true than others, a premise which entirely misses the point of hagiographical construction.

Majumdar correctly observes that scholars in the late nineteenth century, probably under Western influence, were beginning to concern themselves with matters of origins. South Asian culture traditionally has not been particularly interested in precise historical dates. Majumdar believes that the use of dates is a very modern feature; a sixteenth century Bengali writer would most probably not date events.

I, however, do not find the profusion of dates disturbing. The text purports to have been written thirty years after Caitanya's death, that is, five years after Advaita's death, at the request of Sītādevī. By this time the Gauḍīya Vaiṣṇava community had begun to splinter and bicker among itself, and concerns of succession and legitimacy were arising. Other texts in the Advaita corpus *do* mention dates. *Bālyalīlāsūtra* mentions the date of Rājā Gaṇeśa's conquest of Gauṛ (AD 1407), states that Advaita's parents died at the age of ninety, and gives a date of composition. *Advaitamaṅgal* also gives a date of composition, and while its author Haricaraṇ Dās gives no other dates in the text, he tells us when events occurred in relation to each other. Although, as Majumdar points out, this interest in historical precision is unusual in South Asia, it seems to have been important to members of Advaita's branch of Gauḍīya Vaisnavism from the beginning.

The text is regarded as authentic by Haridas Das, Kalikrishna Bhattacarya, Harilal Chattopadhyay, Dineshcandra Sen, and, at least with regard to date and author, by Ahmad Sharif. This group is more interesting for its diversity: three Gauḍīya Vaiṣṇavas and two great scholars of Bengali literature, one Hindu and one Muslim. Since these people do not share a philosophical background, as did the first group, I find their collective opinion more compelling. I am not suggesting that authenticity should be determined by majority vote, but rather that an opinion shared by scholars of diverse philosophical inclinations unmotivated by sectarian loyalties merits attention. Ahmad Sharif, for example, has told me in private conversations that he finds the account of a well-loved household servant quite believable.

Conclusion

Until recently, scholars have approached hagiography as they would approach historical writings, looking for clearly defined statements of truth about a protagonist, and were frustrated to find little agreement among religious narratives. Forced to select the 'correct' account, they then had to reject others.

Majumdar treated the Gauḍīya Vaiṣṇava biographical materials as historical documents, and accepted the set of biographies of Caitanya as the standard of empirical truth against which he measured the remaining compositions. Subsequent scholars seem to have accepted Majumdar's conclusions on faith because of his reputation as a thorough scholar. This situation demonstrates the difficulties one encounters if one attempts to treat religious documents as historical records from which one can extract some sort of truth about the lives of the people they portray.

The truth these texts convey is rather in the faith of their believers, and in the larger issue of the motivations for the creation of the works. Dismissing one set of accounts simply because it differs from previously discovered compositions is overlooking the religious motivation for the creation of such texts. As Tony Stewart has observed, agreement among religious narratives does not of itself constitute historical accuracy, unless the historical events can be confirmed by independent testimony from sources other than the believing community. Such agreement rather demonstrates that the authors all held the same view. Conversely, differences among them do not necessarily reflect differing degrees of accuracy, but rather different purposes among their authors. 'Sacred biography is religiously motivated discourse, not the history of a religious subject' (1991, p. 232).

I contend therefore that the question of authenticity, arising out of a nineteenth-century fascination with origins, is actually a merely peripheral issue with regard to hagiographical material. Religious biographies are constructed for specific politically and/or socially motivated reasons. These reasons can be deduced by examining the patterns which emerge from a study of the entire corpus treating a given figure. The primary motivation for the creation of *Advaitaprakāś* was clearly to highlight Advaitācārya's essential role in the advent of Caitanya. While this role is mentioned in the biographies of Caitanya, that literature provides little information regarding Advaita's own life and character. The *Caitanyacaritāmṛta,* as mentioned above, was constructed to present an orthodox image of the sect's founder. The Advaita corpus was motivated by different concerns, one of which must have been simply to heighten the status of the leader of a shrinking subsect. Further, *Advaitaprakāś* underscores the democratic message of Caitanya's teachings repeatedly, in episodes involving non-

Brahmins. Thirdly, the man whose name means 'Teacher of Nondualism' is clearly shown as advocating dualistic devotion as the best spiritual approach, and the intellectual approach in which both Caitanya and Advaitācārya were apparently originally trained is described as inadequate. Yet his standing as an elder statesman of orthodox Brahmanism grounded the sect in an accepted tradition from the beginning. As the sect established its own legitimacy through the writings of the six gosvāmīs, it would have less need for an Advaitācārya.

Advaitācārya's own subsect was relatively small, compared to those of Caitanya himself or even Nityānanda, and at least immediately after his death was splintered between the followers of Sītādevī and those of Acyutānanda, his eldest son. Nityānanda and Advaita appear to have quarrelled frequently. Clearly Advaita's followers were interested in ensuring their leader's place in sectarian history, in the face of their own possible disappearance. This emerging pattern of sectarian legitimacy in the face of post-Caitanya factionalism has been largely obscured in the secondary literature by the false issue of historical authenticity.

Thus, with all due respect for an elder statesmen of Bengali literary scholarship, I believe that *Advaitaprakāś* was indeed written by Īśān Nāgar, household servant of Advaitācārya's family, and completed in the late sixteenth century as claimed in the text.

REFERENCES

Majumdar, Bimanbihari. *Śrīcaitanya cariter upādān*. Calcutta: Calcutta University, 1939.

Sen, Sukumar. *Bāṅgla sāhityer itihās*. Pratham khaṇḍa. 6th ed. Calcutta: Ananda Publishers Limited, 1991 (1940).

Stuart, Tony. 'When Biographical Narratives Disagree: The death of Kṛṣṇa Caitanya'. *Numen* 38.2(1991): 231-60.

Viṣṇudās and his *Rāmāyan-kathā*

R. STUART McGREGOR

Our knowledge of Viṣṇudās of Gwalior (AD fifteenth century) starts with Garcin de Tassy, who published a passage from his *Mahābhārata* materials in 1849. Search Reports of the Nagari Pracarini Sabha between 1906 and 1941 then mention a few MSS of *Mahābhārata* and *Rāmāyaṇa* adaptations by Viṣṇudās, but it was only in 1972 that the late Loknath Dvivedi of Sagar published his edition of *Rāmāyan-kathā*. This edition consists of a text based on one nineteenth century MS, with very little editorial material, and it seems that Dvivedi died before his work on it was complete. In 1973 Hariharnivas Dvivedi of Gwalior published an edition of Viṣṇudās's *Mahābhārata* materials, with an introductory account of the poet. Dvivedi regarded both these *Mahābhārata* materials, attested from several sources, and *Rāmāyan-kathā* of which he had seen a MS of 1750 not used by Loknath Dvivedi, as authentic works of our poet. In 1976 and 1979 two further studies appeared, entitled *Kavivar Viṣṇudās aur unkī Rāmāyan-kathā* and *Hindī Rāmkāvya aur Viṣṇudās kī Rāmāyan-kathā*, by Mohansimh Tomar and Balbhadra Tivari respectively. I had the advantage of being able to use all this material when writing briefly on Viṣṇudās in 1984 and again in 1991.

Several circumstances combine to focus interest on Viṣṇudās. First, his *Rāmāyaṇa* version of 1442 is a vernacular forerunner of Tulsīdās's *Rām-carit-mānas,* and may predate the Sanskrit *Adhyātma-rāmāyaṇa*: does it, then, show any affinities with these two related works? Secondly, the fact that Viṣṇudās's Braj Bhāṣā versions of the Rām and Kṛṣṇa stories were composed at the very time, and at a place where a Jain Apabhraṃśa tradition of narrative on the same subjects was still flourishing deserves attention. Thirdly, with fifteenth century Gwalior a focal point of political rivalries between the kingdoms of Delhi and Malva, the success of the Tomar ruler Ḍūṅgarendra Siṃh in maintaining independence may be thought likely to have encouraged an independence of outlook, and with that, some readiness for innovation in literature, in the Gwalior community. My 1991 article touched on these points and possibilities. In this paper I attempt to clear some further ground around *Rāmāyan-kathā*, examining first its structure, and secondly the nature of the poet's work as revealed in his statements, and in his treatment of motifs of the story.

Text

There is first a textual question to consider. L.N. Dvivedi's printed edition must be regarded as provisional. I have not yet seen the *Rāmāyan-kathā* MS of 1750 which H.N. Dvivedi saw at Allahabad, though I had expected to do so before writing this paper. However, I have been able to compare the text of about eighty verses from the MS with that of the edition, since H.N. Dvivedi gives them in an appendix. It seems likely that the two sources—the MS and the edition—represent different recensions of an original text transmitted orally and by writing, and liable to show both loss of original material and addition of new material.[1] The edition is obviously a later version showing alteration and modernisation of readings. Neither source appears to provide a complete text of the poems[2] but both agree on presenting essentially the same material, consisting of closely similar or identical verses in the same order, while the edition provides a coherent version of Vālmīki's Rām story in his Books I-IV. I, therefore, decided that it was reasonable to consider the questions addressed in this paper on the basis of L.N. Dvivedi's edition alone.

Structure

The structure of Viṣṇudāsa's poem differs greatly from the usual *kāṇḍa* structure of *Rāmāyaṇa,* for Vālmīki's six *kāṇḍas* are here reduced to only two. The first of these two parts, which is the shorter, contains the subject matter of Vālmīki's Books I-IV, and the longer second part, that of his Books V-VI dealing with Hanumān's expedition to Laṅkā and the battle with Rāvaṇ. The importance of the Laṅkā theme to Viṣṇudās is emphasised by a great imbalance in Viṣṇudās's treatment of the subject matter of Books I-IV as compared with Vālmīki. Viṣṇudās gives only half as much proportionate space as Vālmīki to the important Book II which is the lynch-pin of the narrative, and also very much less space to Book III (on the wanderings, with the major theme of Sītā's kidnapping). To Book IV, on the other hand (the forming of the alliance with the monkeys), Viṣṇudās assigns twice as much proportionate space as Vālmīki.[3] Thus, not only the Laṅkā theme but also the immediate narrative preliminary to it are strongly emphasised. They comprise together about three quarters of Viṣṇudās's material as compared to about one half of Vālmīki's.

The importance Viṣṇudās gives to the subject matter of Book IV throws another structural feature of his version into relief: the great variation in length in the chapters (*sarg*) into which the whole narrative is divided. The variation is from over two hundred verses down to extremely short chapters of twenty, ten or even fewer verses in a *sarg*. It is striking that almost all the very short chapters occur within the Book IV material as printed; while conversely, and distinguishing the treatment of Book IV material from that of all the other Books, only a few of the thirty-odd chapters dealing with Book IV material are of more than twenty verses.

How do we interpret the long succession of short chapters which take the narrative through Vālmīki's Book IV, but are quite untypical of the rest of Viṣṇudās's text? We can deduce that short chapters were originally present in the text, since we find passages in two short chapters (pp. 90.5, 137.25) where the poet refers to himself as author, exactly as in various longer chapters. The shortness of the chapters does not itself indicate such disregard for the content of Books IV and V as to cast doubt on the coherence of Viṣṇudās's treatment of the Vālmīki story, for the Book IV material bulks proportionately larger in Viṣṇudās than in Vālmīki: Viṣṇudās *was* interested in it. The conjunction of small chapters with full treatment of the narrative outline suggests, rather, a clash between conflicting aims of the poet; concern on the one hand, to present the story complete in modern, popular terms, drastically simplified but not omitting too many narrative details, and concern, on the other hand, to reach the important subject matter of Book VI as quickly as possible. Paradoxically in this situation, it was easier to abbreviate the treatment of the well known Book II than the probably less familiar twists and turns of narrative in Book IV, which, with Book V, will have appeared as a kind of prelude to Book VI. The poet wished to give due space, but not too much space, to this material.

References to Viṣṇudās in the text: use of the term bhakti

The second part of this paper deals with the passages where Viṣṇudās refers to himself and to his composition of *Rāmāyan-kathā*. It is also convenient to consider here Viṣṇudās's understanding of the word *bhakti* and of the Name of Rām.

There are at least sixteen mentions of Viṣṇudās in the text, chiefly found in Viṣṇudās's Book II. One interest they have—an editorial one—is that many occur at the beginning or end of chapters or subsections of chapters, or of complete Books, so that they tend to confirm the authenticity of both the work itself, and the form in which we have received it. A second, larger topic of interest is that of the nature of our poet's references to Vālmīki, and to his source and manner of use of it.

Viṣṇudās acknowledges Vālmīki's authority and supremacy: only Vālmīki could describe the vastness of the troop of monkeys, he tells us at one point, *bālamīki bahu kahiyau baina: dala marajāda sakai kahi kauna?* and he goes straight on to ask for the indulgence of knowledgeable persons, the *gunīs*, towards his own attempt to tell the poem: for who can tell a '*purān*' in its fullest sense, he asks (p. 67.13), *ko purāna kahi sakai visek?* The sense of the word *purān* is not clear from this passage alone. Is it not likely that Viṣṇudās is referring here to later, even recent, *Rāmāyaṇa* versions of the kind we would expect him to have been influenced by: to works such as the Apabhraṃśa *Padmapurāṇa* (*Balabhadrapurāṇa*) of Raidhū, of Ḍūṅgarsī's court, or to the *Pāṇḍavapurāṇa* of Yaśaḥkīrti?[4] We find, though, that there are several references in *Rāmāyan-kathā* to Vālmīki himself uttering or telling the '*purāna*', and so we are probably justified in taking all references of this kind as being to the Sanskrit Rāmāyaṇa. One of the most interesting is at the beginning of Viṣṇudās's Book II. Here the poet seems at first to be saying that he goes beyond the *Rāmāyaṇa* in his account (p. 91.1), *bālmīki riṣi kahyo purāna, bāṛhai kathā ju karauṃ bakhāna.* I think however that the second half-line here about the story's 'being extended' refers merely to Viṣṇudās's being about to continue with his Book II at this point: 'the story proceeds as I shall relate'. On this interpretation, the poet's words imply direct dependence on Vālmīki, rather than on post-Vālmīki developments or modern innovations. Elsewhere (p. 125.18) Viṣṇudās refers to himself, with tantalising brevity, as having worked with written Vālmīki materials: thus he has himself seen the *purān, Viṣṇudāsa kabi dekhi purāna,* and has related it as it stands, *taiso kabita kiyo ju bakhāna.* Elsewhere (p. 122.39) we learn that he has gone through the 'vast book', *mathi grantha apāra,* and 'extracted' the tale, *kāṛhi kathā.*

Viṣṇudās stresses the value of telling and hearing the Rām story in ways which in one respect are up to date, but otherwise are essentially traditional. When he lists various benefits of listening to the story, we do not find the gaining of Bhakti included among them; and when he tells us of his own sense of finding inspiration in the story, he adds that telling it was a work of *dharma* (p. 204.184): *rāma-carita dharma hita kahyau.* Likewise, none of the poet's rather few references to Bhakti (pp. 5.18-20, 8.78-9, 190.154, 125.239) seem to bear the later sense of passionate devotion to a deity. The sons of Daśrath follow *dharma* and show Bhakti for their father: Bhagīrath in his asceticism shows Bhakti for Gaṅgā, and the monkeys show Bhakti in fighting devotedly for Rām; Vibhīṣaṇ tells Rāvaṇ to send Sītā back to Rām and then to offer Bhakti to guru and Brahmins. The vulture Jaṭāyu's Bhakti for the gods may seem at first to be of a different order. Jaṭāyu, who had been mortally wounded by Rāvaṇ while trying to stop Sītā from being carried off, is found and, according to Vālmīki's story, comforted by Rām as he dies. Viṣṇudās follows the same story outline but adds that Jaṭāyu responds with a feeling of Bhakti as he goes to join the gods (p. 43.23), *bhaktivanta devani mili kahyau.* After Jaṭāyu's death, however, Vālmīki tells us that Rām praises him for virtues that have nothing to do with the passion of later Bhakti: for righteousness, and the proper tending of sacred fires (III.64.29-30), *yā gatir yajñaśīlānām āhitāgneś ca yā gatiḥ,* etc. Viṣṇudās is likely to be following Vālmīki here also; and Jaṭāyu's Bhakti (III.8.35 and 40) is different from that implied in *Adhyātma-rāmāyaṇa,* where his destination is 'Rām's abode'.

The Name of Rām, however, does have a connotation of fervent devotion for Viṣṇudās. Bharat holds it in his heart and repeats it while ruling at Nandīgrām (p. 31.82), *rāma nāma japu hiyarāṃ dharai,* and the poet in winding up his Book I refers to the two syllables of the name Rām(a) as an axe to fell the trees of greed and sin (p. 90.8), *rāma te dvai accharani kuṭhāra, sirī kahata ati tīchana dhāra.* The metaphor of an axe is of course a traditional one, but the identity of *this* axe of two syllables has everything to do with the early development of modern Bhakti via the Sant tradition.

Contemporaneity in Viṣṇudās

If we ask finally what other indications of contemporary attitudes can be found in *Rāmāyan-kathā* complementing Viṣṇudās's attitude to the Name of Rām, the answer appears to be 'not many'. It might be expected in the light of the recent history of Gwalior that when a story so central to traditional culture was recast—one in which struggle with unrighteous forces is so emphasised—it would be seen as some kind of allegory of the present. Hans Bakker in his paper to this Conference nine years ago noted the suitability of Rām, whose cult had been established before the main Muslim impact, as a new central deity at this time; and Viṣṇudās in his *Mahābhārata* adaptation refers to Gwalior as a 'thorn in the side of its foes' (*vairinī sāl*) and upholder of *dharma*.[5] In *Rāmāyan-kathā* I have not as yet found any remarks of the latter type. It may be that a modern retelling of *Mahābhārata* material proved so apt an allegory in itself of lengthy resistance, reflecting a new mood of cultural self-assertion, that *Rāmāyan-kathā* was freed to serve more broadly, as an expression of cultural confidence rather than a means of specific assertion of identity or values: simply as a modern version of the Rām story for which there was now a new need.

There can be no doubt that Viṣṇudās's intention was to re-create, rather than to reinterpret, Vālmīki's *Rāmāyaṇa*. This can be illustrated from his handling of major and minor motifs of the story. For instance, following Vālmīki, he leaves Mantharā's jealousy unmotivated, whereas *Adhyātmarāmāyaṇa* (Baij Nath 1979, II.2. 44-6), and later *Rām-carit-mānas* (S.N. Caube 1948, II.11.6-7), find an explanation for it in the gods' intervention. Similarly, he (p. 14.159) makes King Daśrath himself, rather than the guru Vasiṣṭha, tell Rām that he will be exiled. Again, like Vālmīki (G.H. Bhatt 1962 and R. Goldman 1984, I. 73) (and *Adhyātmarāmāyaṇa* [Baij Nath 1979, I.7]) Viṣṇudās (p. 11.125-6) has the meeting between Rām and Parśurām take place while Rām is returning to Ayodhya after his marriage, rather than before he leaves Janakpur. Viṣṇudās's dependence on Vālmīki can be suspected even in a case where his innovation seems to be most his own. When Sītā is first imprisoned in the *aśok* grove she receives a visitation from none other than the god Indra, who comforts her. This is unexampled in the other versions that I have checked so far, including Vālmīki's own. The idea could well have been taken, however, from a remark by Vālmīki's Rāvaṇ, who tells Sītā that it is now beyond the power of the gods, and even Indra himself, to rescue her from Laṅkā (p. 41.74-8), *neyaṃ dhārṣayituṃ śakyā sendrair api surāsuraiḥ.* For Viṣṇudās, to reach Laṅkā at least was not beyond Indra! But even here where the idea seems so original, there is room for suspicion that reproducing the sense of Vālmīki was his real narrative purpose.

Lastly though, there *are* cases where Viṣṇudās's treatment of narrative motifs is comparable with *Adhyātmarāmāyaṇa* and even *Rām-carit-mānas* presentation. Thus his Rām is glad to accept exile (pp. 17.16-18.17; G.H. Bhatt 1962 and R. Goldman 1984, II.16.46-60; Baij Nath 1979, II.3.74), as opposed to Rām's compliant acceptance of exile in Vālmīki. Again, the persona of Daśrath is remoulded to make his predicament when the two boons are asked of him somehow more human: rather than face the full horror of exiling Rām, he prevaricates, as in both the later works, and argues with Kaikeyī as a father might, that only one boon should be performed and that Rām should stay in the palace under Bharat's rule (p. 16.203):

रानी मेरौ बचन करेह। यह न देउ औरै बरु लेह॥
अरु पुनि देउ भरथ कहँ राजु। बन जनि राम पठावै आजु॥

I am hoping to continue to work on *Rāmāyan-kathā* to produce an edition if that seems appropriate. This will involve among other things considering Viṣṇudās's narrative technique and the nature and extent of his sources, and also the extent to which he can be seen as a precursor of later attitudes of Bhakti.

NOTES

1. Thus 'old' *tadbhava* words and forms found in MS can be replaced or lost in ed., e.g. MS (p. 185.39)
   ko riṣi siṃgī kabana kau jāu
   kyauṁ āvai yoṁ jaṁpai rāu
   'Who is ṛṣi Śṛṅgī? When was he born?
   How can he (be got to) come here?' says the king.
   [*jāu, OIA jāta-*];

   Cf. ed. (p. 2.27)
   ko sriṃgī riṣi kākau putra
   kyoṁ āvai pura kahau sumaṃtra

Loss of an 'old' word can lead to confusion in an entire line of ed., e.g. MS (p. 184.30)

bauhata bāga maṃdira dvehare
kuvā nivāna sarovara bhare
many gardens, various temples,
well-constructions, tanks filled with water [*dvehare,* fr. *OIA deva-ghara-*];

Cf. ed. (p. 2.17)

bahuta bāga maṭha sara bāurī
kuva nivānani sobhita purī

Here the sense of the final items of the line as given in MS has been taken back in ed. to the first part of the line, with consequent alterations including provision of a makeshift rhyme in the second part, and a new filler phrase containing a *tatsama* word. Oral trans-mission is implied; MS pronunciation-spelling *bauhata* agrees with this; the status of *tatsama* words is shown to be doubtful.

2. For example, twelve couplets of invocation to king and queen, to Vālmīki and legendary persons, and to guru, etc., are absent in MS. On the other hand, ed. omits (p. 30 foll. v. 30a) all but the first line of a MS passage of seventeen lines, an early part of which is needed for narrative continuity (to explain why the *gaṇikās* are to bring the boy-ascetic Śṛṅgī to Romapāda's city); cf. text given in H.N. Dvivedi 1973, p. 155. The idea for the MS passage, which is a *nakh-sikh* description, may arise from Vālmīki's single reference to the *gaṇikās* as (I.9) *rūpavatyaḥ svalaṅkṛtāḥ* 'beautiful and well adorned'.
3. Viṣṇudās's pt. I (*kāṇḍa)* contains 1191 verses, his pt. II 1599 verses, making a total of 2790 verses in these two parts of RK. Almost all these verses are *caupahī* couplets; there are a few verses of other kinds (including some Sanskrit verses (*śloka*). The number of RK verses assigned to the subject matter of Vālmīki's Books I-VI is, respectively, 248, 217, 185, 541, 447, 1152.
4. Information about these unpublished texts, with citations from them, in H. Kochar, 1956, pp. 116-22; R.R. Jain 1974, pp. 645-8.
5. See now H. Bakker 1987, p. 21; H.N. Dvivedi 1973, pp. 5, 71. In Yaśaḥkīrti's *Padmapurāṇa* Ḍūṅgarsī is referred to as 'uprooting the powerful *mlecchas'* (*jiṃ pabalahaṁ micchahaṁ khaṇiü kaṃdu*); text in R.R. Jain 1974, p. 646.

REFERENCES

Baij Nath, trans. *The Adhyātma Rāmāyaṇa.* 2nd ed. New Delhi: Oriental Books Reprint Corporation, 1979.

Bakker, H. 'Reflections on the evolution of Rāma devotion in the light of textual and archaeological evidence'. *Wiener Zeitschrift für die Kunde Südasiens* XXXI (1987): 9-42.

Bhatt, G.H., ed. *Vālmīki Rāmāyaṇa.* 2 pts. Baroda: Oriental Institute, 1962.

Caube, S.N., ed. *Rām-carit-mānas.* Varanasi: Nagari Pracharini Sabha, 1948.

Dvivedi, H.N. *Mahābhārat.* Gwalior: Vidyamandir Prakashan, 1973.

Dvivedi, L.N. *Rāmāyan-kathā.* Allahabad: Sahitya Bhavan, 1972.

Garcin de Tassy. *Chresthomatie hindie et hindouie.* Paris: Imprimerie Nationale, 1849.

Goldman, R.P., ed. *The Rāmāyaṇa of Vālmīki.* Vol. 1 trans. R.P. Goldman, Vols. II and III trans. S.I. Pollock. Princeton: Princeton University Press, 1984.

Jain, R.R. *Raydhū sāhitya kā ālocanātmak pariśīlan.* Research Institute of Prakrit, Jainology and Ahimsa. Department of Education, Government of Bihar: Vaishali, 1974.

Kochar, H. *Apabhraṃśa sāhitya.* Delhi: Bharati Sahitya Mandir, 1956.

McGregor, R.S. *Hindi Literature from its Beginnings to the Nineteenth Century. History of Indian Literature.* Ed. J. Gonda, VIII.6. Wiesbaden: Harrassowitz, 1984.

———. 'An early Hindi version of the Rāma story'. In *Devotion divine: Bhakti Traditions from the Regions of India. Studies in honour of Charlotte Vaudeville.* Ed. D.L. Eck and F. Mallison, pp. 181-96. Groningen: Egbert Forster, Paris, EFEO, 1991.

Tivari, B. *Kavivar Viṣṇudās aur unkī Rāmāyan-kathā.* Allahabad: Sahitya Bhavan, 1979.

Tomar, M.S. *Hindī Rāmkāvya aur Viṣṇudās kī Rāmāyan-kathā.* Delhi: Takshashila Prakashan, 1976.

Bībī Imām Begam and the End of the Ismaili Ginānic Tradition

ZAWAHIR MOIR

Apart from the evidence afforded by her own rather personal and poignant Gināns, very little is known for certain about Sayyida Bībī Imām Begam, the last composer of the Ismaili Gināns in the Indian subcontinent. Contemporary nineteenth-century accounts, printed and manuscript, do not seem to provide any direct evidence for her life and activities. In fact the very sparse sources available, consisting mainly of oral traditions handed down through the Ismaili communities in Bombay and Karachi, and some printed accounts compiled for the community in the early part of this century, only permit us to construct a very sketchy picture of her life.[1]

In this paper I will begin by summarising what is known about her life, and then go on to explore certain aspects of it in more detail so as to draw out her wider significance in the development of the Ismaili Khoja tradition in South Asia. Finally, I will briefly examine her Gināns; their basic forms and features, their main themes and teachings, and their place within the Ginānic literature as a whole.

Bībī Imām Begam appears to have been born in the late eighteenth or early nineteenth century either in Bombay or Cutch. She belonged to the family of the Kaḍīwālā Sayyids (originating from Pir Shams of Multan), who performed preaching and propagating activities for the Ismaili *da'wa* in Gujarat from the sixteenth century onwards. Nothing certain is known about her parents or her early life.[2] A contemporary writer Sachedina Nanjiani, in his book *Khojā vratānt* (1892) does not mention her by name, nor does the author of *Gulzāre Shams* (S. Malick, n.d.), a compilation of the late nineteenth century which registers the descendants of Pir Shams.

From the existing meagre sources of the Ismaili community, it appears that she lived for much of her early life in Thana, in the vicinity of Bombay, where she had a small house. Nobody seems to know her real name except that she is always referred to as Imām Begam, i.e. the Lady of the Imām. This appears as her poetical name in her ten short compositions as printed by the Ismaili community in their official, early twentieth century edition of the Ginān literature rendered in the Khojkī script (Devraj, 1920).

As a member of the official *da'wa* system of the Kaḍīwālā Sayyids (so named because they lived in a town called Kaḍī, about twenty miles from Ahmadabad), she appears to have been well-grounded in the Ginānic tradition and the associated languages. In her compositions she mainly uses the mixed Gujarati/Hindi language with Siraiki, Sanskrit, Persian and Arabic terminology in the usual Ginānic idiom. Her Gināns also display a knowledge of Haṭha Yoga practices, as well as a familiarity with the usual mystical and devotional themes of the Ginān literature (see 258-60). It seems fairly certain that she would also have acquired a knowledge of the Khojkī script, but no manuscripts or documents in her own hand have so far come to light. In addition to the works included in the official canon, a few more of her compositions are reported to have survived in private collections, but so far I have been unable to have access to these (M.T. Sadik Ali 1989, p. 17).

In Bombay, where much of her life was spent,[3] she gradually emerged as a talented preacher and composer of original works of piety and devotion. She learned to play the *sāraṇgī*, and it is reported in the oral tradition that she played her own compositions on her instrument and set them to *rāgs* as well. This appears to have been not uncommon among the early Ismaili preachers in South Asia, who are often said to have sung Gināns, occasionally accompanied by musical instruments, in order to propagate their religious message. Some of her other earlier activities are also mentioned in the traditional accounts, viz., that she preached to Hindus in Bombay, and at one time travelled to Karachi via Cutch. In this connection it has been claimed that she intended to visit the Ismaili Imām (resident in Iran until the 1840s), but could not do so (M.T. Sadik Ali 1989, p. 17).

Although it is clear from several sources that Imām Begam also spent long periods of her life in Karachi, and eventually died there, it is not yet possible to establish any full or accurate chronology for her early connections with that city. One recent account, for example, suggests that she may have spent some time there even before 1814, living at Miran Pir in the Lyari quarter (near Lea Market), and that she may also have returned during the 1830s. In the absence of firm evidence this has to remain conjectural. However, one interesting element common to several traditional accounts of her early connections with Karachi is the story of her romantic attachment to Sayyid Ghulam Haidar Shah, a noted Ismaili preacher who apparently lived in the city during the first few decades of the nineteenth century, along with other Ismaili Sayyids. According to these accounts, he is supposed to have proposed to Imām Begam, and to have regularly ridden out from his home in Kharadhar to visit her and her family near Lea Market. As will be seen a little later on, there is perhaps some material basis for this story, in the shape of their two graves which now lie side by side in the old Ismaili cemetery at Mian Shah near Lea Market (Gh. Allana 1984, p. 13, M.T. Sadik Ali 1989, p. 16 and M. Khoja).

Although the details of her early connections with Karachi thus remain obscure, most of the available sources at any rate seem to agree that (a) she was living again in Bombay by the early 1840s, if not before, and (b) she finally decided to shift her residence from there to Karachi some time after the arrival of Imām Hasan Ali Shah, Agha Khan I, in Bombay in 1845- perhaps as late as 1860. The reasons for her decision are as usual somewhat variously described by the different sources. For instance, in the community's officially published *Collection of Ginans* of 1954 (pp. 9-10), it is reported on hearsay that she had in some unspecified way disobeyed the Imām, but that, though displeased, he had allowed the remuneration she received as a descendant of the Kaḍīwālā Sayyids to be continued on account of the great services they had rendered to the cause of Ismailism in India. Other stories current in Bombay and Karachi allege that she was actually ex-communicated by the Imām and that she incurred his displeasure through her practice of arranging lengthy religious gatherings for women in the city (M.T. Sadik Ali 1989, pp. 16-21).

Having left Bombay for good some time between 1845 and 1860, it appears that Imām Begam finally settled down in Karachi for the rest of her life. A small room near Lea Market is believed to have been her last home. It is known as Dargāh Imām Begam. A few of her personal possessions are on display there but the room itself is almost bare. Here it is popularly remembered that she used to sing her Gināns in a melodious voice, accompanying herself on the *sāraṅgī* or *sitār*.[4]

Two contrary dates are given for her death. Azim Nanji (1978, pp. 94 and 173), citing an unspecified twentieth century publication, puts her death at the beginning of the twentieth century, while another writer (A. Aziz 1974, p. 165) puts it at 1866, at the age of eighty. Unfortunately, no reliable records of the births and deaths of most composers of the Gināns are kept by the community, even amongst the early surviving manuscript copies of the Gināns. However, from the surviving manuscripts it seems that her Gināns began to be copied from 1880 onwards; so it is likely that she may have died in the third quarter of the nineteenth century. As already mentioned, she is buried next to Sayyid Haidar Shah at Mian Shah in Karachi. There a veil is maintained between their two graves, perhaps suggesting that they were not actually married. It is, however, possible that this veil may have been put there more recently.[5] There are no inscriptions on her grave, and male visitors are not allowed. With her death, the line of Kaḍīwālā Sayyids ended, as did the Ginān tradition itself.

In order to appreciate the wider significance of Imām Begam's role in the Ismaili tradition, it is necessary to recall the basic character of the Ismaili *da'wa* system as it existed in the subcontinent before the arrival of the Imām in the early 1840s. As various sources, including British Indian government archives, make clear, the main Khoja Ismaili communities had been controlled since the sixteenth century or so by several branches of Sayyids with their headquarters at Bhuj in Cutch and other parts of Sindh[6] and Gujarat, such as Kaḍī. These leaders were responsible for collecting tithes from the followers of the Imām who then resided in Iran. They and their agents not only collected the dues but delivered them to the Imām, who in turn gave them some remuneration. Besides maintaining the communities' account books for these purposes, many of the Sayyids themselves composed Gināns and either copied them into the Khojkī manuscripts or arranged for their copying. They also performed various other pastoral duties besides preaching and converting. Over the years the Sayyids had thus become largely autonomous, receiving great respect from their followers, especially when they returned from their visits to their Imām with fresh guidance.

From the surviving Khojkī manuscripts and other contemporary records it appears that the Kaḍīwālā Sayyids played a very prominent part in these activities. Sayyid Ghulam Ali Shah (d. 1796) had visited the Imām in Iran, and both he and his wife Ajan Bībī (S. Nanjiani 1892, pp. 232-4) were generally active in preaching and converting in the Kera area of Cutch. Similarly, his successor, Sayyid Muhammad Shah (d. 1813), was active in Bombay and many parts of Sindh, Punjab and Gujarat. Next in line was Sayyid Burhanuddin Shah and it is even possible that Imām Begam was his daughter, and thus the last of the Kaḍīwālā Sayyids in Bombay (S. Nanjiani 1892, p. 236). As mentioned earlier, she was given some remuneration for her duties of preaching and composing Ginān s. But her responsibilities did not include the collection of the dues.

That the Ginān tradition itself should end not with a man but a woman is not as surprising as it may first appear. It was by no means exceptional among the old Ismaili communities for a woman to achieve the kind of position attained by Imām Begam. In fact one of the special features of the Ginān literature—distinguishing it from the rest of the Indo-Muslim hagiographical tradition—is the presence of so many powerful women personalities. Rānī Pālan De, Surājā Rānī and Satī Tārā Rānī are a few such women who appear in the Ginān s, guiding and transmitting religious knowledge, and conducting religious services, as well as being among the earlier notable converts to the *Sat-panth* (true path) (C. Shackle and Z. Moir 1992, pp. 191-2). This feature of the literature may perhaps partly reflect the peculiar Ismaili religious milieu in which certain Hindu ideas and practices were brought together with Islamic themes and doctrines.

Moreover, even before Imām Begam, women had sometimes played a part in composing or inspiring some of the Ginān s. Bāī Buḍhāī, the sister of Sayyid Imām Shah (d. 1513) was co-composer with him of the long Ginān known as *Bāī Buḍhāī*. Also the Kaḍīwālā Sayyid Ghulam Ali addressed his famous long Ginān called *Manahar* to his wife Ajan Bībī (A. Khaki 1971, pp. 10-30). He and his wife are also said to have mixed freely with Hindu Yogis in Cutch. Bībī Imām Begam flourished within this tradition, and as her Ginān s show, was herself well-versed in the yogic idiom long favoured by the composers of the Ginān s, and her compositions were also probably sung by Hindus in Bombay (A. Aziz 1974, p. 165). As such, it is probable that she did not observe the veil, despite reports to the contrary in some oral accounts.

The period of Imām Begam's direct contact with the Imām Hasan Ali Shah in the 1840s was one of considerable social and religious turmoil amongst the Khoja Ismaili community. This unrest was partly occasioned by the Imām's decision to leave Iran and take up residence amongst his Indian followers, but in a wider sense it was also related to the more general upheavals in traditional Indian societies brought about by the spread of British rule in Western India. Within the Khoja community a number of rich Khojas in Bombay Presidency had already started to refuse to pay their customary dues to the Imām as early as the 1820s. To deal with this problem the Imām sent his mother, an eloquent speaker, to Bombay in 1829, accompanied according to one account by Imām Begam amongst others (M.T. Sadik Ali 1989, pp. 16-17). However, despite this effort, the local disputes refused to go away, and indeed began to grow more complex and challenging when the Imām himself arrived in India in 1843, following an unsuccessful attempt to maintain his position in Iran.

Once settled in Bombay, he gradually began to introduce a number of social and religious changes in the set-up of the local community, designed to establish and define his own authority in the new circumstances that had arisen. For instance, he appointed his younger brother Mirza Muhammad Bāqir and other family members to look after the affairs of the community, thus giving them authority to collect dues. This brought him into conflict with the Sayyids of Bhuj who had traditionally exercised these functions. Not only did they then refuse to pay allegiance to the Imām but they also created their own independent order in Cutch (A. Cunara 1936, pp. 615-18).

Meanwhile several court cases involving disputes within the Khoja community were brought before the Bombay High Court. In one of these the right of Khoja women to inherit property was contested. Faced with these new issues, it seems that the British jurists were themselves undecided. In 1847 Justice Perry ruled that the Khoja women were subject to Hindu customary law, thus depriving them of the rights of inheritance enjoyed by other Shia Muslim women (J. Masselos 1976, pp. 97-116).

Perry's judgement also in effect constituted a challenge to the Agha Khan's own position since he himself naturally considered the community to be bound by Shiite Ismaili law and his own authority to be derived from it. Thereafter several Khoja families went so far as to refuse to acknowledge his special position as the head of the community and brought a case to challenge this in 1866. This time, however, after lengthy investigation, Justice Arnould decided the case in Agha Khan's favour. This decision did not affect the validity of Perry's earlier decision about the inheritance rights of Khoja women, but it did have the obvious consequence of strengthening the Imām's authority. After this those who still refused to accept that authority either formed their own breakaway sect or threw in their lot with the larger Sunni or Shia groups; while Agha Khan himself assumed the Pirship of the Ismaili community in addition to his role as Imām (Shihab al Din Shah 1963, p. 19).

It is tempting to look for some kind of connection between these wider Khoja disputes about the position of the Agha Khan in India and the stories about his alleged displeasure with Imām Begam. It must, however, be said that the paucity of evidence hardly lends any weighty support to such speculations. Thus, there is nothing to suggest that the gatherings of women, which Imām Begam is said to have encouraged in Bombay, were in any sense dissident groups sympathetic to such movements. On the contrary, both the oral tradition and Imām Begam's own Gināns imply that whatever disputes may have arisen, and despite her move to Karachi, she herself remained faithful to the Imām and continued to pay allegiance to him. This feeling of devotion comes across very strongly in certain passages of her Gināns, such as in Ginān 1 verse 4 (=1: 4):

kahet imām begam merā pīr hasan shāh

Imām Begam says, My master is (Imām) Hasan Shah.

And in another of her compositions she pleads for a vision of her master and considers herself his handmaiden. Incidentally, these Gināns are even today still very popular in the Ismaili *jamatkhanas* (Pers. *jamā'at-khāna*).

On the other hand, as will emerge later in this paper, there is perhaps a larger connection to be made between the changing relationship between the Imām and the community which follows on his arrival in India, and the ending of the Ginān tradition, of which Imām Begam was the last exemplar. But before going on to consider this last aspect, it seems appropriate at this stage to turn to her Gināns, and examine their form and content in a little more detail.

According to the official compilations of Gināns printed for the community, there are only ten Gināns (see the list in the appendix) attributed to Imām Begam, though it has recently been claimed that she composed as many as thirty-two (M.T. Sadik Ali 1989, pp. 16-21). In the absence of concrete evidence, however, it is difficult to be sure whether the official corpus is incomplete. Unfortunately, too, we have no reliable means of determining exactly how many of her Gināns were extant at the time when the first general edition of the Ginān literature in Khojkī script was printed by Mukhi Lalji Devraj *c.* 1905, since all the manuscripts used by him are reported to have been subsequently destroyed. All we can say is that by that date at least ten of her works were available to him in manuscript form. This would also imply that these particular works had already been accepted as Gināns by the original copyists concerned, presumably on the basis of their awareness of Imām Begam's status as a member of the Ismaili *da'wa* and a descendant of the Kaḍīwālā Sayyids.

After the Devraj edition was issued, her ten Gināns were reprinted several times by the community, which had the effect of spreading knowledge of her works more widely.[7] It is, of course, also possible that copies of other Gināns not included in the official canon may exist elsewhere in private manuscripts, but I myself have only been able to trace nine manuscript versions of her Gināns in the course of cataloguing some of the community's major manuscript collections, and the texts of these are more or less identical with the versions as printed by Devraj.

In their general poetic form, Imām Begam's Gināns largely follow the traditional pattern of Ginānic literature, though, as we shall see, they also exhibit some individual features. All ten of her compositions fall into the category known as short Gināns, consisting of four to fourteen verses each. Altogether, there are eighty stanzas of two lines, excluding refrains. None of her Gināns have separate titles, so, like most of the Ismaili Gināns, they are identified by their first lines. In her case, since all her Gināns begin with refrains, it is these that are treated as their titles; this makes them rather unusual. These refrains are repeated in recitation after each of the main verses, for all her Gināns are meant to be sung and are set to *rāgas.* Most of them begin with the usual Ginānic interjection, *ejī, o,* and end with her poetical name in the last verse.

The style of her expression is very simple, and draws upon the earlier Ginānic forms. particularly those used by Muhammad Shah (d. 1813). She in fact integrates local popular form, rather in the style of folk poetry (A. Asani 1991, p. 10), and does not go in for deliberate artistic effects. The formal structure of the verses follows the usual Indian metres, comprising long and short syllables. Usually both her lines are divided into two unequal syllabic measures, with here and there a few additional words added. It cannot be determined how much of this is in the originals and how much may have entered through faulty textual transmission. Her verses generally maintain rhymes, and occasionally include a few instances of alliteration, metaphor and simile.[8] She favours a very direct form of speech, as illustrated in the line quoted earlier. In one Ginān, where she addresses her own mind, she even adopts a direct conversational style (2: 4):

> tujhe kiyā kahūṅ man merā, tujhe lāj na ātī hae
>
> What should I say to you, O my mind, you have no shame!

Imām Begam's Gināns draw on the composite idiom of the Ginānic literature, using Gujarati, Hindi, Siraiki, Sanskrit, Persian and Arabic terms. On the whole, however, she appears to favour the mixed Gujarati/Hindi language as the basis for the expression of her ideas. Her lyrical and simple verses employ social imagery, often of a rustic and vivid character. Perhaps in keeping with the Khoja community's trading interests, she describes life as a precious jewel (*mānakhā janam ratan hae*) and wonders why waste precious diamonds and pearls (*hīrā ratan motī*). To her the body is like gold (*kancan sarīkhī kāyā*) and she sees worldly life as a bubble of water (*pānī kā parapoṭā*) or a fistful of air (*vāyūn kī muṭhī*) (2: R [refrain] 2: 4, 3: 1, 3: 2).

Her Gināns also evoke certain moods appropriate to certain occasions and are thus sung by the congregation in choral mode. For instance, nos. 4 and 10 are sung for funeral occasions because their imagery reflects the transitory nature of life and the presence of death. But the principal occasion for the recital of her Gināns (nos. 5, 7, 8 and 9) is before the meditation sessions begin. In these she sets the tone either by addressing her own mind or entreating her lord, and sometimes by calling upon her fellow human beings (*bhāī*), thus enhancing the direct personal quality of her appeal.

In the field of themes, Imām Begam's Gināns show a slight departure from the Ginānic mainstream. This is most noticeable in her omission of the concept of *das avatār,* i.e. the ten manifestations of Viṣṇu, a very important theological preoccupation in most Ginānic literature. Otherwise, her Gināns contain the usual teachings about the *satpanth,* or true path, as transmitted by the Kaḍīwālā Sayyids and their predecessors. Overall she emphasises three main aspects or themes.[9]

First, there is the duty to follow the true path and its *sharī'at* or law. This is not actually explained, but to her—as to her ancestor Sayyid Muhammad Shah—it would appear to entail full commitment to the duties of the congregation, i.e. the *gat* (C. Shackle and Z. Moir 1992, pp. 160, 170, 155). Thus she enjoins the payment of tithes and the regular participation in the ceremony of holy water (*aṁīras*) that takes place at the court of the *Imām* (*shāh pīr ke darbār*) (3: 8), that is, in the *jamatkhana,* where the Lord master is everpresent (*hae-zinda*) (3: 11). In one Ginān (no. 3) she simply advises her brethren to observe all the above rituals and duties of the true path. As mentioned earlier, she also stresses the inevitability of death (*maranā hae re zarūr*) (4: R), and (in nos. 4 and 10) of the final reckoning when the Lord will call everyone to account for their deeds in the world. Unlike other Gināns, her compositions do not describe the torments of hell, but she does speak of the dark grave where a heavy weight will lie on the head (*tujhe ghor meṅ sulāve*) (3: 5). There are echos here of the teachings of Sayyid Ghulam Ali Shah (C. Shackle and Z. Moir 1992, p. 118).

The second most important part of her teachings is concerned with the right understanding of human life, which for her is always very precious. Within the body, which is made up of five elements, she says that the human mind (*man*) is like a *rājā* in a city. In its unregenerate state the mind is blinded by the five instinctual thieves (*paṅc cor*), which (like Sayyid Ghulam Ali Shah) she identifies with lust, anger, greed, attachment and pride. Ultimately, these passions lead to human destruction, and it is only by following an upright path, remaining constantly vigilant, and keeping the unregenerate mind under control that life's goal is realised.

For Imām Begam, it is through self-awareness that the mind

and its selfish impulses can be subdued. In Gināns nos. 2 and 3, which perhaps represent her most original contribution, she characteristically seems to wrestle with these problems by addressing and questioning herself (3: R):

tum cet man merā, jug manhe kon terā.

Be warned, O my mind! Who in the world is yours?

The world she depicts as a place of illusion, and the body as transient and insubstantial, like a bubble which bursts in no time. In one day, she says, one expels or loses twenty-one thousand and six hundred breaths: 'O! trader what do you earn?' (*vaṇjārā tuṅ kiyā kamātā hae*) (2: 7). So she urges herself and her brothers to avoid the fate of the worldly, the consequences of which she describes in terms of *pherā,* i.e. the continuous cycles of return from one form of existence to another.

This destructive cycle can only be escaped by opening the heart through loving devotion and daily meditation (*zikar* 'remembrance'). It is for this reason that she places such great emphasis upon the proper practice of *jāp* ('recitation'), in what amounts to the third main area of her teachings. Gināns 7, 8 and 9 deal at length with these aspects. Here, however, she is not concerned with the oral recitation of the word (*sabad*) but with the so-called hidden remembrance (*ajampiā jāp*), in which the Lord's name is repeated internally without the actual movement of the tongue (*bin rasanā*).

Formerly, these three Gināns were sung in full before the meditation services in some of the *jamatkhanas.* Nowadays, however, only a few verses are sung because the other verses make use of yogic terms which are not now approved, In particular, she describes how in meditation, when one's attention and consciousness are focused upon the space between the eyebrows (*bhamar ghuphā*), the body's energy, which lies coiled at the navel (*nābhī*), begins to rise (2: 6):

ejī nābhī se jab uṭhe, vank nār rasatā le,
triveṇī ke tīr par, das mānhe ṭhor rahe.

When it (consciousness) arises from the navel, through a crooked path it reaches the banks of three rivers, and remains fixed at the tenth path.

In verses 7: 6 and 9: 5 she refers to that tenth abode as *dasmā dvār*, and as the cavity between the eyebrows. And *nābhī* and *mūlādhār* (as in 7: 7) according to her are said to be located at the base of the spine, whence the three nerve channels called *iḍā*, *piṅglā* and *suṣumṇā*, rise and meet at the confluence (*triveṇī*). She also urges her brothers to awaken their energies in order to achieve enlightenment (*iyūn karī darsan pāiyeṅ*) (7: 7).

In addition to the practice of meditation, Imām Begam frequently emphasises the need for loving devotion. Thus she sees the Lord as present in every vein of our bodies, like fragrance in flowers. It is through the Lord's grace that enlightenment can be achieved. She prays to her Lord with folded hands, and very humbly, for the vision (*didār*) in very personal terms:

sāmī hūn chūn dāsī mune darasan kī ās jī
sāmī mārī venatī darajo kān (9: 9)

Lord I am your maid servant, I have hopes of the vision
Lord give ear to my supplication.

Here and elsewhere in her texts she uses words like *sāmī*, *sataguru*, *mahārāj*, *nar naklaṅki* as interchangeable terms for Lord (C. Shackle and Z. Moir 1992, p. 22).

From all these passages it appears that she had been initiated into esoteric practices, but it is not clear whether she had any *sataguru* outside the Ismaili tradition though it is known that she mixed with Hindu Yogis in Bombay who are also said to recite her Gināns. In only one of her Gināns does she give us a rare glimpse of her personal religious experience. Here she says that the vision of her '*sataguru*' has dispelled all her illusions and brought her immense bliss; she claims to have achieved high status (*mahāpad*) but does not go into the 'Sufi stages' of ecstasy, simply stating that her experience is beyond description. It is untouched by fear of death and rebirth and there is only eternal light and unstruck music.

Finally, one wider question about the significance of Imām Begam's Gināns in the Ismaili Ginānic tradition needs to be briefly addressed. As indicated earlier, that tradition effectively comes to an end as a living literature soon after the arrival of Imām Hasan Ali Shah in India in the 1840s. Clearly, it is most unlikely (despite the stories of misunderstanding) that Imām Begam's Gināns *per se* were responsible for the closure of the tradition; rather, they may be seen as its last flowering, coincident upon its demise (for a brief discussion of the so-called 'Coronation Hymn', which may possibly have been composed later than Imām Begam's Gināns, see C. Shackle and Z. Moir 1992, p. 165). So this specific question is really about the factors that led to that demise.

Although Ismaili literature itself is somewhat surprisingly silent on this issue, it seems fairly certain that the general explanation is to be found in the new ethos established in the community after the transfer of the Imāmate to India. As we have seen, that event was followed by a new assertion of the Agha Khan's authority as both Imām and Pir, advanced in the face of several dissident challenges. It was also accompanied by a corresponding reduction in the powers previously exercised by the traditional local elites of the Khoja community, the Sayyids, their families and agents, whose position ultimately derived from the great line of Ismaili Pirs whose Indian mission dates from medieval times. Broadly speaking, the position of the former leaders had two complementary aspects: the collection of tithes and the dispensing of spiritual guidance. From the mid-nineteenth century, both these functions were being directly assumed by the Imām; his own agents became responsible for the collections, while he himself took over the spiritual direction of his followers, especially through the regular issue of *farmāns*. Within this new and evolving framework the Gināns as a living tradition had largely become redundant.

It is, however, possible to tentatively offer a parallel, less mechanistic, more metaphorical interpretation of these developments. In the centuries that preceded the transfer of the Imāmate, the physical and mental space that intervened between the Imāms in Iran and their Indian followers was such as to permit and encourage the formation of a largely autonomous Khoja religious tradition in South Asia. Within this tradition the Gināns played a crucial, vitalising role, both in helping to create the first communities of converts to the Satpanth, and later in holding them together in their *jamats* in an environment that was frequently hostile. The Gināns whose authorship was attributed to the charismatic line of Pirs and Sayyids, through whom the Imām's authority in India was mediated, achieved a new kind of religious expression in which the spiritual vocabulary of Hindu converts was used to convey the message of an Islamic mysticism (C. Shackle and Z. Moir 1992, pp. 28-30).

However, though sincerely dedicated to the faraway Imāms and forever yearning for their presence, the Ginānic tradition was also in some sense socially and culturally predicated on their absence. Thus once the Imām crossed that wide divide to make direct contact with his followers, it was perhaps inevitable that much of the old Ismaili Khoja *da'wa,* including the Ginān tradition, would begin to crumble. In this situation, too, it is somehow fitting that the last composer of the Gināns, Imām Begam, should have felt moved to leave the Bombay of Hasan Ali Shah for Karachi, thus restoring a traditional measure of distance between herself and the Imām to whom she had pledged eternal fidelity.

Not, of course, that the Gināns were abandoned by the community or dropped from their *jamatkhanas.* On the contrary, many of the manuscripts containing them were collected and preserved, and, as has been seen, eventually assembled and printed in a number of standard editions dating from the early twentieth century onwards. Even today, they occupy a central place in the services of the *jamatkhanas,* not only in South Asia, but in Western Europe and North America—wherever the Ismaili diaspora has reached. And among these Gināns none are sung with more rapt devotion, especially by women, than the Gināns of Bībī Imām Begam.

APPENDIX I

LIST OF IMĀM BEGAM'S GINĀNS

1. *Āe rahem rahemān.* Refrain + 4 verses.
2. *Uth jāg man merā.* Refrain + 8 verses.
3. *Tum cet man merā.* Refrain + 10 verses.
4. *Maranā hae re jarūr.* Refrain + 8 verses.
5. *Darašan deyo morā nāth.* Refrain + 14 verses.
6. *Satagur maliā mune āj.* Refrain + 6 verses.
7. *Haradam japo pīrshā.* Refrain + 7 verses.
8. *Haradam karo abhiās.* Refrain + 9 verses.
9. *Haradam dharie dhiān.* Refrain + 10 verses.
10. *Saeāṅ jī more ḍar lāgo.* Refrain + 4 verses.

APPENDIX II

TRANSLITERATION OF GINĀN NO. 6

R. ejī satagur maliā mane āj, ānaṅd huṅ pāmī.
1. ejī satagur maliā tāre dhokhāj ṭaḍiyā jī,
 sarve sāriā dāsī nā kāj.

2. ejī daraśan dekhyā man santokhiā jī,
mahāpad pāmī chuṅ rāj.
3. ejī mahāpad kerī bhāī vāt che nyārī jī,
koi na jāṇe e kāj.
4. ejī jo jāṇe so nar navkhaṅḍ māṇe,
ghaṭo ghaṭ dekhe mahārāj.
5. ejī ghaṭo ghaṭ dekhe tāre ek karī lekhe jī,
nar nakalankī nuṅ rāj.
6. ejī kahet imam begam suno morā bhāī jī,
alī nabī che siratāj.

TRANSLATION

R. Today I had the vision of the Lord and I have achieved bliss.
1. When I found the Lord, illusions vanished,
All the endeavours of this maidservant were rewarded.
2. When I beheld the vision, my heart was gratified,
I have attained a high station, a kingdom.
3. The account of this high station is of a different order, O brother,
None can understand this process.
4. Whosoever recognises this, that person enjoys the nine continents,
He sees the Lord in every heart.
5. When he perceives (the Lord) everywhere, he counts Him as One,
This is the kingdom of the Lord Master.
6. Imām Begam says, Listen O my brother,
Ali and the Prophet are the supreme ones.

NOTES

1. No full account of Imām Begam, and of the popular traditions concerning her life, has yet been published. For these traditions I have drawn on the fragmentary materials contained in Bombay Ismailia Association, *Collection of Gināns* 1954, vol. 4, pp. 9-10; G. Allana 1984; A.A. Aziz 1974; and M.T. Sadik Ali 1989. In addition I am especially grateful to Mr. and Mrs. Mahboobali Khoja of Karachi for collecting information from the descendants of the Golārā family in Karachi—Slaves, so-called, because they devoted themselves to looking after Imām Begam in her old age—and from other sources (hereafter M. Khoja).
2. According to some unspecified oral testimony collected by Mr M.T. Sadik Ali, she was born in 1785 in Cutch, the daughter of an Ismaili Sayyid, Hashim Shah of Tando Muhammad Khan in Sindh. Although other testimony (M. Khoja) also records that she was later in the habit of visiting relatives in Tando Muhammad Khan, there does

not appear to be any clear documentary evidence of her parentage and genealogy. See also p. 253 for her possible links with Sayyid Burhanuddin Shah.

3. *Collection of Gināns* 1954, vol. 4, pp. 9-10 and her Gināns appear on pp. 247-55; also A.H. Nanji 1986, pp. 687-8.
4. The room near Lea Market was made available to her by the family of Mukhi Sabz Ali, known as the Golārā family. Some family members still reside in the same building. They have maintained the room in more or less the same condition as it was at the time of her death (M. Khoja).
5. Allana 1984, p. 35 considers the existence of the veil between their graves as evidence for believing that, though engaged, they were not married. However, according to the Golārā family tradition, it is more likely that they were married since otherwise Imām Begam could not have willed to be buried next to Haider Shah's grave (M. Khoja).
6. See, for example (Sindh Archives Karachi) *Selections from the Records of the Commissioner of Sind, no. 113 of 1842-48*: Settlement of a dispute between the Agha Khan and Oomed Ali at Bhooj; also (India Office Records)R/2 Residency Records, Cutch Miscellaneous, 340 of 1848: His Highness the Rao's dealings with the Persian Prince Agha Khan and his followers; also J. Arnould's *Judgment*, 1867.
7. Recently eight of her Gināns have been published in both Gujarati and Perso-Arabic script by HRH the Aga Khan Ismailia Association for Pakistan, in *Ginãne Sharif*. The two omitted Gināns, viz., nos. 2 and 5, may be published in the future, but with certain verses excluded (M. Khoja). These two Ginãns mention both the theory of rebirth and figures who achieved salvation (Pāṇḍavs, Prahlād, etc.).These may be considered objectionable in the present religious climate of Pakistan.
8. For example: *duniyā ke dhandhe meṅ* (2:2); *pānī kā parpoṭā* (3:2); *dān dasoṅd dije* (3:9). Six of her Ginãns were rendered into English verse by Allana 1984, pp. 312-33. Also see C. Shackle and Z. Moir 1992, pp. 24-5 for further discussion of form, style and scansion in one particular Ginān.
9. Dilshad Karim in her article 'Sufi content of the ginans' summarises Imām Begam's teachings. She also comes up with the rather surprising suggestion that Imām Begam may have been a Sayyid writing under a female name.

REFERENCES

Allana, Ghulamali, ed. and trans. *Ginãns of the Ismaili Pirs rendered into English verse.* Karachi: Shia Imami Ismailia Association for Pakistan, 1984.

Arnould, Joseph. *Judgment by the Hon'ble Sir Joseph Arnould in the Kojah Case, otherwise known as the Aga Khan Case, heard in the High Court of Bombay during April and June, 1866.* Bombay: 'Bombay Gazette' Steam Press, 1867.

Asani, Ali S. 'The Ginān literature of the Ismailis of Indo-Pakistan: its origin, characteristics and themes'. In *Devotion Divine, Bhakti Traditions from the Regions of India,* ed. D.L. Eck and F. Mallison, pp. 1-18. Groningen: E. Forsten, 1991.

Aziz, Abualy A. *A Brief History of Ismailism.* Dar es Salaam: The author, 1974.

Collection of Gināns. Vol 4. Bombay: Ismailia Association for Bharat, 1954.

Cunara, Ali J. *Nūrum Mubīn.* Bombay: Ismailia Printing Press, 1936.

Devraj, M. Lalji, ed. *100 Ginān nī copdī bhāg cotho.* Bombay: The editor, *c.* 1920.

Dargawala, Syed M. *Tawārikhe Pir.* Nawsari: The author, 1935.

Fyzee, Asif A. *Cases in the Muhammaden Law of India and Pakistan.* Oxford: Clarendon Press, 1965.

Gināne Sharif. Vol. 2. Karachi: HRH the Aga Khan Ismailia Association for Pakistan, 1979.

Karim, Dilshad. 'Sufi content of the Gināns'. *Africa Ismaili,* 4 (July 1971): 32-51.

Khaki, Ahmad, ed. *Manahar Ginān.* Ahmadabad: Sri Satpanthi Sahitya Seva Mandal, 1971.

Malick, Shuja ul Shamsi. *Gulzāre Shams.* Lahore: Lahore Steam Press, n.d.

Masselos, James C. 'The Khojas of Bombay'. In *Caste and Social Stratification among Muslims in India,* ed. I. Ahmad, pp. 97-116. New Delhi: Manohar, 1976.

Nanji, Azim. *The Nizārī Isma'ilī Tradition in the Indo-Pakistan Subcontinent.* Delmar NY: Caravan Books, 1978.

Nanji, Abdul H. *Pīr padhāriā apane duvār.* Bombay: Darul Ilam Prakashan, 1986.

Nanjiani, Sachedina. *Khojā vratānt.* Ahmadabad: Samasher Bahadur Press, 1892.

Sadik Ali, M.T. 'Sayyida Bībī Imām Begum'. *Hidāyat* (July, 1989): 16-21.

Shackle, Christopher and Zawahir Moir. *Ismaili Hymns from South Asia. An Introduction to the Gināns.* SOAS South Asian Texts No 3. London: School of Oriental and African Studies, University of London, 1992.

Shihab al Din Shah. *Kitāb Khitābāte 'Āliyā,* ed. H. Ojaqi. Bombay: Ismaili Society, 1963.

Some Concepts of Gorakh Yoga through the Analysis of Three Nāthpanthī Manuscripts

MARIOLA OFFREDI

In this paper I will be examining in detail the concept of void, both individually and in connection with other notions, as this makes it easier to draw assumptions about and comment on the link between the Nāthpanth[1] and Buddhism.

The texts on which my discussion is based are three medieval Hindī manuscripts containing three works attributed to Gorakh. I discovered these manuscripts in the library of the Rajasthan Oriental Research Institute at Jodhpur; subsequently, I published an edition and Italian translation of these texts entitled *Lo yoga di Gorakh. Tre manoscritti inediti* (1991). Besides the manuscripts I found and edited, other manuscripts of the same texts have been published by a handful of scholars. Pitambardatt Barthval has carried out the most important work in this field.

The three manuscripts I discovered contained the *Gorakh bodh,* the *Gyān tilak* and the *Sabdī.* Two of the manuscripts are the oldest published to date, while the third was written just over a century later than the one edited by Pitambardatt Barthval. The two oldest manuscripts are the *Gorakh bodh* (saṃvat 1693, AD 1636) and the *Gyān tilak* (saṃvat 1724, AD 1667). The most recent one is the *Sabdī* (saṃvat 1826, AD 1769) (the manuscripts edited by Pitambardatt Barthval are dated, respectively, *c.* saṃvat 1715, *c.* AD 1658; saṃvat 1794, AD 1727; saṃvat 1715, AD 1658).

The manuscript of the *Gorakh bodh* is contained in folios 51-63 (from the first line of folio 51 to the fifth to the last line of folio 63) of Codex 11583 in the Jodhpur collection, which is stored in the library of the Rajasthan Oriental Research Institute. Besides the folio numbers of the codex, there is a further sequence of numbers (18-30) which appears to have been written by the scribe of the manuscript, Udhavdās. Udhavdās also copied two other texts in the codex. The codex was completed in saṃvat 1693

(AD 1636) and the date saṃvat 1745 (AD 1688) written by one of its owners appears at the end. Since the manuscript of the *Gorakh bodh* is itself undated, the *ad quem* date (that is, the date of the codex's completion) is saṃvat 1693 (AD 1636), making it the oldest manuscript of this text hitherto published.

The manuscript of the *Gyān tilak* covers folios 215-17 (from the fifth to the last line of the verso of folio 215 to the fourth to the last line of the verso of folio 217) of Codex 12380 in the Jodhpur collection kept in the above-mentioned library. This codex was completed in saṃvat 1724 (AD 1667). So, although the manuscript of the *Gyān tilak* bears no date, its *ad quem* date is saṃvat 1724 (AD 1667) and is thus the oldest manuscript of the *Gyān tilak* so far published.

The manuscript of the *Sabdī* is found in folios 415-25 (from the ninth line of the verso of folio 415 to the fifteenth line of the recto of folio 425) of Codex 14716 in the Jodhpur collection (referred to earlier). The Codex was completed in saṃvat 1826 (AD 1769). For this reason, while the manuscript itself is not dated, its *ad quem* date is saṃvat 1826 (AD 1769), making it just over a century more recent than the text published by Pitambardatt Barthval.

These manuscripts have little or no aesthetic value. Since they were not copied for wealthy, highly-educated people from either the religious or the secular sphere, they were jotted down somewhat carelessly on ordinary paper.

Dates and works ascribed to Gorakh

Gorakh plays a central role in so many legendary tales that one might wonder if there ever really was such a person. Yet he undoubtedly did exist, for he is mentioned in a work written by the Marathi saint Jñāneśvar or Jñāndev, whose *floruit* was AD 1290. Jñāneśvar proclaims himself to be a disciple of Nivṛttināth, who was in turn a disciple of Gaṇināth or Gahinināth, who was a disciple of Gorakhnāth (see S.G. Tulpule 1979, p. 315). Besides Jñāneśvar's reference to Gorakh, a further, more conclusive, shred of historical evidence proves that he did actually live: in the thirteenth century, the temple and monastery at Gorakhpur, which had been named after him, were both destroyed. While the building of the temple is surrounded by legend,[2] we know for certain that it was demolished and turned into a mosque by Alāuddīn ('Alā'uddīn Khaljī, 1296-1316).[3]

The dates put forward by Indian scholars for Gorakh or, more generally, for the start of the Nāthpanth, range from the ninth to the twelfth or thirteenth centuries. On the basis of historical evidence, the *ad quem* date—and the only certain one—must be the thirteenth century, when the temple and monastery of Gorakhpur were destroyed by the Muslims.

Gorakh is regarded as the founder of Haṭhayoga which was defined by Mircea Eliade (1984, p. 175) as a synthesis of classical Yoga and Tantrism.[4] A number of scholars, including Hazariprasad Dvivedi (1963, p. 53), consider Gorakh not so much the founder of Haṭhayoga as its systematizer, especially with regard to the theory of *cakras*. Some claim that the system was founded by Matsyendra, while others believe its founders to have been Matsyendra and Gorakh (G.W. Briggs 1982, pp. 230-4).

Systematic works in Sanskrit have been attributed to Gorakh, together with non-systematic texts written in mixed Hindī. None of the works that have survived to the present day were written during Gorakh's lifetime. It also seems rather unlikely that Gorakh himself wrote any works in Sanskrit; these were probably composed by learned disciples of the sect who sought to provide a systematic explanation of yoga as practised by Gorakh.[5] These scholars treated Gorakh's asystematic doctrine as the continuation and development of classical Yoga systematized by Patañjali (second century BC or fifth century AD) (see R. Shrivastav 1981, introduction, p. 24), or upheld that the way of life preached by Gorakh was consistent with Patañjali's Yoga. Their approach contrasts with a famous *sabdī*, in which the eightfold Yoga (that is, classical Yoga propounded by Patañjali in the *Yogasūtra*) is described as false:

नौ नाड़ी वहतरि कोठा। ऐ असटांग जोग सब झूठा॥
कूंची ताला सुषमनि करै। उलटि जिभ्यां ले तालू धरै॥

Nine *nāṛīs*, 72 rooms, this eightfold Yoga is wholly false;
The *suṣumnā* must become the key to the lock, the tongue must be rolled and placed on the palate. (*sabdī* 175)

Sanskrit works attributed to Gorakh include the *Haṭhayoga*, a treatise which has been lost, and the *Gorakṣaśataka*.[6] The verses of the *Gorakṣaśataka* are repeated, either verbatim or in their essence, in the *Haṭhayogapradīpikā*, a work in 382 verses by Cintāmaṇi

(Svātmārāma Yogīndra). This is a late work, written no earlier than the fifteenth century (G.W. Briggs 1982, p. 253). It is impossible to date the *Gorakṣaśataka*; according to George Weston Briggs (1982, p. 257), if we accept the unanimous view that Gorakh was its author, then it must date back to the twelfth century. However, J.N. Farquhar (1984, p. 384), who considers Gorakh to be the author, dates it back to the thirteenth century. In any case, the *Gorakṣaśataka* as we know it was written relatively recently.

One of the chief works recognized by modern followers of the sect is the *Siddhasiddhāntapaddhati*, a systematic Sanskrit text which is, needless to say, attributed to Gorakh (in *SSP* I.1, Gorakṣanāth declares himself to be the author of the work). It is impossible to date the *Siddhasiddhāntapaddhati*, which was, however, known in the seventeenth century, when a summa, the *Siddhasiddhāntasaṅgraha,* was compiled in *ślokas* by Balabhadra of Benares (R. Shrivastav 1980, introduction, p. 20). G.W. Briggs (1982, p. 255) mentions one *Siddhasiddhāntapaddhati,* ascribed to Nityānanda Siddha.

Works in Hindī attributed to Gorakh, ·at least in surviving manuscripts, were also definitely written later—four centuries later, if we set Gorakh in the thirteenth century (the *ad quem* date, on historical grounds). Since these were compiled in a mixed language (Eastern Rājasthānī, Braj Bhāṣā, ancient Hindī or ancient Hindustānī but including a few modern forms, as well as Avadhī, Bhojpurī, and occasional Gujarātī forms), dubbed Sadhukkaṛī or 'dialect of the Sādhus' by Ramcandra Shukla (1972, p. 14), it is impossible to say which are the oldest parts. The fact that modern forms are included provides no conclusive evidence for a late date of composition since scribes occasionally modernized forms when copying texts. Conversely, the inclusion of Tantric Buddhist elements cannot be used as definite proof of the text's antiquity, for scribes sometimes inserted apparently older concepts. Gorakh is generally thought to have removed Tantric Buddhist sexual practices from his doctrine, although this may well have been carried out by his disciples who were determined to highlight Gorakh's strong leanings towards Śaivism. In the *Siddhasiddhāntapaddhati* there is a noticeable shift towards orthodox Yoga (Patañjali, the *Gītā,* the Upaniṣads, etc., and even the *Ṛgveda*). While classical Yoga is defined as 'false' in *sabdī* (175 quoted above), in the *Siddhasiddhāntapaddhati* it is regarded as the starting point of Gorakh

Yoga, or as the frame in which the latter evolved (R. Shrivastav 1981, introduction, pp. 22-3).

We therefore have no choice but to accept the Hindī texts as they are. Furthermore, given that Gorakh lived in an age when Buddhist, Śaiva, Śākta and Jain Tantric Yoga practices influenced one another, and that his teachings were addressed to members of all castes and to the masses—amongst whom primitive and magical cults were also widespread—the Hindī works attributed to Gorakh must be regarded as sharper reflections of his practice than the erudite manuscripts penned in Sanskrit. In the *Sabdī*, criticism is often directed at paṇdits who believe they will find the truth in the Scriptures and in other Sanskrit texts which they alone could read.[7]

The Hindī manuscripts may more accurately reflect Gorakh's beliefs and practices than those texts written in Sanskrit because they constitute a *trait d'union* between the Buddhist Siddhas and the medieval Sants—in other words, they form the missing link in a tradition that had apparently been broken. Indian scholars were the first to become aware of this fact when, at the Nagari Pracharini Sabha in Benares in December 1930, Pitambardatt Barthval delivered a paper on the Nāthyogīs, based on Hindī manuscripts he himself had discovered.[8]

Void

Void is variously mentioned in the three manuscripts examined, namely, *Gyān tilak*, *Gorakh bodh* and *Sabdī*. In the *Gyān tilak* the concept is referred to only once—although the negation *nahī* (< *nahĩ*) is used instead of the word 'void' (*suni*):

> Where there is the 'not', there I have seen everything. If I say so no one believes it. Gone are the illusion and fear born of the sentiment of doubt. I have entered the extraordinary state (*GT* 40):
>
> जहां नही तदा सभ कुछ देष्या। कह्या न को पतियाई॥
> दुबध्या भाव़ ज भरम भै भागा। बिरलै पदहि समाई॥

Void is dealt with at greater length in the *Gorakh bodh*, which is written in the form of a dialogue with his presumed master Machindra and which seeks to expound all Gorakh's teachings. First, Void is said to dwell in eternity (*GB* 6) and to constitute the substance of the mind (*GB* 8). The mind, being of the same substance as Void, may dissolve into Void:

Were there no heart, the mind would lie in the Void (*GB* 28):

हिरदा न होता तब सूंनि रहता मन।

Were there no body, the soul would be believed to lie in the Void (*GB* 30):

पिंड न होता तब प्राण पुरिस का सूंनि बिसवासा।

Were there no body, the *jīv* would lie in the Supreme Void (*GB* 36):

काया न होती तब परम सून्य रहता जीव्।

Void is the abode of the Swan (*GB* 44):

सूंनि हंस का बासा।

The *mudā* (< *mudrā*) of knowledge of the Absolute is Void (*GB* 32):

ब्रह्मग्यान का सूंनि मुदा।

Void is the origin of the Originless (*GB* 46):

अमूल का सूंनि मूल।

We are born of Innate Void. Non-dual Void is known through the True Master. Into *atīt* Void we are absorbed (*GB* 66):

सहज सूंनि उतपना आइ। समि सूंनि सत गुर बुझाइ।
अतीत सूंनि मैं रहै समाइ॥

From the Tremendous Void light pours down, from the Fearless Void the word is born, from the Powerful Void comes the essence of the three worlds, with the Void Beyond, one will cross over (*GB* 78):

उग्र सूंनि थैं जोति पलटै। अभै संनि थैं बाचा फुरै॥
प्रभू सूंनि तैं त्रिभव्न सार। अतीत सूंनि तैं उतरिबा पार॥

In the Innate Void the mind is always still (*GB* 86):

सहज सूंनि मन सदा थि(र) रहै।

The mind is the soul absorbed in Void (*GB* 128):

मन स आत्मा सूंनि समाइ।

The *jīv* has faith in Void (*GB* 130):

जीव् का सूंनि बेसास।

The door of Void is inner experience (*parcā*) (*GB* 22):

सूंनि का परचा द्वार।

Ultimately, Void takes on a wide number of meanings, and has many synonyms, as well. The above quotations point to a difference between the various types of Void which is not always clear. According to Nagendranath Upadhyay (1976, p. 163), *atīt* is the highest state; he bases his assertion on couplet 66 quoted earlier. Dharmvir Bharti, however, considers Innate (*sahaj*) Void to be the highest state (see below).

The most common synonym for the term Void (*suni*) is sky (*gagan, gigan* < *gagana*) which we find in the *Sabdī* (and on just one occasion in the *Gyān Tilak*). This sky is not outside the individual; it is the top of the head or, more precisely, it is the 'hole of the Absolute' (*brahmarandhra*) located in the cranium, from which nectar is drunk:

The nectar (is sought) in the sky (*GB* 106):

गिगनि मुषि अमीरस।

That it is within the body is apparent from couplet 118:

The Void is the temple. The mind is god. Seated (in meditation) one must perform the service continually. With the five vessels (i.e. the senses) one enters the *unmanī*:[9]

सूंनि स मंदिर। मन स देव् वैसि निरंतरि कीजै सेव्।
पांचौं पाती उनमनि रहै।

The term Void inevitably calls to mind the Mahāyāna Buddhist concept of Vacuity. The first *sabdī*, which is also the best-known one, seems to be modelled in part on Nāgārjuna's definition of *paramārtha* (absolute truth): 'It may be called neither void, nor non-void, nor both things, nor either of the two, but in order to talk about it we call it Void.'[10] The first *sabdī* states:

Neither inhabited nor void, neither void nor inhabited, it (is) incomprehensible and invisible. In the vault of the sky the child (*bālak*) speaks. What name will you give him?

बस्ती न सुनि सुनि न बस्ती। अगम अगोचर अैसा॥
गगन मंडल मैं बालक बोलै। ताका नांव् धरौगे कैसा॥

The phrase 'neither inhabited nor void, neither void nor

inhabited' recalls Nāgārjuna's definition. The final question, 'what name will you give him?', also echoes Nāgārjuna's affirmation, 'in order to talk about it we call it Void'. The 'child' who speaks in the vault of the sky (the Void within the body) is the Absolute, which is incomprehensible through logical-discursive thinking (this is why Nāgārjuna called it Void) and is also invisible. As is often repeated in the *Sabdī*, knowledge of the Absolute is acquired through inner experience (*parcā* < *paricaya* 'knowledge based on direct encounter').

Sabdī 211 demonstrates how this Void is a positive reality:

> There is being, O paṇḍit, there is not non-being; if there is the extraordinary (knowledge), it reveals itself without interruption:
>
> आसति है हो पंडिता नासति नांही अनभै होइ प्रतीति निरंतरि।

This conception is reminiscent of that of the Vijñānavādin School, which calls supreme truth 'existence' (*bhāva*) in order to distinguish it from nothingness, although it cannot be called 'either existence or non-existence'.

Void is within the body: the word *brahmaṇḍ* ('universe') is used in the *Sabdī* as a synonym for 'hole of the Absolute' (*brahma-randhra*) or for '(the lotus of) 1,000 petals' (*sahasrār*). To quote from a few *sabdīs*:

> The Gaṅgā of the nethermost world (the *kuṇḍalinī* which lies in the lowest *cakra*, behind the genitals) must be lifted into the skull (*brahmaḍ* < *brahmaṇḍ*), where the purest water (nectar) is drunk (*sabdī* 2):
>
> पाताल की गंगा ब्रह्मड चढाइबा। तहां बिमल बिमल जल पीया॥
>
> In this very place is the Everlasting, in this very place is the light, from this very place the three worlds were created. The Imperish-able that remains with (us) always—because of it (to obtain it) many kings have become lords of yoga (*sabdī* 3):
>
> इहां ही अछै इहां ही आलोक यहां ही रचिलै तीनि तिलोक॥
> अछै संगि रहै जू वा ता कारणि अनेक राजो जोगेस्व हूवा॥
>
> In neither the Vedas nor in the Books, in neither the vulvas nor in the words (is it to be found), all (these) did cover it. Ascending to the summit of the sky, the Word revealed itself. There the Invisible-Knowledge is known (*sabdī* 4):
>
> बेदे न कतेबे न षाणी न बांणी॥ सब ढाकी तलि आंणी।
> गगन सिषर्चढ़ि सबद प्रकास्या॥ तहां बूझिलै अलष बिनांणी॥

The mind should be fixed in the Void (sũni man dharai, *sabdī* 18), in the vault of which the waterfall (nectar) flows (suni maṇḍal tahā̃ nījhar jharīyā, *sabdī* 94).

The Void is regarded as the Absolute:

> Therein lies the state of *nirvāṇa*. In the body it is experienced (*parcai*). See (obtain it) from the mouth of the Master, then there will be no transmigration (*sabdī* 166):
>
> तिस अभिअंतरि पद निरबांणी ॥
> पिंड परचै गुरमुष जोई। वहौर्‌यौ आवा़ गवऩ न होई ॥

Liberation is achieved in Void (madhi suni māī baiṭhā jai . . . paramgati pāī, *sabdī* 185); when breath 'merges with the sky . . . the body does not die' (dvādas ā̃gul jahā̃ gag dhar melā̃ . . . kāyā na jampuri jāī, *sabdī* 114).

The Void within the individual is the nectar's dwelling-place: In the vault of the sky (there is) an inverted well. There lies the abode of the nectar. He who has a good master drinks his fill. He who has no master remains thirsty (*sabdī* 26). The inverted well is the thousand-petaled, upside-down lotus from which nectar drips. The nectar is either collected at the top by means of the *khecrī* (< *khecarī mudrā*; turning the tongue over backwards to seal the hollow in the top of the throat. *Khecarī* means 'moving in the heavens'. *Khecarī mudrā* also refers to the ear-rings or cylinders passed through the lobe of the ears of the kānphaṭā [split-eared] Yogī [G.W. Briggs, 1982, p. 11]), or else it is carried upwards from below (sperm), awakening the *kuṇḍalinī*:

> Inverted, the Śakti rises up to the cranium (*sabdī*, 120):
>
> उलटी सकति चढै ब्रह्मंड।

Inner experience is achieved in the Void within the body ('the vault of the sky') and it is superior to discursive knowledge:

> In the vault of the sky the cow has calved, in paper (the Scriptures) they have made yoghurt. After filtering it, the paṇḍits drank (only) the whey. The Siddhas ate the butter (*sabdī* 203).
>
> गगन मंडल मैं गाइ बिया़ई। कागद दही जमाया़ ॥
> छाछि छांणि पंडितां पीवी़। सिधां मांषण षाया़ ॥

To grasp the light of true knowledge, the mind must be stilled by means of meditation without supports—meditation, that is, which concentrates on neither exterior nor interior objects—in order to attain indeterminate ecstasy (*nirvikalpa samādhi*):

> In the sky that has no column (of support) he obtained (the light of knowledge) without oil or wick. (When) he has acquired faith in the words of the master Gorakh, there (is) neither day nor night there (*sabdī* 215):
>
> थंभ बिहूणि गगन रचीलै ॥ तेल बिहूंणी बाती।
> गुरू गोरष के बचन पतिआया़ ॥ तब धौंस नही तहां राती ॥

Void is therefore located at the highest point within the body: it is a sky that is not sustained by columns, in which the light of knowledge shines. Besides being called Void, it is known as 'vault of the sky', 'hole of the Absolute', 'one-thousand petals', 'door of Void', 'tenth door', 'west door', 'west', 'inverted well', 'well', 'beyond-Laṅkā',[11] 'black-bee's cave', 'city of Śiva', 'universe' (i.e. cranium), among other names.

The fact that four types of void are mentioned shows that the concept of Void which appears in the manuscripts analysed derives, at least nominally, from Tantric Buddhism. In Tantric Buddhism (chiefly Vajrayāna) there are four types of void, called *śūnya, atiśūnya, mahāśūnya* and *sarvaśūnya* (meaning, respectively, void, ultravoid, great void and total void). In Nāgārjunapāda's *Pañcakrama,* a text which probably dates from the ninth century, and is therefore fairly close, chronologically, to the older Nāth texts, they are described as follows: (1) *śūnya* is light (*āloka*) and awareness (*prajñā* 'discriminative-appreciative awareness', H.V. Guenther 1972, p. 3), though the mind is active at this stage; (2) *atiśūnya* is the manifestation of light (*ālokābhāsa*). It is *upāya* (means, action), and it, too, is conditioned (*parikalpita*); (3) *mahāśūnya* is intuition of light (*ālokoplabdhi*), it derives from the merging of the first two types of void, it is *prajñopāya,* and it is unconditioned (*pariniṣpanna*), yet *avidyā* (ignorance); (4) *sarvaśūnya* is total void, perfect vacuity. Whereas the first three kinds of void are associated with impure mental states, *sarvaśūnya* is absolutely pure and, as such, self-enlightening. It is beyond being and non-being and it is not even non-dual or a combination of being and non-being; on the contrary, it is beyond non-duality and is indescribable. By yogic practice, one passes through the first three types of void, in which the mind is active in various ways. In actual fact, these are three stages of consciousness, which remain impure because of the activity of vital breath: during the first stage (*śūnya*), breath mingles with thought; in the second stage (*atiśūnya*), thought prevails over breath; the third stage (*mahāśūnya*) is a combination of the first two stages. The fourth stage, while deriving from the previous three, is separate from them. It is not subject to change and, according to the *Pañcakrama* (see S.D. Dasgupta 1997, pp. 46-9), the Omniscient (Buddha) originates from it.

No detailed description of the four voids appears in any of the surviving Nāthpanthī texts in Hindī. A hymn published by Pitambardatt Barthval in *Gorakh-bānī* (1949, pp. 91-2) mentions the yogic practice of absorption in the fourth void—known as *sahaj* (< *sahaja*)—which is performed after the adept has passed through the previous three voids: 'Gold below, gold above, gold in the middle. There is neither sin nor merit in the body of one who knows the three voids . . . when Gorakh, seated (in meditation), sees (his) self, then the gold blends into the Innate (*sahaj*)'.

According to Dharmvir Bharti, the influence of the Tantric Buddhist conception of Void on the Nāthpanthīs was largely nominal. We know of the close relationship between Siddhas and Nāthpanthīs and of their borrowings from one another. The Siddhas claimed as their own the Vijñānavāda conception of void as *tathatā* or Pure Being. After Nāgārjuna (whose concept of 'vacuity' was considered to be negative by the Vijñānavādins, who instead held it to be a positive essence of Pure Being) the notion of 'vacuity' fell on such fertile terrain that each of the various sects conceived of it differently—but always used it to denote the Supreme Reality. Dharmvir Bharti asserts that while the Nāthpanthīs used the term 'Void' to indicate Supreme Reality, they actually modified the Buddhist concept of Void. In Bharti's view, the novelty of the first *sabdī* lies in the declaration that 'in the vault of the sky the child speaks'. This affirmation links the concept of Void with that of the Word or Sound. In the non-Buddhist Tantric sects preceding Gorakh, Śiva and Śakti were conceived of as *Bindu* and *Nāda*. In their view Sound (*nāda*) or *Śabdabrahman* (the Absolute in the form of Sound) was the origin of creation.[12] But even before the Nāths, the Buddhist Siddhas had incorporated the concept of Void into that of Sound: the Caryāpads composed by them mention 'the sound of emptiness' which Munidatta in his commentary to the Caryāpads calls the 'tormentor of all foes'. Sound and Void which, in Nāthpanthī doctrine, are linked might therefore be a conception of Tantric Buddhist origin that derived in turn from a non-Buddhist conception. Nāthpanthī works mention the 'thunder of sound', which they define as 'sound of the *anhad nād*' ('sound of the causeless sound') (D. Bharti 1968, p. 339).

In the *Romāvalī*, which appears in *Gorakh-bānī* (pp. 203-6), Void is associated with Word. The four *bā̃ṇīs* are the master's Word and since they are said to be inside the body, they are perceived as being self-experienced with the aid of the master; since what is to be perceived within the body is Sound, the four *bā̃ṇīs* should be identified with Sound. This interpretation is corroborated by the names and descriptions of the four *bā̃ṇīs*: *sahaj, sañjam, supāi* (*supāv* < *svabhāva* 'own nature'), *atīth* (*atīt*). These are explained as follows: '*sahaj* is the body, *sañjam* (control) is breath, *atīt* is the supreme state' (we are not told what *supāi* corresponds to). In this context, *sahaj* has the sense of 'natural' (*svābhāvika*), while *supāi* must be understood in the technical sense of *sahaj* (innate). Here, *atīt* is the supreme state, the Void of the Beyond, the highest void. It is impossible to reverse the above order, because *atīt* can never be the initial state. The fact that *sahaj* is associated with the body does not mean that the yogī leads an ordinary life, immersed in materiality. Rather it indicates that the body is the natural instrument with which to pursue the supreme state. This initial state corresponds to the state of wakefulness in which the senses and the mind are active. *Sañjam* (control) is said to be breath (*pavan*): breath is described as controlled when, by performing the reverse practice,[13] *prāṇ* and *apān*, instead of being expelled from the body, merge together in the navel, and the mind withdraws from the objects of the senses. This is a 'non-normal' condition that corresponds to the dream-state in which the mind wanders freely because it is considered to be detached from the senses. In the first two states, duality persists; the difference between them lies in the diverse cause and effect relationship (i.e. in the first state the mind is active because of the senses, which also include the mind; in the second state, mental activity is caused by the mind itself). *Supāi* (own nature), for which no explanation is given, is the third state which the Yogī enters. As the term suggests, it is a 'natural' state, but in the yogic—that is to say, technical—sense. In this state, in fact, duality ceases inasmuch as unity of self with the Supreme Self is experienced; it corresponds to the state of dreamless sleep in which 'negative' bliss, lacking any kind of mental or sensory activity, is experienced. *Atīt* (from *ati* 'beyond', 'ultra') is, the ultimate state which is beyond even non-duality; it corresponds to the state called *turīya* (fourth)—the state of attainment, in which the self becomes one with the Supreme Self. In the *Narvai bodh*, edited by Pitambardatt Barthval (see *Gorakh-bānī*, pp. 169-73), the four states of the Yogī are listed as follows: *ārambh, ghaṭ, parcā, nispatī* (*NB* 1). *Ārambh* (beginning) is the initial state, *ghaṭ* (pitcher) is the state in which breath is controlled, *parcā* (knowledge deriving from direct encounter) is the yogic state of inner experience in which duality ceases, while *nispatī* (attainment) is the state beyond non-duality. In the manuscripts analysed here, it is above all the *parcā* state that is described repeatedly.

The concepts of Void and Sound are so closely linked that, just as Sound (*nād* < *nāda*) or Word (*sabad*) was regarded as the Supreme Reality, so Void was defined as mother, father and totality:

> Void is the mother, Void is the father, Void is the Pure (*sabdī* 231, in *Gorakh-bānī*).
>
> सूंनि ज माई सूंनि ज बाप। सूंनि निरंजन आपै आप॥

The substance of the mind was defined as Void (*GB* 8). The Siddhas perceived Void as a 'middle way' beyond being and non-being and, similarly, the Nāthpanthīs described a Yogī who had become 'immortal (and) pure' (that is, whose mind is absorbed into the Void) as a person with 'neither sin nor merit' and 'without *sat, raj, tam*', i.e. devoid of the modalities of the substance *sattva, rajas, tamas* (*sabdī* 70). Yet if the definition of the Yogī whose mind is absorbed into Void as having 'neither sin nor merit' echoes the Siddha concept of Void as a 'middle way', the definition of the Yogī whose mind is absorbed into Void as 'without *sat, raj, tam*' reflects a divergence from Buddhist thought, in which Void is beyond the duality of being and non-being, and reveals Hindu influence.

We have seen how the notion of *prajñā* and *upāya* is predominant in Tantric Buddhism: *śūnya* is *prajñā*, *atiśūnya* is *upāya* and *mahā-śūnya* is *prajñopāya* (a combination of the two), while *sarvaśūnya*, or attainment, is beyond even *prajñopāya*. Although the Buddhist concept of the four voids became an intrinsic feature of Hindu

Haṭhayoga, its disciples rejected the concept of *prajñā* and *upāya*, for which they substituted the identity of Void and Sound/Word. In the *Haṭhayoga-pradīpikā*, a systematic Sanskrit text written towards the end of the fifteenth century, making it comparatively recent, and based on systematic Sanskrit works ascribed to Gorakh—*śūnya*, *atiśūnya* and *mahāśūnya* are regarded as attributes of three types of Sound; the latter are attained in the course of three consecutive stages of yoga practice: *ārambhāvasthā* (initial stage), *ghaṭāvasthā* (the pitcher stage, that is, *kumbhaka* or retention of breath), *paricayāvasthā* (the state of inner experience). In the first stage, the 'Brahmā knot' (*brahmā-granthī*; the knots are the convergence points of the *nāṛīs*, and their names vary from text to text) is pierced until the *śūnya* sound rises within the lotus of the heart; in the second stage, through the blockage known as *jālandharabandha*, the 'Viṣṇu knot' is pierced and the *atiśūnya* sound rises within the lotus of the throat; in the third stage, the *mahāśūnya* sound arises within the lotus between the eyebrows. The points at which these three types of sound occur are known as 'sky' (*ākāśa*, one of the terms used to denote Void) because sound arises in the sky which, in yogic practice, lies inside the body.

The term commonly used by Buddhist Siddhas to express the fourth type of void—the perfect or total emptiness (*sarvaśūnya*) described in the *Pañcakrama*—is *sahaj* (innate). In the Hindī texts attributed to Gorakh, this term is used to connote, among other things, the Siddhas' fourth type of void. As the fourth and highest type of void, the Innate was believed by the Siddhas to be the supreme state, surpassing even the union of *prajñā* and *upāya*. In accordance with Buddhist terminology, it was also called 'middle way'. Statements in the Hindī works ascribed to Gorakh suggest that *sahaj* is the highest form of void. In Dharmvir Bharti's opinion, whereas coming-and-going persists in Void, consciousness becomes stable in Innate Void. He refers to *Gorakh bodh* 78 in Pitambardatt Barthval's edition, which corresponds to *Gorakh bodh* 88 in the manuscript I edited and translated. The couplet gives Machindra's answer to the following question by Gorakh:

> How does it come, how does it go, how does consciousness remain immersed in Void? How do body and mind remain always stable? (*GB* 87):

कैसैं आवैं कैसैं जाइ कैसैं चीया रहै समाइ॥
कैसैं तन मन सदा थि(र) रहै॥

The answer may be translated in three or four ways as follows:

> From Void it comes, into Void it goes, in Void consciousness remains immersed. In Innate Void body and mind remain always stable.
>
> सूंनि ही आवै सूंनि ही जाइ। सूंनि ही चीया रहै समाइ।
> सहज सूंनि तन मन सदा थिर रहै॥

A second possibility is: 'From Void one comes, into Void one goes.' It may also mean, 'In Void it comes, in Void it goes.' In this case, Dharmvir Bharti's interpretation could be accepted, even if 'coming and going' is usually mentioned as *āvāgāvnā* (आवागावना, *GB* 75). But D. Bharti (1968, p. 357) also maintains that the state of non-duality to which the Siddhas subscribed is not mentioned in these verses—a theory which the scholar developed in an analysis that sets out to prove that the Nāthpanth concept of *sahaj* does not stem directly from that of the Siddhas.

In Buddhist and, later on, Śaiva Yoga practices, the term *sahaj* signified 'natural' (*svābhāvika* 'according to one's own nature'). In Bharti's view, the term may have been borrowed from some other tradition. Besides 'natural', however, the word was also used in both doctrines to express the practice involving the union of the female and male principles, termed Prajña and Upāya by the Buddhists, Śakti and Śiva by the Śaivites (or, to be more accurate, the Śāktas) belonging to Yoginīkaulamārga, a sect which, according to Bhārtī, was closely linked to the Nāthpanth. This practice could be either external or internal. In the *Kaulajñāna-nirṇaya* (*Mahākaulajñāna-vinirṇaya,* ninth or eleventh century), a Yoginīkaulamārga systematic Sanskrit text, four Śaktis are mentioned: *sahajā, kulajā, antyajā* and *mahādevī. Sahajā* was the wife (*svakīyā*) of the adherent. In internal practice, the *sahajā śakti* had to be placed inside the body. An adherent practising *sahajā śakti* within his body becomes absorbed in the *sahaj,* abandons duality and obtains *sahajānanda* or innate bliss. In internal practice, the Buddhist and Śaiva-Śākta Innate differed only in the names given to the male and female principles. The *Kaulajñāna-nirṇaya* itself states that, by practising *sahaj,* the adherent becomes stable in the unitary state (that is, he retains no form of duality); he himself is the Absolute, he is Śiva, Soma, Arhant, Buddha (D. Bharti 1968, p. 368).

Since the Nāthpanthīs used the terms Śakti and Śiva rather than Prajñā and Upāya, we may assert that they were influenced by the Yoginīkaulamārga regarded as Śaiva by Dharmvir Bharti, but as Śākta by most scholars. However, we should not overestimate this nominal difference. It is also not possible to prove whether Śaivites/Śāktas and Buddhists actually took the term *sahaj* < *sahaja*, in the sense of 'natural',[14] from an earlier tradition, or whether the concept of Innate as the union of the two principles, male and female, was first adopted by one doctrine and later by the others. But if, as a number of scholars uphold, Tantrism first developed as a system within Buddhism, it cannot be claimed without a shadow of doubt that the Nāthpanthīs' concept of Innate was prompted by Śaiva-Śākta Tantrism rather than Buddhist Tantrism.

There are several references to ritual coitus in the texts attributed to Gorakh but, apart from these, the practice of union is internalised. In what follows, I will discuss the concept of union as described in the *Romāvalī*, which Barthval edited in *Gorakh-bānī*. Comprising a mere 54 verses, the *Romāvalī* is systematic in that it constitutes a kind of summa of Nāthpanth practice and thought (if not specifically that of Gorakh) in the form of brief aphorisms. The text is known from a manuscript dated saṃvat 1743 (AD 1686).

It is stated in the *Romāvalī* that

> he who knows *bā̃ṇī ṣā̃ṇī* (*ṣ* = *kh*) is called Formless; in *AUM* must the light be known.

> जे बांणी षांणीं कौं बिचारै ते निराकार बोलिये, ऊँकार मधे जोति जांणिये।

In other words a person who knows *bā̃ṇī ṣā̃ṇī* actually becomes the Supreme Self. The term *bā̃ṇī* means 'word', 'teaching'. The term *ṣā̃ṇī* means *yoni*, 'vulva'. The *Romāvalī* speaks of 'four vulvas' (*cāri ṣā̃ṇī*), but sets them inside the body, thereby rejecting Tantric Buddhist sexual practice. These four vulvas do not correspond to the four *mahāmudrās* in Tantric Buddhism. Rather, they are the origin of living creatures as classified by Caraka (*c.* sixth to fourth centuries BC): *svetraj/setraj, aṇḍraj, jeraj, udbīraj* (in Sanskrit: *svedaja, aṇḍaja, jarāyuja, udbhijja*); that is, they are born, respectively, from moisture, from the egg, from the womb or placenta and from the earth (sprouting from beneath the ground; vegetation). In the *Romāvalī*, this classification is applied to the human body. The 'four vulvas' are identified as follows: 'bone derives from moisture, sperm derives from the womb or placenta, *netr* derives from the egg (< *netra* = eye, but it can also mean *nāṛī*, which is not necessarily *netrī*), and the *romāvalī* (strands of hair spreading above the navel) derives from the earth/vegetation'. The number four was probably maintained to parallel the four *bā̃ṇīs* and other fourfold principles listed in the *Romāvalī*. Since, however, two components stem from the father (bone and sperm; the third is marrow) and two from the mother (blood, flesh, skin and *nāṛī* are the four listed in the *Romāvalī*; in this case, hair and *nāṛī*), the four *ṣā̃ṇī* in the *Romāvalī* relate to the body. However, a question comes spontaneously to mind: why does the *Romāvalī* lay such emphasis on the fact that the practice of union is internal? This might well prove that at the outset there was a close link between the Nāthpanth and Tantric Buddhism, in which ritual coitus was practised, and late masters revised the doctrine of the sect in order to make it consistent with classical Yoga, thus firmly setting it within Hinduism.

NOTES

1. For the various Nāthpanth sects, see H. Dvivedi 1978, pp. 8-15 and 1966. See also G.W. Briggs 1982; and M. Offredi 1991.
2. For the legends, see G.W. Briggs 1982, pp. 86-7.
3. Another temple, subsequently erected near the site of the original building by the Gorakhnāthīs, was converted into a mosque by Auraṅgzeb (1659-1707; G.W. Briggs 1982, p. 86).
4. In the Sanskrit works ascribed to Gorakh, the word *haṭha* is esoterically explained as formed by *ha* and *ṭha,* which are each identified with a long list of Tantric terms. These terms are grouped in couples, each merging into its complementary principle (*yoga* = union):

   ha: sun, sun-*nāṛī*, Yamunā, *piṅglā*, Śakti, *prāṇ*, menstrual blood, breath, below, left, red;

   ṭha: moon, moon-*nāṛī*, Gaṅgā, *iṛā*, Śiva, *apān*, sperm, mind, above, right, pale.

   For these lists, see Nagendranath Upadhyay 1976, pp. 126, 157.
5. Gorakh may have been a simple Yogī, who did not know Sanskrit. Even the Hindī works ascribed to Gorakh and the other Nāths might not mirror the original doctrine of the sect. According to Hiralal Maheshwari (1980, p. 104), 'It appears that the Nāth-Vāṇīs in the Deśī Bhāṣā were consolidated in the sixteenth century. Amongst many reasons which led to consolidation, one was that around the 16th century there was a strong reaction against the evil aspects of the prevalent forms of Nāthism and the Nāths, therefore, felt it necessary to give their scriptures respectability by consolidating them as the Vāṇīs of recognized masters.'

6. For the English translation and commentary, see G.W. Briggs 1982, pp. 284-304.
7. See, for instance, the following *sabdīs* in the manuscript I discovered and edited: 6, 142 (bis), 152 (bis), 153, 165, 192, 203, 214.
8. Published in the *Nāgrīpracāriṇī Patrikā*, 11.4 (1930). For the manuscripts edited by Pitambardatt Barthval, see Pitambardatt Barthval (ed.) 1979.
9. *Unman*, which I have translated as 'stable', 'still', is a term and a concept on which scholars hold different opinions. In many *sabdīs* and the *Gorakh bodh* we find the injunction to make the *man* (the mind) *unman*. The word *unman* derives from *ud* and *manas*, and thus literally means 'to turn the mind upwards'. In fact, in *unmanī* the Yogī keeps his eyebrows raised upward, gazing at the tip of his nose [see *Mānak hindī koś* and *Hindū dharmkoś*, where *unmanī* is also glossed as 'detached' (*virakt*) or 'indifferent' (*udāsīn*)].
10. Śūnyam iti na vaktavyam 'aśūnyam iti vā bhavet/ubhayaṃ nobhayaṃ ceti prajñaptyarthaṃ tu kathate (*Mādhyamaka kārikā*, XXI, 11).
11. *Palaṅkā* (*par* + *laṅkā*) 'beyond Laṅkā' (Sri Lanka) is a metaphor for 'a very distant place'.
12. The importance that the Nāthpanthīs attach to sound is indicated by the whistle (*sīgīnād*) that Nāthyogīs wear. The whistle, said to have been introduced by Gorakh, is made of antelope, deer or rhinoceros horn (*sīg*, *siṅg* < *śṛṅg* < *śṛṅga*) or of wood, and is about 5 cm long. Yogīs wear it together with a ring called *pavitrī* (sacred) and an Elaeocarpus ganitrus berry (*rudrākṣ* 'Rudra's eye', i.e. 'Śiva's eye'). The whistle is tied by a thread to the *pavitrī*, to which the Elaeocarpus berry is also tied. The *pavitrī* is tied to a thread which the yogī wears around his neck. Some sects consider this thread to be a *janeū* (the sacred or sacrificial thread worn by the orthodox Hindus of the first three *varṇas*). The whistle, which the Yogī blows before meals and daily ceremonies (see G.W. Briggs 1982, p. 12, where it is stated that the Yogī may blow it before defecating), is linked with the phallus (*liṅgam*), and the *pavitrī* is a symbol of the vulva (*yonī*).
13. For the 'reverse practice', see D. Bharti 1968, pp. 413-14; and M. Offredi 1991, pp. 80-4.
14. As D. Bharti points out (1968, pp. 374-85), in Hindī texts attributed to Gorakh, the term *sahaj* is used on the whole to express a variety of concepts: Supreme Reality; Supreme Knowledge; Yoga technique with which to pursue the union of Śiva and Śakti inside the body; Innate Ecstasy; Supreme State; and way of life.

    Let us take a brief look at some of these concepts:

    Sahaj as Supreme Reality. The five elements originate from *sahaj* and are reabsorbed into *sahaj*: 'were there no night, day would come from *sahaj*, when daylight spreads, night is absorbed into *sahaj*'. (*GB* 30).

Sahaj as Supreme Knowledge. By pursuing this *sahaj*, which is devoid of duality, the Indestructible is obtained: 'Inside the fort of the body (are) gods, temples and Kāśī. Naturally pursuing the *sahaj* (there) I obtained the Indestructible'. (*pad* 23.2, in *Gorakh-bānī*, p. 116)

Innate Ecstasy (*sahaj samādhi*). The Nāthpanthīs believed that complete control of the senses, attained by breath control, led to innate ecstasy. Bharti regards this innate ecstasy as a new form of the ecstasy which Buddhist Siddhas achieved from the union of Prajñā and Upāya. In the *Gyān tilak*, innate ecstasy (*sahaj samādhi*) is described as a fire-pot: 'The steam does not come out, the drop does not overflow, having filled the fire-pot (*āgīṭhī*) of the Innate (*sahaj*), (he) uses it. (Practising) innate ecstasy in the house of Yoga (*jog ke ghar mai*) (i.e. with Yoga), with the master's knowledge he has obtained the truth' (*GT* 42).

Sahaj as Supreme State. 'The *sahaj pad* (innate state) is the Supreme nirvāṇa (*param nṛbā̃n*)' (*Goraṣ Datt Guṣṭi* 42, in *Gorakh-bānī*, p. 231).

Sahaj as a way of life. It is the 'natural' middle way, free of external practices, prohibitions, and so on. It was in this sense that, later on, the Sants used the term *sahaj*.

REFERENCES

Manuscripts

Gorakh bodh, Codex 11583, folios 51-63, Rajasthan Oriental Research Institute, Jodhpur.

Gyān tilak, Codex 12380, folios 215-17, Rajasthan Oriental Research Institute, Jodhpur.

Sabdī, Codex 14716, folios 415-25, Rajasthan Oriental Research Institute, Jodhpur.

Catalogues

Rājasthānī-hindī hastlikhit granth-sūcī, III, Jodhpur Saṅgrah, ed. Onkarlal Menariya. Jodhpur: Rajasthan Oriental Research Institute, 1974.

Rājasthānī-hindī hastlikhit granth-sūcī, IV, Jodhpur Saṅgrah, ed. Onkarlal Menariya. Jodhpur: Rajasthan Oriental Research Institute, 1978.

Other

Barthval, Pitambardatt, ed. (see *Gorakh-bānī*).

Bharti, Dharmvir. *Siddha-sāhitya*. Allahabad: Kitab Mahal, 1968.

Briggs, G.W. *Gorakhnāth and the Kānphaṭa Yogīs*. 3rd ed. Delhi: Motilal Banarsidass, 1982 [1938].

Dasgupta, Shashi Bhushan. *Introduzione al Buddhismo Tantrico* (Italian translation of *An Introduction to Tantric Buddhism.* Berkeley: Shambala, 1972.) Rome: Ubaldini, 1977.

Dvivedi, Hazariprasad. *Hindī sāhitya kī bhūmikā.* 7th ed. Bombay: Hindi-granth-ratnakar, 1963 [1940].

———. *Nāth sampradāy.* 2nd ed. revd. and enld. Varanasi: Naivedya Niketan, 1966.

———. *Nāth siddhõ kī bāniyā̃.* 2nd ed., Varanasi: Nagari Pracharini Sabha, 1978 [1957].

Eliade, Mircea. *Tecniche dello yoga* (Italian translation of *Techniques du Yoga.* Paris: Gallimard, 1948.) Torino: Boringhieri, 1984.

Farquhar, J.N. *An Outline of the Religious Literature of India.* 3rd ed. Delhi: Motilal Banarsidass, 1984 [1920].

Gorakh-bānī, ed. Pitambardatt Barthval. 4th ed. Prayag: Hindi Sahitya Sammelan, 1979.

Guenther, Herbert V. *The Tantric View of Life.* Berkeley and London: Shambala, 1972.

Hindū dharmkoś. Ed. Rajbali Pandey. Lucknow: Uttar Pradesh Hindi Sansthan, 1978.

Maheshwari, Hiralal. *History of Rajasthani Literature.* Delhi: Sahitya Akademi, 1980.

Mānak hindī koś. 5 vols. Ed. Ramchandra Varma. Prayag: Hindi Sahitya Sammelan, 1962.

Offredi, Mariola. *Lo yoga di Gorakh. Tre manoscritti inediti.* Milan: Cesviet, 1991.

Rājasthā̃nī sabad kos. 9 vols. Ed. Sitaram Lalas. Jodhpur: Rajasthani Shodh Sansthan & Caupasni Shiksha Samiti (1962-1978).

Siddhasiddhāntapaddhati (praṇetā Gorakhnāth). Ed. Ramlal Shrivastav. Gorakhpur: Gorakhnāth-mandir, 1981.

Shrivastav, Ramlal, ed. (see *Siddhasiddhāntapaddhati*)

Shukla, Ramcandra. *Hindī sāhitya kā itihās.* 17th ed. 1st revd and enld ed. Varanasi: Nagari Pracharini Sabha, 1972 [1940].

Tulpule, Shankar Gopal. *Classical Marāṭhī Literature from the Beginning to AD 1818.* Wiesbaden: Otto Harrassowitz, 1979.

Upadhyay, Nagendranath. *Gorakṣnāth.* Varanasi: Nagari Pracharini Sabha, 1976.

Bārahmāsā in *Candāyan* and in Folk Traditions

SHYAM MANOHAR PANDEY

Bārahmāsā, the description of the twelve months has been a very popular genre in the literature and folklore of northern India dating back to the twelfth century. The first literary *bārahmāsā* was composed by a Muslim Persian poet Sād i Salmān (AD 1043-1131) who lived in Lahore. Sād i Salmān, whose full name was Masū'd ibn Sād i Salmān, lived during the Ghaznavī period of Indo-Muslim history. Masū'd was a wealthy landlord and was made Governor of Jalandhar for some time. His political interests led to repeated periods of imprisonment, but in AD 1107 he was finally set free and lived to an old age (A. Schimmel 1973, p. 11). It was Sanā'ī,[1] the Persian mystical poet from Ghazna, who carefully collected his verses. A little later Jain poets too started writing *bārahmāsā* and the tradition continued for a long time.

Sufi poets writing in Hindi also used the *bārahmāsā* genre, along with *saṭ ṛtu* ('six seasons') descriptions, and my objective here is to discuss the *bārahmāsā* of these Sufi poets. These writers are Maulānā Dāūd (*Candāyan*), Kutuban (*Mṛgāvatī*), Malik Muhammad Jāyasī (*Padmāvat; Kanhāvat)* and Mañjhan (*Madhumālatī*). Later I will compare the Sufi *bārahmāsā* tradition with Masū'd Salmān's *bārahmāsā* and with other *bārahmāsā* current in the folk literature of the Hindi speaking area.

The first Sufi poet to use the *bārahmāsā* genre was Maulānā Dāūd. His composition *Candāyan,* completed in AD 1379 (during the reign of Firoz Shāh Tughlaq, 1351-88), contains a *bārahmāsā* description of the heroine Mainā's *virah* following her husband's elopement with another woman.[2] Mainā's pangs of separation month by month are described in the following sections.

Sāvan

After Candā has eloped with Lorik, his wife Mainā starts suffering from the pangs of separation in the month of Sāvan (July-August). Crying desperately, she watches day and night for her husband's return, and keeps repeating his name (v. 339). She is like a fish out of water.

In the meantime she hears that a caravan of seven hundred traders has arrived whose leader is Surjan. Surjan, a Brahmin, listens carefully to Mainā's *virah* tormented message. Mainā describes her separation through the twelve months, beginning with Sāvan (July-August). In fact, most of the early Sufi texts describe *bārahmāsā* beginning from Sāvan, the only exception being *Padmāvat*, in which the *bārahmāsā* begins in Āsāṛh.

In Sāvan the dry earth becomes drenched with water, and greenery sprouts everywhere. Mainā requests Surjan to tell Lorik that the rainy season has captured her eyes and that they are shedding tears continually, rotting the strings of her garlands, and the kohl on her eyes, a mark of her beauty, has wiped off. Mainā requests Surjan to tell Lorik that ever since Candā took him away in Sāvan, Mainā's eyes have continuously poured water. 'O Surjan! Give Lorik this message that Mainā has been unfortunate and cannot sleep since he went away.'

Kutuban,[3] author of *Mṛgāvatī* (1503), follows *Candāyan* when he describes the earth as wearing a garment of greenery. Rūpmiṇī in *Mṛgāvatī* suffers in the same way as Mainā in *Candāyan*. She requests Dullabh, the leader of the merchants' caravan, to tell her husband Manohar that she has been scorched by *virah*. In *Mṛgāvatī* the bearer of the message is also a leader of merchants but he does not seem to be a Brahmin as in *Candāyan*.

Jāyasī uses more detailed imagery in his *Padmāvat*.[4] Nāgmatī suffers in Sāvan due to the absence of Ratnasen. In her sorrow she sheds tears of blood which fall to the earth as velvet insects (*vīr badhuṭī*). In the month of Sāvan, as is the tradition even now, girls swing on their swings in happiness, but Nāgmatī was overcome by the pain of *virah* and was trembling with agony. Like the author of *Candāyan* and *Mrgāvatī*, Jāyasī describes the earth as having put on a garment of greenery. In *Padmāvat* it is the bird Parevā who is a messenger. Here Nāgmatī, in her message to Ratnasen, says that the whole world is filled with water and that there are impassable mountains and dense forests on the path. 'How could I come to you? I have no wings to fly.' Jāyasī's long and detailed descriptions single him out from the other poets of this tradition of Hindi Sufi poetry.

In *Kanhāvat*[5] which is attributed to Malik Muhammad Jāyasī, milkmaids suffer from *virah* when Kṛṣṇa leaves them and goes to Madhupurī. Their eyes shed water like the eaves of a house during the rainy season. This imagery is also found in *Padmāvat*: the clouds are raining heavily but the milkmaids are drying up. Those women who, united with their husbands, are swinging on swings and wearing nice garments have been described in the same way as in Sufi texts. The milkmaids, like other women suffering from *virah,* are without embellishments and feel that their lives are useless. Here the wind carries the milkmaids' message to Kṛṣṇa.

In *Madhumālatī,* Mañjhan[6] describes the heroines' *virah* as follows: 'Both the thick clouds of the Sāvan month and Madhumālatī's eyes are overflowing with water like the rivers Gaṅgā and Yamunā.' Madhumālatī sheds tears of blood and, as in *Padmāvat,* the tears turn into velvet insects as they fall. As in *Candāyan* and the other Sufi texts, Madhumālatī's eyes shed tears continuously and she is plunged deeply into the agony of separation.

Bhādõ

In Bhādõ (August-September) the nights become deep, dark and fearsome for Mainā, who is still a young girl. Lightning flashes and loneliness seizes her heart in the absence of her husband Lorik. Without a companion she suffers painful isolation. Tears fall from her sorrowful eyes and fill both land and sea. It is impossible for her to cross the mountains and the waterlogged earth to reach her husband. In the last two verses she complains that Lorik listened to a wicked woman (Candā) and ran away with her. Mainā spends her nights crying (*Candāyan,* v. 38).

Mṛgāvatī's description of the month of Bhādõ in the Indian rainy season is more detailed than the description in *Candāyan.* It is continuously raining in torrents and the nights are deep and dark. Lightning is also flashing (v. 318). Like Mainā in *Candāyan,* Rūpmiṇī is also described as being afraid. Her bed is no longer comfortable for her; it bites her like a serpent. Here Kutuban shows his familiarity with Indian myths and legends. Rūpmiṇī's eyes shed water in the same way as rains fall in the Sleṣā and Maghā *nakṣatra.*[7] Rūpmiṇī has become like a *papīhā* bird always calling *piu, piu* ('loved one'). The croaking of frogs which kills Rūpmiṇī has also been described here. She says that she is sinking in the ocean of *virah* and that there is no boatman or rope that she can hold onto. Her eyes are overflowing like the flooded Gaṅgā. Her bed is also floating in the floods.

Malik Muhammad Jāyasī (v. 318) in *Padmāvat* describes the nights of Bhādõ to some extent as in *Candāyan* or *Mṛgāvatī*. Lightning flashing in the deep, dark and cloudy nights is similarly described, and the water flowing from Nāgmatī's eyes is similarly likened to water falling from the eaves of a house. This imagery first appears in *Candāyan* and then in *Mṛgāvatī* and is continued in *Padmāvat*. Nāgmatī is drying up in the rainy season—this is Jāyasī's own imagination. In Bhādõ the land and sky meet but Nāgmatī drowns in the profound water of youth. She says, 'O loved one, come and protect me.'

In *Kanhāvat* (v. 310) the dark night of Bhādõ has been depicted in the same way as in other Sufi texts. In their palaces the milkmaids are suffering and are complaining that Kṛṣṇa has gone away and been enchanted so that he does not care to send them any messages. The earth is filled with water and so are the eyes of the milkmaids; without Kṛṣṇa, who is compared to a boatman, they drown in the deep water of *virah*.

It is needless to say that the poet of *Kanhāvat* also follows *Candāyan* and *Mṛgāvatī* as far as the description of nature is concerned. There is close similarity between *Padmāvat* and *Kanhāvat* in that Nāgmatī is also sinking in the deep water of youth and calls out to her loved one, Ratnasen, to save her. In *Madhumālatī*, Madhumālatī is burning in the forest fire of *virah* during the dark night of Bhādõ. This forest fire of *virah* is her only friend in bed in the dark night of Bhādõ. Siṃh and Maghā disturb her and her eyes shed tears in the same way as water falls from the eaves of a house. Again it can be seen that this description has been borrowed by Mañjhan from his predecessors who wrote *Candāyan* (v. 343/5) and *Padmāvat* (v. 346/4).

Kvār

Now the month of Kvār (September-October) comes and the star Canopus (Agastya) appears.[8] The rains stop but Mainā's husband Lorik does not return. *Kā̃s* (a tall grass) grows and the swans start swimming in the ponds. Cranes, wagtails, and herons also appear. In this month of Kvār young girls are happy with their husbands and start burning lamps in earthen plates. In this new season of freshness, king and poor alike cook nice food in the dark fortnight of the month at the time of Pitṛpakṣa[9] and eat well, but Mainā cannot eat anything. There is no enjoyment for her. She is without her loved one. Mainā expects Lorik to saddle his horse and return home but the *mechu* (*malekṣa*, unclean one) does not return (*Candāyan* v. 345-7); he remains cruel and obdurate.

Kutuban describes Aśvin (Kvār) a little differently. Here the appearance of the star, the stopping of the rains, the appearance of flowers, grass, birds, wagtails, and cranes have all been described in the same manner as in *Candāyan,* but *virah* has become like the Hastī *nakṣatra* (*hathiyā*)[10], thundering and roaring. Rūpmiṇī is alone in her bed. In *Mṛgāvatī* the image of the elephant of *virah* is repeated in lines 5 and 6 of the stanza. The phrase *maimant kuñjar* ('maddened elephant') has been used here for the symbolic elephant who is trampling the body of Rūpmiṇī suffering from the agony of *virah.* In *Padmāvat* the star Agastya and diminishing water have also been described as in *Candāyan* and *Mṛgāvatī.* Wagtails, cranes, and partridges too have been described as in *Candāyan.* The description of the elephant of *virah* tearing Nāgmatī's body into pieces and eating her up is more or less similar to the descriptions in *Candāyan.* However, Jāyasī describes Citrā, Hastī, and Uttarā *nakṣatra* in some detail,[11] displaying his excellence as a poet all the time. 'The elephant of *virah* disturbing Nāgmatī' is not his original idea but the request to Ratnasen to come as a lion to control the elephant (v. 347) is his own creation and adds to the excellence of his poetry.

In *Kanhāvat* (v. 311) the poet describes the happy women whose husbands are at home and who are eating well, but tells us that Kṛṣṇa has tricked the milkmaids Rādhā and Candrāvalī. The star Agastya and the partridge (*khañjan*) are described here as well. The milkmaids lament and say, 'Had we known that Kṛṣṇa would not return we would not have let him go.'

Mañjhan describes, in *Madhumālatī* (v. 404), the festival of Navrātrī, and the wagtails, cranes, and partridges as in *Candāyan.* All the birds are chirping and chanting but Madhumālatī is flying in the forest like a bird. All are happy in this season but Madhumālatī is crying. In Kvār the rains stop and the water begins to subside, but Madhumālatī's eyes are filled with tears; she can neither speak nor describe her sorrow.

Kārtik

In the month of Kārtik (October-November) the nights are pleasant and clear but the moonlight burns Mainā, and she suffers painfully. Other women make beds for their worthy husbands and embrace them. Mainā thinks her loved one will come for Dīvālī to play and sing on this great festival of lights, but he does not return, and the whole world becomes dark for her. Candā took away her bright one (husband), and she suffers in his absence. Her husband has left Mainā and become someone else's. Mainā requests Surjan to plead with him on her behalf and prays that he might return to worship the deity on the festival of *devaṭhān.*[12]

Like Maulāna Dāūd, Kutuban (v. 320) also describes the bright nights of the *śarad* season and the cool moon, all of which disturb Rūpmiṇī since she suffers the pains of separation. In *Padmāvat* the cool nights and bright moon are also described while Nāgmatī burns in *virah.* Kutuban does not describe the Dīvālī festival of lights, but Jāyasī refers to it and the women singing festive songs as in *Candāyan. Candāyan* refers to the worship of *devaṭhān,* but in *Padmāvat, munivar* or *manorā* worship is mentioned.[13] All the women celebrate the festival in *Padmāvat,* but it is a painful occasion for Nāgmatī without her husband.

Kārtik is also painful for the milkmaids in *Kanhāvat* (v. 312) and the moonlight also burns them. Women whose husbands are with them enjoy themselves, but the milkmaids suffer because Kṛṣṇa is away and nobody comes to them from Madhuban with a message.

Madhumālatī (v. 405) is tormented by the cool moon—a standard image found in almost all the Hindi Sufi texts. Other women enjoy themselves, but Madhumālatī suffers in Kārtik. The Divālī festival is referred to here, but Madhumālatī is miserable and flies from one forest to another.

Agahan

In Agahan (November-December) the nights start becoming long and the days, short. Mainā in *Candāyan* (v. 347) says that her own body is decaying day by day. The wind blows slowly and she feels the cold attacking her body, yet her husband Lorik does not return to protect her. She burns with *kām* ('sexual desire') and the pain of *virah* causes wildfire in her body. It burns her to ashes and smears the ashes onto its face and body. *Virah* is clearly personified here as a Śaiva *sādhu* who picks up the ashes of corpses and smears them on his forehead and body. Mainā is deeply anguished and prays to God not to give such suffering to anyone. In contrast Cāndā enjoys the company of the Sun, Lorik, leaving behind her own husband Bāvan. Mainā feels insulted that her husband has abandoned her and laments that in that cold season the shameless Candā sleeps and enjoys herself with someone else's husband.

Mṛgāvatī describes how cold the world feels in Agahan (v. 321). Here Kutuban's Rūpmiṇī sends her message to her husband Manohar and requests him to come and enjoy himself with her as the prime of her youth will never return again. At the end of the stanza Kutuban says, 'One should not forget love even for a moment. This youth declines just as water slowly drips out of cupped palms (*añjali*).'

Following *Candāyan,* Malik Muhammad Jāyasī in *Padmāvat* describes the declining days and the expanding nights. At night hearts tremble as the cold season begins, but Nāgmatī burns in *virah* like the wick of a lamp. Other girls are with their husbands and embellish themselves with fine garments, but Nāgmatī is deprived of all this. Like Mainā in *Candāyan,* Nāgmatī is also burning in the fire of sorrow in separation. She sends her message to Ratnasen and tells him that even bees and crows were burnt black by Nāgmatī's fire of *virah.* Here one sees the universalization of *virah* so typical of Jāyasī (e.g. *Padmāvat* v. 349. 8-9).

In *Kanhāvat* (v. 313), the shortening of the day and expansion of the nights are described in the same way as in *Candāyan.* Here *saur supetī* ('thick quilts and sheets') are being prepared by all the women who are with their husbands, but the milkmaids are shedding tears of *virah* because Kṛṣṇa who used to sleep with them on the bed (*sej suvanār*) is away from them. They are dying of cold and wish Kṛṣṇa could come as the Sun to embrace them and dispel the cold. It is to be remembered that *saur supetī* for thick quilt and sheet first appear together in *Candāyan* when the month of Pūs is described (v. 340) and occur in descriptions of this month also in the works of subsequent Sufi poets (*Mṛgāvatī* v. 322, *Padmāvat* v. 350). The only exception seems to be *Madhumālatī* (v. 406) which describes Agahan as a cold month in which people want to be near the fireplace. The happiness of the daytime has diminished and the sorrows have increased for Madhumālatī whose intense *virah* has been vividly presented here.

Pūs

Now the month of Pūs (December-January) comes and Mainā watches the path for her husband's arrival (*Candāyan,* v. 348). She cannot sleep even for a moment day or night, cannot bear the cold, and feels neither dead nor alive. In every house women arrange thick quilts and sheets (*saur sapetī*) and eat meat of various kinds and ghee (clarified butter), but Mainā's heart burns in separation. She does not want to wear fine clothes or bodices. She thinks that her loved one will return with the arrival of the month of Pūs but that does not happen. Kings and paupers, all enjoy themselves at home with their women in this period, but Lorik has gone away on business (*banij*), and Mainā sheds tears. She requests Surjan to ask Lorik what profit he will gain if he loses his main asset (*pū̃jī*).

In *Mṛgāvatī* (v. 322), Rūpmiṇī is also suffering in the month of Pūs. The frost (*tusār*) has thickened and her cold bed causes her more anguish. She is alone on her bed and the thick quilt and the bed sheets are uncomfortable for her. It is clear that *Mṛgāvatī's* descriptions are distinctive, but Kutuban describes Rūpmiṇī's *virah* as intensely as Maulānā Dāu'd depicts Mainā's in *Candāyan.*

In *Padmāvat* (v. 353), Nāgmatī trembles in Pūs. As in the other works, the sun is weak but her *virah* is great. Even with the thick quilt and sheet she feels cold as if the bed were submerged in ice. A female partridge who is separated from her mate during the night is united with him in the daytime, but Nāgmatī can meet her husband neither in the daytime nor during the night. Nāgmatī is alone and the vulture of *virah* is attacking her. It seems that this vulture of *virah* which is eating her up during her lifetime will not spare her even after her death. Nāgmatī has become thin and emaciated: her flesh has melted and her tears have changed into blood. As these examples reveal, although Jāyasī borrows many themes from *Candāyan,* he surpasses his predecessors in poetic skill.

In *Kanhāvat* also (v. 314) the cold is terrible in Pūs, and cruel (*nichoh*) Kṛṣṇa does not return. The milkmaids' hearts tremble with pangs of separation and they shiver like the leaves of a tree. The firepot of *virah* (*aṅgīṭhī*) burns their bodies to ashes. This image is found in *Candāyan* in the context of the description of Māgh (v. 349.2). The milkmaids say if Kṛṣṇa returns and embraces them, they will revive. They pray to him to come and save them. While the intensity of the *virah* described here is akin to that described in other Hindi Sufi texts, the vulture of *virah* and the image of the partridge and its mate are not found in *Kanhāvat.*

For *Madhumālatī* (v. 407) the night is difficult in this month of Pūs. Other girls desire to meet their husbands, but she flies from one forest to another like a bird, complaining that her husband has left her in the full bloom of youth. Other wives meet their husbands happily, but Madhumālatī is deprived of hers. The biting cold of Pūs has not been mentioned here.

Māgh

In Māgh (January-February), it is frosty and so cold that even the strings of Mainā's necklace tremble on her breasts. Her teeth chatter with cold and tears trickle from her eyes. The firepot of *virah* burns in her heart. First she burns from the pangs of separation, then the frost strikes her. Her life has become burdensome for her. Just as the frost strikes the lotus causing it to decay, so her husband Lorik has caused her to decay in the month of Māgh. In the mornings of this *hemant* season she finds herself without the Sun (Lorik). Candā has eloped with the Sun and that *malekṣa* ('wicked one') has slept with another woman. She requests Surjan to tell Lorik that she is dying, struck by frost, and that he should return soon to comfort her (*Candāyan,* v. 349).

In *Mṛgāvatī* (v. 349) Rūpmiṇī also burns in *virah* even though the cold wind blows. She requests her husband to come and shine like the Sun to remove her cold. The last *dohā* in *Mṛgāvatī* is very interesting; Rūpmiṇī says that *virah* has stolen all her happiness and comforts in the same way as Rāvaṇ abducted Sītā. Her husband should come and kill Rāvaṇ as Rām (Raghunandan) did.

The frost of Māgh strikes Nāgmatī in the same way. Just as in *Candāyan* (v. 349.7) Mainā calls her husband to come in the form of the Sun and warm her up, so in *Padmāvat* Nāgmatī requests Ratnasen to come and do likewise. In the cold season the *virah* burns Nāgmatī to ashes and wants to scatter them all around. Jāyasī uses hyperbole (*atiśayokti*) (v. 351) to intensify the depth of Nāgmatī's *virah.*

In *Kanhāvat* (v. 35) the frost of Māgh disturbs the milkmaids just as it does Mainā in *Candāyan*. Thick quilts and sheets (*saur sapetī*) are cold as ice to them; they suffer from *virah* and complain to their co-wife Kubjā.

For Madhumālatī (v. 408) it is a terribly cold season (*siyāl*), but she sits on the branch of the *virah* tree, which is extremely painful for her. The last verse ('My husband took away all my happiness and besides this, *virah* was attacking my bones and flesh with its sharp knife (*kātī*)') epitomizes Madumālatī's condition.

Phāgun

In *Candāyan* (v. 350) Maulānā Dāūd says that people feel that the cold increases four-fold in Phāgun (February-March) and the wind blows hard, but for Mainā the cold has increased by seven times more. She is dying in the month of Phāg since Lorik is not there to embrace her. In every house girls play Phāg with sticks (*ḍaṇḍāhar*). They are as blessed as princesses; they chew betel leaves, put kohl on their eyes, braid their hair, put vermilion in the part of their hair and a special mark on their forehead. They dance the Phāg dance and their ankle bells ring sonorously. The whole world is overcome with joy, but Mainā sheds so many tears of blood that her bodice and clothes become red. She requests Surjan to tell Lorik that Mainā has been burned to ashes during the period of Holī. In *Mṛgāvatī*, the *virahiṇī* is also burnt to ashes (v. 324). The whole world plays Phāg or Holī and *Mṛgāvatī* puts her life itself in the burning Holikā bonfire, hoping that her ashes might fly to her loved one. The spring season has arrived but *virah* is singing *carcarī* songs to burn her to ashes. She sheds tears of blood and thus her body turns vermilion. The wind also disturbs her, the courtyard and the bed do not please her, and the spring passes in vain since her beloved has left her and become someone else's. The festival of Vasant ('spring') is pleasant for others, but for *Mṛgāvatī* it brings the madness of youth. Leaves fall from the trees and still her husband does not come back home.

In *Padmāvat* (v. 352) the wind of Phāgun blows and the *virahiṇī* Nāgmatī suffers still more. Her body has withered like a dried leaf. Trees have put on flowers and nature is happy, but Nāgmatī is anguished. People enjoy Phāg and women dance and sing Holī songs (*carcarī*, etc.), but Ratnasen has put the bonfire of Holikā into Nāgmatī's heart. Nāgmatī says that she will burn her body and reduce it to ashes and ask the wind to scatter them on the path; maybe her loved one will put his feet on the ashes. She wants to meet him in any way possible.

In *Kanhāvat* as in *Candāyan*, the cold in Phāgun is four times stronger than in the previous month. Women who are with their husbands embellish themselves and play Holī, but the milkmaids dry up in *virah.* The sun also burns them, and Kṛṣṇa has gone away and hidden himself in Madhuban. The milkmaids remember him and suffer (v. 316).

In *Madhumālatī*, the heroine recounts her sorrow. Her burnt body has become like Holikā's bonfire. Autumn has set in and gardens are deserted. Madhumālatī goes to all the trees and sits on their branches in the form of a bird, lamenting and crying. She suffers the pangs of separation as she is away from her husband. Her youth is in full bloom, but in her heart she is dry and deserted (v. 409).

Caitra

In the month of Caitra (March-April) buds appear and the green trees dress in white and red; the lotus blossoms and the sandal trees and other flowers generate sweet fragrances. Bees wander around the perfumed flowers. Mainā says to Surjan that the spring season has arrived, but her husband has seen another creeper and fallen in love with it (*Candāyan*, v. 351). This new season does not please Mainā at all since her husband has not arrived. She requests Lorik to return and see her garden; she is decaying, lonely, making her bed on thorns, and cannot sleep. She requests Surjan to tell Lorik that Mainā does not enjoy his company even for a moment.

In *Mṛgāvatī* (v. 325) new leaves have also appeared and flowers have blossomed. Cuckoos have started singing, but Rūpmiṇī has started burning in the fire of *virah. Candāyan* and *Mṛgāvatī* both contain descriptions of intense *virah,* but in *Padmāvat,* as usual, the descriptions of nature are exhaustive. In this spring season women sing Basant and Dhamār, but for Nāgmatī the world is deserted. Cuckoos sing, and it appears as though Kāmdev, the god of love, is shooting his five arrows. Nāgmatī pours out tears of blood which soak all the trees and their leaves, and the *majith* and *tesū* flowers. Mango trees start to bear fruit; bees buzz around all the flower trees, but they do not please Nāgmatī. They are all like thorns piercing her heart. In the end she requests Ratnasen to be like a homing pigeon and rush back home. The parrots of *virah* have attacked the fruits of her youth. Only he can save her (Padmāvat v. 353).[14]

In *Kanhāvat* women celebrate this spring festival and bring flower garlands home for their husbands. They also decorate their beds with flowers, but for the milkmaids it is not pleasant. All the liveliness of nature burns them in sorrow. Spring is beautiful only when the husband comes home smiling. The milkmaids remember Kubjā and despise her because she has detained Kṛṣṇa and made them suffer. Nights bring death to them, and the whole day they sit and wait for Kṛṣṇa (v. 317).

In *Madhumālatī* (v. 410) the trees have put on new garments of leaves and bees buzz everywhere. The leaves which had fallen in the autumn have appeared again but for Madhumālatī it is still autumn because her husband Manohar has left her. The Sun of *virah* is in the eighth position and shines sharply right upon her head.

Vaiśākh

Mainā says in *Candāyan* (v. 352) that the trees bear fruit in Vaiśākh (April-May). Mainā always thinks of her beloved, keeping him in her heart. She asks Lorik, who lacks good taste, to return and protect his 'mango garden' (i.e. Mainā), and enjoy himself with her. Who else could protect her? It grieves her that she is not able to discover which forest Lorik is living in. She suffers the pangs of separation and, feeling miserable, cries the whole day. She tells the valiant Lorik to return soon, for in his absence the ardent heat burns her badly. The spring season passes but Lorik does not come to her bed. He wanders around another creeper, like a bee enjoying the fruits of another vine.

In *Mṛgāvatī* (v. 326) the trees have also been described as bearing fruit. Rūpmiṇī requests her husband to return and enjoy himself with her, saying that she has protected his mango orchard so far, but it is impossible for her to protect it any longer from wicked ones. The parrot of *virah* wants to eat up all the fruit, and it is impossible to make him fly away.

Jāyasī (v. 354) describes the hot Sun who wants to go towards the Himālayas to cool himself. Instead he drives his chariot towards Nāgmatī who then burns all the more with *virah.* Nāgmatī feels hot despite all her cool clothes, and her heart burns like a kiln. *Padmāvat* does not contain all the descriptions of the mango trees and orchards found in *Candāyan* and *Mṛgāvatī,* but at the end of this section Nāgmatī says that the lotus which had blossomed in the pond of her heart has dried up and that new leaves could sprout in it only after her husband's arrival.

In *Kanhāvat* (v. 318) the Sun is extremely hot and burns Candrāvalī, Rādhikā, and the other sixteen thousand milkmaids. As in *Padmāvat,* cool clothes feel hot to the heroines (here the milkmaids), and sandalpaste fails to cool them down. Akrūr has taken their beloved Kṛṣṇa away to Madhupurī, and he does not care to return.

In Vaiśākh Madhumālatī suffers extremely in contrast to the other girls, who enjoy themselves with their husbands (v. 411). It is still the spring season and trees have put on flowers, but for Madhumālatī everything looks desolate and she is tormented at every moment. Yellow, red, and green leaves and fruit appear on the trees, but the fruits of Madhumālatī's youth, still unripe, fall off in the absence of her loved one.

Jeṭh

After the month of Vaiśākh, Maulānā Dāūd describes the month of Jeṭh (May-June, v. 353). The moon (*cā̃d*) has seized the sun, and the sun, burns the earth. Ardent heat scorches Mainā and tells her the tale of separation. Even cool drinks such as *khaṇḍavānī* and fresh water feel as if they are on fire. Due to the intense heat, she does not apply sandalpaste to her body nor use perfumed grass (*khas*). People start thatching their roofs and repairing the huts in preparation for the rainy season. All the other women enjoy union with their husbands, but Mainā burns in *virah.* She requests Surjan to beg Lorik to return home and to become the water of a river to extinguish her fire.

Kutuban also describes the extremely hot sun in the month of Jeṭh that produces wildfire. Rūpmiṇī invites her husband, Manohar, to come and give her coolness. Since Madan, the god of love, burns her, he must come like the cool wind coming from the Malay mountains. She sends her message through Durlabh, requesting him to tell Manohar to come as a cloud. Otherwise the sun will burn her, and she will crumble to pieces (v. 327).

In *Padmāvat* Malik Muhammad Jāyasī (v. 354) describes the

scorching heat and the dust storms of Jeṭh. Mountains are also extremely hot in this month. *Virah* rises and roars like Hanumān and starts burning Nāgmatī's body like the city of Laṅkā. Winds blow from four directions and fan the flames so that they reach her bed (*palaṅkā*). Nāgmatī burns and becomes black like the Yamunā River (Kālindī). The fire of *virah* has become intolerable for her. Jāyasī says that the hungry ravenous crow, who has started eating her flesh, has struck her bones. Nāgmatī's deep sorrow has been depicted here in detail; no other poet of this tradition surpasses Jāyasī in his use of similes and metaphors, and in his poetic excellence.

In *Kanhāvat* (v. 319) descriptions are simple, without any ornamentation. In Jeṭh the milkmaids have become lifeless. There is scorching heat (*lū*) and the wind blows sharply; wildfire spreads and so does the *virah* of the milkmaids, burning them thoroughly. They pray to Kṛṣṇa to come back from Madhuban to cool them.

In *Madhumālatī* (v. 412) also the month of Jeṭh is extremely hot. The sun spreads fire and Madhumālatī's heart is scorched by *virah.* Her husband is not with her to share her bed; she suffers *viyog* (separation), exile, and loneliness; her form changes from that of a human being into that of a bird. All this makes her desperate. She wants to die, but death does not approach her to take her away.

Āsāṛh

The last month Maulānā Dāūd describes is Āsāṛh (June-July, v. 354) when clouds start thundering and people begin to repair their homes, palaces, and halls; kings as well as ordinary men all start new lives; and traders who have gone to distant islands return home. Everyone who lives away from home is anxious to return, but Mainā's husband remains unconcerned. Her loved one causes her *virah,* and so her body becomes feeble and her flesh decays. She endures a hellish plight and suffers death every day in the absence of her husband. Who could bear the pangs of separation every day? Mainą̄ requests Surjan to tell Lorik that Sāvan has begun again and she cannot control herself and keep herself alive. She looks after the house and store and sheds tears of blood.

In *Mṛgāvatī,* Kutuban follows *Candāyan* (v. 328) when he describes the roaring of clouds in the sky—though here they appear to roar like elephants—and lightning flashing in every direction.

As in the description in *Candāyan,* traders return home. Rūpmiṇī's husband, however, remains in a foreign land. The month of Sāvan begins again and the world is filled with water. Indra and Śani unite to make Rūpminī suffer and cry.

The *bārahmāsā* in *Padmāvat* starts in the month of Āsāṛh and ends in the month of Jeṭh. Āsāṛh comes and the clouds thunder in the sky just as in *Candāyan.* But the *virah* in *Padmāvat* starts a great war and blows its trumpet loudly. Dark, white and grey coloured clouds wander about like soldiers, the flocks of white cranes look like the banners of an army, and the lightning is like the brandished swords of a king. These vivid descriptions in which the king of *virah* launches a war against Nāgmatī are not found elsewhere in Hindi Sufi texts. Peacocks and cuckoos along with frogs all disturb Nāgmatī, and she worries about who will repair the roof of her house. It is interesting to see that Ratnasen is described in the text as a king, but here his wife Nāgmatī, is described as worrying about a roof which needs repairing. In many folktales heroines are described as queens, but they wash their own clothes like ordinary women. In Āsārh Nāgmatī is devoid of happiness without her husband.

Like *Padmāvat, Kanhāvat* also describes the month of Āsāṛh at the beginning of the *bārahmāsā* (v. 308). Clouds thunder and lightning flashes here as well. Cuckoos, peacocks and partridges all call and frogs, who bring the message of rains, croak. Thus the milkmaids suffer agony in separation, saying that Kṛṣṇa is as near to them as a necklace is to the body, but a great mountain like Kubjā has blocked him from coming. It is hard for them to bear this pain and sorrow of separation.

In *Madhumālatī* (v. 413) the thundering of clouds and flashing of lightning are also described, and in this work also people are roofing their houses against the rains. Madhumālatī complains that the earth is turning green and the buds of flowers and fruits are sprouting on the trees and plants, but in her husband's heart love does not sprout. She tells her friend that she spent twelve months in *virah* and asks her to help her come out of it.

It is interesting to see that all the messengers start suffering from *virah* when they listen to the message. Their suffering emphasises a universal cosmic *virah.* Listening to the sad tale of *virah* in *Candāyan,* Surjan himself becomes filled with sorrow; *dvandva* ('conflict and confusion'), *udveg* ('anxiety'), *ucāṭ* ('sleeplessness') all take hold of him as he starts burning in the fire of *virah.* He forgets his own original trade and remembers only the pangs of separation. Not only Surjan, but all his friends and companions also, start burning in the wildfire of *virah.* This *virah* is so strong that all the houses on the path burst into flames. All the animals and birds are blackened by the fire of *virah.* The fish in the sea and the partridges in the lakes suffer from it; the moon's face in the sky is blackish, and the clouds have become dark; both the old and the young have started suffering from the pangs of *virah* (vv. 362-3).

Mṛgāvatī follows *Candāyan* closely in this universalization of *virah.* For example, Nāyak in *Mṛgāvatī* is also plunged into the grief of *virah* and *dvandva* ('confusion', 'conflict'); experiences *udveg* ('anxiety'), and *ucāṭ* ('sleeplessness'). He forgets his own trade and carries the load of all this suffering. Rūpmiṇī's message has deeply affected him. As in *Candāyan,* people who collect taxes on the path (*dānī*) all burn in *virah* along with the houses and forests. In *Mṛgāvatī* even the sea burns up (vv. 332-3).

In *Padmāvat,* when the bird carries the message, the fire of *virah* spreads everywhere and the whole of Siṃhal (Sri Lanka) starts burning. As the fire rises, the clouds become dark, and the earth, sea, fish, forests, and trees all burn from this cosmic *virah.*

In *Kanhāvat* the earth and sky all burn from one spark of *virah* (v. 322). Kṛṣṇa asks the wind why it is burning so intensely, and it replies with the message sent by Rādhā, Candrāvalī and the milkmaids. Kṛṣṇa listens to the message, and love grows in his heart until finally they meet. The suffering of the milkmaids is as intense here as in the other Sufi texts.

It is clear from these descriptions that Sufi poets have a special purpose in describing the *bārahmāsā.* The philosophy of *virah* is central to the Sufi concept of love, and this finds clear expression in the *bārahmāsās.* All the messsengers begin to suffer as they listen to the message of *virah* which the poets make universal and cosmic. They have chosen the *bārahmāsā* theme to convey the *virah* felt by the soul as soon as it separates from the Divine. Love and the pain of *virah* are almost synonymous in Hindi Sufi texts.

Salmān Masū'd's 'Bārahmāsā'

The *bārahmāsā* of Masū'd Sādī Salmān (1043-1131)[15] is the first work of this type in Persian though it does not deal with *virah.* It was composed in praise of King Masū'd who succeeded Mahmūd

Ghaznavī (d. 1030) and reigned for ten years, from AD 1030 to 1040.

This *bārahmāsā* begins with the Iranian month of Parvardīn which begins on 21 March and ends in the month of Spandārmaz (which is called Isfand Māh in modern times). The poet, who lived in Lahore, was probably influenced by Indian folk literature or the literary conventions in which descriptions of the six seasons were very common. In Indian folk literature twelve month descriptions must have been as popular during Salmān's lifetime as they are today, but literary *bārahmāsās* appear at a comparatively late date. The oldest example according to Agarcand Nāhṭā, is *Bārahnāvaū* by an unknown poet, probably composed in the thirteenth century. Vaudeville (1986, p. 18) has analysed the contents of this work which praises Dharma Sūri. It will be interesting to compare this *bārahmāsā* with Salmān's *bārahmāsā,* which is nothing but a eulogy of King Masū'd.

Salmān begins his *bārahmāsā* by asking the people to remain happy. God is great and His commandment is that we should obey the king until the Day of Judgement. King Masū'd is great, and the kings of Rūm send gifts to him. He sits on the throne and possesses various kinds of jewels. All beautiful gardens are symbols of his glory, and he merits praise for them. People taste the good fruits of the trees of his justice. The poet Salmān Masūd wishes him well and prays to God that his glory remain forever and that prosperity and happiness follow him.

The second month that Salmān describes is Ardībahisht, which falls in April. In this month the world becomes a paradise and the enjoyment of wine is permitted. Without wine life is useless. The glory of this month is great: fields, gardens, and mountains have started smiling with flowers and the clouds have started shedding tears, birds have started chirping; the earth has put on different types of raiment; angels have started shaping the earth in beautiful forms; God has given power to the king, and he is enjoying the flowers and perfumes.

Khurdād Māh, which begins in May, looks beautiful with its blooming gardens; the flowers and nature are embodiments of happiness in this season; birds sing sitting on the tree of liberty; slaves and king alike are happy in this season. It is good to drink in this month. King Masū'd is great; his kingdom is superb; he and his people are all happy; he is the custodian of religion; prosperity and generosity are due to him. The poet Salmān prays for him and wishes that he might rule until the Day of Judgement.

With regard to Tīr Māh, the poet declares:

O Beautiful One, with the face of a moon, you should ask for wine in this month. This is a good time. You must enjoy wine. It is through wine that the heart feels fresh. My heart is happy with wine. If you see sins in me, I may tell you truly that I do not have many sins or faults in me. The wine is costly. Even the king feels so when he proceeds for a war with his soldiers. Our king is like a lion. He has captured all the territories; other kings are his slaves.

The poet goes on to say that we are all happy in the month of Murdād, which begins in June:

You must drink wine in this month. The earth has assumed various beautiful colours. The eyes of the clouds are filled with tears. The earth and mountains have all put on new clothes. The city of Rūn looks beautiful with its new garments. Be happy and ask for wine under the protection of our king. King Masūd is the crown of all kings. Jewels obtain brilliance from the king. The throne of the kingdom is stable due to him. O king, I wish you might live long in happiness. Let your enemies die in fear and agony

In the next month, Shahrīwār, people are happy because of the king's justice: 'I am also happy. O my friend, dear to my heart, give me wine and remember the king. He is happy on the throne. There is no other king whose crown is so beautiful.' The poet goes on to say that in the month of Shahrīvūr 'The king has been selected by the sky (destiny). Nobody has ever seen such a good king. In this season camphor has increased on the earth. You should also take perfumed wine in your hand. In this prosperous kingdom you should hold the wine cup since the spring season has now arrived. O king, through your kindness the autumn of the world has changed into spring.'

In the seventh solar month, Mahra,

the moon shows its compassion to the people. If you cannot drink this month, you are unfortunate. In this month the faces of my friends look clean in the daytime but their hearts are black. But the king is the blessed one. He wishes well to others. All other kings are his slaves. There is no other king like him. Mecca and the Kab'ah are very expensive places to see, but our king is easy to approach. He is prosperous; even the sky serves him and bows before him in respect. He has many slaves. His kingdom offers glory to the people.

In the eighth month, Ābān, the rains begin:

They are hidden in clouds. You should drink the water of grapes (wine) at this time. It is good to sleep during this time but it is better to drink and be intoxicated. Have you seen that man who is wise and intelligent and who has broken the backbone of my poverty and removed my sorrow? He has wine, and through this wine he protects others. Pass your time in happiness. Drink wine as you have been set free from sorrows. King Masū'd is sitting down to drink; we must be happy with his justice.

On the arrival of the ninth month, Āzārmāh, the poet says:

Give me strong burning wine. Burn fire. People in the houses are happy. Let this month come with his face as shining as fire. It is true that the gardens are without flowers and the trees are without fruits, but King Masū'd has made this garden like a paradise. People are safe with his justice and generosity. God has given him power. His name is glorious. May the king's glory, kingship, and generosity live—as long as the moon and the sun are in the sky.

When the tenth month, Dei, comes, the wind starts dispersing camphor over the earth. It starts snowing. The autumn wind becomes cold, and the army of cold waves start moving from the sky. 'King Arsalān Masū'd is great; he has changed this earth into a garden. King Alexander and Naushervān have now incarnated in you. Your sense of justice is better than theirs. I wish you a life as long as the sky.'

The poet says that wine is necessary in the month of Bahan:

Wise men infuse new life in the world this month. Minstrels, singers, and wine cup bearers (*sāqī*) appear now and start singing. They play the *rūd* and bring wine for the king in order to celebrate the festival in his presence. The king is sitting and will definitely drink. He is superb, unparalleled, next to none. Sometimes God brings a cold season and sometimes a hot one. The king also sometimes becomes generous and sometimes cruel.

Spandār, the twelfth month of the Iranian solar year, is said to be

the last month for the enemies who are going to die. This month brings a new message of life. Gardens will be green again, flowers will blossom, and beauty will spread everywhere. Birds will start chirping in the plains and in the gardens, clouds will appear and cover the sky, the wind from the north will blow, and fragrance will spread. I thank the king. Through his kindness the new year will bring prosperity and happiness. O king, the sky is beautiful for you. The sea is for you to govern. There are all kinds of gifts and the ornaments for your kingship. May God bless you.

You shine like the Sun and give light to your people. Progress every day and earn more and more prestige from your people.

This poem of Salmān is the first *bārahmāsā* in Persian literature, but its content is neither *virah* nor union of lovers as we find in Indian traditions. In India, literary *bārahmāsās* started appearing in the thirteenth century; before that only the *ṣaṭ ṛtu* (six seasons) descriptions are found. From the Sanskrit poet Kālidāsa to the Apabhraṃśa poet Addahmāṇa of the twelfth century *ṣaṭ ṛtu* are found in large number. Masū'd Salmān is the first and last Persian poet to compose a *bārahmāsā.* It can safely be assumed that he may have been influenced by Indian folk traditions, but his descriptions of nature, praise of his contemporary king, and emphasis on wine drinking is his own creation. The first Jain poet, the anonymous author of *Bārahnāvaū,* describes the greatness of a Jain master, but his *bārahmāsā* is a Jain religious text.

Vaudeville in her *Bārahmāsā in Indian Literature* has made a general study of *bārahmāsā,* including some translations of the original texts. *Virah bārahmāsā* are found in folk traditions in large number. Hindi Sufi poets borrowed their themes from folk tradition, demonstrating the philosophy of *virah* everywhere they could. In *Candāyan* not only the wife, Mainā, but also Surjan, who carries the message of *virah,* begins suffering from the pain, sleeplessness, and anxiety caused by the message. Other Sufi texts follow *Candāyan* in saying that nobody could remain untouched by *virah.*

Krishna Dev Upadhyay has collected fifteen *bārahmāsās*[16] of which eight begin with Āsāṛh,[17] as do four of the eight collected by Ram Naresh Tripathi in *Kavitā Kaumudī* (Bombay: Navnit Prakashan, 1966). It is interesting to see that a large number of *bārahmāsās* begin in the rainy season. In Kālidāsa's *Meghadūta* the Yakṣa sends his message of *virah* in Āsāṛh. This tendency seems to be very common in the folk tradition.

One example of folk *bārahmāsā* beginning with Āsāṛh is given here from the Upadhyay collection. The *virahiṇī* says:

O friend, the first month was Āsāṛh; we could hear the thunder in this month. My cruel husband did not come at all, his heart was obdurate. It was drizzling in Sāvan, but my husband was getting wet in a foreign land. The suffering woman remembered her husband and repeated his name. Peacocks screamed in the forest. In Bhādõ the night was fearsome and it rained heavily in all directions. Partridges were chanting and frogs were croaking. In Kuvār my husband was in a foreign country and my three symbols of vermilion, kohl in my eyes, and youth—all wanted to kill me. Kārtik came, the special bathing (*Kārtik snān*) began, and all my friends bathed in the Ganges; all put on yellow garments, but I put on old tattered clothes. In Agahan my husband brought me home after the *gaunā* ceremony and then left for a foreign land. He did not even send me a letter after he left and did not care to find out news of me. In Pūs it rained, but I was alone, my house was empty, and the night did not pass easily. I did not know when the morning would come. Māgh came. I felt cold. If my beloved husband had been here, I would have made him sleep in my lap, and the winter would not have affected me. In Phāgun Phaguvā was celebrated and all my friends played Holī. If I had played Holī, people would have spoken ill of me. My whole body was burning in *virah.* The month of Caitra was sad for me. My husband had gone away. I was as unfortunate as a black female serpent. It seemed my husband would return in the spring, but he did not come back. Vaiśākh was hot, and I shed tears. How could I blame that Yoginī who had charmed my loved one? In Jeṭh the heat was scorching and the hot wind blew, but still my husband did not return. He was hard and had no tears in his eyes.

This is an example of a simple folk woman's *virah bārahmāsā* with no literary ornamentation. Perhaps this kind of *bārahmāsā* was the inspiration behind the literary versions even though they start in different months. Vaudeville has explained that the literary *bārahmāsā* is indebted to folk literature and not vice versa (Ch. Vaudeville 1986, p. 20). All over northern India such *virah bārahmāsās* are found as an independent genre in folk literature. Their descriptions of external nature through the twelve months are in consonance with the emotions of woman suffering from *virah.* Sufi poets used the *bārahmāsā* to depict the philosophy of *virah* or *firāq,* which was in the origin of creation. Through sexual symbolism these works express the desire of the soul to unite with the divine.

Candāyan begins in Sāvan, and all other early Sufi poets except Jāyasī follow *Candāyan* in this respect. However, it is clear that all these *bārahmāsās* begin in the rainy season, whether in Āsāṛh or Sāvan, because a *virahiṇī* is understood to suffer most when the clouds thicken and lightning flashes. There are some exceptions such as Narpati Nāth's *bārahmāsā* (which begins in Kārtik), but most *virah bārahmāsās* begin in the rainy season.

I would like to add here that the four volumes of oral epics based on the Lorik-Candā tale which I have published so far do not include *bārahmāsā.* Sūfi poets as well as secular poets such as Narpati Nāth, the author of *Vīsaḷdev Rāso,* or the Jain poet

Vinaycandra Suri who wrote *Nemināth Catuṣpadikā,* were influenced by lyrical folk songs. The long oral epics *Lorikī* or *Canaīnī* which I have studied have not used twelve-month descriptions although they have messengers who carry the message of Mainā's *virah* to Lorik. In the Banaras version Jaggū Bañjārā carries the message of Mainā Mājari to Lorik, whereas in the Allahabad version a caravan of traders are the messengers. In the Mirzāpur version the messenger is a barber named Gāṅgī. In all the oral versions of the epic, messengers play an important role in carrying the message of *virah,* even though they all come from different caste backgrounds. In *Cāndāyan* it is the Brahmin Surjan who is the messenger, but he is a trader by profession. An interesting aspect of this *virah,* description is that Mainā Mājari protects her fidelity and faithfulness when faced with adverse situations. But the most important aspect of *Candāyan* is that the poet suggests a philosophy of *virah* to demonstrate the profound nature of divine love.

NOTES

1. Sanā'ī, whose literary activities cover the first half of the twelfth century, was the first Persian author to write an extensive poem elaborating the doctrines of Sufism.
2. For the *bārahmāsā* see verses 343-54 of Gupta's edition of *Candāyan.*
3. For the *bārahmāsā* see verses 317-28 of Gupta's edition of *Mṛgāvatī.*
4. Jāyasī's, *bārahmāsā* in *Padmāvat* begins in Āsāṛh and goes up to Jeṭh-Āsāṛh (verses 344-56 in V.S. Agraval's edition).
5. *Kanhāvat* is a Kṛṣṇaite text attributed to Jāyasī. Its date of composition seems to be AH 947, which corresponds to AD 1540. His *Padmāvat* is also supposed to have been composed in AD 1540. The poet refers to Humāyūn and not Shershāh as the contemporary king. It is difficult to believe that in the same year a poet of Jāyasī's calibre could write two epics, one of which is of such inferior quality. Two different kings are mentioned in these two texts, which also creates some doubts about the authorship of *Kanhāvat.* However, this is the first text in Hindi which deals with the Kṛṣṇa story although it is a Sufi text in which Kṛṣṇa is divine and the women are seekers after love. The *bārahmāsā* occurs in verses 309-19. For details on *Kanhāvat* see S.M. Pandey, 'Kanhāvat a Kṛṣṇaite Sūfi Text', *Orientalia Lovaniensia Periodica,* 26 (1995), 187-8.
6. Mañjhan, who wrote *Madhumālatī* in AH 952 (AD 1545) belonged to the Śattārī order of Sufis. His teacher was Shaikh Muhammad Ghaus, who was a famous saint of this sect. In Gupta's edition of *Madhumālatī,* the *bārahmāsā* is described in verses 402-13.

7. Sleṣā and Maghā *nakṣatra* (verses 315-18) appear in the month of Bhādrapada. It rains in this period very heavily. Maghā is the name of the tenth lunar asterism and contains five stars (*Mṛgāvatī*, v. 318).
8. This becomes visible in northern India at the end of rainy season and heralds the onset of autumn. When Agastya appears, the monsoon withdraws, which is why the sage Agastya, who gave his name to the constellation, is said to have swallowed the ocean (Ch. Vaudeville 1986, p. 67).
9. The dark half of the month of Bhādõ when rites are performed in the honour of the deceased ancestors.
10. Name of the thirteenth lunar mansion. It rains heavily and clouds thunder during this period.
11. Citrā, the fourteenth lunar mansion, is said to be the friend of moon since it is under this *nakṣatra* that the moon begins to shine brilliantly again in a pure sky.
12. The waking of Viṣṇu on the eleventh of the bright half of the month of Kārtik.
13. Agravāl accepts the reading of *munivar* and interprets it as 'the Seven Rishis', whom girls worship at the time of Divālī. According to M.P. Gupta, the correct reading is *manorā* which is a festival celebrated by women after the rains are over (*Padmāvat 348/7*).
14. For a complete and a literal translation of the verse see Ch. Vaudeville 1986, p. 72 and A.G. Shireff, *Padmāvati* (Asiatic Society: Calcutta, 1944), p. 212.
15. See his *Dīvān* ed. Rashid Yasimi: Mu'asasa-yi-cāp wa intiśārāt Pirū 3, Tehrān Hijra Shamsī 1339 (1961), pp. 653-8. Sanā'ī, the mystical poet from Ghaznā, carefully collected his verses (see note 1). See also Annemarie Schimmel 1973, p. 11. I am grateful to Nādir Tanhā for supplying me an Italian translation of Masū'd's Persian *bārahmāsā*.
16. Krishna Dev Upadhyay, *Bhojpurī grām gīt* (Allahabad: Hindi Sahitya Sammelan, vs 2000 [1943]). It was later published under the title *Bhojpurī lok gīt,* vs 2011 (1954). In *Bhojpurī grām gīt* fifteen *Bārahmāsās* were collected, but in the second edition most of them were taken out, leaving only 4; see pp. 407ff.
17. See Shyam Manohar Pandey, 'Bārahmāsā kī paramparā aur Padmāvat' in *Sūfī kāvya vimarśa,* ed. Shyam Manohar Pandey (Agra: Vinod Pustak Mandir, 1968), pp. 97, 104.

REFERENCES

Dāūd, Maulānā. *Candāyan.* Ed. Mataprasad Gupta. Agra: Pramanik Prakashan, 1967.

Jāyasī, Mālik Muhammad. *Kanhāvat.* Ed. Parameshvarilal Gupta. Varanasi: Annapurna Prakashan, 1981.

———. *Padmāvat.* Ed. Vasudev Sharan Agraval. Jhansi: Jhansi Sahitya Sadan, 1961.

Kālidāsa. *Meghadūtaṃ.* Trans. M.R. Kale. Delhi: Motilal Banarsidass, 1969 (reprint).

Kutuban. *Mrgāvatī.* Ed. Mataprasad Gupta. Agra: Pramanik Prakashan, 1968.

Mañjhan. *Madhumālatī.* Ed. Mataprasad Gupta. Allahabad: Mitra Prakashan, 1961.

Schimmel, Annemarie. *Islamic Literature of India.* Wiesbaden: Otto Harassowitz, 1973.

Vaudeville, Charlotte. *Bārahmāsa in Indian Literature.* Delhi: Motilal Banarsidass, 1986.

New Indo-Aryan Poetry in Performance: Metre and Oral Formulae as Exemplified in the Poetry of Harirām Vyās

HEIDI R.M. PAUWELS

INTRODUCTION

This paper is intended as a contribution to an important aspect of the study of NIA literature, namely its oral performance. In order to fully grasp NIA poetry, we cannot remain content with understanding what appears on the written page, but have to take into consideration how it is orally performed and what the audience experiences during that performance. The aesthetic essence or *rasa* of the poetry lies in the interplay between the poet and his audience's expectations. If the poet wants to elicit exclamations of approval from the lips of his audience, he has not only to demonstrate his erudition, but also give his poem an unexpected twist. If we want to do justice to his poetry, we need to study both its technical and creative aspects, that is, the tools and the way they are used in individual poems.

Those steeped in this tradition possess a self-evident understanding of these matters. *Rasiks* or *sahṛdays* don't need words. Nevertheless, there is a huge body of indigenous criticism with elaborate theoretical treatises on the aesthetic experience itself (*ras*), on figures of speech (*alaṃkār*), and on metre (*chandas*), but these *śāstras* do not answer many of the questions of the western student of NIA poetry. Rather, they represent the insider's perspective. Hence, there is a strong need for providing the pedagogical literature that explains the 'hidden conventions' of NIA devotional literature.

One aspect of the oral performance difficult to grasp for the student, yet often neglected in scholarly literature is that of metre. In fact, there is a lack of an analytical framework for talking about metre (K. Bryant 1978, p. 132). Recently, some of the problems have been addressed (see K. Bryant 1992, and for the connection between metre and musical performance, see R. Snell 1983 and 1991, pp. 262-303), but still much remains to be done. It would be useful to devise a way of indicating metrical phenomena with an eye to demonstrating the way the poet can use them creatively.

Another aspect of the oral performance that is difficult to appreciate for the 'outsider' is its repetitiveness. Much NIA devotional poetry leaves the student with a feeling of *déjà vu*: certain phrases and expressions occur again and again, not only within one poem, but in different poems by different authors. These are stock expressions widely used in NIA poetry, and seem to fall under the definition of what is generally called 'oral formulae'. These oral formulae need to be studied together with metre.

So, in order to help understand the 'achieved content', what the audience experiences in oral performance, I propose to study here two aspects of NIA poetry: metre and formulaic expressions. These cannot be studied in the abstract, hence I propose to use the example of an early Braj Bhāṣā poet. I have chosen the sixteenth-century poet from Vrindaban, Harirām Vyās, and have concentrated on two selections from his works, namely the thirty quatrains of his *Rās-pañcādhyāyī* ('The Five Chapters of the Round Dance', referred to here as *R*), and the seventy-one songs of *Mān kī śṛṅkhalā* ['The Series on (Rādhā's) Wounded Pride', referred to here as *M*]. All the references and quotations in this paper are from my scholarly edition (H. Pauwels 1994).[1] On the basis of these carefully established texts, I will present a study of metrical and oral formulaic technique sand the way they are used creatively.

METRE

Obviously, I cannot discuss all metres within the limited scope of this paper. I will therefore concentrate on the most common types of metres in NIA, namely the moric ones. In moric metres the determining principle is not the number of syllables, but the number of morae (*mātrā*), i.e. units of time. One mora is equivalent to a short syllable, whereas a long syllable contains two morae. Moric metres are used frequently for the lyric genre called *pad*, which consists of a refrain (*ṭek*) and a varying number of paired rhyming lines. Each line is divided into two half-lines (*pāds*) by a caesura. For the purpose of this paper, I have concentrated on those metres in which the caesura falls after the sixteenth *mātrā*, or metres of the type 16 *mātrās* + X (with X smaller than or equal to 16 *mātrās*). This group of metres is not only the most prominent in the *pads* of *Mān kī śṛṅkhalā*, but also in other NIA devotional and secular poetry.

General characteristics and use of moric metres

The student who is intent on understanding the metrical dimension of NIA poetry has a hard nut to crack. He may turn to the treatises that contain taxonomies of prosody (*chandaḥśāstra*), but these are not exactly 'user-friendly', cast as they are in a cryptic jargon. Alternatively, he may try to study the character of the metres as they are actually used in other NIA texts. Both approaches, though fraught with problems,[2] are useful in that something can be deduced about the general characteristics and use of the metres.

The student who turns to metrical *śāstras* is immediately confronted with a host of problems. Merely trying to name the metres by using the taxonomies of prosody (*chandaḥśāstra*) is a time-consuming enterprise. A standard scholarly praxis has been to follow Bhānu's *Chandaḥprabhākar* (Rāy Bahādur Jagannāthprasād [1894] 1935), but his nomenclature is not necessarily confirmed by other *śāstras.* Upon comparison, a bewildering variety of names is found. Caution is needed because it is not always clear from the definitions in the *śāstras* whether the same metres are described.

This brings us to the second major problem, namely that of the relation of the *śāstras* to poetic reality. The *śāstras* proffer definitions that cannot always be easily related to the actual metre as used in a poem. On the other hand, important characteristics of the meters, such as the caesura and rhyme, are often not touched upon in the treatises. The *śāstras* say at the same time too much and too little.

The discrepancy between the moric metres and the way they are described is well illustrated by the example of the 'Sāra', Bhānu's name for the metre consisting of 16 + 12 *mātrās.* This metre is described under the name Doaï in *Prākṛtapaiṃgala* (Bh. Vyās, 1.152), a treatise of the end of the fourteenth century. The definition says that this metre should have a 6-*mātrā* foot at the beginning and end of the line, with four 4-*mātrā* feet in between.[3] This internal division does not allow for a caesura after the sixteenth *mātrā*, since it would then fall in the middle of the third

4-*mātrā* foot. One might speculate that the metre described in *Prākṛtapaiṃgala* is different from the 'Sāra', but in fact the examples provided (in 1.155) can be naturally scanned with a caesura after the sixteenth *mātrā*.[4] In any case, the NIA Sāra undoubtedly contains a caesura, and if NIA theoreticians echoed the prescriptions of their predecessors, they did so most likely because of scholastic tradition.

There is a good reason for this striking discrepancy between theory and praxis. The *śāstras* were not written to educate the western student; the intention was rather to record and categorize well-established metres in a scholarly way and link this to the ideal reality of Sanskrit. The historian might speculate that the origin of all moric metres need not be a degeneration of classical Sanskrit metres, but that they came about by a fresh impetus from folk-genres (S. Prasad 1964, pp. 134-57, H.D. Velankar 1933, pp. 33-4). This would explain why they are not mentioned by the Sanskrit theoreticians but came to be incorporated only in later theoretical works, and often explicitly under the heading of *Apabhraṃśa* metres.

That conclusion seems to be reinforced by the study of the actual occurrence of the metres in poetry predating Vyās. Some of the metres of the 16 + X *mātrā* group are attested very early on,[5] but more interestingly many of the songs (*prabandhas*) of Jayadeva's *Gītagovinda* can be analysed as being composed in a metre similar to the 16 + 11 and 12-*mātrā* metres.[6] Moreover, the 16 + 16-*mātrā* metre occurs in the *Bhāgavatapurāṇa* (X, 31) for one of the *virah* songs of the Gopīs. The fact that the two main Sanskrit canons of Kṛṣṇa Bhakti employ the metres under discussion undoubtedly lends them some prestige. Though they are found also in other genres (among others, devotional works by the Buddhist Siddhas, and Punjabi narratives), it is perhaps not arbitrary that they are found so abundantly in the Kṛṣṇa *bhajans*.

Metrical analysis, exemplified by Vyās's use of metre

So far, I have concentrated on some general characteristics and use of the moric metres, but in order to understand the creative aspect of the poetry under discussion, it is also necessary to dwell on the actual techniques which poet had at his disposal.

The basic features of a moric metre are determined in the *śāstras* by the total number of *mātrās* and the place of the caesura.

In addition there is an important factor that the *śāstras* do not mention, namely the underlying stress pattern. K. Bryant (1992) has analysed Sūrdās' moric metres of the 16 + X type, and shown that one metric line frequently can be divided in to four groups of four *mātrās,* with stress on the first *mātrā* of each unit (pp. 216-17). In other words, there is an underlying dactylic rhythm. For easy reference, this meter can be referred to as the *tīn tāl* metre, because of its similarities with the rhythmical cycle of that name in music.

My analysis of the 101 selected poems by Vyās confirms Bryant's results: most lines consistently can be analysed in terms of 4-*mātrā* units, with the same type of exception as noted by Bryant. One of these exceptions I will discuss here in some detail in connection with the poet's creativity. I leave aside the question of word boundaries and the problem of deviation between natural stress accent and the expected poetic ictus for words of short syllables, but concentrate instead on the case where we have an 'inconveniently' located stressed long syllable. This phenomenon is the most interesting, because it constitutes the most audible deviation from the '*tīn tāl*' pattern. Let us take a look at an example in the metre Sāra(16-12) from a poem in Vyās's *Mān kī śṛṅkhalā.* In this and all following quotations, I have provided the metrical transcription (which follows the word boundaries; the vertical bar stands for a short syllable, the curving S for a long; the slanting bar indicates the caesura).

हा राधा विलपत मनमथ डर सुनि री परत पुकारें (*M* 33.0.2)
S SS |||| |||| ||/ ||S ||| |SS
इक इक मूठि पाचंसर वरषत मोंहन गात उघारैं (*M* 33.1.1)
|| ||S |<u>S</u>||| ||||/ S||S| |SS

Whereas the first line of this poem falls neatly within the division of 4-*mātrā* units with beat on the first *mātrā* of each unit, the second line seems to contradict that analysis, at least at first sight. There seems to be an anomaly at the end of the second and the beginning of the third 4-*mātrā* unit, which is underlined in the metrical transcription. In effect, the ictus is shifted forwards by one *mātrā.*

This does not detract from the metrical analysis, but represents a deviation from the expected rhythm which has an audible and quite striking effect. Moreover, a case can be made that it is meaningful too. Here we need to stand back and look at the meaning of the poem. This *pad* describes Kṛṣṇa's longing for Rādhā by means of an extended metaphor. Kṛṣṇa is portrayed as a warrior on the battlefield suffering under the blows of Kāma, the god of Love. The extended metaphor is underlined by rhythm and sound. The two lines quoted above can be translated as:

Wailing: 'O Rādhā', in fear of the god of love, O, listen, he is heard crying. With every fist blow (of the god of love) five arrows are showering down,[7] Mohana's body is exposed.

The first line starts out with a series of long syllables: हा राधा. The long syllables evoke the plaintive character of Kṛṣṇa's sighing, which is underscored by the assonance of *ā*'s, echoing throughout the poem in the end rhyme. In contrast, the second line starts with four short syllables इक इक, expressive of the continual sharp attacks of the god of Love. The sudden shift of the ictus that we have just described illustrates well the sudden strikes of the god of love and the ferocity of his attack in: मूठि पांचसर.

This is not an isolated rhythmic phenomenon, but one that occurs in nearly every *pad* by Vyās, and a cursory reading of other poets provides even more examples. What is needed is an unambiguous term to describe the shifting of the ictus forwards by one *mātrā*, an effect that is caused by the occurrence of the long syllable in an unexpected position, i.e. starting at an unstressed even *mātrā* position. An obvious candidate is 'syncopation', the term from music theory for a beat that starts on an unaccented and continues to an accented part.[8] This phenomenon may be indicated in a metrical transcription, for example, as I have done by underlining the long syllable with the unusual ictus.

At this point we may return briefly to the *śāstras*. The definition of Doaï in *Prākṛtapaiṃgala* specified for the line an initial unit of six *mātrās*. This stipulation may reflect the frequent occurrence of syncopation in the form of a long syllable on the third *mātrā*. In that respect, the *śāstras*' seemingly pointless stipulations may indeed be a somewhat cumbersome way of rendering rhythmic reality in technical terms.

The poet's creativity

What has been established so far is the metrical techniques, the tools of the poet, but it is equally important to investigate the way these techniques can be used creatively. While the stress-pattern remains in place, the poet has the freedom to experiment with rhythmic variations. One way he can do this is by de-emphasizing the expected ictus by inserting a sequence of short syllables. His creativity lies in combining these variations in rhythm with stylistic devices, and thus evoking a musical effect that may be meaningful in context.[9]

In the following examples, rhyme is underlined and alliterating letters are highlighted in bold:

Short syllables with internal rhyme and alliteration:
पटकत **प**द **ल**टकत **ल**ट बाहँ (*R* 23.1.1)
|||| || |||| || S |
'Stamping feet, swaying hair locks and arms'

Short syllables as rhythmic device underscoring excitement and rapid action:
गिरवर तरवर पुलकित गात (*R* 25.3.1)
|||| |||| |||| S |
'Mountains and trees with bristling body'
फरकत उर भुज करत चोव इत जघननि स्वेद चुचानैं (*M* 10.3.1)
|||| || || ||| S | || / |||| S | | SS
'Here, your breast and arms are throbbing with desire, your thighs wet with sweat.'
मदनु दहनु उरु जारतु उमगि वुझावत लोचन नीर (*M* 16.1.2)
||| ||| || S || ||| / | S || S || S |
'A fire of passion singes my heart, tears well up in my eyes to extinguish it'

The poet can also use syncopation in a creative way. As explained earlier, syncopation is an audible and striking device to deviate from the monotonous pulse of the stress accent. It may serve simply to vary the rhythm, but often it is also meaningful. It may emphasize an important point, imitate the sound of what is described, highlight a contrast, be expressive of irritation, etc. This expressive use of the metre is often reinforced by stylistic devices such as alliterations, internal rhyme, and assonance. Some examples are the following:

Syncopation with mimetic sound effect:
तान मान म्रिदंग थके (*R* 27.1.3)
S | S | | S | | S
'Drums get tired, measuring the melodic phrases'
चमकत **द**सन **दां**मिनी मानहु पट घट अरि अरुझांनें (*M* 10.2.2)
|||| ||| S |S S || / || || || ||SS

'Teeth flash like lightning, embraced by their enemy, the cloud like veil of the lips'

Syncopation calling attention to a contrast:
हुँ असाध तुम साध हौ (*R* 14.1.3)
S ISI IISIS
'I am the villain, you are virtuous saints'
ऐेक प्रान दोय देह है (*R* 27.3.3)
SISIS SIS (assuming a monosyllabic दोय)
'They are one breath in two bodies'

Syncopation underscoring the impatience of the speaker or person described (reinforced by rhyme and alliteration):
भूषन वसन सुहात गात नहि विकल जसु रति गांन की (*M* 19.2.1)
SII III ISISI II/ III II IISIS
'His body can't stand jewelry and garments; he becomes distraught by the passion of a song'

Significantly, shifts of rhythm and syncopations occur most often in the final lines of the poems of *Mān kī śṛṅkhalā* (see for example, *M* 2.3.2; *M* 6.2.2; *M* 9.1.2). This is meaningful, because it marks a shift of perspective: whereas the beginning of the poem usually represents direct speech, either the plea of the *sakhī* or of Kṛṣṇa or Rādhā's complaint, the last line describes the happy-ending in the voice of the 'narrator'—*sakhī*, Vyās. In poems where the shift of perspective occurs in the penultimate line, it is often in that line that syncopation is found (see for example, *M* 18.2.1; *M* 19.3.1). The connection between the shift of perspective and syncopation is especially evident in the following poem, where a *sakhī* relates to Rādhā how Kṛṣṇa pleaded with her to become his stand-in and embrace Rādhā. In fact, the *sakhī* is no other than Kṛṣṇa in disguise. Throughout the poem, every line in direct speech is introduced with the spondee of the possessive मेरौ 'mine'. Significantly, in the last line this plaintive rhythm is broken, with the shift in speaker emphasized by the syncopation:

मेरौ कोतौ वडी वेर लहु कुच आंकौं भरि रहियहु
SS SS IS SI II/ II SS II IIII
'As my stand-in, for a long while, keep embracing her breasts and hips'

मेरे दुष सागरहि सोषि सुष सागर जल थल थहियहु
ऽऽ ॥ ऽ ।।। ऽ । ॥ / ऽ ॥ ॥ ॥ ॥॥

'Drain the sea of my sorrow, gauge the waters of the sea of bliss'

इतनौं करत व्यासि स्वामिनि कह पिय हिय वोर निवहियहु
।।ऽ ।।। ऽ । ऽ ॥ ॥ / ॥ ॥ ऽ । ॥॥ ।

'Do this, and tell Vyāsi's Lady to stick with your lover's heart till the end' (*M* 15.1.2-2.2)

Very often syncopations in the final line of the poems from *Mān kī śṛṅkhalā* occur in the poet's signature (*chāp*) itself. The set phrase 'Vyāsa Svāminī' contains syncopation and draws the attention, not so much to the poet's own name, but in good humble Bhakti tradition, to his preferred goddess:

व्यासि स्वांमिनी विहसि मिलतही वाढी प्रीति नई (*M* 4.2.2)
ऽ । ऽ । ऽ ।।। ।।। ऽ / ऽऽ ऽ । ।ऽ

'When Vyāsi's smiling lady met him, new love welled up'

A related phenomenon allows the poet similarly to creatively take liberties with the metrical frame work, in particular with the caesura. This phenomenon may be called 'caesuric enjambment',[10] and be indicated in the metrical transcription by highlighting the slanting bar of the caesura in bold. Alternatively, it can also be described as a case where the caesura falls a *mātrā* or two earlier than expected. Regardless of the term applied, what is important is to recognize that there is no question of a flaw (*doṣ*), but of a purposely constructed figure of speech. In many cases the poet is using the enjambment expressively, as is clear from the following examples with alliteration and repetition as well as internal rhyme:

मेरे दुष**सा**गरहि **सोषि** **सुष/सा**गर जल थल थहियहु (*M* 15.2.1)
ऽऽ ॥ ऽ ।।। ऽ । ॥/ऽ ॥ ॥ ॥ ॥॥

'Drain the sea of my sorrow, gauge the waters of the sea of bliss.' The enjambment hightlights the contrast between joy and pain:

मो देषत अपनैं उर मैं **मों**/हन सूंदरि वदन दुराई (*M* 1.1.1)
ऽ ऽ ॥ ।।ऽ ॥ ऽ ऽ / ॥ ऽ ॥ ।।। ।ऽऽ

'Seeing me, the charmer hid the face of a beauty, at his chest' (Here Rādhā, talking to her imagined rival, stresses that Kṛṣṇa is hers; several other lines in this poem start with मो)

मोहू से **अनु**चर कौ तें **अनु**/राग नही पहिचान्यैं (*M* 12.0.2)
ऽऽ ऽ ॥॥ ऽ ऽ ॥/ऽ । ।ऽ ।।ऽऽ

'Who could be your servant but me? Have you not recognized my affection?' The enjambment highlights the semantic similarity between the words for 'follower' and 'love', both sharing the *upasarga* अनु.

That Vyās is very much aware of the caesura is further illustrated by his device of stressing rhetorical interrogatives by placing them immediately after or before the caesura:

प्रांन मान सौं वैरु वढ्यौ क्यौं / दारुन विपति सहौं (*M* 14.0.2)
S I S I S SI IS S / SII III IS
'In my soul, enmity against her sulking grows stronger, how should I suffer this heart-tearing torment?'

दुष की राति विहाति ना सुष विन/क्यौं करि कूंज रहौं (*M* 14.1.1)
II S SI ISI I IIII / S II SI IS
'A night of sorrow takes forever if devoid of joy. What's the point of my sitting in this bower?'

को तन ताप वुझावै कहि धौ/का के पाइ गहौं (*M* 14.1.2)
SII SI ISS II S / S S SI IS
'Who can put out the fire in my body, tell me? Whose feet should I grasp?'

By now it has become clear that the reader who is alert to syncopation and caesuric enjambment is able to 'taste' the creativity of the poet. However, to grasp a poet's rhythmical creativity, isolated examples cannot suffice, and detailed analyses of expressive use in process are called for.[11]

ORAL FORMULAE

Another aspect of the poet's craft that needs to be understood for grasping what is going on in the poem in performance, is that of 'oral formulae'. The term is to the point, since we are dealing with poems meant to be sung. On the other hand, the very question of whether the songs were composed orally or in writing is irrelevant. There is no way to determine whether for example Vyās worked with or without the help of an amanuensis, whether he scribbled notes while composing his songs, or whether he indeed wrote them down fully, perhaps 'dictating to himself'. The point is rather that he used formulaic techniques similar to those used in what has been termed 'oral composition'. A strict dichotomy between the oral and the written is anyway clearly a fallacy.[12]

Definition and classification

Defining the concept of oral formulae is problematic. It is not easy to know where to draw the line between standard poetic vocabulary and formulae. The question comes down to establishing the minimum length a word group must have in order to qualify as a formula. The length of a formula is obviously language-specific and dependent upon the metrical structures used. Different metrical genres obviously have different formulae. A good example is the discrepancy between the keywords (similar to formulae) of the '*nirguṇī*' distichs (Dohās) and those of the *pads* (W. Callewaert and B. Op de Beeck 1991, pp. 39-47).

The most common metres used by Vyās have a structure based on basic units of four *mātrās,* hence these can be called the minimum 'grammetrical' units (R.F. Lawrence's term, as quoted by C.H. Wang 1974, p. 17). There are many examples of four-*mātrā* words that are the basic building blocks of more complex formulae. They are combined with other elements to suit the semantic and metrical context. Of course, not all formulae are based on four-*mātrā* units. Words of three *mātrās* also serve as the basis for a formula, frequently in combinations of two, as in: कुंज महल (*M* 17.1.2); अंक भरति (*M* 3.3.2); मात पिता (*R* 5.1.1); स्वेद नदी (*M* 3.3.1). Often, the three-*mātrā* words are combined to create formulae with an even number of *mātrās,* e.g. लाज गवाई (*M* 2.3.1); मांनि मनावौ (*M* 20.1.2); कोपु न कीजै (*M* 9.1.1); मान जिनि करै (*M* 13.0.2), except for instance in final position of a *pad* with an uneven number of *mātrās*: see दीन दयाल (*R* 13.1.1). With the latter exception, the total number of *mātrās* in these formulaic combination, is usually divisible by four, as one would expect in a metrical context with the ictus on every fourth *mātrā.*

However, if such basic building-blocks of four *mātrās* are considered to be oral formulae, a list of oral formulae would include nearly every other word in the language. For practical reasons then, I propose to limit the term 'oral formula' to recurring four-*mātrā* units consisting of more than one word and recurring units consisting of more than four *mātrās,* including one-word groups. Most formulae contain a stylistic device such as alliteration, internal rhyme, assonance, or a figure of speech, such as metaphor or comparison. However, they are rarely of great semantic importance. The list of oral formulae would be substantially smaller if we were to apply Parry's criterion that in order to qualify as a formula, a certain group of words needs to express an essential idea (as quoted in C.H. Wang 1974, p. 18). This would further narrow the definition, but it is rather subjective. Moreover, the large category of formulae that it excludes (viz., the narrative formulae, see later) is part and parcel of the poet's craft.

Once the formulae are identified, related formulae can be organized into groups. According to their content, they can be divided into several categories, such as narrative, amatory (with several subcategories, among which 'separation' (*virah*) is the most prominent), domestic, poetic, *nirguṇī*, and mythological formulae.

The most basic category of formulae, which may be termed 'narrative', contains many groups with a verbal element expressing basic actions and feelings. Examples of absolutive phrases are यह सुनि 'upon hearing this' (*M* 6.2.2); इतनौं कहि 'having said so much' (*M* 2.3.1); or the rhyming सुनि धुनि 'having heard the noise' (*R* 1.3.2; *R* 4.4.1), and of adverbial phrases are इतनौं सुनत 'hearing such' (*M* 3.3.1); इतनी कहत 'saying such' (*M* 7.1.2); इतनौ करत 'doing such' (*M* 15.2.2); कर जोरे 'with joined hands' (*R* 14.1.2). Examples of verbal compounds are हिलि मिलि 'having united intimately' (*R* 14.3.3); कहत सुनत 'saying and hearing' (*R* 30.5.1). An example of a combination of absolutive and main verb is हंसि बोले 'he spoke smilingly' (*R* 14.1.1). An example of a compound verb is मिलि रह्यो 'crowded' (*R* 20.1.1), and of a conjunct verb is करत ऊछाह 'create euphoria' (*R* 23.1.2).

The second category of formulae, termed 'amatory', is the largest, divisible into many subcategories. The formulae correspond to stock themes from Sanskrit amatory poetry. Conventional terms relating to the heroine's make-up, attire, and physical beauty include अंजन मंजन 'application of collyrium' (*R* 2.4.1); अंग सिंगार 'make-up' (*R* 2.4.1; *R* 15.3.2); पट भूषन 'garments and jewelry' (*R* 2.4.2; *R* 15.3.3; *R* 28.3.2); अंचल चंचल 'swirling sari-borders' (*R* 15.2.3; *R* 23.1.3); कुंडल मनि ताटंक बिलोल 'pendants with jewels and earrings swinging' (*R* 18.1.1; *R* 23.2.1); कुच तुंबनि 'gourd-like breasts' (*R* 9.2.3); गुर नितंब 'heavy hips' (*R* 19.2.3).

Formulae used to describe the hero's standard traits of astuteness and desire are चतुर सिरोमनि 'paragon of the clever' (*M* 5.1.2); चतुर सुजान 'worldly-wise beauty' (*R* 12.2.1); आतुर कुसल सयानैं 'eager, skillful, and wily' (*M* 10.4.1); जोवन मत्त 'mad with youth' (*M* 14.2.2); बावर 'crazy' (*M* 45.1.1).

The setting of the tryst is described with such formulaic

expressions as कुंज कुटीर 'bower hut' (*M* 16.1.1); कुंज महल 'bower palace' (*M* 17.1.2); किसलय सेज 'bed of tender leaves' (*M* 16.4.1); कुसुमित सेज 'bed of flowers' (*M* 19.1.1).

There are also formulae for every nuance of feeling experienced by the lovers when they meet, such as horripilation: पुलकि तंन 'body bristles' (*R* 27.2.2); obliviousness: सुधि वुधि . . . लई 'from good sense and judgment deprived' (*R* 2.3.3); तन की सुधि गई 'oblivious of the body' (*R* 28.3.2); and joy: सुख लह्यो 'enjoying' (*R* 27.2.3); मन सुष भयो 'joy filled the heart' (*R* 1.1.3); अति सुष भये 'excessive joy came about' (*R* 29.1.2).

Finally, there is quite an inventory for the activities of love-play. Variations for the simple act of kissing are अधर सुधा दे 'bestowing the nectar of the lip' (*R* 10.2.2); अधर सुधा अचई 'sipped the nectar of the lip' (*M* 4.2.1); अधर सुधा . . . चाषि लै 'tasting the nectar of the lip' (*M* 8.1.1); पियत . . . अधर सुधाहि 'drinks the nectar of the lip' (*M* 17.3.2); अधर विधुहि मुष में वरषावै 'sprinkling the nectar of the lip in his mouth' (*M* 18.0.2); वरषावहि विंवाधर जलधरु 'let the cloud-like rosy lips shower rain' (*M* 9.0.2); जलधर अधर पांन 'a sip from the rain cloud-lips' (*M* 19.2.2); दै अधरामृतु 'bestow the nectar of the lip' (*M* 6.0.2; *R* 21.4.2); and simply चुंबनु करि 'kissing' (*M* 27.2.3).

A subcategory of formulae is related to music and dance. Examples are उघटत सबद 'indicate the rhythm' (*R* 22.3.2; *R* 26.4.1); बैन बजायो 'played the flute' (*R* 24.1.1); बाजत ताल मृदंग 'cymbals and drums resound' (*M* 65.1.1; *R* 22.1.1); मुरली मुरंज 'flute and rebeck' (*R* 22.3.1); तिरप लेत 'hops' (*R* 21.1.1); सुलप लेत 'starts the overture' (*R* 27.1.2); अंगु सुधंगु 'the parts of the dance' (*M* 65.1.1; *M* 69.3.1; *R* 22.1.2).

Notwithstanding the general overtones of happiness and merriment, the world of longing in separation (*virah*) is represented in Vyās's songs in formulae describing the heroine's pining for her beloved, the long lonely night, the burning pain of unfulfilled desire, etc. These phrases are reminiscent of the folk genre of 'songs of the twelve months of separation' (*virah bārahmāsā*) that had been adapted for religious purposes by *Apabhraṃśa* Jain poets, Sūfī romance poets, and NIA *bhakta* poets alike (see Ch. Vaudeville 1986, pp. 36-44). They include combinations with the postposition विन, for example प्यारी षिनु 'without the beloved' (*M* 4.0.2); वनिता विनु 'without my lady' (*M* 16.0.2); देखे विनु 'without seeing [her]' (*M* 4.1.2); सुष विन 'without joy' (*M* 14.1.1). A recurring formula about the unending night is

राति विहाति न 'the night doesn't pass' (*M* 14.1.1; *M* 41.0.1; *M* 50.1.1).

Appropriate for the theme of burning desire are formulae about a fire that needs to be extinguished, as in को तन ताप वुझावै 'who would extinguish the burning of my body?' (*M* 14.1.2); मदनु दहनु उरु जारतु उमगि वुझावत लोचन नीर 'A fire of passion singes my heart, tears well up in my eyes to extinguish it' (*M* 16.1.2); अंतर विरह दहन तनु जारतु बरषावहि विंवाधर जलधरु 'An internal fire of separation consumes my body, let your cloud-like rosy lips shower rain' (*M* 9.0.2). An example of a formula with the opposite metaphor, namely drowning in an ocean of longing, is विरह सिंधु हो मगन होतु 'I am drowning in an ocean of separation' (*M* 8.1.2).

Formulae expressing pain and torment are: भयौ दारुन दुष 'welled up heart-rending pain' (*M* 12.2.1); दारुन विपति सहौं 'I suffer heart-rending torment' (*M* 14.0.2); दारुन पीर 'heart-rending suffering' (*M* 16.0.1); दारुंन चिंता 'formidable distress' (*R* 9.1.1); अगनित दुष रासि 'a mass of innumerable sorrow' (*M* 20.0.1); आरतिहि पुकारति ... अकुलात 'desperately calling out ... distressed' (*M* 17.3.1). Formulae with rhetorical exclamations about the unbearable pain of separation are: कैसें कै समाति 'how then can I contain it?' (*M* 20.0.1); अधीर पीर को मेंटै 'who would relieve the pangs of my impatient [heart]?' (*M* 14.2.1); कैसै होतु सुषारौ 'how could he be happy?' (*M* 54.0.2); कैसें जात वषान्यौं 'how can it be described?' (*M* 12.2.1); कैसै जियै/क्यों जीवै 'how/why would he live?' (*M* 59.02; *M* 63.1.1; *M* 4.1.2).

For the person suffering separation, elements that contribute to the erotic mood (*uddīpana*) have not only lost their attraction, but become altogether unbearable. Relevant formulae are सव विपरीति भई 'everything has turned upside down' (*M* 4.0.2); कंटक किसलय सेज 'the soft bed feels thorny' (*M* 16.4.1); कुसुमित सेज भयानक लागत 'the flower bed seems terrifying' (*M* 19.1.1); and the rhyming मालावलि व्यालावलि 'the garland is a string of snakes' (*M* 16.3.2). Moonlight and sandal, referred to with homophonic phrases चंदनु चंदु or चंद्रमां चंदन, usually said to be cooling, are referred to as burning (*M* 12.1.2; *M* 16.4.1). Precedents of these phrases can be found in earlier works, such as Vinayacandra Sūrī's fourteenth-century *Neminātha-catuppadikā* (verse 8, see Ch. Vaudeville 1986, p. 107) and the anonymous probably fifteenth-century *Vasanta-vilāsa* (verse 32 in the short edition, see W.N. Brown 1962, p. 46).

The heroine in the folk-songs often speaks directly to the beloved or to a confidante in set phrases of address and complaint. Examples in Vyās's songs are locutions, such as (तेरे) हाथ विकाने

'sold into your hands' (*M* 10.0.2); (मेरे तू) जिय में वसति 'you dwell in my heart' (*M* 13.0.1); and जानति जुगति न 'don't know a remedy' (*M* 14.2.1). The response of the confidante or lover, who pleads with the heroine to give up her sulking, is likewise formulaic. It may include short phrases such as मांन न करु 'don't be cross' (*M* 9.0.1); मान जिनि कर 'don't be cross' (*M* 13.0.2); व्रत तजि 'give up your vow' (*M* 6.2.2); विनु काजै रूठै 'angry for no reason' (*M* 2.1.2); alternatively, whole *pads* are made up of formulaic expressions, such as: विनती सुनि मुनि व्रतु तजि वलि जांउ 'Hear my prayer, give up your vow of silence, I entreat you' (*M* 8.0.2); विनु अपराधहि कोपु न कीजै दीजै हो प्यारी प्रान दांन 'Don't be angry for no reason at all, bestow, O beloved, the gift of life on me' (*M* 9.1.1); करि अपराध साधु ह्वै वैठे 'He committed an offense, and sits like a holy man' (*M* 1.2.2); मानु दांनु दै री प्रांन राषि लै 'Turn your sulking into a blessing, hey, save my life!' (M8.0.1). Both parties make use of formulaic metrical fillers in the form of interrogatives and vocatives such as कहि धौं 'tell me' (*M* 3.1.1; 14.1.2; 20.0.1); क्यौं करि 'what's the point?' (*M* 14.1.1); क्यौं सषि 'why friend' (*M* 17.0.1); प्रान प्यारी 'beloved of my life' (*M* 13.0.1); and किशोरी 'young lady' (*M* 15.0.2).

A third category of formulae relates to the domestic milieu. They represent the female perspective, tell about the women's world of daily chores, and also reflect on concerns of family honour, all themes prominent in folk songs that are still sung by women today. Devotional poets may well have borrowed formulae from this type of song, just as they adapted the *virah bārahmāsā* genre. This may explain part of the charm and appeal of NIA devotional poetry. Examples are गृह व्यौहार 'domestic chores' (*R* 2.3.2); पति सेवा 'service due to the husband' (*R* 3.3.2); भरता की सेवा 'service due to the husband' (*R* 7.4.1); कुल की नारि 'a noble woman' (*R* 6.3.2); बड़भाग 'happy marriage' (*R* 6.4.1); सुभग सुहाग 'happily married lady' (*R* 6.4.2).

A fourth category of formulae consists of poetic clichés, ranging from set comparisons and hyperboles down to flat expressions that are metaphorical but seem to belong to common speech rather than the poetic register. The comparisons are not always worked out in detail. In fact, many standard formulae are so well-known that the poet only needs to briefly hint at them and can trust that his audience will know what he means. A good example is provided in the following line with conflation of two images: that of the moon-face from which the nectar of immortality trickles, and that of the cloud-like lips that pour reviving rain: अधर विधुहि मुष में वरषावै प्रांननि मरत जिवावै हो 'Pour from your lip moon nectar in his mouth, to revive his dying spirits, hey' (*M* 18.0.2).

For describing the union between fair Rādhā and dark Kṛṣṇa, conventional similes for the contrast between light and dark are used: कनंक नीलमनि मनु 'like a sapphire in gold' (*R* 22.4.2); मरकत कंचन जैसें षच्यो 'like an emerald studded in gold' (*R* 17.2.2); मानहुं नाचत घंन दामिनी 'like lightning dancing in the clouds' (*R* 21.1.2). While describing the charm of the heroine, the poet makes use of formulae with standard complimentary comparisons, such as वदन विधु 'moon-face' (*M* 17.3.2); कर पंकज 'lotus hands' (*M* 6.1.1); पद पंकज 'lotus feet' (*M* 15.1.2); मोहंत गज हंस 'enchants elephant and swan' (*R* 27.1.2). Comparisons that involve the god of love are: वचाई मदन वांन की 'shelter from Madana's arrow shot' (*M* 19.3.1); मदन वांनु संधान्यौ 'Madana has aimed his arrow' (*M* 12.1.1); मनहु मनसिज सर ताने 'it seems, Manasija has aimed his arrow' (*M* 10.1.1); वरषंत ... कांम की चोटहि 'against Madana's raining blows of desire' (*M* 18.1.1). The beauty of a spectacle is said to attract the gods from heaven, who cheer and throw flowers from their chariots, as in सघंन बिमान गगनि 'throngs of chariots in the sky' (*R* 20.1.1); बरषित कसुम करत सुर गांन 'flowers rained down, gods sang in chorus' (*R* 20.2.2).

The perfection of a concert is measured by the appreciation of birds and deer, who have the reputation of being aficionados of music, as in षग मृग सुनि मुनिव्रत धरे 'when bird and deer heard it, they took a vow of silence' (*R* 25.3.3), and similar formulae in a different context: षग मृग सुष भरे 'birds and deer are filled with joy' (*R* 16.3.3). Finally, when all comparisons fail and the poet wishes to express his incapacity to provide an adequate description, he can make use of formulae such as कहि न जाति 'it cannot be expressed' (*M* 19.1.2); न कह्यो परै 'it could not be said' (*R* 22.1.3); परत नहि कही 'it cannot be said' (*R* 29.4.2); कहत नहि आवहि 'it does not get said' (*R* 17.2.3); मो पैं कहत न बनै वषांन 'I cannot manage to describe it' (*R* 16.2.2); कैसें जात वषान्यौं 'how can it be described?' (*M* 12.2.1); रसना ऐक न जाती वषांन 'it cannot be described with one tongue' (*R* 20.4.2).

A fifth category of formulae seems to be borrowed from the devotional vocabulary of the Sants. Phrases that already had currency in a *nirguṇī* context were adapted by *saguṇī* poets in order to convey the erotic Kṛṣṇa legend. A comparative study of the oral formulae as used by the so-called *nirguṇī* and *saguṇī* poets is outside the scope of this paper, but some examples from Vyās's work with a *nirguṇī* ring are the following: कपट तजें छूटै संसारु 'by forsaking deceit, the fleeting world falls away' (*R* 7.4.2);[13] जस बिहुनेहि नरक परै 'without a shred of honor, tumbles into hell' (*R* 8.2.3);[14] चरन सरन 'the shelter of the feet' (*M* 12.2.2);[15] पाइ गहौं 'I grasp the feet' (*M* 14.1.2); पद पंकज गहि रहियहु 'remain clinging to the lotus feet' (*M* 15.1.2);[16] and the common लोक बेद 'worldly and spiritual (injunctions)' (*R* 11.3.2; *R* 14.2.2; *R* 29.3.1).[17]

Finally, there are numerous formulae consisting of names, epithets, and attributes relating to Kṛṣṇa mythology and aspects of *mādhurya* theology, such as, for Kṛṣṇa himself: राधारंमन 'the delighter of Rādhā' (*R* 25.2.3); कुंजबिहारि 'the playboy of the bowers' (*R* 24.3.1); नंदकिसोर 'Nanda's son' (*R* 9.1.2); बंसीबटा 'the banyan tree of the flute play' (*R* 16.4.1); कौस्तुभ मनि 'the Kaustubha jewel' (*R* 18.3.1); उर बंनमाल 'a forest garland around his neck' (*R* 19.1.2); and for Rādhā: राधा/ राधिका प्यारी 'dear Rādhā/ Rādhikā' (*M* 9.0.1; *M* 20.0.1); व्रषभांन नंदिनी Vṛṣabhānu's beloved daughter' (*M* 18.2.1); व्रषभांन दुलारी 'bride of Vṛṣabhānu('s house)' (*M* 20.1.2).

Oral formulaic creativity

At first sight, formulaic poetry may seem to leave little scope for creativity, apart from shuffling around the formulae within the metrical structure of the line. However, a close analysis of Braj Bhāṣā *pads* shows that the formulaic technique does not necessarily stifle creativity, but rather facilitates stringing together sequences of formulae with alliteration and assonance in order to achieve a particular sound effect. In the following example assonating words (highlighted in bold) are combined with a formula (underlined) in order to stress the poetic message. In the first three examples, the combination serves to affirm the basic dactylic rhythm:

<u>राधा **वल्लभ**</u> गहि <u>भुज **पल्लव**</u> दुषितहि कंठ लगावै हौ (*M* 18.1.2)
SS S|| || ||S||/ ||||S| |SS S
'Rādhā, take your darling in your tender arms and embrace the suffering fellow, hey'

<u>चात्रक</u> **कृष्नहि** <u>**तृष्ना**</u> वाढी जल**धर** <u>**अधर**</u> <u>पांन</u> की (*M* 19.2.2)
S|| S|| SS SS/ ||.|| |||S|S
'The partridge, Kṛṣṇa, has grown thirsty for the drink from the rain cloud of your lips'

जल थल क्रीडत ब्रीडत नही (*R* 29.4.1)
ıı ıı S ıı S ıı ı S
'In water, on land, they dallied without restraint'

षग मृग मुनि मुनिव्रत धरे (*R* 25.3.3)
ıı ıı ıı ıııı ıS
'Bird and deer, upon listening, took a vow of silence'

जीव जंतु मयमंतु सब (*R* 25.1.3)
S ı S ı ııS ı ıı
'Mankind and all creation became intoxicated'

The poet may repeat paratactic structures and formulaic expressions in order to stress his message. Vyās makes good use of such formulaic repetition. A formula that reoccurs in the final line of nearly every song of *Mān kī śṛṅkhalā* and also near the end of *Rās-pañcādhyāyī* is कंठ लगा—'to embrace'(*R* 23.4.2; 27.4.2; *M* 2.3.2), frequently in combination with the absolutive (वि)हसि 'smiling' or an equivalent such as (मंद) हास करि 'laughing (softly)' (*M* 1.3.2; 9.1.2). Other common formulaic endings are कंठ लपटां—'cling to the neck' (*M* 10.4.2), अंक भर—'embrace intimately' (*M* 3.3.2; 5.1.2), उरसि लग—'cling to the chest' (*M* 7.1.2), (वि)हसि (पियहि) मिल—'meet (the beloved) smilingly' (*M* 4.2.2; 20.1.2), or कर-विहारु 'sport' (*M* 20.1.2). The repetition of formulae is not accidental, but stresses the main tenor of Vyās's poetry, the recurring happy ending with a smiling Rādhā who embraces Kṛṣṇa. In the catharsis of the final line, all tension is released, all wishes are fulfilled, including those of Vyās himself. He hints cleverly at this by rhyming the formula with his name:

> व्यास आस पुजइ हसि वस कीयो लालनु मोहन मटके (*M* 41.3.2)
> 'Fulfilling Vyās's hopes, smiling, she has captivated her darling with coquettish brows'
>
> व्यासि स्वामिनी सव आसा पुजवति हसि रति रास नचावै हौ (*M* 18.2.2)
> 'Vyāsi's Lady, fulfilling all desires, with your smile make him dance the round dance (*rās*) of love, hey'
>
> व्यास आस कैं बरन्युं रास (*R* 30.2.1)
> 'Vyās described the round dance (*rās*) with aspiration'

Another creative device is to give standard formulae a creative new twist or to postpone the second part of a formula. The latter technique may be called 'splitting a formula'. For example, Vyās changes प्रतिपालय करुनालय 'protector, abode of grace' to प्रतिपालय करुना

वरुनांलय 'protector, ocean (abode of Varuna) of compassion' (*M* 6.2.1); कपोल विलोल '(earrings) swaying on the cheek' (cf. *Gītagovinda* 5.1) to विहसत अधर कपोल औल मनु मांगत नित पहिचानें 'When your lips smile, your cheek looks like a begging-bag, it is always recognized to be begging' (*M* 10.2.1); and नैन सैन 'meaningful glances' to नेंननि तें मेंन निकसिहै 'will Mayana disappear from my eyes?' (*M* 17.2.2). By echoing the formula दै अधरामृतु 'bestowing the nectar of the lip' in the following word, मृतक, which renders a sort of etymological rhyme (common root √*mṛ* 'to die'), Vyās highlights the poem's central contrast between disease and medicine: दै **अधरामृत मृतक** रसाइनि 'Give me the nectar of your lips, alchemy for reviving the dead' (*M* 6.0.2).

In the following lines, Vyās uses the technique of splitting a formula (अंगु सुधंगु 'the parts of the dance' or 'the graceful limbs') and combines this with another standard formula (ताल मृदंग) in order to create a rhythmic effect that echoes the drum-beat of the dance described. Assonance (underlined and bold) and a dactylic rhythm that is sustained for nearly three *pads*, reinforce the effect:

भुषन बाजत ताल मृदंग
S II S II S I IS I
'The ornaments resound along with cymbals and drums'

अंगु दीषावत सकल सुधंग
S I IS II III IS I
'Gracefully, she shows all her limbs'

रंग रह्यो न कह्यो परै
S I IS I IS IS
'This passion cannot be described' (*R* 22.1.1-3)

The poet may also use formulae in an ironic way, by adapting them to a new context. Here creativity lies in a 'tension between the inherited body of meanings in which the formula participates and its special meaning in context' (Stanley B. Greenfeld in the context of Anglo-Saxon poetry, as quoted by C.H. Wang 1974, p. 16). The categories of formulae enumerated earlier are not strictly separate, but frequently overlap, and it is precisely in combining different types of formulae that the poet's creativity lies. Vyās frequently uses formulae from one 'body of meanings' in a different context. This cocktail of formulaic categories is not arbitrary. The enduring irony at the root of the poetry is the adoption of the framework of secular love poetry in the context of devotion. The core of Bhakti theology is that human feelings or attachments can be sublimated into religious fervour. The transplant of formulae from one category to the other is in tune with and serves to underline this basic point.

Perhaps the most interesting type of transfer of formulae occurs where the poet uses '*nirguṇī*' formulae in a '*saguṇā*' context. The result is often ironical. A good example is when Vyās has the Gopīs talk to their lover in terms that would befit any *nirguṇī* poem:

> तुम्हारी क्रीपा विन सब जुग अंधु
> 'Without your grace the whole world is blind
> तुम से प्रीतंम अवर को
> Who is dearer than you?
> तुम सु प्रीत करैं जै धीर
> Those who cherish unwavering love for you
> तिनहि न लोक बेद की पीर
> Are not tormented by worldly and spiritual suffering,
> पाप पुंन्य तिन के नही
> Sin and merit do not apply to them.' (*R* 11.2.2-3.3)

Ironical too is the use of phrases from the context of the guru's or God's grace[18] in a more literal and physical sense, such as for Kṛṣṇa's actions during the love-play with the Gopīs:

> (देइ अधरम्रीत) <u>सिर</u> <u>धरि</u> <u>पांन</u> (*R* 21.4.2)
> 'The hand placed on his head (she bestows the nectar of her lower lip)'

> हरि करुना करि लइ उठाई (*R* 28.4.1)
> 'Hari took pity and lifted her up.'

The idiom used to describe non-believers in Sant poetry, *vimukha*,[19] is ironically applied to Krsna himself in its literal meaning 'turned away.' Vyās has the Gopīs say to Kṛṣṇa: बिमुष भएँ होइ हैं बेहाल 'If you turn away, we will be upset' (*R* 11.4.2). In Sant poetry, major causes of pain (*dukhadātā/ dukhadāī*) are wicked people and lust,[20] but Vyās's Gopīs, in their exclusive devotion to Kṛṣṇa, apply this epithet even to the guru: दुष दाता पति सुत गर बंधु 'Husband, son, guru and brother are providers of sorrow' (*R* 11.2.1). Vyās also has his Gopīs use superficially devout language, with a *double entendre* as in: हरि करिया नहि जानै पीर 'The boatsman, the Lord, cannot fathom our sorrow' (*R* 9.2.2). These are the words of the Gopīs after they have initially been rejected by Kṛṣṇa. By stating that not even Kṛṣṇa himself can fathom the depth of their sorrow upon rejection, they imply that he does not understand the profundity of their love. This is indicative of *mādhurya ras* in that the Gopīs, out of their love for Kṛṣṇa, have become oblivious of his divine nature. Elsewhere too their words have a double meaning. What seems to be emotional blackmail: तुम बिमुषै पिय आतंम हांनि 'If you turn away, beloved, we commit suicide' (*R* 10.4.2), can also be understood with reference to the philosophical oneness of *ātma* and god: 'our very self or *ātma* will be hurt (because you are our very self)'.

To return to *nirguṇ* idioms: the rhyme-words ओट ('cover') and चोट ('blow') are used formulaically to express how God's grace protects from the blows of the world.[21] In Vyās's poetry the fanciful image is that Rādhā's breasts provide the shelter from the arrows of the god of love:

> वरषत मदन कांम की चोटहि उरजनि वोट वचावै हो (*M* 18.1.1)
> 'Against Madan's raining blows of desire, let her shield me with her breasts, hey'

> सुनि पिय उरज ओट दै चोट वचाई मदन वांन की (*M* 19.3.1)
> 'She paid heed and by offering her lover the shelter of her breasts saved him from Madan's arrow shots'

Nirguṇ poets also frequently style themselves as 'helpless', अनाथ, a compound that literally means 'without Lord'.[22] Vyās transports the pun on this word to the *saguṇ* context and has the Gopīs beg their Lord not to leave them 'lordless': निठुर वचंन बोलहु जिनि नाथ—निजु दासी जिन करहु अनाथ 'Do not speak ruthless words, O Lord, do not bereave your own servant of her master' (*R* 9.4.1-2). He goes even further and reverses the roles when he has Kṛṣṇa call himself 'helpless' in the absence of Rādhā: तो विनु मोहि अनाथु जानि अव मदन 'Now Madan knows me to be helpless without you' (*M* 12.1.1).

Of course, Vyās is no exception in applying his craft in such a meaningful way. He is just one exponent of the long tradition of adapting court and folk love-poetry for devotional contexts, similar to Jains and Sūfīs who made use of *viraha bārahmāsā.* One of Vyās's main source of inspiration is the *Gītagovinda* by Jayadeva. As pointed out already, the songs of this work are written in similar metres to those in Vyās's *Mān kī śṛṅkhalā.* It is therefore not surprising that there are many formulae in common with Vyās's works. Some examples are shown in the following table.

Table: Examples of formulae found in the songs of *Gītagovinda* as well as in Vyās's poetry (with abstraction of Sanskrit syntax and orthography)

Formulae	Vyās	*Gītagovinda* (songs)
कुंज कुटीर	*R* 16.1.1	3.1
अंचल चंचल	*R* 15.2.3	5.1
मनि कुंडल	*R* 23.2.1	4.1
अधर सुधा	*R* 10.2.2	5.1; 23.5
मदन दहन	*M* 16.1.2	9.3
उर बनमाल	*R* 19.1.2	2.1
रति रन धीर	*M* 16.5.1	14.7
किसलय सेज	*R* 16.4.1	किसलय शयन 6.3; 11.6; 16.1; 23.1
मांनु न करु	*M* 9.0.1	मा कुरु मानम् 18 (refr)
चंदहि लग्यौ चकोर	*M* 59.2.1	चंद्र चकोर 2.7
चकोर कहा पीयै चंदहि	*M* 63.1.1	

The similarity is not limited to the formulae themselves, but applies also to the way they are used. Only a few examples can be discussed here. The formula अधर सुधा ('nectar of the lip') is a poetic cliché often used by Vyās in the beginning of a line or of a *pād*; hence it seems to be considered a good opener of a *pād.* Indeed, this formula also occurs in the songs of the Sāra meter in the *Gītagovinda* (5.1), and in one instance at the beginning of the first *pād* (in *prabandha* 23.5). Examples from Vyās's songs are the following:

अधर सुधा दे करि विश्राम (*R* 10.2.2)
||| |S S || SS|
'Give comfort by bestowing the nectar of your lip'

पियत किसोर चिकोरि वदन विधु अधर सुधाहि चुचात (*M* 17.3.2)
||| |S| |S| ||| ||/ ||| |S| |S|
'The young man, like a partridge, drinks in her moon-face, her lip trickles with nectar'

नेंक क्रपा करि मुष महि वरषहि अधर सुधा रस धारें (*M* 33.3.1)
S| |S || || || |||/ ||| |S || SS

'Show some mercy: pour in his mouth streams of nectar juice from your lips'

ता के प्रान रहै क्यौं जिहि वह अधर सुधा अचई (*M* 4.2.1)

S S S I IS S II II / III IS IIS

'Why would he still breathe on, who has sipped that nectar from her lips?'

Note how in the last example the cliché has been used in an ironic way: whereas nectar usually is considered to be life bestowing, Vyās ironically questions its life-giving potential, alluding to its side-effect of inspiring weariness of the world. His point is that no one could live on in the world of the senses after having tasted the divine *ras*, after having sipped Rādhā's nectar.

Another formula, रति रन 'battle field of love', is frequently used by Vyās for the beginning of the second *pād*, and often occurs in the *chāp*-line. The alliteration yields a pleasing sound-effect:

व्यासि स्वांमिनीहि मिलि नागरु रति रन कंह भयौ उतारें (*M* 33.3.2)

S I S III S II II / II II IS ISS

'Meeting with Vyāsi's Lady, the sophisticated one was led down to the battle-field of love'

व्यासि स्वामिनी पियहि सुनायौ रति रन कौ जु निसांनु (*M* 71.2.2)

S I S IS III ISS / II II S I IS I

'Vyāsi's Lady has resounded for her lover the drum of the arena of love'

व्यासि स्वांमिनी रति रस वरषति रति रन कीच मची री (*M* 69.3.2)

S I S IS II II IIII / II II S I IS S

'Vyāsi's Lady showered the sensuality of passion. In the mud of the arena, passion splashed [all around], hey'

करुना करि सहचरि लै आई दोऊ रति रन धीर (*M* 16.5.1)

IIS II IIII S SS / SS II II S I

'Graciously the friend has brought the two who are steadfast in the battle of love'

In the three last examples, this formula consisting of four short syllables is immediately followed by a combination of a long and short syllable. The combination with धीर, as in the last example, also occurs in a song in the *Gītagovinda* (*prabandha* 14.7), which is written in a 16-moric metre, called Pādākulaka. In the first example, however, the poet has used the formula creatively by splitting it with the caesura and following it with a tribrach in order to draw attention to the ambiguity of the meaning (for a detailed discussion, see H. Pauwels 1994, p. 200).

Clearly, Vyās's *pads* echo the formulae and formulaic techniques used in the songs of the *Gītagovinda*, which is no surprise if we know that the metres themselves are similar. This study of oral formulae is not intended to show the derivativeness of Vyās's poetry, but rather to understand within which traditions the poet places himself. Vyās uses formulaic expressions from folk and *nirguṇī* poetry, but is clearly also inspired by *Gītagovinda*. If Braj Bhāṣā poets are to be classified on a scale from 'vernacular' or 'folksy' to 'Sanskritic', Vyās, more than most of his contemporaries, would definitely fit towards the latter end of the spectrum.

CONCLUSION

The study of the poetic technique and creativity of Vyās with respect to metre and oral formulaic composition has revealed an unexpected complexity for such apparently simple songs. The analysis has shown that Vyās borrowed from other vernacular genres, as well as from *Gītagovinda*, which was clearly a major source of inspiration. If we take into consideration that Jayadeva's songs in turn may have been inspired by vernacular models, the picture grows even more complex. A Sanskrit work that was inspired by a folk genre has in turn served as a source of inspiration for a vernacular singer. The poems by Vyās, which seemed so simple and straight-forward at first glance, have turned out to be the products of an erudite composer. He must have been equally well-versed in vernacular and Sanskritic literatures in order to be able to purposefully combine both sources. He also appears to have been well aware of the irony underlying such an enterprise. What is more, he has exploited this irony fully in order to enhance his audience's aesthetic delight (*ras*). Whereas Vyās's poetry is indeed *déjà vu* inasfar as it recycles pre-existing materials, it is more than the mere sum of its parts. One way to look at his poetry is to consider it as representation of an erudite return to naiveté, a '*seconde naïveté*'.

NOTES

I would like to express sincere thanks to Professor A. Entwistle, R. Solomon and M. Shapiro of the University of Washington, Seattle and to Professor C. Shackle and R. Snell of the School of Oriental and African Studies,

London for many stimulating discussions and for commenting on drafts of this paper. I am also indebted to the fascinating work of Professor K. Bryant of the University of British Columbia, Vancouver.

1. Though I will refer for convenience to my texts as 'Vyās's', and to the author as 'Vyās', this is of course to be understood in the light of the irretrievability of the original text, and the generic Indian concept of authorship (see J.S. Hawley 1988). For all quotations of the text of my edition, I have omitted the apparatus.
2. A basic problem to be noted at the outset is the lack of reliable text-editions of the *śāstras,* as well as of the works of many NIA poets. Although recently some excellent studies have started appearing, there is still much work to be done.
3. Other metres in *Prākṛtapaiṃgala* are described in the traditional way, indicating the constitution in feet (*gaṇ nirdeśak*), as well as in a more realistic way, with reference to total number of *mātrās* and occasionally to the caesura or *yati.* The latter is, however, not the case in the definitions of the Doaï.
4. This is also true for the metre as it occurs in at least some *Apabhraṃśa* texts (H. Jacobi 1918, as quoted by R. Snell 1991, p. 269).
5. The 16 + 11-*mātrā* metre is attested in Kālidāsa's time (fourth to fifth century), albeit in the controversial *Apabhraṃśa* stanzas from the fourth act of *Vikramorvaśīya* (4.48). The mss. from the northern recension include the songs in the fourth act, those from the southern recension do not. H.D. Velankar (1961, LXXIX) analyses the metre as consisting of 28 *mātrās,* following the practice of counting the last syllable as long. If that is the case, the metre would be an example of the 16 + 12-*mātrā* type rather than the 16 + 11-*mātrā* metre.
6. Nearly one third of the songs seems to be built on a pattern of 16 + 12 *mātrās* (*prabandhas* 3, 8, 11, 17, 20, 22, and 23) and one song on a pattern of 16 + 11 (*prabandha* 15). These references, and all further references to *Gītagovinda* are to the edition by S. Sandahl-Forgue 1977. B.S. Miller (1977, pp. 12-13 and p. 46, nn 15-16) analyses these metres as combinations of 4-*mātrā* measures, whereas S. Sandahl-Forgue (1977, pp. 98-9) analyses them as consisting of lines of 8-8-8-4 *mātrās* and does not find clearly marked caesurae. Likewise, A. Mukherji (1967, pp. 235-7) analyses the metre in term of 'bars' of eight *mātrās,* without indicating the major pause after the first two 'bars'. A. Mukherji (1967, p. 237) rejects an identification of the metres in *Gītagovinda* with the Doaï because of the internal division in *mātrās* associated with the latter metre in the *śāstras.* However, these scholastic stipulations do not necessarily accommodate even the illustrations of the metre given by the pandits themselves. In fact, in quite a few cases, the best examples being songs 11 and 23, there definitely is a main caesura after the sixteenth *mātrā* that coincides

with semantic groups. For a more elaborate discussion, see H. Pauwels 1994, p. 190.

7. The five arrows form the proverbial armoury of the god of love. I have interpreted पांच-सर as a *karmadhāraya* compound. However, it is also possible to read it as a *bahuvrīhi* compound: 'The god with the five arrows showers successively fist blows on him.'
8. Use of this term was suggested by M. Shapiro (course on Hindi poetry, autumn 1991). The term 'syncopation' has been used before in the context of Vidyāpati's poetry (R.A. Hartz 1979, pp. 20-1), where it is also used for cases where the natural word accent does not coincide with the ictus. This may be appropriate for eastern NIA, where the difference between long and short vowels is obliterated and accent plays a more prominent role. However, it does not seem appropriate for Braj Bhāṣā. The term is also used by K. Bryant, who applies it also to sequences of short syllables (1992, p. 220).
9. For similar creative use of rhythm in Sanskrit prose, see R.A. Hueckstedt 1985, pp. 139-48.
10. The term is a translation from French '*césure enjambante*'. From here onwards I will refer to this phenomenon abbreviated as 'enjambment', which should not create confusion because enjambment in the strict sense, namely of lines, does not occur at all in the corpus of poetry under consideration.
11. As this is obviously outside the scope of this paper, I merely refer the reader to my metrical analysis of one poem by Vyās, with indication of patterns of expectation and instances where the pattern is broken (H. Pauwels 1994, pp. 198-201).
12. For references to literature about the continuity rather than dichotomy between oral and written literature, see J.B. Flueckiger and L.J. Sears 1991, pp. 3-5.
13. For references to the formula कपटि छाड- in *nirguṇ* poetry, e.g. that of Kabīr and Dādū, see W. Callewaert and B. Op de Beeck 1991, s.v. कपट and छाड-.
14. For references to the formula नरक पर- in *nirguṇ* poetry, e.g. that of Kabīr, see ibid., s.v. नरक and पर-.
15. For references to the formula चरन सरन in *nirguṇ* poetry, e.g. that of Nāmdev and Raidās, see ibid., s.v. चरन and सरन.
16. For references to the formula पद (पंकज) गह- and variants such as पद लह-, or चरण गह- in *nirguṇ* poetry, e.g. that of Kabīr and Hardās, see ibid., s.v. पद, गह- and लह-.
17. For references to the formula लोक बेद in *nirguṇ* poetry, e.g. that of Kabīr, Nāmdev, Raidās, Hardās, Dādū and Sundardās, see ibid, s.v. लोक and बेद.
18. For references, ibid, s.v. करुना and कर-.

19. For references to *pads* by, e.g., Nāmdev and Raidās, see ibid., s.v. विमुख.
20. For example *durjana* in Sundardās's *sākhī* 23 (see ibid., 1: 526) and *trāsa* in *sākhī* 32 (see ibid. 1: 545).
21. For references, see ibid., s.v. ओट and चोट.
22. For references to *nirguṇ* poets such as Nāmdev, Kabīr, and Raidās, see ibid., s.v. अनाथ.

REFERENCES

Bhānu (Rāy Bahādur Jagannāthprasād). *Chandaḥprabhākar: arthāt bhāṣā piṅgal, sūtra aur gūḍhārth sahit.* [1894] 8th ed. Bilaspur: Jagannath Press, 1935.

Brown, W. Norman. *The Vasanta Vilāsa: A poem of the spring festival in Old Gujarātī, accompanied by Sanskrit and Prakrit stanzas and illustrated with miniature paintings.* New Haven, Connecticut: American Oriental Society, 1962.

Bryant, Kenneth E. *Poems to the Child God: Structures and Strategies in the Poetry of Sūrdās.* Berkeley: University of California Press, 1978.

———. 'Three-three-two versus four-by-four: Metrical Frames for the *padas* of Sūrdās'. In *Devotional literature in South Asia: Current research, 1985-1988,* ed. R.S. McGregor, pp. 209-24. Cambridge: Cambridge University Press, 1992.

Callewaert, Winand M. and Bart Op de Beeck, eds. *Nirguṇ-bhakti-sāgar/ Devotional Hindī Literature: A Critical Edition of the Pañc-Vāṇī or Five Works of Dādū, Kabir, Nāmdev, Raidās, Hardās with the Hindī songs of Gorakhnāth and Sundardās, and a complete word-index.* 2 vols. Delhi: Munshiram Manoharlal, 1991.

Flueckiger, Joyce Burkhalter and Laurie J. Sears, eds. 'Introduction'. In *Boundaries of the Text: Epic performances in South and Southeast Asia,* pp. 1-16. Michigan Papers on South and Southeast Asia, 35. Ann Arbor: University of Michigan, 1991.

Hartz, Richard Alan. 'A Metrical Translation of Selected Maithili Lyrics of Vidyapati'. Master's thesis, Seattle, University of Washington, 1979.

Hawley, John Stratton. 'Author and Authority in the Bhakti Poetry of North India'. *Journal of Asian Studies* 47.2(1988): 269-90.

Hueckstedt, Robert A. *The Style of Bāna: An Introduction to Sanskrit Prose Poetry.* Lanham: University Press of America, 1985.

Miller, Barbara Stoler. *Love Song of the Dark Lord: Jayadeva's Gītagovinda.* New York: Columbia University Press, 1977.

Mukherji, Amulyadhan. 'Lyric Metres in Jayadeva's Gīta-Govinda: Did Jayadeva take over these metres from Apabhraṃśa?' *Journal of the Asiatic Society* 9.2(1967): 232-45.

Pauwels, Heidi R.M. 'Harirām Vyās's *Rās-pañcādhyāyī* and *Mān kī śṛṅkhalā*: A Critical Interpretation. Ann Arbor, Michigan: University Microfilms, 1994.

Prasad, Sivanandan. *Mātrik chaṃdõ kā vikās: madhyakālīn Hindī-kāvya mẽ prayukt mātrik chaṃdõ kā viśleṣaṇātmak tathā aitihāsik adhyayan.* Patna: Bihar Rashtrabhasha Parishad, 1964.

Sandahl-Forgue, Stella. *Le Gītagovinda: Tradition et innovation dans le kāvya.* Stockholm Oriental Studies, 11. Stockholm: Almqvist and Wiksell, 1977.

Snell, Rupert. 'Metrical forms in Braj Bhāṣā Verse: the *Caurāsī Pada* in Performance'. In *Bhakti literature in current research, 1979-1982,* ed. M. Thiel-Horstmann, pp. 353-83. Bonn: Dietrich Reimar, 1983.

———. *The Eighty-four hymns of Hita Harivaṃśa: An Edition of the Caurāsī Pada.* Delhi: Motilal Banarsidass; London: School of Oriental and African Studies, 1991.

Vaudeville, Charlotte. *Bārahmāsā in Indian literatures: Songs of the Twelve Months in Indo-Aryan Literatures.* Delhi: Motilal Banarsidass, 1986.

Velankar, H.D. 'Apabhraṃsa Metres'. *Journal of the University of Bombay: Arts and Law (1).* 2.3(1933): 32-62.

———. 'Apabhraṃśa Metres II'. *Journal of the University of Bombay: Arts and Law (9).* 5.3(1936): 41-93.

———, ed. *The Vikramorvaśīya of Kālidāsa.* New Delhi: Sahitya Akademi, 1961.

Vyas, Bholashankar. *Prākṛtapaiṃgalam: bhāṣāśāstrīya aur chandaḥśastrīya anuśīlan.* 2 vols. Prākṛta-grantha-pariṣad, 2-4. Benares: Prakrit Text Society, 1959-62.

Wang, C.H. *The Bell and the Drum: Shih Ching as Formulaic Poetry in an Oral Tradition.* Berkeley: University of California Press, 1974.

The Gopīs as Role Models: Understanding Paramānand's Function as a Saint

A. WHITNEY SANFORD

Paramānand's *pads* lead the *bhakta* through a ritual of transformation or a cognitive pilgrimage in which the *bhakta's* perspective shifts from the *laukik* to the *alaukik.* The *pads* which present Kṛṣṇa's *līlā* in Braj arouse the *bhāv* which facilitates this transition. In many of these *pads,* however, the Gopīs, the cowherding women and girls of Braj, act in ways which clearly violate social norms and conventions of Indian society. The question is how do we interpret their apparently licentious behaviour, and what devotional role does this behaviour play for the *bhakta*? This paper examines the Gopis' actions looking at interpretive differences between the *laukik* and the *alaukik* realms and how the *pads* can then mediate between the two realms. Paramānand's *pads* and this mediation constitute one element contributing to his designation as a saint; understanding the *pads*' mediatory and transformative role offers insight into Paramānand's function as a saint in the community.

Paramānand and his pads *as rituals of transformation*

The Puṣṭimārg tradition considers Paramānand to be one of Vallabha's *aṣṭasakhā* (eight companions) and one of Vallabha's converts to his *sampradāy* (doctrinal community).[1] According to the *Caurāsī vaiṣṇavan kī vārtā,* a Vaiṣṇava hagiography, Vallabha initiated the poet-singer into the *sampradāy* in 1521 and convinced him to turn his talents towards praise of Kṛṣṇa's childhood life in Vrindavan and the Braj area as depicted in the *Bhāgavatapurāṇa.* Paramānand then devoted his life to performing *sevā* (service) for the *svarūp* (self-manifestation) of Śrī Govardhannāthjī established by Vallabha. In the *līlā,* he assumes the *ādhidaivik* form of the *sakhā* Toka and the *sakhī* Candrabhāgā. The Vārtā states that Paramānand's assigned *darśan* period is *maṅgalā-āratī*, and his favoured *bhāv* is *bāl-līlā*.[2] Each of the Aṣṭachāp guarded one of the eight gates into Govardhan Hill; Paramānand's gate was near Surabhīkuṇḍ.[3]

Paramānand's *pads* are known throughout north India; they are sung in homes and in temples and are part of most everyone in the Braj area's mental repertoire. The *pads*, sung by Paramānand and his contemporaries, the other *Aṣṭachāp* poets as well as other Braj poets, were instrumental for cultivating appropriate emotional and cognitive states in the *bhakta*. These *pads* are generally short dramatic episodes in Krṣṇa or Rādhā's life or vignettes which present a typical Braj scene but without the dramatic action; as 'verbal icons'—to use Kenneth Bryant's phrase—they offer the *bhakta* an insight into Krṣṇa's life and his Braj environs which enables the *bhakta* to develop a cognitive and emotional approach to Kṛṣṇa and place him or herself within Kṛṣṇa's entourage. As rituals of transformation, the poems shift the *bhakta's* perspective from the *laukik* to the *alaukik* ; this is not a substantial change, but a perspectival one in which the *bhakta* invests a person or object with *bhāv*, thus essentially making the profane sacred. The *bhakta* assumes the identity and emotions appropriate to one of the Braj characters and develops an intimate relationship with Kṛṣṇa patterned on the human relationships in the Kṛṣṇa-*līlā*. The characters in the *līlā* are then the models for the *bhakta*. This quotation from a female Puṣṭimārgī from Owen Lynch's article ('Pilgrimage with Kṛṣṇa') is illustrative:

> There are two types of Bhakti: that like the milk maids and that like Yaśodā. The milk maids are our model here. They do not take the path of knowledge. They experienced a feeling of love for Lord Kṛṣṇa. We try to do the same with the *bhāv* as the milk maids have done. (O. Lynch 1988, p. 179)

The *pads* help to create the ambience which allows the *bhakta* to forge an emotional bond with Kṛṣṇa. It is important to consider that when Paramānand sang these *pads*, he was actually seeing the eternal Kṛṣṇa-*līlā*. Though the *Bhāgavatapurāṇa* and other sources first informed him of the *līlā* and shaped the 'theatre of memory' from which he derived the *līlā*, he was not merely recreating the *pads* from memory; instead, he was having *darśan* of the actual events and scenes. When Paramānand and the other Aṣṭachāp sang *kīrtan* for Kṛṣṇa,[4] they saw, or had *darśan,* of the *līlā.* The poems are not remembered or fabricated but considered accurate depictions of the *līlā.* The tradition holds that these poems are descriptive visions, not creative or imagined accounts.[5]

Traditional accounts state that Paramānand himself experienced all the *līlās* of the tenth *skandha* of the *Bhāgavatapurāṇa* after he had been instructed by Vallabha (R. Barz 1976, p. 150). Paramānand was communicating to the *bhaktas* aspects of Kṛṣṇa's life from first-hand experience. The richness of detail and sensual perception come from actual experience. According to his *vārtā,* Paramānand, more than any of the other Aṣṭachāp poets, had reached a plane of spiritual awareness and being which enabled him to live and function almost exclusively within the Kṛṣṇa-realm. He had little awareness and interest in mundane, or *laukik,* affairs, but, having reached the pinnacle of Kṛṣṇa devotion, remained within the *alaukik* realm of being. Thus, he could communicate to *bhaktas* in the *laukik* realm exactly what he was 'seeing' in the *alaukik* realm of existence. Through the *pads,* Paramānand makes manifest the *alaukik,* bringing the sacred into the profane.[6]

In the *līlā* as presented by Paramānand's *pads,* the Gopīs violate almost every conceivable social norm to meet with Kṛṣṇa. They are irresistibly drawn to Kṛṣṇa and long to see him; they plot to catch a glimpse of him, telling lies and making up excuses. They are jealous of anyone or anything close to him, including his flute which continually tastes the nectar of his lower lip. To see him these women (many of them married) shirk their household duties, set up assignations whenever they can slip away and ultimately abandon their families when Kṛṣṇa calls them for the *rās-līlā* dance on his last night in Braj. Their illicit love of Kṛṣṇa is special and free from constraints of duty that comes with familial or spousal love.

Rāg-sārang[7]

He took the flute in his hand and laid it upon his lower lip.
Look at the sport of the greatest lord, the thief of the hearts and minds of the Braj-women.
When they heard the sound of the flute, they abandoned their homes;
Madan's powerful body was multiplied;
Whose love made them forget their husbands and sons;
Hey Hari, hey Hari, your flute brought them to you.
His face laughing, eyes blooming like the lotus bud at sunrise.

Paramānand's love for the one with lotus feet; meeting with Kṛṣṇa is a good thing.

These women are seen as the ideal *bhaktas,* but how are we to reconcile this behaviour with traditional social standards?

Different realities: laukik *and* alaukik

Several questions emerge which, I believe, can be answered by understanding the terms '*laukik*' and '*alaukik*' and how qualities and behaviour are perceived differently in the two realms. These *pads* are guides for the *bhaktas,* though not in a physical and worldly sense. Instead, they are guides in emotional and cognitive approaches to Kṛṣṇa, and the activities are only really undertaken in the *alaukik* realm when one has achieved the *ādhidaivik* body (the perfected form).[8] *Laukik* and *alaukik* derive from the Sanskrit word '*loka*', which can be loosely translated as 'world' or 'the profane realm'. *Laukik* indicates being of the world, something normal and customary. *Alaukik* is beyond the world, in the realm of the sacred or the 'other'.

In the Braj interpretation of these words, the gap is not substantial or geographical, but cognitive and perceptual; the *alaukik* world of Kṛṣṇa is accessible here and now, in this world. The two are different perspectival aspects of reality, the physical and the supramundane. Though the *bhakta* may exist in the *laukik* realm, he or she lives in the *alaukik* realm. Every sound, sight, and feeling—all perception—relates the *bhakta* to Kṛṣṇa; what might by a non-*bhakta* be perceived as merely a tree or a cow, to a *bhakta* is resonant with awareness of Kṛṣṇa, provoking memories and images of Kṛṣṇa's Braj sport. Through the investiture of *bhāv* which is aroused by the *pads,* the memory and the senses, the *bhakta* renders the *laukik alaukik.*[9]

Paramānand's Gopīs

Paramānand mediates between the eternal *līlā* of Kṛṣṇa in the *alaukik* world and the *bhakta* in the mundane, *laukik* realm, leading the *bhakta* to the ultimate goal of following the *mādhurya,* or erotic, approach: participation and service of Rādhā and Kṛṣṇa in the *nikuñj-līlā,* when Rādhā and Kṛṣṇa meet in the forest at night. His *pads* lead the *bhakta* inward on a cognitive pilgrimage which arouses the *bhāv* and transforms the *bhakta*'s vision and emotions, allowing the *bhakta* to 'see things as they really are'.[10] As an actor in the divine drama of Braj, the *bhakta* forges an emotional bond with Kṛṣṇa based on human relationships depicted in the *pads*, originally seen in the *Bhāgavatapurāna*: the four primary emotional and aesthetic approaches are: *mādhurya*/erotic, *vātsalya*/parental, *sakhya*/friendship and *dāsya*/servanthood. The first two are the most important in the Braj devotional tradition and, in particular, in Paramānand's *pads*.[11]

The *bhakta* conceives of him or herself as one of Kṛṣṇa's entourage and cultivates the appropriate emotions.[12] For example, the *bhakta* cultivating a relationship with Kṛṣṇa of a Gopī would develop the appropriate intimate feelings as a Gopī towards Kṛṣṇa, as a young girl would feel towards her lover, regardless of the gender of the *bhakta*; for example, the *bhaktas* should feel the joys of union and the burning pains of separation, feel the anticipation and longing for even a short meeting with their beloved Kṛṣṇa.

Rāg-sārang[13]

Why doesn't he speak of Braj?
Without Kamalnayan, now we burn with misery,
As if crores of the sun's rays sear our hearts.
Without the beautiful Śyam, the moon of Gokul is stolen,
just like an eclipse.
This pain of separation: who can erase it? Such is my fortune.
Paramānand says, without the lord, my eyes flow with tears.

These Gopīs are fierce in their devotion to Kṛṣṇa; they are willing to risk their social standing and the shame of their families. They happily trade their *loklāj* (the honor of their families) for any interaction or meeting with Kṛṣṇa.

Rāg-rāmkalī[14]

Oh friend, what should I do now?
After my eyes fell upon Nandanandan, I can't remain apart from him
even for a moment.
My mother and father frighten me; they invoke the
honor of the family.
Outside all voices speak harshly: here comes the lover of Kānha.
Night and day do not pass easily for me; I do not like the house and
the courtyard.
The lord of Paramānand laughs, he has stolen my mind.

They often sneak away in the middle of the day or abandon their work to meet with him. When Kṛṣṇa calls for the *rās-līlā* the Gopīs show up in all states of undress and unpreparedness; they drop whatever they are doing to join Kṛṣṇa. Pots are left boiling, and sentences half-spoken. But none of these worldly things matters as much as Kṛṣṇa.

These are the Gopīs whom Paramānand praises; his implicit praise of their actions is evident in the poems. Yet, how should we understand these poems and the Gopīs' behaviour? These actions—as manifest in the *pads*—violate social norms and heap shame upon the Gopīs and their families.[15]

Interpretations

One answer might be found in Vallabha's understanding of the Gopīs' character types and its role in devotion. Vallabha's *Subodhinī* discusses the different types of characters one may have.[16] These character types are based upon the three *guṇas* of Indian thought: *sattva* (lightness); *rajas* (passion); and *tamas* (dullness and stubbornness). Each person has a primary and a secondary *guṇa* so there are nine different possibilities. Traditionally *sattva* has been considered the most exemplary of the character types, the most likely to achieve some sort of liberation or able to practice austerities. The Gopī's clearly embody what is normally the least desirable of the *guṇas*: the *tamas*. They are stubborn in their devotion and will let nothing stand in their way. No amount of argument or shame will deter them in their goal; they turn deaf ears to the complaints of their families and the rest of society.

Vallabha considers them the ideal *bhaktas*, for it is not their intelligence or skills in meditation and practice of austerities that makes them ideal, but precisely their faults. The much-criticized obstinacy and single-mindedness of the Gopīs earns them high praise from Vallabha and Paramānand for their devotion. These qualities are to be revered not censured, but we must distinguish between the *alaukik* and the *laukik* realms here. These ignoble qualities are esteemed because they are understood in the *alaukik* realm, not the *laukik*. The qualities have been purified by their participation in the *alaukik* realm. Stubbornness and obstinacy in general are not particularly valued in the world, but the fires of the *alaukik* have burned away the low status of the qualities.

A second perspective is that this behaviour does not occur in the so-called 'real' world, the world as we see it, but in the sacred or *alaukik* realm. Yet, it must be emphasized that the *līlā* is not considered to be merely allegorical or metaphorical; there is nothing allegorical about Kṛṣṇa's Braj activities. Although they occured once historically upon the earth, they continue in perpetuity 'on a plane that transcends our everyday experience'.[17] Those who do not see it are blinded by the *laukik* world; their perception is faulty. Ignorance and mis-perception hide the eternal *līlā* from people; wisdom and devotion will reveal it.

These *pads* were intended for an audience of *bhaktas*; Paramānand was not aiming to convert or convince; he was singing for Kṛṣṇa and in service of Kṛṣṇa. His audience was present to serve Kṛṣṇa and receive his *darśan*. Paramānand's audience were 'insiders' who were familiar with the episodes and natural settings mentioned in the *pads*. These *pads* evoked responses heightened by a previous familiarity with and affection for the material.[18] Thus, his contemporary audience and *bhaktas* today are unlikely to misinterpret the *pads*; the *bhakta* is able to contextualize them and see beyond face value.

The *bhakta* truly participates in the *līlā* when he or she is summoned by Kṛṣṇa to play and receives the *ādhidaivik* body which the Yamunā River bestows. When the *bhakta* has achieved the proper devotion to Kṛṣṇa, he or she participates in the *līlā* by assuming this body which is *alaukik* and eternal. So when the *bhakta* ultimately follows the actions which appear anti-social, they are not being performed in the *laukik* world, under *laukik* auspices and standards, but in the *alaukik* world in which these actions are sacred and good. Paramānand and Vallabha are not advocating that *bhaktas*—particularly women—should go out and commit egregious social acts but that they should internalize the emotions and ultimately participate in the *alaukik līlā*.

The qualities of stubbornness and obstinacy which characterize the maligned *tamas* type are good and right when applied to Kṛṣṇa devotion and when they appear in the *alaukik līlā*, not when they appear in the *laukik* world. The apparent anti-social behaviour of the Gopīs in the *līlā* is not proper in the *laukik* world. Instead the *bhakta* must appropriate the emotions arising from the behaviour and apply them to Kṛṣṇa Bhakti, mentally and emotionally acting as a Gopī. Through the *pads*, the *bhakta* places him or herself within the *līlā*, using the situations and the emotions which arise in the Braj drama to arouse and enhance the transformative *bhāv*. The love of union, the pain of separation and the fires of longing all deepen the *bhaktas*' feelings towards Kṛṣṇa and bring the *bhakta* closer to the *alaukik līlā*.

Vallabha's ideas on renunciation also instruct the *bhakta* in the proper behaviour towards Kṛṣṇa devotion as well as offering insight into the role of the Gopīs' behaviour. Vallabha never made provisions for renunciation in the *sampradāy* and himself married—a departure for a man in his situation. According to an article by Fred Smith on the *Saṃnyāsanirṇaya,* he stated that one could perform all duties as a householder and vows of *saṃnyāsa* were unnecessary.[19] But, if one were so taken with the *līlā* that one could no longer perform one's worldly duties, then that individual could remain absorbed in the *līlā.* This guide, in the *Saṃnyāsanirṇaya,* one of Vallabha's treatises in the *Sodaṣagrantha,* can also apply to the situation of women; he has made provisions for the *bhakta* (like Paramānand himself) who is totally absorbed in the *līlā* and can no longer participate in the duties of the mundane world. The Gopīs, too, are unable to participate in the social world; they think of Kṛṣṇa, nothing else.

Paramānand as a saint

Paramānand acts as a saint in two ways here: first, he composed the poems which enhance the *bhāv* and enable the *bhakta* to create intimacy with Kṛṣṇa. He mediates between the *alaukik* and *laukik* realms, leading the *bhakta* to a relationship with Kṛṣṇa and participation in the eternal *līlā*; and second, the *pads* provide norms of behaviour for the *bhakta,* both in this *laukik* realm and the *alaukik.* Though the Gopīs are seen as the ideal *bhakta*s, he does not advocate that women—or men—run off and leave their families to meet a lover. These behaviours are not to be followed *verbatim* in the *laukik* world. Rather, he presents the *līlā* so that the *bhakta* might internalize and develop the emotions, creating an intimacy with Kṛṣṇa that might ultimately lead to the assumption of the *alaukik* body.

Saints' behaviour often violates worldly standards. In an essay in *Saints and Virtues,* Jack Hawley terms that situation 'morality beyond morality';[20] as saints, their behaviour is exempt from conventional social standards. Paramānand himself does not violate any norms, although he did leave his marriage to devote himself totally to Kṛṣṇa-*sevā.* But the Gopīs do appear to violate social convention until one understands that their behaviour and qualities must be interpreted and understood through the *alaukik* realm. In the *laukik* realm, the Gopīs' behaviour still appears to violate social convention, but when understood as *alaukik* their behaviour is appropriate and laudable. The *alaukik* world purifies the qualities and behaviours of the Gopīs and the others of Braj. Similarly, as Hawley explains in *Kṛṣṇa, The Butter Thief,* Kṛṣṇa's pranks and his stealing the butter appear like theft when understood in the *laukik,* but as *alaukik* his actions depict his free dispensing of love (see J.S. Hawley 1987, pp. 52-72).

Paramānand's Gopīs should be judged by *alaukik* standards, not *laukik.* What appears as wrong by *laukik* standards (the Gopīs' obsessive attachment to Kṛṣṇa), through *alaukik* standards is valued; the Gopīs' constant and stubborn love for Kṛṣṇa is a model for the *bhakta.* Just as the Gopīs only think of Kṛṣṇa, the *bhakta* should place devotion to Kṛṣṇa before anything else. Love for and total awareness of Kṛṣṇa should supplant all else. The Gopīs' determined behaviour gives a message to the *bhakta* about proper devotion to Kṛṣṇa. Yet, this message is only understood through the *alaukik* perspective. In the *laukik* perspective, it seems nonsensical or even wrong-headed—just as without *bhāv,* a pilgrim-age site or a *svarūp* has no real meaning to a non-*bhakta* or one who knows nothing of Braj. Thus, the Gopīs only make sense to the informed *bhakta*; to all else, they are, at best, misunderstood or, worse, seen to promote a licentious lifestyle.

The *pads* focus the *bhakta's* thoughts and feelings on Kṛṣṇa. A *pad* illustrating the Gopīs' desire for Kṛṣṇa focuses the *bhakta's* thoughts on Kṛṣṇa which, in response to the content of the *pad,* encourages the appropriate *bhāv.* The Gopīs' actions are a vehicle to the bliss of Kṛṣṇa; eroticism or sensuality is not an end but a means to evoke the relevant *bhāv* so that the *bhakta* can experience *ānand,* or bliss, which results from intimacy with Kṛṣṇa.[21] The *pads,* in this case, function in a similar capacity as sites on a pilgrimage; they promote and facilitate *bhāv* and *darśan* of Kṛṣṇa's *līlā.* Paramānand, like a good *caube,* or pilgrimage guide, leads the *bhakta* on this journey within, a cognitive and internal pilgrimage rather than a physical or geographical trip. This is not to deny the importance of the sacred geography of Braj. Indeed, the sites and images are crucial for the *bhakta* to experience the *līlā* and *darśan* of Kṛṣṇa, but the *pads* can offer similar enticement to the stimulation of *bhāv*. They—just as the pilgrimage sites—present vignettes of the *līlā* to which the *bhakta* can add the narrative and context. Paramānand then through his *pads* leads the *bhakta* to participation in the *alaukik* realm.

The original question was how can we resolve the issue of the Gopīs' licentious behaviour with their status as ideal *bhaktas*? And, through the *pads*, how does Paramānand function as a saint in the Braj devotional community? The Gopīs' activities—full of what appear to be faults (if not sins)—are rendered virtuous when understood as *alaukik*. The *pads*—as 'verbal icons'—arouse the *bhāv* in the *bhakta* which transforms the *bhakta's* consciousness from *laukik* to the *alaukik*. The *bhakta* can understand the *pads* in their *alaukik* capacity and feel *prem* (not *kām*) for Kṛṣṇa. Paramānand's *pads* are the agents in a ritual of transformation in which 'things are seen as they really are'; they guide the *bhakta* on a cognitive pilgrimage so that the *bhakta* can participate in the reality of Kṛṣṇa's *līlā* and realize the sacred within the profane.

NOTES

1. There are several sources for biographical information on Paramānand. Nābhādās' *Bhaktamāl* ('Garland of *Bhaktas*') gives biographical information on a number of *bhaktas*. The Vallabhan *vārtās* tend to be more hagiographical and less reliable. The *vārtās* in R. Sampandit (1981) give no dates.

   The *vārtās* are the first hagiographical material regarding the Aṣṭachāp and their role within the Vallabha *sampradāy*, but only present information from the sectarian point of view. The *Caurāsī vaiṣṇava ki vārtā* was first written by Gokulnāth (1552-1641), Viṭṭhalnāth's fourth and probably most influential son, and later edited and commented upon by Harirāy (1591-1716) with the *Bhāvprakāś*. These *vārtās* present hagiographical material written in simple Braj Bhāṣā appropriate for a mass audience, to be used as a teaching material to spread the '*sampradāy*' version of the Aṣṭachāp lives as well as other Vallabha initiates among the *bhaktas*. Unfortunately, there is little external evidence regarding their lives, so we must rely, though cautiously, on these texts. The *vārtā* of each member of the Aṣṭachāp describes his pre-Vallabha life, the meeting and their role within the *sampradāy*. Also see R. Barz 1976, Shyam Das 1985, D. Gupta 1970 and G.N. Shukla 1963 for biographical information about Paramānand and the other Aṣṭachāp. They are hagiographical writings, presented so as to be easily accessible to the *bhakta*. The prose is straightforward and the vocabulary basic. These are not philosophical texts, but instead are meant to educate the *bhakta* about the Aṣṭachāp and the progression from *laukik* to *alaukik*. The Aṣṭachāp are exemplary *bhaktas* and models to follow; their *vārtās* are used congregationally by Puṣṭimārgīs to inspire the *bhāv* (R. Barz 1976, pp. 101-2). There are also other *vārtās* which discuss the lives of Vallabha and Viṭṭhalnāth.

Born in 1494 to a family of Kannauj Brahmans, Paramānand had a well-off and traditional Brahman upbringing. He died in 1585, making him remarkably long-lived (R. Barz 1976, p. 104).

2. Paramānand has been linked by some scholars primarily to *bāl-līlā*, but his poetry is more complex than that. Though externally, many of his *pads* appear as *bāl pads*, many, upon closer examination, lead the *bhakta* into the *bhāv* of *mādhurya līlā*.
3. See R. Barz 1976, p. 104. Inside these gates at night is the *līlā* of Rādhā and Kṛṣṇa in which only the *sakhīs* have a role; each of the *Aṣṭachāp* also has a *sakhī* form.
4. *Kīrtan* are songs of praise to the deity. The *Bhāgavatapurāṇa* mentions nine types of *bhakti* expression: *kīrtana; śravaṇa;* (hearing the lord's name); *smaraṇa;* (remembering the lord) *padasevanā* (worshiping the feet); *arcanā* (offering ritual worship); *vandanā* (praising the lord); *dāsya* (being the lord's servant); *sakhya;* (being a friend of the lord) and *ātmanivedana* (offering absolute surrender) (R. Barz 1976, pp. 83-4). The first eight are preludes to *ātmanivedana*, although taking the *Brahmasambandha mantra* assumes absolute surrender (B.M. Parekh 1943, p. 141).
5. This idea of seeing the *līlā* certainly accords with the Indian tradition of *darśan* in which the actual deity is seen in the image. For a discussion on the idea of seeing the deity, see D. Eck 1981.

O. Lynch's discussion of *darśan* is helpful regarding the transformative nature of the *bhāv*. *Darśan* also has the connotation of arousing feeling as well as having a visual component. Lynch, in this article discusses *darśan* as the attempt to an 'experiential and practical means . . . to change one's perception of reality'. With *darśan*, the *bhakta* has a vision of the divine, not a symbol, but the divine itself, but here the focus is perceptual transformation through vision. Lynch presents the feeling dimension of *darśan* in which the sight produces a religious emotion. A pilgrimage—just like the *pads*—as an extended *darśan*, is less an attempt to see, than it is an attempt to feel. *Darśan* has a tripartite structure: *bhāv*, *bhāvnā* and *ras*.

Sights or experiences stimulate the feelings, or *bhāvnās*; these then transform the *bhāv* to the higher *ras*. The *bhāv* which are emotions innate in all human beings are the means to seeing the divinity in what would otherwise be ordinary material (O. Lynch 1988, p. 188).

An anecdote about Govindsvāmī's *vārtā* depicts the relationship between the poetry and *darśan* of the *līlā*. He was singing *pads*, then suddenly stopped. When asked why, Govindsvāmī replied that he could no longer see the *līlā*.

6. Vallabha's *Siddhāntarahasya* presents a relevant analogy regarding the merging of gutter water with that of the Gaṅgā. Once the gutter water flows into the Gaṅgā, it is part of the Gaṅgā and no longer distinguishable. Once merged, the two—the pure and the impure—are inseparable.
7. *Paramānand-sāgar*, 777.
8. There is a bodily transformation, but this is something apart from the adoption of the *alaukik* consciousness. When Kṛṣṇa particu-larly favors a *bhakta*, he can give that person the *ādhidaivik* body (divine and purified body) which is just like Kṛṣṇa's. That *bhakta* then can participate in the *nitya līlā*; this is the highest stage of devotion, beyond even absorption in the *akṣara brahman*. The Yamunā River bestows this body. This body, just as the *bhakta's* ability to perform *sevā*, comes only through Kṛṣṇa's grace and not through any effort on the part of the *bhakta* (G.H. Bhatt 1984, p. 17).

   See also J. McDaniel 1993, pp. 80-1, in which she discusses the *siddha-deha* which is comprised of consciousness and bliss (*cidānanda*).
9. To a non-*bhakta*, the sights and sounds of Braj, *līlā* and *sevā* are meaningless or worse, appear as 'vicarious epicureanism, . . . People unsusceptible to the *bhāv* may react in the same way Babbitt did to French Romanticism, in which he saw a tendency to a hyper-trophy of sensation and an atrophy of ideas . . . a quest that may at any time assume the guise of heavenly idealism' (A.W. Entwistle 1993, p. 100).
10. Both David Haberman (1994, p. 73) and Owen Lynch (1988, p. 188) describe the perspectival shift from the *laukik* to the *alaukik* as 'seeing things as they really are'. Pilgrimage focuses the *bhakta's* thoughts and emotions to foster this shift of awareness from the mundane to the *līlā*.
11. Of the four relationships, all of the *ras/bhāvs* appear only in *śṛṅgār*. The others can all be subsumed under the category of erotic love, but the reverse is not true. For example, erotic love should not manifest itself within the context of parental love.
12. We should distinguish between *kalpanā*, imagination, *bhāvnā*, the emulation of the *bhāv* and the *bhāv* itself. *Kalpanā* does not give the sense of having insight or knowledge; it is fairly superficial; *bhāvnā*, on the other hand, indicates the emulation of the ways of Braj by the Braj *bhakta*. Kṛṣṇa is himself *bhāv*, and the *bhāvnā* is the emulation of those who realize Kṛṣṇa's identity with *bhāv*, particularly those characters in the Braj *līlā*. *Bhāvnā* suggests an awareness and

participation in the *līlā*, while *kalpanā* is only what one might produce in the imagination. Paramānand's participation in the *līlā* exemplifies this distinction. When Paramānand sang of the *līlā*, he was actually seeing it; he was not just recreating it from memory or basing it upon something he imagined to be happening. *Bhāvnā* indicates an awareness of the *līla* that is actually occuring and suggests the *bhakta's* participation in it.

13. *Paramānand-sāgar,* 1028.
14. *Nitya kīrtan: Ras ratnākar,* 367.
15. Uddhava and Kṛṣṇa also criticize the Gopīs for their behaviour at different times. After Kṛṣṇa has summoned the Gopīs with his flute, he insults them for abandoning their families and acting in such a shameful manner. Uddhava also criticizes the Gopīs' behaviour in the *Bhramargīt.* For a discussion of the *Bhramargīt,* see W. Sanford 1994, pp. 113-40.
16. See J. Redington 1983, pp. 44-7 for a discussion of the ideal *bhakta* types and requisite *guṇas.*
17. A.W. Entwistle 1987, p. 71. Kṛṣṇa's *alaukik* activities are *aprakaṭ* (unmanifest) on the *laukik* plane, but none the less they are real and accessible to *bhaktas.* Activities manifest in the *laukik* realm are considered *prakaṭ* (manifest).

    Western categories of sacred and profane cannot adequately account for the concept of the reality of the *līlā.* The West traditionally assumes a substantial gap between the sacred and the profane and so any incursion of the sacred into the profane must be understood in terms of metaphor, allegory or symbol. Possibly Lynch's term 'divine metonymy' might be the best way to under-stand the ontology of the *svarūp* and the presence of the sacred within the profane. The important issue is to narrow, if not close, the gap between the signifier and the signified in understanding the *svarūp* and the physical Braj. Though this gap might adequately serve much of the Western tradition of thought and religion, it does a dis-service to our understanding of Braj devotionalism. The point of this discussion is to 'deconstruct' assumptions about the sacred which naturally follow from a discussion about the sacred image and *svarūp.*
18. Vallabha, too, intended his material for those who had already achieved a certain spiritual level. *Jana,* normally means people or women; here, Vallabha refers to those who already have *bhakti* as a result of Kṛṣṇa's *anugraha.* Vallabha had selective criteria for his *sampradāy* and, though a prostelytizer, did not accept everyone. Today, the Puṣṭimārg community, excepting such groups like the *Svadhyāya* movement, does not actively seek converts. *Jana* also indicates those who will not be born again: *ja na,* short for *na jayanti.*
19. Vallabha himself had a non-traditional attitude towards marriage.

While many in his position would have taken vows of *saṃnyāsin*, Vallabha married, believing that Kṛṣṇa-*sevā* could and should take place from within the stage of householder. He did not disallow renunciation but made no provisions for it in the *sampradāy*. He apparently did accept some form of renunciation of worldly duties if a *bhakta* became so entranced by service of Kṛṣṇa that he or she could no longer fulfill his or her duties. For a discussion of the *Saṃnyāsanirṇaya*, see F.M. Smith 1993.

20. See J.S. Hawley 1989, pp. 261-87, for discussion on the economy of love as opposed to the economy of the world in regard to Kṛṣṇa's stealing the milk and curd from the Gopīs.

21. Vallabha himself realized that this *mādhurya bhāv* could be misinterpreted by ignorant people, so he states that the *rās*, though real, is 'devoid of sensualism'. It should not be understood in the worldly, or *laukik* sense (G.H. Bhatt 1984, p. 23). One should distinguish between *prem* and *kām* in this case. *Kām* is the profane, lusty love which produces children; *prem* is a purified and *alaukik* love which characterizes the *bhakta's* love for Kṛṣṇa (O. Lynch 1988, p. 181) quotes a pilgrim who claims the *rās* had no real food or sex; only the bliss of Kṛṣṇa's non-physical activities were present. Kṛṣṇa's *līlā* takes place not in the physical world but in the realm of pure bliss, and the *alaukik* Braj is comprised of bliss.

REFERENCES

Barz, Richard. *The Bhakti Sect of Vallabhācārya.* Haryana: Thomson Press (India) Limited, 1976.

Bhatt, G.H. *Śrī Vallabhācārya and His Doctrines.* Baroda: Shri Vallabha Publications, 1984.

Das, Shyam. *Aṣṭachāpa: Kṛṣṇa's Eight Poet-Friends.* Baroda: Shri Vallabha Publications, 1985.

Eck, Diana. *Darśana: Seeing the Divine Image in India.* Chambersburg, PA: Anima Books, 1981.

Entwistle, Alan W. *Braj, Centre of Kṛṣṇa Pilgrimage.* Groningen: Egbert Forsten, 1987.

———. 'Synaesthesia in Poetry and Ritual of the *Puṣṭimārga*'. *Journal of Vaiṣṇava Studies.* 1.3 (Spring 1993): 84-103.

Gupta, Dindayalu. *Aṣṭachāp aur Vallabha-sampradāy.* Prayag: Hindi Sahitya Sammelan, 1970.

Haberman, David. *Journey through The Twelve Forests.* New York: Oxford University Press, 1994.

Hawley, John S. *Kṛṣṇa, The Butter Thief.* Delhi: Oxford University Press, 1989.

———. 'Morality Beyond Morality in the Lives of Three Hindu Saints'. In

Saints and Virtues, ed. John S. Hawley, pp. 52-72. Berkeley: University of California Press, 1987.

Lynch, Owen. 'Pilgrimage with Kṛṣṇa, sovereign of the emotions'. *Contributions to Indian Sociology*. 22. 2 (1988): 188-94.

McDaniel, June. 'Dancing in the Hidden Vṛndavana: The Ritual Service of Caitanya'. *Journal of Vaiṣṇava Studies*. 1. 3 (Spring 1993): 72-83.

Nitya kīrtan: Ras ratnākar. Ed. Giridhardasji Mundhara. Bikaner: Mundhara Foundation.

Parekh, Bhai Manilal C. *Shri Vallabhacārya: Life, Teachings and Movement*. Rajkot: Harmony House, 1943.

Paramānand-sāgar. Ed. Sribrajbhushan Sharma. Kankaroli: Vidya-vibhag.

Redington, Thomas. *Vallabhācārya on the Love Games of Kṛṣṇa*. Delhi: Motilal Banarsidass, 1983.

Sampandit, Ramdasji. *Dosaubāvan vaiṣṇava kī vārtā*. Bombay: Kalyan, 1981.

Sanford, A. Whitney. 'An Evolution of Emphasis: A Comparison of the Story of "Uddhava's Message" in the *Bhramargīt* in the *Bhāgavata-purāṇa* and the *Bhramargīt* of Nandadās'. *Journal of Vaiṣṇava Studies*. 2. 3 (Summer 1994): 113-40.

Smith, Frederick M. 'The *Saṁnyāsanirṇaya*'. *Journal of Vaiṣṇava Studies*. 1. 4 (Summer 1993): 135-56.

Shukla, Govardhan Nath. *Kavivar Paramānand aur Vallabha Sampradāy*. Aligarh: Bharat Prakashan Mandir, 1963.

Sacred Biographies and Profane Lives: 'Bhāratendu' Hariścandra's *Uttarārdha bhaktamāl*

SAGAREE SENGUPTA

Bhāratendu Hariścandra (1850-85) composed his *Uttarārdha bhaktamāl* as a modern continuation of Nābhādās's well-known work. My paper closely examines the style of the latter-day 'hagiography' to show what, besides the content, makes it modern despite Hariścandra's flawless Braj Bhāṣā.

My aim in this paper is to look at some of the elements of sacred biography and autobiography that connect Bhāratendu Hariścandra's clearly marked religious writing with his secular works. Vasudha Dalmia-Lüderitz (1992, pp. 281-97) has very ably shown in her research on the nineteenth-century Hindi writer's Vaiṣṇava affiliations how missionary and orientalist methods were appropriated in order to assert a revived base for Hinduism. She has also pointed out the importance of the text of Hariścandra's *Uttarārdha bhaktamāl* for propagating Benares's (usually thought of as a Śaiva stronghold) and his own family's identification with Vaiṣṇava tradition.

Hariścandra's version of nationalism relied on a generalized Vaiṣṇava philosophy along with a vision of revivified Hindi language and literature. Still, there are times when the writer announced a desire to keep his Vaiṣṇava faith protected from 'the world'. One signal of the separation he felt had to be maintained between pious Vaiṣṇava works and profane consumption are the warnings—against the revelation of 'the mystery' to crass-minded non-believers—with which he felt compelled to preface his books of erotic devotional poetry. Such were the perils of expanding the world of *kīrtan* and private poetic gatherings into printed forms. In *Uttarārdha bhaktamāl*, first published 1876-7 in *Hariścandra candrikā*, however, Hariścandra is able to build a bridge between world of Rādhā-Kṛṣṇa and his own historical one; the connection between divine and worldly consists of the habits of devotion—

namely service to the deity, charity, gifts to temples and the composing of didactic and poetic Vaiṣṇava works, and these activities are the stuff of the long poem's narrative. *Uttarāradha bhaktamāl* (*Bhārtendu Granthāvalī* [*BG*], pp. 221-70),[1] is his labour of love for his fellow believers and a 'completion' in the same *chappāī*[1] verse form, one per devotee, of Nābhādās's seventeenth century *Bhaktamāl*, or catalogue of great Vaiṣṇava devotees. In bringing Nābhā's hagiography 'up to date', Hariścandra is inducting non-mythologized figures—his contemporaries, as well as himself—into, what is, at least formally, a religious rhetoric.

Nābhādās also included devotees from all sects for the greater glory of Vaiṣṇava faith. His work provides a ready model for Hariścandra's wide net. If the degree of compaction makes Nābhā hard to follow without commentary, Hariścandra's verses seem quite rangy and accessible—partly because he packs less into each *chappāī*, and partly because many of his subjects were still alive and thus had not yet been able to give rise to the standard hagiographies that followed the death and apotheosis of a famous *bhakta* in earlier times. Many of Hariścandra's verse accounts can be supplemented with information from other sources, including his other writings.

Translated, many of the *chappāīs* are reduced to pious bibliographies rather than biographies, as one of the ways to gain a place in Hariścandra's 'Garland' was by doing your own propagating through doctrinal texts or songs. Another method of induction into the 'Garland', familiar from Nābhā, is the recounting of incidents and habits from the life of the devotee. In a way, this points to what is remarkable about the 'new' *chappāīs*: Hariścandra puts into fluent, easy Braj meter accounts of modern Vaiṣṇavas, some of them perfectly ordinary-sounding devotees; he iconizes these examples of piety without removing them entirely from the realm of the ordinary. There is far less ellipsis in Hariścandra's Braj Bhāṣā than in 'classical' Bhakti lyrics, and his syntax is generally more straightforward; as in his other Braj Bhāṣā production, there is a morphological uniformity in the language that is obviously 'modern'. All of this makes for greater accessibility, but perhaps for less spiritual mystique.

नरायनदास प्रभु-पद-निरत अम्बालय में बासत रहे।
नृप नौकर अवसर न पावते प्रभु दरसन कों॥

उत्कठित दिन राति धन्य धनि जिनके मन कों॥
कब जैहौ भैया श्री वल्लभ के दरसन हित।
चाकर राषे सुरति देन कों यों छन छन तिन॥
बहु भेंट पठावत हे प्रभुहि ऐसे ये भागवत हे।
नारायनदास प्रभु-पद निरत अम्बालय में बसत हे॥46॥

(*BG,* vol. 2, p. 254)

Narāyandās, devoted to the feet of the Lord, lives in Ambālay.
Servant of a king, he has no time to receive *darśan* of the Lord.
In his heart 'blessed thanks' is sung out day and night.
'When will you go, brother, to see Vallabha?' Instead,
He placed three servants to provide entertainment at every moment.
He sent many gifts to the Lord, such a Bhāgavat is he.
Narāyandās, devoted to the feet of the Lord, lives in Ambālay.

Hariścandra praises Nābhā himself for 'stringing together verses', the implicit merit-claim of which action as favorably reflecting on himself cannot be ignored:

बनमाली के माली भए नाभा जी गुन-गन-गथित।
नाम नरायनदास बिदित हनुमत कुल जायो।
अग्र कील्ह गुरु-कृपा नयन खोयोहू पायो॥
गुरु-आयसु धरि सीस भक्त-कीरति जिन गाई।
भक्तमाल रस-जाल प्रेम सों गुथि बनाई॥
नित ही नव-रूप सुबास सम सुमन-संत करनी कथित।
बनमाली के माली भद्द नाभा की गुन-गन-जन-गथित॥184॥

(*BG,* vol. 2, p. 264)

Stringing together [verses about] virtuous people, Nābhā became the garland maker of the wild-garlanded Kṛṣṇa.
He was born in the Hanumata clan under the name of Nārāyandās;
He lost his eyesight but got it back through the grace of his Guru Agra Kīlha—
Holding the command of his guru on his head, he sang the fame of devotion,
And wove together the *rasa* soaked net of *Bhaktamāl* with great love.
He told of a garland of saint-flowers, always fragrant as if newly blossomed;
Stringing together [verses about] virtuous people, Nābhā became the garland maker of the wild-garlanded Kṛṣṇa.

Hariścandra's poet-father, Gopālcandra or Giridhardās, appears in the same roster, his Vaiśya caste identity pointed out with pride:

गिरिधरदास कवि-कुल-कमल वैश्य वंश भूषण प्रगट॥
रामायन भागवत गरग संहिता कथामृत।
भाषा करि करि रचे बहुत हरि-चरित सुभाषित॥
दान मान करि साधु भक्त मन मोद बढ़ायो।
सब कुल-देवन मेटि एक हरि-पंथ दृढ़ायो॥
लक्षावधि ग्रन्थन निरमये श्री वल्लभ विश्वास अट।
गिरिधरदास कवि-कुल-कमल वैश्य वंश भूषण प्रगट॥ 188॥

(*BG*, vol. 2, pp. 265-6)

Giridhardās, a lotus among poets and the ornament of the Vaiśya caste, was born.
He composed commentaries on the immortal books of the *Rāmāyaṇa, Bhāgavata, Garg saṃhitā,*
And many epigrams on the deeds of Hari and collections of sayings.
By giving gifts and respect he increased the joy in the hearts of holy devotees,
And he put an end to all the family gods and firmly established the exclusive worship of Hari.
He wrote more than a *lakh* of books and was immovable in his Vallabhan beliefs.
Giridhardās, a lotus among poets and the ornament of the Vaiśya caste, was born.

In his geographic and intergenerational reach, Hariścandra is defining not only a new kind of Vaisnava roster, but also claiming a wider and wider portion of India as his own cultural area. His inclusivism can be seen as a mild sort of proto-nationalism. Hariścandra's gradually moving the focus of the poem from deities to deified gurus, and traditionally accepted saints to ordinary human beings still entangled in the world despite their devotion, creates a sacralized world, a contemporary scene justified with mythology. It is a kind of strategy that would continue to be relevant in Indian social and political life.

Last but certainly not least, Hariścandra describes himself both as devotee and as poet, in a long string of *dohās* (distichs) that is the *locus classicus* of his self-presentation as a member of several traditions. Here are the last few of these *dohās*:

हरि-चरित्र हरि ही कह्यो हरिहि सुनत चित लाय।
हरिहि बडाई करत हरि ही समुझत मन भाय॥
हम तो श्री वल्लभ-कृपा इतनो जान्यौ सार।
सत्य एक नँदनंद है झूठो सब संसार॥

तासों सब सों बिनय करि कहत पुकार पुकार।
कान खोलि सबही सुनौ जौ चाहौ निस्तार॥
मोरौ मुख घर ओर सों तोरौ भव के जाल।
छोरौ जग साधन सबै भजौ एक नँदलाल॥

(*BG*, vol. 2, pp. 269-70)

Hari himself tells the story of Hari and Hari himself listens with an intent mind—
Hari himself sings praises and Hari himself understands with pleasure.
As for us, through Śrī Vallabha's mercy we know this to be of essence,
That there's only one Truth and it is the Son of Nanda—the rest of existence is false.
That is why I humbly call out to everyone—
Open your ears and listen, all of you, if you want to be saved.
Turn your face away from your home, and slash through the net of existence,
Stop serving the world, all of you, and repeat only the name of Nanda's son!

The Prakritization common to words transferred into Braj Bhāṣā renders Hariścandra's name Haricanda or Harīcanda depending on the metrical need—Hariścandra also uses this to change the meaning of his name in Kṛṣṇa Bhakti contexts. To have 'Hari' as the first element of a devotee's name is conveniently auspicious indeed, and in works such as his colophon to *Uttarārdha bhaktamāl* he uses it extensively in his reverent punning. The line *hari-caritra hari hī kahyau harihi sunata cita lāya* can mean both 'Hari (Kṛṣṇa) himself related the story of Hari (Kṛṣṇa) and Hari (Kṛṣṇa) himself hears it with hearfelt emotion', or 'Hari (Hariścandra) related the story of Hari (Kṛṣṇa) and Hari (Kṛṣṇa) hears it with heartfelt emotion.' When we go on to the second line of the couplet—*harihi baṛhāī karata hari hī samujhata mana bhāya,* 'It is Hari who does the praising and Hari who, pleased in his heart, understands'—the purport becomes that the relater of the narrative, its subject, its audience, and connoisseur are all Kṛṣṇa. The deity is behind the poet's impulse to praise and tell as he is behind all the actions of the world.

Composing *Uttarārdha bhaktamāl* was hardly the rote exercise it may seem to readers now though admittedly it is not the most esthetically interesting of Hariścandra's works. Writing in a more obviously modern spirit (and perhaps his non-Brahmin background made this easier) he generously admits in *Vaiṣṇavatā aur Bhāratvarṣ*

(1884) that ancient Vaiṣṇava practice may have not been like its modern counterpart:

Dhruv and Prahlād were certainly Vaiṣṇavas, but did they wear *tulsī* beads, markings on their foreheads and *mudrās*, and did they abstain from meat etc.? There is no reliable proof of these matters. In the same way, judging from the religious preferences of India now, it is clear that in the future the sanctions about eating and drinking in Vaiṣṇava practice will disappear and many changes will certainly take place. (*BG*, vol. 3, p. 796)

He further admits that contemporary practices contained much that was not ideal, such as concern over untouchability even between different sects of Vaiṣṇavas; hence an attempt at unifying and liberalizing Vaiṣṇava tradition through a new, eminently recitable text complemented his other efforts.

As far as his own reputation and character, in *Uttarārdha bhaktamāl*, Hariścandra's worldly 'vices'—or tendency to indulge in *kām*—are subsumed under the idea of *prem* due to the heroic volume and fame of his versification; but as vices unmutated, they also increase the piteousness of his appeal to God as a 'sinner', a favourite way for *bhaktas* to sign off verses. Hariścandra's 'bad reputation' fits in neatly with this requirement of devout poetry, and his devotional rhetoric disarms his human critics.

If Hariścandra was bringing the world into his Vaiṣṇavism, he could also borrow from devotion to pay tribute to the world. His 1884 cycle of eight *chappāīs* in tribute to Lord Ripon—*Ripanāṣṭak*—sing the glories of the Viceroy in a style just one remove from the accounts of the *Uttarārdha bhaktamāl*: Ripon's *āṣṭak* is a garland just for one personage, and only the omission of the repeated last line makes the verses different in form from those in the *Uttarārdha bhaktamāl*. Ripon is praised as treating *setāset* or white and non-white people equally, as able to enchant feuding parties with his words and as able to resolve impossible problems. In his persuasive talents, Ripon is a cousin of divinely inspired poets, whose ranks included Hariścandra himself. Ripon could be seen as especially beneficial to Hindus, and this may be why he is practically deified by Hariścandra while other viceroys in the lineup are damned with faint praise.

जदपि बाहु-बल क्लाइव जीत्यौ सगरो भारत।
जदपि और लाटनहू को जन नाम उचारत॥

जदपि हेसटिंग्ज आदि साथ धन लै गए भारी।
जदपि लिटन दरबार कियो सजि बड़ी तयारी॥
पै हम हिंदुन के हीय की भक्ति न काहू संग गई।
सो केवल तुमरे सँग रिपन छाया सी साथिन भई॥ 9॥

(*BG*, vol. 2, p. 817)

Although Clive won all of India with the might of his arm,
Although the names of the other Viceroys are on people's lips,
Although Hastings and others took away huge amounts of treasure,
Although Lytton made great preparations for the Durbar,
The heartfelt devotion of us Hindus did not go to anyone else,
Except with you, O Ripon, where it is a companion close as a shadow.

Hariścandra's claim to the lineage of *bhaktas* lies in his dedication of copious amounts of poetry to Kṛṣṇa. On the other hand, he emphatically follows the convention of self-denigration when describing himself in his devotional poetry. No reconciliation of these two aspects were necessary for him, because there was no felt contradiction between being a poet of renown and being something of a famed sensualist around Benares; his appeals to Kṛṣṇa's grace seem actually heightened by the resonant correspondence between the 'fallen one' of his colophons and his known life. Ironically, the encomiast biographers of Hariścandra who wrote after his death were far more disgruntled by the necessity of acknowledging his lifestyle—Hariścandra left too much evidence for it to be ignored—along with his contribution to Khaṛī Bolī and Braj Bhāṣā literature. Shivnandan Sahay's chapter 'Gulāb mẽn kā̃ṭā' (The Thorn on the Rose [1905] 1975, pp. 331-6) is one of the earlier attestations of the perceived contradiction between Hariścandra's virtues and vices. The moral requirements of an Indian national hero, which is the mold later writers try to fit Hariścandra into, had become quite stringent. Thus Hariścandra is remembered in a new set of hagiographies, which couch the facts of his colourful life in pious regret and rationalization, in gestures which attempt to associate him with the type of the exemplary cultural reformer derived from other, more sedate, Indian national heroes. Despite the difficulties, a degree of apotheosis has been reached in the secondary material on Hariścandra that contrasts sharply with the frankness of his own writings.

NOTE

1. A six-line verse form, the first four lines of which usually have twenty-four measures each (*rolā*), and the last two, twenty-six measures each (*ullāl*).

REFERENCES

Dalmia-Lüderitz, Vasudha. 'Hariścandra of Banaras and the reassessment of Vaiṣṇava bhakti in the late nineteenth century'. In *Devotional Literature in South Asia: Current Research, 1985-1988,* ed. R.S. MacGregor, pp. 281-97. Cambridge: Cambridge Univercity Press, 1992.

Hariścandra ('Bhāratendu'). *Bhāratendu granthāvalī.* Edited by Brajratan Das. 3 vols. Kasi: Nagari Pracharini Sabha, 1935, 1954-5.

Sahay, Shivnandan. *Hariścandra: Bhārat Bhūṣaṇ Bhāratendu Bābū Hariścandra kā jīvan-caritra.* 1905. Reprint. Lucknow: Hindi Samiti, 1975.

'. . . in this bushy land of Salsette . . .': Father Thomas Stephens and the *Kristapurāṇa*

HUGH VAN SKYHAWK

Historical context and reception

On 29 April 1616, Father Thomas Stephens, S.J., wrote in the dedication of his *Purāṇṇa da Vinda e Vida do Christo* ('Treatise on the coming of the Redeemer into and his life in the world') to the Bishop of Goa and Primate of India, D. Fr. Christovao de Lisboa, the following summary of his *magnum opus* (S. Bandelu 1956, pp. 942f):

> I offer your Lordship this poor gift which is a work written after the fashion of this country, and in a style most acceptable to the natives. It contains a catechetical course of instruction, not such, however, as would satisfy your holy zeal, nor even such as this new Christian flock stands in need of, but only such as I with my poor talent have been able to prepare here in this bushy land of Salsette: and the more lengthy it is, treating of many and various things of our Holy Faith, the more timidly is it presented to the public.

It soon became clear, however, that Father Stephens's retelling of the Old and New Testaments in the '*Brahman-Mahratta*' language (Old Marathi) had won the hearts of the people of seventeenth century Goa. Hardly two years subsequent to Stephens's death in 1619, the *Kristapurāṇa* is mentioned with great enthusiasm in the *Lettere annue del Giappone, China, Goa et Ethiopia* (Naples, 1621) (S. Bandelu, pp. 35f):

> This work is so delightful that not only do the Christians derive much profit from it, but even the non-Christians speak of it with pride. On Sundays and feast-days this book, or Puranna, as it is called, is being read in the churches with as much profit as it gets applause.

Thomas Stephens, born in Bushton, Wiltshire in the year 1549, was the first Englishman to make Goa his home. Moreover, he was the first (and to this day only) European to make a lasting contribution to the literature of the Marathi-speaking people. Even more importantly, with the exception of Saint Francis Xavier (d. 1552), Thomas Stephens was the missionary whose life and works contributed most to the shaping of Christianity in Goa.

When 'Phadar Estevan' reached Salsette in 1579 the Christian community counted approximately 8,000 souls of a total population of 80,000. When he died in 1619 the entire community had converted to Christianity. Even under 'normal conditions' in sixteenth century Goa Thomas Stephens's achievements would represent significant contributions to the history and culture of India. But the conditions under which Father Stephens pursued his mission in Goa were anything but 'normal'. For, just as Stephens won the hearts of the Goans by his humility and self-sacrifice, other Jesuits and their Portuguese troops sowed a bitter harvest of hate and dread among the Hindu population by resorting to oppression and atrocities to establish their rule. In this connection, an appalling series of events, which occurred in 1582, four years subsequent to Thomas Stephens' arrival in Goa, is related in detail by Stephen Neill. The following summary will serve as a brief contextualization of the historical setting in which Stephens lived and in which the *Kristapurāṇa* was written (S. Neill 1984, p. 239, quoting G. Goldie, *The First Christian Mission to the Great Mogul* [Dublin, 1987]):

Two villages in the extreme south of the peninsula of Salsette—Cuncolim and Assolna in the spelling used by the Portuguese—had been specially obstinate in holding fast to the Hindu way and its ceremonies. Early in 1582, in reprisal for injuries done to a messenger who was carrying despatches from Cochin to the Viceroy, a fleet of boats sailed down from Goa and destroyed the temple at Assolna. At the same time, the captain of Rachol marched down with troops to Cuncolim; a Jesuit, Fr. Berno, set fire to the large temple in the village; a number of smaller shrines was also destroyed. Then Fr. Berno, with incredible folly, 'killed a sacred cow on the spot, with the double object of defiling the holy places and destroying the object of superstition, and he profaned a sacred tank by casting into it the intestines of the slaughtered animal'.

The authorities seem to have been unaware of the lasting fury occasioned by the outrage. In 1583 a visit was paid to Salsette by the new provincial Rudolf Aquaviva, formerly of the mission to the Great Mogul, accompanied by a number of priests, some Indian Christians, and a group of Portuguese gentlemen. On 15-25 July, the anger of the people broke out in open violence. Aquaviva, who stood forth as the acknowledged leader, was the first to suffer. Then the mob fell on Fr. Berno, the object of their special animosity; the other two priests followed soon after. A lay brother, Aranha, though terribly wounded, survived in hiding till the next morning, when he was discovered, killed and horribly mutilated. Altogether fourteen others were killed, the bodies were stripped by outcaste menials, thrown together into a large pit which, this being monsoon time, was full of water, and covered over with branches to prevent discovery.

When, the same evening, news of the disaster reached Goa, there was no limit to the distress and dismay caused by events for which there was no precedent in the history of the missions. Many Christians had died at the hands of pirates or in sporadic outbursts of violence. But so ruthless a massacre, carried out by the generally kindly and gentle Hindu population, was unexpected and alarming. It was decided that the bodies of the martyrs must be recovered and given Christian burial.

It fell to Thomas Stephens as rector of the college at Rachol to set about the recovery of the bodies. At first the people denied all knowledge, but before long were tricked into agreeing to the surrender; the menials carried the bodies to the north bank of the river, where they were received by the group from Goa and reverently carried to the church. It was found that the bodies were so swollen by their immersion in water that it was not possible to array them in Jesuit robes; but with such order and ceremony as was possible they were laid to rest.

What follows is far from edifying. Though the Fathers pleaded that vengeance should not be taken on the guilty, fifteen of the leading men who came in to plead for pardon and to promise friendship were immediately cut down by the soldiery; others were pursued to the mainland and done to death. The five villages concerned were deprived of their liberty, two being handed over in fief to one Portuguese, and three to another.

Content and literary form

Thomas Stephens, who was a contemporary of the Maharashtrian Bhakti reformer Śrī Sant Ekanāth of Pratiṣṭhān (1533-1609), lived the greater part of his life in Goa (1579-1619). In the course of the thirty years prior to the composition of the *Kristapurāṇa* he gained an intimate knowledge of the Bhakti traditions of the Marathi-speaking Hindus and thus the ability to express Christian beliefs and teachings in the images of folk Hinduism.

In contrast to his successor in Goa, Father Etienne de la Croix (1579-1643), Thomas Stephens refrained from disparaging or ridiculing Hindu beliefs. Rather, he put Hindu patterns of thought in the service of Christianity. In this way Stephens and his Purāṇa won the hearts of the Marathi-speaking Indians, while de la Croix's *Saint Peter Purāṇa* is now known only to historians of the church in Goa and specialists of Old Marathi literature.

In keeping with the devotional nature of Bhakti, Stephens rendered the contents of the Old Testament in brief (4,035 quatrains) and expanded upon the life of Christ in the New Testament (6,686 quatrains). Instead of using the religious terminology of Latin or Portuguese, he chose or coined corresponding terms from Sanskrit and the regional language, Marathi. Similarly, the metre and the rhetorical devices used in the *Kristapurāṇa* derive from Bhakti literature in Old Marathi. Only with regard to its specifically Christian contents and intention does the Purāṇa from the quill of the first Englishman in Goa differ from the works of Ekanāth or Śrī Sant Jñāneśvar (d. *c.* 1294), not, however, in its literary form and composition. In this connection, mention should be made of Thomas Stephens's glowing praise of the regional language, Marathi, as the proper vehicle for conveying the teachings of Christ in India (S.G. Tulpue 1979, p. 381):

> To enlighten the masses on the Holy Doctrine (*parama śāstra*),
> Is narrated here the story (of Jesus) in the Marathi language.
> As the gem among the pebbles, or the blue diamond among gems,
> Or the *mogarī* among flowers, or musk among perfumes,
> Or the peacock among birds, or the *kalpataru* (wishing tree) among trees,
> So is the pure, elegant and respected Marathi among the langues Indian.

Religious syncretism in the Kristapurāṇa

Stephens begins his rendering of the story of the birth of Christ in keeping with the classical structuring of a *bhakti-kathā:* first, the *namana,* or homages. From the outset the text reflects an intimate knowledge of Old Marathi as a literary language. The *namana* consist of 6 *ovīs,* or quatrains, in two units of 3 *ovīs* each, in total, 24 *caraṇas,* 24 being a number associated with completeness or perfection in medieval India. In form as well as content the number three emerges as the organizing principle of the *Kristapurāṇa* (hereafter *KP*): In the *namana* three persons are praised: (1) Jesus;

(2) Maria; (3) the unnamed Santa-*bhaktas*. The proportioning of the 24 *caraṇas* is elegant: Jesus is praised in 12 *caraṇas*, Maria in 8, and the Santa-*bhaktas* in 4, respectively. The total numbers of *ovīs* in the seventh and eighth *avasvarus* (chapters) of the *KP*, in which the story of the birth of Christ is told, are 91 and 111, respectively. Ninety-one is the product of thrice thirty plus one, the supplementary one being in use in India since Vedic times as a symbol of wholeness and perfection (see J. Gonda 1974, pp. 5-23). While 111 as the product of thrice thirty-seven is less rich in mystical signification, the sum of the numerals 1+1+1=3 again alludes to a triad. For Father Thomas Stephens of the Society of Jesus, however, the triad had another, more immediate meaning: the Holy Trinity.

While mystical numbers determine the underlying structure of the *KP*, antithesis is the dominating syntactical ornament of its textual surface: *jari* . . . *tari* (if . . . then; 7.27 and passim); *jaisi* . . . *taisi* (as . . . just as; 7.50, 7.84, and passim); *jetukẽ* . . . *yetukẽ* (how much . . . so much, 8.26 and passim).

The sources of this finely crafted literary style may be found in the *Ekanāthībhāgavat* (hereafter *EBh*) of Śrī Sant Ekanāth of Pratiṣṭhān (whose *magnum opus* was completed in 1573, six years previous to Stephens's arrival in Goa[1]), in the *Jñāneśvarī* of Śrī Sant Jñāneśvar, or in the *Śrīkṛṣṇacaritrakathā* of Kṛṣṇadāsa Śyāmā (1526), a part of which Thomas Stephens transliterated into Roman script (see S.G. Tulpule 1979, pp. 366f). Stephens uses the short final *caraṇa* typical of Jñāneśvar, but is as expansive as Ekanāth in his metaphors taken from everyday life. The *pālṇa-gīt* (cradle song) sung by Maria to baby Jesus at 8.20 of the *KP* bears a striking resemblance to Ekanāth's famous *abhaṅga* 'Jo, jo, jo Saguṇa . . .' ('Sleep, sleep, sleep baby Kṛṣṇa . . . '):

> jo, jo, jo jesu bāḷaka / namo tuja visvatārakā /
> namo vaikuṇṭha-nāyakā / svargīceā rāyā //
>
> 'Sleep, sleep, sleep, baby Jesus. Honour to you, O rescuer of the world, lord of Vaikuṇṭha, king of *svarga*!'

While the structure and the literary devices used in the *KP* are familiar features of Bhakti literature in Old Marathi, Stephens's use of spiritual terminology is clearly innovative. For the most part, the spiritual *termini technici* of the *KP* are borrowings from Bhakti literature in Old Marathi. That Thomas Stephens found a ready-made genre of literature with concise composita for describing spiritual phenomena may account for his choice of literary Old Marathi interspersed with words of Konkani rather than the spoken vernacular of Goa, which he chose for his catechetical book *Doutrina Kristā̃*.

For a Jesuit in Hindu Goa in the late sixteenth and early seventeenth centuries, the decision to use terms borrowed from Bhakti literature in Old Marathi was a bold spiritual strategy indeed. To what extent did Stephens succeed in redefining or replacing the world-view, self-understanding, and religious experience of medieval Hinduism, which is inherent in the borrowed terms of Bhakti literature with specifically Christian content? To what extent did he become the prisoner of his own borrowings and, thus, contribute unwillingly to a syncretism of Hinduism and Christianity that was to continue in Goa up to the present day? The remainder of this paper will be concerned with examining these questions on the basis of the seventh and eighth *avasvarus* (chapters) of the *KP*, in which the Christmas stories of Matthew, 2.1-12 and Luke, 2.1-22, are retold in a medieval Indian setting:

jayā namo sālvādorā / namo virjeṃceā kumarā /
krupānidhī karuṇākarā / jesu, kristā svāmiyā // (7.1)
jayā jayā vaikuṇṭhanāyekā / svāmiyā visvatārakā /
bhaktajanāṃ pratipāḷakā / krista rāyā // (7.2)

The Bhakti specialist will recognize immediately such epithets as *kṛpā-nidhi* (a mine of grace), *karuṇākara* (a quarry of compassion), which will be attributed to any holy man in India. More specific is *vaikuṇṭhanāyaka* (the lord or leader of Vaikuṇṭha, the heaven of Viṣṇu) and '*Viśvatārakā*' ('who brings the world over [the sea of rebirths]), *bhakta-jana-pratipāḷakā* (who cares for and nurtures the *bhaktas*). Especially striking in this passage is the introduction of the word *virje,* from Latin *virgo*, and three *ovīs* later, its Old Marathi paraphrase *sadā aṅkuvāri* (7.4; eternal virgin). Similarly, the virgin birth is juxtaposed with a familiar theme from Bhakti literature in Old Marathi.

taise nhave jesucī jananī / spiritā sānta varuni /
puruṣasaṅgevāñconi / saṃbhavlā garbhī // (7.47)

This was not the way for the mother of Jesus (i.e. the pains of labour). The Holy Spirit had chosen her. The foetus was conceived without contact with a man.

The phrase *puruṣasaṅgevāñconi* calls to mind the story of the prostitute Piṅgalā in *EBh* 8.188-306, who describes Puruṣottama (Kṛṣṇa) as *vīryacyutīviṇa ramavitu* (*EBh* 8.244) (He who gives pleasure without the movement of semen). Just as Jesus is named the *vaikuṇṭhanāyaka* (7.39) or *vaikuṇṭhapatā* (7.81), *vaikuṇṭhapati* (8.105), *vaikuṇṭhanātha* (7.20, 7.80), *mahācakravartī* (8.105), and, at the same time, *israēlicā rakhyaṇā* (8.2) (protector of Israel), so also, Maria is adorned with the epithets *vaikuṇṭharāṇī* (7.43) (the queen of Vaikuṇṭha, i.e. Lakṣmī) and *vaikuṇṭhamaulī* (8.3) (the mother of Vaikuṇṭha, i.e. Lakṣmī). Moreover, Maria is equipped with an *amṛtadṛṣṭi* (7.66) (a look or vision that conveys the nectar of immortality). Especially striking in this connection is the passage 7.82-6:

> 'In order to give us the treasure of Your Grace,
> O Lord of Vaikuṇṭha, you have taken birth as
> a poor man. (7.81)
>
> 'Now accept the clothes of a poor man
> to cover the nakedness of your immaculate body
> and ward off the harshness of the winter.' (7.82)
>
> Thus spake Maria to Jesus. She brought freshly washed
> clothing, and covered him. (7.83)
>
> Then she took out her well-formed breast,
> which was purer than crystal and like a precious pearl,
> to nurse him. (7.84)
>
> She held the infant Jesus to her breast
> and gave him her nipple.
> He drank: '*ghuṭu-ghuṭām, ghuṭu-ghuṭāṃ*' (onomatopoeia) (7.85)
>
> Jesus drank Maria's milk,
> while Maria had *dhyāna* of Jesus
> and enjoyed the *amṛta* of Vaikuṇṭha in her heart. (7.86)

Though in modern Marathi the word *dhyān* can be translated as meditation without specific technical connotations, its meaning in the outgoing sixteenth century was still closely bound up with popular notions of Yoga, specifically, with the sixth part of Pantañjali's system, or with Bhakti-yoga variations of this phenomena. The term occurs frequently in the *EBh*, and always signifies a connection in the subtle matter of the inner organ (*antahkaraṇa*) of the *bhakta* with the *svarūpa* of the god Kṛṣṇa. As in the system of

Patañjali, so also in the *EBh*, the *antaḥkaraṇa* of the *bhakta* penetrates the object of contemplation and takes on its form. It is highly unlikely that Father Stephens had this in mind. For, the notion of taking possession of the subtle body of Christ by *dhyāna* would have amounted to heresy in the eyes of the Roman Catholic church. On the other hand, it is just as unlikely that Stephens' listeners in Goa in the early seventeenth century would have been able or inclined to dissociate themselves from the inculturated meaning of *dhyāna* with which they were familiar from Bhakti literature.[2] As the first member of a compound the term *dhyāna* occurs in several passages in the story of the birth of Jesus: the *bhaktas* (the pious listeners) are *dhyānasta* (7.50) (abiding in *dhyāna*), Maria is *dhyānasti devamātā* (7.51) (the Mother of God abiding in *dhyāna*), and the pious listeners are *dhyānasta-jana* (8.78) (the people who abide in *dhyāna*).

Though the personalities and themes of Hindu mythology are not mentioned in the *KP*, its structure, terminology, and metaphors attest to an intimate familiarity with Bhakti literature and with the world-view of medieval Hinduism. A conspicuous passage in this connection is *KP* 7.54-8, in which the narration of Christ's coming into the world takes on—albeit contrary to the author's intention—the appearance of a story of the birth of an *avatāra*:

When the second watch (*prahara*[3]) of the night began,
the Devamātā was in *dhyāna*.
She waited, filled with *prema*. (7.51)

The downpour from the clouds ceased.
The heavens became clear.
Light filled the firmament. (7.52)

Impatient to see the immaculate birth,
Candra could hardly wait
for the time of delivery to come. (7.53)

The constellations of the second *prahara*
were straining to remain firm in their positions
in order to see the wonder. (7.54)

The constellations that arrive in the third *prahara*
were straining to move backward through time.
And the constellations of the first *prahara*
could only think of the second *prahara*. (7.55)

All the angels (*bhoḍ've*) in *svarga* were
striving to see how their *svāmī* would arrive
in new vestments (*vastra*). (7.56)

Countless *devadūtas* jumped down from Vaikuṇṭha
onto the earth. (7.57)

While the Virgin gave birth, the angels abided there
and praised the event of this Holy Night. (7.58)

Just as the abundance of terms borrowed from Bhakti literature leads inevitably to an overlayering of the popular religious concepts of sixteenth century Goa onto the story of Christ's birth, so also the shifting of Indian herdsmen (*gopāḷs*) to Bethlehem (*Beleāpūr*) gives the story a strong resemblance to the story of the birth of Kṛṣṇa. Even the three kings of the East and the evil intentions of King Herod (Luke, 2.8) have correspondences in the Purāṇic stories of King Kamsa's foul schemes to kill baby Kṛṣṇa. Father Stephens may have been aware of the similarity of the two holy traditions, for, in contrast to his treatment of the remaining narrative material from Matthew and Luke, the story of Herod's attempt to use the three kings as police informers to lead his henchmen to the place at which the prophesied Messiah would be born is conspicuously absent in Stephen's rendering in chapters eight and nine of the *KP*. The story of the three kings is taken up again later, in the tenth chapter, thus separating these narrative events from the focal point of the Christmas story and minimizing the likelihood that Christ would be identified as an *aṃśavatāra* (partial incarnation) of Kṛṣṇa:

Some *devadūtas* set out from *svarga* toward the East,
where they met three kings
and conveyed this message to them: (8.49)

'Hear me, O wise kings! In this night in Judeyā
a child was born. He is of the tribe of Jacob. (8.50)

'A star has risen in *samsara*!
The earth is filled with light.
Come ye, to see the child!' (8.51)

And on this night on a mountain in Beleā
goṃvaḷe (cowherds, here: herdsmen) were
keeping watch over their sheep
in the *vana* (wilderness). (8.52)

Many foreigners came there.
They would have stolen the sheep.
So, the *gopāla* kept watch in the night. (8.53)

An angel came there, and the shepherds saw him.
The light of the Svāmī was all around them. (8.54)

When they saw the light, the *goṃvaḷe* were afraid.

The angel granted them the condition of fearlessness. (8.55)
(The angel spoke): 'We shall give you such good news
that all over the earth a festival will be celebrated.
Hear my words! (8.56)

'Today, in the city of David, your charioteer (*sārathī*),
Svāmī Kristu, the *viśvatārakā* of *samsara* was born. (8.57)

'If you want to set out to have *darśan* of Him,
I will tell you the sign by which he can be known.
Know ye, that the child will be found
wrapped in a *lugaḍī*, lying in a feeding trough (*gavaṇī*).' (8.58)

As the angels spoke to the *gopāḷas*,
a wonder occurred in the heavens. (8.59)

Countless other *svargavāsīs* joined the multitude of angels,
offered their *namaskāra* to the Svāmī,
and exalted him. (8.60)

They said: 'Praise be to Parameśvara in *svarga*,
and in *saṃsāra* peace and welfare (*baravī vāsanā svasta hoū*)
among the people.' (8.61)

Such was the exaltation of the *devadūtas*.
Thus spake the *Vajelisti* (the evangelists, i.e. Matthew and Luke).
'Let us go now together with the angels
to praise baby Jesus', said the *gopāḷas*. (8.62)

'From the East, where Sūrya rises, to the West,
Kristu, the son of the Virgin, is the king.
Let us go to serve Him.' (8.63)

'The creator of the universe, the Svāmī,
has taken on a human body (*manusya deha kelem pairaṇa*)
to destroy the *akarma* (evil deed, i.e. the original sin)
of the *ādipuruṣa* (i.e. Adam).' (8.64)

The *gopāḷas* go to the manger, and at the first sight of the infant Jesus they experience the well-known *sāttvika bhāvas* of Bhakti literature (8.75ff.): (1) their eyes fill with tears; (2) their throats contract; (3) the hair on their bodies stands on end; (4) streams of sweat roll down their faces; (5) finally, they become mute in bliss and fall repeatedly at Jesus' feet.

At this point Stephens embellishes and expands upon the story of the adoration of Jesus by the *gopāḷas*. His free poetic composition betrays the hand of a master of literary Marathi. Some verses even equal the elegance of Jñāneśvar, and, at the same time, are as abundant with metaphors of daily life as the *ovīs* of Ekanāth:

'We are low people, *gopāḷas*,
who have come to see your *caraṇa kamala* (foot-lotus, i.e. lotus feet).
That's why you're here now in this humble house. (8.81)[4]

'We are humble *goṃvaḷe* for the mute *jātis* (i.e. beasts).
There isn't a spark of Bhakti in us!
That's why you've taken birth among the mute beasts.
To let us have *darśana* of your holy feet. (8.82)

'Or, perhaps you want to be a *goṃvaḷā* like one of us.
Is that why you've called us here? (8.83)

'Have mercy on us, who have fallen at your feet!
See to it that we don't turn back again!
O granter of all things! (8.84)

'We have all come to you.
May our *manas* always be fixed on your feet! (8.85)

'If only you had already grown a little!
We could have played with you in the forest (*vana*)! (8.86)

'We *goṃvaḷejan* ('shepherd folk') would have worshipped you
like a king!
We would have served you lovingly everyday. (8.87)

'We would have made necklaces of cowrie shells (*kavadi*)
and laid them around your neck.
We would have made hung earrings of *guñja* (red berries) on
your ears. (8.88)

'We would have woven garlands for you
so that they would have reached from your neck to your chest.
We would have bound them around your forehead too! (8.89)

'We would have adored you so much!
We would have put you in the middle (of our circle)
and played around you (*kheḷateuṃ subhavaṃte*). (8.90)

'But you're just a baby! A little boy as lustrous as the sun!
We see that you can't keep watch over the sheep! (8.91)

'The light of your lotus-face shines like a pearl.
And your mother has this appearance too!
She is not an ordinary woman. (8.92)

'But the *devadūtas* didn't tell us
that you would watch over our sheep this night. (8.93)

'They only said that he who will be the *tārakā* (rescuer)
has taken birth in samsara this night,
as foretold by Moise (Moses) and the prophets. (8.94)

'You have put us in your debt.
Now we will celebrate your birth.
Now you shall grow up quickly in days and months,
O Samarathā (8.95)

'You are our *tārakā*! You are the hope of Israel!
You will fulfil our hopes, O manorathu! (8.96)

'You have called us through the angels.
You are the *jagatra-jivanu* (life of the world)' (8.97)

Then the *gopāḷas* of Beleā touched the feet of Jesus
with their foreheads. (8.98)

Then a Brahmin said: 'After hearing the wondrous story
of the birth of Jesus, I was filled with bliss. (8.102)

'That's why I didn't ask any questions.
And whatever questions I would have asked,
such matters you relate to us
so beautifully in the story. (8.103)

'We don't want to ask any questions.
But, we are very surprised that the Svāmī
has such great intelligence. We carry
his *buddhi* on our heads. (8.104)

'We are surprised that the king of kings, the *vaikuṇṭhapati,*
the lord of the angels, the *cakravartī,*
has taken such a low birth on this earth (*khitī*).' (8.105)

Then the *pādrī* replied: 'O Lord!
Your wondrous deeds are infathomable!
No one can comprehend you!' (8.106)

The composition of the *Kristapurāṇa* attests to Thomas Stephens' intimate knowledge of devotional religion in medieval Maharashtra. For, the belief in the manifestation of a god through the passionate narration of his characteristics and deeds, that is, of his life-story, underlies all Bhakti literature. The pious audition of the narration of a Purāṇa has been described by Stephens's contemporary Śrī Sant Ekanāth as the highest form of Bhakti, a 'rest-house' in the form of hearing, in which the karma of the *bhaktas* is destroyed.[5] By means of such hearing with devotion the devotee fuses his mental organ with the divine consciousness-substance (*caitanya*, *EBh* 29.76) for Bhakti means: to be or have part of God in a material sense, that is, as a fusion of the subtle matter of the devotee and God. Only in the course of subsequent generations did specifically Christian contents gradually replace the notions normally associated with such terms as *vaikuṇṭhanāyaka* ('the lord of Vaikuṇṭha, the heaven of the Hindu god Viṣṇu') in the religious experience of Hindu converts to Christianity who heard Stephens's narration.

It is highly unlikely that the Portuguese translation of the *Kristapurāṇa*, which Paulo Mascarenhas on 3 April 1614 attested to be a true and correct rendering of Stephens's Purāṇa (S. Bandelu 1956, pp. 943f.), was understood in the same way by the European churchmen as the original text in Old Marathi was understood by the Goans themselves. The terminology of Latin or Portuguese is as inseparable from the religious traditions of Europe as the terminology of Bhakti from the religious traditions of India. For the Goans of the sixteenth century, who first came into contact with Stephens's Purāṇa, *Vaikuṇṭhapūtra* or *-suta* could only have meant a divine being who was an incarnation or *avatār* of Viṣṇu, and not the birth of the son of God as a mortal being.

Hermaneutics

Placing ourselves for a moment on the cutting edge of Paul Ricoeur's 'hermeneutical arc', we might say that Father Stephens's 'object-sign-interpretant triangle' was not the same as that of his audience. For the Goans of the late sixteenth and early seventeenth century the 'sign' '*dhyāna*' had as its object a spiritual phenomenon of Hinduism. Thus, the sign evoked in the contemporary listener an interpretant (i.e. a gloss, commentary, or definition on the sign in its relation to the object) within the Hindu community of experience. This interpretant, which is a part of the chain of interpretations within Hindu tradition, was incorporated by the contemporary audience into their understanding of Stephens's text. Together with the numerous other interpretants belonging to Hindu tradition that are evoked by Stephens's use of the conventions of the literary genre of the Purāṇa, *dhyāna* firmly anchors his discourse in the Hindu world of ideas and grafts it onto preceding discourses regarding the births of *avatāras.* The sum of these Hindu interpretants leads to an 'intended meaning' of Stephens's text that was not the intention of its author. For an understanding of the semantic complexities involved here, Ricoeur's thoughts on the interpretation of a text as an objective process form a useful point of departure (P. Ricoeur 1961, pp. 161-4):

> . . . the intended meaning of the text is not the presumed intention of its author, the lived experience of the writer, but rather what the text means for whoever complies with its injunction. The text seeks to place us in its meaning, that is—according to another acceptation of the word *sens*—in the same direction. So if the intention is that of the text, and if this intention is the direction which it opens up for thought, then depth semantics must be understood in a fundamentally dynamic way. I shall therefore say: to explain is to bring out the structure, that is, the internal relations of dependence which constitute the statics of the text; to interpret is to follow the path of thought opened up by the text, to place oneself en route towards the orient of the text. We are invited by this remark to correct our initial concept of interpretation and to search—beyond a subjective process of interpretation as an act on the text—for an objective process of interpretation which would be the act *of* the text.

With regard to the *Kristapurāṇa* and Hindu-Christian syncretism in Goa, a fascinating area of research now emerges: When, to what degree, and for which sections of the population did the orientation of the interpretants change from the Hindu to the Christian tradition? When did such terms as *dhyāna,* Vaikuṇṭha, *amṛta, bhakti, bhakta, cakravartin,* etc., acquire specifically Christian interpretants and thus become semantic outposts of Christianity? When and to what degree did they cease to be terms of popular Hinduism pressed into the service of an alien system of beliefs in which they were glossed with radically different contents? Again, we are reminded of Ricoeur's thoughts on the interpretation and 'appropriation' of a text (ibid., pp. 943f.):

> . . . the series of interpretants is the chain of interpretations produced by

the interpreting community and incorporated into the dynamics of the text, as the work of meaning on itself. Within this chain, the first interpretants serve as tradition for the final interpretants, which are the interpretation in the true sense of the term. . . . The idea of interpretation as appropriation is not, for all that, eliminated; it is simply postponed until the termination of the process. It lies at the extremity of what we called above the *hermeneutical arc:* it is the final brace of the bridge, the anchorage of the arch in the ground of lived experience. But the entire theory of hermeneutics consists in mediating this interpretation-appropriation by the series of interpretants which belong to the work of the text upon itself. Appropriation loses its arbitrariness insofar as it is the recovery of that which is at work, in labour, within the text. What the interpreter says is a re-saying which reactivates what is said in the text.

The enthusiastic reception of the *KP* by the Goans of the early seventeenth century is a striking example of what Ricoeur (p. 159) has called 'appropriation': 'the struggle against cultural distance', 'against the estrangement from meaning itself, that is, from the system of values upon which the text is based'. [Appropriation] is 'a making one's own of that which was initially alien. . . .'

ACKNOWLEDGEMENT

With deep sorrow I acknowledge here the last in a long series of intellectual debts to the late Professor Shankar Gopal Tulpule, without whose thorough introduction to the peculiarities of Thomas Stephen's Old Marathi usage and orthography this paper could not have been written in its present form.

NOTES

1. Ekanāth gives *śake* 1495 and *vikram* 1630, i.e. AD 1573, as the date of the completion of his monumental Marathi commentary on the *ekādāśa skandha* of the *Bhāgavatapurāṇa.* See *EBh* 31.552. For a discussion of Ekanāth's use of literary devices see my *Bhakti und Bhakta: Religionsgeschichtliche Untersuchungen zum Heilsbegriff und zur religiosen Umwelt des Śrī Sant Ekanāth* (Stuttgart: Franz Steiner Verlag, 1990), pp. 31ff. On Ekanāth's use of mystical numbers, see pp. 24f. of the same publication.
2. In an article that has unjustly fallen into academic oblivion, A.K. Priolkar presents two confidential letters written by Thomas Stephens to the General of the Jesuit Order in Rome, which shed light on the situation which followed upon the rapid conversion of Hindus in Goa in the latter half of the sixteenth century:

The first of these letters is dated 6 December 1601. It was written at Margaon (Goa) where Fr. Stephens was at that time working as the Rector of the Jesuit College. It is a document of undoubted historical importance for the light it throws on the contemporary social conditions in Goa. Fr. Stephens complains bitterly of the ignorance of the new converts in matters of religion, and the general atmosphere of bickerings, mutual hatred, and malice prevalent among them. . . . Behind an outward pretence of Christian practice they tended to hold fast to Hindu belief and practice. This deplorable state of affairs came to be the chief concern of the Inquisition (Priolkar cites da Cunha Rivara, J.H., *Ensaio Historico da Lingua Concani*, Goa, 1857: 65), which was established in Goa in 1560. Persons suspected of leanings towards Hinduism were clapped in prison and, in the last resort, burnt in the *Auto de Fé*. It was, however, soon clear to thinking minds that coercion and force could not go far in weaning people from the religion of their forefathers. It was, therefore, decided to supplement these by persuasion and education and the importance of the native languages for this purpose was fully appreciated. (A.K. Priolkar, 'Two Recently Discovered Letters of Father Thomas Stephens'. *Journal of the University of Bombay,* 35.2 [September 1956]: p. 116.)

3. Stephens's text shows *prāhāru* in nominative and *prāhārīṃ* in locative. I have standardized the orthography to *prahara* throughout this paper.
4. The notion of an inn or public house seemed to require a paraphrase in the language of sixteenth century Goa. Thus, we read in 7.41 that Joseph and Maria found accommodations among the foreigners in a hut near the house of a female cook (*rāndhayeṇiceā grahāpāsīṃ*).
5. ghara righona bhakti niṣkāma / bhaktāṃce nirdaḷī sakaḷa karma / yā nāṃva parābhakti parama/viśramadhāmaśravaṇārthyāṃ//(*EBh* 29.67)

REFERENCES

Bandelu, Santram, ed. *Phādara Stephanskṛta Kristapurāṇa.* Punem Prasada Prakashan, 1956.

Gonda, Jan. 'Triads in Vedic Ritual'. *Ohio Journal of Religious Studies* 2.2 (1974): 5-23.

Neill, Stephen. *A History of Christianity in India: The Beginnings to A.D. 1707.* Cambridge: Cambridge University Press, 1984.

Ricoeur, Paul. *Hermeneutics and the Human Sciences: Essays on Language, Action and Interpretation.* Edited, translated and introduced by John B. Thompson, 1961. Reprint: Cambridge: Cambridge University Press and Paris (Editions de la Maison des Sciences del'Homme, 1982 and 1983).

Tulpule, Shankar Gopal. *Classical Marathi Literature from the Beginning to A.D. 1818.* Weisbaden: Otto Harrassowitz, 1979.

Text and Context: Two Versions of Tulsīdās's *Rām-lalā-nahachū*

DANUTA STASIK

The text of Tulsīdās's *Rām-lalā-nahachū* (hereafter *RN*) in its most popular printed version (hereafter *RNP*) consists of twenty *sohar* stanzas (forty couplets).[1] Its authenticity has been doubted, especially on the account of the 'unseemly' reaction of King Daśrath at the sight of a young *ahirini* (a woman belonging to the caste of *ahīr,* i.e. herdsmen)[2]:

अहिरिनि हाथ दहेंड़ि सगुन लेइ आवइ हो।
उनरत जोबनु देखि नृपति मन भावइ हो॥

(*RNP*/5B)[3]

Among other reasons for doubting its authenticity are the mention of Kauśalyā's *jeṭhi* (husband's elder brother's wife) (*RNP* 9A), as well as compositional faults appearing in the text (*RNP* 8B and 10A; 11A and 11B; M. Gupta 1972, pp. 133 and 235-7).

Mataprasad Gupta in his work on Tulsīdās revealed to the scholarly world the existence of the oldest known copy of *RN*, which differed from the widely known *RNP*. In the discussion of *RNP* and the version as received from the old manuscript found by him (hereafter *RNG*), M. Gupta showed a very strong bias towards the latter one and finally considered it to be authentic, thus denying the authenticity of *RNP* (M. Gupta 1972, pp. 208-11 and 234-40).[4] However, in his book he gave only a selection of couplets (sixteen couplets out of twenty-six). The full text was published after M. Gupta's death by his son in an article entitled 'Tulsīdās aur Rāmjī kā nahachū' (Sh. Gupta 1974, pp. 437-42).

It seems very interesting and promising to compare these two versions for features common to both of them, as well as for points of differences, because such inclusions and omissions most likely conceal particular visions of social reality manifested during the rite of *nahachū* (nail-paring ceremony). It is hoped that the analysis may help us answer whether any one version offers a more genuine, poetical vision of Rām's *nahāchū* and which of them, if any, can be viewed as the authentic one.

Let us first consider the course of events presented in both versions.

TEXTS

(a) RNP

As it has already been mentioned, *RNP* consists of forty couplets arranged in twenty *sohar* stanzas. It depicts the rite of *nahachū* and *māyan* performed in the house of King Daśrath in Ayodhyā (*RNP* 1A, 2A and 13A). First, we witness the erection of a wedding canopy and the washing of Rām in Ganges water (*RNP* 3). The ceremonial square (*cauk*) is prepared and Rām is seated on the throne (*RNP* 4). Next, beautifully dressed women of different menial castes come for the *māyan* rite (*pūjā* of the Seven Mothers or goddesses by women) and bring with them different requisites. A *loharini* (blacksmith's wife) brings an iron ring (*barāyan*) and an *ahirini*, an auspicious pot of curds (*dahẽṛi*) (*RNP* 5). A shapely *tābolini* (betel-seller's wife) appears with betel in her hand and a *darajini* (tailor's wife) with a suit of clothes nicely smelling of saffron (*RNP* 6). A *mocini* (cobbler's wife) enters the courtyard with a pair of shoes (*RNP* 7A). A *maliniyā* (gardener's wife) comes with a marriage crown (*maur*) (*RNP* 7B); and a *bariniyā* (a woman of the *bārī* caste, members of which produce leaf-cups and leaf-plates and also act as attendants) with a *chātā* (parasol) in her hand (*RNP* 8A). Finally, a *nauniyā* (barber's wife) appears and sings joyously a *gāri/gālī*[5] in the *ranivās* (women's apartments; *RNP* 8B). Then Kauśalyā is instructed by her *jeṭhi* to start performing the *nahachū* rite (*RNP* 9A). Kauśalyā sits with Rām in her lap and covers his head with the end of her *sārī* (*RNP* 9B). Then the barber's wife is called again and she approaches Rām with a *naharnī* (nail-parer) in her hand (*RNP* 10). She sings a *gālī* in which she teases Daśrath's family:

काहे रामजिव साँवर लछिमन गोर हो।
कीदहुँ रानि कौसिलहि परिगा भोर हो॥
राम अहहिं दसरथ कै लछिमन आन क हो।
भरत सत्रुहन भाइ तौ श्रीरघुनाथ क हो॥

(*RNP* 12)

Why is Rāmjī dark and Lakṣmaṇ fair?
There must have been some deceit by Kauśalyā.
Rām is Daśrath's, Lakṣmaṇ, someone else's,
Still Bharat and Śatrughna are Śrī Raghunath's brothers!

The barber's wife, proud of her role, touches Rām's nails with her hand, washes his feet and having cut his nails applies *jāvak* (red colour) (*RNP* 13B-15).

Nichāvar (ceremonial) gifts follow the rite (*RNP* 16). The barber loads them on the cart and takes them home. His family rejoices over the gifts and sleeps undisturbed by troubles (*RNP* 17).

In the meantime, all those gathered in the women's quarters sing *gālīs* addressing Rām, and play together mimicking one another, their hearts filled with joy (*RNP* 18). At this sight, the Queen feels happy at heart and gives presents in abundance (*RNP* 19A).

(b) RNG

RNG is shorter than *RNP* and consists of twenty-six couplets. At the beginning of the text Gaṇeś is addressed and the title of the work *Rām jī kā nahachū* is given. In the opening couplet, women gather together for the wedding and for the *nahachū* rite, which is said to be held in Janakpur (*RNG* 1). Pots with Ganges water for washing Rām are ordered and the *cauk* is prepared (*RNG* 2). The barber's wife is sent for and she comes smiling (*RNG* 3). Then it is said that Avadhpur(!) looks beautiful in dazzling lights (*RNG* 4). The very fortunate barber's wife touches Rām's feet with her hand, feeling proud to perform the rite (*RNG* 6). Five women sit together, and turmeric is applied (to Rām); the barber's wife sings *gālī* in almost the same manner as in *RNP* 10 (*RNG* 8-9). Kauśalyā answers back in a very witty manner:

मे तोहि पुछो नउनिया दुइ कर जोरि हे।
तोहरे नउआ काहे सांवर तोह काहे गोरि हे॥

(*RNG* 10)

I'm asking you, barber's wife, having folded both my hands,
Why is your barber dark and why are you fair?

The canopy of green bamboo, *dubi* grass (*Panicum* or *Cynodon dactylon*) and mango leaves is sprinkled with camphor (*RNG* 12). Four princes sit under it on a *jājim* (red silken cloth) spread on the carpet and the Brahmin is called (*RNG* 13). The barber's wife prepares the wedding altar and smears it with sandalwood paste (*RNG* 14). When Kauśalyā sits on a *maciā* (low stool) the following song begins:

केहि एहे पोखरा खनावल घाट बधावल हे।
काकर भरीहै कहार तौ केहि नेहाएब हे॥
राजा दशरथ पोखरा खनावल घाट बधवाल हे।
कोसिला के भरीहै कहार तौ प्रभु को नेहाएब हे॥

(*RNG* 16-17)

Who dug a tank and made the steps?
Whose water-carrier will fill it and then who will be washed?
King Daśrath dug the tank and made the steps.
Kauśalyā's water-carrier will fill it and then Prabhu will be washed.[6]

The barber's wife pares Rām's nails and applies red colour (*RNG* 18-19). The *nichāvar* gifts follow in abundance (*RNG* 20-2)[7], but the barber's wife considers them to be meager and demands a horse (*RNG* 23). Although Kauśalyā says that she will give her a horse when Rām comes home after the wedding, she insists on a horse for her husband and a silken *sārī* for herself immediately (*RNG* 24-5).

It may be added here that in the colophon, which has also been printed, the name of the scribe, Kiśordās of Gayājī in Sonaut district, and the date, Monday, the fifth day of the bright half of *Māgh*, 1665 Vikram era (AD 1608) are given.

RNP AND *RNG*: CONTEXTUAL COMMENTS

M. Gupta (1972, pp. 209-10 and *HSK*, vol. 2, 1986, p. 520), comparing the two versions of *RN*, wrote that they had twelve couplets in common,[8] and elsewhere (Gupta's article '*Rāmkāvya*' in Dh. Varma 1959, vol. 2, p. 313) he wrote that they shared thirteen couplets. But when they are scrutinized one finds six couplets that they share with almost the same wording, i.e., *RNP* 10A and *RNG* 3, *RNP* 11A and *RNG* 5, *RNP* 12A and *RNG* 8, *RNP* 12B and *RNG* 9, *RNP* 13A and *RNG* 1, *RNP* 13B and *RNG* 6. These couplets are as follows:

	RNP		*RNG*
10A	नाउनि अति गुनखानि तौ बेगि बोलाई हो।	3	नाउनि अति गुन आगरि बेगि बोलाइअ।

	करि सिंगार अति लोन तौ बिहसति आई हो॥		करि सिगार नउनिआ बिहसति आइअ॥
11A	कानन कनक तरीवन बेसरि सोहइ हो।	5	कानन पेन्हु तरिवन नक बेसरि सोभिअ।
	गजमुकुता कर हार कंठमनि मोहइ हो॥		गले सोभै गजमोती कै हार कंठहि मन मोहिअ॥
12A	काहे रामजिव साँवर लछिमन गोर हो।	8	काहे राम तुम्ह सांवर लछुमन गोर हे।
	कीदहुँ रानि कौसिलहि परिगा भोर हो॥		कीदहु रानी कोसिलहि परिगौ भोर हे॥
12B	राम अहहिं दसरथ कै लछिमन आन क हो।	9	श्रीराम भए दशरथ को लछुमन आन को।
	भरत सत्रुहन भाइ तौ श्रीरघुनाथ क हो।		भथ्र चतुरगुन भए दोउ चतुर सुजान को॥
13A	आजु अवधपुर आनँद नहछू राम क हो।	1	आजु जनकपुर ब्याह नहछू राम को।
	चलहु नयन भरि देखिय सोभाधाम क हो॥		चलहु सखी सब देखन सोभा स्याम को॥
13B	अति बड़भाग नउनियाँ छुऐ नख हाथ सों हो।	6	धन नउनिआ को भाग चरन छुवहि हाथ सो।
	नैनन्ह करति गुमान तौ श्रीरघुनाथ सों हो॥		मुख भरि करहि गुमान श्री रघुनाथ सो॥

There is also one couplet (*RNP* 10B and *RNG* 18) and six separate lines (in *RNP* 3A and *RNG* 12, *RNP* 3B and *RNG* 2, *RNP* 4B and *RNG* 15, *RNP* 15B and *RNG* 19, *RNP* 16B and *RNG* 21/22, *RNP* 20B and *RNG* 26) which are more or less similar. They are as follows:

	RNP		*RNG*
10B	कनक-चुनिन सों लसित नहरनी लिय कर हो।	18	हाथहि सोभित नहरनी नाउनि अति सुंदरि हे।
	आनँद हिय न समाइ देखि रामहिं बर हो॥		प्रभु को बदन निरेखहि हँसी मुख मोरि हे॥
3A	आल हि बाँस के माँड़व मनिगन पूरन हो।	12	काचहि बास कर माडव हरिअर दुबि हे।
3B	गंगाजल कर कलस तौ तुरित मँगाइय हो।	2	कनक कलसा गंगा जल भरि लाइअै।
4B	मानकदीप बराय बैठि तेहि आसन हो।	15	सोने का कलसा उपर बरही मानिक दीप हे।
15B	जावक रचि क अँगुरियन्ह मृदुल सुठारी हो।	19	पातरि अगुली महाउरि अति छबि छाजिआ।

16B	भरि गे रतनपदारथ सूप हजार हो।	21	के दीहल रतन पदारथ भरि गएउ सूप हे।
		22	कोसिला दीहल रतन पदारथ भरि गएउ सूप हे।
20B	जे यह नहछू गावैं गाइ सुनावइँ हो।	26	जो एहि नहछू गावही गाए सुनावही।

It is thus clear that in both versions there are twenty lines which can be seen as close or more distant equivalents. Their sequence is as follows:

RNP	*RNG*
3A (line 1)	12 (line 1)
3B (line 1)	2 (line 1)
4B (line 2)	15 (line 1)
10A	3
10B	18
11A	5
12A	8
12B	9
13A	1
13B	6
15B (line 1)	19 (line 1)
16B (line 2)	21 (line 2)/22(line 2)
20B (line 1)	26 (line 1)

Thus sixty lines in *RNP* and thirty-two in *RNG* differ either because they are too dissimilar to be considered equivalents or because they introduce themes absent in one of them. The most prominent of the latter type in *RNP* are those that describe the women of different castes who come for the rite (5-7B), that mention Kauśalyā's *jeṭhi* (9A), the special significance of the barber's wife in the rite of *nahachū* (14), and the barber who takes home the gifts and shares happiness with his relatives (17), as well as those that describe the joyful play in the women's quarters after the rite (18). In *RNG* the most important unique lines are those that concern the five women attending the rite (7, 11), the preparation of the wedding altar by the barber's wife (14), the song about the tank dug by Daśrath (18), and the demanding of more payment by the barber's wife for her service (23-5).

The language and the composition of these two versions are different. The language of *RNP* is similar to that of other works by Tulsīdās written in Avadhī, and especially to the language of the *Barvai-rāmāyaṇ* (D. Śrīvāstav, 2014 [1957], especially pp. 347-8 and

352]. He considers the language of these two works to be Eastern Avadhī). It is also a good example of a narrative poem preoccupied with a single event (*khaṇḍ-kāvya*; cf. *HSK*, vol. 1, pp. 212-13 and M. Gupta 1972, p. 379). After the introduction, the narration gradually develops until the culmination, i.e. the paring of Rām's nails and the applying of red colour to his feet, after which the distribution of *nichāvar* gifts follows. And they are royal indeed; the barber's family is fully satisfied and the family of Daśrath may indulge in joyful play. Daśrath sits on his throne and those who sing about Rām's *nahachū* are promised different blessings.

The language of *RNG* is clearly influenced by Bhojpurī. It is organized in the form of a dialogue between singers or groups of singers which is a characteristic feature of folk songs in general, and marriage folk songs in particular (cf., e.g. W.G. Archer 1985 and A.K. Agarwala 1982). It ends in a very abrupt manner; the barber's wife dissatisfied with *nichāvar* asks for more gifts. This conflicting situation has no solution. The story ends here; only those who sing about Rām's *nahachū* are promised blessings. This difference becomes very meaningful when the *nahachū* rite is set in its wider social context, which will be discussed later.

As has been mentioned above, some errors in the text of *RNP* have been pointed out. One of them is the appearance of Kauśalyā's *jeṭhi* (*RNP* 9A), which by M. Gupta and other authors (M. Gupta 1972, pp. 235-6; Sh. Gupta 1974, p. 438 and V. Garg 1974, p. 43) was understood as 'husband's elder brother's wife'. Indeed, if we apply such meaning to the term *jeṭhi*, the statement would be incorrect according to the *Rāmāyaṇa* tradition; no source mentions any *jeṭhi* of Kauśalyā who was the chief queen at the court of Daśrath. However, the term *jeṭhi* also designates a person who is elder/senior (cf. 'जेठि भरत कहँ ब्याहि' from *Jānakī-maṅgal* [172]) and is synonymous with a noun *jyeṣṭhā*, i.e. 'a senior female relative' (cf. B. Avasthī 1990, vol. 1, p. 363). Such persons are entitled by the right of their age to give instructions; advice is sought from them, but the right to perform the ceremony is reserved for the mistress of the house, i.e. Kauśalyā (cf. Bh. P. Simh 1976, p. 138). In fact, the *jeṭhi* just instructs Kauśalyā to start performing the rite.

Another error pointed out by M. Gupta occurs in the couplets 8B and 10A. In the first of them the barber's wife sings a *gālī* in the *ranivās*, and in the second one it is said that she is ordered to come. If these couplets are taken out of their contexts and put together they may seem inconsistent. But the fact is that between the couplet 8B and 10A there are two couplets of stanza number 9 in which Kauśalyā approaches the throne and sits on it with Rām. In view of this change of place, it seems quite natural that the barber's wife, whose presence is indispensable in the rite but who was left behind, has to be ordered to come near (cf. also Bh. P. Simh 1976, p. 139).

In discussing the couplets 12A and 12B quoted above, which start with the 'barber's wife's question', 'Why is Rāmjī fair and Lakṣmaṇ dark?' and end with the reference to Bharat and Śatrughna, M. Gupta (1972, p. 236) wonders: 'When once it is said that Kauśalyā was misled, then how can it be said further that Rām is Daśrath's [son] and Lakṣmaṇ someone else's? Then, how Bharat and Śatrughna could be both called Rām's brothers? Bharat and Rām were resembling each other but Śatrughna was resembling Lakṣmaṇ. . . . ' To corroborate his point he quotes the appropriate lines from the *Rām-carit-mānas* (1.311.3B-4A) (M. Gupta 1972, p. 236). It is clear that M. Gupta is overlooking the fact that the barber's wife is singing a *gālī* in which she teases the whole family of Rām—four brothers, the queens and Daśrath. As a result he comes to a conclusion that is faulty (cf. Bh. P. Simh 1976, pp. 139-40).

Another point which has been discussed in connection with *RN* is whether it deals with the rite preceding Rām's wedding or the ceremony of investiture with the sacred thread (*upanāyan*). The question was raised because of the place in which the rite is performed. In *RNP* it is said to be performed at the house of Daśrath, in Avadhpur (Ayodhyā). In the beginning of *RNG* Janakpur is mentioned but afterwards it is said to be performed also in Ayodhyā. It stands in obvious contradiction to the fact that Rām, after breaking Śiva's bow and thereby winning Sītā's hand in Janakpur, stayed there for the wedding rites. The *nahachū* is customarily performed in the groom's house before the departure of the *barāt* (the bridegroom's party) but because Rām was already in Janakpur, it could not take place in Ayodhyā. Some authors (cf. S.P. Bahadur 1980, pp. 47-8.) have presumed that it could be performed in the place assigned for the groom's party to stay (*janvās*) or some other temporary camp, but why should it be called Ayodhyā? In this context, another question arises: how to explain the presence of Kauśalyā and the other women of Ayodhyā? We know from the *Rām-carit-mānas* (*RCM*, I.345.4-346) and the *Jānakī-maṅgal* (207-11) that the queens waited impatiently for the return of the *barāt* and greeted their sons in Ayodhyā. We should also remember that women usually did not go (and still do not go) with the procession. If we consider the temporary camp solution valid, it can be explained that it was provided for women eager to perform the rite and that they did not form a part of the *bārāt* (S.P. Bahadur 1980, pp. 47-8). However we solve these problems, there should be no doubt that *RN* describes the rite preceding the wedding (cf. Bh. Mishra, 1974, pp. 289-90). In *RNP* Rām is referred to as a bridegroom four times, twice as a *bar* (9B, 10B) and twice as a *dūlah* (9B, 19A).[9] *RNG* also explicitly refers to the context of marriage, using such words as *byāh* (marriage, 1) and *biāhi* (the absolutive form of the verb 'to marry', 24).

Let us now make a few remarks on the social context of *nahachū* seen as a preliminary rite of the wedding. Marriage has always been considered as one of the most important events in the life of a Hindu. It is also an occasion for a long series of rituals (*nahachū* and *māyan* being two of them) in which the services of many castes are indispensable and these services are, in turn, liberally compensated (L.M. Fruzzetti 1990, pp. 16, 18, and 43-5; L. Dumont 1980, pp. 98 and 109-10).

As L.M. Fruzzetti (1990, p. 44) aptly observed in her book on Bengali marriage:

> The ritual achieves its goal through the proper observance of the various actions, the use of required objects, and the participation of the prescribed persons. Since peace and harmony should reign in the performance of an auspicious rite such as marriage, the *paonas*[10] must not only be given but should also be graciously accepted. A refusal is in itself inauspicious (*amaṅgal*). Although there should be no nagging, a *ginnimā*[11] will try to increase the *paona* should it be found meagre.

As a social event marriage is also a splendid occasion for sharing joy and happiness during various rites and the preparations for them. It is especially true in the case of the women of a community who to a greater extent than men are involved in carrying out different duties connected with them. The congenial and joyful atmosphere necessary to make such an event a success is best expressed in marriage songs sung by women.[12]

In view of the foregoing ramarks it seems that *RNP* is not only more exhaustive but also renders a better image of a social occasion which involves Rām, the hero and God, as well as his family. The prevailing atmosphere is full of joy, happiness, and satisfaction. No conflict arises. While still being deeply rooted in folk tradition, it also displays the unusual (royal and divine) character of the event. Bamboo is used for the erection of the canopy, but it is decorated with jewels and garlands of pearls; the *cauk* is drawn not with *candan* as in *RNG*, but with diamonds;[13] Rām sits not on a *jājim*, but on a throne set among golden columns; also Kauśalyā sits not on a *maciā* (low wooden stool), but on a throne. In addition to all this, not only people witness the rite—gods are also present (2A). In other words, *RNP* when compared with *RNG* appears to be a poetical work that is more accomplished and refined in its character.

CONCLUSION

Comparison of *RNP* and *RNG* indicates that they have enough features in common to suppose that either one of them could have been the source for the other or that they had some common source about which we have no information. In either case, the main concern of this paper is not the age of the *RN* manuscripts (although very important in itself), but rather which of them could have been composed by the poet. The foregoing discussion implies that the genius of the poet is more visible in *RNP* than in *RNG*. There are also not as many faults in *RNP* as M. Gupta (1972, p. 238) indicates. Of course, to be able to pass a sound judgement, further work with the manuscripts is indispensable, especially in view of the fact that in both versions there are many printing and editing errors. As pointed out in the foregoing discussion, M. Gupta's judgement of *RNP* seems unjust. Often one gets the impression that the real reason for Gupta's opinion was, in his own words, the text's *amaryādit śṛṅgāriktā* (unconventional or immodest erotic sentiment). Whether we are inclined to call it *amaryādit* or not, it should be justly weighed against the relevant evidence and in no case should its role be exaggerated (cf. Bh. Mishra 1974, p. 290).

The present analysis testifies also to the need for preparing a new, critical edition of *RN*,[14] a small but very distinctive work by

Tulsīdās, which may add to our understanding of his poetical world.

NOTES

1. *Sohar* is a kind of an auspicious song sung by women on joyful occasions such as the birth of a son or marriage. All references in connection with *RNP* are, if not otherwise stated, to the text as published in R. Shukla *et al.,* 1958, pp. 3-5.
2. Cf., e.g. Mishrabandhu, *Hindī navaratna,* pp. 82 and 99; quoted in M. Gupta 1972, p. 133; see also Gupta's own opinion, op. cit., p. 320.
3. In reference to *RNP* a number designates a full *sohar* stanza, a letter, a couplet within it: A is the first one, and B, the second one.
4. Cf. also Gupta's article in Dh. Varma *et al.*, 1986, *Hindī sāhitya koś* (hereafter *HSK*), vol. 2, pp. 520-1.
5. *Gāri/gālī* songs are bawdy and mockingly insulting in their character. They are an essential element of marriage rituals. As William G. Archer observes: 'In these sexual jokes is a release of repressed energy which when applied to the marriage must necessarily make it fertile' (W.G. Archer 1985, p. 7).
6. It is reminiscent of a very similar song noted by William G. Archer in Bihār in the 1940s, sung during the preparation of the bride when she was washed (W.G. Archer 1985, p. 38):

   Who dug a tank and made the steps?
   Who brings water for Rām to wash?
   King Daśrath dug the tank and made the steps
   Rām's mother brings water for him to wash.

7. Cf. the couplets given in *Grāmya sāhitya,* R. Tripathi (ed.); quoted in Bh. Simh 1976, p. 127.
8. This number (twelve) is repeated by other authors; see, e.g. V. Garg 1974, p. 43 and Sh. Gupta 1974, p. 438.
9. See also the discussion in Bh. P. Simh 1976, pp. 129-36 and 138.
10. *Paonas* means 'dues for services'.
11. *Ginnimā* means 'mistress of the house'.
12. In this context Agarwala (1982, pp. 23 and 24; cf. also Bh. P. Simh 1976, p. 126) makes a very important observation:

    The essence of the caste system . . . lies in certain boundaries being adhered to. Yet with social events like marriages one finds occasional instances of what one would say is an infringement of these boundaries.

He further remarks:

> . . . within cultural and geographical unit of a village marriages (and festival to the village deities) are the only occasions that permit an unusual degree of freedom in communication between various castes. This may be the reason why they occupy such a permanent place in the life of village India.

13. For similar elements in decoration cf. *RCM*, 1.287-9.
14. We should note that this was already postulated by M. Gupta (1959, p. 314, and 1972, p. 211). See also V. Garg 1974, p. 43 and Bh. P. Simh 1976, pp. 143-4.

REFERENCES

Agarwala, Atul Kumar. 'Marriage Songs in Harauti', Doctoral Dissertation, Kiel: Christian-Albrechts-Universität, 1982.

Archer, William G. and Barbara Stoler Miller, eds., *Songs for the Bride: Wedding Rites of Rural India*, New York: Columbia University Press, 1985.

Arya, Ramsvarup and Girirajsharan Agraval, eds., *Tulsī mānas sandarbh.* Sambhal: Manas Catushshati Ayojan Samiti, 1974.

Avasthi, Bacculal. *Tulsī śabda-koś.* Delhi: Books & Books, 1990.

Bahadur, S.P. *Complete Works of Goswami Tulsidas*, Vol. 6, Varanasi: Prachya Prakashan, 1980.

Dumont, Louis. *Homo Hierarchicus: The Caste System and Its Implications.* Complete revised English edition. Chicago: The University of Chicago Press, 1980.

Fruzzetti, Lina M. *The Gift of a Virgin: Women, Marriage, and Ritual in a Bengali Society.* First Indian edition; Delhi: Oxford University Press, 1990.

Garg, Vedprakash. 'Tulsīdāsjī kī kṛtiyā̃'. In *Tulsī mānas sandarbh*, eds. R. Arya and G. Agraval, pp. 40-57. Sambhal: Manas Catushshati Ayojan Samiti, 1974.

Gupta Mataprasad. 'Rāmkāvya'. In Dh. Varma, ed. 1959, pp. 300-1.

———. 'Rām-lalā-nahachū'. In Dh. Varma, ed. 1986, pp. 520-1.

———. *Tulsīdās.* Allahabad: Hindi Parishad Prakashan, 1972.

Gupta, Shaligram. 'Tulsīdās aur Rāmjī kā nahachū'. In *Tulsī mānas sandarbh*, eds. R. Arya and G. Agraval, pp. 437-42. Sambhal: Manas Catushshati Ayojan Samiti, 1974.

Mishra, Bhagirath. 'Aiśvaryarūpopāsak maryādā Rāmbhakt Kavi'. In *Hindī sāhitya kā bṛhat itihās*, eds. Devendranath Sharma and Vijayendra Snatak, vol. 5, pp. 270-313. Varanasi: Nagari Pracharini Sabha, 1974.

Shrivastav, Devakinandan. *Tulsīdās kī bhāṣā.* Lucknow: Lucknow Vishvavidyalay, 1957.

Shukla, Ramcandra *et al.* eds., *Tulsī-granthāvalī*. Vol. 2. Varanasi: Nagaripracarini Sabha, 1958.

Simh, Bhagavati Prasad. 'Rāmlalā nahachū: punarvicār'. In *Tulsī: Sandarbh aur samīkṣā*, ed. Tribhuvan Simh, pp. 126-44. Varanasi: Tulsi Shodh Sansthan, 1976.

Varma, Dhirendra, ed. *Hindī Sāhitya*. Vol. 2. Allahabad: Bharatiya Hindi Parishad, 1959.

———. ed. *Hindī sāhitya koś*. Vol. 1. Varanasi: Jnan Mandal Limited, 1985.

———. ed. *Hindī sāhitya koś*. Vol. 2. Varanasi: Jnan Mandal Limited, 1986.

Transformations in Kabīr Hagiography: Pre-modern to Modern Texts

DAVID C. SWAIN

In this paper I will be examining how the authors of more recent Kabīr hagiographies have transformed earlier material by shaping the narratives according to their own sectarian theological and political agendas. The earliest sources of information about Kabīr's life, such as the Sikh *Ādi Granth* (compiled AD 1604) and Nābhādās's *Bhaktamāl* (*c.* AD 1600), are quite stingy in the clues they provide about Kabīr's domestic life, etc. However, within about a quarter of a century after these were composed/compiled, a full cycle of legends had evolved and been recorded in Anantadās's *Kabīr paracaī.* These stories were spread further by Priyādās's commentary, *Bhaktirasbodhinī* (AD 1724), on Nābhādās's *Bhaktamāl.* The more recent accounts (late nineteenth century to present) from the Kabīr Panth are complex cycles of legends woven together in continuous narrative form, and filled out with sectarian apologetics. It seems to be a rule that the further the hagiographies are removed from Kabīr's time, the more elaborate and embellished they become.

From several Kabīr hagiographies, I have chosen two as being fairly typical of the Kabīr Panth's current representations of Kabīr. These texts are the *Kabīr jīvan caritra* by the present Mahant of the Kabir Chaura, Gangasharan Shastri; and Madhavacarya's Hindi translation of the *Kabīr manśūr* by Paramānand (long version, originally composed in 1887), which is particularly popular among the Dharmadāsīs.[1] Both the *Kabīr manśūr* and the *Kabīr jīvan caritra* appropriate certain key words from Hindu theology, however, they do this quite differently. The *Kabīr manśūr* subsumes preexisting Hindu terminology. For example, it rejects the '*sthūl Vedas*' (i.e. the four Hindu Vedas) of the Brahmins, while substituting its own '*sūkṣma Vedas*' (i.e. the words of Kabīr). The *Kabīr jīvan caritra,* on the other hand, moves in a bold effort to make Kabīr Panth theology conform to traditional Vaiṣṇava theology—going so far as to equate Rām (both *saguṇ* and *nirguṇ*) and Kabīr.[2]

Primary texts

The authors of the *Kabīr manśūr* and the *Kabīr jīvan caritra* rely on a variety of sources for their material. In providing evidence (*pramāṇ*) for Paramānand's life of Kabīr, Madhavacarya's Hindi version of the *Kabīr manśūr* cites several panthic texts, such as the *Anurāg sāgar, Bṛhat Kabīr kasauṭī, Kabīr caritra bodh,* etc.[3] It may, however, be anachronistic to refer to the latter two texts as sources for Paramānand's Urdu *Kabīr-i-manshūr.* In any case, the basic outlines of the principle narratives discussed below can be found in Rāghavdās's *Bhaktamāl* (AD 1660) and even earlier in Anantadās's *Kabīr paracaī* (sans adoption narrative). Gangasharan Shastri has made extensive use of this latter text throughout. The *Kabīr paracaī* of Anantadās is worthy of separate mention as the oldest extant cycle of Kabīr legends. However, what most of the Kabīr Panthīs know of Anantadās's text, is restricted to what has been incorporated in the popular texts. As David Lorenzen himself has stated (1991, p. 20): 'Anantadās's text is now virtually unknown to the sadhus of the Kabīr Panth, its *versions* of the Kabīr legends are to them much less important than the versions found in popular texts such as the *Kabīr manshur.*' For present purposes, I will refer those interested in the *oldest* hagiographies to the work of Lorenzen, Callewaert and others. My objective here is to provide a complementary study by focusing on two texts which are in *current* widespread use among Kabīr Panthīs.

The Kabīr manśūr

The *Kabīr manśūr* first drew my attention while I was doing field research among the Dharmadāsīs. Several of the Panthīs mentioned it as required reading for understanding the life of Kabīr and the teachings of the Kabīr Panth. According to the Hindi translator, Pandit Madhavacarya (Paramānand 1933, p. 32), the first version of the *Kabīr-i-manshūr* was written in 1880 and comprised about 350 pages. Paramānand did not rest on the great popularity of this work, but rather composed the *Tālīm Kabīr kaliyug* (1885) which was in essence a revised and expanded edition of the original *Kabīr-i-manshūr.* But he was not satisfied with this either, so in 1887 he composed a much longer version (over 1500 pages) also titled *Kabīr-i-manshūr.* The work of translating this version into Hindi was begun by Yugalanand Bihari (first 272 pages) and completed by Pandit Madhavacarya (ibid., p. 12). Today relatively few Kabīr Panthīs read Urdu, though the Hindi *Kabīr manśūr* is still immensely popular.[4] I have used a 1988 edition of Madhavacarya's Hindi translation throughout since it was recommended to me by the Panthīs, and was being sold at their *maṭhs* during their biggest annual celebration, the *Kabīr Jayantī.*

The *Kabīr manśūr* is a fascinating compendium of Kabīr Panthī mythology, theology, hagiography, doctrines and discipline. It contains several stories of Satpuruṣ's previous incarnations before his manifestation as Kabīr.[5] The body of the text is mainly prose, but there are long passages of verse quoted from other Kabīr Panthī works. In overall character, the *Kabīr manśūr* is somewhat of a sectarian encyclopedia of religious knowledge. Thus, one finds in it such diverse topics as comparisons of various religions; stories of various heroes and prophets of Hinduism, Islam, and Christianity; accounts of the *Vedas,* the Koran, and the Bible; Puranic stories; stories about Hindu philosophers (e.g. Śankarācārya, Rāmānuja); accounts of famous *bhaktas* (e.g. Mīrābāī, Garībdās, Dādū Dayāl); and treatises on *karma,* rebirth, Yoga, etc. But there are also such diverse topics as the English alphabet and a strange bestiary of various mythological animals, including many half human half animal creatures.[6]

The Kabīr jīvan caritra

The present Mahant of the Kabir Chaura, Gangasharan Shastri, has set forth his understanding of Kabīr's life in the *Kabīr jīvan caritra.* This work was first published in 1976, when Amritdas was still the Ācārya or head Mahant of the Kabīr Chaura *maṭh.*[7] In a preface, Amritdas praises the book as being thoroughly researched and filling a long time need. He hopes that, 'this book will help people to understand Sadguru Kabīr'.

In contrast to the *Kabīr manśūr,* the *Kabīr jīvan caritra* focuses on a single incarnation of Satpuruṣ, that of Kabīr. The text is about 360 pages (including introduction). Its language is a highly Sanskritized form of Hindi, sometimes referred to as '*śuddh Hindī*'.[8] This also happens to be the language spoken by the educated *sādhus* in the Benares *maṭhs,* though it is no one's mother tongue. Except in passages where there is an obvious attempt to mimic Muslim speech, Urdu vocabulary has been avoided. The language issue is not purely incidental. Both the form (including vocabulary) and content of this text are closely linked to a Vaiṣṇava portrayal of Kabīr. This view of Kabīr as Vaiṣṇava is made clear from the very outset in the text's introduction (G. Shastri 1991, p. 4):

> On the basis of such books as the *Kabīr paricayī* it seems that in regard to Nīru's religion, for some reason he had already converted to the Muslim religion, Gurudev Kabīr again caused him to be consecrated (*saṃskṛt karāyā*) into *Ārya* religion, and his entire family became members of the Vaiṣṇava religion.

Gangasharan Shastri seems to have thoroughly researched what *he* regards as the most authoritative sources: traditional hagiographies, stories of elderly *sādhus*, and stories told to him by Sri Gurudev Ramvilasdas, the twenty-first Ācārya of the Kabir Chaura (loc. cit.). Obviously, he considers his guru, Ramvilasdas, to be the greatest authority. In this connection, it is interesting to read about Ramvilasdas's source (loc. cit.):

> Gurudev [i.e. Ramvilasdas] said one more thing, 'In Magahar I saw the *Kabīr jīvan caritra* by the Kabir Chaura's third Ācārya, Śrī Jñandāsjī Sāhib, but unfortunately some thief has stolen that book. Several books were collected in it that had been written in old Devanāgarī script. Therefore, I will tell you only the stories I remember that were written in it.' Thus, I am writing the following stories, taking Gurudev's words as authoritative.

It is truly unfortunate that the above mentioned book is not available for study. According to traditional guru genealogies, such a text would probably predate both Anantadās's *Kabīr paracaī* and Nābhādās's *Bhaktamāl.* For a Panthī of the Kabir Chaura, the existence of such a text is unquestionable since it was reported by a head Mahant. Few scholars, however, would be willing to base any arguments on the alleged existence of this text since, for all practical purposes, it has been removed from any possibility of examination. In fact, I have not seen it mentioned outside of Gangasharan Shastri's *Kabīr jīvan caritra.* This instance illustrates different valuations of authority—scholars requiring evidence that can be examined (i.e. empirical evidence); Panthīs relying on the infallible words of their gurus—with obvious practical implications for knowledge about Kabīr.

Accounts of three crucial events in the life of Kabīr

To facilitate a comparison of the texts, and to show how specific sectarian agendas shape the portrayal of Kabīr in various directions, I will concentrate on three focal points in Kabīr's hagiography:

the epiphany and adoption of Kabīr, his alleged initiation by Rāmānand, and his passing from this world. These stories illustrate how the two major branches of the Kabīr Panth have variously assimilated or rejected certain aspects of the Hindu religious, social, and cultural milieu. They also demonstrate a definite concern not only with legitimating a given sect by providing a reputable etiology, but also with establishing a particular group's hegemony over rival branches of the Kabīr Panth.

Appearance and adoption of Kabīr

The earliest version of Kabīr's adoption legend is that found in a Dādū Panthī text, Rāghavdās's *Bhaktamāl* (1717 [Vikrama Saṃvat]/ CE 1660). Lorenzen translates as follows (1991, p. 44; cited as Rāghavdās 1965, p. 177 [vs. 349]):

> There appeared in the eastern region the man (*jan*) Kabīr, a devotee of the Absolute without attributes (*nirguṇ bhagat*). One day a Muslim weaver went outside of Kashi on his way somewhere. Under a tree someone had left a child who was calling out. The weaver took it home with him and entrusted it to his wife. All their clansmen were called, and a big celebration was held. When Kabīr had grown up, he worshipped Ram and had no attachment to anything else.

From this basic plot, some rather elaborate narratives have been woven. The versions found in the *Kabīr manśūr* and *Kabīr jīvan caritra* are fully embellished. Although the outline of the appearance and adoption narrative is similar in both the *Kabīr manśūr* and the *Kabīr jīvan caritra,* there are significant differences. For a start, the author of the *Kabīr jīvan caritra* is much more apt to rely on 'a voice from heaven' (*ākāśvāṇī*) to settle disturbing questions, whereas in the *Kabīr manśūr,* Kabīr himself makes these proclamations. For example, when Nīmā finds Kabīr floating in a giant lotus in Lahartara Pond, Nīru objects to bringing the unknown child home due to the scandal it would cause—from this point the stories diverge. In the *Kabīr manśūr,* the infant Kabīr tells the couple not to worry, that he has come to preach the message of liberation. On the other hand, in the *Kabīr jīvan caritra,* Nīmā petitions 'Bhagvān Hari' (very strange for a Muslim woman!) to make her husband agree to take the child home. Then, suddenly there is a voice from heaven that explains Kabīr's true identity. This 'voice from heaven' is just one of the many devices used by Shastri which cause his narrative to resonate with the Sanskrit epics. Shastri's Kabīr is reminiscent of the forgetful Rām, who from time to time must be reminded of his true identity. The Kabīr of the *Kabīr manśūr*, on the other hand, retains much more of his omniscience and omnipotence during his earthly incarnation. While this difference may appear to be merely a matter of literary convention, it actually goes to the heart of a crucial theological difference between the *Kabīr manśūr* and the *Kabīr jīvan caritra*.

The Dharmadāsī theology of the *Kabīr manśūr* expresses a theological antipathy toward the traditional *avatārs* of Hinduism. These are considered to be products of the delusion that has been created by the great deceiver, Nirañjan, and his agents Māyā, Brahmā, Viṣṇu, Maheś. Satpuruṣ (the absolute transcendent godhead), from time to time becomes incarnate to preach the way of liberation from this delusion. During an interview in 1991, the present Mahant of the Dharmadāsīs, Udit Nam Sahib, told me in a lowered voice, as if it were some great scandal, that the Mahant of the Kabir Chaura was a '*Rām upāsak*', ('worshipper of Rām', obviously referring to *saguṇ* Rām). In fact, Gangasharan Shastri does quite openly sympathize with the *saguṇ upāsanā* view that *nirguṇ* Rām and *saguṇ* Rām are one, and that Kabīr and Rām are one, as will be shown later.

The *saguṇ upāsanā* commentatorial tradition of the *Bījak*, which identifies Kabīr's Rām with Daśrath's son, and thus expresses the identity of *nirguṇ* and *saguṇ* Rām, is not something totally new in the Kabīr Panth. The *saguṇ upāsanā* commentary of Viśvanāth Siṃh, King of Rewa (ruled AD 1833-54) is one of the earliest published commentaries (litho. 1868) on the *Bījak*. In the introduction to his own commentary on the *Bījak*, Shastri divides fourteen or fifteen extant (in 1981) commentaries into three categories: first, the *saguṇ upāsanā* tradition; second, the strictly *nirguṇ upāsanā* tradition (Shastri calls these '*pārakhī*', and derides them), which is best represented by Pūraṇ Sāhib's commentary (*c.* AD 1837); and finally, various 'new' types of commentaries, including one Garībdāsī devotee's Sanskrit *advaitavedānta* commentary, Ahmad Shah's English commentary, a Radhasoami 'sectarian' (*sampradāyvād*) commentary, etc. (Lorenzen 1991, pp. 41-7).[9] Shastri makes no secret of his own leanings, and awards much praise to the *saguṇ* commentary of 'param Vaiṣṇav Sant Śrī Jayrām Dās Jī', which also propounds the unity of *saguṇ* and *nirguṇ* (Lorenzen 1991, p. 42). So, it is no accident that Shastri's life of Kabīr constantly evokes images, and uses literary devices, of the *Rāmāyaṇa* and other Vaiṣṇava mythological and literary traditions in ways which are inconsistent with a purely *nirguṇ upāsanā* agenda. This tendency sets the *Kabīr jīvan caritra* in sharp contrast to the *Kabīr manśūr*. It also indicates a major shift within the Kabir Chaura from the situation which existed as late as 1970. According to Vaudeville (1993, p. 359), in 1970, Pūraṇ Sāhib's *nirguṇ upāsanā* commentary on the *Bījak* was 'the standard text for the Kabīr Chaurā branch of the Kabīr-panthīs'.

Kabīr's initiation by Rāmānand

Harirām Vyās's *vāṇī* (*c.* AD 1561) and Nābhādās's *Bhaktamāl* (*c.* AD 1600) list Kabīr among Swami Rāmānand's disciples, however, these do not contain the story of his initiation. The earliest account of Kabīr tricking Rāmānand into bestowing the 'Rām' mantra appears the Nirañjanī recension of Anantadās's *Kabīr paracaī*, though it is not found in most manuscripts of the Dādū Panthī recension (Lorenzen 1991, pp. 23-4). It also appears in Priyādās's *Bhakti rasa bodhinī* (AD 1712). Several scholars have suggested that the story of Kabīr's initiation by Rāmānand was a fabrication of later *bhaktas* in an attempt to clear Kabīr of the stigma of being *nirguru* ('without a guru'). The question occurs for Kabīr Panthīs, 'Why did Kabīr need this seal of approval if he were himself Satpuruṣ incarnate?' Two Dharmadāsī Mahants have addressed this question directly, 'In order to honour the traditional concept of initiation by a Guru, he [i.e. Kabīr] decided to be a disciple of Swami Ramanand, who was an accomplished Vaiṣṇava saint in those days' (J.D. Shastri and Ramswarupdasji 1990, p. 22).

Though Panthic tradition has it that Rāmānand, a Vaiṣṇava, was Kabīr's guru, the *Kabīr manśūr* goes to great lengths in refuting traditional Vaiṣṇava theologies. On the other hand, one of the dominant concerns throughout the *Kabīr jīvan caritra* is in establishing Kabīr's Vaiṣṇava identity. This point is given special stress in the story of his initiation by the leading Vaiṣṇava guru of his day, and in the story of the Hindu-Muslim quarrel over how to dispose of his remains. Gangasharan Shastri makes explicit his view that Kabīr was the founder of a Hindu renaissance, in a section entitled 'The Resurrection of Vaiṣṇava Religion by Sadguru'.[10] This view not only shapes the biography, it is critical to the current identity of the Kabir Chaura branch as a whole. For example, when questioned about their top-knots (*choṭī*), sectarian forehead marks, white *vairagī* costume, etc., several of the Kabīr Panthīs told me that they considered themselves Vaiṣṇava in Rāmānand's lineage, since the great Svāmī was Kabīr's guru. Shastri has himself stated (D. Lorenzen 1981, p.162), 'I am a Hindu, I am a Vaiṣṇava'.

In the *Kabīr manśūr,* Kabīr decides, of his own volition, to become a disciple of Swami Rāmānand. Knowing of Rāmānand's caste prejudice, Kabīr thinks up a way to trick the Swami into giving him a mantra, which, according to the text, would be equivalent to *guru-dīkṣā* ('initiation by a guru'). The *Kabīr jīvan caritra,* on the other hand, has the goddess Śakti, by means of a mysterious *ākāśvāṇī,* instructing Kabīr on how to trick Svāmī Rāmānand into bestowing the mantra.

Gangasharan Shastri is not content with merely demonstrating Kabīr's inclusion into the Vaiṣṇava fold. He also uses this story as a platform for some fairly mild Hindu nationalist rhetoric. This emerges at two points, first just after Nīmā sees her adopted son in his Vaiṣṇava outfit; second, in a contrived mental soliloquy by Rāmānand. In the first case, Nīmā reminds her audience that 'for two generations' no one has chanted the name of Rām in her family. This serves to remind the reader of a point made in Shastri's introduction, that the weavers of Kashi were relatively recent converts to Islam. This point is followed by gossip from the citizens of Kashi that reiterates Kabīr's non-Muslim origin. The reader is also reminded of 'strict Islamic religion' (*kaṭṭar islām dharm*)[11] and its opposition to the 'Aryans' (*āryõ kā* [sic] *khilāfat*). The icing on the cake is Shastri's use of the term 'Sanātan Dharm' to describe the 'special faith' (*viśeṣ viśvās*) of the Brahmins and merchants who gather to complain to Rāmānand about his initiation of Kabīr. They also report to Rāmānand that the Muslims are up in arms about Kabīr's conversion—now a full scale communal row is brewing.

Anyone having lived in Benares in the past few years may feel that Shastri's account of communal tensions is suspiciously modern. Nevertheless, precedent for Shastri's version of the story can be found as early as the *Kabīr paracaī* of Anantadās. What is striking about Shastri's account, is how the language and terminology he uses makes the narrative seem more contemporary, almost as if he were describing events surrounding the '*śuddhi*' (Hindu reconversion) movement, and tends to give the text something of a Hindu nationalist tone. It is necessary to be cautious about drawing too many conclusions from a single passage such as this. Never-theless, another passage occurring in the same story provides further and more explicit examples of the religious and political leanings hinted at above.

The second passage referred to is a contrived mental soliloquy on Rāmānand's part in which he remembers Aṣṭānanda telling what he had seen at Lahartara Pond. This includes a Vaiṣṇava etiology of Kabīr, the 'partial incarnation' (*aṃśāvatār*) of 'Bhagavān Nārāyaṇ', '. . . about whom Vedavyās wrote in the *Bhaviśyapurāṇa* that, in order to give protection (salvation, *trāṇ*) to the sons of God invaded by the barbarians (*mlecchõ se*), Hari himself, by the name of Kabīr, becoming incarnate without being born from a womb, will protect the Eternal True Religion (*sanātan satya dharm*). . .' (G. Shastri 1991, p. 26). This passage is explicit enough without going into who the 'barbarians' are. Though attributed to Rāmānand, there is little doubt that these thoughts represent Shastri's own views. The introduction to Shastri's commentary on the *Bījak* (G. Shastri 1991, pp. 13-15), especially his account of the Muslim invasions and their consequences for the Hindus, bears this out.

The earlier passage again shows Shastri's identification of Kabīr with Hari (Viṣṇu). This is in sharp contrast to the Dharmadāsī theology of the *Kabīr manśūr,* which views Hari as part of the Hindu trinity born from the union of Nirañjan (the great deceiver) and Māyā.[12] The differences between these two theologies come into even sharper relief in the story of Kabīr's passing from this world.

Kabīr's passing from this world

The *Kabīr manśūr* reminds the reader at the beginning of this story, 'this [i.e. Kabīr] is Parameśvar himself, neither can he be killed by another's hand, nor can he be cut, nor drowned, nor burnt, nor will any weapon be successful against him, nor can humans, animals or gods, etc. harm him in any way. . . .' Since Kabīr Panthīs believe Kabīr to be immortal, yet he is clearly no longer on this earth in bodily form, the sect is stuck with the difficult question of what happened to him. The answer given in the *Kabīr manśūr,* and in the *Kabīr jīvan caritra,* is that Kabīr voluntarily withdrew from the world when he was nearly one hundred twenty years old. He went to his own abode in bodily form. However, there is much more to the story than a mere apology for his absence. In all the sectarian accounts, before Kabīr's Muslim and Hindu followers realized that his body was missing, they quarreled over which funeral rites to perform. According to the hagiographies, Kabīr saved them from a bloody battle by taking his body with him and leaving in its place only a pile of flowers and a sheet (or two sheets). These were divided equitably, and the Hindus and Muslims performed their respective funeral rites over their shares of these items.

The *Kabīr manśūr* has a much shorter version of Kabīr's disappearance than the *Kabīr jīvan caritra.* This can be largely attributed to three factors: (1) Shastri waxes literary with his flowery descriptions, much of which resonates with the style of the Sanskrit epics, (2) Shastri describes his concept of 'true religion' (*satya dharm*) in the course of the narrative, whereas this topic is treated in separate chapters in the *Kabīr manśūr,* and (3) Shastri uses the story as a platform for the promotion of the Kabir Chaura as the chief seat of the Kabīr Panth. The *Kabīr manśūr* is not without theological and sectarian expositions, however, these are found in different chapters and not so much woven into this particular segment of Kabīr's hagiography. For example, in the *Kabīr manśūr,* immediately following the story of Kabīr's disappearance is a chapter titled 'The Kabīr Panth's Religious Observances' (*Kabīr-panth ke dhārmik niyam*), a list of fifty articles of faith and religious observance.[13]

As in the other narratives, the *Kabīr manśūr* contains no *ākāśvāṇī,* but has Kabīr himself as the central actor and power behind the scenes. Dharmadās is given special mention in the *Kabīr manśūr*—he is one of two disciples that Kabīr appears to after vanishing from Magahar. Śrutigopāl, alleged founder of the Kabir Chaura *maṭh,* is not mentioned in the *Kabīr manśūr's* version of this story. The Dharmadās branch is also alluded to when Kabīr, 'explained clearly the observances of the forty-two generations'. This is a reference to Kabīr's alleged prophecy that the descendants of Dharmadās would hold office for forty-two generations.

In Shastri's much enhanced version, the reader is given a clear definition of 'true religion' (*satya dharm*) (G. Shastri 1991, p. 244):

All the people became worshippers (lit. 'priests') of *Rām Nām.*[14] In order [for people] to cross the ocean of the world (*saṃsār rūpī sāgar*), Sadguru Kabīr made the bridge of Rām Bhakti, which has become everlasting from age to age for the deliverance of people. Having ascended this, people will easily (*sahaj mẽ*)[15] continue to cross the ocean of existence (*bhavsāgar*).

As noted earlier, Shastri's Rām Bhakti includes *saguṇ* as well as *nirguṇ* Rām—a view which is anathema to the Dharmadāsīs. The *Kabīr jīvan caritra* also repeats the proposition that Kabīr and Rām are one. Kabīr says to Mahārājā Vīrdev Siṃh and Avid Ali Khān (G. Shastri 1991, pp. 246-7):

Know that I am the cause of the world. I am the beginning and end of creation. It is my name that is Rām,[16] which is the supreme name. When from time to time it becomes necessary, then I, becoming enveloped with my power of illusion (*māyā*), come into the world and show the path of truth to straying creatures. I take on an appropriate form according to the need. I am omnipotent. There is no jurisdiction above me.

This doctrine of incarnation is a fairly standard Hindu view, see for example the *Bhāgavadgītā*, 4.7, 8:

Whenever a decrease of righteousness
Exists, Descendant of Bharata,
And there is a rising up of unrighteousness,
Then I give forth myself, (7)
For the protection of the good
And the destruction of evil doers;
For the sake of establishing righteousness,
I come into being from age to age. (8)[17]

Though not readily apparent in the English translations, Shastri's Hindi mirrors the relative clause construction of the Sanskrit to produce an effect that strongly resonates with the above passage from the *Bhāgavadgītā*, one which would be familiar to most educated Indians. Compare the Hindi, *jab jab āvaśyaktā hotī hai tab-tab maĩ* . . . with the Sanskrit, *yadā yadā hi dharmasya glānir bhavati . . . tadā 'tmānaṃ*. . . . I have little doubt that this parallelism was intentional. Furthermore, Shastri's description of Kabīr (during his ascension) also echoes a well-known conceit used to describe Kṛṣṇa's cosmic manifestation; Kabīr 'with the radiance of many suns' goes flying off to his World of Truth. Several other devices and poetic conceits are borrowed from the Sanskrit epics. For example, upon his ascension there is 'a rain of flowers from the sky', 'the songs of *apsarās* (celestial nymphs) and *gandharvas* (celestial musicians) were heard'. It seemed as if the entire sky were filled with celestial cars (*vimān*)' (G. Shastri 1991, p. 248)'. Kabīr travels in a *vimān* shaped like a swan. Then there is the classic personification of Nature's *virah* (longing) (ibid., p. 249):

> Meanwhile, all the creatures on earth were filled with grief. The wind ceased blowing. The leaves of trees and plants stood drooping.[18] Animals and birds cried a stream of tears. The earth was overcast with a deathly pallor. To everyone, the entire world appeared desolate. The sky turned red. The directions started to spin, the five elements began to weep, the ground began to tremble.

Similarly, Shastri describes the impending battle between Hindus and Muslims over the body of Kabīr in terms which harken back to Kurukṣetra.

Ironically, sectarian politics are also voiced in this narrative, whose moral points beyond such rivalries. Shastri uses Kabīr's parting words for a rather blatant promotion of the Kabir Chaura. In the *Kabīr jīvan caritra* (ibid., p. 245) Kabīr says, 'Śrī Śrutigopāl Dāsjī, Śrī Padmanābhā Dāsjī, and Śrī Kamāl Dāsjī, etc., are my chief disciples.' The internecine rivalry between the Kabir Chaura and the Dharmadās branch is apparent by the conspicuous omission of Dharmadās's name from the list of chief disciples. Not satisfied with Śrutigopāl being listed as one among other chief disciples, the text further states (ibid., p. 246):

> Sāhib said expressly to Śrī Śrutigopāl, 'You are the best among my disciples. You, with the help of your other guru-brothers, are to run the Kabir Chaura, the chief service-ashram situated in Kashi, because it is that which is the centre of the promulgation of the religion (*dharm pracār*). So, maintain a hut for service and preaching in that ashram.'

Of course, taken at face value, this would conveniently establish Shastri's position as head of all Kabīr Panthīs, not merely the Kabir Chaura branch.

Conclusion

Within the Kabīr Panth there is a certain assumed epistemological ladder of authority.[19] At the top level is knowledge that is revealed in the life and teachings of Kabīr. Because of this, those who have, through office and trust, the ability to shape the portrayal of Kabīr's life, also exercise tremendous power in transforming the knowledge which is considered most essential to their disciples. I am referring, of course, to the Mahants, who are next down in the hierarchy of authority, and who exercise extraordinary discretionary power in shaping this knowledge of Kabīr's life and teachings. In a 'régime of truth' (Foucault) the Mahant is dictator for life. He is not answerable to the scholars, whose authority rests largely on their ability to demonstrate their arguments by means of the lower knowledges (based on empirical evidence and reason)[20] though he may draw from their findings, or cite them as references at his convenience.

The *Kabīr manśūr* and the *Kabīr jīvan caritra* both draw on earlier hagiographies for their material, and both share some crucial assumptions about the nature of knowledge and authority. Yet, very different Kabīrs emerge in the course of the narratives. At first this might seem paradoxical, but on closer examination one finds that it is because of, rather than in spite of, their common presuppositions that the images of Kabīr differ as much as they do. These shared assumptions are the constants on which the diverse variables of sectarian politics and theological differences operate. Thus, the emergent portraits of Kabīr are, to a large extent, functions of the interaction of a constant epistemological hierarchy with variable political and religious agendas.

The element of sectarian rivalry in these texts is no more surprising than what one would expect of sects locked in competition over membership, financial means, and the authority to interpret and thereby control the official theology of the Panth. This competitive antagonism surfaces in the texts in both subtle and not-so-subtle ways. The simple omission of the name of one of the founding disciples, Dharmadās or Śrutigopāl, can become a glaring attack when placed in the context of Kabīr naming his 'chief disciples'. Both sides play this game. Besides the earlier example from the *Kabīr jīvan caritra,* a mythological account in the *Kabīr manśūr* has Kabīr, *in illo tempore,* creating four disciples and distributing the four *sūkṣma Vedas* among them for the sake of bringing salvation to the world. Dharmadās receives the *Kotjñān kī vāṇī,*[21] which corresponds to the *Ṛgveda*—Śrutigopal is not mentioned (Paramānand 1988, p. 60). The Kabīr *jīvanīs* become ready weapons in the arsenal used to contend internecine quarrels. Consequently, these quarrels exercise their own marked effects in shaping the narrated lives of Kabīr.

Competing branches of the Kabīr Panth are not the only

opponents to which these texts answer. In the course of its 1300 plus pages, the *Kabīr manśūr* takes on various Hindu *sampradāys*, Islam, Christianity, etc. The text is concerned with defining its own theological positions over and against the others. In contrast to this, the *Kabīr jīvan caritra* is not confrontational with regard to Vaiṣṇava theology, but makes every effort to reconcile it with the Panth's earlier sectarian views. On the other hand, it is not so generous with Islam.

Both the *Kabīr manśūr* and the *Kabīr jīvan caritra* attempt to come to terms with the Hindu cultural milieu in which they are immersed. However, the *Kabīr manśūr* does this by subsuming the language and terminology of a pre-existing Hindu culture. It rejects the '*lok Vedas*' or '*sthūl Vedas*' (i.e. the four Hindu Vedas) which have fooled the Brahmins into praising Nirañjan; and it substitutes its own '*sūkṣma Vedas*', which are parts of the '*Svasaṃveda*', that is, the words of Kabīr. Mythologically, Nirañjan meditates and inhales the '*sūkṣma Vedas*'. He takes their essence and exhales their husks, which are mixed with his own bad ideas (*jāti* [caste] comes from these *Vedas*). These corrupt shells of the true Vedas were spread by Brahmā among the inhabitants of the earth. To save the people from Nirañjan and his evil influence spread by these false Vedas, Kabīr comes from age to age and re-establishes the true Vedas (Paramānand 1988, pp. 57-61). In this way, the revelation of Kabīr, as expounded in the *Kabīr manśūr,* supplants even the Hindu Vedas—however, it adopts and revalorizes the terms of a Hindu cultural medium to do so.[22]

The *Kabīr jīvan caritra,* on the other hand, endeavors to make Kabīr Panth theology conform more to conventional Vaiṣṇava theology. In the story of Kabīr's initiation, the *Kabīr manśūr* does not have the voice of a goddess directing Kabīr on how to obtain Rāmānand's initiation. Kabīr is omniscient in himself and needs no such help. The *Kabīr jīvan caritra,* however, models its life of Kabīr along the lines of the epic lives of Rām and Kṛṣṇa. The author of the *Kabīr jīvan caritra* accepts much of the traditional Panthic theology, as is readily apparent from his commentary on the *Bījak,* however, he also makes every effort to reconcile this with *saguṇ* Vaiṣṇava theology. For Shastri, ultimately *saguṇ* and *nirguṇ* are one, and Kabīr and Rām are one.[23] His project in the *Kabīr jīvan caritra* is not so much to re-interpret and hegemonize Vaiṣṇava theology and mythology in Kabīr Panthī terms, but to make Kabīr Panthī theology and hagiography conform more to conventional Vaiṣṇava standards.

Most, if not all, of the participants in this conference have worked with medieval texts, and are familiar with the impact that different sectarian agendas may have on various recensions of a common corpus of legend. The texts I have analysed give a modern twist to earlier hagiographic materials. That is, they illustrate the more contemporary concerns of the Kabīr Panth in the transmission and transformation of knowledge about Kabīr. The information I have provided here is intended to be complimentary to studies of pre-modern Kabīr hagiography, and thus, add one more perspective in the attempt to understand the complex dynamics of human agency and the transmission of texts and knowledge about Kabīr.

NOTES

1. The long version was published in Urdu in 1891. Though I have seen a microform copy of the Urdu version (original held by the British Library), for this study I have relied primarily on the Hindi translation which is in current use among the Kabīr Panthīs: Paramānand, *Kabīr manśūr: arthāt Svasaṃvedārtha prakāś*, translated from Urdu to Hindi by Madhavacarya (1988 edition).

   The earliest Hindi translation of this work that I have been able to locate is by Makanjī Kubera (1903). The earliest edition of Madhavacarya's translation I have come across is 1933. Both are held by the British Museum Library.
2. G. Shastri (1991, p. 247) has Kabīr saying: 'My name is Rām, which is the supreme name. . . . Look, I have two forms. There is one which is beyond illusion and ignorance, people call this *nirguṇ* (without attributes). My other form is that which comes from time to time, and does the tasks of this world, and which is constrained by ignorance, which in the world is referred to as creature (*jīv*).'
3. P.D. Barthwal (1936, p. 282) dates the composition of the *Anurāg sāgar* during the first quarter of the eighteenth century. The latter texts are probably late nineteenth or early twentieth century productions of Yugalānand Bihārī.
4. There are more than just differences of language between the Urdu *Kabīr-i-manshūr* and its Hindi translation. For example, the Hindi version has long passages quoted from the *Anurāg sāgar* which do not appear in the Urdu version. The sequence of some chapters has also been altered.
5. Satpuruṣ (a.k.a. Satyapuruṣa) is the Kabīr Panthī designation for the supreme godhead.
6. My edition is replete with illustrations of these bizarre creatures.
7. I will be using the 1991 edition throughout.

8. This trend of Sanskritization can be said to have reached its culmination in the Sanskrit biography by Brahmalinamuni, *Sadguruśrīkavīracaritam* (1960).
9. Dates supplied from Keay (1931, p. 132) and Lorenzen (1991, p. 16).
10. *Kabīr jīvan caritra* (G. Shastri 1991, p. 57): 'sadguru dvārā vaiṣnav dharm kā punarutthān'.
11. '*Kaṭṭar islām*' is a stock derogatory phrase akin to 'fanatic Muslims'.
12. Das Gupta 1969, pp. 322-37, compares the Dharamdāsī cosmogony with ideas found in Vedic literature, in the Upaniṣads, the Sāṅkhya system, Puranic literature, etc. (especially the Prajāpati Brahmā cosmogony).
13. A full translation appears in Keay 1931, pp. 145-9.
14. *Sabhī log rām nām ke pujārī ho gae.*
15. The narrator may be punning on '*sahaj*', meaning 'easy' or, in Kabīr's terminology, 'the natural way'. '*Sahaj*' is a technical term in the Sants' vocabulary, indicating the inner path or 'intuition' as P.D. Barthwal (1936, p. 57) translates it.
16. Rām and Kabīr are one, it cannot be said they are other.
    But if someone says he is other, then he will not find Sadguru.
    Sākhī granth
17. Sargeant 1984, pp. 207-8.
    yadā yadā hi dharmasya glānir bhavati bhārata /
    abhyutthānam adharmasya tadā 'tmānaṃ srjāmyaham //7//
    paritrāṇāya sādhūnāṃ vināśāya ca duṣkṛtām /
    dharmasaṃsthāpanārthāya saṃbhavāmi yuge yuge //8//
18. A similar description is met with in the *Rāmāyaṇa* when Rām, Lakṣmaṇ and Sītā leave Ayodhya to go into forest exile.
19. For a more in-depth treatment of the interaction of human agency and hierarchies of knowledge in Indology, see R. Inden 1990.
20. I am temporarily putting aside the politics of academic hierarchies of authority.
21. H. Dwivedi (1990, p. 28) renders this, '*Kūt-vāṇī*' (language of riddles).
22. N. Cutler (1987, pp. 7-10) discusses a similar dynamic found among the devotees of the Tamil saints. The devotional songs of these saints are called the 'Tamil *Vedas*'.
23. See note 2.

REFERENCES

Barthwal, Pitambar Datta. *The Nirguna School of Hindi Poetry: An Exposition of Medieval Indian Santa Mysticism.* Foreword by Syam Sundar Das. Varanasi: Indian Book Shop, 1936.

Brahmalinamuni. *Sadguruśrīkavīracaritam.* Baroda: The author, 1960.

Cutler, Norman. *Songs of Experience: The Poetics of Tamil Devotion.* Bloomington: Indiana University Press, 1987.

Das Gupta, Shashibhushan. *Obscure Religious Cults.* 3rd ed. Calcutta: Firma K.L. Mukhopadhyay, 1969.

Dwivedi, Hazariprasad. *Kabīr.* 6th ed. New Delhi: Rajkamal Prakashan, 1990.

Gosvami, Vasudev. *Bhakta-kavi Vyās Jī.* Ed. Prabhudayal Mital. Mathura: Agraval Press, 1952.

Harirām Vyās. See Gosvami, Vasudev.

Inden, Ronald. *Imagining India.* Oxford: Basil Blackwell, 1990.

Kabīr. *Bījak Kabīrdās saṭīk.* With commentary of Viśvanāth Siṃha, King of Rewa. Lucknow: Munshi Newal Kishore Press, 1883.

———. *Bījak Śrī Kabīr Sāhab,* with 'Trijyā' commentary by Pūraṇdās. Lucknow: Ganga Prasad Varma Press, 1872.

———. *Bījakṭīkā manoramā,* edited, with modern Hindi translation and commentary by Gangasharan Shastri. Varanasi: Kabir Vani Prakashan Kendra, 1989.

Keay, F.E. *Kabīr and His Followers.* Calcutta: Association Press, 1931.

Lorenzen, David N. *Kabir Legends and Anant-Das's Kabir Parachai.* Albany: State University of New York Press, 1991.

———. 'The Kabīr Panth: Heretics to Hindus'. In *Religious Change and Cultural Domination: XXX International Congress of Human Sciences in Asia and North Africa.* Edited by David N. Lorenzen, pp. 151-72. Mexico, D.F.: Colegio de Mexico, 1981.

Nābhādās. *Śrī Bhaktamāl.* With the verse commentary of Priyādās, *Bhaktirasbodhinī,* and a prose commentary by Sītārāmśaraṇ Bhagvānprasād Rūpkāla. Lucknow: Tejkumar Press, 1962.

Paramānand. *Kabīr manśūr: arthāt svasaṃvedārtha prakāś.* Translated from Urdu to Hindi by Madhavacarya. Bombay: Lakshmivenkateshvar Steam Press, 1988.

———. *Kabīr manśūr.* Translated from Urdu to Hindi by Madhavacarya. Bombay: Gangavishnu Srikrishnadas, 1933.

———. *Kabīr manśūr.* Translated from Urdu to Hindi by Makanji Kuber. Bombay: Srivenkateshvar Steam Yantralay, 1903.

Priyādās. See Nābhādās.

Pūraṇ Sāhib. See Kabīr. *Bījak Śrī Kabīr Sāhab,* 1872.

Rāghavdās. *Bhaktamāl.* With the verse commentary of Caturdās. Edited by Agarachand Nahata. Jodhpur: Rajasthan Oriental Research Institute, 1965.

Rāghavdās. *Bhaktamāl.* With the verse commentary of Caturadās and a prose commentary by Nārāyaṇdās. Jaipur: Sri Dadu Mahavidyalaya, 1970.

Sargeant, Winthrop (trans.). *The Bhagavad Gītā.* Rev. ed. Edited by Christopher Chapple. Albany: State University of New York, 1984.

Shastri, Gangasharan. *Kabīr jīvan caritra.* 2nd ed. Varanasi: Kabirbani Prakashan Kendra (1976), 1991.

———. ed., trans., comm. See Kabir. *Bījak ṭīkā manoramā,* 1989.

Shastri, Jagdish Dasji and Ramswarupdasji. *Glimpse of the Life of Sadguru Kabir.* Edited by J. Das. Jamnagar: Shri Kabir Ashram, 1990.

Siṃh, Viśvanāth, King of Rewa, comm. *Bījak Kabīrdās saṭīk.* See Kabīr. *Bījak Kabīrdās saṭīk,* 1883.

Vaudeville, Charlotte. *A Weaver Named Kabir.* Delhi: Oxford University Press, 1993.

The Oral Tradition of *Rāmkathā* in Gujarātī Folk Songs

HASU YAJNIK

The great epics, *Mahābhārata* and *Rāmāyaṇa,* exist in both oral and written form in almost all the modern languages of India. In Gujarātī the stories of Kṛṣṇa and Rām have been rendered in prose traditions referred to as 'rural *Mahābhārata*' and 'rural *Rāmāyaṇa*', in the rural areas, and as 'tribal *Mahābhārata*' and 'tribal *Rāmāyaṇa*' in the hill or tribal areas. It is taken for granted that these oral traditions are for illiterate people and have come into vogue as simplified adaptations of the written tradition. However, the oral traditions found in the villages and hill areas of Gujarat also preserve features of their own that are distinct from the written tradition. This became clear to me from the study and editing of folk songs of Gujarat. The Gujarat State Folk Literature Committee has collected 3,964 folk works in fourteen volumes under the general editorship of H.C. Bhayani. From this basic collection, I have edited Gujarātī folk songs dealing with Kṛṣṇa, the Pāṇḍavs, and Rām and have found 606 of them to be based on *Kṛṣṇacarit,* 121 on *Rāmkathā,* and 20 on *Pāṇḍavkathā.* This work in narrative songs enabled me to compile statistical data relating to the various kinds of story-based songs and the interaction between oral and written tradition. If the total of 3,964 collected folk works is taken as the basis for a sample survey, we can see that the percentage of *Kṛṣṇacarit* in Gujarātī oral tradition is 15.28 per cent and of *Rāmkathā* 3.05 per cent. On comparing the oral works with the written ones it was found that against 606 folk songs on Kṛṣṇa we have 211 medieval poets who have composed works based on *Kṛṣṇacarit,* and against the 121 folk works on Rām nearly a hundred medieval poets have created nearly 350 compositions on *Rāmkathā.*

These figures show that in both oral and written traditions *Kṛṣṇacarit* is more popular than *Rāmkathā.* The reason for this lies in the differences between the stories and the images of the characters concerned. The story of Kṛṣṇa has narrative force from the very beginning, whereas *Rāmkathā* acquires dramatic impetus only after the abduction of Sītā. The birth of Kṛṣṇa itself is dramatic and his childhood and adolescence are full of dynamic, heroic, and mischievous events. The second difference lies in the image of these two heroes. Lord Kṛṣṇa is not only a divine incarnation to be worshipped, but a near and dear one in the form of a son, friend, or lover. He has all the characteristics required for being loved, such as manliness, zest for life, and love of music and dance. The whole concept and dimension of love and the love story appear to be transformed: love, generally a bond between two individuals turns out to be a bridge between one and many.

It should be noted here that both *Kṛṣṇacarit* and *Rāmkathā* are connected with the Indian life cycle and season cycle. Although both heroes are incarnations of Viṣṇu, their respective styles of devotion and worship are somewhat different. Kṛṣṇa's worship, especially in the Puṣṭimārg, expresses itself in dance and music. Most Vaiṣṇava families conduct their own *pūjā* and possess images of 'Lāljī' (Kṛṣṇa as a child) which in being woken up in the morning, bathed, dressed, offered different foods, and swung in a cradle are treated just like a child of the family. All these rituals are accompanied by specific songs. In the temple (*havelī*) a daily schedule of *śayan, maṅgalā, snān, vāghā,* etc., is observed. Seasonal songs are sung and rituals, such as *horī* and *hiṇḍol,* celebrated. Also, devotional songs by the Aṣṭachāp poets are sung in the Dhrupad-Dhamār style of Indian classical music. In contrast, the worship of Rām is simple and includes no varieties of dance or music, which is why fewer folk songs based on *Rāmkathā* are available.

In his *Rāmkathā: Utpatti aur vikās,* a deep comparative study of Indian and foreign versions of *Rāmkathā,* Camille Bulcke noted the following two main differences in the Indian versions:

1. Most of them say that Rām was banished at the behest of Kaikeyī: she asked Daśrath to send Rām away to the forest for fourteen years and to offer the throne to her own son Bharat.
2. Most of them (except the Buddhist, Jain, and Kashmiri ones) narrate that Rām deserted Sītā because of the scandalous remarks of a washerwoman. Some of the plentiful 'non-Vedic' (i.e. non-Brahminical) traditions explain that he deserted her because she drew a picture of Rāvaṇ and Laṅkā.

Almost all the written versions in Gujarat follow the Brahminical tradition and reject the heterodox variations. However, the oral versions, although they fall within the Hindu tradition, accept the Buddhist, Jain, and Kashmiri deviations. This shows that oral traditions, since they are concerned with the narrative and its variations, are willing to accept anything that has a striking and appealing story element, regardless of whether it is acceptable to the orthodox Hindu tradition. Bulcke concluded that the character of Kaikeyī and Rām's abandonment of Sītā are later elements in the story. He even pointed out that they are later additions to Vālmīki's *Ādi-rāmāyaṇa*. Oral tradition in Gujarātī not only supports this conclusion, but also helps us formulate a clear-cut idea of the basic *Rāmkathā*.

The rural prose *Rāmāyaṇa* and some songs also narrate that Sītā's abduction took place just after her *svayaṃvara* and that Kaikeyī is not the cause of Rām's banishment. It is also possible that, as Jainism spread in Gujarat during the time of Kumārpāl Solāṅkī (1142-72), the Jain version of the Rām story (*Paümacariu*) may have influenced the Gujarātī oral tradition. In spite of this influence, the rural *Rāmāyaṇa* and some of the songs from the oral tradition help us to gain an impression of the basic structure of the original (*ādi-*) *Rāmāyaṇa*. However, because the editing and preservation of oral literature began in 1851, the main difficulty in using it as a source of study is that we have no specific, acceptable method or source for deciding how old an oral version is. In the case of the written tradition, we can determine the dates of any alteration or addition to the story because the date of the author and manuscript can be fixed. This is not possible for the oral narrative, though with the help of cross-references between oral and written compositions some light can be shed on the evolution of a specific episode. Kaarle Krohn (1863-1933) was the first to apply the historical-geographical method to the study of the folktale (S. Thompson 1946, p. 396). We may likewise make a comparative study of a story that has its roots in both oral and written traditions. *Kṛṣṇacarit*, *Pāṇḍavkathā*, and *Rāmkathā* are widespread in all regions of India in different languages. Needless to say, most of the ancient and medieval stories of India are available in both oral and written traditions, even today.

The oral tradition of *Rāmkathā* is widely prevalent in all regions of India, sometimes in a form different from that of the written tradition of Gujarat, but at the same time it tallies with the remote tribal tradition. According to the prose rural *Rāmāyaṇa*, Sītā is not the daughter of the Earth, as she is said to be in the written traditions, but is the daughter of Rāvaṇ. The story goes that Rāvaṇ did penance to please Śiv and became king. When he ordered *ṛṣis* to pay a penance tax, eighty-seven of them filled a pot with their blood, sealed it, and then gave it to Rāvaṇ, asking him not to open it for nine months. From that pot a girl was born, and it was prophesied that she would be the cause of the destruction of Rāvaṇ and his kingdom. He therefore put her in a wooden box which he had set afloat in a river. A washerman found her and gave her to King Janak. This story prevails among the Kurvar and Velor tribes of Kerala (See B. Mishra 1987, pp. 189-90). The reason for Sītā's abandonment, according to the Prakrit *Upadeśapada,* Hemacandra's Jain *Rāmāyaṇa,* the *Rāmāyaṇa* of Kṛttibās of Bengal and Cīramān of Kerala, the Kashmiri *Rāmāyaṇa,* and the Sanskrit *Ānandarāmāyaṇa,* was her drawing of a picture of Rāvaṇ. This bears a close relationship, and perhaps owes its origin, to Jain sources that have influenced the oral tradition of Gujarat.

Prominent incidents in the written tradition do not have such a dominant place in the oral tradition. Out of 121 folk works, 33 songs (that is, nearly a quarter of them) deal with Sītā's *svayaṃvara,* 19 (15.7 per cent) deal with Rām's forest exile, and 15 (12.39 per cent) with Sītā's abduction, while 10 works (8.26 per cent) narrate the *Rāmkathā* in brief. This gives us a clear idea of which episodes had appeal for the folk tradition and why. Let us look at the comparative data:

Incident	*Oral*	*Written*
1. Śravaṇa	8	—
2. Śabarī	3	—
3. Hanumān	—	6
4. *Rāmkathā* in brief	10	30
5. *vār, tithi,* etc., misc.	18	5
6. Birth of Rām	—	3
7. Sītā's *svayaṃvara,* abduction, abandonment	70	33
8. Battle between Rām and Rāvaṇ	12	5
9. Rāvaṇ and Mandodarī		11
10. Laṅkā	—	5
11. Lav-Kuś and *aśvamedha*	—	2
TOTAL	121	100

It appears that, unlike the oral tradition, the written one has more compositions on *svayaṃvara,* Hanumān, and Aṅgad-Viṣṭi.

The *aśvamedha* has attracted some attention in the written tradition, but none in the oral. The basic difference between oral and written forms is seen in Sītā's abandonment, as noted above. Almost all written traditions follow the canonical versions of Vālmīki and Tulsīdās, while oral traditions, which have a preference for the story element, accept the Jain versions.

In the basic structure of *Rāmkathā* Kaikeyī is not the cause of Rām's banishment, and Sītā's abandonment is included in the main story at the second stage of its development. If one therefore has to study the basic structure of *Rāmkathā*, the oral tradition provides something additional and very useful. The reason is that oral tradition, even of a religious story or myth, is not merely secondary or an echo of written tradition, but sometimes has a direct relation to the root or birth of the story. Secondly, the story usually becomes fixed once it has entered the written tradition and has obtained a definitive and perfected literary form. We may say that in oral tradition the story is free to flow like river water, whereas in written tradition it is like water stored in a pond.

Oral tradition has preserved themes that are found in the oldest extant Indian literature. For example, the main source for the theme of love between a mortal man and an immortal *apsaras* (viz., the tale of Purūravas and Urvaśī) is a hymn in the tenth *maṇḍala* of the *Ṛgveda*. Later, a definitive literary version of the tale was provided by Kālidāsa in his *Vikramorvaśīyam*, but in the oral tradition the seeds continued to develop, eventually to be reborn in stories such as Lākhā-Fulānī of Kutch.

The oral tradition of *Rāmkathā* also helps us to study the 'how it happened and why' type of story, as exemplified by incidents during the forest exile featuring the Tanner's Cassia, the crow, the vulture, and the squirrel. The Tanner's Cassia tried to rescue Sītā and so won the boon of flowering in all seasons. However, it rebuked Rām for his inability to protect Sītā and so Lakṣmaṇ condemned it to be mixed with leather. Thanks to boons from Sītā, the vulture acquired its ability to eat stones, the squirrel acquired the stripes on its back, and the little black crow acquired its red anus. Such aetiological anecdotes are based on observation and are drawn from folklore.

It is interesting and useful to mention here the occasions and opportunities on which folk songs based on *Rāmkathā* are connected with the individual's life cycle and the social and seasonal cycles of Gujarat:

1. Folk songs based on Sītā's *svayaṃvara* (nos. 9-34)[1] are generally sung at Gujarātī marriages.
2. Folk songs based on the forest exile (36-54), Sītā's abduction (55-69), the battle between Rām and Rāvaṇ (73-84), and Sītā's abandonment (85-93) are mostly sung by married women during a vigil (*jāgaraṇ*) for the Jayā-Pārvatī Vrat, and by unmarried girls observing Gaurī Vrat.
3. The prose rural *Rāmāyaṇa* (94) and other works narrating the Rām story in brief are generally recited before an audience at night.
4. *Salokas* (99-101) are generally recited by one or sometimes two people in question-answer form at a public meeting place. Sometimes two shepherds or farmers also recite in question-answer form to pass the time and relieve the monotony of grazing herds or protecting fields from birds.
5. Miscellaneous folk songs (104-21) are mostly sung by groups of women observing the *agiyāras* fast (i.e. the eleventh and twenty-second days of the month). Some of them, such as lullabies, *kīrtan, pad-bhajan, vār, tithi,* and *mās,* are sung in Rām temples.
6. *Śravankathā* songs are generally sung by wandering beggars in train compartments.

Such are the occasions when *Rāmkathā* songs are sung in a continuing oral tradition that has maintained its connection with the life and seasonal cycles of Gujarat. This continuous oral tradition provides an opportunity for studying the origin and development of *Rāmkathā* and also reveals the 'give and take relationship' between the oral and written traditions.

NOTE

1. These numbers are given as per H. Yajnik 1992.

REFERENCES

Bulcke, Camille. *Rāmkathā: utpatti aur vikās.* Allahabad: Hindi Parishad, 1962.

Mishra, Bhagirath. *Rāmkathā: vividh āyām.* Delhi: Dr. Ramnath Tripathi Abhinandan Samiti, 1987.

Thompson, Stith. *The Folktale.* New York: The Dryden Press, 1946.

Yajnik, Hasu, ed. *Lok gito mā̃ Rāmcarit ane Pāṇḍavkatha.* Gandhinagar: Gujarat Sahitya Akademy, 1992.

The Householder Saints of Maharashtra

ELEANOR ZELLIOT

T.N. Madan has shown us that non-renouncers can be legitimate holy persons, and noted that the *bhakta* saints Basava, Nānak, Vallabha and Caitanya 'extolled domesticity as the good life as long as it was an affirmation of the bliss of the union of the devotee and the deity and not a contradiction of it' (T.N. Madan 1987, p. 9). The Bhakti movement in Maharashtra goes much farther than this. Almost all the Saint-poets are householders; most members of the family join with the Saint in devotion to Viṭṭhala, the God of Pandharpur, who himself came to that place because of the devotion of a son to his parents; the legends of Mahīpati (Mahīpati 1933-4, 1935; C.A. Kincaid 1919) stress family not only for the Maharashtrian Saint-poets but also for the northern Saints Mīrā and Kabīr. The Bhakti movements in India would seem to be a natural ground for the householder Saint, since the Bhakti way was open to all genders, classes and castes, but this seems to be stressed only in Maharashtra.

In the Marathi tradition, Saint-poets with families who are very much part of their lives and legends abound in the creative 500 years of the movement. Indeed, it is difficult to think of very many Saint-poets in the Vārkari Sampradāy[1] who did not live as householders. The pilgrimage of the Vārkarīs is to Pandharpur, and the coming of the God Vitthala or, affectionately, Viṭhobā, the object of Bhakti devotion in Maharashtra, to that town is due to the devotion of Puṇḍalik to his mother and father. Too busy caring for his parents to look up, the reformed rake Puṇḍalik threw the waiting God a brick to keep his feet from the mud, and Viṭhobā still stands on a brick in Pandharpur, an object of devotion for hundreds of thousands of pilgrims.

Asceticism and its counterpoint eroticism both are largely absent in the songs and the lives of the Vārkarīs. On the contrary, the householder tradition is present throughout the history of the

Bhakti movement in Maharashtra. The greatest exception is Kānhopātrā, the daughter of a courtesan, who merged with Viṭhobā in the temple at Pandharpur rather than become the concubine of the local sultan. It could also be said that the legendary founder of the Vārkarī Panth, Dnyāneśvar, is an exception to the idea of the importance of the household in Maharashtrian Bhakti since he was not married (probably could not marry since his father had been declared an outcaste for returning from his *saṃnyāsī* state to his wife and fathering four children, all at the behest of his guru). But Dnyāneśvar, his brothers and his sister formed a family unit, living together as a group, even travelling together as, one by one, each took *samādhi* at the end of his or her productive life. The most telling evidence of householder Saints may be found in the *abhaṅgas* of Nāmdev and Cokhāmeḷā, two of the many Saints in the early fourteenth century pantheon gathered around the pilgrimage to Pandharpur. The material on their householder lives may be found in Mahīpati's *Bhaktavijaya,* as well as in the extant *abhaṅgas* found in the basic collection of the Sants' work, the *Sakala santa gāthā* and a nineteenth century collection of Marathi poetry, the *Navanīt.*

It was Nāmdev, Dnyāneśvar's travelling companion and disciple, who not only began the tradition of the pilgrimage to Pandharpur in the company of all the Saints and (probably) travelled north (his poems were eventually included in the Sikh Granth) but who also illustrates almost to excess the family tradition.

Nāmdev's immediate family consisted of his mother and father, his wife, his four sons and their wives, his sister and his daughter—his wife complains that she has fourteen mouths to feed. We have over 2000 *abhaṅgas* from Nāmdev and a few each from his mother Goṇāī, his wife Rājāī, his sons Goṇḍobā, Nārā, Viṭhā, and Mhādā, his sister Aubāī, his daughter Limbāī, and his daughter-in-law Lāḍāī; and most famous of all but Nāmdev himself, his serving-maid Janābāī. An *abhaṅga* of Nāmdev's recounts the family members with pride and makes it clear all are *bhaktas*:

Goṇāī-Rājāī, both mother and her daughter-in-law,
Dāmā and Nāmā, the father and his son,
Nārā, Mhādā, Goṇḍā, Viṭhā—four sons
born in this holy lineage,
Lāḍāī, Godāī, Yesāī, Sākarāī—look, Nāmā' daughters-in-law
Nimbāī his daughter, Aubāī his sister,

crazy Janī his servant—
every one has sung *abhaṅgas*—Nāmā says,
God has fulfilled us all.[2]

Not all of the many *abhaṅgas* of Nāmdev's family are in praise of Viṭhobā or a celebration of joys of the pilgrimage. The Saints in their total devotion to the God could be very trying; both Nāmdev's mother and wife sang *abhaṅgas* so totally irreligious that one wonders why they were kept in the Vārkarīs' memory. Nāmdev's mother Goṇāī sings:

Goṇāī says, 'Nāma, stop being god-crazy.
Because of your stubbornness you're ruining your family.
Look how other peoples' sons behave—
but you! the bright light of my family!
Blessed is the son who is a husband, a householder.
The unlucky ones get Pandurang in their heads.
Nothing remains of those who follow him—
He is not God; he destroys families.
What outlandish devotion is this, Nāma,
Setting your own affairs on fire? .
Goṇāī says, Nāma, this is not good,
You're ruining your household, your lineage too.[3]

Abhaṅgas by Nāmdev's wife are equally critical but are not even addressed to Viṭhobā but to the non-Sanskritic goddess Mesāī:

My husband has found this guru,
Oh, what should I do now?
I have a family but I don't have a family—
that's 'divine miracle'?

Oh Goddess Mesāī, come quickly, help,
No one else can fix this;
You have the power, please make this go away.

He has taken to chanting mantras,
Devotees turn up at the house—
servants of the Lord, indeed!
May they all come to grief.

They are all goners; they're not coming back.

What can I tell you—the things they do:
They wash each other's feet and drink that water.
Deranged, they merrily dance away

They fall down at each others' feet—
all useless for this world.
They call Viṭṭhala's name
They rock and sway, Brahma-blissed.

My poor mother-in-law Goṇābāī, unsuspecting,
Gave birth to this bright gem.
He is hooked on the Sleeper-on-the-Snake—
What should I do? asks Rājāī.[4]

The mood of Nāma's sister and daughter is far different from that of his mother and his wife. While wife Rājāī in the middle of the night pleads with the wife of Viṭhobā, 'Lady Rukmiṇī', to find a way to release her husband from the thrall of 'Lord Viṭṭhala' so that she can feed her family, daughter Limbāī addresses Rukmiṇī's Lord in conventional terms, using a familiar Purāṇic story as a reference:

Save me now, Rukmiṇī's Lord,
Pandhari's Lord, O Mother-and-Father.
Sages like Sanaka have called you
the refuge of the forlorn, so I have heard.
Trusting them, I have come to you, Panduranga.
Nāma's daughter Limbāī says
Merciful God, protect me.[5]

Sister Aubāī's single *abhaṅga* reveals the *nirguṇ* God who is as familiar to the Maharashtrian *bhaktas* as the *saguṇ* Viṭṭhala:

I have come to see
the Great Void revealed.
Form ceases to be
and Nothing takes its place.
The voice is the essence, it is the essence,
it contains all that moves
and all that does not move.
Nāma's sister Aubāī is contained in that void,
her mind at rest in Viṭṭhala.[6]

A second Saint of the fourteenth century, Nāmdev's contemporary and his close friend, the Untouchable Mahār Saint Cokhāmeḷā, had a smaller family, but each member had a religious message and distinctive tone and we have a record of number of *abhaṅgas* ascribed to each. His wife, Soyrābāī, is credited with sixty-two *abhaṅgas*; his sister Nirmalā with twenty-four; her husband Baṅkā (probably Soyrābāī's brother) with thirty-nine; his son Karmāmeḷā with twenty-seven. Untouchability, the problems of treatment by society, the battle against the concepts of purity and pollution are subjects that trouble all of them, but in addition, each has a style all his or her own.

Soyrābāī did not complain about her husband in the fashion of Nāmdev's wife and mother, even when legends tell us he walked away as she was about to bear her son. Her poems are not about household matters but about her joy in devotion, her pain in separation from God, her grief over the treatment meted her as an Untouchable—and about her sister-in-law Nirmalā, whom she clearly adored. Curiously enough, she longs for the cessation of Samsara, but she does not ask God to release her husband from His grip, and she finds that the recitation of the Name comforts her in all her troubles. Her search for God is very personal, even though she signs herself often simply as the Mahār wife of Cokhāmeḷā. The following *abhaṅga* seems to me to be about her own efforts at meditation:

House and home are meaningless;
Samsara is meaningless, the body is meaningless.
Your Name is meaningful, all else is meaningless; if people don't drown [in this world] it is only because of the Name.
All things are meaningless, ideas are meaningless, great wisdom is meaningless; who cares?
The science of words is meaningless, words themselves are meaningless, knowledge is meaningless; why speak of these things?
If your mind is not steady, that's also meaningless, and how then will you come to Hari?
'Till then there's no meaning in speaking speech, says Cokhā's Mahārī.[7]

A second *abhaṅga* by Soyrābāī (no. 37 in *Sakal santa gāthā*) offers an idea of the way *bhaktas* combined devotion and the household through *nāmasmaraṇa*, the reciting of the Name of God (see Sh. G. Tulpule, 1991):

I have relied on the Name, regarded it as Truth, been carried to the other side of the river.
The Name is easy, so easy; the Name is easy when you sing it.
I love the Name every moment of my life; there is no one time to sing Your Name.
People are rescued from samsara by the Name, says Cokhā's Mahārī.[8]

Nirmalā, Cokhāmeḷā's sister, is perhaps the most deeply spiritual of the family; her husband Baṅkā is the story-teller. Nirmalā does not identify herself as Baṅkā's wife, but as Cokhāmeḷā's sister. Baṅkā, on the other hand, tells at length the story of the God Viṭṭhala going to Soyrābāī at the time of her delivery in the form of Nirmalā. Although Cokhāmeḷā clearly is the centre of the family and the chief devotee among them, all seem to have their own individual voices. The son of Cokhāmeḷā and Soyrābāī, Karmāmeḷā, is the most bitter, expressing the greatest anger over the treatment God and society mete out to him. Although all of the Untouchable Saints question the idea of purity and bemoan their low status, no one reaches the heights (or depths) of despair that Karmāmeḷā does. Much of his anger is over his low status, but the following *abhaṅga* is both a tribute to his father's closeness to Viṭhobā and his own 'dark night of the soul' complaint to God:

My father was your ward, Viṭṭhala,
How can you forget?
You bathed me when I was small
Why are you hard-hearted now?
Keep your vow, Viṭṭhala;
Only then will you keep your good name!
Cokhā's son Karmāmeḷā says,
You ought not forget me, God.[9]

Unlike Nāmdev, Cokhāmeḷā does not sing of his family, nor are there dialogues between members, as there are for Nāmdev and his mother. However, the number of *abhaṅgas,* the references back and forth to other family members, the stories of Cokhāmeḷā's family found in Nāmdev and Eknāth's works, and even the folk legends of the region in which Nirmalā and Baṅkā lived[10] indicate that this was a genuine family.

* * * *

Although the family members of others of this early circle of Saint-poets in the Maharashtrian tradition are not recorded poets, the legends about them do involve family. Gorā the potter tramples his child along with the clay in his ecstasy of devotion (his wife forgives him, and of course, eventually the child is restored to life). Although Janābāī as a child is left behind in the pilgrimage centre of Pandharpur because she refuses to leave her God, she does not enter the temple but instead becomes a serving maid in the bosom of Nāmdev's enormous and devout family, and is counted by him as a family member. When Rākā the potter decides to give up all worldly pursuits and go into the forest, his wife and daughter go with him. Santobā Pawār becomes a hermit only to live on the alms begged for him by his wife!

Even when Mahīpati, the eighteenth-century biographer of the Saints, wrote of the Hindi Saints' lives, he managed to reflect this sense of the family as centre, the family as the natural environment for *bhaktas.* Mahīpati's legend of Kabīr includes a loving stepmother and a wife as well as a son. Mīrābāī is not given a husband who poisons her, but a royal father who gives her poison, to the sorrow of her mother. The absorption of the poison by Kṛṣṇa (who turns green) converts the king to Vaiṣṇava piety, and Mīrā happily continues to worship Kṛṣṇa in the palace. This version of the Mīrā legend is a far cry from the wandering rejected princess we know from Northern stories.

* * * *

The reasons for the stress on not only the *bhakta* as householder but the entire family as a unit are probably many. No one writing about Maharashtrian character seems to have uncovered any special emphasis on family life. And indeed one great hero of Maharashtrian Brahmins, Rāmdās, often mistakenly considered a Saint-poet in the Vārkarī Bhakti tradition, was celibate and founded a celibate order, which perhaps prophetically has not continued in any strength. The Nāth Yogīs were also important in Maharashtra; Dnyāneśvar's brother and Nāmdev's guru were Nāths, and the name of Eknāth may be related to their influence, but this *saṃnyāsī* tradition does not seem to have affected the emphasis on *bhakta* householders; many of the Nāth establishments such as the one at Paithan are in disrepair and the Nāths who still wander the area are from the North.

I would suggest three possible reasons for the importance of the family to the Vārkarī Sampradāy:

(1) Maharashtra was a rural area with few big cities. There is an exception in Paithan, a large trading centre and former capital, where Eknāth (and his loving wife and difficult son) flourished in the sixteenth century. However, most of the Saint-poets come from

villages or, as in the case of Cokhāmeḷā, practice their traditional occupation in Pandharpur, where they live with their families. The family is essential to the farm and the village and traditional crafts, and the Vārkarī Sampradāy was predominantly a rural village tradition.

Not only is the basis of the Vārkarīs' life a rural one, but the Desh area of Maharashtra, from which most of the *bhaktas* come, is a rain shadow area, with frequent famines. The seventeenth century Saint-poet Tukārām lost his first wife and child in the 'Great Mahādurgā' famine of 1630. There is a saying that out of five harvests, two will be good, two will be just barely enough, one will be bad. The hardiness of rural life required in such an area may well lead to a stress on the total family and an inability to support those who do not perfom householder duties.

(2) The Vārkarī Sampradāy was and is a movement centered chiefly on one temple, the one in Pandharpur. And while this is a large and impressive temple in a small and dusty town, it has a strange place in the Bhakti movement. The priests of the temple, the Badve, are by and large not Vārkarīs in the Bhakti tradition. While the temple is the focal point of the pilgrimage, the pilgrimage itself seems to be more important than the temple. A Saint did not come to live a renouncer's life in the temple; he or she would not have been welcome. Cokhāmeḷā's *samādhi* is at the foot of the stairs leading to the great door; Nāmdev's is on the steps. Kānhopātrā, the courtesan's daughter who merged with the image, is the only saint memorialized inside, a phenomenon I do not understand. The movement was not a movement of renouncers; the temple had no place for them; the land could not support them. Almost as an illustration of how all *bhaktas* were expected to live, the Saint-poets lived in their households, did their normal daily work, and in most cases their wives and their children joined them in devotion to the God.

(3) The Vārkarī Sampradāy is not dominated by Brahmins, the group which, according to Madan, most value the ascetic tradition. Dnyāneśvar, the author of the most beloved text of the Vārkarīs, a commentary on the *Bhāgavadgītā,* was the child of an outcasted Brahmin. Eknāth, it is true, was a highly educated Brahmin, but one who chose to share his Brahminical knowledge in Marathi with all castes and classes. The other two most important *bhaktas* in the tradition are Nāmdev, a tailor, and Tukārām, a

grocer in the Śūdra *varṇa*, and the range of Saint-poets chiefly includes those from artisan castes. The combination of rural life in a rain-shadow area, a lack of the kind of temple centre found in the south, and leadership from either Śūdra or unorthodox Brahmins may be most reponsible for Maharashtra's householder *bhaktas*.

NOTES

The late Dr. Tulpule worked with me on the study of Cokhāmeḷā and his family for many years; much of my understanding of Bhakti owes a debt to him, although the interpretations are my own.

1. The most thorough account of the Vārkarī Sampradāy (the tradition of the pilgrims) is still Deleury's *The Cult of Viṭhobā* (1960).
2. *Navanīt*: 19, *abhaṅga* 22: *goṇāī rājāī doghī sāsū-sunā.* Translated by Jayant Karve with some changes by the author. The *abhaṅga* is a flexible form of poetry used in Marathi Saint poetry. Its literal meaning is 'unbroken'.
3. *Navanīt*: 32, *abhaṅga* 1. A longer version is in *Sakala santa gāthā* 1267: *goṇāī mhane nāmyā soḍī devpise.* Translated by Jayant Karve with some changes by the author. Pandharang is another name for (Viṭṭhala) or Viṭhobā.
4. *Navanīt*: 32: *don prahar rātra pāhoni ekant.* Translated by Jayant Karve, as are the *abhaṅgas* by Limbāī and Aubāī which follow.
5. *Sakala santa gāthā* 1: *tārī maj ātā.*
6. *Sakala santa gāthā* 1: *śūnya sākārale.*
7. *Sakala santa gāthā* 10: *vāuge ghardār vāugā saṃsār.* Translated by Vijaya Deo and Eleanor Zelliot, as is the one which follows.
8. *Sakala santa gāthā* 37: *nāmācā bharaṅvasā mānilāse sār.*
9. *Sakala santa gāthā* 1: *āmucā bāp tujhā poṣnā.* Translated by Vijaya Deo with changes by Jayant Karve and Eleanor Zelliot.
10. N.R. Śenḍe records legends from the area in *Loksāhityasampadā* (Nagpur: Vidarbha Sahitya Sangh Prakashan, 1964). Dr. Prabhakar Made, Sudhir, Waghmare and I found strong memories of Nirmalā and Baṅkā when we visited Mehenpuri in 1992.

REFERENCES

Deleury, G.A. *The cult of Viṭhobā*. Poona: Deccan College Postgraduate and Research Institute, 1960.

Godbole, Parshuram Pant Tatya, ed. *Navanīt.* 1882 Reprint. Pune: Vasudev Ganesh Joshi, 1910.

Joshi, Kashinath Anant, ed. *Śrīsakala santa gāthā*. Pune: Srisantwangamaya Prakashan Mandir, 1967 (1923).

Kincaid, C.A. *Tales of the Saints of Pandharpur*, Bombay: Oxford University Press, 1919.

Madan, T.N. *Non-Renunciation: Themes and Interpretations of Hindu Culture.* Delhi: Oxford University Press, 1987.

Mahīpati. *Bhaktalīlāmṛta (Nectar from Indian Saints)*. Translated by Justin E. Abbott and N.R. Godbole; Poet Saints of Maharashtra Series 9. Poona: J.F. Edwards, 1935.

———. *Stories of Indian Saints: An English Translation of Mahīpati's Marathi Bhaktavijaya.* Justin E. Abbott and N.R. Godbole. 2 vols. Poet Saints of Maharashtra Series 9-10. Poona: United Theological College of Western India, 1933-4.

Tulpule, Shankar Gopal, *The Divine Name in Indian Tradition,* Shimla: Indian Institute of Advanced Study, 1991.

Contributors

VIDYUT AKLUJKAR is currently Research Associate at the Centre for India and South Asia Research, University of British Columbia. Her areas of research include classical and contemporary Indian literature, the Indian diaspora and its literature, *bhakti* literature, and women's literature. She teaches courses in Hindi and on Indian literature. In addition to her academic publications, she has also published many works of poetry, fiction, and journalism.

H.C. BHAYANI has worked in the postgraduate and research departments of the Bharatiya Vidya Bhavan (Bombay), Gujarat University (Ahmedabad), and L.D. Institute of Indology (Ahmedabad). His numerous publications span a vast array of topics, including Early, Middle, and Modern Indian languages, particularly Prakrit, Apabhraṃśa, and Old Gujarati, folklore, religion and linguistics. Among his many recent publications are *Gujārātī Bhāṣānuṃ Aitihāsik Vyākaraṇ* (1988) and *Rāula-Veda of Roḍa* (1994). He has recently published editions of the *Dohā-gīti-kośa* and the *Caryā-gīti-kośa* (Prakrit Test Society, 1997).

NETTY C. BONOUVRIÉ is affiliated with Documentation Centre of South Asia at the Kern Institute at the Rijks Universiteit Leiden.

MANDAKRANTA BOSE is Acting Director of the Centre for India and South Asian Research, and Lecturer in Classical, Near Eastern and Religious Studies at the University of British Columbia. Her publications include *Movement and Mimesis: The Idea of Dance in Sanskritic Tradition* (1991), a critical edition of the *Nartananirnaya* by Puṇḍarīkaviṭṭhala (1991). Two edited volumes, *Captive Subjects: Images and Voices of South Asian Women* and *The World My Mother Gave Me: Asian Women's Intergenerational Perceptions in Literature* are in press.

THOMAS DE BRUIJN is currently affiliated with the International

Institute for Asian Studies in Leiden. His publications, in both Dutch and English, deal with both Bhakti literature and the Indo-Sufi *masnavī*.

KENNETH E. BRYANT is Associate Professor of Hindi at the University of British Columbia. His many publications include *Poems to the Child-God: Structures and Strategies in the Poetry of Sūrdās* (1978).

RICHARD J. COHEN is Associate Director of the South Asia Regional Studies Department of the University of Pennsylvania. His research interests include Middle and Early New Indo-Aryan languages and literature, Jainism, early Indian Sufism, and Indian illustrated manuscripts. He is currently preparing a critical edition, translation and analysis of *Cāndāyan*.

ALAN W. ENTWISTLE at the time of his death in 1996 was Associate Professor of Hindi at the University of Washington. His research specializations were early Hindi language and Indian religions, particularly Hinduism and Sufism. Although he has published widely on many aspects of north Indian literature, language, and culture, he is best remembered for his *Braj, Center of Krishna Pilgrimage* (1987).

PETER GAEFFKE is Professor of Modern Indian Literature at the University of Pennsylvania. He studied at Mainz University, where he took an M.A. in Classics and German and a Ph.D. in Indo-European comparative linguistics. He works in Hindi, Bengali, Urdu and Dakanī Urdu and has published books on Hindi linguistics and literature. He has worked recently on such issues as the rediscovery of Buddhism in India, the press in India, and the comparative rhetoric of Hindus and Muslims.

DANIEL GOLD is Professor of South Asian Religions at Cornell University. His teaching and research specialization include pre-modern north Indian religion, especially the Sant and Nāth traditions; urban religion, in contemporary India and problems in the study of religion. Among his publications are *The Lord as Guru: Hindi Saints in North Indian Traditions* (1987) and *Comprehending the Guru: Towards a Grammar of Religious Perception* (1988).

DAVID L. HABERMAN is Associate Professor of Religious Studies at

Indiana University. He is a student of northern Indian Hinduism, and specializes in the religious culture of Braj Vaishnavism. He has contributed numerous articles to academic journals and encyclopaedias and is the author of *Acting as a Way of Salvation* (1988) and *Journey Through the Twelve Forests* (1984).

NASEEM HINES is Senior Lecturer in Hindi and Urdu at the University of Washington, from where she obtained her Ph.D. in 1997. Her fields of specialization are medieval Hindi poetry and the Indo-Sufi *masnavī*, particularly *Cāndāyan*, by Maulāna Dāūd, classical and modern Urdu poetry and modern Urdu short stories and novels.

ALLAN M. KEISLAR is currently Assistant Professor of South Asian Religions at the Institute for Vaiṣṇava Studies, Berkeley. He is also Adjunct Professor of World Religions at the Graduate Theological Union, Berkeley. His interests include medieval Vaiṣṇava texts, especially those of the Gauḍīya commentarial tradition, inter-religious dialogue and developing an interfaith liturgy.

TIMOTHY LENZ is a doctoral student in Sanskrit at the University of Washington. His M.A. thesis dealt with the *Rāul Vela* inscription. His Ph.D. dissertation will deal with early Buddhist texts from Gandhara.

DAVID N. LORENZEN is Professor at El Colegio de Mexico. His current research interests are Nirguṇī and Nāth literature, particularly the *gosṭhī* texts of the Kabīr Panth. His recent publications include *Kabir Legends* and Anantadās's *Kabir Parachai* (1991), *Bhakti Religion in North India* (edited, 1995) and *Praises to a Formless God* (1996).

REBECCA J. MANRING is currently Visiting Assistant Professor of Religious Studies and Indian Studies, Indiana University, where she teaches courses on Hindi, Sanskrit, Asian religions, and South Asian literature. Her research interests are Gauḍīya Vaiṣṇavism (especially the hagiographical literature) and Bengali tantra.

R. STUART MCGREGOR, until his recent retirement, was Lecturer in Hindi at the University of Cambridge. His main research interests are Hindi language and literature and lexicography. His publications include *Outline of Hindi Grammar* (1972), *The Round Dance of Krishna and Uddhav's Message* (1973), *Hindi Literature of the Nineteenth and Early Twentieth Centuries* (1974) and *Hindi Literature from its Beginnings to the Nineteenth Century* (1984). He edited the *Oxford Hindi-English Dictionary* (1993).

ZAWAHIR MOIR is Retired Research Associate of the Ismalia Association for Pakistan and Member of the Academic Faculty of the Institute of Ismaili Studies, London. Her main interest is in the modern history and Ginan literature of the Ismaili community. Her principal publications include (with Christopher Shackle) *Ismaili Hymns of South Asia: An Introduction to the Ginan Literature* (1992), (with J. Robson and M. Moir) *Writings on India by John Stuart Mill* and a forthcoming study of Pir Shams as reflected in the Ismaili Ginans.

MARIOLA OFFREDI is Associated Professor of Hindi Language and Literature at the University of Venice. Her research interests include contemporary Hindi literature (novel, poetry, journalism), medieval Hindi literature (Gorakh, Jāyasī), contemporary Indian art and the socio-economic history of India. Some of her recent publications have dealt with the Hindi press, the Hindi novel and Hindi poetry.

SHYAM MANOHAR PANDEY is a member of the Department of Asian Studies, Istituto Universitario Orientale, Naples. After receiving his Ph.D. from Allahabad University, he taught for some years at the University of Chicago and the School of Oriental and African Studies, University of London. His publications include *Madhyayugīn premākhyān, Sūfī kāvya vimarś, Sūfī Mansūr Hallāj kī bānī, Hindī aur fārsī sūfī kāvya* and a series of volumes presenting versions of the oral epic of Loriki and Canainī.

HEIDI R.M. PAUWELS is currently Assistant Professor of Hindi at the University of Washington. Her research interests include early and modern Hindi literature and Hinduism. After earning her Ph.D. in 1944 from the University of Washington, she taught at the School of Oriental and African Studies, University of London. She is the author of *Kṛṣṇa's Round Dance Reconsidered: Harirām Vyās's Hindī Rās-pañcādhyāyī* (1996).

CAROL SALOMON is Affiliate Assistant Professor of Bengali at the

University of Washington. She obtained her Ph.D. in 1983 from the University of Pennsylvania. Her fields of specialization include Bengali literature, both modern and medieval, the Bauls and their songs, and Islam in West Bengal and Bangladesh.

A. WHITNEY SANFORD is Assistant Professor of Religion at Iowa State University. She is currently working on a project on Balarāma, co-editing a volume on issues of text *versus* experience in Indian religions, and completing a manuscript on Paramānand. She received her Ph.D. from the University of Pennsylvania in 1995.

SAGAREE SENGUPTA is Visiting Assistant Professor at the University of Wisconsin at Madison. Her area of specialization is the language and literature of north India. Currently she is completing a book on Bharatendu Harischandra and translating from modern Urdu fiction. Her bibliographic essay on the Tagore family was published in the Winter 1997 issue of *The Library Chronicle of the Harry Ranson Research Center.* She received her Ph.D. from the University of Pennsylvania in 1992.

MICHAEL C. SHAPIRO is Professor of Hindi at the University of Washington. He obtained his Ph.D. in 1974 from the University of Chicago. His fields of interest include Hindi language, literature and linguistics, and comparative Indo-Aryan linguistics.

HUGH VAN SKYHAWK is Assistant Professor in the Department of Indology, South Asia Institute, Heidelberg University. His main research interests are the hagiographies of Hindu and Muslim medieval sants of the Deccan, in old Marathi and Dakanī, and in the oral traditions of the Central Asian epic of Gesar in Surushaski. He has published *Bhakti und Bhakta: Religionsgeschichliche Untersuchungen zum Heilsbegriff und zur religiöses Umwelt des Srī Sant Ekanāth,* edited 'Minorities on Themselves' (*South Asia Digest of Regional Writing,* 1986), and written many articles.

DANUTA STASIK is Reader in Hindi in the Department of South Asian Studies, Oriental Institute, University of Warsaw. Her research interests are the *Ramayana* tradition in Hindi literature (from Viṣṇudās and Tulsīdās until the present), the Indian diaspora in the West (particularly as represented in Indian writing) and Hindi literature. In 1992 she published (with T. Rutkowska) *Outline History of Hindi Literature* (in Polish).

DAVID C. SWAIN is Lecturer at Loyola University (Chicago). His areas of teaching and research are the history of religions, Sant traditions, and nirguṇa bhakti.

HASU YAJNIK is Managing Director of the Meghani Folklore Research in Ahmedabad. Previously he was Lecturer in Gujarati at the Government College. His publications include *Madhya-kālīn gujaratī prem-sāhitya* (1972), *Madhya-kālīn gujaratī kathā sāhitya* (1988) and *Gujaratī lok-sāhitya.*

ELEANOR ZELLIOT is the Laird Bell Professor Hindi emerita, Carleton College. Her primary fields of research specialization are the Dalit movement in India and Maharashtrian medieval saint-poets. Her publications include *From Untouchable to Dalit: Essays on the Ambedkar Movement* (1996) and *The Experience of Hinduism* (co-editor, 1988).

Index